A
BRIEF HISTORY
OF THE
WESTERN WORLD

VOLUME II
FROM THE LATE MIDDLE AGES TO THE PRESENT

EIGHTH EDITION

A
BRIEF HISTORY
OF THE
WESTERN WORLD

VOLUME II
FROM THE LATE MIDDLE AGES TO THE PRESENT

EIGHTH EDITION

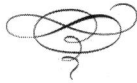

THOMAS H. GREER
MICHIGAN STATE UNIVERSITY

GAVIN LEWIS
JOHN JAY COLLEGE
CITY UNIVERSITY OF NEW YORK

WADSWORTH
™
THOMSON LEARNING

Australia • Canada • Mexico • Singapore • Spain
United Kingdom • United States

WADSWORTH
✦ ™
THOMSON LEARNING

Publisher: Earl McPeek
Executive Editor: David Tatom
Market Strategist: Steve Drummond
Developmental Editor: steve Norder
Project Editor: Louise Slominsky

Art Director: Carol Kincaid
Production Manager: Linda McMillan
Compositor: Progressive Information Technologies
Cover Printer: Lehigh Press, Inc
Printer: R.R. Donnelley, Crawfordsville

Cover Image: Pable Picasso, *Three Musicians*, Fontainbleau, summer 1921. Oil on canvas, 6'7" × 7'3" (200.7 × 222.9 cm). The Museum of Modern Art, New York, Mrs. Simon Guggenheim Fund. Photograph copyright © 2001 The Museum of Modern Art, New York.

Printed in the United States of America
1 2 3 4 5 6 7 05 04 03 02

For more information about our products, contact us at:
Thomson Learning Academic Resource Center
1-800-423-0563
For permission to use material from this text, contact us by:
Phone: 1-800-730-2214
Fax: 1-800-730-2215
Web: http://www.thomsonrights.com

Library of Congress Catalog Card Number: 2001088694

ISBN: 0-15-507501-2

Asia
Thomson Learning
60 Albert Street, #15-01
Albert Complex
Singapore 189969

Australia
Nelson Thomson Learning
102 Dodds Street
South Melbourne, Victoria 3205
Australia

Canada
Nelson Thomson Learning
1120 Birchmount Road
Toronto, Ontario M1K 5G4
Canada

Europe/Middle East/Africa
Thomson Learning
Berkshire House
168-173 High Holborn
London WC1 V7AA
United Kingdom

Latin America
Thomson Learning
Seneca, 53
Colonia Polanco
11560 Mexico D.F.
Mexico

Spain
Paraninfo Thomson Learning
Calle/Magallanes, 25
28015 Madrid, Spain

For Margarette and Nadia

PREFACE

Those who cannot remember the past are condemned to repeat it.

George Santayana
1863–1952

What is the nature of the Western world? How has it shaped the men and women who are its heirs? Many of today's young people, in search of their own identity, are asking such questions. The search is not new; it traces back to the ancient Greeks. Inscribed on the temple of Apollo at Delphi were the words of the god: *Know yourself*. And one way to self-knowledge is to learn of the past experiences of humans like ourselves. As William Shakespeare observed, *What's past is prologue*.

Our aim in *A Brief History of the Western World* is to present a clear, concise account of truly meaningful human experiences relevant to the society in which we live. Following this aim, we have focused on the outstanding institutions, ideas, and creative works that have formed (and expressed) Western civilization. Both volumes are designed also as a guide and companion for further and deeper explorations of the human past. These can best be accomplished, we believe, by reading original sources and worthy interpretative works. To this end, we have prepared a selection of books for Recommended Further Reading that can be found at the back of this book (pp. A-1 through A-19). It is followed by a list of Recommended Videocassettes (p. A-19 through A-21).

Throughout the book we have sought to illuminate the narrative by means of various visual features. These include completely revised and updated *maps* of the places and areas under discussion in the text; *time charts* (also geared to the text) showing the chronological relationships of notable individuals, events, and works of architecture, art, and music; and *time lines* (at the top of certain pages) showing the sequence and duration of particular historical periods. The duration of these periods is indicated by the length of the respective line segments; the darkest segment normally corresponds to the period discussed on the same or nearby pages. In addition, we have provided an *illustration* of each work of art described in our narrative.

Other special aids for the student include the identification of *important historical terms*. These are marked by an asterisk (*) placed before selected entries in the *Index*; the *meaning* of each term is explained on the pages shown for that entry. Also shown in the Index are the years of birth and death, or years of reign, for each person named in the text. And we have provided numerous *cross-references* to help point out the *interconnections* of ideas and events that occur in the various times and places.

We have made extensive changes in this eighth edition to meet the developing needs of teachers and students, while maintaining full continuity with the content, organization, and features of earlier editions.

An entirely new feature is the overviews that begin each chapter. Rather than simply summarizing the contents of each chapter in advance, the overviews are written as introductory "mini-essays," designed to enhance understanding of the chapter contents in two ways. First, the overviews explain how the general theme of each chapter fits into the pattern of development of Western civilization as a whole; second, they make clear how the individual topics covered by each chapter relate to each other and to the chapter's general theme. Where appropriate, the overviews include general introductory material additional to the contents of the chapters themselves. The coverage of individual topics generally follows the sequence of the main chapter sections, but rather than listing the contents of each section, the overviews concentrate on conveying understanding of the topics themselves.

Also with the aim of conveying the overall pattern of Western development, we have added dates to the part titles and divided the old Part Four into two. The new Part Four, "The Changing West, 1600–1850," includes chapters 10 through 12, and chapters 13 through 15 now form Part Five, "The West in the Contemporary World, 1850–2000."

In addition, the reader will find many more illustrations than before. There is double the number of color plates, in three inserts relating respectively to ancient and medieval times, the early modern period, and modern times. (In this two-volume version, the first insert appears in Volume I, the second in both volumes, and the third in Volume II.) Also, the number of black-and-white illustrations has been increased by one-third. All existing color plates and black-and-white illustrations of art objects dealt with in the text have been retained; the new illustrations include many different types of images that give a visual dimension to subjects discussed in the course of the book.

We have extensively revised and expanded our treatment of various topics in response to the changing interests of teachers and students as well as recent scholarly findings.

Throughout the book we have given greater prominence to the development of technology and its impact on government, society, and culture. We have added material on technical innovation in many ancient civilizations, on the beginning of the Iron Age, and on present-day "high technology." The historic innovations of the later Middle Ages—firearms, printing, mechanical clocks, and new types of sailing ships—and their wide-ranging impact on Western civilization are dealt with in a new section of chapter 7, "The New Technology."

Further, we have placed additional stress on military factors at various key points in Western development: the impact of the needs of warfare on the rise of Greek city-state government; the role of the army in the power structure of the Roman republic and empire, and in Rome's "decline and fall"; and the part played by new technologies of warfare and the increasing burden of armaments in both the rise of absolute monarchy and the seventeenth- and eighteenth-century revolutions.

We have made significant changes in our treatment of prehistoric and an-cient times. The discussion of women in prehistory and ancient civilizations has been much increased, including the possible origins of women's subordinate status in the course of the Agricultural Revolution. Prominence is given to the crisis and recovery of the international world of ancient Middle Eastern civilization be-tween 1200 and 900 B.C. and the way in which the crisis was a prelude to the Iron Age, the spread of alphabetic writing, and the rise of universal empires. The treat-ment of the beginnings of Greek civilization has been rewritten so as to stress the way in which the rise and fall of Aegean civilizations was part of this same inter-national crisis and recovery. This, in turn, enables us to take a position on the much-discussed question, which books dealing with Western civilization can hardly leave unanswered, of whether Greek civilization was "stolen" from earlier peoples.

There is additional discussion of the spread of Christianity within the Roman Empire, its replacement of traditional polytheism, and its separation from Judaism. The treatment of Judaism has been rewritten to explain how most of the general features of monotheistic religion arose out of the experience of the ancient Jews, and also to cover the development of Judaism as a monotheistic religion in its own right.

In the treatment of the medieval period, we have given greater prominence to the Balkans, both to explain the region's role as a frontier area of Western civiliza-tion, and also in order to provide understanding of the historical roots of the present-day ethnic and religious conflicts in the region. The final chapters have been updated to cover the continued aftershocks of the tumultuous events of the early 1990s in the former communist countries, the Middle East, and elsewhere, as well as pursuing into the twenty-first century the themes of ethnic conflict, democ-ratization, globalization, and postmodernism in thought and art.

In this two-volume version of *A Brief History of the Western World*, Volume I, *From the Beginning to the Enlightenment*, includes chapters 1 through 10, and Vol-ume II, *From the Late Middle Ages to the Present*, includes chapters 7 through 15. (The book is also, of course, available in a single-volume version). A printed In-structor's Manual/Test Booklet, as well as computerized testbanks in Windows and Macintosh formats, accompanies the full textbook and volumes. The Instructor's Manual/Test Booklet, as well as many other instructor and student resources, are also available on Thomson's Web site *A Brief History of the Western World Online*. The material can be accessed at

http://www.harcourtcollege.com/history/greer_lewis

For more general information on Western civilization and other history-related topics, go to

http://www.harcourtcollege.com/history

Our warmest thanks go to the editorial staff at Harcourt, in particular to David Tatom, steve Norder, Louise Slominsky, Carol Kincaid, and Linda McMillan, who contributed their editorial and production expertise to this book. And it is a plea-sure to acknowledge the help of our colleagues Donald R. Abbott (San Diego Mesa

College), Melissa Bonafont (College of the Siskiyous), and Michael A. Zaccaria (Cumberland County College) for their excellent advice and suggestions.

We hope that our readers will find a measure of excitement, challenge, and pleasure in this book!

Thomas H. Greer
Gavin Lewis

CONTENTS

PART FOUR
THE CHANGING WEST: 1600–1850   445

CHAPTER 10 Science and a New Cosmology   448

CHAPTER 12 **The Impact of the Machine   551**

PART FIVE
THE WEST IN THE CONTEMPORARY WORLD: 1850–2000   593

CHAPTER 13 **Imperialism, World War, and the Rise of Collectivism   597**

CHAPTER 14 **Global Transformation: Dawn of a New Age   646**

CHAPTER 15   The Revolution in Western Culture   711

MAPS

TIME CHARTS

A
BRIEF HISTORY
OF THE
WESTERN WORLD

VOLUME II
FROM THE LATE MIDDLE AGES TO THE PRESENT

EIGHTH EDITION

III-1 Hans Holbein the Younger. Detail from *The French Ambassadors*, 1533. Oil tempera on wood, approx. 6′8″ × 6′10″. National Gallery, London.

PART THREE

THE COMING OF MODERN TIMES

1300–1650

	POLITICAL, SOCIAL, AND ECONOMIC DEVELOPMENTS	RELIGION, SCIENCE, AND PHILOSOPHY	HISTORY AND LITERATURE	ARCHITECTURE, ART, AND MUSIC
1300	Travels of Marco Polo			Florence Cathedral
				Giotto
		"Babylonian Captivity" of papacy (1309–1376)		
	Black Death (bubonic plague) Hundred Years' War (1338–1453) Decline of feudal and manorial systems	Renaissance humanism (1350–1600)	Petrarch Boccaccio	
	New weapons of war: longbow and crossbow	Great Schism (1379–1417) Wiclif		Madrigals (polyphony) Renaissance style of architecture: Brunelleschi
1400	Domestic system of production (1400–1750)	Hus		Donatello Masaccio van Eyck Ghiberti
	Age of despots in Italy: Cosimo de' Medici Francesco Sforza New-style armies: cannon and muskets	Platonism (Florentine Academy) Ficino Pico della Mirandola Machiavelli	Valla Gutenberg	
	Fall of Constantinople to Ottoman Turks			
	Christian reconquest of Spain			Botticelli
	Jacob Fugger			

	POLITICAL, SOCIAL, AND ECONOMIC DEVELOPMENTS	RELIGION, SCIENCE, AND PHILOSOPHY	HISTORY AND LITERATURE	ARCHITECTURE, ART, AND MUSIC
1500	Overseas exploration: Columbus, da Gama, Magellan Establishment of European colonial empires: Cortéz, Pizarro Rise of national monarchies: Henry VIII, Francis I Charles V, Holy Roman Emperor Philip II Elizabeth I Spanish Armada	Luther (beginning of Protestant Reformation) Calvin Pope Paul III (beginning of Catholic Reformation) Copernicus Loyola and Society of Jesus Council of Trent	Erasmus Castiglione More Rabelais Cellini Montaigne	Leonardo Michelangelo Titian Holbein St. Peter's Basilica Brueghel Escorial Palace Baroque style
1600	Religious wars (Thirty Years' War in Germany)	Bacon Kepler, Galileo Descartes	Cervantes Shakespeare Jonson	Globe Theater Rubens Rembrandt Bernini
1650	Peace of Westphalia Louis XIV			Taj Mahal Versailles Palace

CHAPTER 7

❧ ❧ ❧

THE TRANSFORMATION AND
EXPANSION OF EUROPE

Overview

U nlike the Roman world, medieval civilization did not "fall." There were
no waves of invading barbarians, no collapse of civic order and commerce. On the contrary, western Europe at the "close" of the Middle Ages
displayed a remarkable vitality and an expansive spirit. It moved, without a
noticeable break, into "modern" times. Thus, we cannot point to any historical event or series of events and say, "Here ended the Middle Ages." We
might even say that our present civilization is an extension of medieval
times, for the evolution of Western institutions has been continuous over the
past thousand years, and the seeds of each new era have been nurtured in the
old. All the same, a great shift in civilization took place between the fourteenth and seventeenth centuries: the medieval synthesis began to dissolve
not long after 1300, and by 1650 a new and more recognizably modern pattern of civilization had come into being. The new cultural and religious developments of these centuries are discussed in chapters 8 and 9; this chapter
deals with the social, economic, and political changes with which modern
Western civilization began.

In the late Middle Ages—that is, the fourteenth and fifteenth centuries—the advanced civilization that had grown up in Europe since 1000
was shaken by a series of crises: famine, social conflict, and peasant revolts;
the disaster of the Black Death, the famous mid-fourteenth-century pandemic outbreak of the plague which ravaged the entire Eastern hemisphere;
and attacks by powerful Asiatic peoples that led much of eastern Europe to
fall under the rule of the Muslim Tartars and Turks.

But these crises did not stop the continuing evolution of western European civilization; in fact, in some ways they even spurred it on. As merchants reinvested their profits in industry and banking as well as trade, a

capitalist sector of the economy began to appear alongside the agrarian and guild-based economy of the Middle Ages. With capitalism, there appeared a new, "modern" attitude to life, geared to the "rational" pursuit of material gain. Partly in order to serve the needs of this new economy, and helped by its ability to mobilize resources and create markets, late medieval inventors came up with a series of world-changing devices: three-masted sailing ships, firearms, printing presses, and mechanical clocks. Though all these inventions built on inspirations from Islam and the Far East, for the first time they gave Europe technological leadership among the civilizations of the world. Feudal methods of government were made obsolete by money and credit, new infantry weapons overthrew the battlefield supremacy of mounted knights, and *cannon* made noble castles vulnerable, as well as being too expensive for anyone but major rulers to afford. The governments of the Italian city-states provided examples of efficient organization and the competitive pursuit and use of power, which the rulers of western European countries followed as they began to build up centralized governments and armed forces responsible to themselves alone.

Finally, increased contact with the Far East, the renewed Muslim threat, the capitalist pursuit of profit, and the competitive ambitions of powerful western European rulers led on to the single most momentous undertaking of late medieval Europe: the exploration of new routes to distant continents. The explorers not only succeeded in their original goal of finding new routes to the Far East; they also came into contact with the civilizations of the New World, which were less advanced than those of the Old World and therefore easy to conquer. The capitalists of western Europe gained worldwide profits, and the region's governments won worldwide power. The Christianity of western Europe, both Catholic and Protestant, became a worldwide religion. And Western civilization broke out of its European homeland to spread its influence across the globe.

DISSOLUTION OF THE MEDIEVAL SYNTHESIS

The forces that dissolved the old synthesis and created the new were varied but related to one another. When a change began in one sphere of human affairs, it was reinforced by changes in others. The primary force appears to have been economic. In the thirteenth century, out of the bustling towns and cities and the increasingly populous and productive countryside that had developed since 1000, a truly commercial and capitalist economy was emerging. New social ranks appeared, serfdom grew obsolete in western Europe, and the entire class structure became more fluid. The bonds of caste and group were thereby loosened, and the freedom of the *individual* was enlarged. With economic and social change came political change.

When stability and prosperity returned to Europe, monarchs found that they could exert a larger measure of direct authority over their kingdoms. Feudal states gradually gave way to centralized national states.

With the world changing in so many ways, ethical and philosophical views were bound to change, too. In the sharpened competition for wealth and power, the medieval ideals of asceticism, poverty, and humility were thrust aside by the "modern" aspirations for pleasure, money, and status. In formal thought, the scholastic approach to knowledge was challenged and discredited (pp. 299–302). (We will discuss the new view of human nature and its expressions in philosophy, art, and literature in chapter 8.)

The breakup of the medieval pattern proceeded, during most of the transitional period, in a gradual, undramatic fashion. Many of the changes were hardly noticed when they took place, and few people could tell where they were leading. But one change was observed by all: the seamless garment of Western religious faith was torn by the Protestant movements of the sixteenth century. These movements set in fairly late in the course of the medieval dissolution, and they served to convince reflective men and women that a new age had indeed arrived. For, if the Catholic Church had been the core of western European life, its division confirmed the end of the traditional synthesis. We will consider forces underlying this religious upheaval in chapter 9. In the present chapter we will examine the economic, social, geographic, and political factors that changed the face of Western civilization.

The Calamitous Fourteenth Century

Deep-running historical currents were already transforming European institutions by 1300, but the events of the years that followed hastened the process. The fourteenth century was a time of turmoil and disaster, comparable to the late fifth century B.C. in Greece (pp. 98–101) and the turbulent third century A.D. in Italy (pp. 149–151). Social unrest, growing out of the deprivations and indignities that the common people had suffered for centuries, grew acute in western Europe after 1300. Revolts by peasants against their feudal masters had occurred at various times and places throughout the Middle Ages, but they had always been crushed by the feudal nobles. In the fourteenth century, however, social unrest threatened the very foundations of the political and economic order.

The trouble started with the weather. Early in the century Arctic cold and heavy rains swept across Europe, flooding farmlands and shortening the growing season. For the three preceding centuries, the population had grown, and more and more land had been taken under the plow to feed it (pp. 257–260, 262). But now there was no more wild territory that could be turned into productive fields, and the available farmland had reached the limit of what it could produce with the methods in use at the time. The combination of bad weather and population increase that strained the limits of resources led to widespread hunger and starvation. (These natural disasters are a reminder that all societies live within a delicate ecological balance. A climatic shift of a few degrees can upset that balance, as it did in

7-1 Manuscript illustration showing the crushing of an uprising in fourteenth-century France. A town has been captured, and foot soldiers hack at rebels and throw them into a river; mounted knights patrol the streets, and noble ladies look on.

the fourteenth century.) The resulting famine had further effects: lower human resistance to disease, severe dislocations in agriculture and commerce, and fiercer competition among individuals, classes, and nations.

In 1320 a peasant uprising started in northern France. Its leaders expressed the grievances of the poor and a religious hope that the lowly would overthrow the highborn and establish a "Christian commonwealth" of equality for all. Farmers and poor people from the cities joined excited mobs as they made their way across the countryside (Fig. 7-1). The rebels seized arms, attacked castles and monasteries, and destroyed tax records. As tales of atrocities circulated, the nobility and the clergy grew alarmed. Finally, after Pope John XXII had condemned the outlaws, mounted bands of knights took to the field and ruthlessly slaughtered the weary peasants. But the resentment and anger of the poor persisted.

Another uprising occurred about a generation later, in 1358. It was called the "Jacquerie," from Jacques, the popular catch-name for a peasant. Kindled in a village near Paris, the revolt spread like wildfire across the country. At its peak, perhaps one hundred thousand men, women, and children were on the rampage.

Though better equipped and organized, the Jacquerie suffered the same fate as the earlier rebels. For two months both the peasants and the avenging nobles engaged in burning, looting, and killing.

France was not alone in her ordeal. During the century similar uprisings occurred all over Europe. In England the Peasants' Revolt of 1381 followed the pattern of the Jacquerie. Marked by murders and burnings, it was finally crushed by the ferocity and treachery of the nobles and the king.

Adding to these miseries were the drawn-out struggles between the English and French monarchs. (This prolonged conflict, which began in 1338, was later referred to as the Hundred Years' War.) Though combats were limited mainly to the noble class, they brought ruin to the farms and towns of France, the principal battlefield. The long-term political consequences of the Hundred Years' War will be discussed later in this chapter (pp. 347–349); the widespread physical damage was the immediate and most distressing result.

The cruelest blow of all to fourteenth-century Europeans was the bubonic plague, or Black Death, which struck in 1348. The plague was part of a pandemic (universal) outbreak of the disease that had begun in the Far East about 1340, and spread in a few years throughout the Eastern hemisphere. The infection, which is carried by black rats and their fleas, had already devastated much of Europe in the sixth century (p. 215). For several centuries thereafter, there were no massive outbreaks; but now the rats carried the plague to all parts of the continent and to the British Isles. Having had slight prior contact with the infection, people were highly susceptible, and their capacity for resistance had been weakened by widespread malnutrition. The first symptoms of the disease appear as ugly sores, or buboes, at the spot of the flea bite. Fever and chills follow, along with dark spots on the skin. (Since the dark spots usually precede death, the pestilence came to be known as the "Black Death.") After the primary form of the plague has become established in humans, it can be transmitted directly by breath to other humans. This second form, which invades the lungs, is even more lethal than the first and causes death within a few days.

The plague was at its height during its first two years and then continued to flare up from time to time. It killed perhaps a quarter of all the inhabitants of Europe during the fourteenth century (twenty-five million out of a population of one hundred million). In addition to its toll in death and suffering, the plague had drastic economic, social, and psychological effects. *Death* became a universal obsession. Many people interpreted the plague as a punishment from God that called for severe personal penitence; some thought the end of the world was at hand.

By the close of the century the effects of the plague had diminished, and life returned more or less to normal. But the medieval patterns of society had been severely strained by the plague and by the other catastrophes that had struck the people of Europe. The bonds holding people and institutions together were close to the breaking point: between serf and lord, journeyman and master, noble and king, lay person and priest, priest and pope. The bonds held, for yet awhile. But new forces, new ideas, and new relationships were on the rise; with the gradual recovery of European strength and confidence, the new ways would shortly overcome the old.

EASTERN EUROPE: WESTERN COLONISTS, ASIAN INVADERS

The crisis of the later Middle Ages affected eastern Europe even more severely than western Europe. Whereas the western countries mastered the crisis and rebuilt European civilization, those of the east never completely recovered. Instead, they took on the role in European civilization that they have retained down to the present day: that of "junior partner" to the western European countries and of bulwark against threats to Europe from further east.

The differences between western and eastern Europe were partly religious and cultural, originating in the divergences between Roman and Byzantine civilization and the schism between the Latin (Catholic) and Greek (Orthodox) churches (pp. 183–184, 312–313). The capture of Constantinople by western crusaders in 1204 led to more than two hundred years of chaos in the Balkans, a region that Byzantium had earlier dominated, but which the Latin Empire of Constantinople and the restored Byzantine Empire after 1261 were both too feeble to control (p. 246). Serbia and Bulgaria, both already important earlier in the Middle Ages (p. 246), reappeared for a time as powerful independent kingdoms, but eventually they disintegrated as a result of disputes over the succession to their thrones and rivalries among their nobles. Other rulers held power over less prominent Balkan ethnic groups—the Slavic Bosnians, and the non-Slavic Albanians and Romanians (p. 219)—which thereby took their first steps toward independent nationhood. Meanwhile on the outskirts of the Balkans, powerful neighbors—Venice, Hungary, and most menacingly, the Turks (pp. 327–328) took advantage of the situation to gain power and influence in the region.

Yet the spiritual and cultural hold of Byzantium over the Orthodox peoples of eastern Europe was as strong as ever. The most successful Bulgarian and Serbian rulers took the title of *tsar* or "emperor" (p. 246), surrounded themselves with Byzantine pomp and ceremony, and dreamed of ruling in Constantinople. They established national "Bulgarian" or "Serbian" Orthodox (as opposed to "Greek Orthodox") churches, and appointed "autocephalous" (independent) patriarchs to run these churches. They built splendid cathedrals and monasteries, where glowingly colored frescoes and icons (holy pictures) seemed to give believers a glimpse of the other world, and where monks wrote chronicles and lives of saints in the ancient Slavic religious language and the Cyrillic alphabet used by all the national Orthodox churches (p. 220). In many ways, the late Middle Ages were the golden age of Slavic Orthodox culture.

As a result of the disaster of 1204, this flourishing Orthodox world now viewed the Catholic Church as an enemy and a traitor to Christianity. The Bulgarian, Serbian, and restored Byzantine rulers sometimes struck bargains with the popes, submitting to papal religious authority in return for Western military and political support. But these bargains never lasted, for suspicion and hatred of Rome were firmly anchored in the hearts of the Orthodox faithful. Thus, the estrangement between the Catholic and the Orthodox churches hardened into bitter religious hostility.

The divergence between western and eastern Europe was also social, economic, and political. With the rise of a dynamic urban trading and industrial economy from 1000 on, western Europe forged ahead of the east. While the ruling families of western Europe came to accept the principle of primogeniture (p. 242) in the eleventh and twelfth centuries, those of eastern Europe continued to divide their dominions among numerous heirs until the end of the Middle Ages, thereby weakening their dynastic power. Europe came to be divided into a group of stronger and more highly developed western countries and a group of weaker and less highly developed eastern countries. The second group included not only the Orthodox countries but also Catholic Poland and Hungary, and the eastern territories of the Holy Roman Empire (map, p. 243). This division has persisted down to the present day.

In the Middle Ages, the western countries gained many advantages from the presence of a group of less advanced countries on their eastern borders. For western Europe, the east provided territories for colonization and emigration, and sources of foodstuffs and raw materials. In the twelfth and thirteenth centuries, crusaders from the Holy Roman Empire conquered many still pagan tribes on the southern and eastern shores of the Baltic Sea (map, p. 243). Throughout these eastern borderlands of the Holy Roman Empire and on into Poland and Hungary, masses of German colonists moved in, clearing the land for agriculture and founding new towns and cities—a migration that nationalist-minded German historians centuries later christened the "Drive to the East." Along with the migration of Germans, there was also a mass movement of Jews, fleeing eastward from western European anti-Semitism (p. 314).

In the newly colonized territories, and throughout much of the rest of northeastern Europe, farmers grew grain and flax, and lumberjacks logged timber, for export westward. The towns of eastern Europe functioned as trading outposts of the important German coastal cities that headed the dominant commercial organization of northern Europe, the Hanse (p. 330). Farther south, the commerce of Hungary, Serbia, Bulgaria, the Byzantine Empire, and the Black Sea regions (map, p. 246) was controlled in the same way by the Italian city-states (pp. 341–344).

Sometimes this western expansion into eastern Europe led to conflict. For more than two hundred years, the rulers of Poland vied for control of the Baltic coastlands with the Teutonic Knights, a group of crusading warriors that had led the German conquest of the pagan tribes of that region. The kings of Hungary likewise contested the hold of Venice on the eastern shores of the Adriatic Sea, Hungary's main outlet for seaborne commerce. In Bohemia, which was inhabited mainly by the Slavic Czechs, resentment at German immigration, along with religious disputes, led eventually to a bitter internal and international struggle, the Hussite Wars (pp. 410–411).

But these conflicts were exceptional. So long as the rulers of eastern Europe did not feel directly threatened with the loss of their local power and independence, they usually accepted western immigration and commercial domination. The kings of Bohemia, Poland, and Hungary welcomed and even invited Germans and Jews to settle in their countries, for the sake of the increased prosperity —and increased tax revenues—that the newcomers brought. Noble landowners were glad to supply foodstuffs and raw materials to the West; and with the kings weakened by the division of their territories and family disputes, it was often the nobles who wielded the greatest share of power. Their main concern was to ensure that they and not the peasants would pocket the profits to be made from trade with the West, and that (with far fewer peasants on the land following the Black Death), enough labor would be available to grow the profitable crops. For this reason, from the fifteenth century onward, the nobles of eastern Europe began to reimpose the burdens of serfdom, which had earlier been loosened there as in the western countries (p. 262). As a result, from the eastern territories of the Holy Roman Empire through Poland, Hungary, and on into Russia, serfdom persisted down to the nineteenth century (pp. 416–417, 461, 480–481, 544, 625).

In these ways, the government system and the social structure of the eastern countries began to diverge from those of western Europe. In the East, the ordinary person remained unfree, and the nobles retained a great deal of governing power in their own hands. Moreover, in eastern Europe social differences were also ethnic. In any particular region, the peasants belonged to one ethnic group, and the townspeople to other groups—usually German, Jewish, and in the Balkans also Greek—and it was not unusual for the nobles and rulers to belong to yet another ethnic group. In the Middle Ages, eastern Europe was on the whole more tolerant of ethnic and religious diversity than western Europe. But in modern times, under the impact of religious, nationalist, and class ideologies of western European origin—combined, in the Balkans, with the lasting effects of Turkish conquest (pp. 332–334)—eastern Europe would be torn by savage strife.

There was another important difference between eastern and western Europe: the eastern countries, unlike the western ones, were constantly exposed to Asiatic attack, for the increasingly advanced nomadic peoples of the steppes (pp. 54–55) were an ever more formidable threat. This threat reached its height in the thirteenth century when a pagan nomadic people from the Far East, the Mongols under Genghis Khan, built an empire that stretched from China to Europe. Between 1237 and 1240, Genghis' grandson Batu Khan devastated much of eastern Europe and conquered Russia. It was not long before the Mongol empire broke up, but Russia's ancient capital city of Kiev and most of the country's southern territories (present-day Ukraine) remained under the rule of the Tartars, a Muslim people allied with the Mongols. The northern regions, however, were held by native Russian vassals of the Tartars, most prominent among whom were the rulers of the city and surrounding territory (principality) of Moscow. Over the generations, even while acknowledging Tartar overlordship, Moscow extended its power over most of northern Russia. The new state was in close contact with the Byzantine-influenced Slavs of the Balkans, and shared in their flourishing religious and cultural life; but its rulers already controlled far more people and territory than the Bulgarian and Serbian monarchs who so proudly called themselves "tsars." Eventually, the Russian rulers would take—and keep—that title (pp. 458–459).

Meanwhile, another Asiatic empire was forming that would be not much smaller than that of the Mongols and last for far longer—that of the Turks. By origin yet another nomadic people of the steppes, the Turks had entered the Middle East and become Muslims in the ninth century (p. 309). Under the

Seljuk dynasty in the eleventh and twelfth centuries, they had already conquered most of Asia Minor. Then, in 1299, they came under the rule of a new dynasty, the Ottomans. Combining the warlike prowess of their nomadic ancestors with highly civilized diplomatic and governing skills, the Ottoman Turks expanded their empire by stages rather than all at once—and their first target was the chaotic and divided Balkans. They first landed in Europe in 1352, and quickly took over most of the limited territories that the restored empire of Byzantium still possessed. Within fifty years, the Bulgarians and Serbs were conquered, and the Albanians not much later. There followed Byzantium's final destruction. In 1453, the last outpost of the thousand-year-old empire, Constantinople itself, was taken. The city founded by Rome's first Christian emperor became the capital of the Ottoman sultan, and Justinian's cathedral of Hagia Sophia was turned into a mosque (pp. 155, 216–218). Outlying areas of the Balkans, such as Greece and the Romanian territories, still had to be "mopped up," but by 1500 the Turks were ready to turn their attention to new targets: Hungary, the lands surrounding the Black Sea, and a huge swath of Arab countries stretching right across the Middle East and North Africa. Once again, Christian Europe confronted a vast and expanding Islamic empire.

For the Christian peoples of the Balkans, life as subjects of this empire had its advantages. The Turks brought unity and peace such as the region had hardly ever known since Roman times, and with unity and peace came prosperity and low taxes. Trade flourished and towns burgeoned. Constantinople, where a shrunken population had lived amid abandoned buildings at the time it was conquered, grew to a size of three-quarters of a million, thereby regaining its long-lost position as Europe's largest city. Turkish rule even brought religious benefits, for the sultans, in accordance with Muslim principles (p. 223), tolerated other monotheistic religions. The Orthodox majority not only could practice their religion freely, but were sheltered by Turkish power from Catholic efforts to make them accept the supremacy of the pope. Furthermore, under Muslim law the Orthodox faithful constituted a separate community, governed in secular as well as spiritual matters by their own religious leaders. As a result, the Orthodox bishops, headed by the patriarch of Constantinople, actually wielded greater worldly power under the Turks than they had ever enjoyed under the Christian emperors. Jews, too, fleeing Christian persecution around 1500 in Spain and Portugal, found the Turkish-ruled Balkans a haven of tolerance, and were far more prosperous and respected there than those who fled western Europe for Poland and Hungary.

All the same, most non-Muslim ethnic groups in the Balkans now had a status of second-class citizens from which there was only one way of escape: conversion to Islam. Most noble landowners in the Bulgarian, Serb, Bosnian, and Albanian territories seem to have accepted the new religion so as to maintain their privileged status, and eventually became Turkish in language and customs as well. Christian heretics, who were numerous in Bosnia (p. 282), probably also converted in large numbers, without losing their ethnic identity; so did Albanians moving eastward, out of their mountainous homeland along the Adriatic Sea, into the nearby Serb-inhabited plain of Kosovo.

There was one non-Muslim group that was highly favored: the wealthy Greek upper class, which became almost a second ruling group of the Balkans under the Turks. Now that Venice was kept at bay by Turkish power, Greek merchants and bankers controlled the region's trade and finance, and provided men and ships for the Turkish merchant and war fleets. Likewise, Greek patriarchs and bishops held religious and worldly power throughout the Balkans, regardless of whether the local faithful were Greek or not. The other Orthodox nations of the Balkans now consisted almost entirely of peasants, with no leadership apart from their parish priests, and little literate culture except what survived in monasteries. What mainly kept their national identities alive was a flourishing oral culture of epics and folk tales, telling and retelling of the tragic events and defeated heroes of the struggle against Turkish conquest.

In all these ways, new religious and national divisions, coupled with inward-looking ethnic identities and long memories of defeats to be avenged, grew up throughout the Balkans. When Turkish rule grew weak and oppressive in the eighteenth and nineteenth centuries, and finally disappeared early in the twentieth century, this mixture would flare into frequent murderous conflicts.

Throughout the centuries of Mongol and Turkish expansion, the western European countries on the whole left eastern Europe to its fate. The popes generally strove for friendship with the pagan Mongols, in hopes of converting them to Latin Christianity and turning them against the Muslims. Such western help as came to the Balkans against the Turks was generally too little and too late—and was usually coupled with highly unwelcome demands that Orthodox rulers and their subjects submit to the pope. Up to the end of the Middle Ages, what prevented the invaders from advancing still further into Europe was above all the huge size of their empires: both the Mongols and the Turks found their territories difficult to control, and they had to fight wars on many other fronts besides Europe. Later, in the sixteenth century, powerful central and eastern European rulers emerged who mounted effective resistance to the Asiatic conquerors (pp. 353, 458–460). Thus, with little effort of their own, the western countries were insulated from attacks from the east as they pursued the innovations that would create modern Western civilization.

THE NEW ECONOMY

We have already pointed out that the rise of trade and towns was a crucial development of the eleventh and twelfth centuries (pp. 262–269). But from 1200 onward European commerce began to take on a new look. Medieval guilds and merchants had generally operated within limited areas and had been subject to local regulation (pp. 268–269). The system fostered the growth of trade and industry while Europe was still relatively backward, but by 1200 its very success was beginning to reveal its limitations. The masters of the workshops paid money wages and hoped to make a profit from their enterprises, but most prices were fixed, and the scale of business was small. As a result, the master's profit was seldom large, and whatever he made usually went to the upkeep of his shop and the care of his family. Though capital was used in trade and industry, very little capital *surplus* could be built up. The *entrepreneur* (organizer of a business) still thought primarily in terms of "production for use" in a limited market; he had not yet grasped the idea of the unlimited accumulation and expansion of capital. The *true capitalist* had not yet emerged.

The Birth of Modern Capitalism

Italian merchants had taken the lead in the revival of trade in the eleventh century (pp. 264–265), and in the thirteenth century they pioneered the development of capitalism. They dominated the profitable trade of the Mediterranean, and many of them made quick fortunes in their dealings. Finding that they could not spend all their profits immediately, they hit upon the idea of *reinvesting* the surplus.

This novel idea made it possible for the successful trader to launch new, more ambitious enterprises. Soon he was no longer traveling about as an ordinary merchant but was minding his account books at home as a "capitalist." He directed his energies to extracting profits from his varied enterprises and reinvesting them to gain *more* profits. Thus emerged the features that have characterized the "capitalist system" for the past five centuries: its boundless profit-seeking and its dynamic spirit.

For merchants to accumulate really substantial capital surpluses, they had to expand their trading activities constantly. What the Italians achieved as the middlemen between Europe and the Orient, the merchants of the port cities of Germany achieved in the Baltic Sea area. They found that by pooling their resources they could build fleets and win joint trading privileges abroad, and by the fourteenth century, the leading towns of northern Germany had formed an effective commercial league (the *Hanse*). The cities of the Hanseatic League monopolized the foreign trade of northern Germany and set up outlets in the trading centers of Russia, Poland, Norway, England, and the Low Countries. From these far-flung outposts, rich profits flowed in to the capitalists of northern Germany (p. 326).

The merchants of the Low Countries prospered, too. The wharves of Antwerp and Bruges saw a steady stream of Italian ships carrying oriental spices and silks, and vessels from the Baltic loaded with furs, timber, and herring. The industries of England and the German Rhineland also sent their products into the Low Countries. By the fifteenth century a truly international commerce had developed—extensive enough to provide for the accumulation of profit surpluses and for the growth of a capitalist class.

Innovations in Business Organization

The new leaders of enterprise scrapped many of the traditional methods of doing business. In the eleventh and twelfth centuries, the masters of each guild, collectively, had served as its directing force; and within a framework of rules, individual masters had run their own shops. After 1200, several industries cast off the shackles of the guilds. Still, entrepreneurs found that they could seldom go it alone. Commerce was becoming more extensive and complex, requiring a pooling of capital and of managerial talent. Gradually the *partnership* came into favor as a unit of business organization. A special form of partnership, the family firm, was the most common. A group of relatives could best handle matters demanding secrecy and mutual trust and could assure the continuance of the enterprise.

The displacement of guild control is best illustrated by the woolens industry, in which the traditional association of master weavers, journeymen, and apprentices had disappeared in most areas by 1400. The industry was taken over by enterprising merchants, who bought the raw wool and put it out to semiskilled laborers for processing—first to spinners and then to weavers, dyers, and cutters in succession. The workers were paid by the piece or by measure, but ownership of the materials stayed with the merchants. They sold the finished cloth (or garments) in the international market at whatever price they could get.

The wool merchants thus reaped the profits of both industry and commerce. They paid the laborers at a low rate and permitted them no say in the conduct of the business. Moreover, the laborers were forbidden by law to organize or strike. This "putting-out" or "domestic" system was the principal mode of production in early modern Europe. It destroyed the close relationship between master and journeyman that had existed in the medieval guilds. It made profit the sole concern of the entrepreneur and diminished the worker's sense of creativity. The antagonisms that grew up between these entrepreneurs and the workers foreshadowed the fierce conflicts that were to mark the later industrial world.

The Rise of Banking and Bankers

As Europe moved from a largely self-sufficient economy to an economy geared to trade, the old techniques of exchange and finance proved inadequate. Relatively little money had circulated in the early Middle Ages; most exchange was by barter. From the thirteenth century onward the supply of coins grew steadily. However, the expansion of enterprise depended not so much on money itself as on new instruments of exchange and credit.

Perhaps the most important substitute for money payments was the *bill of exchange*, which was similar to a modern bank draft or check. A merchant with branch offices in various countries usually made a side business of selling drafts that were payable by his firm in some other city. A Venetian who bought linen from Antwerp, for example, would find it inconvenient to ship money to the Low Countries every time he placed an order. Instead, he could go to a Venetian firm that did business in Antwerp and purchase a draft payable by its office there. The seller of the linen in Antwerp was perfectly willing to accept this bill of exchange, for he knew he could collect on it in his own city. Rather than demand cash for it, however, he would probably endorse the bill and use it as a means of payment in a later business transaction.

The first bankers were successful merchants who had accumulated a profit surplus and who wished to reinvest it. They found that the business of moneylending,

7-2   Manuscript illustration showing fourteenth-century Italian bankers doing business. At right, money is being counted; at left, the manager of the bank listens to a report from one of his clerks.

though risky, could bring high returns. Commencing in the thirteenth century, large-scale moneylending became normal. It had been practiced in earlier times, but on a smaller scale—partly because the economy was not so prosperous, and partly because the Church condemned all interest-taking as usury (lending at an *excessive* rate). In consequence lending at interest had been done chiefly by Jews, whose faith did not forbid it. This particular role of the Jews no doubt contributed to the periodic anti-Semitic outbursts in Europe (pp. 313–314).

With the expansion of commerce, however, many people came to realize that lending was a useful and acceptable activity. The traditional argument against interest payments was based on a revulsion against taking high rates from individuals "in distress." But loans to businessmen engaged in profitable enterprises, or to kings and popes, were obviously of a different sort. These loans could be *productive,* and they exposed the lender to risks that justified some reward. Many theologians agreed that this kind of lending was not sinful, and the popes themselves were among the biggest borrowers. Consequently, small-scale Jewish moneylending came to be overtaken by large-scale Christian banking.

Italian merchants first moved into the banking business during the thirteenth century *(Fig. 7-2)*. In the next century Florence became the leading center of international finance. The Bardi and Peruzzi families, for example, advanced huge loans to Edward III, king of England. Later, Edward refused to repay the loans and thereby forced those families into bankruptcy. But in the fifteenth century a new house of bankers, the Medici, emerged in Florence. This family restored the financial power of the city and came to dominate its political and cultural life.

Banking spread north from Italy to the rest of Europe. Jacques Coeur, a French merchant who had made a fortune in trading with the Orient, was appointed royal treasurer by Charles VII, king of France (1439). Taking advantage of his position at the court, Coeur acquired extensive holdings in mines, lands, and workshops and thus became one of Europe's most powerful international bankers. He used his enormous wealth for the benefit of his family and built a palace worthy of a king in his native town of Bourges.

The wealthiest and most famous banker of the period was Jacob Fugger of Augsburg. Southern Germany, in the fifteenth and sixteenth centuries, was sharing in the prosperity of growing commerce—and had the added resource of copper and silver mines. Some years earlier, capital had been put into the mining industry for the first time, permitting miners to dig more deeply and more efficiently with improved tools. The leading entrepreneurs of the industry soon took control of smelting and metalworking as well as mining, concentrating the direction of all operations in a few hands. The workers, who formerly had been independent producers, now became voiceless employees of the capitalists.

The Fugger family drew immense wealth from these and other enterprises and channeled their surplus into banking. Jacob pushed the family business beyond Germany by opening branch offices in the major commercial centers of Europe. He ventured into buying, selling, and speculating in all kinds of goods, and he provided financial services to merchants, high clergy, and rulers. One of his more spectacular operations was to lend half a million gold coins to Charles I, king of Spain. Charles wanted to "buy" the office of Holy Roman emperor through payments to the imperial Electors (pp. 352–353). A good capitalist, Jacob was also a good *philanthropist*. He and his brothers built, as evidence of their piety and generosity, an attractive group of dwellings for the "righteous" poor of Augsburg. It still stands, near the center of the city, as a memorial to the Fuggers' wealth and charity.

THE IMPACT ON SOCIAL STRUCTURE AND VALUES

The forces released by the rise of capitalism disrupted western European society and economic life by undermining the guilds and weakening the manorial system (pp. 260–262, 268–269). The customs associated with manorialism had seemed almost unbreakable, even in the later Middle Ages; they survived long after the reasons for their existence had vanished. Even so, important features of manorialism were soon altered by the capitalistic economy.

The most far-reaching change, which affected all relationships between nobles and peasants, was the substitution of *money* for payments in goods or services. Earlier in the Middle Ages the lord of the manor had received, as rent, a share of the *crops* from his peasants' strips. In addition, the serfs had been required to cultivate the lord's "demesne," the land reserved exclusively for his benefit. This forced labor was not very efficient, however, and the lord himself usually cared little about better land management. Toward the close of the medieval period, the nobles often found it advantageous to rent out their demesnes to *free tenants*, who were now able to sell their produce at nearby markets and pay their rents in cash (pp. 262,

265). The feudal landlords had also been entitled to extra labor in return for the serfs' use of their "common" fields and woodlands (p. 259). This service, too, was gradually converted into money payments. The serfs preferred this arrangement because it released them from extra work; the lords preferred it because they could usually find cheap day labor and still have cash left over from the serfs' payments.

The next step was the emancipation (freeing) of the serfs. Now that the nobles no longer depended on forced labor, they were willing to grant the serfs freedom. In most instances, the freedman remained on the land as a tenant, and in exchange for his freedom paid his lord a lump sum or extra rent. But in so doing he normally lost his former hereditary right to stay on the land, which meant that he could be ousted when his lease expired.

By 1500 serfdom had disappeared from England and had become a rarity in western Europe. The medieval lord, with his rights to the produce and services of the peasantry, had become a capitalist landowner living off his *rents*. Though many of the great estates remained intact, the pattern of relationships had been changed. In short, the spirit of commercial enterprise had spread to the countryside. Merchants began to buy estates and play the role of landed aristocrats, while intermarriage between bourgeois and landed families further blurred the old distinctions. Serfs were becoming freemen, merchants were becoming landholders, and noblemen were becoming capitalists. (The different development in eastern Europe, where trade and capitalism actually strengthened the bonds of serfdom, is discussed on pp. 326–327.)

This social change, like other significant changes in history, brought loss as well as gain. The sense of personal security and community solidarity declined, but no longer was one class arbitrarily subjected to another. Equality of opportunity did not arise immediately, for the new circles of privilege were tightly drawn; but there was greater freedom of movement, both upward and downward.

Dislocations in society led to dislocations in ethics. Capitalism has been called the major heresy of the Middle Ages—by those who see it as opposed to some of the central teachings of Jesus. The merchants and bankers of the early modern period made profit their immediate and constant concern; they separated commercial dealings from Christian ethics. In their desire for gain they differed only in degree from the landlords and rulers of medieval times. The latter, however, could cover their activities under the cloak of feudal and royal rights and customs; the upstart bourgeois had no such camouflage at hand. Materialism came to be openly approved and systematized, leading to the overturn of traditional values. Pride, envy, and greed—branded by the Church as cardinal sins—were now regarded as the mainsprings of economic life. The religious ideals of meditation, prayer, and giving were overtaken by the goals of hard work, punctuality, and saving.

One might suppose that the Church would have mobilized its forces against this challenge to its ancient ideals. With its widespread organization and its control over public opinion, it could certainly have done so. But it no longer wanted to. Though it continued to profess its attachment to spiritual goals, the Church itself had in large measure succumbed to materialism. Nowhere was this more apparent than in the top ranks of the clergy. The popes, like almost everyone else in

Europe, were dazzled by the new riches and became obsessed with wealth, elegance, and power.

The active carriers of the new morality were the bourgeois, or middle class. Some members of this class, like Jacques Coeur and Jacob Fugger, attained high levels of influence, equal to that of counts or princes. The position of the class as a whole, however, advanced much more slowly. The bourgeois enjoyed one long-run advantage in their competition for power with the landed nobility: they controlled the *movable* assets of the economy (commodities, ships, and money), and these assets were growing in value, while the nobility controlled the *fixed* assets (mainly land), and these assets were declining in value. Money, furthermore, was infinitely more flexible than land, and with it the middle class could buy the goods and services that secured influence.

Several centuries were to pass before the bourgeois attained social dominance. The nobility maneuvered to retain its inherited privileges, and the weight of tradition slowed the advance of the middle class. But from the sixteenth century onward bourgeois ideals had a growing influence on society as a whole. Bourgeois "virtues" included, in addition to the habits of work and thrift, the qualities of reliability and inventiveness. These competed successfully against the "romantic" ideals of the nobility: physical prowess, courage, and chivalry. Middle-class ideas, dress, and manners, by the middle of the nineteenth century, would become the main standards of Western civilization.

THE NEW TECHNOLOGY

The rise of capitalism, like the rise of trade and towns earlier in the Middle Ages (pp. 265–266), went hand in hand with technical progress. Now, however, increased contact, both peaceful and warlike, with the intercontinental civilization of Islam exposed Europe to the often superior technology not only of the Arabs but of the Far East as well (pp. 226–227). Like many earlier peoples, the Europeans adapted and improved on advances that they learned from other civilizations, and in this case the result was a whole series of world-changing technical innovations. Sea transport, warfare, book production, the measurement of time—all were revolutionized by the Europe of the late Middle Ages.

One of the basic needs of growing medieval trade, in an age when transport was far more efficient by water than by land, was for reliable methods of navigation—for sailors at sea to be able to know where they were, and what direction they must sail in to get to the ports for which they were bound. Building on geographical techniques developed by the Greeks and transmitted and improved on by Arab scientists, European mapmakers began to produce accurate charts of the Atlantic and Mediterranean coastlines. New instruments of navigation came into use. One was the north-pointing *magnetic compass*, of Chinese invention, which helped the navigator set and hold the course of his ship. Another was the astrolabe, a sighting instrument devised by Arab astronomers, which enabled the navigator to calculate his latitude (his position north or south of the equator) by determining

7-3   Sixteenth-century engraving showing a carrack, the "workhorse" ship of European overseas exploration. The two forward masts carry square sails for speed, and the mast nearest the stern carries a triangular sail for maneuverability; the vessel is armed with cannon along the sides and at the stern.

the height of the sun and stars above the horizon. All these aids to navigation were in common use on the seaways of Europe by the early fifteenth century. Soon they would help guide sailors across oceans to distant continents.

Growing trade also needed ships that were large, strong, and easy to handle. Shipwrights in Venice and Genoa, whose craft had to be able to carry goods to and from western Europe, combined features of ship design from both the Mediterranean and the stormier Atlantic waters. They borrowed the stout hulls and square, wind-catching sails of Atlantic ships, and the triangular sails of the Arabs (with whom they shared the Mediterranean) which made for easier maneuvering. The result was a new kind of vessel, the *carrack*—the first type of three-masted sailing ship, which appeared about 1400 and would soon become the "workhorse" of overseas exploration (*Fig. 7-3*). These ships had a combination of speed, maneuverability, and seaworthiness that was unmatched by the vessels of the most advanced non-European civilizations. And eventually, three-masted ships would also become unbeatable fighting machines, once they were equipped with another late medieval invention—cannon.

The Chinese invention of gunpowder first became known to Europeans in the twelfth century, when Christian warriors in North Africa and Spain found their Muslim foes using the quick-burning substance against them as an incendiary (fire-starting) weapon. The idea of confining the powder so that it would actually explode, and using the force of the explosion to hurl a projectile, seems to have been a European one. At any rate, "fire-pots" or "tubes" (Latin, *canones*) are first mentioned in Italian documents of the 1320s. Up to around 1400, cannon were too small, inaccurate, slow to operate, and dangerous to their users to make much real difference to warfare, but in the fifteenth century improvements came quickly. Makers of church bells began using their knowledge of large-scale bronze casting methods (p. 265) to manufacture guns that were solid and safe to use. Ironworks started turning out cannonballs that were heavier in proportion to their size, more accurately spherical, and far quicker to make than stone ones. Carpenters devised wheeled gun carriages that made the weapons mobile and absorbed the recoil when they were fired. Water-powered hammermills (p. 265) were adapted to crush charcoal, sulfur, and dried animal droppings so as to produce gunpowder by the ton. Mathematicians tackled the problems of weight and motion involved in accurate aiming. By 1500, cannon could be relied on to smash any stone castle or town wall—let alone the wooden hulls of sailing ships—and scaled-down versions of the big weapons were beginning to appear, which were small and handy enough for a single soldier to load, aim, and fire.

European traders and warriors earlier in the Middle Ages had learned from the Muslims of peaceful as well as warlike Chinese inventions—most notably, of paper and of woodcut printing. Paper, made mainly from rags that were beaten to a pulp with water and various chemicals (p. 265), and then dried into sheets in special frames, was much faster and cheaper to make than parchment (the skin of lambs or calves), the traditional European writing material. Likewise, printing with woodcut blocks was faster than writing out books by hand. The process involved carving a whole page of text and illustrations in mirror image out of the surface of a single block of wood, then smearing the block with ink, and pressing a sheet of paper onto the block with a roller. By 1400, small books and items such as playing cards (an Arab pastime that had spread to Europe) were commonly produced in this way. But woodcut printing was an expensive way to produce large books with a great deal of text, since hundreds of blocks had to be painstakingly chiseled and then thrown away when the job was finished. Supposing, however, that each individual letter was made in mirror image on its own tiny block, many such blocks could then be put together to form the text of a page, and taken apart and reassembled any number of times to make new pages. The printing process would become fast and cheap, even for the largest books.

This had already occurred to printers in China and Korea, but the idea had never caught on there—partly because of the large number of characters in Far Eastern writing systems, which made it hard to manage all the different blocks. When the same idea struck a businessman in the German city of Mainz, Johann

Gutenberg, he had the basic advantage of belonging to a civilization that used an alphabetic writing system with relatively few characters (p. 45). Even so, it took twenty years of tinkering and much technical wizardry to put the idea into practice. Gutenberg's greatest inspirations were to make the tiny single-letter blocks ("types") out of metal, so that they could be quickly cast in molds rather than laboriously carved; and to adapt the centuries-old olive or grape press (p. 131) to apply quick and accurate pressure to the paper lying on the ink-smeared type. By about 1450 he had developed a reliable system of printing with "movable" (reusable) type.

The new method of printing, with its drastically reduced costs, for the first time made it possible to mass-produce books; and the international trading and credit networks of early capitalism enabled books to find a mass market. By 1500 there were more than a thousand printers at work in Europe, and nearly ten million books had been printed. The earliest printed books (incunabula or "cradle books," as they are called) were of excellent quality in type, paper, and binding. As the reading public grew and price competition in the mass market became more pressing, the general quality of printing declined. Still, the influence of the printed word was infinitely greater than that of the written word had been before. The spread of religious and cultural movements like Renaissance humanism and the Protestant Reformation, as well as the growth of powerful centralized governments with their need for law books and many kinds of standardized paperwork—all were helped along by the Gutenberg printing process. In the long run, it was the invention of movable type that made possible the free public libraries, universal education, and cheap newspapers and magazines of the modern world.

Along with printed books and firearms, the late Middle Ages also saw the introduction of history's first widely used automatically operating machine, the mechanical clock. The basic idea of the clock seems to have come from astrolabes, which used dials with revolving pointers as sighting devices to measure the motion of the sun, moon, and stars across the sky. Sometime late in the thirteenth century, inventors in various countries began tinkering with ways to make the pointer actually "imitate" these heavenly bodies—in particular the sun—by moving around the dial. Since the hours and days were reckoned by the motion of the sun, the effect would be that the motion of the pointer would measure the passage of time.

Of course, for this to happen, the pointer would have to be made to turn by itself. A falling weight, attached to a cord wound around a spindle, could provide the necessary turning power. But there would also have to be mechanisms to slow the weight's fall and "wind it up" again when there was no more cord left to unwind, and gearwheels to slow the turning motion still more, so that the pointer would move round the dial no more than once in a day. It seems to have been mechanically minded English monks, looking for improved ways of regulating their communities' complex daily routines of work and prayer (p. 198), who first came up with practicable solutions to these problems around 1300. But it was not long before the lives of townspeople, with their hours of work fixed by guilds or settled privately between capitalists and their employees, also came to be regulated by the new time-measuring machine. High in a tower of town hall or cathedral, it was visible to all as its hand (usually only one of them) moved, with no human intervention, in step with the movement of the sun itself; and all could hear its tones as, thanks to an improvement that was not long in coming, it struck the changing hours of the day.

In these ways, late medieval Europe took the first steps toward the modern age of automation, mass production, mass communications, and firearms. And already by the end of the Middle Ages, firearms and the new sailing ships were helping rulers to build powerful centralized governments, and sailors to explore and conquer across the world.

THE NEW POLITICS

Intimately bound up with economic evolution and expansion were new developments in the patterns of government. The fact that all classes of society now made payments in money, coupled with the rise of trade and banking, made it easier than before for rulers to mobilize the resources of their countries. They could collect rents from peasants on their personal landholdings (pp. 251, 333–334) like other landowners. They could levy tariffs on trade, or even get involved in commerce themselves. They could find ways to collect money from their subjects who lived on the lands of other lords, by way of national taxation. And if the money from all these sources fell short or was slow in coming in, wealthy bankers like the Bardi, the Peruzzi, or the Fuggers could come up with loans that were big enough to tide them over. With all this money available, rulers no longer had to rely on personal service from independent-minded vassals. Instead, they could do government business through officials who were bound to obey orders; and they could apply capitalist methods to warfare, making contracts with mercenary captains to supply trained soldiers complete with weapons.

In practice, these new methods were often no more efficient than those of feudalism. Most officials were not paid from the central government treasury, but were expected to charge the public fees which they put directly into their own pockets—a license for every kind of fraud and corruption. Military contractors might take the money but not provide the soldiers—or they might provide the soldiers but not get their money, in which case the soldiers would mutiny for lack of pay. But the new system did have one great advantage over feudalism: it put control of the government and the armed forces directly in the hands of the major rulers.

This growth of centralized government was also furthered by dramatic new developments in warfare (*Fig. 7-4*). Up to about 1300, mounted knights had been virtually invincible in battle against foot soldiers, and the castles of nobles had been difficult to capture, even with the aid of advanced stone-throwing machines (p. 265). So long as rulers needed knights to win battles and nobles could rely on their castles as safe refuges, neither the independence nor the lands of the feudal elite could be touched. But during the fourteenth and fifteenth centuries new weapons came into use that acted as "equalizers" between foot soldiers

7-4   Early sixteenth-century woodcut showing "state-of-the-art" warfare. In front, opposing masses of foot soldiers wielding pikes and halberds (axes on poles) have come to grips; where they meet, there is a grim "killing zone." Behind them, cannon are emplaced to bombard a walled town; to left of the town, more pikemen are shown leveling their weapons for the charge. At rear, armored knights charge against each other in the traditional way.

and horsemen. First was the longbow, which could penetrate the armor of knights and disable their horses at a distance. Then came the pike (a long spear against which horses would refuse to charge), and various types of axes, knives, and hooks on long poles, which could be wielded against men on horseback. Finally, by 1500 cannon were becoming mobile enough to be used in battle. As a result, battles were fought by *combined* forces of infantry, cavalry, and artillery, in which the infantry was the single most important arm. Meanwhile, cannon had revolutionized siege warfare by their ability to smash stone fortifications. In these ways, the feudal nobles lost their ability to win battles or to hold out in their castles. Furthermore, the new weapons, particularly siege cannon or cannon-armed ships, were so expensive that only governments, supported by taxation and loans, could afford them.

None of these developments deprived the nobles as a group of their leading place in society and government. Bourgeois officials and bankers usually invested their profits in land, and expected to be rewarded for their services to rulers with titles of nobility; nobles did not find it beneath their dignity to be royal officials or captains of mercenary soldiers. Sometimes, nobles were able to prevent the growth of centralized government, as happened in the Holy Roman Empire in the sixteenth century, or to roll it back for a time, as in France at the same period (pp. 352–353, 415–417, 455). But countries that remained without strong central government for any length of time were bound to become dominated by more powerful neighbors, or even to be swallowed up by them. From the late Middle Ages on, the successful European countries would be ones where feudalism, with its divisions into small, loosely centralized units, gave way to larger units of centralized power.

Absolutism in Practice: Italy

Ironically, it was in one of Europe's most politically fragmented regions that the new politics began, for the theory and practice of strong government were pioneered by the Italian *city-states*. It was here, too, that the modern practice of *diplomacy*, and the development of the body of law that would one day govern *international relations*, first began. A tribute to the early ambassadors is the portrait by Hans Holbein the Younger (*Fig. III-1*, p. 316).

One reason for the late unification of Italy was the long struggle that took place between the popes and the Holy Roman emperors. Each party wanted to win overlordship of the Italian peninsula and was willing to sacrifice the country and its people to gain that end. The state under the direct rule of the popes began with the Donation of Pepin (p. 232), which had granted the papacy a substantial portion of Italy. With Rome as its capital, the States of the Church cut across the peninsula, dividing it in two (*map*, p. 342). Lesser states were to rise and fall in Italy, and the Holy Roman emperors were often busy north of the Alps. But until near the close of the nineteenth century the pontiffs of the Roman Church proved to be constant foes of Italian *unity*.

Reinforcing the popes' opposition to unification were Italian "localism" and factionalism, forces deeply rooted in history. Like the ancient Greeks, the Italians identified strongly with the *city* of their region, rather than with any broader territorial unit. The city was near and familiar; it was worthy of reverence and sacrifice. Dante, for example, was more a Florentine than an Italian. Furthermore, in northern Italy, with its commercial and industrial wealth (pp. 264–265), many cities had the resources to defend and govern themselves. Thus, northern Italy had come out of the Middle Ages as a collection of rival city-states struggling against each other for survival and mastery. By the middle of the fifteenth century the stronger ones had expanded their boundaries, absorbing weaker neighbors. A kind of "balance of power" developed among the three leading city-states, Milan, Florence, and Venice, together with the States of the Church, and in the south of the peninsula, the feudal Kingdom of the Two Sicilies.

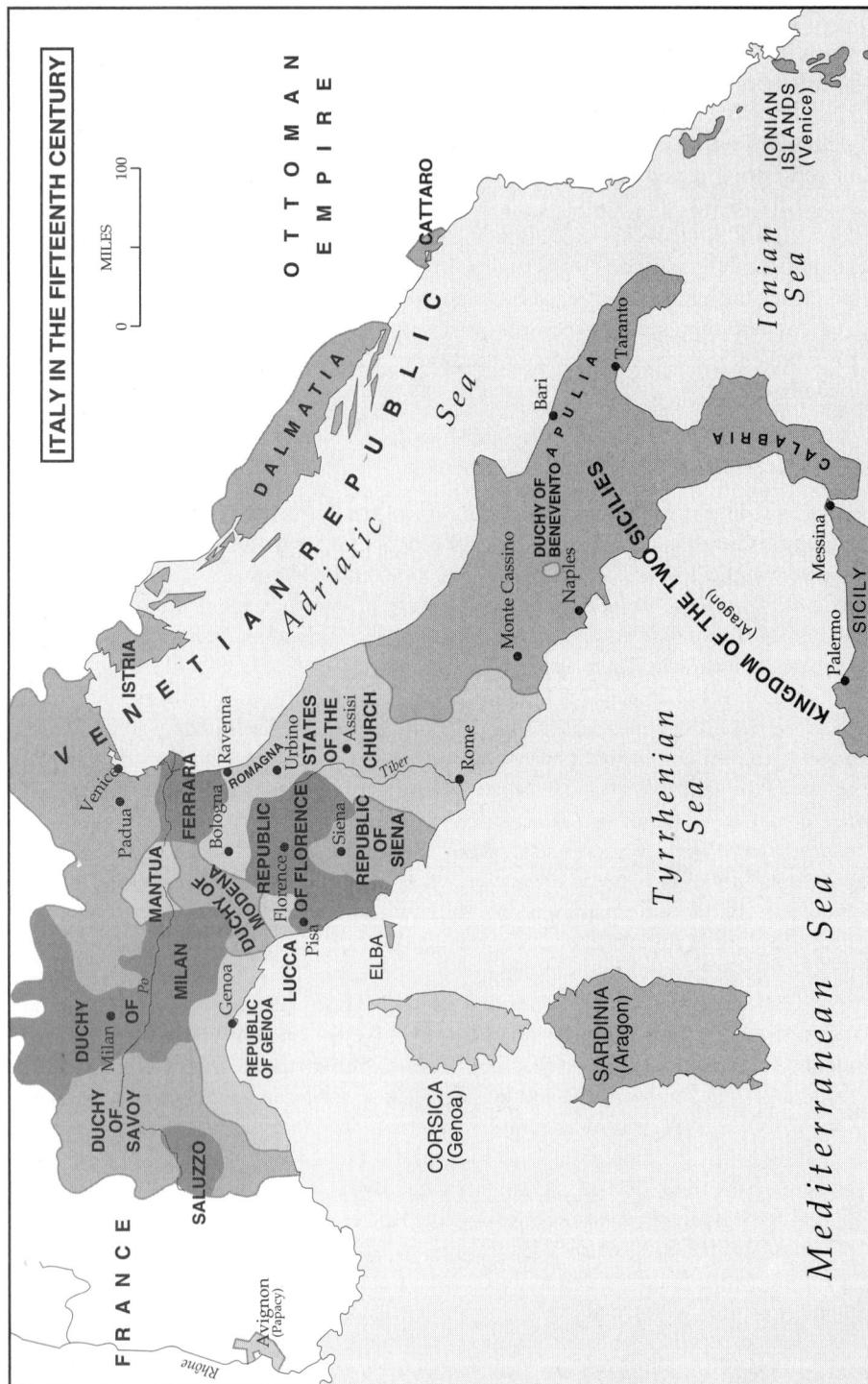

ITALY IN THE FIFTEENTH CENTURY

MILES
0   100

FRANCE

Rhône

Avignon
(Papacy)

SALUZZO

DUCHY
OF
SAVOY

DUCHY
OF
MILAN
Milan

Po
OF

REPUBLIC
OF GENOA

Genoa

LUCCA

DUCHY
OF
MODENA

MANTUA

FERRARA

Padua

Venice

ISTRIA

V E N E T I A N   R E P U B L I C

DALMATIA

OTTOMAN
EMPIRE

CATTARO

Adriatic Sea

Ravenna

ROMAGNA

Bologna

Urbino

STATES
OF THE
CHURCH

Assisi

REPUBLIC
OF FLORENCE

Florence

Pisa

Siena

REPUBLIC
OF
SIENA

ELBA

Tiber

Rome

Monte Cassino

DUCHY OF
BENEVENTO

Naples

PULIA

Bari

Taranto

KINGDOM OF THE TWO SICILIES
(Aragon)

CALABRIA

Ionian
Sea

IONIAN
ISLANDS
(Venice)

Messina

Palermo

SICILY

Tyrrhenian
Sea

CORSICA
(Genoa)

SARDINIA
(Aragon)

Mediterranean Sea

During these turbulent years significant changes occurred in the internal politics of the Italian cities. By the end of the thirteenth century most of the cities had won self-rule from the feudal nobility and had emerged as *sovereign* (independent) republics. Their citizens, however, proved incapable of stable self-government. The usual source of trouble was the rivalry among factions: the bankers and capitalists, rising rapidly in wealth, tried to take political control from the more numerous small merchants, shopkeepers, and artisans. At the same time, wealthy families competed with one another for special advantage.

Out of the struggle, which was marked by corruption and violence, political "strong men" had emerged during the fourteenth century. Sometimes they were invited to assume power by one or another of the factions looking for an alternative to chaos; sometimes they invited themselves. In the main they supported, and were supported by, the bankers and capitalists. The rest of the citizens submitted (except for occasional plots and uprisings), for they, too, preferred stability to the disorders of freedom.

The new rulers, generally known as "despots," had been schooled in the arena of Italian politics. Men of few illusions, they trusted no one, yielded nothing, and resorted to any means to advance their interests. They put power first. In the past, weak governments had given rise to rebellion and disorder; the despots used an iron hand to restore peace and economic well-being and relied on hired soldiers to preserve their power. Since there was no citizen militia to speak of during this period, professional warriors decided the conflicts within and between cities.

The soldiers were organized in armed bands led by enterprising captains (*condottieri*). The condottieri, in the spirit of the times, were a special sort of "merchant"—their merchandise was military service. With no sentimental attachments, they generally sold their services to the highest bidder. (The bankers usually made the best offers.) On occasion they turned down all bids and seized power for themselves. These hardened and crafty adventurers, thirstier for money than for blood, remained an unpredictable force in the politics of Italy.

One of the most famous was Francesco Sforza, who made himself ruler of Milan in 1450. Assuming the title of "duke," which a preceding despot had purchased from the Holy Roman emperor, he governed from his moated *castello* (fortress-palace). Under the shrewd policies of Sforza and his heirs, Milan enjoyed a half-century of peace and prosperity. In the fashion of the times, the despot supported the arts and attracted scholars to his city.

The city of Florence, though it had experienced numerous upheavals and short-lived tyrannies, remained a republic. In 1434 authority settled in the hands of Cosimo de' Medici, heir to a wealthy banking family. He and his successors generally held no major political office, but through persuasion, manipulation, bribery, and force they controlled the machinery of government. The Medici advanced their own financial interests and the interests of their supporters and treated rival groups harshly. Despite their methods, they enjoyed the support of most citizens—for they put an end to a previous period of rioting and confusion in the city. The most illustrious member of the family, Lorenzo the Magnificent, was a man of extraordinary ability and artistic taste. Under his rule, in the latter part of the fifteenth century, Florence reached its peak as the cultural center of Italy.

The States of the Church belonged to the popes, but the pattern of despotism there was barely distinguishable from that in the rest of the country. The popes hired condottieri to reduce subject cities to obedience, engaged in wars and alliances, and used their office to further the wealth and rank of their families. The Borgia pope, Alexander VI, was notorious for his faithlessness and immoral behavior; Julius II had a fondness for waging war; and the Medici Leo X was noted as an elegant connoisseur of the arts. Such qualities were hardly those of Peter the fisherman, but they were typical of the despots of the new era.

South of Rome, the development of commerce had been interrupted by successive military conquests. The Byzantines and Muslims had invaded this area (including Sicily), and the Normans had established a feudal state there in the eleventh century. French and Spanish claimants had fought over the territory during the thirteenth and fourteenth centuries, and at last, in 1435, the larger portion of it (the kingdom of Naples) was taken by Alfonso of Aragon, who already held Sicily. His joint realm, called the Kingdom of the Two Sicilies, was equal in area to all the rest of Italy (*map,* p. 342). Though the south Italian countryside was agrarian and backward, under Alfonso's "benevolent" despotism cultural life flourished in the capital at Naples.

The only major city to escape the trend toward absolutism was Venice, whose government had been stable since the beginning of the fourteenth century. A small group of rich merchants managed to keep political control over the city and saw to it that the rest of the citizens were excluded from participation. The constitution of Venice, the envy of its less fortunate rivals, provided that the city be governed by councils and committees elected from and by the merchants. The "official" head of state was a *doge* (duke), who was chosen for life by the leading families. Though the doge was treated with respect, he had no independent authority.

The Theory of Absolutism: Machiavelli

Fifteenth-century Italy was throbbing with individualism—in commerce, in learning, in the arts. And yet in politics there was a pronounced tendency, as we have seen, to curb individual freedom. The citizens of the city-states were proud and competitive men who by no means relished submitting themselves to absolute authority. But their long experience with factional rivalries and political instability had been disheartening. And so one city after another had accepted the rule of a despot. This submission to political authority did not check individualism in other spheres, however; Italy's "age of despots" was also the age of its greatest artistic flowering.

In the judgment of many Italians, their whole nation would benefit from a unified, absolute government. Despotic rule had put down internal dissension in Milan and Florence, for example, but in relations between city and city anarchy still reigned. If a despot could bring all of Italy under his rule, these wasteful conflicts would cease. After 1500 the argument for unity grew stronger. The French and Spanish monarchs found that they could sweep into the Italian peninsula and easily subdue the divided cities, which were protected only by corrupt mercenaries. The invaders, with their loyal, well-equipped armies, kept Italy in turmoil for a century.

The most able spokesman for Italian unification and political absolutism was a Florentine, Niccolò Machiavelli, a one-time diplomat and a close observer of Italian affairs. He set down his basic views in a kind of manual, which he intended as a guide for the despot who would one day liberate Italy. *The Prince*, written in 1513, was dedicated to the Medici rulers of Florence.

Machiavelli's book marks a sharp turning in Western political thought. Medieval philosophers had seen government as one aspect of God's administration of human affairs: the Church and its officers direct Christians toward *spiritual* salvation, which is eternal; the state looks after their physical well-being, which is *temporal* (limited in time). Yet both branches of authority are subject to divine law.

Thomas Aquinas had discussed this matter in his *Summa Theologiae* (p. 301). He reasoned that temporal power is invested by God in the people as a whole, who delegate it to suitable persons. The state, then, whether monarchical, aristocratic, or democratic, is not a power in itself. It receives its authority from God (through the people), and it must exercise the power for *Christian* purposes and in a Christian manner. To be sure, medieval practices often seemed to contradict this doctrine, but these were explained away as the result of human frailty or error.

Machiavelli met the doctrine head on, rejected it, and stated the "modern" view of politics and the state. He felt no uneasiness in breaking away from traditional Christian teachings. He blamed the papacy for keeping Italy divided and felt that Christian teachings, in general, did not contribute to good citizenship. In his commentary on the ancient Roman Republic *(Discourses)*, Machiavelli observed that the pagans had encouraged civic pride and service, whereas the early Christians had urged people to turn away from public affairs.

The state, he thought, does not rest on any *supernatural* authority. It provides its own justification, and it operates according to rules that have grown out of the "facts" of human nature. He thereby removed politics from Christian ideology and placed it on a purely secular (worldly) level. As noted earlier in this chapter, economic life had already become secularized, and literature, art, and science were soon to follow. This trend toward the *secularization* of life heralded the arrival of a new age.

Machiavelli's view of government won general acceptance in European thought and practice. Largely through his influence, the word "state" came into use to mean a sovereign political unit. And the evolution of European states from the sixteenth century onward moved in the direction outlined by Machiavelli. The state was to become the central force of modern times, a law unto itself, subjecting both institutions and individuals to its will.

Means, as well as ends, were a matter of concern to Machiavelli. As he saw it in *The Prince*, the central problem of politics is how to achieve and maintain a *strong* state. Much depends on the character of the citizens. He admired the

Romans of the ancient republic and the self-governing Swiss of his own day, but he concluded that a republican form of government could prosper only where the citizens possessed genuine civic virtue. This he found lacking in sixteenth-century Italy. And, in giving advice to his ideal despot, he wrote in the context of his own time and place. His book was not a blueprint for utopia; it was a manual for present action.

His advice to rulers is geared, therefore, to a particular view of human nature. The Italians of his day were evidently people of exaggerated defects and exaggerated virtues. Machiavelli regarded them as corrupt beyond correction (except, possibly, by a strong prince). He wrote that they were, in general, "ungrateful and fickle, fakers, anxious to avoid danger, and greedy for gain; they offer you their blood, their goods, their life, and their children, when the necessity is remote; but when it approaches, they revolt."

With citizens of such character, how was a state to be founded and preserved? Machiavelli advised that a ruler first turn his attention to military strength. The prince, he believed, must devote himself to the training and discipline of his troops and must keep himself fit to lead them. He must practice maneuvers and study the decisive battles of the past; it was thus that Caesar had learned from Alexander. Machiavelli had only contempt for the condottieri and their hirelings, for they had proved ruinous to Italy and incapable of defending the country from invasion. He advised the prince to build an army of citizens drawn from a reserve of qualified men under a system of compulsory military training, for their interests would be bound up with his own. Machiavelli thus introduced to modern Europe the ideas of universal male conscription (draft) and the "nation in arms."

Military strength is not enough in itself, however. For the prince must be both "a lion and a fox." The lion, Machiavelli explained, cannot protect himself from traps, and the fox cannot defend himself from wolves. A ruler, in other words, must have *both* strength and cunning. Machiavelli noted that the most successful princes of his time were masters of deception. They made agreements to their advantage, only to break them when the advantage passed. He declared that the ruler should hold himself *above* normal rules of conduct, Christian or otherwise—that the only proper measure for judging the behavior of a prince is his *power*. Whatever strengthens the state is right, and whatever weakens it is wrong; for power is the end, and the *end* justifies the *means*.

Machiavelli cautioned the prince never to reveal his true motives and methods, for it is useful to appear to be what one is not. Though the prince must stand ready, when necessary, to act "against faith, against charity, against humanity, and against religion," he must always *seem* to possess those qualities. Machiavelli summarized his advice to the ruler as follows:

> Let a prince therefore aim at conquering and maintaining the state, and the means will always be judged honorable and praised by everyone. For the vulgar [common people] is always taken in by appearances and the result of the event; and the world consists only of the vulgar, and the few who are not vulgar are isolated when the many have a rallying point in the prince.

Building the National Monarchies: France and England

The rising monarchs of Spain, France, and England were cut to the Machiavellian pattern. Often building on the inheritance left by strong rulers of feudal times (pp. 251–256), they were aided in their efforts to extend state power still further, in each country, by growing national sentiment. In Spain, the spirit of patriotism had been ignited during the fierce struggle to expel the Muslims. When the kingdoms of Castile and Aragon, which had led the fight, were linked through the marriage of Queen Isabella of Castile and King Ferdinand of Aragon in 1469, the way was open for a unified Spain. Though the Portuguese remained independent, the other peoples of the peninsula welcomed this consolidation of territories once ruled by the Muslims. With popular backing, Ferdinand and Isabella broke the independence of the feudal lords, who had taken over most of the lands from the defeated enemy. They also reformed the Spanish Church, gaining the right to name its bishops. So vigorous were the centralizing efforts of the two rulers that the foundations of royal absolutism were completed by the close of Ferdinand's reign (1516).

In France, the nobles were more firmly rooted, and the challenge to the monarchy was therefore greater. France was also the richest and most populous kingdom of Europe, with some twelve million inhabitants. As France became increasingly unified, it would move irresistibly to the forefront of European power and culture. The most powerful stimulant to national feeling was the Hundred Years' War (1338–1453), an off-and-on struggle with the English that arose out of conflicting feudal claims. The English rulers had long resented the loss in 1204 of their northern French fiefs (p. 253); in the fourteenth century, stronger than they had been before, they decided to regain these territories. Their king, Edward III, laid claim to the throne of France as well. (The succession was in doubt, as Edward was the grandson of an earlier French king.) And so the long campaigns began. By 1420 the English had triumphed, and most of France north of the Loire River (*map*, p. 348) was given to Henry V, now the English king. The French forces also agreed to accept Henry as heir to their throne.

This humiliation at the hands of foreigners brought forth a surprising reaction among the French people, who traditionally had been indifferent toward feudal struggles. After the throne fell vacant, they found an inspiring leader in a peasant girl called Joan of Arc, who in 1429 persuaded Charles, the disinherited son of the former French king, to march to Reims (the ancient crowning place of French monarchs). Claiming divine guidance, Joan herself took command of a small military force and vowed to drive the English from the soil of France. The young prince, responding to Joan's appeal, was crowned in Reims Cathedral as Charles VII and went on to lead his armies to final victory over the English. Joan did not live to see that day, however. Soon after Charles' coronation she fell into the hands of the English, who tried her as a witch and burned her at the stake. The martyred Joan has been revered for centuries as the glorious symbol of French patriotism.

The Hundred Years' War was frightfully destructive to France (p. 324) and interrupted the growth of royal authority. But when it was over the French monarchs

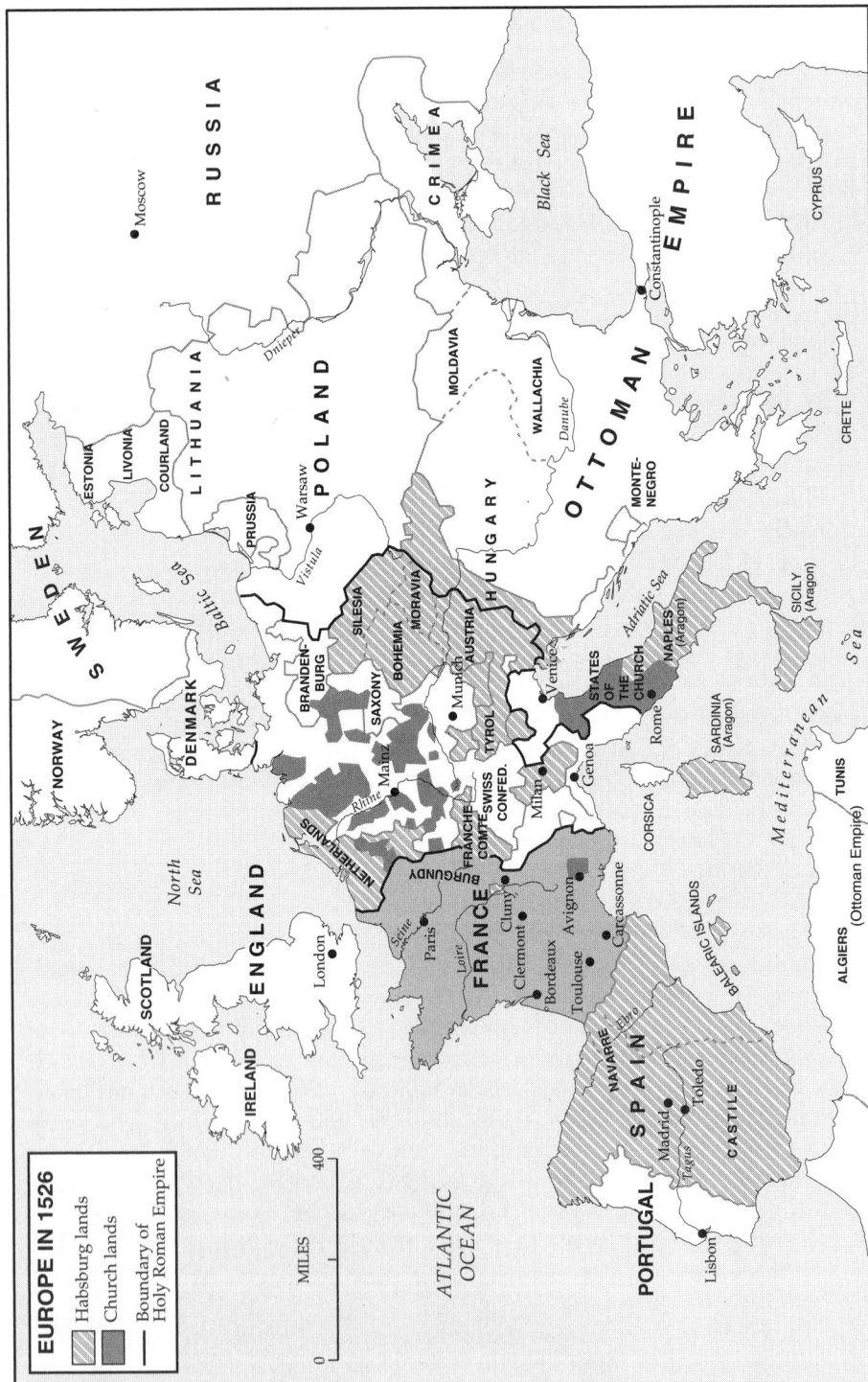

EUROPE IN 1526

Habsburg lands
Church lands
Boundary of Holy Roman Empire

751	987	1328	1589
Carolingian Dynasty (Frankish Kingdom)	House of Capet (Kingdom of France)	House of Valois	

Hundred Years' War
(1338–1453)

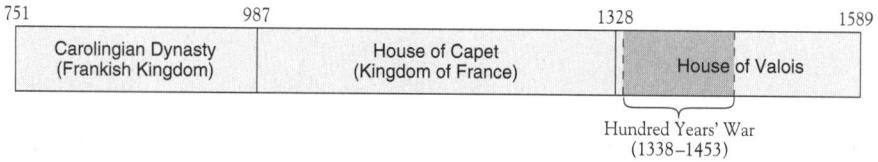

were able to proceed more rapidly than before with the work of political centralization. The nobles, great and small, had been reduced in number and power, and a
new spirit of national consciousness had spread through the land. The majority of
the people, especially the bourgeois, now looked to the king for security and economic well-being. Charles VII and his son, Louis XI, completed the building of a
strong national state.

In their struggle with the feudal nobility, the kings of France were able to take
advantage of the new developments in warfare to build armies that were more than
a match for any aristocratic opponent. Such armies required more revenue than
the monarch had ever received through ordinary feudal dues, but Charles succeeded in raising this revenue. In preparing for his final thrust against the English,
he summoned the Estates-General of France in 1439. This body, which represented
the three estates, or classes, of France (p. 257), had the sole power to authorize
new taxes. In a burst of patriotic fervor, the Estates-General approved Charles' national army and voted a permanent tax for its support. This tax was called the *taille*
(cut); it was a kind of income tax levied on all persons in the country. With this
substantial new revenue, supplemented by income from his own lands, Charles
could now afford to act independently of the nobles. He acted by deception,
threats of force, and marriage alliances to bring the great fiefs back into the royal
domain (his personal holdings). He permitted the lesser nobles, if they were cooperative, to remain on their ancestral estates and to keep their inherited titles. But
he eliminated feudal officeholders and replaced them with *royal* administrators recruited from the nobility.

Charles' son, Louis XI, pursued his father's methods and more than doubled
the size of the royal domain. His final victory was to win back the duchy of Burgundy, which had long been independent even though it was legally subject to the
French crown. Its last duke, Charles the Bold, had tried to expand his holdings
into a major state between France and Germany. But his plans had miscarried; and
when he died without a male heir, Louis took over the duchy (1477).

In their contest with the resisting nobles, the kings of France enjoyed the support of the middle class. The merchants and capitalists had much to gain from a
secure national market, and they despised the pretensions and arrogance of the
aristocracy. Wealthy individuals gave financial aid to the monarchs. (Jacques
Coeur, it will be recalled, was treasurer for Charles VII and financed his later military campaigns—p. 333.) And the expanding towns became firm allies of the king.

The success of the monarchy in consolidating its power changed the role of
the nobility. The nobles had no choice but to submit to these new conditions. By
the end of the fifteenth century, most of them had adjusted and had begun to seek

favored positions as military or civil officers of the king. The monarch, for his part, now had at his command the services of an *elite* class.

The Estates-General lingered on, meeting from time to time at the request of the crown. It might have developed into a constitutional body of importance, as did Parliament in England, but class and sectional rivalries, coupled with skillful manipulation by the monarchy, prevented this from happening. The Estates-General never became a serious challenge to royal authority, and it was to be swept into the dustbin of history in 1789 (pp. 511–512).

Nothing now checked the king's control over secular matters. But absolute power, to be absolute, must embrace ecclesiastical matters as well. While taming the nobility, Charles did not overlook the clergy. In some respects the spiritual lords were more powerful than the lay aristocracy. The archbishops, bishops, and abbots held vast properties in France and had a strong influence over the people. They generally supported the king in his efforts to centralize authority and end feudal warfare. They were jealous, however, of their own privileges, and they wavered in their loyalty between king and pope.

After the extreme ambitions of the papacy collapsed at the end of the thirteenth century (p. 284), the French clergy had tended to act independently of Rome. Although the French bishops and abbots had no thought of overturning traditional Church doctrines and institutions, they resented papal interference in local administrative affairs. The popes, however, continued to insist on the right to fill important ecclesiastical offices, a privilege that brought them handsome fees. They also siphoned off a substantial proportion of Church revenues to Rome.

As national feeling grew in the country, there was mounting sentiment for establishing a self-governing "Gallican" (French) Church. In 1438 the clergy, with Charles' approval, formally declared its *administrative* independence of the pope at the Council of Bourges. The decree limited papal interference and forbade payments and appeals of local decisions to Rome. This move gave clear control of the Gallican Church to the French bishops under royal protection. Louis XI revoked the decree, however, and his successor, Francis I, struck a bargain with the pope that extended the influence of the crown over the Church. In a treaty with the pope (the Concordat of 1516), Francis secured the right to appoint French bishops and abbots. In return for this right, the papacy was granted the first year's income of Church officeholders in France. The pope thereby gained additional revenue and the alliance of a powerful monarch; the king, outflanking his own clergy, brought the Church within his grip.

The rise of absolute monarchies contributed to the general rise of secular forces in Europe. During the Middle Ages, when governments were weak and decentralized, the popes had sought supremacy over them. Having failed then, they had lost their chance forever. Rulers of the new states were growing in power and tried to remove every sort of external influence; they therefore became increasingly hostile to a *universal* Church, which could not be put under their control.

The despots were also good Machiavellians, however. They had themselves crowned with religious pomp and declared their zeal for a unified Christendom. But behind these ceremonial demonstrations they nourished their real interests

c. 900		1066	1154		1399	1461	1485
United Anglo-Saxon Kingdom		Norman Kings	House of Plantagenet			House of Lancaster	House of York

Hundred Years' War
(1338–1453)

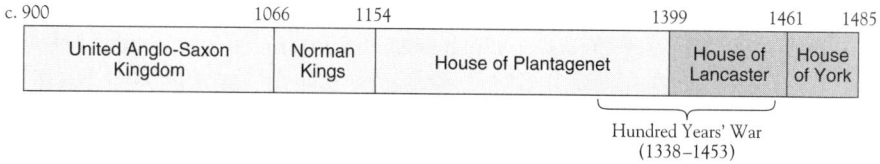

and intentions. Thus, Francis, the "Most Christian King" of France, allied himself with the infidel Turks against Charles, "His Most Catholic Majesty of Spain." Henry VIII of England, whom popes had named "Most Christian King" and "Defender of the Faith," denounced the papacy in 1534 and proclaimed himself the supreme head of the Church of England (pp. 426–427).

Before Henry became king, however, England had suffered through a long period of struggle for power. The Hundred Years' War had had an effect on England quite different from its effect on France. Though it had strengthened the national feeling of the English, it had weakened the position of the monarch. For one thing, it had permitted the nobles to build up large bands of armed men, who subsequently became their personal retainers. Moreover, in order to raise the substantial sums of money needed for the expeditions to France, the kings of England had been compelled to make concessions to Parliament.

The origins of Parliament go back to the thirteenth century. Already in 1215, the Magna Carta had expressed the idea that the king needed the advice and consent of his barons before taking measures such as the levying of unaccustomed taxes (p. 256). Later in the century, as both king and barons sought to enlarge their bases of support in the country, the custom grew up of inviting representatives of the shires (counties) and boroughs (towns) to such meetings. In 1295, Edward I held the precedent-setting "Model Parliament," and during the next century Edward's successors called Parliament frequently in their need for additional funds to carry on the war in France. Parliament evolved into two chambers: the House of Lords and the House of Commons. In the former sat the great barons and clerics of the country—lords who held fiefs and offices directly from the crown. In the latter sat representatives of the shires, and of certain towns. The Lords were the more important house for several centuries, but the Commons would ultimately have the upper hand in lawmaking.

The king had to turn to Parliament for approval of new revenues, and its members took advantage of that to gain privileges and redress of their grievances. It will be recalled that the Estates-General, a similar body in France, voted a royal income tax without demanding concessions from the monarch. Parliament did not agree so readily to the desires of the king and kept a firm hold on the purse strings.

Its control over lawmaking and general administration came only slowly, however. By 1399 Parliament had won the right to determine the line of succession to the throne. It chose the Lancaster house (family), and the monarchs of that line (who reigned from 1399 to 1461) worked closely with Parliament. At the close of the Hundred Years' War, however, England suffered a series of calamities. Confidence in the crown was shattered by the defeat in France, and the nobles proceeded to slaughter one another in a *civil* war led by the house of York against the house of Lancaster (Wars of the Roses). Henry Tudor, who would become Henry VII, was a relative of the Lancasters. When he at last emerged victorious from these wars in 1485, the strength of the nobles had been broken, and the nation was yearning for peace and unity.

Henry restored law and order and put an end to private warfare. Aware of the value of the bourgeois to the nation, he supported measures to protect home industries and commerce from foreign competition, and, by means of treaties, he extended markets abroad. As the influence of the old nobility declined, that of the middle class rose. And the English middle class, like the French, rallied to the service of the king as its position improved.

The sixteenth century, the century of Henry VIII and Elizabeth I, was an era of despotic power in England. Parliament, however, unlike the Estates-General, did not disappear. In fact, in the century to follow it would replace royal absolutism with *parliamentary* government.

The Eclipse of the Universal Empire: Germany

Strong central government did not come for centuries to other parts of Europe. Neither Germany nor Italy became a unified state until 1870. The reasons for this contrast with the rest of western Europe are many and complex, but the main one is the failure of the Holy Roman emperors to turn their territories into an effectively governed feudal state during the Middle Ages (p. 254). As a consequence, while Spain, France, and England were growing into strong centralized powers, Germany lingered on as a patchwork of hundreds of fiefs. It was a pleasant and prosperous country (except for the endless quarrels) but politically out-of-date. There were landed nobles with a bewildering array of ranks and titles, wealthy officials governing "free" cities under imperial charters, and powerful Church lords. The ranking princes of the empire had won the status of permanent "electors" as the result of an imperial decree of 1356 (known as the Golden Bull). Three of these electors were ecclesiastical: the archbishops of Cologne, Mainz, and Trier. Four were lay: the Count Palatine of the Rhine, the Duke of Saxony, the Margrave of Brandenburg, and the king of Bohemia. When an emperor died, these seven men met to choose his successor. This was often an occasion for lengthy bargaining—even bribing (p. 333); for the imperial office, though its power was declining, remained the political position of highest prestige in the West.

Dynastic (family) considerations, more than concern for national feeling, guided the politics of central Europe. The family that played the dynastic game most skillfully was the Habsburgs, whose influence on the continent endured for centuries. Rudolf of Habsburg, a south German prince, had been elected Holy Roman emperor in 1273. The main reason for his being chosen was that he was a minor figure who could be counted on not to create trouble for the independent-minded barons and bishops. And, in fact, he took his imperial responsibilities lightly, choosing to concentrate on expanding his family holdings. In a struggle

Otto the Great 962		1438	Dissolution by Napoleon 1806
Holy Roman Empire			
Germanic Dynasties		Habsburg Dynasty	

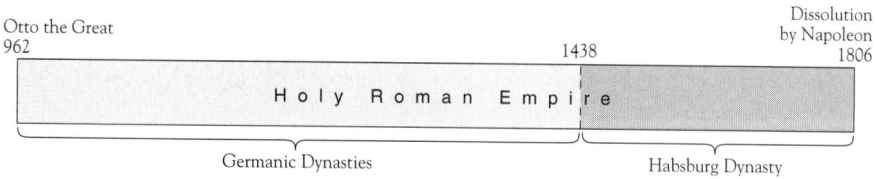

with a defiant vassal (Ottokar of Bohemia), Rudolf won the duchy of Austria and surrounding territories. He assigned these lands to his sons as imperial fiefs, and Austria thus became the base of the family properties.

The Habsburgs' mounting power worried the electors, who, when Rudolf died, chose an imperial successor from another, less affluent family. For nearly two centuries the Habsburgs were then passed over, but in 1438 another member of the family (Albert) was elected emperor. Thereafter, until the end of the Holy Roman Empire in 1806, the Habsburgs managed to keep the office in their possession, while extending their wealth and power by means of carefully arranged marriages.

The family holdings reached their greatest extent when they passed to the young man who was to become Emperor Charles V. His inheritance included the ancestral lands on the Danube River, Luxembourg, and the Netherlands, as well as Spain (with Hispanic America), Sardinia, Naples, and Sicily. When he secured the imperial title in 1519 (by buying the votes of the electors), he added to his family's domains the overlordship of Germany and northern Italy (map, p. 348). In 1526 the death (in battle against the Turks) of the king of Hungary and Bohemia, to whom Charles was related by marriage, brought him the title to those two kingdoms as well. This was by far the greatest aggregation of territory, both in and outside Europe, that any European monarch had ever ruled.

But the aggregation proved exceedingly hard to control. Charles' empire was a hodgepodge of holdings, like those of the Middle Ages. The emperor encountered an endless series of political, military, and personal frustrations, and he at last retired to a monastery in 1556. Before abdicating, Charles divided the Habsburg properties into an eastern and a western portion. The western portion consisted of Spain, the family's other territories in western Europe and the Mediterranean, and the vast Spanish overseas empire. The eastern portion included Austria, Bohemia, Hungary, and the rule of the Holy Roman Empire.

Far from weakening the Habsburgs, the division of their territory into more manageable portions actually strengthened them. Working closely together, the Spanish and Austrian branches of the dynasty dominated Europe for a hundred years. The Europe of today still feels the effect of their power: it was they who sustained the Roman Catholic Church against the Protestant revolt, and who finally fought the Turks to a standstill (pp. 329, 432, 458). Yet in the long run, the far-flung Habsburg territories, assembled by conquest and marriage and united only by their ruling dynasty, were destined to crumble. The future lay with the rising national states and their despotic monarchs.

THE NEW GEOGRAPHY

The expansion of Europe came about as a combined result of all the other changes that took place toward the end of the Middle Ages. The need to respond to the renewed challenge of Islam, the vision of ever-growing markets and fathomless riches supplied by capitalism and materialism, and the competition of powerful centralized governments in western Europe all provided incentives for exploration and empire building in distant continents. Cannon-armed sailing ships provided the means for exploration; printed books and maps publicized the explorers' discoveries and stirred up public opinion for yet more voyages. In addition, the expansion of Europe was the climax of the outward political, cultural, and religious thrust of European civilization that dated back to the tenth century, and the final outcome of the gradual strengthening of Europe's links with other civilizations which had been going on since the time of the Roman Empire (pp. 128, 206, 226–227).

Had the mariners of ancient Greece or imperial Rome made their way across the Atlantic to America, it is almost certain that their journey would have had no results. The reported landing by the Norwegian Leif Ericson around 1000 (p. 240) made only a slight impression in Europe. Likewise, a fifteenth-century non-European venture, in which the Ming emperors of China sent several powerful fleets ranging across the Indian Ocean from the East Indies to the African coast, came in the end to nothing. Neither earlier Western civilizations, nor non-Western ones of the fifteenth century, were ripe for sustained exploration leading to domination of distant parts of the world.

But in the fifteenth and sixteenth centuries, Europe—or at least, a group of leading western European countries—was hungrier than ever before for contact with the outside world. The hunger of these countries was sharpened by a significant feature of their common civilization, the urge to compete with one another (pp. 207, 247). In the technology of sailing and fighting at sea, they were ahead of the other civilizations of the Eastern hemisphere; and they enjoyed a much wider margin of technical supremacy over the civilizations of the Western hemisphere. Nothing in the history of world relations proved more fateful than the resulting far-flung encounter between Europe and other continents.

The Impulse to Overseas Expansion

The expansion of Europe was partly the result of internal developments, and partly also of changes in the wider community of civilizations of which Europe had come to be a part. Ever since the rise of Islam and of the nomadic peoples of the steppes had linked the civilizations of the Eastern hemisphere, Europeans had benefited in many ways from membership in this wider community. They had tasted sweets, spices, and other luxuries from afar; they had enjoyed exotic pastimes such as card games and chess; and they had made use of non-European knowledge and extensive inventions (pp. 227, 335–339).

But Europeans had for long known little or nothing of the distant lands from which these things came to them. The crusades (pp. 308–313) had carried them to the Middle East and excited their curiosity about the lands beyond. They knew the Black Sea and, of course, the Mediterranean. But the areas beyond were great blanks on their maps—reaching eastward and westward, perhaps to the "edges of the earth." Popular conceptions about the uncharted world were full of fanciful suggestions. Tales of sea monsters abounded, and sailors, fearful of the unknown, hugged the coasts in their tiny vessels.

In the thirteenth and fourteenth centuries, this European ignorance of the outside world began to change. The main reason was the rise of the intercontinental empire of the Mongols. As devastating as the Mongol conquests were to their victims in eastern Europe and the Middle East (p. 327), once established, their empire maintained peace and secure communications across the steppes for a hundred years. The civilizations of the Eastern hemisphere were drawn together as never before. For the first time, Europeans were able to visit the lands beyond Islam, and return to tell what they had seen.

Marco Polo, a thirteenth-century merchant of Venice, contributed more than anyone else to Europe's awareness of these lands. Members of the Polo family, after establishing trading contacts with the Mongol empire in western Asia, decided to journey to the far side of the empire. A long trek by caravan took them from the Black Sea to the Chinese capital of Beijing, where the Mongol ruler Kublai Khan held court as emperor. The Polos were welcomed with courtesy, and Marco remained there for many years before returning by way of Southeast Asia and the lands of the Indian Ocean. Once back in Italy, he wrote of his travels and revealed to astonished Europeans the fabulous wealth of the Orient.

Not long afterward, Europe received the same revelation about another, hitherto unknown, part of the world with which it did indirect business—West Africa (that is, the lands in the bulge of Africa south of the Sahara). Early in the fourteenth century, the ruler of the powerful Islamic empire of Mali, fulfilling his obligation to visit Mecca (p. 225), passed through Cairo, where there was a large Italian trading community. Soon the news reached Europe that the wealthy pilgrim had handed out so much gold, by way of gifts, that the gold-based Egyptian coinage had temporarily lost a quarter of its value. Much else was reported about the ruler, his empire, and its resources. From this, as well as the reports of Marco Polo and other travelers, Europeans began to get a distinct idea of the distant lands and peoples of the Eastern hemisphere—together with the uncomfortable but enticing feeling that among the intercontinental family of civilizations to which they belonged, they were, so to speak, poor relations.

In the middle of the fourteenth century, the Black Death swept through Asia, Africa, and Europe (p. 324), leading to an intercontinental decline in prosperity and trade. Disputes among the successors of Genghis Khan led to the gradual collapse of the Mongol empire, and the rising power of the Turks (pp. 327–328) blocked off the western end of the overland routes to the Far East. Trade and other contacts between Europe and the Orient came to be channeled mainly through Egypt. Thus, as Europe gradually recovered from the Black Death, it found the door to the outside world partially closed. But in the countries of western Europe, the effect was actually to increase their hunger for contact with distant lands.

Among the Italian city-states that had traditionally dominated the routes to the Middle East (pp. 264–265, 330), competition to control the chief remaining link with the Orient grew intense. The two largest cities, Venice and Genoa, fought a series of wars that ended in the victory of Venice. That city now became Europe's main gateway to the rest of the world. Venetian strongpoints and harbors were scattered through the coasts and islands of the eastern Mediterranean, guarding the sea routes, attracting the commerce of neighboring areas, and creating a Venetian trading monopoly in the region. But the Venetians not only traded, they also developed new resources. In the Venetian-owned island of Cyprus, a fabulously profitable crop of Middle Eastern origin, sugarcane, was grown on plantations worked by gangs of slaves imported from countries to the north of the Black Sea. In these ways, Venice set an example of empire building and colonial exploitation that was carefully studied by the increasingly powerful and prosperous countries of western Europe—even while they envied the city's newfound monopoly of links with the East. As for Genoa, it consoled itself with control of the western Mediterranean and the sea routes leading from there to the lands of Europe's Atlantic coast. It was no coincidence that Christopher Columbus came from Venice's Atlantic-oriented rival city.

Furthermore, the fifteenth century saw a hardening in western European attitudes toward the neighbor and rival civilization of Islam. The Muslim world, for so long the connecting link between Europe and other civilizations of the Eastern hemisphere, came to seem an irksome obstacle, now that western Europeans had some idea of what lay beyond it. At the same time, the Turkish drive into eastern Europe left no doubt that Islam was a stronger and more dangerous enemy of Christendom than ever before—one against which it would be most desirable to find non-European allies.

In Portugal and Spain, France and England, dreams began to grow of acquiring the luxuries of the Orient direct from the producers—and paying for them with the gold of West Africa, obtained in return for European goods also sold on the spot. In this way, the middlemen's profits of Venice and Islam would be eliminated, going instead into the pockets of the western European nations. Besides, somewhere in the world beyond Islam, there might be powerful Christian rulers, or non-Muslim ones ripe for conversion to Christianity, who would join Europe's struggle against the followers of the Prophet. To bypass Venice and Islam, it would be necessary to find new routes to distant destinations, leading through waters to which the western European countries had direct access—the Atlantic Ocean. No doubt this would be a difficult task, but at the same time as the western European countries were becoming hungry for access to distant lands, the development of three-masted sailing ships and cannon, as well as the improvement of aids to navigation, were giving them the knowledge and technical abilities necessary for exploration at sea.

By the fifteenth century a race was under way to find sea routes between western Europe and the Far East. Europeans knew that no water passage existed between the Mediterranean and the Indian Ocean; hence, only two possibilities lay open. One was to try the way *south*, around Africa, then eastward to India. This was a relatively conservative plan, since ships could hold close to land during most of the voyage. The other was a much bolder, more theoretical plan: sailing due *west* across the open Atlantic. Though Africa and the Indian Ocean appeared on existing maps of the world, the Atlantic was uncharted. Geographers agreed that China must lie on the farther side, but none knew for sure what distances or barriers might have to be crossed before reaching it.

The prizes to be won by whoever solved these geographical riddles were glittering indeed. The merchants of each western European nation hoped to win control of any newly discovered sea route, each excluding the merchants of the other nations, just as Venice monopolized the existing Mediterranean route. But the alternative possible routes were costly and risky to test, and merchants were often reluctant to finance voyages of exploration on their own. In any case, this could be better done by governments, because to set up commercial routes and bases, as the Venetian example also showed, would require political and military power.

The ambitious monarchs of western Europe grasped the opportunity. They hoped that by bringing wealth to their lands they could strengthen the economic base of their countries and hence their own personal power and glory—not least, of course, against each other. In backing exploring ventures, the kings had the blessing and encouragement of the Church. Not only did the clergy support the idea of finding non-European allies against Islam; in addition, responding to the Scriptural obligation to spread Christianity (pp. 174–175), they were eager for new converts. Indeed, in the European religious turmoil of the sixteenth century (see chapter 9), both Catholic and Protestant missionaries, and even different Protestant churches and Catholic religious orders, would each strive against the other to baptize the maximum number of converts.

Thus, three central motives combined to launch the brave sailors and their ships: the desire of the clergy to combat Islam and spread the gospel, the ambition of the monarchs for power and glory, and the hunger of the merchants for gold— all sharpened by the spur of competition. That was why the expansion of Europe, once started, spread so far and so fast.

THE VOYAGES OF EUROPEAN DISCOVERY: THE NEW WORLD

The little kingdom of Portugal took the lead in sponsoring exploration. It had only a short history of independence, having emerged when the Muslims were being expelled from the Iberian peninsula. Portugal had been a fief for a period, subject to the Christian rulers of Castile, but in the twelfth century its count proclaimed himself a king. The Portuguese monarchy, with its capital at Lisbon, reached the height of its power during the sixteenth century. With astounding will, enterprise, and ruthlessness, the Portuguese exploited vast territories and peoples overseas. Portugal became the early model of that form of worldwide cultural aggression known as Western imperialism.

The Portuguese favored the proposed route around Africa. In the course of developing it, their forces occupied the nearby Madeira Islands and the Azores, and opened trade for gold, ivory, and slaves along the coast of West Africa. At last, in 1498, Vasco da Gama rounded the Cape of Good Hope and sailed across the Indian Ocean to the west coast of India (*map*, p. 359), thereby linking Europe with the Orient. The Portuguese, having won that race, moved swiftly to secure their prize.

Prior to this achievement, a Genoese mariner named Christopher Columbus had sought support for a plan to sail *west* to China and Japan. The son of a weaver, he had turned to the sea and to dreams of fame and fortune. Finding his way to Lisbon, the center of activity in geography and navigation, Columbus went into the business of making maps and sea charts. On occasion he accompanied ship captains on voyages down the African coast. He also gained sufficient social status to marry a daughter of the governor of Madeira, thereby gaining access to the royal court of Portugal.

When Columbus described his bold project to the king and asked ships and provisions, the royal advisers pronounced his plans unsound. Columbus' scheme was based on the inaccurate calculations of Ptolemy and on an exaggerated notion of Asia's eastward projection; the king's advisers correctly reckoned that China was too distant to be reached by sailing westward across the Atlantic. Columbus believed China to be about three thousand nautical miles west of Lisbon, while his critics put the figure at about six thousand. The actual distance is more than twelve thousand miles.

Though disappointed, Columbus was not a man to give up. He turned next to the Spanish rulers, Ferdinand and Isabella, who were now driving the last of the Muslims from the Iberian peninsula (p. 347). His proposal was at first rejected by a commission of experts, for the same reason that had been advanced by the Portuguese. However, when the queen learned that Columbus was journeying north to offer his plan to the French king, she called him back. Attracted by his winning personality, Isabella decided to give him her personal support and agreed to an extravagant contract whereby Columbus was to become governor of all the lands he discovered and was to receive one-tenth of the wealth he extracted from them. Further, he was to be known as "Admiral of the Ocean Sea, Viceroy, and Governor."

Columbus personified the early modern spirit. A modest capitalist, he invested some of his own money in the venture. When his tiny vessels dipped below the horizon in 1492, they carried with them a high faith in the individual—and a passion for wealth, power, and glory. His courage brought him to the "discovery" of the New World, though he never understood the true nature of what he had found. By a bizarre coincidence, he sighted land (the Bahama Islands) at precisely the point where he expected to find the shores of Asia (*map*, p. 359). This convinced him that his geographical theories and calculations were correct and that he had reached his true destination. Yet if a continent unknown to him had not lain across his path, the admiral would have returned to Spain empty-handed—or sailed on to his death.

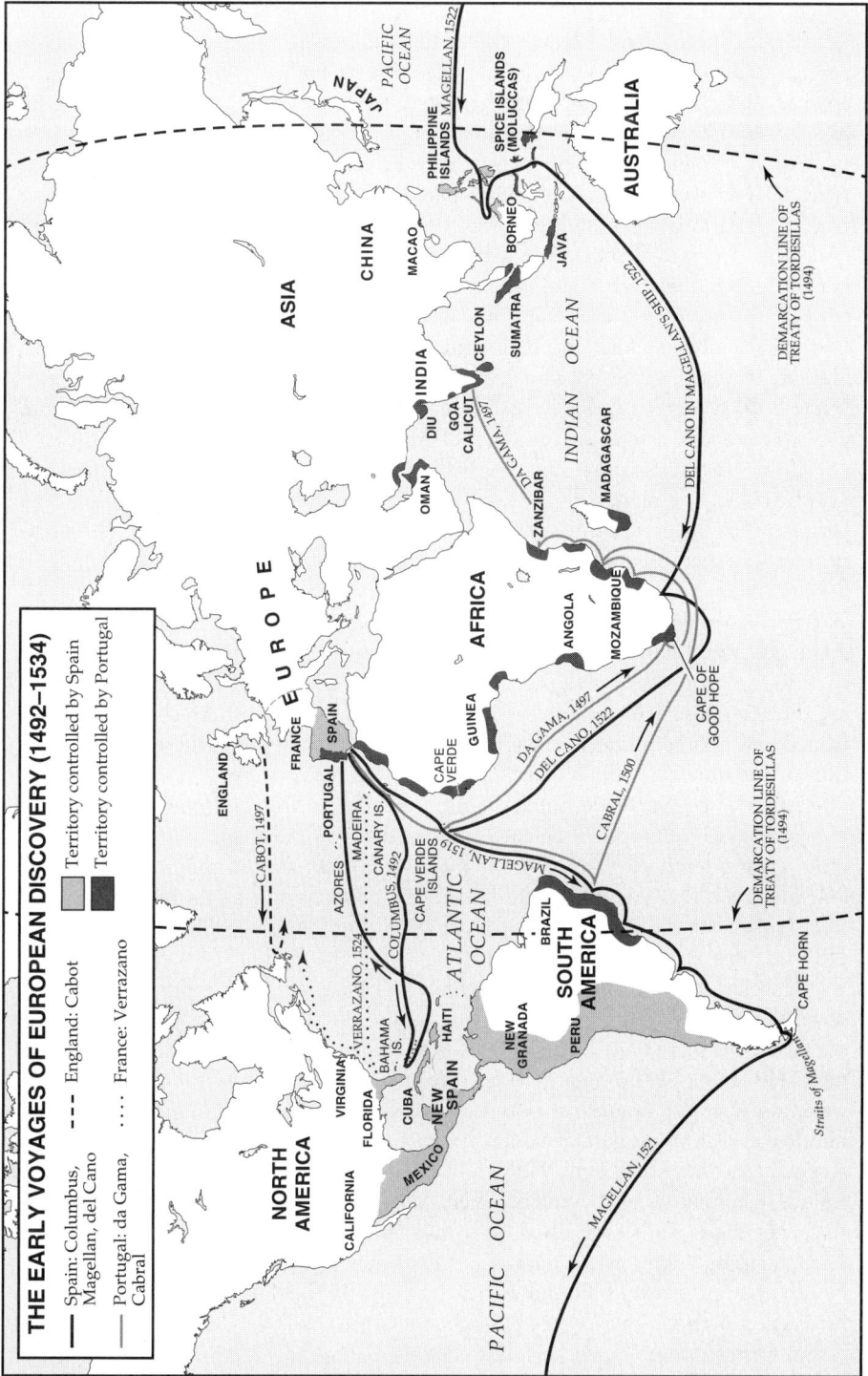

THE EARLY VOYAGES OF EUROPEAN DISCOVERY (1492–1534)

—— Spain: Columbus, Magellan, del Cano
- - - England: Cabot
······ France: Verrazano
—— Portugal: da Gama, Cabral

☐ Territory controlled by Spain
■ Territory controlled by Portugal

PACIFIC OCEAN
JAPAN
CHINA
ASIA
MACAO
PHILIPPINE ISLANDS
SPICE ISLANDS (MOLUCCAS)   MAGELLAN, 1522
BORNEO
JAVA
SUMATRA
CEYLON
INDIA
DIU
GOA
CALICUT
OMAN
AUSTRALIA
DEMARCATION LINE OF TREATY OF TORDESILLAS (1494)
INDIAN OCEAN
MADAGASCAR
ZANZIBAR
AFRICA
ANGOLA
MOZAMBIQUE
DA GAMA, 1497
DEL CANO IN MAGELLAN'S SHIP, 1522
CAPE OF GOOD HOPE
DA GAMA, 1497
DEL CANO, 1522
CABRAL, 1500
DEMARCATION LINE OF TREATY OF TORDESILLAS (1494)
EUROPE
ENGLAND
FRANCE
SPAIN
PORTUGAL
CABOT, 1497
AZORES
MADEIRA
CANARY IS.
CAPE VERDE
GUINEA
CAPE VERDE ISLANDS
VERRAZANO, 1524
COLUMBUS, 1492
MAGELLAN, 1519
ATLANTIC OCEAN
NORTH AMERICA
CALIFORNIA
FLORIDA
VIRGINIA
BAHAMA IS.
CUBA
HAITI
NEW SPAIN
MEXICO
NEW GRANADA
PERU
SOUTH AMERICA
BRAZIL
CAPE HORN
Straits of Magellan
MACELLAN, 1521
PACIFIC OCEAN

Still seeking Japan or China, Columbus spent several months exploring the Caribbean, whose islands he mistook for the "Indies." He sighted and claimed Hispaniola (Haiti) as well as Juana (Cuba). On three subsequent voyages, he strengthened Spain's claim to the Western hemisphere. He died in 1506 still believing he had opened a westerly route to Asia.

After 1500 most geographers were convinced that Columbus had not reached Asia but had stumbled across a land mass hitherto uncharted. They decided to name it for another explorer, one who first grasped the true nature of Columbus' discovery. Amerigo Vespucci was a Florentine adventurer and mapmaker who was once connected with the banking firm of the Medici (p. 332). Although knowledge of his activities is uncertain, he apparently took part in several Spanish and Portuguese voyages along the mainland coasts of the hemisphere, from Brazil to Florida. Vespucci wrote colorful letters about what he saw and coined the term "New World." Copies of his letters were widely circulated in Europe, and literate persons were soon discussing the "land of Amerigo" (America).

Conflicts quickly arose over the rival overseas claims of Spain and Portugal. To avoid trouble, the monarchs of the two countries agreed, in 1494, to draw a line between their spheres of interest. In the form of a circle of longitude, the Demarcation Line of the Treaty of Tordesillas passed through a point approximately fifteen hundred miles west of Cape Verde, the westernmost tip of Africa (*map*, p. 359). The Portuguese were to confine their claims to territories *east* of the line, while the Spaniards would limit themselves to areas *west* of the line. The Spaniards believed that this division would give them all the lands in the area of Columbus' discoveries; they had miscalculated the eastward extension of the southern continent. As it turned out, a large portion of it (Brazil) reached into the Portuguese zone. Lisbon thus gained, unexpectedly, a claim in the Western hemisphere.

After Vasco Núñez de Balboa sighted the Pacific Ocean, from the isthmus of Panama (1513), Europeans came to realize that beyond the New World lay another great stretch of water. The Spanish were disappointed that Columbus had failed to reach the Orient and still hoped that portions of it might fall within their treaty sphere. It was mainly with this in mind that Ferdinand Magellan set out in 1519 to find a *passage* to the Pacific through which he might sail on to Asia.

Magellan, a Portuguese in the service of Spain, guided his fleet of five ships down the coast of South America. After a false start up the broad Plata River, he continued his search until he entered the straits near the southern tip of the continent. He managed the hazardous passage into the Pacific and then sailed northwestward into the greatest of oceans. Following a frightful crossing of about one hundred days, during part of which his men lived on leather and rats, Magellan reached the island of Guam. With fresh provisions, he sailed on to the Philippine Islands, claiming them for Spain. There he was killed in a skirmish with the natives, but the expedition pushed on to the Spice Islands (the Moluccas), and the one remaining vessel, with a remnant of the original crew, finally returned to Spain by continuing westward around Africa (*map*, p. 359). Magellan's expedition thus revealed that there was a water passage *around* the New World and demonstrated that a westerly route could be followed from Europe to Asia. More significant, it demonstrated conclusively that the earth was round, it dramatized the vastness of the Pacific, and it gave a truer idea of the globe's size.

Though Spain and Portugal felt that the overseas world was to be shared by them alone, the northwestern countries of Europe did not intend to stand idly by. The English, the French, and the Dutch were also seeking routes for direct trade with the Orient. A Genoese mariner, whom the English called John Cabot, was sent out in 1497 to seek a "northwest passage" to the Indies. Cabot touched the shores of the New World somewhere around Labrador and Newfoundland and thereby provided England with a claim to North America (*map*, p. 359).

Shortly afterward a Florentine, Giovanni da Verrazano, explored the North Atlantic coast for the king of France. Neither he nor anyone else ever discovered another water passage, but the search led to a close examination of the hemisphere's eastern shores from Labrador to the Straits of Magellan. It was only after hope of finding a shorter passage had been abandoned that the French and English took steps to settle the northern lands.

THE COLONIAL EMPIRES

The Portuguese had won the race to the Orient when Vasco da Gama brought his ship into the harbor of Calicut, India. They had seen their goal clearly, attained it, and exploited their victory to the full. What they wanted was a monopoly over the richest trade in the world, and this they held for more than a century.

When the Portuguese arrived in India, they found a heavily populated land with substantial resources. India's civilization dated back to 3000 B.C., when settled communities first appeared in the Indus River valley (p. 17; *map*, p. 51). Indian culture was not firmly established, however, until after Indo-Europeans (Aryans) from the north had completed their conquest of the subcontinent about 1500 B.C. (pp. 56–57). The civilization that evolved came to dominate not only India but all of southeast Asia. It was marked by profound religious and philosophical teachings, an imaginative and moralistic literature (Sanskrit), and a sensuous art and architecture.

Though most Indians held to a common faith (Hinduism) and lived under a common caste (class) system, they had enjoyed only brief periods of *political* unity—and that unity was usually imposed by foreign conquerors. The conquerors, after the tenth century A.D., consisted of successive armies of either Turks or Mongols, all converts to Islam. A Muslim sultan (ruler) at Delhi controlled most of India from about 1250 until 1398, when Delhi's power was smashed by yet another Mongol raider, Tamerlane (Timur).

At the moment of the Portuguese landing in 1498, India was divided into a number of separate kingdoms and was torn by hostility between Hindus and Muslims, friction among the various castes, and warfare among local warlords. Even so, the local rulers were too strong for the Portuguese to conquer. With their superior warships, however, the newcomers were able to exploit the local turmoil so as to establish permanent trading settlements along the western (Malabar) coast.

The next strategic step for the Portuguese was to get control of the trade in luxury goods from the Indian ports to the Middle East and Africa. Having seized much of this trade from the Arabs, they extended their operations eastward to the Spice Islands and entered the ports of China and Japan. Here, too, they sought to gain control of the commerce in goods such as silks, lacquer, and spices. By about 1530, the coastlines of the Eastern hemisphere from western Africa to the Far East were dotted with Portuguese-controlled harbors, naval bases, and trading stations. It was a repetition of what Venice had done in the eastern Mediterranean, only on an enormously larger scale—and, of course, to the great disadvantage of the Italian city. For it was the Portuguese who now monopolized the trade between Europe and the East; and it was Lisbon, not Venice, that had become Europe's gateway to the Orient (*map*, p. 359).

The cost of maintaining naval vessels, bases, and men was high, but the crown and a few chosen companies reaped sensational profits—for a time. The Portuguese were too few in number to colonize the oriental lands, and their grip on key positions was insecure. When the Dutch and English cut into the spice trade during the seventeenth century, the golden empire began to crumble. Nevertheless, Portugal managed to cling to the remnants of its overseas possessions for nearly five centuries after da Gama's initial voyage.

The Spanish looked on enviously as the Portuguese piled success on success. The demarcation treaty of 1494 had tied their hands east of the dividing line, and Columbus' failure in the west had for the time being destroyed their dream of breaking through from that direction. True, Magellan had finally arrived in the Orient, and Spain was eventually able to reach across the Pacific and acquire the Philippines as a foothold in Asia. But at first, the New World appeared to the Spaniards as a monstrous obstacle to their ambitions.

The Caribbean natives were peaceful enough, but they offered little of value to European traders. The only hope left to the Spanish adventurers was to fall upon some precious store of wealth—gold, silver, or gems. This they did in a manner and on a scale that surprised even those hardy soldiers of fortune. It was Hernando Cortéz who first struck it rich. Attracted by rumors of wealth on the mainland, he organized and equipped a small expeditionary force in Cuba. He sailed off in 1519, without authorization from his superiors, and made for Mexico; there he had his soldiers proclaim him the legitimate ruler of the land, subject only to the king of Spain. Then he scuttled his ships, so that his men had no means of escape.

Cortéz' conquest of the Aztec empire was both daring and cruel. The Aztecs, like the Mayas before them (and the Incas of Peru), were by no means primitive; their civilization boasted rich cities, splendid temples and palaces, and superb artistic creations. In the Caribbean islands the Spanish had looted and destroyed as they pleased, but in Mexico they faced an organized power, capable of resistance. The Aztecs suffered serious disadvantages, however. They had not invented the wheel, could not make iron utensils or weapons, and lacked horses and cattle. The government was oppressive and constantly threatened by tribal unrest. Finally, like the other natives of the Western hemisphere, the Aztecs had not been exposed to the European diseases; they were therefore open to the deadly germs that the invaders brought with them.

Cortéz played upon the natives' superstitious fears, drew up his cannon (recently developed in Europe), and set one tribe against another. In the face of constant personal danger, he succeeded in overthrowing the emperor, Montezuma. While the defenders were falling ill with smallpox, Cortéz then destroyed the Aztec capital and laid out a new one on the old site, which later became Mexico City. Rich prizes were sent back to the Spanish court, and the king recognized Cortéz as captain-general and governor of "New Spain." Within a decade his lieutenants had taken over most of Central America, from the Rio Grande to Panama (*map*, p. 359).

This caesar of the New World had many freebooting companions and rivals, though none surpassed him as a conquistador (conqueror). South of the Panamanian isthmus, the most notorious adventurer was Francisco Pizarro. Learning of gold and silver in the Inca territories, he organized an expedition with royal approval. The Inca empire, like that of the Aztecs, rested upon an advanced society; it stretched southward along the Andes Mountains from Ecuador through the modern states of Peru and Bolivia. Pizarro discovered, however, that the empire was torn by internal unrest and infected with smallpox — to which his own soldiers were resistant. Like Cortéz, he made the most of the situation. Armed with superior weapons, Pizarro's men captured the ruler (Atahualpa) and held him for an extravagant ransom. After Pizarro had received tons of gold and silver, carried in from all parts of Peru, he had his prisoner baptized a Christian and then had him strangled. He next marched to the magnificent Inca capital of Cuzco, looted it, and took over the empire (1534).

The exploits of these European adventurers were to be repeated over and over again in the New World. Small bodies of armed and determined men were able to overturn impressive civilizations. They did so under exceedingly difficult conditions, operating far from home and with little knowledge of the strange lands, languages, and cultures. But they had decisive advantages on their side. While the native leaders and peoples were usually divided among themselves, the conquistadors were united by their purpose of plunder.

Their greed was accompanied by a driving sense of superiority and a fanatical conviction that Christianity was the one true faith and that they were responsible for spreading it. Priests came with the invaders; missionaries and bishops soon followed. The superior weapons of the Europeans provided them with the tools of victory, and through a combination of force, terror, treachery, and infectious disease they subdued the New World.

The court of Spain was delighted with the wealth taken from Mexico and Peru. The king received his royal share, and nobles close to the throne were granted vast estates in America. But soon it became evident that the quick-and-easy prizes of the New World had been consumed. The Spaniards came to realize that Columbus' discovery was an asset of unmeasured dimension, richer than all of Europe. But that wealth — which existed in the form of land and people — had to be cultivated in order to be harvested. By 1550 the monarchy had begun to lay the foundations of royal administration in the Americas. The era of conquest and plunder was over, and the long period of *construction* and *development* had begun. Thus, driven by the twin desires for material gain and Christianization, the Spanish set out to impose the institutions of Western culture on the New World. (Most legal experts and philosophers of the time justified these actions with arguments based on Christian teaching, "natural law," and ancient Roman law.)

After 1600 the Portuguese, too, turned their attention from commerce alone to the longer, harder task of developing the wealth of America. They established in Brazil a system of autocratic control similar to that of the Spanish. In both colonial empires the natives were forced into virtual serfdom, working huge estates (*encomiendas*) for the white landlords. In Brazil and the Caribbean, which were thinly populated by less advanced peoples than those of Mexico and Peru, the Native Americans quickly succumbed to the maltreatment and disease of the whites. They were replaced, over time, by millions of Africans, brought to the Western hemisphere as slaves (pp. 367–368). As a result, blacks and mulattos today make up about one-sixth of the total population of Latin America, while whites constitute about one-quarter; most of the remainder are mestizos (mixed white and Native American). From early times, the Spanish and Portuguese permitted intermarriage between Europeans and Christianized nonwhites.

For much of the sixteenth century, the efforts of the English, French, and Dutch to explore, trade, and colonize overseas were overshadowed by the fabulous successes of Portugal and Spain. Yet these northwestern European countries were just as ambitious in this respect as the southwestern countries. France and England were powerful national monarchies whose rulers, nobles, and merchants were all eager for land and profits overseas. The Dutch, who rebelled against Spanish rule and formed their own independent republic (the Netherlands) in the second half of the sixteenth century (p. 451), were now the most dynamic commercial nation of Europe. Three such competitors could not forever be kept on the sidelines.

As the sixteenth century drew to a close, the English, French, and Dutch redoubled their efforts to gain a share of world trade and world empire. They explored the coastlines of North America and northern Europe, vainly searching for northwest or northeast sailing passages—routes not dominated by Spain and Portugal, which could take them to the Indies. (Though such routes do exist, they are too icebound to have been used by sixteenth- and seventeenth-century ships.) More successfully, the northwestern countries began to *settle* in areas not yet occupied by Spain and Portugal, chiefly in North America. In addition, the new competitors began to encroach on the trade and territories held by the Spanish and Portuguese themselves. An era of "world wars" began, in which European armies and navies fought for control of distant overseas lands.

By the end of the seventeenth century, England, France, and the Netherlands had successfully stepped into the inheritance of Portugal and Spain. They now dominated the trade of the Far East, and most of Portugal's possessions there were now in the hands of the Dutch or English. The northwestern countries had driven the Spanish from much of the Caribbean, and Dutch ships carried much of the overseas trade of the Portuguese and Spanish empires in South and Central

America. English, French, and Dutch colonies in North America were thriving, with those of the English already harboring tens of thousands of settlers.

The northwestern countries struggled as fiercely with each other for trade and empire as they did with Spain and Portugal. During the eighteenth century, with the Dutch exhausted by wars within Europe, the overseas struggle narrowed to one between France and Britain (from 1708 on, Britain was the name for the union formed by England and Scotland—p. 498). Every major eighteenth-century war, including those of the American and French revolutions (pp. 506, 515–516, 520–521), was part of a worldwide conflict between these two most powerful western European nations. By the end of the eighteenth century, in spite of the loss of its American colonies, Britain had come off best. It had won the position it was to keep down to the twentieth century as the world's leading commercial and imperial nation.

OVERSEA CONSEQUENCES OF EUROPE'S EXPANSION

In the long run, the European discoveries and conquests were to have a profound impact throughout the world. As Europe became the heart of an expanding system that reached into all parts of the globe, changes occurring at the center of the system reverberated in far-off places. In the sixteenth century, however, the impact of the Europeans was felt above all in the Western hemisphere. The European conquest of the Americas was, in fact, more devastating than any other invasions of recorded history. The killing, burning, looting, raping, and enslaving were not unusual. But there was, in addition, a rare psychological shock, arising in part from the clash of very different cultures.

The trauma was intensified by the suddenness and strangeness of the encounter. The dark-skinned natives had no knowledge of the existence of the white men and no warning of their coming. When the conquerors stepped ashore from the great ocean—with their pale skin and unfamiliar dress—it was as if they had descended from another world. They rode animals never before seen, wore armor stouter than anything known to the natives, and spoke in the name of the "one true God," who was stronger than all the rest. The astonished natives readily became believers when they observed that the white Christians stayed relatively healthy while they themselves died in terrifying numbers from smallpox and other diseases.

In fact, the confrontation between the Europeans and the Americans was really a clash between the Old World and the New World, in which the advantage was overwhelmingly on the side of the former. Europe was but *one* among many Old World civilizations, which over the centuries had influenced each other in many ways, and which had a longer and broader history than those of the New World. At the time of the European discovery of America, about forty-five hundred years had passed since the civilizations of Sumer and Egypt had first arisen, whereas it was only about twenty-five hundred years since the earliest civilizations had appeared in the Western hemisphere (p. 17). The European horses that amazed the Indians had first been domesticated in central Asia; the invaders' armor was made of iron, a metal first worked in the Middle East; and the gunpowder for their terrifying firearms had been invented in China. Thus, the Europeans had behind them the collective achievement of all the Old World civilizations. Furthermore, the diseases that the Europeans brought with them were common throughout the Old World but unknown in the New. It is believed that, having no resistance to these diseases, the native population of the Americas was reduced by as much as ninety percent in the first hundred years of European rule—a staggering blow to their ability to resist.

After the conquests were over, the routine of exploitation was less painful (except for the continuing outrage of the slave trade and the persisting toll of Old World diseases). The Spanish and Portuguese monarchies, in intimate partnership with the Church, endeavored to bring a new order of existence and Christian salvation to their subject millions. On the whole, considering the immense geographical distances involved, they succeeded remarkably well. The *Pax Hispanica* (Spanish Peace) covered an area far broader than the Roman Empire. And, while Rome imposed its civilization upon only a portion of its domain, Spain (and Portugal) determined to Christianize and Westernize the *whole* of the Americas.

The Spaniards, in a sense, carried the historic Roman mission to the New World in the sixteenth century. Heirs to Rome, they would build as well as or better than their forebears. During three centuries of rule they organized new cities and towns, churches and missions, plantations and industries. They constructed fine bridges, aqueducts, and highways. While destroying the native civilizations, the Spanish (and the Portuguese) brought to America, long before anyone else did, the Western legacy of art, literature, and learning. These contributions were enjoyed mainly by a privileged few—the European-born whites. For the colonial administrations differed from those of the Roman Empire in one vital respect: Rome permitted the native peoples to participate in the imperial prosperity (p. 131); Spain viewed them primarily as "wards" of the monarchy—to be Christianized and "civilized"—but to serve the interests of the crown and its supporters.

While the impact of the Europeans in the Western hemisphere was catastrophic, in Asia it was at first hardly noticeable. The reason, once again, was that Asia and Europe both belonged to the same community of civilizations. The Europeans had most of their knowledge and skills, and even their diseases, in common with the peoples they encountered; indeed, the wealth of India, the statecraft of China, or the military organization of Japan, for example, were all superior to their own. Thus, the Europeans held no massive advantage that would have enabled them, as a handful of newcomers, to undermine and destroy the Asian civilizations. The most they could do was to use their superiority in the single area of sea warfare to corner the trade in luxuries between Asia and Europe itself, and to make inroads into the regional commerce of the Orient. But apart from the Spanish in the relatively backward Philippines, Europeans were unable to conquer and Christianize any Asian territories other than their tiny commercial footholds.

Heroic missionaries, like the Jesuit father (pp. 431–432), and later saint, Francis Xavier, traveled incredible distances and learned many (to Europeans) extraordinarily difficult languages, so as to preach the Gospel throughout the

East. But without the help of conquering armies, cultural shock, and deadly diseases, as in the New World, the missionaries had little effect on the great religions and flourishing cultures of Asia. True, in the seventeenth century the rulers of China and Japan began strictly controlling contact with the newcomers, as well as (in Japan) viciously persecuting Christian converts. This was a sure sign that in those countries, the elites took the Europeans seriously as a potential threat. But it was not until the eighteenth century and, especially, the nineteenth century, that the Europeans gained a margin of superiority sufficient to turn the potential threat into a real one (pp. 601–602).

In the last major area of the world where the Europeans were newcomers, black Africa south of the Sahara, they also encountered civilizations and cultures that they could not destroy. In West Africa, civilized Islamic states with a literate elite had existed for centuries, and at the time of the arrival of the Europeans, pagan central and southern Africa were also advancing in prosperity and sophistication. Stable governments and powerful tribal chiefdoms, centered on permanent capital cities like Timbuktu in western Africa or Zimbabwe in the southeast, were an increasingly common feature of the region. Iron, horses, and of course Old World diseases were more or less familiar throughout most of Africa. Even with their firearms, when Europeans tried to conquer black African nations, they were generally defeated. Thus, they had to treat the states and kingdoms of the region as partners to be dealt with on the basis of mutual interest rather than as victims to be destroyed.

Above all, this mutual interest lay in trade. Black African rulers had traditionally built their power partly on the control of those resources of their region that were most highly valued in the outside world, namely gold, ivory, and slaves. European traders had originally been attracted to Africa above all by the lure of gold, but following Venice's example, they had soon begun buying slaves to work on sugar plantations—in this case, located in various newfound islands of the Atlantic. Then, in the sixteenth century, the rulers of the new European empires in the Americas turned from plunder and commerce to developing new sources of wealth. In Brazil, the Caribbean, and North America there was endless land suitable for growing not only sugar but other profitable crops like tobacco, coffee, and later cotton; but there were few, if any, natives who could be compelled to grow them. However, all along the Atlantic coast of Africa were densely populated regions where states and chiefdoms were rising in power, conquering land and people as they did so. The result was the appearance of the most massive and systematic traffic in human beings that the world had ever seen: the African slave trade.

The African slave trade was one of the most extensive population movements in human history, second only to the later European emigration to the New World. Between 1523, when the first Africans were shipped across the Atlantic, and the 1880s, when the trade finally came to an end, at least twelve million people were transported from Africa to the Americas. This was also the most systematically brutal of all forms of slavery. Although many civilized societies have made widespread use of slavery, it has often been moderated in practice—for example, by the close association of slaves and owners in ancient Athens (p. 73). African slavery had none of these moderating features. Captured by enemy warriors in the course of plundering their villages, the victims—mostly young men, though young women were also taken—were marched down to the nearest coastal trading station and sold to European (mainly Portuguese, English, and Dutch) dealers. They were packed lying down into the holds of the slave ships for a voyage of many weeks: at least one in six could expect to die on the way. Once arrived and sold to a plantation owner, another one in three could expect to be dead of overwork and underfeeding within three years. But that did not matter to the owners. Until competition among traders drove up the price in the late eighteenth century, new slaves could always be bought cheaply from the African suppliers.

For Africa, the result of the slave trade was a debilitating loss of human resources. Many other warlike and rapidly advancing societies, including that of medieval Europe (pp. 263–264), had profited by selling captives to foreigners as slaves. But to do so on such a vast scale helped bring to an end several centuries of social and political advancement in black Africa. For the Americas, the result was a corresponding gain, especially from the late eighteenth century when the African survival rate began to rise. In the end, a distinctively African element emerged in the culture of many nations from Brazil to the United States. For the western European countries that ran the slave trade, the result was enormous profits that helped make them the economic center of the world. In addition, the unchecked exploitation of Africans led to the growth of the belief in white racial superiority, and the related feeling that the rest of the world was at Europe's disposal to do with as it wished. It was these notions that fueled the intensive imperialism of the nineteenth and twentieth centuries (pp. 602–607).

CONSEQUENCES FOR EUROPE

What effects did the overseas expansion have on Europe itself? The most immediate *motive* for the explorations had been economic, and their first *effect* was economic: expansion nourished the roots of capitalism. As trade with the Orient and the Americas increased, profits accumulated; and the huge investments required for the long voyages and the colonial ventures brought handsome gains to bankers and capitalists. The flow of gold and silver from the New World stimulated general business activity. By 1600 the volume of money in existence in Europe had risen to nearly one billion dollars (in today's terms). This more adequate supply of coins promoted trade and strengthened the incentive of all classes to produce for the market, and it also made for *price inflation*. This, in turn, gave an added push to business, for merchants and investors are eager to buy goods and properties when they see that prices are moving upward.

The overseas trade brought an abrupt shift in the geographical distribution of prosperity and power. Venice, Florence, Genoa, and the smaller Italian cities had long enjoyed a strategic position between the Middle East and northern Europe. Italy had sparked the revival of trade in the eleventh century and had helped the growth of early capitalism (pp. 263–330). But after the Portuguese reached the sources of oriental commerce in the sixteenth century, the Mediterranean routes dwindled in importance; for the countries of western Europe facing upon the Atlantic now had the advantage of geographical position. Venice, the queen of the Adriatic, fell into decline.

As Britain, France, and Holland became the main trading gateways between Europe and the rest of the world, the center of prosperity and power shifted to northwestern Europe. Antwerp, Amsterdam, and London were to become, in turn, the leading financial centers of expanding world commerce. These cities had the first organized "money markets" in which large private and government loans were arranged. Exchange houses arose there for trade and speculation in commodities, currencies, bonds, and stocks. Stocks began to appear in the seventeenth century with the creation of "joint-stock companies," the forerunners of the modern corporation; these companies made it possible to raise large sums of capital for long-term investment. Though limited at first to commercial ventures, joint-stock companies were later formed in the mining and manufacturing industries.

The triumph of capitalism was assured by the acceleration of trade and production. The wealth of Europe mounted steadily, and the variety and quantity of goods increased with every day. Commodities and habits (like tobacco), formerly unknown in Europe, were introduced from both America and Asia. New foods added nourishment and novelty to European diets, notably potatoes, Indian corn, tomatoes, citrus fruits, chocolate, coffee, and peanuts. (Syphilis was also introduced from America—in exchange, perhaps, for the European gift of smallpox to the Native Americans.) Chinaware, oriental furnishings, and art objects began to appear in the homes of the privileged classes. The taste for luxuries had been whetted by medieval commerce, and the well-to-do could now indulge it to the full.

In these ways, overseas penetration triggered the expansion of capitalism into a *worldwide* system. The fact is that after 1500 the world became a treasure house for the West. Europe, whose people made up a tiny fraction of humanity, was in a position to seize and exploit vast areas of the globe. In no other period of history has a major cultural group enjoyed so favorable a ratio between its population and its available resources. Although the Europeans were to squander this advantage on endless wars, it served to lift their standard of living and their sense of power.

Just as important as the economic results of the expansion of Europe were its religious and cultural ones. All of a sudden, though not quite in the way that the earliest explorers had expected, the position of Christianity among the world's great religions was transformed. After many centuries in which Christianity had been almost entirely confined within the narrow limits of Europe (pp. 276–277), between 1500 and 1600 it replaced Islam as the world's farthest-flung intercontinental religion.

In addition, the growth of Europe's worldwide power had the effect of strengthening the nonreligious elements in Western culture. Europe's newfound success had a profound effect on the outlook and psychology of Western men and women. By confirming the usefulness of curiosity, daring, and ruthlessness, it raised the value they placed on these traits. The success also strengthened *materialism* by making more widespread the enjoyment of wealth and the chances of acquiring it. It broadened the intellectual horizons of Europeans to some degree, but contributed little to their respect for non-Western ideas and institutions. On the contrary, the startling victories of the Europeans fortified their optimism and strengthened their faith in their own *superiority*.

Both in its religious and its nonreligious aspects, Western civilization now became a *worldwide* civilization. For the first time in history, a civilization was to leap every barrier of race and geography and spread its influence around the globe. Some areas, of course, would be touched only superficially, but European values and ideas would become familiar almost everywhere. And within the emerging world of associated cultures, the West would continue to serve as the chief carrier and transformer of ideas and institutions.

CHAPTER 8

● ● ●

THE RENAISSANCE:
UPSURGE OF HUMANISM

Overview

The political, social, and economic changes that swept over Europe from the late Middle Ages onward were accompanied by spectacular new developments in thought and culture, many of which involved a break with existing traditions. From about 1300, scholars, thinkers, artists, and writers appeared who turned away from the prevailing literary and artistic styles, and to some extent even from the accepted values, of medieval civilization. Instead, they sought inspiration in a deeper knowledge and understanding of Europe's forerunner civilization, that of pagan Greece and Rome. To those who took part in this revival of classical antiquity, it seemed so exciting that they spoke of literature, thought, and the arts as having been "reborn" after many centuries of "barbarism." In fact, the medieval culture that the admirers of Greece and Rome despised was itself a highly civilized one, which was strongly influenced by classical literature and thought. All the same, the revival movement rediscovered a great deal of the past of Greece and Rome that had been neglected or forgotten over the centuries, and that is why we still call the movement by the French word for "rebirth"—the Renaissance.

The Renaissance involved far more than simply resurrecting the past, for there was no way that the admirers of Greece and Rome could separate themselves from the living European civilization of their own day and age. Scholars pored over the works of ancient authors and rediscovered the classical ideal of the fully developed human being whose character was formed by literary study and education—but then they had to grapple with the implications of this ideal for the *otherworldly* values of the Christian faith. Architects studied the ruins of Roman temples and imperial palaces—and applied what they learned to building cathedrals, or townhouses for bankers. Artists gazed in wonder at ancient statues of gods and busts of emperors—and were inspired to paint portraits of popes, or to carve nude statues of Old Testament kings. Writers longed to "equal or surpass the ancients" in eloquence— but sharing as they did in the national cultures that had grown up during the Middle Ages, they wrote eloquently not just in Latin and Greek, but in English, Spanish, French, and every other vernacular (native) language of Europe.

Out of this encounter between the pagan Greco-Roman past and the Christian European present came an extraordinarily diverse cultural achievement. In Italy, "pagan" despisers of Christian morality analyzed human behavior in terms of what *was* rather than what *ought to be,* and idealistic philosophers inspired by Plato sought for an ultimate truth that would reconcile pagan wisdom and the beliefs of Christianity; meanwhile, in northern Europe, earnest believers sought to renew Christianity by bringing it back to its roots in the ancient world. Painters depicted the naked female body sometimes as an emblem of worldly sensuality, and sometimes as a symbol of divine beauty and truth. Writers revived ancient literary forms such as satire and drama, but most often, they used these to display and comment on the life and characters of their own times—for example, the alleged hypocrisy and corruption of monks, the foolishness of a would-be knight errant, or the tragic flaws of an all too thoughtful prince of Denmark.

Today the specific ideals and strivings of the Renaissance no longer seem as urgent as once they did. For modern civilization, it is not a matter of vital cultural importance to recover the reality of ancient Greece and Rome beyond what is already known. Not many people today, even among the most educated, believe that the best way to perfect themselves as human beings is to read the classical authors in the original languages. But the shift in culture that the Renaissance brought about was a permanent one, whose effects are still felt five centuries later. The belief in the ennobling effect of education and exposure to literature and art—widened to include ancient, medieval, and modern, Western and non-Western—remains a basic value of present-day civilization. And this widening of what is considered valuable in literature and art is itself a long-term result of the Renaissance, for by revering pagan culture alongside Christianity, the scholars and thinkers of the Renaissance set a precedent of understanding and appreciation between different cultures and civilizations that has lasted to the present.

In many other ways, too, the scholars and thinkers of the Renaissance contributed to the shifts in civilization that began in the later Middle Ages. By criticizing the religious practices of their own time in the light of what they discovered about the Christian past, they helped to bring about both the Protestant Reformation and the reform and reaffirmation of Catholicism. They brought back into circulation a vast mass of ancient ideas and knowledge, from the theorems of Hellenistic mathematicians to the tactical formations of the Roman legions, without which the changes of later centuries in such fields as science, government, and warfare would hardly have happened. In the process of looking behind the myths of the present to the reality of the past, they developed a distrust of received wisdom and preconceived ideas that eventually helped the growth of knowledge in every field. And though the writers and artists of today have traveled far from the aims and methods of their Renaissance forerunners, the best of Renaissance literature and art provides an understanding of the human condition and an ideal of beauty that will never cease to console and inspire.

THE RENAISSANCE VIEW OF HUMAN NATURE

At the core of the Renaissance as a movement of cultural change was an upsurge of *humanism*. The humanist way of thinking can be most broadly defined as any view that puts the human person *(humanus)* at the center of things and stresses the individual's creative, reasoning, and aesthetic powers. Such a view is at least as old as the Greeks and Romans. Although the word "humanism" was not used in the classical age, Cicero (p. 134) referred to *humanitas* as the quality of mind and spirit that distinguishes human beings from mere animals. That quality, he thought, is best nurtured and expressed through literature (including history, philosophy, and oratory). Renaissance scholars, following Cicero's lead, identified the study of classical literature (both Greek and Latin) with humanism, and they applied the term "humanist" exclusively to classical scholars.

The Revival of Interest in the Classical World

Interest in the classics had not altogether disappeared during the Middle Ages. By the twelfth century many scholars had made themselves familiar with works of antiquity, and Dante and Chaucer drew heavily from the Latin poets. Before the fourteenth century, however, there had been little to equal the enthusiasm of Renaissance scholars for classical writings. It was in those works that they caught their "new" vision of humanity. Moved by this vision, they searched eagerly for ancient documents and developed a deep respect for the literary culture of antiquity. Their enthusiasm was not caused primarily by dramatic finds of "new" documents; it resulted, rather, from a quickening change in the European *state of mind*.

The medieval intellect, steeped in a God-centered, otherworldly view of the universe, had been largely closed to the naturalistic, pagan spirit. The schoolmen fingered classical manuscripts through thick gloves, so to speak; their religious training normally kept them from a truly sympathetic contact (p. 303). But with the passing of the Middle Ages, the ideals of asceticism and Christian poverty receded before advancing worldliness.

Caught up in this trend were many groups among the educated elite of Europe. In the developing towns, the bourgeois found medieval ideals increasingly unattractive, and were looking for standards closer to their hearts. Kings and nobles glimpsed through the classics the worldly elite of Greece and Rome, whose elegance, refinement, and heroic achievements they hoped to imitate. Even popes and bishops, coming as they mostly did from bourgeois and noble families, often dropped their suspicion of the pagan ancients and became patrons of humanist learning. Bourgeois, aristocrats, and high churchmen all hoped, by imitating the best in ancient thought and behavior, to re-create classical standards in their own times. They failed to bring back the past, or even to imitate it faithfully, but their efforts to do so helped shape modern values.

To most Renaissance thinkers the classical view of humanity was the proper view. They, like the ancients, saw human beings as active *egoists* whose interests were centered in the *here* and *now*. Though they seldom renounced religion, they regarded it as a formality or as an extension of *human* knowledge and power.

The good life, they thought, is the life that is pleasing to the senses, intellect, and aesthetic capacities. Human desires are generally good, though they need to be cultivated and kept in balance. The greatest wrong, to most Renaissance humanists, was *negation*, the absence or repression of spontaneous expression. Well-born and educated individuals, they believed, should be free and proud. They should strive for mastery of all the worthy arts, because their ultimate value as human beings would be measured not in humility, but in talent and accomplishments. Successful individuals, as the Italian humanists put it, possess the quality of *virtù* (strength, virtuosity). Their minds are so filled with thoughts of *this* world that they have little time (or desire) to think about the next.

The ideas of the humanists plainly ran counter to many Christian teachings. They seemed to reject the doctrine of Original Sin and *natural* human sinfulness. They suggested that individuals could perform mighty deeds without divine assistance. And yet (especially in northern Europe) a Christian humanism developed alongside this secular humanism. Some pious scholars shared the growing enthusiasm for the classics and ancient languages. They shared, too, the heightened appreciation of human capabilities, especially the powers of reason and creativity. But they insisted that all human powers were a gift of God — and that this life, though rewarding, fell short of the glory of heaven.

THE NEW SCHOLARSHIP: PETRARCH, BOCCACCIO

It is no accident that the Renaissance arose in Italy (as did capitalism and absolutism). The forces of social change were most advanced there; the development and spread of urban life, for example, had progressed further in Italy than in northern Europe. There was another reason, however, independent of those forces: the growing consciousness of *nationality*. While this consciousness did not produce a unified state in Italy (as it did in Spain and France), it caused Italians to embrace their past more warmly than ever before. As Italian humanists studied the Latin classics, they began to dream of restoring the grandeur of ancient Rome. Few Italians had forgotten those glories, for their land offered eloquent architectural reminders. The humanist "road back to Rome" was shortest in Italy, and it was traveled by *patriotic* pilgrims.

Francesco Petrarca (Petrarch), who is regarded as the founder of Renaissance humanism, was born in 1304 of an exiled Florentine family. Urged by his bourgeois father to study law, he came upon the works of Cicero in the course of his reading. His admiration for Cicero's thought and style led to a passion for all the classics, and when his father died Petrarch gave up his study of law and turned to a life of scholarship.

It was Petrarch who first undertook the collection of ancient manuscripts. He persuaded others to join him in a search through monastic and cathedral libraries that took him all over Italy and into France and Germany as well. Among his finds were some lost orations and letters of his beloved Cicero. He employed copyists in his home and built up an admirable collection of pagan documents and books. His private library, the first of its kind, became a model for scholars and other intellectuals.

Petrarch's enthusiasm was contagious. Following his example, many of the well-to-do took up the search and began to build their own libraries. Wealthy patrons became interested and by the fifteenth century had founded such famous libraries as the Laurentian in Florence, St. Mark's in Venice, and the Vatican in Rome.

Petrarch set the style as a scholar as well as a collector. Though he led a busy life and spent much of his time in cities and at the courts of aristocrats, he expressed a love of solitude and the peace of nature. But this was a different solitude from that prescribed by the ascetic ideal; it was closer to the ancient Roman model. He spent his private hours not meditating and praying, but studying literature; for isolation without books, he declared, was "exile, prison, and torture." He alternated writing with reading, in the fashion of the modern scholar. What a glory it was, thought Petrarch, "to read what our forerunners have written and to write what later generations may wish to read. . . ."

He preferred to write in classical Latin, because he had only contempt for the vernacular tongues (p. 304) and the corrupted Latin of the Middle Ages. Many of his writings were in the form of epics, dialogues, and letters patterned after the style of Cicero and Vergil (pp. 134–135). He is hardly remembered for those efforts. More successful were his love poems (sonnets), which he wrote in Italian. He addressed most of them to Laura, a beautiful young married woman whom he loved and idealized (though she was unaware of his passion). A record of his most intimate thoughts upon seeing her and thinking of her, these sonnets to Laura became a model for many generations of romantic poets.

Petrarch lived only a generation after Dante, the supreme poet of the high Middle Ages (p. 307), but in these two figures we can see the shift from medieval to modern times. Although Dante knew the classics, he remained a medieval man. Petrarch knew them better, and, while continuing to profess the Christian faith, he warmly embraced pagan values. His irrepressible pursuit of fame led to his being crowned with the *laurel wreath* in 1341; he thus became the first *poet laureate* of modern times. Originally the laurel wreath had been placed upon victors in the ancient Greek "Pythian" games honoring the god Apollo; later it was conferred upon outstanding public officials and artists. The Romans had adopted the custom, and it was revived late in the Middle Ages. Dante, significantly, refused the offer of a laurel crown, but Petrarch was pleased to strengthen his link with antiquity and to bask in the "immortal glory" of the prize. After the formal examination before King Robert of Naples, he was crowned in a classic ceremony in Rome.

One of Petrarch's followers, Giovanni Boccaccio, was among the first Westerners of modern times to study the Greek language. The son of a Florentine banker, Boccaccio grew bored with the humdrum of credits and debits and set out to learn Greek. Once he had done so, he instructed his tutor to translate Homer into Latin and thus helped to introduce his generation to their first reading of the *Iliad* and the *Odyssey* (p. 87). Like Petrarch, Boccaccio searched far and wide for ancient manuscripts. One of his prized discoveries was a work of the historian Tacitus, which he uncovered in the monastery library at Monte Cassino. When he first saw the neglected condition of the archives there, he broke into tears.

Though Boccaccio was nominally a Christian, his own writings are markedly pagan in spirit. *Fiammetta*, which is sometimes called the first psychological novel of the West, makes no reference to the world of Christian faith and morals. When the heroine is torn by the question of whether to give herself to her lover, she is answered not by the Virgin, but by Venus. The characters in the *Decameron*, Boccaccio's best-known work, are similarly un-Christian in outlook and behavior. The tales in this collection, which Boccaccio borrowed from various countries of Europe and the Middle East, feature sensual escapades, deceits, and clever revenges.

Now other Italian scholars began to study Greek. They were aided by refugee scholars from Constantinople, who had begun to flee the city before its fall to the Turks in 1453 (p. 328)—bringing with them Greek manuscripts, and offering instruction in the language. By 1500 nearly all the Greek authors had been recovered by the West and translated into Latin and Italian. This was an accomplishment of lasting importance. While medieval scholars had become familiar, through Arabic, with many of the writings of Aristotle and the Hellenistic scientists, they had no direct knowledge of Greek *literature*. It was the humanists who restored to our Western heritage the works of Homer, Herodotus, Thucydides, Aeschylus, Sophocles, Euripides, and Plato.

Humanistic Education and the "Gentleman"

This new body of knowledge challenged traditional patterns of education and thought. Along with new social forces and the rising secular spirit, it set off a revolution in European schooling. Medieval education had been almost exclusively by and for the clergy. Professional training in law and medicine had been introduced into Italian universities during the Middle Ages and had spread to the north. But for medieval Europe as a whole, religion remained the focus of higher learning. The *trivium* and *quadrivium* centered on scriptural texts, the writings of the Church Fathers, and the logic of Aristotle (p. 298).

The Italian humanists made up the first substantial body of *secular* (nonreligious) scholars in Europe. Most of them were sons of the middle class or the nobility and had no connection with the clergy. Nor had they any use for the tiresome scholasticism that still dominated education (pp. 299–302); in fact, they regarded it as irrelevant to the new society. In Greek and Roman literature they saw the means of providing students with a truly *liberal* education.

It was fairly easy to eliminate scholasticism from the Italian universities, for it had never taken deep root there. The new learning was introduced in its place by humanist professors of rhetoric (speaking and writing), whose lectures drew enthusiastic students from all over Europe. The humanists were not welcomed at most northern universities, however. In the scholastic strongholds of Paris, Cologne, and Heidelberg, the faculties looked with disdain upon the unfamiliar Greek studies. Some Oxford masters condemned them as "dangerous and damnable." Not until the end of the sixteenth century did Greek and Latin literature—the "classics"—supersede philosophy as the foundation of liberal education in the north.

Humanism reached into elementary as well as higher education. The private schools that arose in the towns to serve the sons of the well-to-do were secular in tone and concentrated on Latin and Greek studies. But they aimed at more than the cultivation of the intellect. The schoolmasters saw the ancient statesmen (like Pericles and Cicero) as models to inspire young men to lives of fruitful citizenship. The Greeks and Romans had lived in cities and had enjoyed a sophisticated social life; so it was their example, rather than that of the monks and saints, that seemed relevant to the new society. Literature and moral instruction were balanced by training in music and athletics. The Greek ideal of the well-rounded man, mentally and physically fit, was at the heart of humanistic education.

During the sixteenth century this pattern of education spread from Italy throughout western Europe. The private secular school largely replaced monastic and cathedral schools in the education of Europe's leaders. Like the classical model on which it was based and the privileged society it served, the private school was aristocratic in purpose and style. (Its most famous descendants are the "public"— actually, private—schools of England, notably Eton, Harrow, and Winchester.)

Although the curriculum of Greek and Latin studies often became rigid and sterile, it helped shape a new type of personality: the "gentleman." As an ideal, the gentleman now took the place of the medieval knight or the ascetic holy man. Whether of noble or bourgeois background, the ideal gentleman was a man of refinement and self-control. Just as chivalry had tamed the warriors of the Middle Ages (pp. 250–251), humanistic education taught the new landowners and capitalists the ways of urbane living.

The true gentleman possessed a disciplined mind, graceful manners, and excellent taste. For those impatient to acquire such virtues, manuals of proper behavior began to appear; the most influential of them, *The Courtier,* was published in 1528 by an Italian nobleman, Baldassare Castiglione. As Machiavelli was advising rulers on the art of statecraft, Castiglione advised young aristocrats, both male and female, on education and manners. The gentleman and the lady would flourish as admired types in the West for some four hundred years. In the twentieth century the gentleman seems to have disappeared as a model—replaced, perhaps, by the "expert" or the "organization man."

Philosophy: The Appeal of Platonism

Although the recovery of Greek learning revolutionized European education, its influence on philosophy was comparatively modest. Its main effect was to put Plato (pp. 83–85) in Aristotle's place as the foremost philosopher. Aristotle had ruled over the medieval universities because his methods of logic proved so useful to the scholastic thinkers (p. 299). His works were better known than Plato's, and his moderation appealed to men like Aquinas. But the humanists found his writings difficult and without literary appeal. As the complete dialogues of his teacher, Plato, became available during the fifteenth century, the humanists were struck by their charming style as well as their ideas. Here was philosophy that was at the same time literature, and literature that was philosophy. Plato became the new master.

Florence was the leading center for Platonic studies. Cosimo de' Medici, a scholarly ruler who was keenly interested in Plato, founded the Platonic Academy there about 1450. The Academy served as a center for the translation of Platonic writings and for discussions of Plato's philosophy. Just as thinkers of the Middle Ages had sought to reconcile Aristotle with Christian doctrines, so the Italian humanists tried to do the same for Plato.

The Academy was more of an intellectual club than a school. It consisted of only a few select scholars, subsidized by the Medici, and their circle of friends. Their talk and writings were of a rarefied sort that meant little to ordinary people. And yet the influence of the Academy was substantial—especially in art and literature. Almost every artist of the later Renaissance was influenced by Platonism, and some, like Botticelli and Michelangelo, became deeply absorbed in it. Through them the Platonic influence passed on to later generations—ultimately to such nineteenth-century writers as Wordsworth and Goethe (pp. 530–532).

Marsilio Ficino was the shining light of the Academy. Chosen by Cosimo at an early age, he was carefully educated and then installed in a villa in the hills near Florence. From that time until his death, he devoted himself to translating Plato's writings and explaining his doctrines. He presided over polite seminars at the villa and corresponded with notables all over Europe, seeking to demonstrate that Platonic teachings were in agreement with Christianity. For those who could not accept religion on the basis of "revelation," he suggested that Plato could open another way.

Pico della Mirandola, a disciple of Ficino, went beyond his master and attempted a synthesis (bringing together) of *all* learning, Eastern and Western. This genius of the age knew Arabic and Hebrew as well as Greek and Latin, and he studied Jewish, Babylonian, and Persian records. He refused to ignore any source of truth merely because it was not labeled Christian. He felt that by employing all the records and resources of scholarship he had achieved a comprehension of humanity and the universe beyond that of scholastic philosophy. Actually, Pico added little to the view of the world shared by others of his times. He did, however, emphasize human freedom and capacity for learning, and, by breaking through the bounds of medieval theology, he opened a door to the study of *comparative* religion and philosophy.

Like the other members of Cosimo's circle, Pico embraced the Platonic view of creation and existence, which held that by some accident of prehistory humans had become separated from their divine home of pure spirit. Though each soul (spirit) had fallen prisoner to matter (the body), it struggled for liberation and a return to God. This view corresponded to the Christian doctrine of the Fall and the human longing for salvation.

An interesting offshoot of this idea had a profound effect on the arts. The feeling for *natural beauty*, said the Platonists, came from the soul's remembrance of the *divine beauty* of heaven. Hence, aesthetic expression and enjoyment took on a religious connection. Finally, the Platonists linked the emotion of physical love to the higher urge that moves individuals toward their divine source (Platonic love). These teachings raised the arts, even when they dealt with secular subjects, to a higher level. According to the Florentine intellectuals, *art* stimulates appreciation of beauty, and *love* brings the individual closer to the ultimate goal of spiritual reunion with God.

The widespread acceptance of this idea helps to explain the Renaissance "cult of beauty" and the toleration by devout Christians of a frankly sensual art. It reinforced the naturalistic thrust of humanism and the rising secular taste of the times. Thus, by the fifteenth century most painters and sculptors had turned their backs on the "otherworldly" style of art and had plunged eagerly, sometimes ecstatically, into *realistic* representation.

THE CRITICAL SPIRIT AND THE BEGINNINGS OF EMPIRICISM

Beyond its influence on aesthetics, the Platonic revival had only a limited effect on European philosophy. Of greater importance were the methods of scholarship that were introduced by the humanists, although the philosophical implications of those methods were not fully recognized at the time. Petrarch, Boccaccio, and the others who collected classical manuscripts sought to recreate, from the various documents, *correct* texts of the ancient authors. Their intention was simply to reassemble old learning, but their method led to a more *critical* attitude toward the written word and greater attention to *observed facts*. The downfall of scholasticism, with its system of knowledge based on authority and reason, encouraged later scholars to find truth by *empirical* methods (observation and experiment—p. 468).

The Roman humanist Lorenzo Valla was a pioneer of modern textual criticism. An expert on Latin style, he abhorred the carelessness of medieval writers and was bold enough to attack even the Latin of the Vulgate (the Bible as translated by Jerome—p. 196). He also challenged the popular belief that the Apostles' Creed, the traditional confession of Christian beliefs, had actually been composed by the apostles. His most shocking discovery, in 1440, was that the Donation of Constantine (p. 232) was a forgery. This document, which served as a basis for papal claims to secular supremacy over the West, had stood unchallenged for centuries.

Using his new tools of scholarship, Valla demonstrated that the *language* of the Donation could not have been that of the fourth century but was more likely that of the eighth or ninth. Going beyond grammatical analysis, he also pointed out (as a careful scholar should) that the manuscript contained terms of a period later than the date when it was supposedly written. In the words of the Donation, the Emperor Constantine assigns vast powers to Pope Sylvester *before* leaving Rome to build a new capital at Byzantium. Yet he declares that the pope shall have supremacy over all patriarchs, including the one at "Constantinople." How could this be, asked Valla, when at that time Constantinople was not yet a city and there was no such patriarch? So conclusive was Valla's criticism that the Donation was recognized by all as a fraud.

It speaks for the spirit of the age that the popes made no move to punish Valla. On the contrary, they asked for the scholar's services. He was secretary to King Alfonso V of Naples when he published his exposé of the forgery. Afterward, Pope Nicholas V hired him away and brought him back to Rome to translate the ancient Greek historian Thucydides (p. 92). Nicholas, a patron of humanism, also founded the Vatican (papal) Library as a depository for ancient manuscripts.

Valla was bold, critical, and independent, but, as a practicing humanist, he limited his attention to what could be learned from the literature of the past. The methods of Niccolò Machiavelli went further. He wanted to see what could be learned through direct observation of the world around him. As we noted in the preceding chapter (pp. 344–346), Machiavelli's work was a watershed in the history of political thought. We have seen how his view of the state contrasted with that of Thomas Aquinas, but even greater was the contrast in the *methodology* of the two scholars. Aquinas, the scholastic philosopher, had sought truth mainly by reasoning from authority *(deduction)*. Machiavelli sought it mainly by generalizing from collected data *(induction)*. He drew his facts from recorded history *and* personal experience. Though he lacked the system, precision, and control of modern social scientists, Machiavelli was clearly moving toward a new conception of knowledge and its verification.

He was not alone in this. Leonardo da Vinci, a fellow citizen of Florence, grew discontented with bookish learning and determined to see things for himself. Although Leonardo is best known for his great paintings (pp. 394–395), his love of art was matched by a desire to unlock the secrets of nature. In order to improve his skill in drawing human and animal bodies, he dissected cadavers and set down his on-the-spot sketches and comments in notebooks. He found dissection difficult and distasteful, but he insisted that observation was the only means to true knowledge. He also experimented with mechanics and drew up plans for ingenious practical inventions. A man of his times, Leonardo both typified Italian humanism and foreshadowed the age of empiricism.

CHRISTIAN HUMANISM: ERASMUS

So far we have spoken about humanism only in Italy, without tracing its spread beyond the Alps. During the fifteenth century a number of northern scholars journeyed to the Italian centers of learning and carried home with them the seeds of the new scholarship. But the soil of the northern countries produced a different variety of humanism—the pagan flavor, so strong in Italy, was missing.

When humanism came to the north, the intellectual leaders there were filled with Christian piety (deep reverence), and were eager to reform the Church. Dissatisfied with scholasticism, they seized on the rediscovered classics of antiquity. Unlike the scholars of Italy, however, they were not looking for models of sophisticated secular life. Rather, they sought guides to a purer religion and found in the ancient writings those ideals that would encourage *spiritual* reform.

Humanism as represented by Pico and his circle was an outlook based upon many faiths and systems. In the north, however, it emerged as a strictly Christian framework. The northern leaders believed that the example of disciplined and balanced living found in Cicero and the Stoics (pp. 137–138) could well be followed by Christians. Above all, they sought to use the new linguistic and textual skills developed by the Italian humanists as a means of establishing a "truer" Bible. They hoped with these tools to cut away the "false growths" of medieval religious practice and to restore thereby a "pure" Christianity.

There were many devout and vigorous humanists in the north, especially in Germany and England. But the greatest of them all was Desiderius Erasmus. Born in Rotterdam in 1466, he became a cosmopolitan scholar, at home in many lands. His learning and scholarship won him acclaim throughout Europe as the "prince of humanists."

Erasmus, an illegitimate child, had little knowledge of his family background. His father, of middle-class origin, was a priest at the time of Erasmus' birth. Little is known of his mother. Sent off to school as a boy, he lacked the comfortable bourgeois background characteristic of the Italian humanists. His school was supervised by an order of devout laymen, the Brethren of the Common Life. The Brethren, who were dedicated to a pious, mystical Christianity, taught that individual lives should be modeled on the example of Jesus. While subjecting themselves to rigid spiritual discipline, they emphasized the ideals of service and love. Erasmus was deeply touched by this early influence, and he adopted the "philosophy of Christ" as his lifetime ideal.

After Erasmus left school, he was persuaded to enter an Augustinian monastery, where he received little formal instruction but was free to read as he pleased in the classics, both Christian and pagan. At the age of thirty, looking to wider and deeper scholarship, he secured a release from his monastic vows. He went to the University of Paris, where he completed a course in theology. From then on he devoted his life to research and writing, visiting the major centers of learning. Though he was ordained a priest, Erasmus never served a parish. He lived, sometimes meagerly, on the support of patrons and on income from his books.

In the classics Erasmus found models of behavior that could well be followed by genuine Christians. Socrates, Plato, and Cicero were worthy, he thought, of a place among the saints. But he read the ancient writings as a firm believer, and he was persuaded that such studies should serve to strengthen faith, not undermine it. He mastered Greek, for example, not in order to find a truer Homer or Thucydides, but to discover a truer Christ.

Erasmus used his scholarly skills to prepare a more accurate version of the New Testament. Like Valla, he felt certain that the Vulgate Bible, respected though it was, contained errors. After collecting a number of the earliest available New Testament manuscripts in the original Greek, he produced a fresh Greek version based on a comparison of texts. He finished this work in 1516, along with his own Latin translation and commentary, hoping that these efforts would lead to a clearer understanding of the message of Christ—and to translations in the vernacular tongues. He was one of the first to believe that the Bible should be read by the *people* themselves.

Erasmus also prepared improved texts of the writings of the Greek and Latin Church Fathers as well as revised editions of pagan authors. He carried on an extensive correspondence with fellow scholars, and the influence of his ideas, expressed in clear, polished Latin, was extraordinary. He was feared by suspicious conservatives among the clergy but was welcomed everywhere by admiring humanists. Unlike many of them, however, Erasmus was not content to bask in the adulation of an elite; he wanted to make his thoughts available to all literate people.

He published a great many works, often satirical, through which he tried to call attention to the need for reform. He wished to cleanse the Church and society of selfishness, cruelty, hypocrisy, pride, and ignorance—and to replace them with tolerance, honesty, wisdom, service, and love. Repelled by violence and disorder, he hoped that appeals to *reason* would bring about peaceful change. But he sometimes questioned if reform could be achieved peacefully. His most widely read and most entertaining work, *In Praise of Folly*, is filled with doubts and double meanings. Paraded before the reader are the lovers of Folly, a character who personified for her creator the strongest forces in human nature.

Erasmus has Folly sing her own praises: "Without me the world cannot exist for a moment. For is not all that is done among mortals, full of folly; is it not performed by fools and for fools?" People find happiness in light-heartedness and light-headedness—in spontaneous, animal-like behavior. They delight in deceiving and in being deceived. Society rejects the person who pulls off the masks in the comedy of life; the "well-adjusted" person adapts to the game, mixes with others, and encourages their delusions.

At one point Folly observes that sober reason puts an unwelcome damper on natural impulses. The preacher's congregation yawns when he discusses a serious matter but perks up when he tells some silly anecdote. And human behavior is governed less by reason than by the emotions. According to Folly, anger holds the fortress of the breast, and lust rules "a broad empire lower down."

Erasmus spoke of the foolishness of war and war-makers and of the peculiar conceits of individuals and nations, but he reserved most of his barbs for the clergy. The Church, he thought, had grown unduly fond of Folly and had drifted far from the teachings of Christ. He criticized the hair-splitting theologians, the vain and ignorant monks, and the power-loving bishops and popes. He also ridiculed the excesses of the popular cult of the saints and their relics (pp. 274–277), and the purchase of indulgences (p. 413).

In Praise of Folly was written in 1509. Although Erasmus spoke with tongue in cheek, contemporary events tended to confirm what he said. The literate men and women who read his books were impressed and amused, but neither they nor the

Church nor society at large were much changed by his sharp words. His criticism of clerics, it is true, helped to bring on the Reformation, but that religious revolt took a shape that he despised. What he hoped for was a *peaceful* reform of Christianity as a *whole*. He wanted a purified Church, not a divided one.

Erasmus was just as critical of the passions and violence aroused by Martin Luther as he was of the errors of the popes. This made him appear to be, in the eyes of Protestant reformers, a moral and physical coward who would not stand up for his convictions. Actually, Erasmus stood fast upon his own convictions—that Christian unity should be upheld, reason promoted, and rebellion shunned.

THE REVOLUTION IN ART

The spirit of humanism could not be confined to literature and philosophy, and as early as the fourteenth century it burst forth splendidly in the visual arts. It appeared first, as one might expect, in Italy—in Florence, the capital of humanism, which remained for some two hundred years the leading center of European art. Few places on earth, over a comparable period, can match that city's output of painting, sculpture, and architecture.

THE PIONEER OF NATURALISM: GIOTTO

In point of time, Giotto di Bondone was a medieval man, living at the same time as Dante. But he was, in fact, a transitional figure who foreshadowed the modern spirit. In his own day (the early fourteenth century) Giotto was hailed by the citizens of Florence for having achieved a revolution in artistic technique.

In 1305 he was commissioned to paint, on the inside walls of the Arena Chapel in Padua, the New Testament story of Mary and Christ. This was an enormous task, calling for some thirty-five separate scenes. Giotto worked in a common technique known as fresco. Each morning a small area of the wall, covering the space the artist planned to finish that day, was plastered fresh (*fresco*). The paint, consisting of powdered pigment mixed with water, was applied to the wet plaster and became part of the wall surface when it dried. Because of its size and excellence, Giotto's work in the Arena Chapel was a milestone in European painting. Later artists would be commissioned to follow Giotto's grand example; their efforts reached a peak in Michelangelo's stupendous fresco on the ceiling of the Sistine Chapel (pp. 395–396).

Giotto's paintings reveal the new techniques that were just beginning to emerge. He was not satisfied with the flat look of medieval altar panels and the painted figures of manuscripts. These served well enough to tell a story, and they were often superb in color and design. But Giotto wanted to re-create an actual scene, to give the viewer the feeling of being an eyewitness. In order to accomplish this, he sought to produce the illusion of "depth" (perspective) on a flat surface and to make the figures look solid and real. This he did by skillful use of light and shadow and by *foreshortening* the hands and feet. He also gave careful attention to

8-1   Giotto. *Lamentation*, c. 1305. Fresco. Arena Chapel, Padua, Italy.

the *composition* of each scene, arranging individual figures and groups as in a stage setting. Finally, he suggested the emotional state of his subjects through careful attention to facial expression and gesture (*Fig. 8-1*).

Later painters were to go beyond Giotto in the development of naturalism. But he was the pioneer and was recognized as such. His tomb, in the cathedral of Florence bears this inscription: "Lo, I am he by whom dead painting was restored to life, to whose right hand all was possible, by whom art became one with nature. . . ." Giotto's influence touched every artist of the Renaissance and extended beyond mere technique. He established himself as a model to follow: the artist as hero, a famous individual. Medieval painters and sculptors had rarely put their names on their works, but Giotto, in the new spirit of the times, signed his paintings and amiably accepted popular acclaim. He demonstrated, further, the humanist ideal of the many-sided genius, the person of *virtù*. A man of many skills, he became the official architect of Florence and designed the graceful campanile

8-2   Arnolfo di Cambio. Cathedral of Florence. Tower by Giotto, dome by Filippo Brunelleschi. Florence, Italy. Begun 1296.

(bell tower) of the cathedral. Rising some four hundred feet, it overlooks his beloved city and the valley of the Arno River (*Fig. 8-2*).

NEW ARTISTIC TECHNIQUES: BRUNELLESCHI, VAN EYCK

Giotto left a technical challenge to his successors: How could painting be made *more* naturalistic? It was not until a century later that a significant advance in this direction was made. Again it was a Florentine, Filippo Brunelleschi, who pointed the way. A master of sculpture and architecture as well as painting, he designed a stunning Gothic dome to match Giotto's tower (*Fig. 8-2*). But he shared with his fellow humanists a distaste for medieval forms and, after a close study of Roman ruins, set out to create a new style. Adapting classical forms to the needs of his day, Brunelleschi set the tone of Renaissance architecture. His distinctive style marks many of the churches and palaces of Florence; proofs can be seen in his own work (*Fig. 8-3*) and in the work of architects influenced by him (*Fig. 8-4*).

Brunelleschi made a unique contribution to drawing and painting through his study of *perspective*. He was the first to lay down the mathematical rules governing the reduction in size of pictured objects, according to their placement toward the

8-3   Filippo Brunelleschi. Interior, Church of Santo Spirito, Florence, Italy. Begun 1436.

8-4   Michelozzo. Medici-Riccardi Palace, Florence, Italy, 1444–1464.

rear of a scene. The ancient Romans, and Giotto, had been skillful in suggesting depth and distance, but they did not have at their command precise mathematical laws. Brunelleschi formulated them by means of observation and measurement, the "new tools" of Renaissance learning.

One of the first painters to make use of the laws of perspective was Masaccio, some years younger than Brunelleschi. In 1427 he finished a fresco in the church of Santa Maria Novella (Florence). It was a startling innovation. The subject matter was common enough: the Holy Trinity, with the Virgin, St. John, and the donors of the painting (*Fig. 8-5*). What was striking about it was that it presented the illusion of a Roman tunnel vault reaching back through the church wall. The placement and handling of the figures increased the sense of depth. Perspective drawing is familiar to us today, but its unveiling in the fifteenth century provoked amazement. As viewers stood back from the wall, they must have gasped at what seemed to be a group of sculptured figures placed within a classical, three-dimensional chapel.

In northern Europe, artists were taking a different approach to naturalism. Among the most influential was Jan van Eyck, a painter of Flanders (in the Low Countries). The Flemish towns, it will be recalled, were thriving in the fifteenth century as centers of the expanding international trade (p. 330). Well-to-do

8-5 Masaccio. *Trinity with the Virgin, St. John, and Donors*, c. 1428. Fresco, 21' × 10'5".
Soprintendenza alle Galerie, Florence, Italy.

patrons began to appear there, as in Italy, and Flemish art set the style for northern
Europe during most of the Renaissance period.

Van Eyck, less radical than Masaccio, observed most of the traditions of late
Gothic painting. But he carried to an unprecedented degree the recording of precise detail. He worked, for example, on the famed Ghent Altarpiece (completed in
1432). It contains twelve separate panels, with *The Adoration of the Mystic Lamb*
the central subject. The painting was conventional in style, but van Eyck was far
more exact in his treatment than any previous painter had been.

Van Eyck's realism was distinct from that of the Italians. Giotto and Masaccio
sought to give their figures roundness and solidity, set against a receding and dark-
ened background, whereas van Eyck treated objects in the background of his paintings with the same close attention that he gave to those in the foreground. His
work has been described as both microscopic and telescopic. In the detail from one
of his portraits, *Giovanni Arnolfini and His Bride* (Fig. 8-6), he seems to have
counted every hair on the little dog, and he shows each one in a precise gradation
of light and shadow (Fig. 8-7).

8-6   Jan van Eyck, *Giovanni Arnolfini and His Bride*, 1434. Oil on panel, 33″ × 23″. National Gallery, London.

8-7   Jan van Eyck. Detail from *Giovanni Arnolfini and His Bride*.

In his efforts to achieve such effects, van Eyck experimented with various paint materials. He was among the first to develop and use *oil* paints. Before this time, painters had mixed powdered pigments with water, or with a white-of-egg liquid (called tempera). The latter gave fairly good results, but it dried out rather quickly. Van Eyck discovered that by mixing his pigments with linseed oil he could work more slowly and produce the special effects he desired. The quality and brilliance of his painting, as well as its accuracy, soon led most European artists to follow his lead.

THE LIBERATION OF SCULPTURE: DONATELLO

Sculpture, even more than painting, can be used for the faithful reproduction of nature. Sculptors have no need to create an illusion of depth, for they work in *three* dimensions. Yet medieval sculptors usually had to fit their figures into the narrow spaces assigned to them by architects and were therefore unable to realize the full potential of their art. Donatello, a contemporary of Masaccio and Brunelleschi, restored sculpture to an independent status and gave to his art the character of naturalism and humanism.

Donatello made a careful study of the remains of Roman sculpture. Discarding the copybook methods of medieval workmen, he also began to work (as the Romans and Greeks had done) from live models. One of his earliest (1416) statues, a marble *St. George (Fig. 8-8)*, reveals the contrast between the new technique and that of the Middle Ages. The young warrior, standing firmly by his shield, does not have the "otherworldly" gaze of most medieval figures; he looks straight ahead with an expression of readiness. This realistic appearance reflects Donatello's painstaking observation of the human body.

Donatello's fame spread swiftly from his native Florence. Just as Giotto had been called to Padua to paint the murals of the Arena Chapel, so Donatello was commissioned to work in one city after another. (The rival city-states of Italy competed with one another not only in arms and politics, but in art as well.) Near the close of his life, Donatello spent some ten years in Padua, which was then part of the Venetian Republic. There he produced a monumental equestrian statue in bronze *(Fig. 8-9)*. The rider, Gattamelata, is a Venetian general (condottiere) with the assured bearing of a Caesar. One of the first equestrian statues to be made since ancient Roman times, it was modeled after a monument to the emperor Marcus Aurelius. That splendid work, the only one of its kind to survive from the ancient world, was discovered by humanists in the fifteenth century *(Fig. 3-8, p. 148)*.

The *Gattamelata*, which still stands in the cathedral piazza (public square), was Donatello's largest free-standing statue. He created smaller carvings and *relief* sculptures as well. His most striking relief is *The Feast of Herod*, a bronze panel *(Fig. 8-10)* for the baptismal font (holy-water basin) of Siena's cathedral. In the biblical scene shown, King Herod is being presented with the head of John the Baptist. Herod had ordered John's beheading reluctantly, at the urging of his stepdaughter, Salome. (She wanted John killed, because he had condemned the king's

8-8   Donatello. *St. George*, 1415–1417. Marble. From Or San Michele, Florence, Italy.

8-9   Donatello. *Gattamelata*, 1447–1453. Bronze. Approx. 11′ × 13′. Padua, Italy.

8-10 Donatello. *The Feast of Herod*. San Giovanni, c. 1425. Gilded bronze. Approx. 23′ × 22′. Siena, Italy.

unlawful marriage to Salome's mother.) Now Herod and his guests, seated at the banquet table, recoil in horror. Though Donatello's panel measures only about two feet on each side, it is rich in dramatic detail. Having learned the trick of perspective from his friend Brunelleschi, he created a marvelous illusion of *depth*. One can look through the rounded arches to Herod's musicians and beyond, through other archways, into the far background.

Though less revolutionary, Lorenzo Ghiberti surpassed Donatello as a sculptor of reliefs. His fame rests on the gilded bronze doors of the cathedral baptistry at Florence, on which he labored for nearly thirty years. Michelangelo later called the doors fit to stand as the "Gates of Paradise," and so they have been known ever since. They are divided into ten large panels, each presenting a scene from the Old Testament. One of the panels, *The Meeting of Solomon and the Queen of Sheba (Fig. 8-11)*, shows the artist's mastery of composition, perspective, and dramatic effect. The "Gates of Paradise" were hung in 1452, an event that may be regarded as the crossing point in Renaissance art between the period of revolution and the period of fulfillment.

8-11   Lorenzo Ghiberti. *The Meeting of Solomon and the Queen of Sheba.* East doors, baptistry. Bronze. Florence, Italy.

ART TRIUMPHS OVER NATURE: BOTTICELLI, LEONARDO

The painters and sculptors of the late fifteenth and early sixteenth centuries were challenged by a task even greater than that of their predecessors. Masaccio, van Eyck, and Donatello had shown the way to naturalistic representation—an impressive achievement, made possible by intensive study and technical innovation. But once naturalism had been established, it revealed its own limitations. A "literal" presentation of subject matter did not necessarily result in harmonious composition. It did not always carry a message, mood, or emotion in the most effective way. Finally, if it was a perfect imitation of reality, it could not, as art, *transcend* (go beyond) nature.

Sandro Botticelli, a fifteenth-century Florentine, wanted to preserve the liveliness and realism typical of the work of the Renaissance pioneers, and yet he wanted to create an art that would be more appealing than nature itself. This meant taking liberties with the actual appearance of things, subordinating realism to *form* and *color*—even injecting elements of *mystery*. One of his most successful efforts was the *Birth of Venus (Color Plate B1)*.

Botticelli was among the first painters to use figures from classical mythology in a major work. During the Middle Ages the Church, the chief patron of art, had forbidden the glorification of pagan traditions. The humanists admired antiquity, however, and during the Platonic revival in Florence (pp. 378–379) the Greek myths rivaled the Christian stories in popularity. In fact, Botticelli

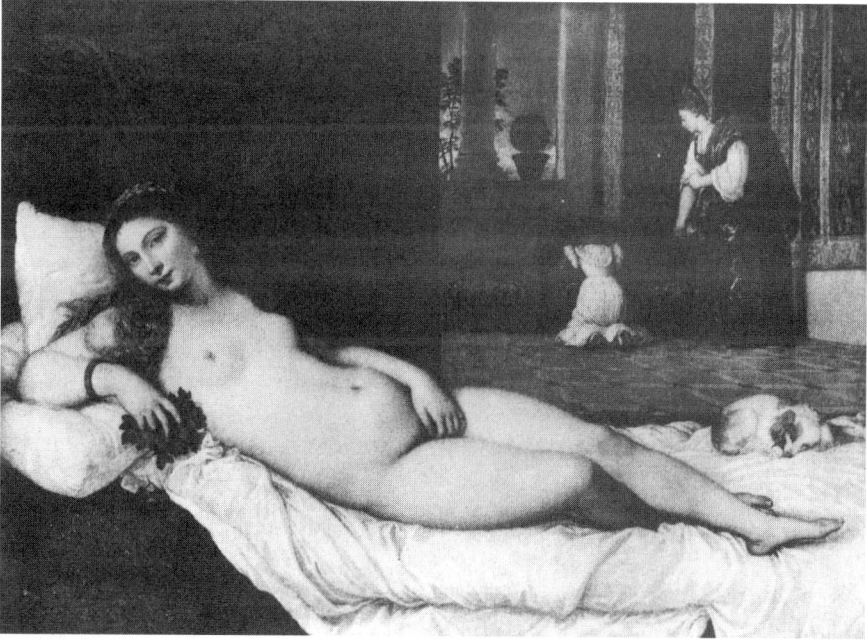

8-12 Titian. *Venus of Urbino*, c. 1538. Oil on canvas, 48″ × 66″. Uffizi Gallery, Florence, Italy.

was commissioned by one of the Medici to paint the *Birth of Venus* for his private villa.

The work is full of color, movement, and grace. In the center, being wafted to shore on a seashell, stands the goddess of love. The picture is harmonious and unified, and it conveys the mystery of beauty that so fascinated the Florentine intellectuals. It will be recalled that they associated love of beauty with man's desire for reunion with the divine. Venus, symbolically, was the fountain of beauty and love. Though Botticelli used a flesh-and-blood model, his Venus appears detached, unearthly—an *idealized* beauty.

The cult of beauty encouraged patrons and artists alike to select pagan themes. Even when the myths were not completely understood, the humanists assumed that they contained hidden wisdom. Under this cloak of intellectual respectability, some artists went on to portray their subjects in a frankly sensual manner. The Venetian painter Titian is a notable example. His *Venus of Urbino* (Fig. 8-12), which he painted in 1538, concentrates the viewer's attention on a reclining, seductive nude. This is not the spiritlike Venus of Botticelli, but an enticing woman who seems aware of her naked loveliness and the eyes of the viewer. Titian's remarkable technique is revealed in his flesh tones and textures. His works were to serve as models for every painter of nudes who followed him.

The innovations in treatment and technique were, indeed, more significant than changes in subject matter. And the leading experimenter, in both art and

8-13   Leonardo da Vinci. *Mona Lisa,*
1500–1505. Oil on panel, 31″ ×
21″. Louvre, Paris.

nature, was Leonardo da Vinci, who fulfilled the humanist ideal of the "universal genius" (p. 374). His notebooks demonstrate the astonishing breadth of his curiosity. He began his artistic training toward the end of the fifteenth century as an apprentice in a Florentine workshop, where he learned, under the guild system of supervision, the standard methods of observing and sketching models and objects. He studied the optics of perspective, the mixing of colors, and the techniques of metalwork. But when he left the shop of his master, Leonardo had only started his education. For he was less interested in the surface appearance of things than in what lay underneath, and so he undertook his ceaseless exploration of anatomy, physiology, and nature (p. 380).

He left many of his projects unfinished. We have only a few of his major paintings, and some of these are in poor condition. In those we have, his genius is clear. He resolved the difficulties of combining lifelike representation with artistic form and an element of mystery. By comparison, the mirrorlike paintings of van Eyck appear rigid and lacking in focus. In his use of light and shadow, Leonardo found that shading lends grace and softness to facial features and reduces stiffness of line. By blurring his contours, especially at the corners of the mouth and eyes, he left something to the imagination of the viewer. Each time we look at his *Mona Lisa* (*Fig. 8-13*) her expression (and thought) seems to change.

Leonardo's most famous painting is *The Last Supper,* completed in 1497 (*Color Plate B2*). This sacred subject had been treated countless times before.

How could an artist do anything special or original with it? Most earlier paintings had shown Christ and his disciples quietly seated around the supper table in varying settings and kinds of dress. Leonardo introduced drama and excitement. He chose the precise moment after the Lord had said, "One of you will betray me" (Matt. 26:21). While Christ sits calmly at the center of the picture, waves of disbelief, amazement, and distress sweep to the right and left of him. Only Judas, among the disciples, is motionless. And, even with the agitation and tension of the recorded instant, the painting forms a harmonious whole.

The Artistic Climax: Michelangelo

Although Leonardo was the most versatile of Renaissance figures (artist, musician, and scientist), he was overshadowed as an *artist* by Michelangelo Buonarroti. Leonardo observed and investigated nature as a whole; Michelangelo concentrated on anatomy, convinced that the inmost urges and sensitivities of human beings could best be expressed through the human figure.

Michelangelo preferred to represent the body in three dimensions of sculpture, but he was required to do numerous works as a painter. In 1503 he was called to Rome from his native Florence by the pompous and militant Pope Julius II. The pontiff, desiring a monumental tomb for himself, had turned to Michelangelo, the best sculptor of his day, to make it. Complications arose, however, and Julius asked Michelangelo to paint the ceiling of his private chapel instead. The chapel had been built by Pope Sixtus IV (hence, the name Sistine), and its walls had been painted by an earlier generation of masters (including Botticelli). The ceiling vault, however, remained blank.

Michelangelo, disappointed when his sculpturing commission was put off, accepted the new task with reluctance. But, having once decided to undertake it, he plunged into the work with his customary vigor. Some four years later the fresco was finished. It covers about ten thousand square feet and includes more than three hundred figures. In plan, execution, and magnitude no other painting in history (by a single individual) has surpassed it.

In the Sistine Chapel painting, as in all his creations, Michelangelo expressed his deep religious concern about humankind. Tormented by a sense of sin, his own and that of the human species, he suffered from a feeling of personal frustration, of unfulfilled ambitions. His conviction that individuals struggle helplessly against destiny led him to a tragic view of life. He felt that the human spirit, of divine origin, desires to return to God but is held fast by the flesh and by the sins of the flesh. In *The Last Judgment*, which he painted late in life on the end wall of the Sistine Chapel, he portrayed a severe and muscular Christ condemning crowds of sinners to the eternal fires of hell.

Michelangelo was clearly influenced by the Platonism of the Academy (p. 378). In an effort to reconcile his Christian convictions with the teachings of the Platonists, he merged the two in his pictorial layout for the chapel vault. The main feature, on the ceiling proper, is a series of nine panels showing the

Hebrew-Christian stories of the Creation and the Flood. (The story from Noah to Christ had already been painted on the lower walls.) Perhaps the most appealing of these panels is *The Creation of Adam (Color Plate B3)*. The Father, borne by the heavenly host, is about to bring the inert Adam to life by the touch of his finger. Evident here is Michelangelo's ability to suggest *latent* (reserved) power and to inject light and movement.

After finishing his backbreaking labor on the Sistine scaffolds, Michelangelo returned to his first love, sculpture. From solid blocks of marble, he began to carve several figures for the projected tomb of Julius II. The special quality of his sculpture can be understood in part by his attitude toward the stone: before taking up his chisel, he always visualized the human form within each block. He then proceeded, with furious energy, to "liberate" the form from the stone.

One of his finest works, carved some years earlier, expresses the spirit of athletic youth. His eighteen-foot-tall *David (Fig. 8-14)* was at first placed in the main piazza of Florence. A copy stands there today, but the original is housed in a Florentine museum. The *David* shows the influence of Greek sculpture on Michelangelo's work. Later creations, such as the figures for Julius' tomb, show the influence of Platonism. In one of these, known as the *Dying Slave*, Michelangelo shows a mature, powerful body falling into repose as death approaches, releasing the slave from life's futile struggle. Among Michelangelo's other sculptural works are a *Pietà* (the sorrowing Virgin mourning for the dead Christ) and a wrathful, monumental *Moses*.

Later in life, having won fame as a painter and a sculptor, Michelangelo turned his attention to architecture. Here, too, he was without peer. He continued the development of the Renaissance style that had been initiated by Brunelleschi. Much of his work was done in Rome, and the touch of his hand is revealed there in countless places: the Farnese Palace, the church of St. Mary of the Angels (which he converted from a great hall that had once been part of the Roman Baths of Diocletian), and the Campidoglio (a piazza atop the Capitoline Hill, enclosed by civic buildings).

His last masterpiece was the dome of St. Peter's. The new St. Peter's (replacing the original church of the fourth century) was planned early in the sixteenth century by the tireless Julius II. He wished to erect, over the tomb of the first apostle, a structure that would surpass all others in Christendom. Several architects had a hand in the design, but in 1547 Michelangelo was put in charge. During the remaining years of his life he devoted most of his energies to planning the mighty basilica (church of special distinction).

The floor plan was for a colossal structure laid out in the form of a Greek (square) cross. A central dome was to be the crowning feature. Earlier schemes had called for a shallow dome modeled on that of the Pantheon *(Fig. 3-4, p. 142)*, but Michelangelo wanted something greater for the "capitol" of Christendom. Inspired by Brunelleschi's dome in Florence *(Fig. 8-2)*, he planned one even steeper and higher—one that would tower over every other building in the Eternal City.

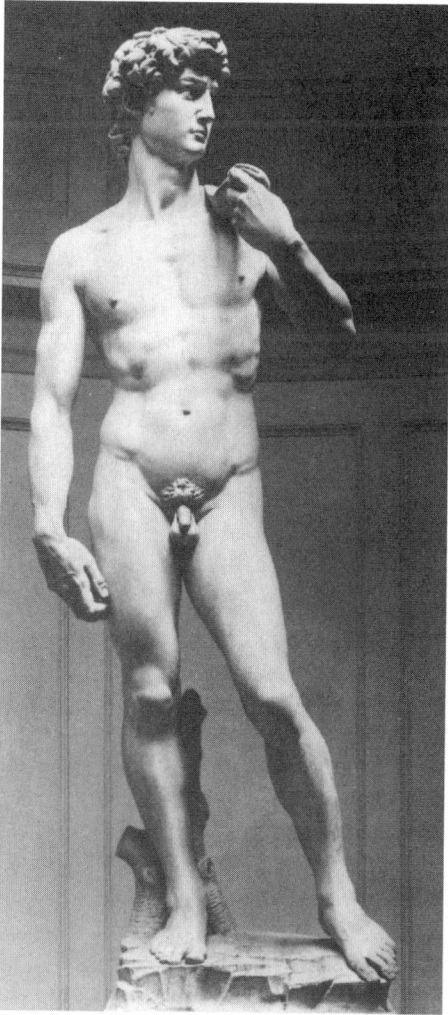

8-14 Michelangelo. *David*, 1501–1504. Marble, height approx. 18'. Accademia, Florence, Italy.

Although he died before St. Peter's was completed, the dome was finished according to his designs. The square plan of the basilica, however, was altered into a Latin (oblong) cruciform plan (*Fig. 6-2,* p. 287), which meant that a long nave (central aisle) had to be constructed. As a result, the view of the dome from the front of the church is partially blocked. The view of St. Peter's from the *rear (Fig. 8-15)* shows the dome as it would have appeared from all sides had the original plan been carried out.

The magnificent dome, the largest in the world, has been copied by architects everywhere. Equal in diameter to that of the Pantheon, it rises *three hundred feet* higher. It stands as a splendid symbol of Christianity and a fitting monument to Michelangelo.

8-15   Michelangelo. St. Peter's Basilica, Vatican, Rome, c. 1547.

LITERATURE AND DRAMA

While the visual arts of the Renaissance reached their climax in Italy, striking accomplishments in literature were appearing beyond the Alps. The north could not match the best painting and sculpture of the south. It proved equal or superior, however, in the *written word*—the impact of which was enormously increased by the invention of printing with movable type (pp. 337–338). Erasmus probably had more contemporary readers than any previous writer, and now that there existed a mass market for books, he was soon joined by other humanist authors whose works became "bestsellers."

THE LIBERTARIAN HUMORIST: RABELAIS

In France the most popular author was François Rabelais, an enthusiastic humanist with a talent for satire and parody. Though his books were condemned by religious and civil authorities (the issue of censorship arose soon after the invention of printing), they had a warm appeal to readers. Rabelais was (and still is) a most popular author.

Like Erasmus, who was born a generation earlier, Rabelais knew the Church and the universities from the inside. From a middle-class family, he had entered a Franciscan monastery in order to become a scholar. But he was a rebel from the beginning; his absorption in the classics disturbed his superiors and led to trouble. He switched from one religious order to another, for a time wore the garb of a priest, studied at various universities, and later took up law and medicine. His career, like his writing, followed no visible plan. With a vast appetite for life and learning, he was the personification of a vigorous and spontaneous humanism.

Although Rabelais loved the classics and knew them intimately (especially the Roman), his own temperament was by no means classical. It was the content, not the style, of the classics that appealed to him. He wrote in vernacular French, rather than classical Latin, and he detested all rules and regulations. One should follow, he insisted, one's own inclinations. Rabelais thus represented a humanism that did not copy classical models (or any other) but stood as a purely *individualistic* philosophy. Rejecting the doctrine of Original Sin (and most other doctrines), he stressed *natural goodness;* he held that most people, given freedom and proper education (in the classics), will live happy and productive lives.

This idea is central to Rabelais' great work, *Gargantua and Pantagruel.* The story, about two imaginary giant-kings, was published in several volumes over a period of years (beginning in 1538). Rabelais often used the giants, father and son, as spokesmen for his own views. He wrote the work primarily for amusement, because he believed that laughter (like thought) is a distinctively *human* function. However, in telling of the heroes' education and adventures, he voiced his opinions on the human traits and institutions of his time. In a tumble of words, learned and playful, he mingled serious ideas with earthy jokes and jibes.

Monasticism was a prime target for Rabelais, as it was for most humanists. Its stress on self-denial, repression, and regimentation was to him inhumane and hateful. He had Gargantua give funds to a "model" institution that *violates* monastic practices in every possible way. At this "abbey of Thélème," with its fine libraries and recreational facilities, elegantly dressed men and women are free to "do as they please." Monks, hypocrites, lawyers, and peddlers of gloom are barred from the abbey; only handsome, high-spirited people are admitted.

Rabelais disliked pretense and deception and praised the natural instincts and abilities of free persons. Rejecting the ascetic ideal, he expressed secular humanism in its most robust and optimistic form. In doing so, Rabelais also reflected the views of the ancient Greek *hedonist,* Aristippus (p. 82) — and he anticipated the modern appetite for unlimited experience and pleasure (p. 732).

THE SKEPTICAL ESSAYIST: MONTAIGNE

Michel de Montaigne, born a generation after Rabelais, lived through the same troubled times of religious struggle between the Protestants and Catholics and shared Rabelais' keen interest in the classics. But some critical difference of personality turned him toward quite another kind of humanism. His temperament was

c. 1350   1520   1650

Era of Renaissance Humanism	Reformation and Religious Wars

c. 1600

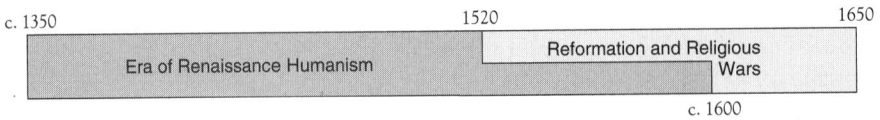

nearer that of Erasmus (pp. 380–383). Both men remained loyal to the Roman Catholic Church and both were dedicated scholars, but Montaigne was more secular-minded and detached than Erasmus. He had no strong desire to reform society, and he was not concerned with what others thought of him. (His *own* opinion was all that mattered.) The son of a landowning family near Bordeaux, Montaigne received a superb education. His father held public office, traveled abroad, and believed in a humanistic upbringing for his children. When his parent died, Michel inherited the family estate and was able to retire at the age of thirty-eight to his library of a thousand books.

Privacy and leisure, which Montaigne treasured above all else, gave him an opportunity to read and think. He chose only those books that gave him plea-sure—pleasure in the Epicurean sense (pp. 135–137). These were the Latin au-thors (and some Greeks in translation), whom Montaigne considered superior in style and content to other writers. From his reading he developed a desire to live his personal life according to classical ways, and, like Petrarch, he began to record his own thoughts and observations.

Out of this activity came the first two volumes of *Essays* (1580). Unlike Ra-belais' books, these were models of clear French prose. They were immediately popular, and Montaigne was encouraged to publish a third volume soon afterward. Altogether, he wrote more than a hundred essays on such topics as the emotions, superstition, customs, education, marriage, scholarship, and death. His usual man-ner was to begin with the opinions of traditional authorities on the topic, inserting quotations from their works, and then to explain his own views. Sometimes he would present opposing answers to a given question and then suggest a compromise solution—or, perhaps, no solution at all.

Montaigne's essays were a new form of literature, though they owed much to the example of Seneca, a Roman writer of the first century A.D. (p. 135). They were not systematic studies of the sort written by scholars but were simply *essais* (personal views). Montaigne did not attempt to change the minds of his readers, but wrote, in large measure, for his own satisfaction. And, because the essays were based on his own experiences and thoughts, they were also a form of *autobiography*. The notion that every person of worth should pass on some record of that person's life and ideas became widespread during the Renaissance. The boastful Florentine artist Benvenuto Cellini was among those who accepted this idea; he dictated his *Autobiography* in 1560. Gradually the *essay* and the *memoir* became standard liter-ary forms, further expressions of the individualism and self-confidence of the age.

In one of Montaigne's most notable essays on the subject of knowledge and reason (Vol. II, Essay 12), he showed himself to be a philosophical *relativist* (pp. 81–82). He spoke of the limits of reason in efforts to comprehend the universe: neither theology, classical wisdom, nor science can provide final answers to the "big questions"; all knowledge is subject to *uncertainty* and *doubt*. The human mind, observed Montaigne, is erratic; and the senses, which are unreliable, often control the mind. Beliefs, no matter how firmly held, cannot be regarded as constant, for they, too, have their seasons, their birth and death. He thus challenged the self-assurance of both Christians and earlier humanists.

Montaigne did not suggest that people should not use their minds. On the contrary, he thought that every individual capable of reason should seek answers satisfactory to that individual. The thinking person should never embrace the ready-made views of others, no matter how impressive their authority; rather, one ought to consider various ideas and then make a choice. And if one feels unable to make a choice, one should remain in doubt. The uncertain character of knowledge ought to teach us, above all, that *dogmatism* (absolute self-assurance) is unjustified—and that persecuting people for differing beliefs is wrong.

Montaigne made his eloquent plea for tolerance in the midst of the frightful struggle among religious fanatics that raged through sixteenth-century France. He could see that war and homicide are often the outcomes of absolutistic thought and belief. Like Erasmus, Montaigne was a *political conservative* and opposed to violence; he felt that firm authority was indispensable to peace and order. Although he cherished independence of thought, he did not rebel against established institutions, hoping that those who held power would see the light, ultimately, of moderation and decency. In any event, he stuck to his personal philosophy—a blend of skepticism, Epicureanism, and Stoicism (pp. 135–138)—and remained aloof from other people. In the quiet and security of his library, Montaigne could meditate on one of his favorite sayings: "Rejoice in your present life; all else is beyond you."

Rabelais and Montaigne were among the few writers on the continent whose devotion to humanism was not disturbed by the religious upheavals that broke out around 1520. Another was Miguel de Cervantes, the greatest author of Spain. He began his masterpiece, *Don Quixote*, well past midlife (about 1600). It was a satire on the tales of chivalry (pp. 304–305) that were still being written (and read) in his native land. Cervantes' hero is a caricature of the romantic *knight*; he imagines windmills to be evil giants and vainly charges against them. While Don Quixote is a hopeless idealist, his squire, Sancho Panza, sees the world in simple, down-to-earth terms. (As the story unfolds, the dialogue between them produces a reversal of values in each.) Cervantes succeeded in ridiculing chivalric literature and revealed, through the Don's adventures, a panorama of the Spain of his day. On the philosophical level, the contrasting and shifting values of Panza and Quixote remind one of the *relativity* of truth that Montaigne had noted in his essays.

THE MASTER DRAMATIST: SHAKESPEARE

Humanism came late to England. It had hardly been established there by 1500, and it might even have vanished in the religious turmoil that erupted shortly thereafter. One of the casualties, indeed, was Sir Thomas More. A dedicated scholar and a friend of Erasmus, he wrote the visionary *Utopia*, in which he set down the humane features of a decent, planned society (pp. 568–569). But he later paid with his life for refusing to swear loyalty to the king as head of the Church of England (p. 426). Humanism and the secular spirit proved hardy, however, and attained their full expression in literature around 1600. The leading genius of this expression was William Shakespeare.

Shakespeare was not a classical scholar. As his friend (and rival playwright) Ben Jonson said, he knew "small Latin and less Greek." But he was familiar (in the original or in translation) with many of the ancient authors. Moreover, he was filled with the *spirit* of humanism, which characterized the Elizabethan age (1550–1600). For England this was a period of rising national strength, bourgeois prosperity, and lusty living. Shakespeare's plays contain elements of the classical and the timeless, but they speak in the voice of the Renaissance.

The roots of Elizabethan drama go back to the Romans and the Greeks, for during the Middle Ages there had been only religious pageants and "Passion" and "morality" plays. But the classical revival of the fifteenth century stimulated the reenactment of Roman dramas at the courts of Italian rulers, and in time a new form of *secular* drama, based on the Roman model, came into being and spread across Europe.

Although the Italian playwrights followed the classical tradition of lengthy recitations, a chorus, and little action, the English introduced modifications to suit their national taste. They also began to build permanent theaters for dramatic performances; none had existed in medieval times. When Shakespeare arrived in London about 1590, both the new drama and the new way of designing theaters were approaching maturity.

The Globe Theater of his day is a good example of the Elizabethan playhouse. Octagonal in outward plan, it faced inward on a large courtyard (*Fig. 8-16*). The stage, or platform, was built on one side of the inner circle and projected some ten feet into the yard; ringing the yard were three tiers of balconies, or covered boxes. Those who could not afford boxes stood or sat in the yard itself.

The stage lacked the scenery and equipment available to our contemporary theaters. A curtained area in the rear could serve as a chamber or an inner room; when closed off, it became the backdrop for a setting on the main stage. The front of the platform often served as a street or passageway. Because there was no main curtain, the script had to provide action to clear the stage at the end of each scene.

A balcony directly above the stage could represent the window of a house, the deck of a ship, or the top of a castle wall, while trapdoors in the floor and roof of the stage enabled witches and spirits to ascend and descend. Lighting was no problem, since this was an open-air theater and performances were given in the afternoon. Though much of the setting was left to the viewer's imagination, the Elizabethan theater proved remarkably flexible and enabled the actors to establish close contact with their audience. As in classical drama, all the roles were played by men or boys. (The stage was not considered a fit place for females, and "respectable" women were seldom seen in the audience.)

The dramas themselves still bore the mark of the classical tradition. The length of the plays, their division into acts, and the types of characters and themes

8-16 The Globe Theater, London.

came from ancient comedy and tragedy. Greek plays were known in Elizabethan times only through their Roman versions, particularly those of Seneca (p. 135). Drawing from well-known Greek myths, Seneca had written gruesome dramas peopled by crudely drawn characters, ghosts, and phantoms, and dealing with themes of betrayal, revenge, and madness.

Renaissance drama differed from ancient drama in significant ways, however. It was not associated with religious festivals, as Greek drama had been (pp. 88–89), and, though it often dealt with moral issues, its spirit was markedly secular. Supernatural touches were occasionally introduced (the audience expected them), but the plays were emphatically "of this world." Though Shakespeare himself was nominally a Christian, his dramas lack any doctrinaire Christian tone; in some of them there are even hints of religious doubts and fatalism.

The range of Shakespeare's themes and locales is greater than that of the classical dramatists. "All the world's a stage," declares one of his characters (Jaques, in *As You Like It*) — speaking to an audience that had daily reports of adventures in newly discovered lands. Many other features of his work reflect the values and concerns of humanism. The urge to *power* is the central theme in many of his plays, and the rising sense of *nationality*, or patriotism, fills his historical dramas.

Shakespeare's deep interest in character and inner psychological conflict reflects the Renaissance concern with *individualism*. Many of his passages reflect, too, an emphasis on *materialism* and *sensuousness*. Finally, he demonstrates the same concern for *realism* displayed by the humanist painters and sculptors.

Hamlet, one of Shakespeare's greatest tragedies, illustrates his dramatic methods. The story comes out of a medieval Danish history book, though Shakespeare probably based his work on an English dramatic adaptation of the early sixteenth century. *Hamlet* is a tragedy of *revenge*, a type of drama popular at the time. Shakespeare gave it the elements of conflict, suspense, violence, and poetic imagery that his audience enjoyed. Since the audience consisted chiefly of well-read individuals, he was able to bring moral and philosophical ideas into the course of the dramatic action.

As a character, Hamlet typifies the ideal "gentleman" of the new Europe (p. 377). He also embodies the conflict between meditation and action that fascinated the intellectuals of the age. Hamlet knows that it is his *duty* (by custom) to avenge his murdered father, but he insists on using the humanistic tool of *reason* to guide his actions. While he delays *acting*, a series of miserable deaths occurs. Shakespeare leaves it to his audience to decide whether reason should bow to custom, and whether humans are the masters of their destiny.

We know little about Shakespeare's life except that he prospered in London and retired to his native Stratford some years before his death (1616), but we do have the legacy of his works. No one has had a surer feeling for the sense and sound of the English language. In addition to his poetry, he left some forty plays, among them several masterpieces. These make superb literature as well as good theater; his collected writings have been referred to as the "English secular Bible." The Renaissance, which admired the individual genius, produced one in Shakespeare. Moreover, as Ben Jonson observed, he was "not of an age but for all time."

CHAPTER 9

❂ ❂ ❂

THE REFORMATION:
DIVISION AND REFORM IN THE CHURCH

Overview

The breakup of medieval civilization was completed in the sixteenth and seventeenth centuries by the explosive force of religious revolt and reform. Since the thirteenth century, Christianity had been divided in two by the schism of the Latin (Catholic) and Greek (Orthodox) churches (p. 325). About 1520, the struggles of the Reformation broke out in the territories dominated by the Latin Church—struggles that were mainly over religion, but were all the longer and more bitter because they also involved political, social, and economic matters. By the time that the conflict died down about 1650, a third branch of Christianity had arisen: Protestantism.

Although the Reformation began suddenly, its roots lay far back in the Middle Ages. Throughout the fourteenth and fifteenth centuries, increasingly powerful Catholic rulers had struggled with the popes for control of the Church hierarchy (organization). Heretical movements had arisen that in various ways tried to weaken or eliminate the priests in the name of Christian equality; these movements were often allied with peasant movements of protest and revolt against inequality and oppression in general. At all levels of society, contempt for the Church's wealth, power, and corruption had grown, at the same time as Renaissance scholars had contrasted the Church's worldly present with the purity of its ancient past.

Shortly after 1500, all these sources of discontent were tapped by the German monk Martin Luther, whose personal quest for spiritual peace had led him to an understanding of how souls were saved that differed from the official view of the Catholic Church. Human beings, Luther believed, were completely helpless to enter heaven by their own efforts, let alone to help other humans into heaven; rather, they must have complete faith in the mercy of God, which alone could save them. The Church's traditional belief was that humans could play at least some part in their own salvation by pleasing God (e.g., by contributing money for pious or charitable purposes or by becoming monks and nuns), and that God had given some human beings (e.g., the saints in heaven, the priests, and the pope) a role in helping others into heaven.

Thus, having shifted his belief on the basic issue of how to cope with consequences of sin, Luther was led to oppose Church fund-raising practices, monasticism, the veneration of saints, the Catholic priesthood, the authority of the pope, and countless other traditional beliefs and practices. In time he found himself at the head of a movement of "reformation" in Germany, backed by all classes of society, that sought to put his ideas into practice.

But Luther's answer to the problem of salvation also raised a great many questions. If no human being was more pleasing to God than any other, and all were equal so far as they shared in God's mercy, did that mean that there was no need for any kind of clergy or Church organization? Did the religious equality of Christians apply also to worldly affairs, so that peasants were the equals of nobles, servants the equals of their masters and mistresses, and subjects the equals of their kings and queens? And if God's power, not their own efforts, enabled humans to enter heaven, did that mean that God had decided in advance who would be saved and who would be damned, regardless of any individual's character and deeds?

Different Protestant leaders and groups answered these questions in different ways. As a result, Protestantism soon ceased to be what Luther and other early leaders had originally wanted—a united movement of reform throughout the whole Church. Instead, by 1600 Protestantism had split into many different "churches," each with its own theology and beliefs, which have lasted down to the present day. There were the Evangelicals (Lutherans); the Reformed (Calvinists or Presbyterians, who followed the theology of Protestantism's second "founding father," the Frenchman John Calvin); the Anglicans (Episcopalians); the Anabaptists (Baptists); and others. Meanwhile, the largest of the "churches" remained the Roman Catholic Church. By 1600, in response to the Protestant challenge, it had rallied around its traditional beliefs and practices, and the traditional authority of the papacy; it had abolished some of the worst abuses that had brought its hierarchy into contempt; and it had developed new religious orders, above all the Jesuits, that were powerful instruments of Catholic education and propaganda.

By 1650, after more than a century of controversy, propaganda, persecution, and war, it was clear that none of the parties in the Reformation conflict could defeat the others. The various "religions," as they came to be called, settled down in the territories of Europe and the New World that they still occupy today. Mutual acceptance very gradually set in. In the eighteenth century, religious minorities ceased to be repressed and gained toleration (though only as second-class citizens); in the nineteenth century, they gained full civil equality; and in the twentieth century, something like reconciliation finally came about. As always, division had its positive side: the arts and architecture, for instance, were enriched by the Protestant stress on simplicity and individual character, and by the magnificence and drama of the Catholic Baroque.

In two respects, the Reformation had the same results throughout both Protestant and Catholic Europe. Of the questions raised by Luther's ideas about salvation, one was answered definitely in the negative: religious equality was not to be extended to the economic, social, and political order, which remained unchanged and in some respects became more oppressive. And though religion remained a dominant force in the life of individuals and communities, the churches that emerged from the Reformation did not wield the independent power that the medieval Catholic Church had wielded. Whether a country remained Catholic, or what kind of Protestantism it turned to, depended mostly on the decisions of its holders of secular power, above all its rulers. Accordingly, in Catholic and Protestant countries alike, the balance of power between Church and state swung decisively in favor of the state.

BACKGROUND OF THE REFORMATION

From the view of the established Catholic organization, the Protestant reformers were *heretics* who defied the pope. Differences on matters of doctrine had arisen early in the life of the Church, but for many centuries unity had been maintained in the West. (Differences between the Latin [Catholic] and the Greek [Orthodox] churches had arisen following the breakup of the Roman Empire; the final separation occurred following the capture of Constantinople by Catholic crusaders in 1204—p. 312.) To preserve Western unity, the popes and bishops had exercised continuous watchfulness and strong discipline. During the Middle Ages thousands of heretics had been burned at the stake in the name of Christian purity and unity. How was it that the Protestant heretics survived where their predecessors had perished? One reason is that the late medieval Church had suffered a fateful decline.

Decay of the Church

During the thirteenth century the medieval Church had reached the height of its power. This was when the great cathedrals were built, when powerful reform orders were founded, and when scholastic philosophy achieved its greatest influence. Under Pope Innocent III the papal monarchy had dominated the rulers of Europe as well as the Church organization (p. 284). But the fourteenth and fifteenth centuries saw a steady fall in the condition of the Church, and by 1500 the organization had reached its low point.

The fortunes of the Church as a whole were closely tied to those of the papacy. Medieval popes like Gregory VII and Innocent III had done much to strengthen the Church structure. But the popes of later centuries had been less

1303	1417	1520	1650

Avignon Papacy and Great Schism	Continued Spiritual Decline of Papacy	Reformation and Religious Wars

1534

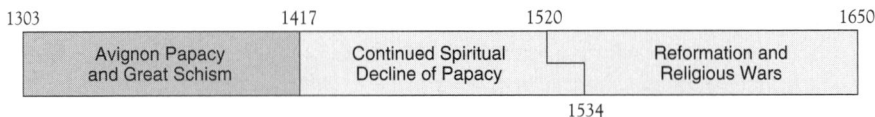

successful in their undertakings, and their failures affected the entire institution. Boniface VIII, for example, was defeated in his struggle with the French king Philip the Fair (p. 284). After Boniface's death (in 1303) Philip moved to avoid future trouble with Rome by forcing the election of a French bishop as the new pope. Thus, the papacy was drawn into French politics. The new relationship was demonstrated shortly thereafter when the pope (Clement V) transferred his court from Rome to Avignon.

Avignon was a papal holding on the lower Rhone River, just east of the border of the French kingdom. Clement went there voluntarily, chiefly because conditions in Rome were unsafe. But his move confirmed a widespread feeling that the papacy had become a *captive* of the French monarchy. Clement secured a French majority in the College of Cardinals (p. 280), and for some seventy years a succession of French popes reigned at Avignon.

Outside France, these popes were looked upon with suspicion and hostility. Because the pope holds office by virtue of his being the bishop of Rome, it seemed improper that he should reside anywhere but in the Eternal City. The English, who were then at war with the French, regarded the papacy at Avignon as the ally of their enemy. Actually, the popes acted quite independently during these years, but that did not prevent the Italian humanist Petrarch from labeling their stay at Avignon as the "Babylonian Captivity," a reference to the forced removal of ancient Jewish leaders to Babylonia (p. 166).

More serious embarrassments to the Church were yet to come. In 1377, Gregory XI decided to return the papal court to Rome; upon his death there, the Roman populace pressured the cardinals into choosing an Italian as pope. But the French cardinals then fled the city, pronounced the election invalid, and chose another pope. This one, with his supporting cardinals, moved to Avignon, while the Italian pope, with *his* cardinals, stayed in Rome. Each declared the other to be a *false* pope and excommunicated him and his followers.

The Great Schism (split), as this division was called, lasted some forty years (from 1378 to 1417). Europe now endured the spectacle of a Church divided into opposing camps, with *two* popes and *two* colleges of cardinals. Conscientious Christians were distressed, for they had no way of being certain who was pope and who was "antipope." Civil rulers supported whichever side seemed more useful politically. Thus, France and its allies recognized Avignon, while England and the German princes recognized Rome. The schism was at last settled by a general council of the Church (at Constance), which deposed both rival popes and elected a new one. But by this time the papacy had suffered serious damage. The foundation of papal power had previously been its immense *moral* authority. That position was now gravely weakened, opening the way to contempt and defiance.

The humiliation of the papacy contributed to the decline of the clergy as a whole—a decline that had begun after 1300. Worldliness and abuses had swept the Church once more, and the brave reform efforts of earlier centuries were forgotten (pp. 277–279). The monastic orders, traditionally the conscience of the clergy, fell into scandal, corrupted by comfortable living. Many of the seculars (priests and bishops) also slipped into self-indulgence, lust, and greed. While there doubtless remained thousands of honest, chaste, and pious clerics, the general situation was nevertheless distressing.

Vigorous reform of these abuses became urgent. But the popes of the fifteenth century, themselves deep in worldliness, were not interested in reform. The "princes" of the Church were more interested in politics, wealth, and art than in spiritual affairs. The Medici Pope Leo X is reported to have said, after his election in 1513, "As God has seen fit to give us the papacy, let us enjoy it!"

THE AWAKENING REFORM SPIRIT: WICLIF, HUS

Many devout Christians realized that moral reform of the Church would have to start at the *top*, but they feared that the papacy lacked the will to reform. As a consequence, they began to turn *inward* in their devotions. In northern Europe, the fifteenth century saw a revival of *mysticism* (p. 279) and *pietism* (deep reverence). One response there was the founding of the Brethren of the Common Life (p. 281), whose members turned away from the formalism of established rituals. They joined together in semireligious communities stressing Christlike simplicity, purity of heart, and direct communion with God. Other Christians were moving, at the same time, toward a new idea of what the Church should be. Their model was "primitive" Christianity as practiced during the first century after Christ.

John Wiclif, a leading Oxford scholar and teacher, was among the first to question openly the need for a *priesthood*. His ideas, preached late in the fourteenth century, provided a foundation for later Protestant doctrines. After a lifetime of study, Wiclif concluded that the Church was suffering from more than just the misbehavior of some of its clergy. He challenged the established role and powers of the clergy itself—arguing that God and the Scriptures are the sole sources of spiritual authority.

Wiclif made an English translation of the Vulgate Bible (p. 196). In doing so, he sometimes chose English words that supported his own scriptural interpretations, as opposed to those of the Church authorities. (Later translations of the Bible into the various languages of Europe would often, in a similar way, bear significantly on doctrinal disputes.)

More important, Wiclif urged laymen to read the Bible for themselves. Every individual, he said, can communicate directly with the Lord and can be saved without the aid of priests or saints. For challenging the accepted doctrines of authority and salvation, he was condemned and forced to retire from teaching. (Civil disturbances in England and the Great Schism in the Church saved him from more drastic punishment.) Wiclif was thus silenced, but his ideas were not.

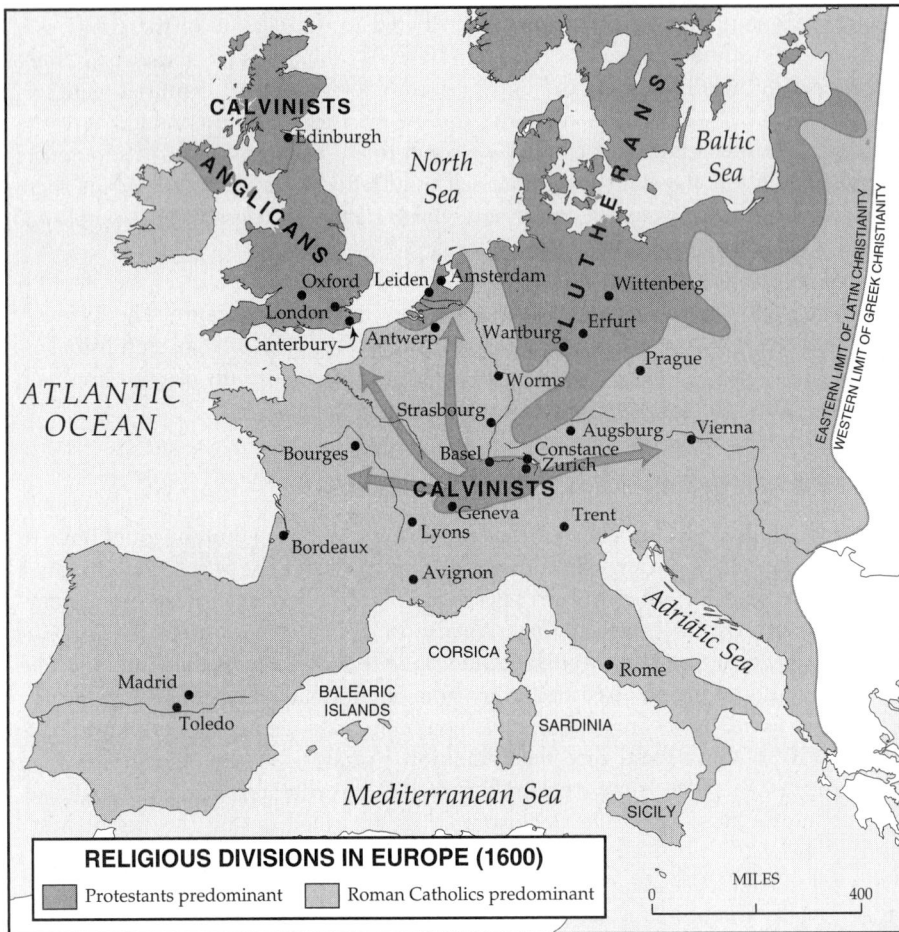

RELIGIOUS DIVISIONS IN EUROPE (1600)

Protestants predominant   Roman Catholics predominant

MILES
0   400

Most of Wiclif's followers in England (who were known as Lollards) were exe-cuted as heretics. Jan Hus, the hero of Bohemia, met the same fate. Hus was a priest and a professor at Charles University in Prague (*map*, shown above), in the kingdom of Bohemia. Already active in efforts to reform the clergy, he was inspired by the writings of Wiclif to launch stronger, more radical attacks. Hus had the sup-port of most of his compatriots, partly because many of the clerics he criticized were Germans, whereas the majority of the population in Bohemia were Czechs (pp. 245, 326). (National feelings, here and elsewhere, showed themselves in the religious disputes.)

Bohemia was part of the Holy Roman Empire, and the Emperor Sigismund had grown disturbed by the mounting agitation among the Bohemians. When Hus was summoned by the Council of Constance in 1414 to stand trial on charges of heresy, the emperor promised him safe conduct to and from the trial. After a long

9-1   Sixteenth-century woodcut showing the Czech heretic Jan Hus being burned at the stake in 1415. Hus is shown calm and dignified amid the flames, as befits a martyr, which is how the Protestants of the Reformation period regarded him.

and cruel imprisonment in Constance, Hus was tried and found guilty. The emperor did not keep his promise of protection, and Hus, refusing to recant (withdraw) his beliefs, went to his death at the stake *(Fig. 9-1)*. The reaction in Bohemia was instantaneous. Anti-German and antipapal sentiments were inflamed, and a bloody uprising erupted in the country. This was but the beginning of a long series of political-religious wars in Europe.

During the fifteenth century, the criticisms by heretics like Wiclif and Hus were reinforced by the writings of the Christian humanists (pp. 380–383). Erasmus poured ridicule on the high clergy, monasticism, and popular devotional cults. But his intellectual approach did not stir the common people, and he never challenged the authority of the Church. For these reasons, and because of the humanistic leanings of the Renaissance popes, Erasmus escaped personal harm.

Nevertheless, there was a link between the Christian humanists and the rebels against authority. The leaders of the Protestant revolt found justification for their actions in Erasmus' call for a purer religion, one freed from ritualism and superstition. They were prepared, of course, to go much further than Erasmus: they would defy authority and split the Christian community if necessary in order to achieve their goals.

THE INFLUENCE OF POLITICAL AND SOCIAL FORCES

By 1500 ideas for religious reform were in broad circulation. All that was needed was the opportunity to start an effective *movement*. A century after Hus, the political, economic, and social conditions in Europe were shifting in such a way as to present that opportunity. The new situation would permit the rise of religious *founders* instead of religious martyrs.

National sentiment and political absolutism, whose growth was discussed in chapter 7, were working against the principle and practice of the universal Church. As distinctively national cultures took shape, people grew increasingly conscious of belonging to a particular *nation*—a nation independent of all others. The citizens of the northern countries, especially, came to regard the popes as "foreigners" who had no proper business outside Italy.

This popular feeling supported the desire of kings and princes to gain control over the Church in their own territories and to build *state* churches. By 1520 the monarchs of Spain and France had virtually achieved this end by securing the right to appoint the bishops within their kingdoms. One reason for the failure of heresies in those two nations is simply that their kings had nothing to gain from religious changes. In Germany and England, however, where the kings and princes expected to enlarge their powers in the event of a religious break with Rome, heresies were to prove successful.

The higher social classes also began to sense that they might benefit from a break with Rome. In Germany the Church was immensely wealthy, holding from one-fifth to one-third of the total real estate. The landed aristocrats looked on those holdings with covetous eyes, and members of the middle class, though not particularly interested in acquiring land, disliked the fact that Church properties were exempt from taxes. Their own tax payments would be reduced, they reasoned, if Church holdings were shifted to private hands. And all classes of German society deplored the flow of Church revenues to Rome; the feeling that the "foreign" papacy was draining the homeland of wealth thus created another source of support for a religious revolt.

These economic, social, and political factors must be kept in mind if we are to understand the nature and success of the Protestant reform movements. The reformers, to be sure, did not act upon a *calculation* of these factors; they acted, rather, in response to their religious thoughts and feelings. But this had been true also of the less fortunate heretics who preceded them. The success of the Protestant leaders was due primarily to the new political and social forces. The time was ripe for religious revolt in northern Europe; the division of the Roman Church was at hand.

THE REVOLT OF LUTHER: "JUSTIFICATION BY FAITH"

The reformers did not intend, at the outset, to *divide* the Church or to start new churches. Each believed that he had the correct vision of the *one true* church, and he set out to convert (or force) all Christians to his point of view. (The Protestant leaders, to the disappointment of Erasmus, were to prove as intolerant as the papacy.) But, because no one of them managed to dominate the others, the end result was the division (and subdivision) of the Church.

THE PROVOCATION: THE SALE OF INDULGENCES

In 1517 Martin Luther struck a spark that set religious passions aflame. The event did not appear at the time to have far-reaching significance, but it started a chain reaction of dissent and rebellion. A Dominican friar (p. 279) named Tetzel, who was selling papal *indulgences* (p. 281) in Germany, had located himself near the Saxon town of Wittenberg (*map*, p. 410). In Catholic teaching, indulgences may reduce or eliminate penalties due for sins, both on earth and in purgatory. (Purgatory, in Catholic doctrine, is a temporary state or condition, after death, for the cleansing of *pardoned* souls on their way to heaven.) Tetzel, however, made extravagant claims for indulgences, implying that they would *automatically* remove a sinner's *guilt* as well as the penalty.

Tetzel's claims were unacceptable to the local professor of theology, a priest named Martin Luther. In protest, he prepared a long list of criticisms of the sale of indulgences (the "Ninety-five Theses") and reportedly nailed it to the door of the Wittenberg Castle church. Luther charged that the money from Tetzel's sale of indulgences was going to Rome for the building of a new St. Peter's church (pp. 396–398). (He resented having Germans pay for an undertaking that would be of no benefit to them.) He also challenged indulgences in general, implying that they were of doubtful value. His charges brought an immediate attack from the clergy, but they struck a sympathetic chord with the laity. Copies of the "Ninety-five Theses" were distributed throughout Germany; the revolt from Rome, aided by the new technique of printing, was under way.

The pope, Leo X (a Medici), directed that a reply be made to Luther's theses (arguments). In answering this reply, and in the series of exchanges that followed, Luther began to question the basic authority of the papacy and the whole Catholic system. When it became clear that his radical views could not be reconciled with the doctrines of the Church, Luther chose to stand by them, rather than recant. Unlike Erasmus and other humanists, he did not hesitate to defy authority in matters of personal belief. He would obey only his conscience. When he was warned that his unyielding position might lead to "division, war, and rebellion," Luther answered that *one cannot compromise on what one believes to be true*.

Luther's Spiritual Search: His Doctrine of Salvation

The force of Luther's personal conviction was due in part to his temperament. He relished a fight and was capable of quick, violent, and sustained anger. He was also a man of instinctive frankness and courage. But his beliefs were mainly the product of a long spiritual pilgrimage marked by doubt, agony, and, finally, conviction.

Luther was of peasant stock. His father, who had once been a miner, made wise investments and became a respected bourgeois. He wanted his son to study law in preparation for a career as a middle-class civil official. But Martin, who had attended a school run by the Brethren of the Common Life (p. 381), had fallen into deep spiritual fears in his early years. By the time he completed his liberal arts course at the University of Erfurt (in Saxony), he had decided to abandon secular life and enter a monastery. His decision was sealed, he later explained, when he was caught in a violent thunderstorm and, terrified, interpreted the thunder as a call from God.

Luther took vows at an Augustinian monastery in Erfurt. Fearing that his soul was in danger of damnation, he hoped that an ascetic life would afford him a better chance of salvation. But he found no peace of mind either as a monk or as a priest. No matter how strictly he fasted, prayed, and punished himself, his sense of unworthiness persisted. The Church taught that salvation could be achieved only by God's grace (p. 273), known through faith, and by "good works," including the partaking of the sacraments. Luther despaired of doing *enough* good works to gain God's favor. While he was in this torment, he was sent by his superior to a new university in Wittenberg that had been founded by Frederick, the Elector (Duke) of Saxony. After receiving his doctor's degree there in 1512, he stayed on as professor of theology.

At Wittenberg Luther began to discover his path to spiritual peace. While preparing some lectures on the Bible, he was struck by certain passages that seemed to suggest an answer. In Paul's Epistle to the Romans, for example, Luther read, "The just shall live by faith" (1:17). After days and nights of pondering, he concluded that "by grace and sheer mercy God *justifies* [saves] us through *faith*." The whole of the Scripture, he explained later, then took on new meaning for him. Whereas the "justice of God" had formerly filled him with hate, it now became "inexpressibly sweet in greater love. This passage of Paul became to me a gate to heaven. . . ."

Now Luther understood why his own self-punishment and works as a monk had gained him nothing. Man, by his nature, cannot please God without faith; but faith, a free gift of God's mercy, "justifies" a person and ensures salvation. We are saved not by works, concluded Luther, but by *faith alone*. Those of us who accept Christ as our Savior have the right to feel that true faith has been given us. From our love of God, we will freely perform good works—not because we *need* to, but because we *want* to.

Ideas of this kind had a long history in Christianity. The apostle Paul had been the first to proclaim justification by faith, and Augustine, the leading Christian thinker of the later Roman Empire, had adopted the belief and found it consoling (pp. 176, 192). But although these ideas brought Luther immense personal relief, when he began to apply them to the institution of the Church he grew troubled. If people received faith according to God's secret judgment, of what use was the ordained priesthood? If every Christian was, in effect, a priest, were not the claims of the clergy absurd and hateful? And what good were the special vows and way of life undertaken by monks and nuns? If *works* were no help to salvation, what was the benefit of sacraments, pilgrimages, and papal indulgences?

In 1517, Tetzel's selling of indulgences brought Luther face to face with what he regarded as a flagrant distortion of religious teachings. Up to this point he had shared his views only with his students; now he felt compelled to speak out. And so it was that he prepared, in traditional form for academic debates, his "Ninety-five Theses."

THE WIDENING SPLIT WITH ROME

As the dispute over indulgences dragged on, Luther busied himself with writing theological pamphlets in which he broadened his attack on the Church, especially the papacy. At the same time he appealed to the German nobles (*Address to the Christian Nobility of the German Nation*), and to the laity in general, by speaking of the "priesthood" of *all* baptized Christians. Ordained priests and bishops, he argued, had no more *special* powers than other Christians; they were simply fulfilling the duties of their office (as princes fulfilled theirs). He also attacked monasticism and declared that priests should be permitted to marry.

In addition to challenging the doctrines of apostolic succession (pp. 181–182) and "good works," Luther struck directly at the number and meaning of the holy sacraments (pp. 272–273). Of the seven traditional sacraments, he asserted that only *two* were called for by Scripture: baptism and the Eucharist. And, contrary to Catholic doctrine, he insisted that in the Eucharist there is no miraculous *change* of substance (*transubstantiation*) from bread and wine into the body and blood of Christ. Luther taught, instead, the "Real [Corporeal] Presence" of Christ *along with* the bread and wine; and the Presence, he insisted, is not brought into being by the priest, for God is *everywhere* present *always*.

Pope Leo, whose main interests appeared to be in art, hunting, and politics, was annoyed by the excitement Luther had stirred up in Germany. He referred scornfully to the dispute over indulgences as a "squabble among monks." But when he realized how serious the implications were, he moved against Luther—cautiously. One reason for this caution was that Luther, as a professor at Wittenberg, enjoyed the protection of the Elector Frederick of Saxony; and the pope, for political reasons, was trying to stay on friendly terms with Frederick.

Ultimately, however, Leo had to act. In 1520 he ordered Luther excommunicated. Luther responded by burning the *bull* (the papal document of excommunication) before the city gates of Wittenberg, thus demonstrating his defiance of Rome. The clergy now called on the Holy Roman emperor, Charles V, to seize Luther (it was considered the duty of the civil ruler to punish confirmed heretics), but Luther had such strong support among all classes of the laity that the emperor hesitated.

The Elector Frederick then insisted that Luther receive a hearing before the imperial Diet (assembly) of princes. At the Diet of Worms in 1521 Luther was afforded a last chance to recant his heresies. He refused, declaring eloquently that Scripture was the sole source of authority and that he must obey his conscience. The Diet then condemned Luther and issued a decree prohibiting *all* new religious doctrines within the Holy Roman Empire.

Luther had been guaranteed safe conduct on his journey to Worms. After he left the assembly, however, the emperor ordered him put under the ban—which meant that he was branded an outlaw. Subjects of the empire were forbidden to shelter him, and, if seized, he could be killed. Frederick, however, had planned for Luther's safety in advance. His soldiers kidnapped Luther as he left Worms and took him secretly to Frederick's castle at Wartburg, where Luther remained for about a year working on a German translation of the Bible. His "people's" version of Scripture helped shape the modern German language as well as Protestant doctrines.

BUILDING THE LUTHERAN CHURCH

When Luther thought it safe, he returned to Wittenberg to lay plans for a reformed church. He spent the rest of his life not as a rebel, but as an organizer and administrator. It was in this part of his career that he met some of his severest tests. Many of his followers had responded in unexpected ways to his teachings of the "priesthood of all believers" and the sole authority of Scripture. Some developed disturbing notions about Christian practices and about the relation of religion to society. Numerous sects began to appear, not only in Germany but in Switzerland and Holland as well.

The principal group went under the general name of Anabaptists—a name derived from their views on baptism. They insisted that baptism was meaningful only after someone old enough to comprehend Christian doctrines had made a voluntary confession of faith. They therefore opposed infant baptism and held that grown-up Christians who had been baptized as infants must accept the rite *again* (*ana*baptism). The sects within the Anabaptist group varied considerably in their social ideas, which often proved troublesome to established laws and customs. Applying New Testament teachings *literally* to their own times, they refused military service and sought to establish a more egalitarian community. Some, including a group of Mennonites in Holland, resisted all forms of *modernization;* like the Amish (their descendants in America) they considered the acceptance of new fashions as a "compromise with the world." Still other sects advocated acts of violence against "ungodly" persons and against officials who declined to punish them.

Luther, who was extremely conservative in his views on the social order, was alarmed by such proposals. He believed in unquestioned obedience to the *state* and opposed any sort of rebellion against established *political* authorities. In 1524 Luther responded angrily to a peasant revolt that swept over Germany; the serfs were seeking relief from new burdens laid upon them by their feudal lords, especially in eastern Germany where, as in the rest of eastern Europe, serfdom was growing more oppressive at this time (pp. 327, 457). He urged the aristocracy to put down the violent uprising without mercy, to slay the rebels as they would "mad dogs." He later admitted that it was he who had commanded the slaughter of the peasants: "All their blood is on my head. But I throw the responsibility on our Lord God, who instructed me to give this order." (Luther also urged harsh measures against Jews, reinforcing the popular anti-Semitism of his times.)

He was equally severe with preachers who disagreed with his doctrines. He considered them "blasphemers" and believed that they, like persons guilty of rebellion against the state, should be executed. Though claiming for himself the freedom to interpret Scripture, he denied it to those whom he judged to be not properly "qualified." The Lutheran Church developed an orthodoxy of its own, resting on the "Augsburg Confession" of 1530. This document, largely the work of Luther's friend and disciple Philipp Melanchthon, was a moderate statement of Luther's doctrinal views, including those on justification (salvation), sacraments, and the relation of faith and works.

The Emperor Charles, though busy with war and politics outside Germany, still hoped to suppress the Lutheran Church by force. In 1529 Charles and the Catholic members of the imperial Diet reaffirmed the earlier Worms decree prohibiting all new religious doctrines in Germany. The Lutheran princes (of northern Germany) *protested* this action and thus acquired the name "Protestant." In time, this name came to be used for all the rebellious creeds.

Soon Germany was split into armed alliances; Catholic states lined up against Lutheran states. By the time the emperor could send his forces against the Lutheran princes, he found them too powerful to overcome. The result was a truce, known as the Religious Peace of Augsburg (1555), in which the members of the imperial Diet agreed to leave each prince free to choose either Catholicism or Lutheranism for his realm. (Other doctrines were still prohibited.) Under the Peace of Augsburg, religious warfare among the German states was suspended for some sixty years.

The people living in the Lutheran states found no great difficulty in accepting the decisions of their respective princes. Though the peasants had been embittered by Luther's harsh attitude toward them, their bitterness softened with time. For their part, the princes, nobles, and bourgeois enthusiastically supported the reformed church. It appealed to German patriotism by rejecting the Roman papacy, and its support of the established order pleased all who held office or wealth. The laity as a whole tended to feel comfortable in Luther's church. According to his doctrine, all baptized Christians were on the same spiritual level as their ministers; the devout man of property could feel equal, before God, to the ascetic, propertyless cleric. Secular society and values had won the approval of the church.

The kings of Scandinavia recognized the advantages of a state church, and they, too, established the new faith as their official religion. In each Lutheran country the ruler appointed superintendents to oversee his religious establishment — thus subordinating church to state. The formerly Catholic religious buildings and grounds were assigned to the new churches, but the extensive landholdings of the bishops and abbots were seized by the crown.

In accordance with Luther's views, monastic orders were abolished in all these states, and ministers were permitted to marry. Luther himself married a former nun, who bore him six children. By his acts and teachings he raised the value placed on marriage and upheld the rights of wives to sexual satisfaction; he did not, however, urge any basic changes in the social role of women. The veneration of saints and relics (pp. 276–277) and all manner of formal "good works" were rejected. Luther did, however, retain the principle of church *authority* and many semblances of medieval religious practice. The worship service, in German, was not much different from the Catholic service. Unlike some other reformers, Luther also kept art and music in his church; he composed a notable book of hymns as well as several *catechisms* (handbooks for oral expression of church teachings).

CALVIN AND THE ELECT: "PREDESTINATION"

Luther was by no means the only religious rebel at work during the 1520s. And, though he tried to impose his doctrines on the others, he failed to do so outside northern Germany and Scandinavia. The logic of his own thought, in fact, worked against a unified reform movement. He had taught that each individual, guided by the Holy Spirit, must see the truth of Scripture according to his or her own conscience. While the papal theory of Petrine supremacy (p. 183) had offered a logical basis for *one* interpretation of truth and for *one* church, Luther's view led naturally to *many* churches. Once papal authority had been overthrown, there was no logical limit to the number of creeds and denominations.

Of the countless separations that followed Luther's revolt, two require special attention because of their far-reaching historical impact. One of these is the Church of England, the most conservative of the major splits from Rome. The other, initiated by John Calvin, departed most radically from the Catholic tradition—in doctrine, spirit, organization, and ritual.

CALVIN: THE INTERNATIONAL REFORMER

Younger than Luther by some twenty-five years, Calvin (*Fig. 9-2*) was born and raised a Frenchman. Fear of persecution by the Catholic king forced him to flee to Switzerland, however, and he settled down in the city of Geneva in 1536. The city, which had just revolted from its feudal overlord (a bishop), was in the midst of political and religious turmoil. Within a short time Calvin and his version of reformed Christianity achieved dominance in the community. For some twenty years, until his death in 1564, he guided the church, the state, and the Academy (university) of Geneva (*map*, p. 410).

Calvin's influence extended far beyond the boundaries of his city. He corresponded with rulers and theologians alike, and reformers from all over Europe came to Geneva to study his doctrines. When they returned to their homelands, they carried Calvinism with them. Calvinism thus became the leading Protestant

WARE BILD ·NVS IOHAN·
NIS CAL· VINI WEI·
LAND P· PFARRHER
ZV GENF IN SOPHOI

B-H
1574

IOHAN HVSS HAT DIE BEHMEN BKERT
VND LVTHER HAT DIE DEVTSCHEN GLERT
SO HAT DIESER CALVINVS GMERT den
DEN GLAVBEN IN FRANCKREICH ·V GWER
DEM ANTECRIST · DARVM ER MORDT
WIE DER TEVFFL · IST NIE ERHORT

9-2 Woodcut portrait of John Calvin, 1574. The German caption at the top identifies the picture as one of Calvin. The lower caption carries a powerful propaganda message: it claims Calvin as the successor of Jan Hus and Martin Luther, and declares (untruthfully) that he was murdered on account of defending the Protestant faith against "Antichrist" (the pope).

force in France (the Huguenots), Holland (the Reformed Church), Scotland (Presbyterianism), and England (Puritanism).

Calvinism is important not only because of its international influence but because of its special appeal to the bourgeois. Born to a middle-class family, Calvin accepted business as a normal Christian vocation. He took for granted (as Luther and the Catholic theologians did not) the functions of capital, banking, and large-scale commerce. Though urging entrepreneurs to be honest and reasonable in their dealings, he did not question the correctness of their occupation. He was the first theologian to praise the capitalistic virtues: hard work, thrift, and the accumulation of money. He praised the creation of wealth through industry so long as that wealth was not used for self-indulgence. The businessman should be sober and disciplined, dedicated to the "service of the Lord."

It is not surprising that these ideas were warmly received in such commercial centers as Amsterdam, Antwerp, and London. (In Switzerland, the mountain regions remained Catholic, while the urban centers embraced Calvinism.) Calvin's faith suited the economic realities of the day and was attractive to the most progressive and venturesome class of Western society. Carried to New England in the seventeenth century, Calvinism (Puritanism) contributed significantly to the shaping of American life.

As a young man, John Calvin had prepared for the priesthood in Paris and then, at his father's urging, had turned to the study of law. His legal training sharpened his logic and strengthened his ability to express himself; but he found a career in law distasteful. He became active in humanistic scholarship (p. 374) and, after receiving his law degree, took up the study of Greek and Hebrew. His taste for the classics was reflected in a book he wrote about a work of the Stoic philosopher Seneca (p. 135). A year later (in 1533) Calvin had a sudden conversion to the idea of religious reform. France, like the rest of Europe, was the scene of heated disputes about the Church; the writings of Erasmus and Luther had stirred the youthful Calvin. He remained a keen scholar all his life, but after his "conversion" Calvin the humanist gave way to Calvin the *reformer*.

He turned to a systematic explanation of his religious views and finished the first edition of the *Institutes of the Christian Religion* when he was only twenty-six years old (1536). He wrote the original in Latin but soon made a translation into French. This work was to stand as the principal statement of Protestant theology for some three hundred years and as such is comparable to the Catholic statement by Thomas Aquinas (*Summa Theologiae*, p. 301).

THE DOCTRINE OF GOD'S OMNIPOTENCE

Calvin was very close to Luther in his basic theology. He saw the Bible as the sole source of authority and rejected a priesthood based on apostolic succession. (Though Catholic teaching upheld the Bible as supreme, it insisted that its interpretation be reserved to the *Catholic authorities*.) Calvin agreed, too, with Luther that salvation was determined by God's grace alone, unaffected by man's works. Like Luther, he scorned monasticism and such "Romish" practices as pilgrimages, indulgences, and the veneration of saints and relics (pp. 276–277, 281).

The difference between the two men, and it was a real one, lay in what each chose to emphasize. Luther was obsessed with his soul's salvation, and it was this that led him to his doctrine. Calvin, on the other hand, was obsessed with a sense of God's *omnipotence* (unlimited power) and human *depravity* (wickedness). He argued that everyone must do what God wills not as a means to salvation, but *because God wills it*. Calvin's position may well have been a reaction to his contact with humanism, which *praises* human abilities. But he drew his vision of God's glory and perfection directly from the Old Testament, and no other theologian has followed through with such relentless logic the implications of that vision.

The best known and most controversial of Calvin's doctrines is that of "predestination" and "election." Like justification by faith, this doctrine was not a new one, but dated back through Augustine to the apostle Paul (pp. 176, 192). More than any other Christian thinker, however, Calvin made it the center of his system

Color Plate B1   Sandro Botticelli, *The Birth of Venus,* c. 1482. Tempera on canvas, approx. 5′8″ × 9′1″. Uffizi Gallery, Florence, Italy.

Color Plate B2   Leonardo da Vinci, *The Last Supper,* c. 1495–1497. Fresco, 15′4″ × 29′4″. Convent of Santa Maria delle Grazie, Milan, Italy.

Color Plate B3 Michelangelo, *The Creation of Adam*, 1508–1512. Fresco, Sistine Chapel, Vatican City.

Color Plate B4 Pieter Brueghel the Elder, *The Wedding Dance*, c. 1566. Oil on panel, 47″ × 62″. Detroit Institute of Arts.

Color Plate B5 Peter Paul Rubens, *The Rape of the Daughters of Leucippus*, c. 1617. Oil on canvas, approx. 7'3" × 6'10". Alte Pinakothek, Munich.

Color Plate B6 Jean-Antoine Watteau, *Music Party*, c. 1719. Oil on canvas, 26" × 36". Wallace Collection, London.

Color Plate B7   Jules Hardouin-Mansart and Charles Le Brun, Hall of Mirrors, Palace of Versailles, France, c. 1680.

of religious belief. God, declared Calvin, foreknows and determines everything that happens in the universe—even those events ordinarily credited to *chance*. It follows that he certainly determines who shall be saved and who shall be forever lost. All individuals, because of Adam's sin and their own wickedness, would disobey God if left to their own puny powers. But God gives to those he "elects" the ability to persevere in his service. The rest, for his own reasons, he allows to fall. Calvin unflinchingly defined this doctrine in his *Institutes*:

> Predestination we call the eternal decree of God, by which he has determined in himself, what he would have become of every individual of mankind. For they are not all created with a similar destiny; but eternal life is foreordained for some, and eternal damnation for others. Every man, therefore, being created for one or the other of these ends, we say, he is predestinated either to life or to death.

In his discussion of predestination, Calvin warned that the subject is dangerous and delicate, since it touches on a guarded *secret* of the Almighty. To the charge that God could not be so unfair as to condemn most of humankind to damnation, Calvin answered that *no one* deserves salvation and that it is only through God's gracious mercy that *some* are saved. Further, it is wrong to question the plans and judgment of God. Man has only a worm's-eye view of Creation. Whatever God has willed is right, because he has willed it. Calvin admitted that the Lord's predestination was an "awesome decree," but he held that all must nevertheless accept it.

But many would not accept so harsh a doctrine. Luther accepted it, though he did not stress it in his teachings. Most Protestant groups, in time, would turn away from the doctrine for two reasons: it is very gloomy, and it denies free will. The Roman Catholics (including Erasmus) condemned Calvin's teachings, declaring that they reduce human beings to mere puppets. Catholics did not deny that God's grace is indispensable to salvation, but they believed that it is offered more generously than Calvin suggested. They also insisted that each individual can either cooperate (through good works) in achieving salvation or can *refuse* to cooperate. By refusing, a person chooses the path to hell, but this is the person's own doing. Calvin answered that the Catholic argument is an insult to God's majesty. It suggests that God's will is not all-powerful and that his grace, alone, is insufficient.

In reply to the charge that his doctrine would destroy all incentive for following a worthy Christian life and cause some people to throw themselves into reckless indulgence, he declared that nothing in the doctrine of predestination excuses any person from striving to obey God's commandments. On the contrary, argued Calvin, no one knows for certain who is of the "elect" and who is "reprobate" (condemned). All individuals, therefore, should act as if they enjoy God's favor. If they do enjoy that favor, they should want their lives to be shining examples to others; if they do not enjoy it, they should obey God anyway. It is surely the duty of those who feel moved by the Spirit to do God's will themselves and to see that others, whether or not they are to be saved, also honor God. The divine will can be clearly read in Scripture; all should shape their lives accordingly, regardless of the decree of predestination.

CALVINIST ETHICS: THE PURITAN DISCIPLINE

Calvin applied this line of reasoning with strict logic to the entire field of Christian morals. Although a person's behavior is not the means of his salvation, it must nonetheless be subjected to close scrutiny. *Puritanism* as a social discipline was thus developed by Calvin, for he wanted the behavior of all Christians to be held under tight control. To Calvin, God is a righteous, demanding judge, under whose searching eye Christians should conduct themselves humbly and soberly.

Calvin gave a further justification of his ascetic doctrine. For the faithful to truly *glorify* God, they must first rid themselves of the "distractions" of the flesh. This belief followed that of Paul, Augustine, and the medieval ascetics; it was opposed to the humanism of Calvin's day. Yet his acquaintance with humanism gave him some appreciation of its values. He was even willing to tolerate a moderate enjoyment of the fruits of the earth, such as wine, since they are part of God's creation. But, because moderate indulgence often leads to excess, he urged *abstinence* as a practical policy.

Calvin criticized any form of decoration lest it lead to vanity and pride — and any form of cardplaying lest it lead to gambling. The theater, because of its historical associations with paganism, was closed down in Geneva; art was seen as a distraction from God's word. Drinking was condemned as a prelude to intoxication, and dancing was prohibited as a stimulant to desire. The clothing of women had to be plain and ample; he regarded the display of personal ornament or the exposure of flesh as a signal to sexual instincts. In living a "puritanical" life, concluded Calvin, one follows the teachings of the Lord, who "condemned all those pleasures which seduce the heart from chastity and purity."

To Calvin, a person's *conscience* is the prime defense against ungodly distractions and against sin itself. But conscience must ever be on guard. One should not yield to "natural" inclinations to sin; they are in all probability the temptings of Satan, and God wants us to overcome them. This compelling, inward sense of sin is difficult for most modern minds to comprehend. But in the sixteenth century the sense of sin and the fear of its consequences haunted God-fearing men and women. Luther himself confessed that he was harassed by the Devil and once threw his inkpot at him.

If the individual could not avoid wrongdoing, Calvin believed, it was up to other Christians to be their "brother's keeper." As chief pastor in Geneva, he used his pulpit to warn and frighten potential sinners. When his sermons failed, he resorted to force in prohibiting unseemly acts and words. The Consistory of Geneva was a special body of pastors and lay elders responsible for public morals and discipline. Alleged offenders were called before this court, which might reprimand the accused or impose bread-and-water sentences upon them. Common offenses were profanity, drunkenness, dozing in church, criticizing ministers, dancing, and other "immoral" acts.

More serious offenses were handled by the town council. One man, accused of placing an insulting placard on Calvin's pulpit, was tortured until he confessed; later, he was beheaded on a further charge of conspiring against Calvin.

Accused heretics were also brought before the council. The most notorious trial was that of the Spaniard Michael Servetus, who challenged the Christian doctrine of the Trinity. Calvin, after warning Servetus to stay away, had him arrested when he visited Geneva. Calvin then charged him with heresy and supported his conviction and execution (1553). With firm logic, Calvin justified the destruction of "false prophets" by referring to the harsh thirteenth chapter of Deuteronomy:

> God makes plain that the false prophet is to be stoned without mercy. We are to crush beneath our heel all affections of nature when his honor is involved. The father should not spare his child, nor the brother his brother, nor the husband his own wife, or the friend who is dearer to him than life.

The Protestant reformer had come full circle to the papal position of *intolerance* toward dissenting doctrine. By excommunicating "wrongdoers" from his church, Calvin drove most of his critics from Geneva; refugees from Catholic persecution, meanwhile, kept slipping in from other lands. By the end of Calvin's rule (1564), most of the citizens of Geneva supported his principles and policies. They admired and respected him for defending Christian doctrine and imposing strict rules of conduct upon all the residents of the city.

RELATIONS OF CHURCH AND STATE

Although Calvin dominated both religion and government in Geneva, he held no public office. He opposed the union of spiritual and civil authority. But he desired legal separation as a means of safeguarding the independence of the church and of assuring its position *above* the state. In this he again followed papal policy, especially as conducted by Gregory VII (pp. 283–284): ministers of the Church must stand as *teachers* and *judges* of civil rulers. To Calvin, the purpose of government was to regulate society according to the will of God, and the *Church* was the appointed interpreter of God's will: "Great kings ought not to think it any dishonor to humble themselves before Christ, the King of Kings, nor ought they to be displeased at being judged by the church. . . . They ought even to wish not to be spared by the pastors, that they may be spared by the Lord."

Geneva was legally a republic whose principal governing organ was the elected town council. As we have seen, the council served to protect Calvin's church against critics, rebels, and heretics. And in the manner in which Pope Gregory VII had held the threat of excommunication (and disgrace) over kings and princes (p. 284), so Calvin held it over the politicians of Geneva. His Consistory watched their public and private behavior for the slightest evidence of anything "improper."

For some twenty years Geneva served as a model of theocracy (church-controlled state). The organized church, Calvin asserted, is essential for the supervision of the state as well as for the salvation of souls. This view, too, paralleled the papal pronouncement that individual salvation is possible only within the Church. The idea of dependence on church membership may seem to contradict Calvin's doctrine of predestination and election. If God has already determined that a person is to be saved, why must that person remain in Calvin's church (or any other church)? This was a difficult question for both Luther and Calvin because their very doctrines suggested that they themselves were not essential. Yet "inner voices" told them that this could not be. Calvin's explanation was simple: it is God's will that the elect be saved *through* the True Church. And through its inspired teaching and discipline the ways of Heaven might be reflected on earth.

CALVINIST MINISTRY AND RITUAL

Calvin saw nothing inconsistent in holding to certain Roman Catholic principles. But he differed sharply from them with respect to the ministry and ritual of the Church. Calvin accepted, with Luther, the principle of the "priesthood of all believers"; his church gave to its ministers no special powers that set them apart from baptized laymen. Their authority came only from their assigned *office*, as did the authority of civil officials.

Calvin guarded against preaching by self-proclaimed ministers. A "legitimate ministry," he declared, is formed when suitable persons are appointed by the lay elders, subject to the approval of the congregation and the pastors of the community. In the administration of each church, the minister was assisted by elders elected by the congregation. Thus developed the *presbyterian* form of church government. (The word *presbyteros* is the Greek word for "elder.")

Today, at each level of most Calvinist churches (local unit, district, and nation), control rests in the hands of ministers and elected elders. Thus, the ultimate authority in these churches (and others that follow its model) is the highest "presbytery" of baptized believers. Some other Protestant denominations leave control with each local congregation (*congregational* form of government).

Calvin insisted that Church ritual be based exclusively on Scripture. He found, with Luther, that only baptism and the Eucharist are clearly established there as sacraments. (But, unlike Luther, he held that the presence of Christ in the Eucharist is *spiritual* only.) Beyond the administration of these two rites, Calvin permitted little except the singing of psalms and the preaching of sermons. He regarded *images* of the saints as a distraction from the exclusive worship of the Almighty, and he therefore barred their use.

He believed that music, art, and ornamentation had no place in the Church; the awesome Catholic cathedrals, with their stained glass, gilt, and statuary, he branded as pagan temples. Jesus and Paul, according to Scripture, had conducted their ministries in simple fashion by preaching. And preaching was the core of the Calvinist service. There were no processions, genuflections (bending of the knee), embroidered garments, incense, or Latin chants. The minister wore simple black and spoke only in the ordinary language of his congregation (as Jesus had). The typical Calvinist service was once described by a critic as consisting of "four bare walls and a sermon."

HENRY VIII AND THE CHURCH OF ENGLAND

Calvinist austerity found little acceptance among Lutherans or among English reformers. While Protestant ideas from the continent influenced the doctrine of the Anglican Church (Church of England), organization and ritual remained close to the Catholic tradition. Thus, the Anglican Church came to represent a sort of compromise between extreme Protestantism and Roman Catholicism. Radical reformers would criticize it as a muddled and illogical institution, subservient to the state; Roman Catholics would condemn it as divisive and heretical. The Anglicans, however, insisted that theirs was the True Church, that it was both Catholic *and* reformed. This is still the view of the worldwide Anglican churches, including the Protestant Episcopal Church of America.

Although John Wiclif had preached reform during the fourteenth century (p. 409), there was no English counterpart to Luther or Calvin in the sixteenth century. Religious reform in England, though supported by numerous critics of the Catholic Church, was carried through by its monarchs. From the time of Henry VIII, who initiated the reform, to the time of Elizabeth I, who completed it, changes were prompted primarily by the wishes of the crown. The reformed Church of England does not bear the mark of any one spiritual leader, though many devoted clergymen helped establish it.

The first Tudor monarch, Henry VII, had laid the foundations for royal absolutism and bourgeois prosperity (p. 352). His policies were vigorously pursued by his son and successor, the youthful Henry VIII. Henry proved to be a popular king, a robust Renaissance despot. He had some training in theology, for, as a younger son in the royal family, his father had started him on a career in the Church. The plan was dropped on the death of his elder brother, Arthur, which left Henry heir to the throne. His interest in religious matters continued, however, and after his coronation he formally defended the Catholic view of the sacraments against Luther's public attack (1521). As a reward, Leo X gave Henry the title "Defender of the Faith."

Henry's Desire for Independence

Henry accepted Roman Catholic doctrine, but he soon came to resent Roman interference in the affairs of his kingdom. The rising tide of national feeling had already stripped the pope of much of his influence in European states. In Spain and France the monarchs controlled the Church within their borders, but in England the pope still confirmed the appointment of high-ranking clergy. Appeals from Church courts (in keeping with canon law) and a portion of Church revenues continued to go to Rome.

But it was a personal matter, related to the welfare of the state, that led Henry VIII to break with Rome. In order to preserve the alliance between the ruling families of England and Spain, he had married Catherine of Aragon, the widow of his elder brother. Because it was contrary to canon law to marry so close a relative, he had sought and received a papal dispensation (p. 281) permitting the union. In the course of their marriage, Catherine bore six children, but all except one were still-born or died in infancy. The single survivor was a girl (Mary). The English had only recently emerged from a bloody civil war over the succession to the throne, and they feared that a female ruler might prove unable to maintain national strength and unity. When it appeared that Catherine would have no more children, Henry and his advisers began to think about his taking a new wife.

Henry's sense of duty was accompanied by his fondness for Anne Boleyn, an attractive young lady-in-waiting to the queen. In 1527 he decided to marry her and directed his chancellor (chief minister) to have his marriage to Catherine *annulled*. The Church did not permit divorce; but if it found a marriage to be invalid, both partners were free to marry again. It was thought that Pope Clement VII, a Medici, would grant Henry's request, just as a previous pope had approved the original union. Because the marriage to Catherine had been contrary to canon law, it would have been easy enough for papal lawyers to find some *defect* in the earlier dispensation.

But the infatuated Henry was to be disappointed. The Habsburg emperor, Charles V, was Catherine's nephew. He informed the pope that there were no proper grounds for annulment and that such action would be cruel and insulting to his aunt and his family. Charles did not wish Henry to remarry, for Henry's daughter, Princess Mary (Charles' cousin), was heir to the English throne. If Henry had no son, Mary would ultimately become queen, bringing another state into the Habsburg circle of power.

Charles was busy at the time in a campaign to win control of Italy, and his army happened to be in Rome when Pope Clement received Henry's appeal. Charles added to the pressure on Clement by offering to restore the Medici family to power in Florence if the pope would refuse to grant the annulment. But Clement decided to do nothing, hoping that something would happen to spare him from making the choice. After nearly six years of waiting, Henry's patience ran out. He married Anne Boleyn in 1533, after his newly appointed archbishop, Thomas Cranmer, had declared his marriage to Catherine annulled. Clement promptly excommunicated the king and released Henry's subjects from their obligation of obedience to the crown.

BREAK WITH ROME: THE ACT OF SUPREMACY

Infuriated by the pope's delaying tactics and by what he considered to be Clement's interference in state affairs, Henry determined to free himself of the pope once and for all. He was backed by both Parliament and the people, for the papacy had become exceedingly unpopular in England. Having first submitted the issue to the assembled English clergy, Henry had the Act of Supremacy passed by Parliament in 1534. This act declared that the king was the "only supreme head on earth" of the Church of England and approved his power to "repress, redress, and reform" all errors, heresies, and abuses in religion.

A series of supplementary acts made the break with Rome complete. Communication with the pope (who was now referred to as the "Bishop of Rome") was forbidden; payments to Rome were stopped; the crown was given sole right to appoint bishops and abbots; and any denial of the king's supremacy was labeled as treason. Sir Thomas More, a Christian humanist (pp. 401–402) and former chancellor, refused to take the required oath of supremacy and was beheaded. Other men of strict principle followed More to the cutting block, and some minor rebellions had to be put down. But Henry imposed his will on the clergy, Parliament, and his subjects.

Henry's taking control over the Church of England did not mean that he wished to reform its *doctrine*. On the contrary, he disliked the Protestant tendencies in the country and had Parliament pass the notorious Six Articles, which defined heresy. Individuals who denied any of the "test" articles of faith could be executed. These articles included belief in transubstantiation, celibacy of the clergy, and the necessity of oral confession in the sacrament of penance (p. 273). Henry thus showed his determination both to rule the Church and to keep it "true." Those who challenged his authority were sent to the block as traitors; those who questioned Catholic doctrine were sent to the stake as heretics.

Henry's only important departure from Catholic tradition was his suppression of monasticism. The monks had acquired an unfavorable reputation, and as leaders of the pro-papal faction they had aroused Henry's anger. Further, the religious houses possessed great wealth and extensive lands, and Henry was hard pressed for money. His obedient Parliament voted to close the monasteries and to turn over their property to the crown. The income from a portion of this property was assigned to the support of older ("retired") monks, some of the property was taken for the king's own purposes, and the rest was distributed to his favorites and supporters.

Henry—a shrewd manipulator of people and institutions, a true Machiavellian prince (pp. 344–346)—was thus able to create new ranks of landed noblemen who now had a vested interest in his break with Rome. In those troubled times, moreover, many of the English (like many Italians) preferred despotic power to liberty and disorder. The success of Henry's undertakings, as well as his hearty manner, endeared him to most of his subjects despite his greed, cruelty, and marital misadventures.

Three years after marrying Anne, he accused her of adultery and treason, had her beheaded, and then went on to take, in succession, four more wives. Anne Boleyn had borne him a daughter (Elizabeth), and Jane Seymour gave him a son at last. But the boy proved frail. He came to the throne as Edward VI when only ten years old (1547), and his powers had to be exercised by a guardian *regent* (an appointed officer acting for the crown). He died before coming of age, and the crown passed, after all, to his elder sister Mary (the daughter of Catherine of Aragon).

THE STRUGGLE OVER DOCTRINE: PROTESTANT ADVANCE AND CATHOLIC REACTION

During the regency period of Edward, Protestant factions in England brought about significant changes in the Anglican Church. Cramner, the archbishop of Canterbury, had Lutheran leanings; after Henry's death, he led the way to reform by

1485	1509	1547	1553	1558	1603
Henry VII (House of Tudor)	Henry VIII	Edward VI	Mary	Elizabeth I	

persuading Parliament to repeal the Six Articles and to pass an Act of Uniformity (1549). This act required that all church services follow a uniform text, composed in English by Cranmer himself; this was then put into the *Book of Common Prayer*, which is still (as revised) the basis of Anglican ritual. All subjects of the kingdom were required by the act to attend services regularly; other forms of public worship were outlawed. Cranmer also issued a summary of doctrine, the Forty-two Articles, which was a moderate statement of Protestant doctrines.

When Mary succeeded Edward in 1553, the religious pendulum swung back. Mary, who had been raised a devout Catholic, was determined to restore the nation to allegiance to Rome. She replaced Protestant-minded bishops with Catholics and compelled the clergy to give up their wives. (Under Cranmer, priests had been allowed to marry, in keeping with the Lutheran practice.) Latin replaced English in the services of the Church. When Mary invited Cardinal Reginald Pole to England as papal ambassador, he ceremoniously pardoned her subjects from "heresy" and restored England to communion with Rome. Mary's most unpopular act was to wed her relative, Philip, heir to the Spanish throne and a bitter enemy of Protestantism.

In the face of Mary's ruthless policy against dissenters, most people adjusted their beliefs to avoid execution; but several hundred, including Cranmer, went to the stake for their convictions. The monarch thus earned the name (among Protestants) of "Bloody Mary." She was no more ruthless than her father, Henry, but she offended national feeling by subjecting the country once again to the pope and by marrying a despised foreigner. As Mary bore no child, her reign proved to be only a reactionary interlude whose net effect was to make Catholicism more unpopular than before.

THE ELIZABETHAN COMPROMISE

Elizabeth, the daughter of Anne Boleyn, inherited the crown upon Mary's death in 1558. She had been raised a Protestant but, unlike her half-sister, was neither devout nor fanatical. During her early years she could observe for herself the frequent shifting of loyalties in religion and politics. As queen, she stood firmly for a Protestant church and independence from Rome. But her first concern was for the security of the crown and the unity of her subjects.

A true child of Henry, she managed Parliament and her ministers with shrewdness. She had Mary's Catholic legislation repealed and the Act of Supremacy reenacted (1559). But she avoided giving unnecessary offense to those of her subjects who were pro-Catholic. Her new laws established the "Elizabethan Compromise" (or Settlement), which remains to this day the foundation of the Anglican Church.

Parliament, with Elizabeth's approval, enacted a revised summary of official doctrine known as the Thirty-nine Articles. Similar to Cranmer's earlier statement, it was designed to satisfy all but extremists. The Thirty-nine Articles were Lutheran or Calvinist on certain matters, including the exclusive authority of Scripture, salvation by faith alone, the number of sacraments, and the freedom of the clergy to marry. But on many points the language was obscure, leaving a wide range of interpretation. There was also a firm insistence upon respecting the *traditions* of the Church, except those that were clearly "repugnant to the Word of God." Under the cover of tradition, pro-Catholics would continue to venerate the saints, go on pilgrimages, and engage in other "Romish" religious practices.

In internal organization the Anglican Church was very like the Roman Catholic. The monarch was its "Supreme Governor," but only in the sense that she was responsible, under God, for ruling all classes (religious and secular) in the country. This idea was similar to the priestly role of kings David and Solomon in the ancient Jewish state and to the position of Constantine, Theodosius, and Charlemagne in relation to their empires (p. 236).

The actual ministering of the Word and the sacraments was restricted to the ordained priesthood, in accordance with the doctrine of apostolic succession. The Anglican bishops traced their authority back to the twelve apostles, as did the Roman Catholic bishops (and those of the Orthodox Church). They rejected, however, the theory of *Petrine supremacy*, which was the cornerstone of papal claims to universal authority (p. 183).

It is in the theory and role of bishops that Anglicanism differed most sharply from other Protestant denominations. This distinction is reflected in the designation "Episcopal Church" in America (*episcopus* is the Latin word for "bishop"). Most other Protestant groups developed a presbyterian form of church government, a form we encountered in our discussion of Calvinism (p. 424). The presbyterian form may be characterized as *representative*, the episcopal form as *aristocratic*. Roman Catholic government (to complete our comparison) is *monarchical*.

The Elizabethan Settlement brought stability because most of the English (who by this time were weary of religious quarreling) were prepared to conform. Only a handful of the clergy—who had called themselves Catholic under Mary— now refused to accept the new Act of Uniformity. Elizabeth, who cared little about the *private* views and doubts of her subjects, was content with outward obedience. She would not tolerate open dissent, but penalties were softened and offenders were few. Not until the seventeenth and eighteenth centuries would new religious stirrings disrupt the established Church. These would lead to further divisions of Christianity in England and elsewhere: Baptists, Quakers, Methodists, Congregationalists, Unitarians, Mormons, and many others. But all that lay in the future. For the rest of the queen's long reign, her firm hand brought internal peace and prosperity.

The age of Elizabeth also brought England to the threshold of world power. Philip of Spain, who had become Philip II in 1556, sought the hand of Elizabeth after the death of his wife, Mary. Elizabeth had held him off, so Philip finally decided to take her kingdom by force. (The pope excommunicated Elizabeth in 1570, declared her deposed, and thus opened the way to Philip's adventure.) In 1588

Philip sent a mighty fleet (the Spanish Armada) against England, expecting that once his soldiers had landed on the island, the thousands of unhappy Catholics in the country would rally to his banner. But the Armada was routed in the Channel by the English navy and was smashed by storms on its return home. With Spain, the leading power of the continent, thus humbled, the English became conscious of their strength on the seas. Elizabeth's reign marked a turning point in the nation's history. Thereafter, English sea power, commerce, and diplomacy were to exercise a mounting influence over European and world affairs.

THE ROMAN CATHOLIC RESPONSE: REFORM AND REAFFIRMATION

The Protestant movements — the revolt of some religious leaders and civil rulers against the Roman Catholic Church — grew out of a mixture of motives and were shaped by varying political and social conditions. But they all led to one result: the division of Western Christendom. Within half a century after Luther's challenge at Wittenberg, most of northern Europe had broken away from the papacy. Protestants dominated the cities of Switzerland; they formed a militant minority in France; and a few had even penetrated the Catholic strongholds of Spain and Italy.

Finally the Roman Catholic Church, after hesitation and uncertainty, moved to check the spreading revolt. Too late to reverse the major losses, these efforts did recover some ground and kept the remainder of Europe loyal to Rome. The response took two main courses: reform within the Catholic Church and *counter* measures against Protestanism.

RELATION TO PROTESTANT MOVEMENTS

Catholic reforms were inspired, in part, by the same ideas and ideals that had motivated Luther and the other religious rebels. As we have seen, the condition of the late medieval Church had caused widespread discontent and sharp criticism. The Christian humanist Erasmus was the most eloquent spokesman for reform without rebellion. Other sincere Catholics, both lay and clerical, worked for correction of abuses. A groundswell of reform, similar to that which had started the Cluniac movement in the tenth century (pp. 277–279), now began to rise. There can be no doubt, however, that Catholic reform in the sixteenth century was also prompted by the Protestant actions. The papacy, whose leadership was essential to effective action, had long remained indifferent. But when Paul III became pope in 1534 he was forced to respond to the events in both Germany and England.

Though some aims were common to both the Catholic and the Protestant reform movements, there were important differences between them. Both conservatives and liberals among the Catholic leaders accepted the central doctrines, traditions, and organization of the Church. What the Catholic reformers desired was a purer Christian life within the established Church, in keeping with its historic tradition of *self*-reformation. The Protestant leaders, on the other hand, were not content with purification alone. As we have seen, they wanted a *reconstruction* of the Church, in accord with different theories of authority, priesthood, and salvation.

While the Protestant movements arose in the north, Catholic reform efforts were centered in Spain and Italy. The Spanish reformation had begun in the late fifteenth century, led by Cardinal Ximénes (Archbishop of Toledo), with the full support of the monarchy. The Spanish reform served as a model for Catholic action elsewhere in Europe. This was reform distinctly in the medieval tradition: it included a rigorous campaign to improve the morals and education of the clergy, military action against infidels (the Muslims, p. 307), and a strong effort to wipe out heresies.

In Italy, too, some churchmen had urged similar actions. But the Renaissance popes had dampened the hopes of reformers, and the princes of Italy were either indifferent or unwilling to make the necessary effort. As in the Middle Ages, however, new and reformed religious orders now arose to improve the quality of Christian life. One was the priestly order of Theatines, which was dedicated to education. Another was the order of Capuchins, a reformed branch of the Franciscan friars (p. 279). The Capuchins modeled themselves upon Francis of Assisi and carried his message of love, piety, and simplicity to the common people.

LOYOLA AND THE SOCIETY OF JESUS

One man and one order above all others, however, were to play a decisive role in the Catholic reformation and in stemming the Protestant tide. Ignatius Loyola, a Spanish nobleman and soldier of the king, was the founder of this new order. At about the time Luther was standing before the Diet of Worms (1521), Loyola was seriously wounded in a battle. His leg was shattered by a cannonball, and he lay for months in painful convalescence, during which time he experienced a profound spiritual conversion.

Loyola was burdened, as Luther had been, by a sense of sin and unworthiness. After a lengthy period of confession, fasting, and nightly vigils (watches), visions of Christ and Mary appeared to him and relieved him of his fears. Now he resolved to give up all thought of resuming his former life and enlisted himself as a "soldier of the Lord." He turned the strong military and chivalric traditions of his country to a spiritual purpose, dedicating his services to the Virgin, as a knight to his lady. And he held also to the Spanish tradition of religious orthodoxy, finding satisfaction not in revolt but in absolute obedience to God and the pope.

Loyola realized that if he was to save souls from heresy or indifference he would need a thorough religious education. After preparing himself in Latin, he went on to the University of Paris, where he studied for some seven years, gathering about him a small band of devoted followers. Working at first as an informal association bound by common vows, they formed a regular religious order in 1540.

The order was named the Society of Jesus, and its members were commonly called Jesuits. Loyola was elected its general, or commander, for life, and he placed himself and his society at the service of the pope. The general shaped the internal organization along strict military lines, with a "chain of command" reaching down to the ordinary Jesuit "soldier."

The Jesuits took the usual monastic vows of chastity, poverty, and obedience and required, in addition, absolute acceptance of orthodox doctrines and the authority of the pope. In his manual for members, Loyola laid out both "spiritual exercises" and rules of conduct. One of the rules stated, "To be right in all things we ought to adhere always to the principle that the white which I see I will believe to be black if the Church so rules. . . ."

The organization and discipline of the Society of Jesus were well suited to its broad purpose: "to employ itself entirely in the defense of the holy Catholic faith." The Jesuits sought to accomplish this goal chiefly through widespread education and preaching. They founded schools and colleges to inculcate young minds with the "true" doctrine, and they sent out missions to convert heathens and heretics (pp. 366–367). The Jesuits also tried (mainly through oral confessions) to keep wavering Catholics on the path to *correct* belief. And, by serving as confessors and advisers to civil rulers, they tried to guide states in policies favorable to the Church. Though the Jesuits were highly effective in their education and preaching, these political activities ultimately brought heavy criticism and attacks.

THE REFORMING POPES AND THE COUNCIL OF TRENT

When Loyola died in 1556, the Society of Jesus had grown to nearly fifteen hundred members. All were carefully selected men, well trained and well disciplined, who could be counted on to support the pope without question. They proved especially effective in imposing papal control over the important Council of Trent (*map*, p. 410) in the mid-sixteenth century.

Paul III was the first of the reformation popes. Unlike his Medici predecessor, Clement VII, he was seriously committed to reform. He found a report by a committee of cardinals on abuses among the clergy so shocking that he decided to keep it secret. He did, however, launch an overhauling of papal administration, and he summoned a council to deal with reform and heresy.

Many Catholics, as well as Protestants, felt that a church council might help settle the deep troubles of Christendom. The conciliar (council) tradition was long established; the first general council, held at Nicaea in 325 (p. 187), had successfully faced a serious division over doctrine. The Council of Constance (p. 408) had faced an equally trying problem in 1414 with respect to the Great Schism of the Church. Some believed that another meeting of all the high clergy might once again restore unity and purity to the Church.

Others, however, though they favored a reform of practices, feared that a council might be drawn into a compromise on *doctrine*. The pope was hesitant for an additional reason: past councils had tried to limit the papal monarchy and to establish the council itself as the supreme authority in the Church. Although Paul III at last summoned a council, he made sure that the papacy would control it.

The Council of Trent met, with interruptions, over a period of some twenty years (1545–1563). The Jesuits at the council sought to keep a balance favorable to Roman policies; they were aided in this by the facts that papal ambassadors presided over the sessions and that Italian bishops outnumbered those of any other nationality. (The French clergy, who were committed to a "national" church, did not participate fully.) Because the Italians (and Spaniards) were loyal to Rome, they could be relied on to support the papacy.

By the time the council opened, the pope had decided on a definite course of action. Earlier, a few of his advisers had recommended that some effort be made to bring about reconciliation with the Protestants, but this had proved futile. The pope settled instead on a program of reform and reinvigoration, while refusing to compromise on doctrine. He was willing, apparently, to accept the Catholic setbacks for the time being and to concentrate on holding the line against further losses. This, he thought, could best be done by correcting abuses and by restating beliefs.

The Council of Trent sent its final decrees to the pope for approval, thereby reaffirming the supremacy of his authority. In general, the decrees gave the papacy what it wanted. They fell into two main parts: reform decrees and statements of doctrine. Bishops were ordered to regain strict discipline over their clergy in such matters as keeping vows, morals, behavior, and dress. (Special attention was given to the problem of restoring chastity and putting aside concubines.) And they were required to provide better education for the priesthood by establishing a seminary (theological school) in each diocese. Among the higher clergy, the practice of *simony* was forbidden. (This was the selling of Church "offices" [positions] that had regular incomes attached.) Also forbidden was the holding of more than one office at a time. The Council of Trent, in addition, outlawed the *selling* of papal indulgences, while affirming that the spiritual grace granted by indulgences was genuine and worthy of continued belief and practice. Had these reforms been launched fifty years earlier, they might have blunted the criticisms of Erasmus and other conscientious Christians. In any case, Trent was a turning point in Catholic history, and the clergy and laity both experienced a reawakening of piety and devotions.

Although the Protestant revolt no doubt stimulated the reform and revival of the Church, it also prompted a hardening of Catholic doctrine. The Council of Trent made no compromise with Luther or Calvin on theological issues; in responding to the Protestant challenge, it not only reaffirmed traditional doctrines but stated them more distinctly. The result was to make orthodoxy clearer and narrower and to leave Catholic theologians with less freedom of interpretation than they had had before Trent.

The special powers of the priesthood, the necessity of the Roman Church and the seven sacraments, the doctrine of transubstantiation (p. 415), the veneration of saints and relics, the belief in purgatory and indulgences (p. 413)—all were specifically confirmed by the council. At the same time, the council condemned the opposing Protestant doctrines. Headed by the papacy, the Church was now prepared to carry out the reform decrees of Trent and to restore "correct" doctrines throughout Christendom. Under the zealous popes of the second half of the sixteenth century, the Roman Church moved from stagnation and defensiveness to a bold offensive.

In addition to the Jesuits, two other agencies worked to crush heresy and to keep the faithful safe in "true" beliefs. The first was the Inquisition, of medieval origin (pp. 282–283), that was now revived in Spain, Italy, and the Low Countries. Directing its efforts against those accused of heretical ideas, its secret trials, torture, and burnings aimed at *conformity* through *terror*.

The censorship of books had been ordered by the Council of Trent as another means of checking "false" beliefs. The council authorized an Index (list) of prohibited books, including all those that attacked the Roman Church or contained ideas contrary to its doctrines; and it established a Congregation of the Index to publish the list and keep it current. Church members were forbidden to read any work named in the Index, which soon came to include much of the serious literature of Europe. Censorship, of course, had long been used by both Catholics and Protestants, but the new effort was more comprehensive and was executed with greater energy than ever before. Although the prohibited books continued to circulate even in Catholic countries, the Index no doubt contributed to a narrowing of the exchange of ideas. It remained in force until 1965, when it was dropped by order of the Second Vatican Council (p. 730).

The vigorous response of the Roman Church to the Protestant challenge prevented further Catholic losses. Switches in religion among Europeans have been few since 1570, and the divisions of that time (*map*, p. 410) generally remain today.

HISTORICAL SIGNIFICANCE OF THE REFORMATION

Viewed from the perspective of the twentieth century, the struggles of the Reformation period seem strange in some respects. In the first place, it appears odd that theological issues should have called forth so much attention, energy, and bloodshed at a time when religion generally was a declining force in European affairs. In the second place, while looking *backward* to early Christianity, the Protestant movements actually drew strength from *new* social developments and gave them strength in return. The growing sense of *nationality*, for example, helped Luther's cause in Germany and was, at the same time, stimulated by Luther's revolt. The turning away from Rome helped the power-seeking princes of northern Europe, while putting the church under state control (in Lutheranism and Anglicanism) was both a response and a stimulus to *secularism*. Also, Protestantism and *capitalism* tended to be mutually reinforcing. Calvin, for instance, though urging businessmen to behave ethically, gave his blessing to their occupations. And by praising hard work and thrift, he supported bourgeois morale and encouraged the accumulation of capital.

Perhaps the leading trend in Western culture from the close of the Middle Ages onward was toward *individualism*. It can be observed in the breaking down of the medieval social order, the growth of commercial enterprise, and in overseas exploration (see chapter 7). The trend continued in the Renaissance—in art, literature, and society. The Protestant movements, too, reflected this tendency and gave it new force. Luther and Calvin stressed the right and power of all believers to read the Bible for themselves and to communicate directly with God. True, both soon came to the position of placing their authority over others. But the initial thrust of Protestantism—its spirit of rebelliousness and its appeal to individual conscience—could not be checked.

Moreover, the Reformation radically altered the position of Christianity in Western civilization. The Christian Church, after the sixteenth century, could no longer speak with a single voice, and thoughtful individuals found it hard to accept absolute truth and absolute authority when the claimants to that truth and that authority contradicted and fought one another. This division brought dismay to many and led some to atheism or skepticism (p. 475).

More than a century of wars over religion ended eventually in stalemate in 1650 (p. 453). The surviving religious denominations did not abandon their claims to absolute truth, but most people in western Europe came to agree that "truth" should no longer be imposed by force. And religious toleration, which thus emerged as a by-product of the Reformation, created a new intellectual climate of open questioning and reasoning. The binding faith of medieval Christendom, with its intensity and its ecstasy, was gone forever. Religious doubt had made its mark on modern Western culture.

ART DURING THE REFORMATION

For many Protestants, sacred paintings and sculpture were associated with Rome, and the revolt against "popery" was often accompanied by attacks (physical and verbal) on art images. Calvin, as we have seen, saw works of art as a distraction from the word of God. He objected to any attempt to "paint or carve" subjects that went beyond ordinary observation: "God's majesty, which is too exalted for human sight, may not be corrupted by fantasies which have no true agreement therewith."

The Protestant reformers (and some pious Catholics as well) were also offended by the *sensuality* in some Renaissance art. The "cult of beauty" (pp. 379, 392–393) had produced works that were shocking to puritanical viewers, and a reaction now set in against the portrayal of nudity. Reforming popes of the sixteenth century ordered artists to paint clothes on the figures in numerous Renaissance masterpieces, and many of these works simply disappeared from public view.

THE IMPACT OF PROTESTANTISM: HOLBEIN, BRUEGHEL

The Protestant artists of the sixteenth century faced two problems: they stood in the shadow of the Renaissance giants, and their main source of patronage had been cut off by the Reformation. In many areas, especially those under Calvinist influence, works of art were banned from the churches, and even for private homes paintings and decorations were frowned upon as frivolous. Erasmus, writing from the Netherlands in 1526, reported, "The arts here are freezing." For individual painters or sculptors, the chill was often fatal. They might lose income, acceptable subjects, and useful work—which could be a psychological as well as a financial blow. The sense of "alienation" (feeling "left out"), familiar to artists today, had its beginnings in the period of the Protestant Reformation.

The career of the German painter Hans Holbein is illustrative. Born in 1497, he mastered the techniques of his day and produced works that combined the best of the Italian and the northern styles. Most of his early paintings were designed for church altars, but with the coming of the Reformation Holbein had to turn to portrait painting. By good fortune and with the help of Erasmus (p. 381), he was able to move to England, where he secured commissions from the aristocracy; eventually, he became court painter to Henry VIII. He produced hundreds of lifelike portraits of the monarch, his family, and the royal courtiers (close officials of the king). Working with oils and in the realistic tradition established by Jan van Eyck (pp. 386–389), Holbein usually showed his subjects in their customary setting and surrounded by the symbols and tools of their office or profession. A notable example is *The French Ambassadors* (Fig. III-1, p. 316).

Other Protestant painters explored the possibilities of landscapes and scenes of *ordinary* life ("genre" painting). The Flemish master of genre was Pieter Brueghel; though he produced many splendid landscapes, he is best known for his pictures of common folk. Brueghel was himself a townsman, but he showed a keen understanding of plain, unsophisticated peasants. His interest in rustic subjects is evident in his paintings of peasants at work and at rest, and in his scenes of hunting, feasting, and playing.

Brueghel's *The Wedding Dance* (Color Plate B4), painted in 1566, near the end of his life, is a striking example of *perspective* and *organization*. With its lively movement and rhythm, it suggests the healthy animal spirits of the dancers. Brueghel was one of the first artists to break with the aristocratic tradition of Renaissance painting to show us, bluntly and honestly, the ordinary men and women who made up the bulk of European society.

THE DEVELOPMENT OF THE BAROQUE: RUBENS, REMBRANDT

Although many Catholic painters were also skillful at treating secular subjects, they were encouraged to direct their talents to religious art. The Catholic Church, after the Council of Trent (pp. 432–433), was eager to check the spread of Protestant ideas, and one way was to bring the teachings of the Church directly to the faithful. Art had provided religious instruction during the Middle Ages; it was now called upon to renew its role in defense of Catholic teachings.

The response was an outpouring of magnificent art ranging from the mystical to the sensual. Though the new artists built on Renaissance models, they threw off the restraints of classical rules. Their work came to be called *baroque*—meaning excessive or ornate. But the movement generated its own standards and must not be measured by classical norms. At its best, baroque has an impressive originality and impact.

The leader of baroque art is the Flemish painter Peter Paul Rubens. In 1600, as a young man of twenty-three, he journeyed to Italy, where he learned to create heroic, large-scale canvases. After returning to his native Antwerp, Rubens combined the traditional Flemish attention to detail with his newly learned Italian style. He worked chiefly for the court of the ruling Habsburgs, the Flemish aristocrats, and the Church. A man of enormous energy and versatility, he created fine portraits, altar paintings, and huge murals for palaces and religious houses. His subject matter ranged from romantic and mythological themes to the central mysteries of the Catholic faith.

Rubens was one of the few painters in history who were successful, prosperous, and generally respected in their own day. So great was the demand for his work that he set up a well-organized workshop in which he trained specialists to paint certain elements—heads, hands, animals, or backgrounds. He supervised the production of each work and finished the key features with his own hand. His paintings are notable for their organization, color, and texture.

He was blessed by good fortune and a happy disposition, and his paintings are charged with movement and vigor. His well-nourished nudes reflect the spirit with which he viewed the world. In his treatment of a traditional subject from Greek legend, *The Rape of the Daughters of Leucippus (Color Plate B5),* he arranged powerful men, horses, and women into a tight group of solid figures. There is little "philosophical" intent in this kind of painting, but it combines exciting elements of form and action.

As Rubens was the artistic master of Catholic Flanders, Rembrandt van Rijn was the master of Protestant Holland. But a greater contrast in personalities can hardly be imagined. A generation younger than Rubens, Rembrandt won substantial recognition early in his career. After his beautiful and well-to-do wife died in 1642, however, his fortunes began to decline. He fell into debt, his popularity vanished, and he turned more and more *inward* in his thoughts.

Yet it was in the dark days of tragedy and self-examination that Rembrandt did his most profound work. He painted no longer for rich patrons, but for himself. Although he often painted religious subjects, all his works possess a mysterious spiritual quality. Unlike Rubens, he usually took his subjects from the middle or lower classes. He portrayed them with remarkable economy of line and without affectation, shunning bright colors and extravagant movements and relying on contrasting lights and shadows. His colors appear dark or drab to those who see his paintings for the first time; Rembrandt favored browns, dark reds, and golds. He

9-3   Rembrandt. *Portrait of the Artist*, c. 1660. Oil on canvas, 46″ × 40″. Greater London Council, The Iveigh Bequest, English Heritage, London.

did not wish the surface of his canvases to blind the viewer to the "inner" person. When we look closely at a Rembrandt portrait, we sense the essential *character* of the subject *(Fig. 9-3)*.

Rembrandt spent most of his life in Amsterdam, but he put into his work many of the qualities of Italian painting. These included careful organization and balance and, above all, *psychological interest* (as stressed by Leonardo, p. 395). An illustration of Rembrandt's religious painting is the *Supper at Emmaus (Fig. 9-4)*. A good Protestant, he was a devout reader of the Bible, and in this picture he dramatized a moment from the life of Christ as recounted in Luke (24:13–31). The Gospel states that on the day of the Resurrection Jesus appeared, unrecognized, along a road. There he joined two of his disciples, who invited him to eat with them at an inn. Rembrandt shows Jesus at the moment when he blessed and broke the bread and was revealed to his disciples as the risen Christ.

9-4   Rembrandt. *Supper at Emmaus*, 1648. Oil on panel, 27″ × 26″. Louvre, Paris.

BAROQUE SCULPTURE AND ARCHITECTURE: BERNINI

The main source of the baroque style was Rome, where the Catholic Reformation was centered. The climax of that style came during the seventeenth century in the work of the sculptor and architect Giovanni Lorenzo Bernini (who died in 1680).

A leading characteristic of baroque artists was their effort to *fuse* architecture, sculpture, and painting into a single structure of grandeur and "truth." Bernini was trained as a sculptor, but he thought of himself as an artist who combined several talents. "I render marble as supple as wax," he declared, "and I have united in my works the resources of painting and sculpture." Bernini's most distinctive contribution was the revival of the Italian sculptural tradition, which had fallen into decline with the passing of Michelangelo (pp. 395–397). In the cold and hard medium of stone, Bernini succeeded in catching the fleeting instant, the throbbing passion, the rhythm of movement.

He learned much from the muscular, twisting figures of Michelangelo, but his work displayed even wider range and inventiveness. By means of extraordinary technical skill, he brought sculpture to new heights of drama and emotion. *The Ecstasy of St. Theresa (Fig. 9-5)*, which Bernini prepared for a chapel in a small

9-5   Giovanni Lorenzo Bernini. *The Ecstasy of St. Theresa*, 1644–1652. Polychrome marble and bronze, height 11′6″. Cornaro Chapel, Church of Santa Maria della Vittoria, Rome.

Roman church, shows the mystical Spanish nun after her heart has been pierced by the arrow of divine love. As a smiling angel looks on, the face and body of the saint express indescribable rapture.

Bernini skillfully blended sculpture with architecture. Under Michelangelo's dome in the great basilica of St. Peter's he created an elaborate decoration for the apse (p. 286); and directly above the central altar (which rests over the tomb of Peter) he built a huge bronze canopy, or baldachin (*Fig. 9-6*). The scale and character of its swirling columns capture the spirit of Catholic baroque.

Some years later, Bernini fashioned a dramatic setting for the *exterior* of St. Peter's to match what he had done inside. He designed the vast oval piazza that stands before the largest church in Christendom. (More than a hundred thousand people crowd into this space on special days to await the blessing by the pope.) To enclose its two sides, Bernini constructed a huge, curving colonnade (*Fig. 9-7*), consisting of 284 Greek-style columns. They carry a roof more than sixty feet high, surmounted by seventy giant-sized statues. Visitors

9-6   Giovanni Lorenzo Bernini. Baldachin, 1624. Gilded bronze, approx. 100′ high. St. Peter's Basilica, Vatican, Rome.

entering the piazza from its open end are embraced, symbolically, by the "arms" of the Church.

    Baroque architecture (like baroque painting and sculpture) was an *adaptation* of Renaissance models. Such classical elements as columns, pediments, and arches were used freely, but without following strictly the ancient "rules" for their use. From the late sixteenth century to our own day, many of the public buildings of the West have been designed in this flexible style.

    The Catholic monarchs of Europe were quick to adopt the style for their own purposes. Philip II of Spain, the most powerful ruler of his time (pp. 429–430),

9-7   Giovanni Lorenzo Bernini. Colonnade, St. Peter's Basilica, Vatican, Rome.

started in 1563 to build a new royal palace, choosing for its site the village of Escorial, in the mountainous country near Madrid. Philip's architects laid out a vast complex of buildings and courtyards, with an elegant church at the center. Beneath its main altar was placed a burial vault in which the Spanish kings and queens have since been entombed. The Escorial complex also included a monastery, a seminary, and a library. Its architectural style is generally restrained, but its plan is baroque.

A better-known monument to royal conceit is the Versailles palace, built a century later by Louis XIV. The French monarchy had by then replaced the Spanish as the leading royal house of Europe, and Louis wanted to erect a residence and a center of government and the arts that would surpass all existing palaces. Like the Escorial, Louis' residence was built in the countryside (about twenty miles southwest of Paris). It was a high point of the secular baroque style, combining architecture, landscaping, sculpture, painting, and the minor arts into a grand synthesis.

Built at staggering cost, Versailles matched Louis' love of display. The enclosed areas cover seventeen acres and housed some ten thousand people. The formal gardens, courts, parade grounds, and surrounding woods stretch over many square miles. The overall plan is a masterful realization of the baroque idea of "integrated" design. While the exterior of the Versailles palace is relatively modest, the interior is lavish in the extreme. One of the most dazzling chambers is the Hall of Mirrors *(Color Plate B7)*, a shimmering room designed to overawe visitors to the French court.

In many respects, Versailles proved to be highly "functional." Though wasteful of the nation's resources, it helped the king to centralize his authority within France, and it strengthened the role and image of France as cultural leader of the West. A milestone in politics as well as in civic planning and the arts, Versailles called forth a hundred imitations by the monarchs and princelings of Europe.

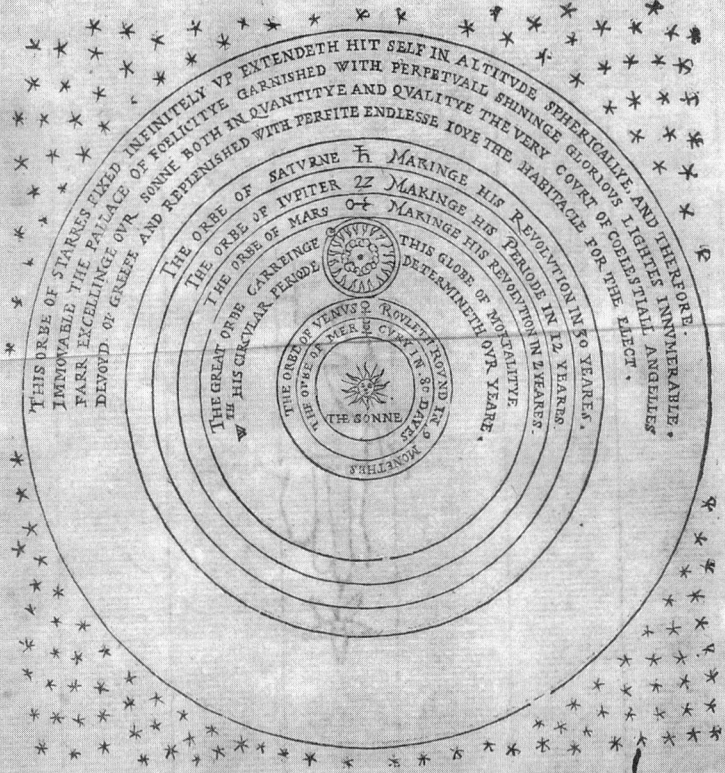

IV-1 Diagram of the universe by Thomas Digges, an English follower of Copernicus, 1576. The earth is shown as one among the planets circling the sun; beyond the planets, the stars are said to extend "infinitely" in every direction, and to be "far excelling our sun both in quantity and quality."

PART FOUR

THE CHANGING WEST

1600–1850

	POLITICAL, SOCIAL, AND ECONOMIC DEVELOPMENTS	RELIGION, SCIENCE, AND PHILOSOPHY	HISTORY AND LITERATURE	ARCHITECTURE, ART, AND MUSIC
1600	Religious Wars: Thirty Years' War in Germany Grotius and emergence of international law Peace of Westphalia	Copernicus (dies 1543) Bacon Kepler Galileo Descartes		Baroque style of architecture Monteverdi (opera)
1650	English Revolution Cromwell Mercantilism Louis XIV Age of absolutism	Royal Society founded Hobbes Bossuet Locke Newton		Versailles Palace Wren
1700	Rise of Prussia and Russia: Peter the Great Frederick the Great Enlightened despotism	The Enlightenment: Deism Montesquieu	Age of classicism: Racine Pope	St. Paul's Cathedral Handel Rococo style: Watteau Boucher Fragonard Reynolds

	POLITICAL, SOCIAL, AND ECONOMIC DEVELOPMENTS	RELIGION, SCIENCE, AND PHILOSOPHY	HISTORY AND LITERATURE	ARCHITECTURE, ART, AND MUSIC
1750	Industrial Revolution and beginnings of factory system American Revolution U.S. Constitution French Revolution	Rousseau Smith Kant Condorcet Burke	Voltaire Diderot Jefferson	Classical revival style of architecture David Jefferson Hayden Mozart
1800	Napoleon I and empire of the French Conservative reaction Congress of Vienna Metternich System "Concert of Europe" Spread of political and economic liberalism Growth of nationalism Early Industrial Revolution in Britain	Ricardo Hegel Dalton Schwann Utopian socialists: Saint-Simon Fourier Owen Comte Mazzini	Goethe Age of romanticism: Wordsworth Scott Byron Shelley Keats Balzac	Beethoven Schubert Chopin Romanticism in art: Goya Gothic revival style Houses of Parliament Turner, Constable Delacroix
1850		Marx, Engels, Bakunin Darwin	Dickens	Berlioz Wagner Tchaikovsky

CHAPTER 10

● ● ●

SCIENCE AND A NEW COSMOLOGY

Overview

B y 1650 the shift from the medieval pattern of civilization had been completed, but that did not mean that the West settled down into a new era
of stability. On the contrary, the changes that had begun about 1300 continued even faster than before, producing not a single new pattern of civilization but a whole series of further shifts in the pattern, each following
swiftly after the one before it, right down to the present day. The seventeenth and eighteenth centuries were the era of the rise of absolute monarchy, of the beginning of modern science, and the emergence of a new,
secular worldview. These centuries were also the era of the first great revolutions, which led in the nineteenth century to the replacement of Europe's
traditional social and political power structure with a new one based on the
principles of liberalism and nationalism. And in the nineteenth century
also, far-reaching changes in technology replaced the agrarian economy and
society that had emerged from the Agricultural Revolution (pp. 12–17)
with a new, urban and industrial civilization. This chapter deals with the
seventeenth and eighteenth centuries; chapters 11 and 12 cover the political, social, economic, and technical changes that came to a head in the
nineteenth century.

In the seventeenth and eighteenth centuries, Europe still consisted
mostly of peasant nations in which agriculture was by far the most important
sector of the economy; hereditary monarchs, privileged nobles, and established churches still dominated most countries; and Western civilization was
not yet far enough ahead of the civilizations of Asia and Africa that it could
conquer and change them, as it had done with those of the Americas. All
the same, the pace of change continued to be swift.

In the field of politics, government, and warfare, exploration and
the growth of strong centralized government since the late Middle Ages
had intensified the established competitiveness of European civilization

(pp. 247, 339–353). In the late sixteenth century a long-lasting struggle got under way among the seagoing west European nations for trade and territory worldwide (pp. 364–365). In Europe itself the wars were just as fierce, fueled as they were by the religious disputes of the Reformation as well as by the rivalries of increasingly powerful rulers. When the religious conflict ended in stalemate about 1650, the rulers continued on a vastly larger scale the competitive pursuit of territory and power that had been practiced by the Italian city-states of the Renaissance.

Largely in order to fight these wars at home and overseas, most of the centralized royal governments of late medieval western Europe evolved into absolute monarchies, and the governments of central and eastern Europe followed suit. The rulers cast off restrictions on their decision-making power and tightened their grasp on their countries' resources—at the price of guaranteeing legal privileges to the nobles and the established churches. Absolute monarchy has a bad name today on account of its arrogant rulers, its upholding of privilege, and its suppression of freedom. But at the time, it was praised by both Catholic and Protestant theologians as a God-given institution; and the influential nonreligious thinker Thomas Hobbes declared that the discipline of absolute monarchy was necessary in order to form masses of selfish and mutually destructive individual human beings into functioning societies. In practice, absolute rulers enabled their countries to survive and prosper within Europe's highly competitive civilization; they harshly enforced obedience to the government; and they often encouraged economic progress. In these ways, absolute monarchy was an important stage in the evolution of the modern state.

Meanwhile, some of the intellectual changes that had begun with the Renaissance were leading to a momentous and unexpected result: the Scientific Revolution. Renaissance humanists had revived a great deal of ancient thought that had a bearing on science—for instance, Plato's notion that ultimate truth must be simple and beautiful, and must be expressed not in words but in the "language" of geometry and numbers. Under the influence of the revived ideas and knowledge of the Renaissance, investigators from Nicholas Copernicus to Isaac Newton brought about a revolution in one particular field of natural knowledge: astronomy. They did not just prove that the earth moved around the sun, but developed a whole new understanding of the universe that followed logically from this original insight. The universe, they found, consisted of an unimaginably vast extent of empty space, in which stars, planets, and moons moved in predictable and self-regulating paths according to mathematical laws. In the course of arriving at this new view, astronomers and mathematicians devised new methods of mathematical reasoning, and of gaining knowledge by observation and experiment. These methods applied not just to stars, planets, and moons but to many other aspects of nature. Thus, in addition to revolutionizing astronomy, the sixteenth- and seventeenth-century investigators launched the whole modern enterprise of scientific discovery.

This new understanding of the natural universe led, in turn, to a new understanding of humanity and God—that of the eighteenth-century Enlightenment. The pioneers of the Scientific Revolution had not intended to make basic changes in philosophy or religion. But the philosophes—the writers and intellectuals who led the Enlightenment—mounted the first serious challenge in many centuries to the Christian worldview, on which the traditional Western understanding of humanity and God was based. To the philosophes, it seemed that the new scientific discoveries made God more distant, and human beings less evil and helpless, than Christianity proclaimed. In place of Father, Son, and Holy Spirit, the philosophes put a remote deity who had created the universe, established its laws, and left it to itself. He did expect righteousness from human beings—but he had set no forbidden fruit in the Garden of Eden, had sent no Savior to redeem fallen humanity, and had established no Church to help people into heaven. In place of faith in the unseen the philosophes put human reason which could limitlessly discover the unknown; in place of original sin and redemption, they put the ideas of progress and human perfectibility; in place of the Church's sacraments as protection against spiritual evil, they put education to do away with earthly ignorance and poverty.

In some ways, the Enlightenment was a divisive new ideology that would bring bitter conflict to Europe like the Reformation before it. But it was also an attractive way of thinking that influenced all classes of society. Few people shed their traditional religious beliefs, but many came to feel that within the limits set by ignorance and sin, there was more room for improvement in the human condition than had been generally believed in the past. Even many nobles, bishops, and absolute monarchs came to believe in such things as widespread education, religious toleration, and the abolition of serfdom. In time, the ideas of the Enlightenment, softened and without their antireligious edge, would become prevailing values of Western civilization.

In the cultural field, Europe continued its Renaissance encounter with ancient Greece and Rome—but as Europe itself changed, creative styles and themes changed as well. In literature and architecture, the passion and drama of the baroque style, inspired by the revived Catholicism of the late sixteenth and early seventeenth centuries (pp. 436–443), gave way to the order, clarity, and precision of *classicism*. It was a style that was actually more faithful to ancient models than the baroque or even the Renaissance—but it was also suitable to an age of reason and exact science, when even the human passions were believed to be subject to universal laws. Likewise, in tune with the luxurious court and noble life of the era, painting moved from Renaissance grandeur and baroque drama to the elegance and refinement of the eighteenth-century rococo style.

Alongside the writer, the architect, and the painter, there also appeared a new kind of creative artist, the musical composer. Though music is known to have played an important part in every civilization, in the Middle Ages and the Renaissance reliable methods of writing it down were developed, together with more complex styles of composition and new instruments that could produce a greater variety of sounds. As a result, music for the first time became an art form comparable to literature or painting. Otherworldly Catholic mysticism, heartfelt Protestant piety, the splendor of royal courts, the passions of classical tragedy, the Enlightenment hope of a better future—these were only some of the impressions and emotions that the great composers from the Renaissance to the eighteenth century were able to evoke in the language of music.

NATIONAL AND INTERNATIONAL DEVELOPMENT

A miniature model for the new European state system had appeared in Italy during the Renaissance, when city-states such as Florence, Milan, and Venice had worked out a system of relationships among themselves as sovereign powers. They established embassies and agreed on diplomatic rules for peace and war; they made alliances and sought to maintain a "balance of power" inside Italy (pp. 341–344). The increasingly powerful states beyond the Alps drew on the Italian experience in shaping their own international relations.

FOUNDATIONS OF THE EUROPEAN STATE SYSTEM: THE PEACE OF WESTPHALIA

The European state system grew out of a combination of forces, including dynastic ambition, national sentiment, and religious antagonism. In the Dutch revolt against Spain, for example, all three forces were present. Calvinism had won many converts in the Netherlands, which formed a rich part of the Habsburg domains; the Catholic rulers had responded in 1567 by imposing repressive measures in the Netherlands. In addition to admitting the Inquisition (p. 434) to the area, the Habsburgs had introduced harsh political and economic restrictions. The northern (Dutch) provinces reacted by declaring their independence in 1581; leading their struggle was William "the Silent," prince of the house of Orange. When Philip II of Spain (the Habsburg ruler) tried to bring the provinces back under his control, he met with armed resistance. The defiant Dutch, with English help, fought the Habsburg forces on land and sea and at last forced them to withdraw. In 1648 the United Provinces of the Netherlands (Holland) was formally recognized by the principal powers of Europe as an independent state (p. 453).

Religion and politics were similarly mixed in France, where the Catholic monarchy viewed the Calvinist minority (known there as Huguenots) as disloyal to the crown. After the death in 1547 of Francis I, the country had a series of weak rulers, and an aristocratic reaction against the monarchy had set in. Many nobles, seeking to regain their independence from the crown, had associated themselves with the defiant Huguenots.

1555   1618   1648

Growing Religious Tension	Thirty Years' War

Peace of   Peace of
Augsburg   Westphalia

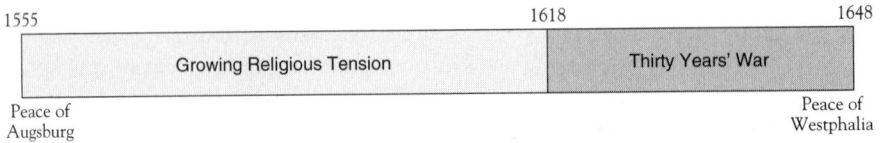

The resulting civil strife was mainly a contest between monarchists and the aristocratic faction in France; the religious convictions held by many on both sides tended to become submerged in the struggle. King Henry IV, seeking a truce in the political-religious warfare, secured civil rights and a limited religious tolerance for the Huguenots by his Edict of Nantes (1598). In the course of the seventeenth century, however, the royal government broke the military power of the aristocratic Huguenot faction, and Louis XIV canceled the edict in 1685.

In Germany, religion and politics combined to produce the most tragic consequences. As we have seen, the Lutheran military revolt had ended in 1555 with the Peace of Augsburg (p. 417), which left each German prince free to decide whether the religion of his subjects would be Lutheran or Catholic. This settlement had brought a kind of peace for sixty years, although divisive pressures mounted steadily. Guided by the Jesuits (pp. 431–432), the Catholic princes during these years stamped out the remnants of Protestant dissent in their territories. The zeal of the Lutheran princes, on the other hand, was weakened by bitter squabbles with Calvinist minorities. Sensing danger, some of the Protestant princes joined together in an armed league in 1608, an action promptly countered by the formation of a Catholic league.

As each camp eyed the other, watching for any move that might upset the religious and territorial balance, revolt exploded in Bohemia, which was part of the Holy Roman Empire. Most of the population of Bohemia were Czechs who were both anti-German and antipapal, and the trouble there had its roots in the Hussite rebellion of the fifteenth century (pp. 326, 410–411). During the sixteenth century the Protestants of Bohemia had enjoyed toleration under moderate Catholic rulers. But when Ferdinand of Styria, a Habsburg and a fanatical Catholic, was forced upon them as king, they feared that their religious and political rights were in jeopardy. Accordingly, in 1618 the Bohemian nobles announced their open defiance of Ferdinand and chose a Calvinist prince of the Rhineland to be their king. The Catholic league of princes moved swiftly to help Ferdinand crush the poorly organized rebellion, and Ferdinand's election as Holy Roman emperor in 1619 gave him added strength.

But as he proceeded to destroy Protestantism in Bohemia, other anti-Catholic and anti-Habsburg countries became alarmed. The king of Denmark decided to intervene in Germany in order to protect Lutheranism and to acquire territory for himself. He was promised help by the English and the Dutch, who for their own reasons, also wanted to check the advance of Habsburg (and Spanish) power. Later, Sweden and France joined the struggle against Emperor Ferdinand, chiefly for political reasons. During this Thirty Years' War (1618–1648) Germany was turned into a ghastly battlefield, fought over by mercenary armies. As time passed, the aims of the warring powers grew ever more blurred.

The Peace of Westphalia, which concluded the war, is a landmark in European history. With the militancy of both Catholics and Protestants reduced by the long struggle, the so-called religious wars came to an end. In Germany the terms of the Peace of Augsburg were restored and extended to include Calvinism as well as Lutheranism and Catholicism. Each prince retained the right to prescribe one of these faiths for his subjects, but conditions throughout the country were so wretched that none of them used force to compel conformity. Thus, a kind of religious "coexistence" emerged from the exhausting struggle.

The end of the wars left Germany in a desperate condition. Having long suffered from political disunity, the country had then endured the ravages of warfare, plunder, famine, and pestilence (typhus). The population had been cut by a *third*, and the loss of property had been severe. At the Peace of Westphalia, the German princes won recognition as independent sovereigns, and the Holy Roman Empire was thus reduced to a shell. Switzerland and the Netherlands, which had once been subject to the Habsburgs, were also recognized as independent states. With the decline of Germany and of Habsburg power, the Bourbon dynasty (founded by Henry IV) took the lead in Europe, and a century of French dominance was at hand.

Thus, Westphalia marked a shift in the balance of dynastic power and the emergence of the modern European state system. Gone were the remains of imperial and papal claims to authority over the political life of Europe; gone was the medieval idea of a unified "Christian commonwealth." The settlement, whose principal provisions held until the Napoleonic Wars (1800), transformed the continent into an area of independent states (*map*, p. 454), with each free to wage war or make peace and generally to act in a sovereign manner. The earlier Italian practices of diplomacy, alliances, and balance of power were now followed throughout Europe.

The seventeenth century also saw the emergence of the idea and practice of international law, aimed at regulating relations among these independent states. Some rulers, of course, were more careful in following the law than were others, but the law at least provided *standards* that were widely respected. The classic statement of those standards is the *Law of War and Peace* (1625), written by the Dutch lawyer Hugo Grotius—partly in response to the atrocities committed during the Thirty Years' War. Though Grotius recognized war as a "legitimate" state of affairs, he distinguished between just and unjust conflicts and laid down some guidelines for "humane" methods of waging war. Grotius condemned such acts as poisoning wells, mutilating prisoners, and massacring hostages. Drawing on the ancient Roman principles of natural law (pp. 139–140), he also spelled out the rights of neutral states and of *civilians* in war zones.

With later extensions and refinements, Grotius' statement remained the recognized authority on international law until the global upheavals of the twentieth century. The introduction of "total" war and weapons of mass killing have largely bypassed the "law of war and peace" and traditional notions of sovereignty and neutrality.

In addition to beginning a new phase in the endless rivalry of European countries and rulers, the Thirty Years' War and the decades that followed it saw a

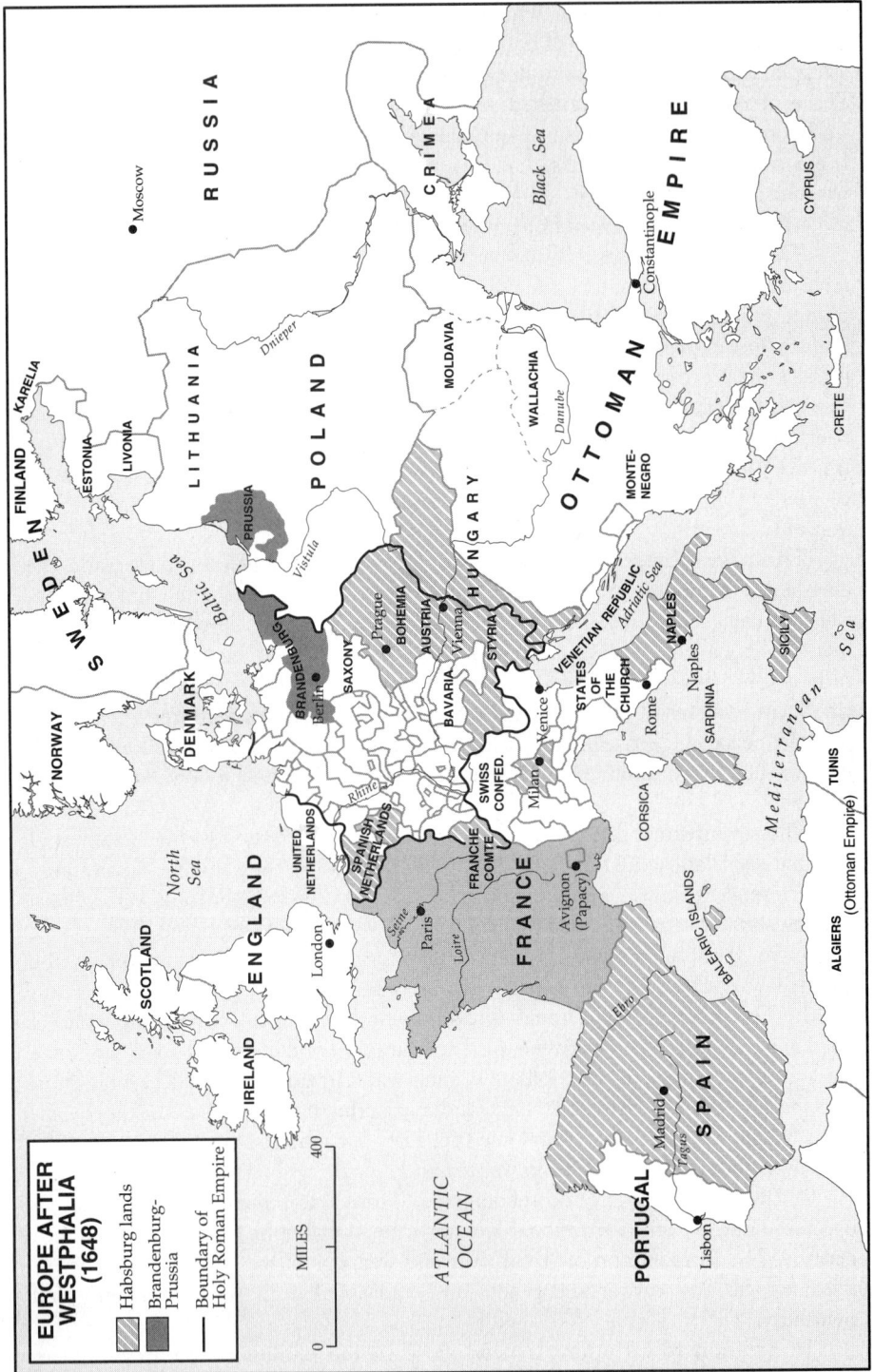

EUROPE AFTER
WESTPHALIA
(1648)

Habsburg lands

Brandenburg-
Prussia

Boundary of
Holy Roman Empire

renewed strengthening of royal government throughout most of Europe. The main reason was that only by increasing their power to control their countries could rulers hope to maintain or increase their weight in the balance of power—and this, in turn, was to a large extent because only powerful governments could mobilize the resources necessary to fight wars.

The changes in methods of warfare that had begun in the late Middle Ages (pp. 337, 339–340) had gone on into the sixteenth and seventeenth centuries, making warfare ever more costly. Shipbuilders had learned to build vessels large enough to carry whole batteries of artillery; engineers had devised cannon-resistant methods of fortification; gunsmiths had developed small firearms (muskets) that were handy and reliable enough for foot soldiers to use effectively. Already in the sixteenth century, the long time it took to build ships and train their crews had led governments to maintain standing navies. Late in the seventeenth century, the unreliability of the mercenary armies that had fought the Thirty Years' War, and the advantages of having forces ready to move the instant that war broke out, meant that governments began to keep standing armies as well. From now on, the increased cost of war had to be borne also in peacetime.

The result was that rulers began to tax their countries ever more heavily, and to do so at their own discretion. Where representative assemblies like the French Estates-General existed, which were supposed to give their consent to taxation (p. 349), the rulers stopped calling them together, or reduced them to rubber-stamp bodies. Though there was resistance, it was mostly weak and ineffective. This was partly because the rulers bought off the most powerful likely opponents, the nobles and church leaders, by leaving untouched their traditional privileges: tax exemption; favored access to government, military, and church positions; the power to repress religious minorities; and authority over the peasants. And unquestionably, many subjects felt that they had a real interest in their rulers' being strong, so that their countries could survive and prosper in the intensified European "struggle for existence." It was in this way that *absolute monarchy*—"absolute" in the sense of "unrestricted"—rose to be the predominant European form of government. (The very different development in England is discussed in chapter 11, pp. 498–503.)

THE ABSOLUTE MONARCH: LOUIS XIV

Of all the seventeenth-century absolute monarchies, the most powerful, and for a long time the most successful, was that of France. The wealthiest and most prosperous of the west European nation-states, France had moved steadily toward political centralization during the fifteenth and sixteenth centuries (pp. 347–350). After a temporary setback following the death of Francis I, the trend toward absolute monarchy proceeded steadily during the seventeenth century. Cardinal Richelieu, the astute minister of Louis XIII, led the way in crushing provincial and aristocratic revolts and in fashioning effective instruments of royal power. His aim, he declared simply, was "to make the king supreme in

1328		1589		1792
	House of Valois		House of Bourbon	

Louis XIV
(1661–1715)

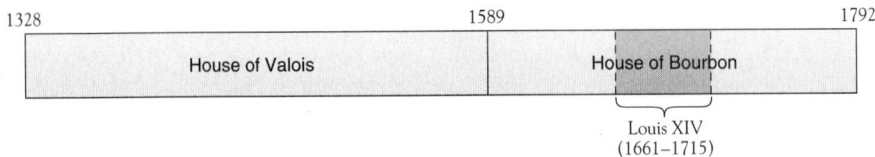

France and France supreme in Europe." Richelieu died in 1642, but his work was completed during the reign of Louis XIV.

The idea of absolutism was not new, but in Louis it found its most spectacular fulfillment. Having come to the throne as a boy in 1643, he took personal charge of state affairs in 1661. Louis held firm control for half a century, laboring ceaselessly at perfecting his royal image and performing his royal tasks. His style of governing became the model for all Europe, as did the French army, language, manners, and culture.

Louis ignored the traditional checks on royal power as he concentrated all authority in the *crown*, which became the symbol of national power. (He is credited with having declared, *"L'état, c'est moi,"* or, "I am the state.") Louis overawed the nobles (whose fathers had notions of regaining their independence), though he maintained their privileges and surrounded himself with men and women of the oldest and wealthiest noble families at his magnificent court. His minister of finance, Colbert, strengthened the tax system and promoted economic development. Internal trade was aided by improved roads and waterways; colonies and trading companies were founded overseas; and French industries were sheltered by protective tariffs and export subsidies.

The purpose of Colbert's program was to increase employment, profits, and state revenues—and to secure for France a "favorable balance of trade" with other countries. (This means *selling* goods abroad whose total value is more than that of goods *purchased* abroad; the balance due must then be paid with gold or silver, which were thought to be especially useful by the monarchs of that day.) Regulation of business was not novel in Europe, for the towns and guilds had practiced it for centuries (pp. 268–269). But the chief economic controls now shifted to the *national* governments; this system came to be called "statism" or "mercantilism." It was well-established in seventeenth-century France and was also practiced, with similar measures, in Spain, Holland, and England.

Louis had a passion for territorial expansion and a love of war and glory. By siphoning off the nation's wealth and manpower into costly military adventures, he spoiled many of the accomplishments of his long reign. His driving desire was to gain and hold France's "natural" frontiers—the Rhine River, the Alps, and the Pyrenees—and he tried, beyond that, to bring Spain under French control. This bold challenge to the European balance of power gave rise to a Grand Alliance of the other leading states against France. Despite the brilliance of his generals and the sacrifices of his subjects, Louis failed to realize his grandiose ambitions. On his death in 1715, France lay exhausted, its military power spent.

Eastern Europe: Prussia, Austria, and Russia

From the sixteenth to the eighteenth centuries, as in the Middle Ages, eastern Europe remained a distinctive region, although closely linked to the dominant western countries. During the Middle Ages, two powerful forces had tied eastern and western Europe together: immigration and trade (p. 326). In the following period, the rulers of Hungary, Poland, and Russia continued to welcome German settlers, but by the eighteenth century, most western European emigrants preferred to seek land and religious freedom in North America. On the other hand, the trading links between the two halves of Europe grew stronger than ever. Barred by geography from ready access to worldwide trade and empire, the eastern countries looked to western Europe for overseas products; to pay for these, they sent grain, timber, and cattle westward in ever larger quantities. The rulers and nobles of the region, for whom these exports were their main source of income, redoubled their efforts to control and exploit the producers of these valuable resources: the peasants. By the beginning of the eighteenth century, *serfdom* in eastern Europe, far from dying out, had become more oppressive than it had ever been in the Middle Ages.

In eastern Europe as in the western countries, the leading rulers worked to build up absolute monarchies and struggled with each other for control of territory. Their task was complicated by the facts that the nobles were stronger and more independent-minded than those of western Europe, and that the mixture of religious and ethnic groups in the region made it hard to build truly national states (p. 327). Some rulers, unable to overcome these domestic problems, became vulnerable to external attack. From the late seventeenth century, the formidable Turkish empire went into decline and lost part of its European territory. Poland, a leading contender for power in eastern Europe until the eighteenth century, was actually swallowed up by its rivals (pp. 460–461).

But the ruling dynasties of three other states, the Hohenzollerns of Brandenburg-Prussia, the Habsburgs of Austria, and the Romanovs of Russia, proved more successful. By the end of the eighteenth century they dominated eastern Europe; they built up states that, at least in terms of military power, could stand comparison with the wealthy imperial countries of western Europe.

The Hohenzollern dynasty rose to power from comparatively small beginnings in the Middle Ages, as vassals of the Holy Roman emperors. The center of their properties was the north German princedom of Brandenburg, but the family also held the territory of Prussia, to the east, and claimed several smaller territories in western Germany. Through the Peace of Westphalia, Prince Frederick William gained additional lands and then spent the rest of his life tightening his control over the family's holdings. Following the example of Richelieu in France, he built up a centralized treasury and civil service and greatly strengthened his army. By 1688, when Frederick William died near his capital of Berlin, Brandenburg-Prussia had become the most efficient state in Germany. His successor joined the coalition against Louis XIV, and the Holy Roman emperor awarded him the title of "King in Prussia" (in addition to Prince of Brandenburg). The higher title soon displaced the lesser one, and the name, Prussia, soon was applied to the whole of the Hohenzollern lands.

During the eighteenth century the Hohenzollern rulers continued to increase their power—regulating economic activities, raising larger and better-equipped armies, and demanding *strict discipline* from their soldiers and subjects. Prussia's landed aristocrats accepted the monarch's authority in return for complete control over their serfs. They also supplied the king with a hereditary officer class. Since the army was essential to the survival of the Prussian state, it enjoyed high status and special privileges. It was at this time that the extreme militarism—"Prussianism"—emerged that was to mark modern Germany's destiny.

Frederick II (the Great), who was crowned king of Prussia in 1740, personified the new ideal of power. A product of the international anarchy and the political cynicism of his time, he became a master of the arts of war and diplomacy. With Machiavellian keenness, Frederick expanded his possessions to the east at the expense of the less efficient Habsburgs of Austria, and the dissolving state of Poland. He proved shrewder than Louis XIV, whom he first looked to as a model. In his palace at Potsdam (whose design had been inspired by Versailles), he could boast at the end of his reign that he had made Prussia a power of the first rank in Europe.

In Austria, the Habsburg rulers of the sixteenth and seventeenth centuries succeeded in maintaining control of their various possessions in spite of rebellions by Protestant nobles and peasants, and in gaining territory at the expense of the Turks in Hungary and the Balkans (pp. 353, 452). However, their position was weakened by the declining power of the Spanish branch of their family (p. 353), which died out at the end of the seventeenth century. They also suffered from the increasing feebleness of the Holy Roman Empire, of which they were the nominal rulers. Increasingly, they were forced to depend on the resources of the other central and eastern European territories that they ruled; the government of these lands, however, was unwieldy and inefficient. In the eighteenth century, defeats at the hands of Frederick II of Prussia galvanized the Austrian Habsburgs into making administrative and social reforms. Empress Maria Theresa and her son Joseph II made considerable progress in centralizing control of their territories, improving the administrative and tax systems, and limiting noble exploitation of the serfs so that the latter would be able to pay higher taxes to the government (p. 480). In this way, the Austrian rulers hoped to build up an army that would be a match for Prussia's. Though Habsburg Austria never achieved the degree of unity and discipline to be found in Prussia, it nevertheless counted as one of the leading European powers.

Perhaps the most spectacular change in eastern Europe was the rise of Russia. At the end of the Middle Ages, the principality of Moscow, from which modern Russia originated, had been a tributary state of the Asiatic Tartars (p. 327). But the Muscovite princes were ambitious men, with a strong sense of mission. The Russians, like the other eastern Slav peoples, were Orthodox Christians with strong religious and cultural ties to Constantinople (pp. 218–220, 246–247, 325). Throughout the Middle Ages, powerful, Byzantine-influenced Slav rulers had from time to time taken the title of *tsar* ("caesar"), thereby setting themselves up as rivals of the emperor in Constantinople (pp. 325, 327). Following the Turkish capture of that city and the end of the Byzantine Empire in 1453 (p. 328), the Muscovite ruler Ivan the Great (who died in 1505) married Sophia, the last emperor's niece. It was natural that Ivan should assume the title of tsar, no longer as a rival of the Byzantine rulers, but as their heir. The Byzantine rulers had themselves been regarded as the legitimate successors of the emperors of ancient Rome, and accordingly, a Russian writer of Ivan's time referred to Moscow as the "third Rome." Thus, from early times Moscow was driven by a sense of imperial mission.

Over the generations, in spite of many setbacks, Ivan's successors were true to this mission. In the sixteenth century, they first threw off the overlordship of the Tartars, and then made the Tartars their subjects. Russian colonists penetrated ever farther east into the wilderness of Siberia, until by the beginning of the eighteenth century the tsar's dominions stretched all the way to the Pacific Ocean. (Together with contemporary conquests by the powerful Ching emperors of China, this brought to an end thousands of years of nomad domination of the steppes, and nomad invasions of the settled peoples of Europe and Asia—pp. 54–55.) At the time, this vast land empire was not nearly as profitable to its owners as the overseas empires of the western countries. All the same, it made Russia what it has remained ever since: a country that dwarfs (geographically) all the other countries of Europe, and whose sheer size has made it impossible to conquer.

From the accession of the Romanov dynasty in 1613, however, the efforts and ambitions of the tsars were mainly focused on Europe. They struggled with two principal competitors, Poland and Sweden, for control of the territories lying between the Black and Baltic seas. Though not always the aggressors in this struggle, the tsars were ultimately the victors. By the end of the seventeenth century, they had reached the coasts of the Black Sea, and were pressing forward to the Baltic. In the eighteenth century, Peter the Great, the most energetic and ruthless of the Romanov tsars, at last broke through.

Russia's rival in the Baltic area itself was Sweden. The Swedes for centuries had sought power beyond their home in Scandinavia: during the Viking era they pushed successfully into the east Slavic heartland (p. 241); later, having absorbed Finland, they fought for control of the Baltic shore across from Sweden. By the sixteenth century, under the Vasa dynasty, the Swedish monarchy had succeeded in making itself the dominant power of the Baltic region. But a grand alliance of eastern states, including Russia, at last put a hold on Swedish imperialism. After a lengthy war, in 1721, Peter took from Sweden the eastern Baltic provinces of Karelia, Estonia, and Livonia (*map*, p. 454). In this region, close to the border of Finland, he built a new capital, St. Petersburg. This "window on the West" was a symbol of his determination to make his empire into a well-organized state on the western European model, and if possible to make his subjects themselves into Westerners (*Fig. 10-1*).

When Peter died, a bitter struggle broke out between those Russians who supported a Western orientation and those who opposed it. Catherine II ("the Great"), who became tsarina in 1762, looked toward Europe. She had gained the throne after marrying a grandson of Peter; and though she was the daughter of a

10-1   Official propaganda for Peter the Great's Westernization of Russia. A traditionalist Russian has seen the error of his ways: he has taken to wearing Western-style jacket, breeches, and cloak as the tsar has ordered, and has come to a barber for a Western-style shave. "Cut off my beard, barber," he says—"if you don't do it, I'll call the police!" But the barber takes pleasure in obeying the tsar. "I'll be glad to give you a shave!" he replies. Woodcut, c. 1700.

German nobleman, she devoted herself to the interests of her adopted country. Within the limits of her subjects' tolerance, Catherine followed Peter's lead in encouraging Westernization. Forced to compromise with stiff-necked nobles, she never managed to secure the same degree of internal control that prevailed in France and Prussia. (Her sprawling empire embraced many nationalities, and nine-tenths of its population were serfs.)

In external affairs, Catherine continued the Romanov policy of expanding their power further into Europe. In wars against the Turks, many of whose subjects shared the Orthodox Christianity and Slavic ethnic origins of the Russians (pp. 218–220, 246–247, 325, 328), she extended her territories to the south. On Russia's western frontier, Catherine intervened in the neighboring country of Poland. Once one of the strongest powers in eastern Europe, Poland had gradually been reduced to anarchy and helplessness as a result of the overweening power and endless factional disputes of its nobles, whom the rulers could never bring under control. Between 1772 and 1792, Poland was "partitioned" (divided up) among its neighbors. Russia gained the largest share, and the rest was taken over by Prussia and Austria (partly so as to prevent Russia from advancing still farther westward). By the end of the eighteenth century, Russia had become a major force in the power balances of Europe and the Middle East.

For all their successes, Prussia, Austria, and Russia remained in some ways weak and vulnerable. This was partly because the rulers of these eastern European states had built upon societies that were backward and poor compared with the western countries. In spite of the efforts they put into reorganizing their governments, increasing the yield of taxes, and recruiting and training soldiers, the eighteenth-century Hohenzollern, Habsburg, and Romanov rulers could not fight a war for any length of time without massive financial help from Britain or France. (Because these western countries were worldwide rivals—p. 365—an eastern European ruler could generally get money from one of them, in return for using his or her armed forces against the other.) In spite of their autocratic government, the eastern rulers could not overcome the resistance of their nobles to abolishing serfdom. And this was a reform, as the wiser of these "enlightened despots" (pp. 480–481) well understood, that offered the main hope of modernizing their economies and making their countries truly wealthy and powerful.

A further handicap, for the Habsburgs and Romanovs in particular, was linked to the fact that they had expanded into regions of eastern Europe that were ethnically very mixed. Once-powerful independent nations—Poles, Czechs, Hungarians, Ukrainians, and many others—were now under the rule of foreigners. Russia and Austria were not *national*, but *multinational* states, in which no single ethnic group formed the overwhelming majority.

In the seventeenth and eighteenth centuries, serfdom and the subjection of nations to foreign rulers were generally accepted as legitimate, but in time this would change. Already in the seventeenth century, changes in another area, that of religion, had brought widespread suffering to eastern Europe. The Protestant Reformation and the Roman Catholic countermeasures (chapter 9) had disrupted the relative religious harmony of the region; tens of thousands had suffered exile or death as a result of systematic campaigns of expulsion and massacre directed by Catholics, Protestants, and Orthodox against each other—and by Catholics and Orthodox against Jews. In the serf societies and multinational states of nineteenth- and twentieth-century eastern Europe, social and national conflicts would arise that would dwarf these earlier religious struggles; instead of tens of thousands, millions of people would be expelled or killed.

JUSTIFICATIONS FOR ABSOLUTISM: BOSSUET, HOBBES

Absolutism was the predominant form of government in the seventeenth and eighteenth centuries. In those times it appeared superior to other forms for very practical reasons: despots were able to check civil strife within their realms, and in the struggles with competing rulers they could command the full resources of their states. Nevertheless, no form of government enjoys the unquestioned respect of every subject, and absolutism, by its very nature, aimed for total control. Consequently, the despots sought ideological *justification* for absolutism. They wanted to show why it was *right* for subjects to submit to them—no matter what their policies or demands.

The seventeenth-century monarchs might have turned to the absolutist theory of Machiavelli, who had viewed politics as a purely secular art and science (p. 365). This was, indeed, the thought and practice of the new monarchs, but they were themselves too Machiavellian to admit holding to his theory. (Machiavelli had advised rulers to cloak their purposes in piety and religion.) For personal and political reasons, the despots preferred a "higher" justification for their authority; they found it in the doctrine of *divine right*.

This was not, however, a return to medievalism. In the Middle Ages all authority was thought to be sent from heaven, but authority was believed to be *distributed* and *limited*. The theorists of the seventeenth century went further: they sought to reconcile *absolutist* concepts and practices with traditional Christian doctrine. James I of England, the Stuart king who succeeded Elizabeth I in 1603, did not hesitate to speak out for himself. "The state of monarchy," he lectured Parliament, "is the supremest thing on earth, for kings are not only God's lieutenants upon earth, but even by God himself are called gods." Parliament, however, was not to be won over; in fact, time was running out for English defenders of absolutism. (The English Revolution will be discussed in chapter 11.)

It was in the France of Louis XIV, the "Grand Monarch," that divine right truly held sway. The theory was stated most precisely by a favored bishop of the court, Jacques Bossuet. In a booklet prepared about 1670 for the instruction of Louis' heir (*Politics Drawn from Holy Scripture*), Bossuet set down the royalist arguments. Referring to the Bible as the ultimate truth, he supported his points with appropriate quotations. Royal authority, he concluded, is sacred, fatherly, and absolute. The king's judgment is subject to *no* appeal on earth, and the king must be obeyed for reasons of religion and conscience. Whoever resists the king's command in reality *resists* God. For, declared Bossuet, "the royal throne is not the throne of a man, but the throne of God Himself."

The monarchs of France and other European states found these ideas appealing and, having heard them from childhood, probably believed them. They were less enthusiastic about the *secular* argument for absolutism developed by Thomas Hobbes. An English scholar and philosopher, Hobbes was a royalist who supported the Stuart kings. His writings (around 1650) did them little good; nevertheless, his analysis proved significant for later generations.

Hobbes broke completely with religious traditions and drew instead on the mathematical and scientific advances of his time. (These will be discussed in the next section of this chapter.) In a sense, Hobbes took up where Machiavelli had left off; accepting politics as a purely secular matter, he tried to make of it a deductive *science*. His philosophy rests on materialism and mechanism and reduces the human being to a mere physical machine, the product of complex motion and countermotion. From this it follows that the physiology and psychology of human beings are the true bases of political organization and, consequently, the true bases of the state.

Hobbes held that every organism has an instinctive drive for self-preservation. Individuals cannot achieve this goal once and for all, but they can move constantly to enlarge their *means* of security. As Hobbes wrote in his classic study, *Leviathan*, "I put for a general inclination of all mankind, a perpetual and restless desire of power after power, that ceases only in death." In a "state of nature," with no governing (coercive) authority, the general human condition is a "war of every man against every man." To Hobbes such a life was "solitary, poor, nasty, brutish, and short." He did not look at history or primitive cultures to prove his generalizations; his method was logical rather than empirical, *deductive* rather than *inductive* (p. 468). His dismal picture of the original (precivilized) condition of human beings arose from his assumptions regarding their physical makeup.

Fortunately, said Hobbes, humans have a power of *reason* that enables them to provide an alternative to the *anarchy of nature*. Because they are selfish egoists, unable to trust one another, they cannot create a cooperative society of equals. What they can do is agree to surrender their personal strength to a higher authority, which alone will have the power to curb individual aggression. Hobbes believed that human society, the state, and civilization itself arose from this imaginary "contract" of each individual with all others:

> I authorize and give up my right of governing myself, to this man, or to this assembly of men, on this condition, that you give up your right to him, and authorize all his actions in like manner. . . . This is the generation of that great Leviathan, or rather (to speak more reverently) of that Mortal God [king] to which we owe under the Immortal God, our peace and defense.

Once civil government is established in this manner, all subjects are bound by their contracts to *obey* it. They do so not for moral or religious reasons, but, again, because of the underlying motive of *self*-interest. *Law* is preferable to anarchy—because it better serves the *individual*. Hobbes supported absolute monarchy, or any other authority, on these grounds. But it is clear why his logic was not appreciated by the monarchists of his day. He demolished their claim to divine right and brushed aside all moral arguments, appeals to tradition, and personal sentiments. Though a royalist, Hobbes was, in fact, a most radical Englishman. While defending the *old* (monarchy), he turned people's minds to the *new* (in politics). His thought contains some errors and confusions, but it was a breakthrough in the study of human behavior. And it provided a justification for the modern *authoritarian* state.

THE SCIENTIFIC REVOLUTION OF THE SEVENTEENTH CENTURY

We will turn now to the intellectual changes that influenced Hobbes' ideas and that would have such a profound effect on Western life and thought. By comparison with these changes, the development of political institutions (which absorbed the attention of kings and ministers) was of passing importance. The scientific revolution of the seventeenth century produced a radically different *view of the universe* and a new *mode of thinking*.

The methodology of modern science seems natural enough to educated persons of the twentieth century. Because we are accustomed to it, we do not appreciate how *unnatural* it is and how difficult it was to achieve. Yet our scientific method is unique in world history, a very special creation of the human mind. Science may be defined as a series of interconnected concepts and conceptual patterns related to "stubborn facts." It is a fruitful union of precise observation, mathematics, and general principles. Through science, we have penetrated the "mysteries" of nature and have learned to predict and manipulate it.

Our unaided "common sense" could never have produced science (any more than it could have produced theology or philosophy). In fact, one of the greatest barriers to scientific thinking was the tendency of human beings to accept as truth the judgments of their senses. The fantastic world that science reveals to us is often concealed under natural appearances. Through countless centuries, in every corner of the globe, people accepted the "obvious": that the earth, for example, stands still, while the sun and stars wheel past overhead. It was only through a rare combination of circumstances and high creative impulse that science was "invented." The methodology has not been perfected even yet, but it had its principal beginnings during the seventeenth century. The fertile minds of that time produced a stunning intellectual triumph and made the West the teacher of the world.

This achievement rested, of course, on a rich intellectual heritage, starting with the science of the Greeks, which had been recovered in the late Middle Ages (pp. 80–81, 227). The medieval philosophers added refinement in *logic*; strengthened the idea of an *ordered* universe, and made modest contributions in some scientific fields (p. 302). Then Renaissance men undertook geographical exploration and stressed the precise observation of nature. During the sixteenth and seventeenth centuries instruments for observation were invented or improved; and mathematics, that indispensable tool of the mind, was sharply advanced. Equally important, the founders of science displayed the ability *to see old things in new ways*. The result was the overthrow of a universe—that of Aristotle and Aquinas. As the new universe took form (*Fig. IV-1*, p. 444), the methods that produced it became a new way of thinking.

Discoverers of a New Cosmos: Copernicus, Kepler, Galileo

Aristotle's system must be looked at before the revolution of the seventeenth century can be understood. That system was far more in harmony with the world of *appearances* than was the system that would take its place. As adapted by Ptolemy, a second-century Greek astronomer (p. 138), Aristotle's scheme placed the solid, immovable earth at the *center* of things. Rotating about the earth, in perfect circular motion, were the luminous heavenly bodies, each embedded in a transparent sphere (globe). Closest to earth was the sphere that carried the moon; then, at successive intervals, were the spheres of Mercury, Venus, the sun, Mars, Jupiter, Saturn, and the fixed stars. Beyond the sphere of the fixed stars was the Primum Mobile (Prime Mover)—a sphere whose daily rotation from west to east drove all the other spheres in the opposite motion, from *east* to *west*. Beyond the Primum Mobile was the Empyrean (the highest heaven).

This ancient view was accepted into Christian thought and went unchallenged until the sixteenth century. It fitted everyone's ordinary observations, and by means of clever adjustments it could be made to correspond to observed data. Moreover, it suited people's awe of the heavens and their instinct for "rank" by placing the heavenly bodies in a "higher" zone, distinct from the earth. Scholars taught that imperfection and decay ruled over the human zone but that the revolving spheres were governed by a *superior set of laws*. This explained the apparent permanence of the heavenly bodies (in contrast to the temporary nature of things on earth)—and the regularity and harmony of their motions.

Now, Ptolemy was aware of a heliocentric (sun-centered) theory of the universe that had been taught by Aristarchus, an earlier Greek astronomer, in the third century B.C. According to his theory, the apparent motion of the heavenly bodies was due to the *earth's rotation* on its axis. But Ptolemy rejected this theory, as did other astronomers, because it did not fit his recorded observations so well as the geocentric (earth-centered) theory. Further, it was impossible to reconcile Aristarchus' notion of earthly rotation with existing beliefs about *motion*. Again, the authority of Aristotle was decisive. He had held that *earthly* objects remain in a *state of rest* unless they are moved by a *force* and that continued motion requires continued force. Because it was held that these rules did not apply in the heavenly zones, the rotation of the crystalline spheres presented no difficulty. But in the earthly zone, motion depended on force; and the astronomers could find no existing force strong enough to keep the earth's mass *turning*. Because of this, and because of the *appearance* that the earth stood still, the heliocentric theory had failed to convince the ancient thinkers.

Nevertheless, Nicolaus Copernicus revived it in the sixteenth century. A learned Polish cleric with a passionate interest in astronomy, Copernicus grew dissatisfied with the geometrical complexities and discrepancies of Ptolemy's system. He allowed himself to imagine various patterns and found that the *heliocentric* one offered the simplest geometrical explanation of observed movements. His major work, *Concerning the Revolutions of the Celestial Bodies*, was published in the year of his death (1543). Although other astronomers of the time shared his dissatisfaction with the Ptolemaic system, they did not accept the Copernican theory.

Copernicus' book was condemned by religious leaders, including Luther and Calvin, on the grounds that it contradicted Scripture and thus offended God. In one respect his theory was but a limited departure from the accepted view; it did not challenge the "motion mechanics" of Aristotle. Copernicus accepted the idea of the revolving spheres and only exchanged the positions of sun and earth. This alteration, however, upset the traditional view, for it shifted the earth into the *heavenly* zone of laws and forces—and that made his theory unacceptable.

A further objection was that Copernicus could furnish no observational proofs of his belief. If, as he thought, the earth revolved around the sun, then the position of the fixed stars should show a shift when sighted from opposite sides of the earth's orbit. As astronomers know now, they do shift; but the shift is so small (because of the enormous distances) that Copernicus could not detect it. Copernicus also faced a problem that had baffled the ancients: How could he account for a force sufficient to keep the earth in rotation? He offered an answer, but it was hardly persuasive. He argued that it was the "nature" of spheres to rotate and that the earth could not keep from doing so.

It was more than a century before the Copernican theory gained substantial acceptance. Religious criticisms were not the only obstacle; a great deal of observational work had to be done before its correctness could be properly checked. We should remember that Copernicus had no telescope to use in seeking proof for his theory; he worked from the ancient observational data handed down by Ptolemy. His mathematical mind constructed a neater system into which to fit the data, but he failed to reconcile his system with the prevailing physics of his day.

Though Copernicus did not overcome the limitations of traditional science, he inspired later generations to resume the search for a simpler and more satisfying truth. Toward the end of the sixteenth century a Danish astronomer, Tycho Brahe, made new and more comprehensive observations of the skies. These were assembled and analyzed by his coworker, the brilliant German mathematician Johannes Kepler. As a test of the Copernican theory, Kepler tried to fit Brahe's data on the planets to *circular* courses (orbits) around the sun. When that effort yielded a negative result, he tried fitting the data to *elliptical* orbits. This gave him a positive result, and his finding came to be known as Kepler's First Law (1609).

Kepler next studied the data in order to find if there was *consistency* in *all* planetary motions. His resulting Second and Third Laws hold that every planet, though traveling its course at varying speeds, sweeps out equal areas of its "elliptical plane" in equal times, and that the *square* of the time a planet takes to complete its orbit is proportional to the *cube* of its mean distance from the sun. Kepler thus appears as the first man to work in the manner of modern scientists: he first formulated hypotheses and then tried to check the deduced consequences empirically (by observation). He also bridged the supposed gap between heavenly bodies and the earth by demonstrating the consistency of mathematical relationships *throughout* the solar system. Of still broader significance, he was the first to glimpse the universe as a vast, intricate machine subject to *exact and knowable* laws.

Although Kepler described the movements of the planets in precise mathematical terms, he was less successful in explaining what *made* them move. He assumed that some force might be holding the planets in orbit and moving them continuously along their courses. This force he concluded to be the *sun*. Basing his view largely on the experiments of William Gilbert, an English physicist, Kepler suggested that the planets were magnetic. The sun, he held, was a giant rotating magnet; as it turned it pulled the planets along in their orbits. Here Kepler was clearly reaching toward the modern concepts of *universal gravitation* and *inertia*. But it was left to the Italian genius Galileo Galilei to complete the overthrow of

Aristotle, confirm the heliocentric theory, and bring the laws of motion to the point of a grand *synthesis*.

Galileo, a contemporary of Kepler, was less a mathematician and more an observer and experimenter. An astronomer as well as a physicist, he was the first, in 1609, to construct a *telescope* that could be used to examine the heavens. (The instrument had been invented a few years earlier by Dutch lensmakers.) Galileo's telescope was a lead tube about three feet long, with a two-inch glass. Crude and low-powered by modern standards, it nonetheless revealed a world previously unknown to earthlings.

To his excitement, Galileo saw that the planets were not mere points of light but bodies of dimension like the earth and the moon. Venus showed "phases" that corresponded to its position with respect to the sun and earth; this disproved the older notion that the planets were self-lighted and gave further support for their heliocentric arrangement. By discovering the moons of Jupiter, Galileo provided support for the idea that there could be more than one center for heavenly orbits. And as he peered into the depths of space, looking past the fixed stars, he was overwhelmed by the incredible distances revealed by his telescope. Tens of thousands of stars, previously unseen, came into view, and he was convinced that uncounted millions lay beyond. The "familiar," closed universe of the Greek and Christian worlds vanished forever; earth and humans were now seen as wanderers through dark and boundless space.

The Catholic Church was quick to challenge Galileo's proofs and to condemn his conclusions. Because its authority and doctrines were linked to the Ptolemaic system, it regarded the new ideas as a menace to Christian truth and salvation. To the Church authorities (Catholic *and* Protestant) it mattered not that Copernicus, Kepler, and Galileo were deeply religious men, awed by God's wonders; their teachings contradicted both Scripture and sacred tradition.

Warned to give up his view that the "earth moves," Galileo had managed to keep his convictions private for some time. But he fell into trouble after publishing his *Dialogue on the Two Chief Systems*. In 1633 he was charged with heresy and brought before the Roman Inquisition; threatened with torture, he formally recanted. Through the *Dialogue*, however, his devastating attack on the conventional astronomy continued to spread. The book was placed on the Index (p. 434), along with the works of Copernicus and Kepler, where it remained until 1835. But the banning of a book could not alter the order of the heavens.

After his ordeal before the Inquisition, Galileo was allowed to work quietly in a villa near Florence. During these years he turned to a subject that in itself would not disturb the authorities—but that opened the way to the ultimate victory of the new view of the universe. The subject was *motion*. Though Aristotle's picture of the *heavens* was by now entirely discredited, his beliefs about motion were still accepted. It was clear that the overthrow of his universe must include the rejection of his "motion mechanics," but no one had yet shown how that was to be done.

Earlier in his life Galileo had experimented with *falling bodies*. He later built special structures in order to study the acceleration of polished balls rolling down frictionless wooden surfaces. These permitted him to make more precise measurements of time and distance than he could make when objects were dropped through the air. In 1638 he published the results of his experiments and set forth his general conclusions on the subject of mechanics. He rejected the traditional beliefs that objects are "normally" in a state of rest, that there are "natural" directions of motion for certain substances, and that heavy objects fall faster than light ones.

His observations convinced him that a body in motion (with friction disregarded) continues at a constant speed without any continuing force; a *change* in either velocity or direction *requires* a force. He also found that the distance covered by any falling body is proportional to the square of its time of descent. These conclusions, known today to most schoolchildren, were revolutionary in the seventeenth century. Galileo did not quite see that his "law of falling bodies" was the same law that kept the planets in their orbits. But he completed the overturn of Aristotle's universe and contributed the important new idea of *inertia* (the tendency of objects to remain in their *existing* state of either "rest" or "motion").

Makers of Scientific Method: Bacon, Descartes

Although the most striking accomplishments of the scientific revolution were in astronomy and mechanics, swift advances were taking place along the whole frontier of knowledge. One of the most significant was the development of science itself as a *methodology*. Here two men stand out: Francis Bacon and René Descartes.

Bacon, born in England in 1561, was a man of wide interests, a public official as well as a scholar. But his chief concern was the advancement of learning. He complained of the stagnation of knowledge, blaming the condition on undue reverence for the ancients—above all, as we have seen, on the authority of Aristotle. While Aristotle's ideas were being upset by Kepler and Galileo, Bacon struck at the *root* of his system—its *methodology*—thereby adding force to the intellectual revolution.

Bacon favored the practices of observation and experiment that had sprung up during the Renaissance (pp. 379–380). Experiments in themselves were not new, but he saw in them the foundation for a planned structure of useful knowledge. He criticized Aristotle's reliance on *deduction* (p. 301), which he viewed as a mere manipulation of words. Bacon's proposed system called for *induction*—that is, repeated experiments that would lead to a *general* statement or conclusion. Following each induction, new observations and experiments would be undertaken that would permit further inductions to be made. In this fashion a *total system* of descriptive truth could be built up, he thought, in a relatively short time.

Bacon was mistaken in many of his own beliefs about nature, but he was confident that future experiments would correct his errors. He also urged scientists to *record* their experiments and to exchange data, in the interest of mutual assistance. Bacon's philosophy and practical suggestions stimulated the budding science of the seventeenth century. True, he subordinated the role of mathematics in scientific activities, but that fault was remedied by the Frenchman, René Descartes.

The advance of science requires, indeed, *two* modes of thought. One of these is induction, stressed by Bacon; the other is deduction, emphasized by Descartes.

Descartes' classic *Discourse on Method* appeared in 1637; along with Bacon's writings, which had been published somewhat earlier, this book gave new direction to both science and philosophy. Descartes and Bacon had at least one thing in common: they were dissatisfied with traditional learning and sought to construct a completely new methodology of knowledge.

Descartes was a brilliant mathematician, and his accomplishments in mathematics affected his approach to knowledge as a whole. A private scholar of independent means, he was disgusted by the absence of certainty and precision that he found in most areas of study. He therefore tried to apply to other subjects the methods of *geometry* and *arithmetic*, which start with "clear and simple" propositions of unquestioned truth. From these propositions, all consequences are *deduced*; plane geometry, for example, is built upon a single axiom (self-evident assumption): "A straight line is the shortest distance between two points."

In adopting the method of mathematics, therefore, one must commence by *doubting* all present ideas ("Cartesian doubt"); the slate must be wiped clean, so to speak. If an idea can be questioned for any reason at all, it must be discarded. Descartes did just that, reducing knowledge to a single idea that he could accept absolutely: "I *think*" —from which he deduced, "therefore, I *exist.*" Upon this foundation he set out to construct, by a series of *logical* steps, a complete picture of the universe (including God).

In this ambitious effort, Descartes committed errors and fell short of success. But his rejection of existing knowledge, intellectual authority, and traditional ways of reasoning undermined those old ways of looking at the world. Especially challenging was his vision of a *mechanical* universe governed by *mathematical* rules, a vision that would profoundly influence philosophy and religion as well as science.

THE GRAND SYNTHESIZER: NEWTON

The final statement of seventeenth-century science was left to Isaac Newton, who perfected and refined the new cosmic system first outlined by Kepler and Galileo. It was Newton, also, who established the rules of scientific method as a union of Baconian and Cartesian theory. Genius though he was, he could not have accomplished what he did without the knowledge and techniques developed by countless predecessors.

Newton was a simple country youth whose rare talents won him a place at Cambridge University. After earning his degree, he became deeply absorbed in mathematics and shortly developed the system of *calculus*, which is essential for the continuous measurement of complex variable quantities. While still in his twenties, he was appointed professor of mathematics at the university, where he continued his far-ranging research. Motivated by the pure love of knowing, he had little interest in publishing the results of his work. He soon turned his inquiring mind to the puzzles posed by the new astronomy.

Galileo had virtually established the principles of earthly motion but had failed to demonstrate how those principles applied to bodies beyond the earth. Why did the planets move in curved orbits rather than in straight lines? Galileo mistakenly answered that curved motion was as "natural" as straight-line motion and therefore had its own kind of *inertia*. The solution to the mystery, of course, lay in the pull of gravity. While Galileo recognized and gauged the earth's gravity in his observations of falling bodies, he had not made the stupendous leap to the concept of universal gravitation.

Ideas about the magnetic attraction of physical masses had begun to be formulated during the seventeenth century. Around 1600 William Gilbert had built a spherical magnet and had noted that its properties were similar to those of the earth. He reasoned that the heavenly bodies must also resemble the earth in this respect, each one exerting a pull toward its own center. The moon, he said, keeps the same face toward us because of its magnetic attraction to the earth. But the sun, the largest body in the solar system, is the *focus* of magnetic power. It will be recalled that Kepler also held this belief and said that the motion of the planets is due to the sun's rotation (p. 466).

Suspecting that the relation between inertia and gravitation was the key to understanding planetary motion, Newton studied the problem over a period of years. In order to prove his theories, he had to translate masses and motions into mathematical terms. He succeeded in calculating the masses of the sun, the planets, and their satellites. One of the first important consequences of these calculations was his discovery that each planet would travel according to Kepler's laws only if the gravitational pull upon it was inversely proportional to the square of its distance from the sun. He next applied this gravitational formula to the motion of the moon around the earth. Treating the moon as a body with inertial movement in space, he theorized that its curved orbit was due to a continuous "falling" toward the earth. And, after making due allowance for its distance from the earth, he concluded that the moon behaves in the same way as do falling bodies on earth. Newton thus linked Galileo to Kepler, eliminated the barrier between forces acting in space and those on earth, and established by *empirical and mathematical proof* the existence of *universal* laws.

Such was the message of Newton's *Principia (Mathematical Principles of Natural Philosophy)*, published in 1687. In this work he unraveled the mysteries of planetary motions and demonstrated the fact that human beings have the means to achieve far greater understanding. For he demonstrated that, on the basis of experiments conducted in a tiny corner of the universe, and aided by the lever of mathematics, he had discovered the nature of gravitation *everywhere*. Newton was able to express this discovery in the most precise terms: "Every particle of matter in the universe attracts every other particle with a force varying inversely as a square of the distance between them, and directly proportional to the product of their masses." Newton also set down *rules of scientific reasoning* to guide others in finding the fundamental principles embodied in nature, stating those principles mathematically and verifying them through observation and experiment.

Not surprisingly, Newton was hailed by his generation as a lawgiver, a scientific Moses. As Alexander Pope put it:

> Nature and nature's laws lay hid in night;
> God said, "Let Newton be," and all was light.

Although the *Principia* was not so widely read as Descartes' more literary *Discourse on Method*, it soon became the undisputed source and symbol of science—the new testament of a new faith. Most of Newton's ideas about matter and motion have been modified by twentieth-century physicists (pp. 577–578, 716–720), but his methodological principles remain a model.

THE ORGANIZATION OF SCIENCE

The story of science since Newton has been one of continuous acceleration in the growth of knowledge. Even in Newton's time, discovery was proceeding in numerous fields, and findings in one subject suggested and aided investigations in others. Robert Boyle identified physical "elements" and thereby fathered chemistry. William Harvey explained the function of the heart and the circulation of the blood, thus beginning the science of physiology. The Greek physician Galen (p. 138), whose authority had ruled for centuries, fell from favor; medicine and pharmacy now achieved a scientific foundation.

Rapid strides were also made in optics, and the development of the microscope (as well as the telescope) opened promising new areas of exploration. The microscope paved the way for the sciences of botany and zoology and made it clear that human beings stand near a midpoint on the scale of *size* in the universe—halfway between the giant stars and the tiniest particles of matter. Along with optical devices, various types of instruments were invented for *measurement*—to give experimenters the *precision* they needed. And the idea of the *laboratory*, where experiments could be conducted under controlled conditions, took shape by the end of the seventeenth century.

These developments reflected the growing *interdependence* of scientific investigators and their equipment. The isolated, casual experimenter of the Renaissance (like Leonardo—p. 380), had given way to a new type. No matter how proud or self-centered scientists might become, they fully recognized that science was a *social* enterprise. No one individual or nation was alone responsible; the advance of science was an international achievement that depended on generally accepted procedures and continuous communication among investigators. Curiously, while religion and politics were breaking down into *national* and subnational units, science took the *opposite* direction.

The universities were painfully slow in promoting the new learning. Still in the grip of religious and humanist traditions, they were generally hostile or indifferent to science. In the education of young men, two centuries were to pass before the "classical" curriculum (pp. 376–377) would make room for scientific subjects, and new institutions had to be created for the support and coordination of experimental studies.

The earliest societies for the advancement of *research* were founded in Italy. Rome set up an academy in 1603, of which Galileo was a member; a half-century later the Medici established a scientific institution in Florence. More influential and longer lasting, however, was the Royal Society of London, which was chartered in 1662. It consisted of scientists and mathematicians as well as interested merchants, nobles, and clerics. In an effort to support Francis Bacon's idea for

c. 1350	Copernicus c. 1543	Newton c. 1687	c. 1789
Era of Renaissance Humanism		Scientific Revolution	The Enlightenment

c. 1600

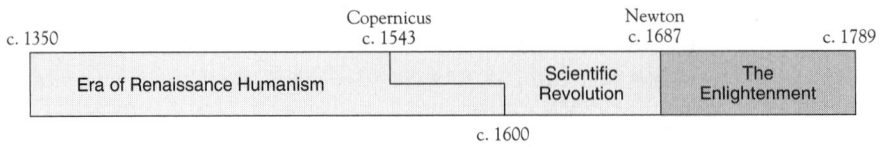

building up a total system of knowledge (p. 468), the society aided experiments, listened to learned discussions, corresponded with foreign societies, and published a scientific journal.

The society was interested in the *practical applications* of science as well as in "pure" research. Bacon himself had declared that the true goal of science was to give human beings greater *power* for human benefit. And Robert Boyle, an early member of the Royal Society, confessed that he did not desire merely to talk and write about nature—he wanted to learn to *master* it. Traditional philosophy, he pointed out, had been barren of practical advantage to humanity. Science, properly understood, would strengthen the useful arts and raise the people's standard of living.

This emphasis on practical applications attracted support from commerce, industry, and government, on the continent as well as in England. Louis XIV, at the suggestion of his finance minister, Colbert, endowed the Academy of Science in 1666, and similar institutions were founded in other European states. Thus, science (the search for *understanding* of nature) and technology (the search for ways to *control* nature) began to experience a mutual attraction, though the actual marriage of the two had to wait until the nineteenth century (p. 557–558).

THE IMPACT OF SCIENCE ON PHILOSOPHY: THE ENLIGHTENMENT

The link between science and technology could soon be observed in the increased output of workshops and military arsenals. More subtle and complex was the influence of science on the general ideas, values, and attitudes of society. For science gave to educated Westerners a radically new view of their universe and the forces that move it. While only a few intellectuals were trained scientists, most of them accepted (sooner or later) the scientific depiction of the natural order. Since their way of looking at life came from their underlying beliefs about the nature of the universe, from this new base they proceeded to construct a new philosophy and a new society.

Of course, the new scientific vision of the universe, as well as the philosophical ideas derived from it, penetrated much more slowly among the general population. Even among the educated, many did not totally accept the new views, and some actively opposed them—mainly because these views conflicted with established religious teachings. But even opponents could not help being affected by the consequences of the change. A new intellectual climate enveloped Europe in the eighteenth century, which in the long run affected all classes, and spread outward to the ends of the earth.

A Revised Cosmology: The "World-Machine"

The scientists themselves had little to do *directly* with the philosophy that took shape during this era. Men like Kepler and Newton tended to be conservative in their religious and social views; Descartes, though a promoter of intellectual doubt, urged people to conform to traditional habits of life. Nor did professionally trained philosophers play a very significant role. The shift in thinking was mainly the work of gifted amateurs—"literary" persons. Most of them were French, and although they did not establish any formal system of philosophy, they came to be known in their country as the *philosophes* (philosophers).

The philosophes were so dazzled by Newton's brilliance that they considered themselves living in an unprecedented age of "light." It was this notion that gave rise to the term "Enlightenment" as a name for the period that reached from 1687, the date of Newton's *Principia*, to 1789, the start of the French Revolution. Those who glimpsed the new vision of the universe thought of themselves as the "enlightened" ones, and they were eager to spread the light to others.

The universe they held up to view contrasted sharply with the traditional Christian one. The most evident and disturbing differences were that the new universe was heliocentric and that it extended through boundless space. The devoutly religious mathematician Blaise Pascal had confessed, "I am terrified by the eternal silence of those infinite spaces." But the humanist as well as the Christian felt humbled: the human being was no longer the *center* of nature's plan. The architecture of Newton's universe made humans appear insignificant, both in time and in space. It was still possible to believe that a personal God existed, that he had a special plan for humanity, and that human life had supreme value. But such a faith was no longer supported by the evidence of astronomy. It seemed, rather, to be *contradicted* by the extravagant dimensions of the cosmos.

Other supports for traditional beliefs collapsed. With Aristotle's laws of motion overthrown, no role remained for a Prime Mover (p. 465), or for Moving Spirits. The hand of God, which once kept the heavenly bodies in their orbits, had been replaced by universal gravitation. Miracles had no place in a system whose workings were automatic and unvarying. Governed by precise mathematical and mechanical laws, Newton's universe seemed capable of running itself forever.

People had long been familiar with such complex machines as watches and clocks. Was it not logical, after Newton, to believe that the universe itself was a grand machine? Not all its rules of operation had yet been discovered, but scientists knew enough to be able to sketch the nature of the whole. The French astronomer Pierre Laplace expressed the mechanistic idea of the eighteenth century when he said, "Give me the present location and motion of all bodies in the universe, and I will predict their location and motion through all eternity."

THE VIEW OF GOD: DEISM

If the "enlightened" concept of the universe had profound implications for the meaning of human freedom, responsibility, and ethics, it raised even more disturbing questions about religious convictions. What was to become of the beliefs of Christianity? Many scientists and intellectuals found it extremely difficult to bring together the Newtonian system and Christian theology, to fit Christian teachings and practices into the new cosmology. The "world-machine," it seemed, had no *need* for supernatural guidance, prayer, priests, sacraments, or penance; these appeared superfluous, if not contradictory. The philosophes, therefore, persuaded that they could not logically reconcile Christianity with scientific truth, rejected the former.

This did not mean that they necessarily gave up the idea of God. Newton had explained the *operation* of matter in motion, but he gave no demonstration of its *origin*. Because common sense still made it difficult for people to think of something as existing that had not been *made*, the question of creation remained unanswered. Here was a role for God that appeared reasonable to the philosophes. It also satisfied the urge to believe, which remained a part of their cultural inheritance.

Newton himself stated that the First Cause is not mechanical and suggested that God, "in the beginning," had formed matter in the particular way he desired. Thus, God was referred to in scientific circles as the Creator, the Maker, or the Author. It was equally logical to believe that he had established the governing rules of the universe as well as its substance; hence, he was given such alternative names as the Great Mathematician, the Great Engineer, and the Governor. Though some scientists suggested that the Divine Watchmaker might occasionally intervene to correct an irregularity in the operation of the world-machine, their belief was that God had long since removed himself from the affairs of the physical universe. Only *nature* remains, so it is nature that must be understood and respected.

This was a religion of sorts, but it was clearly not Christianity, Judaism, or any other revealed system of belief and worship. Vaguely labeled "Deism," this new religion had been started in the seventeenth century. An Englishman, Lord Herbert of Cherbury, tried to make of it a universal faith that would include and surmount all the others. He posed five basic truths as common to the foremost religions of the world—and not incompatible with science. These were: the existence of a Supreme Power, the necessity of worship, the requirement of good conduct, the benefit of repentance of vices, and the existence of rewards and punishments after death.

Lord Herbert's efforts failed to bring all believers together. He had dreamed of an end to sectarian strife and the beginnings of accord among all people of good will. Though Deism became popular with such eighteenth-century intellectuals as Voltaire, Franklin, and Jefferson, for most churchgoers it was an inadequate substitution for traditional religion. It lacked mystery, ritual, emotional appeal, and discipline. And it was offensive to the clergy of all denominations, for it challenged the authority of their sacred books, doctrines, and offices.

Deism gradually lost its appeal even to the converts of science. By the close of the eighteenth century many of them had decided that there really is no need even for a Creator. Newton had shown that motion is as natural as non-motion. Is not matter, then, as natural as non-matter? Was it not old-fashioned to think that things must be *created?* The universe and its motion had always been and always would be. This line of reasoning led some to deny God absolutely *(atheism)*; others said they could not or did not know whether God existed *(skepticism* or *agnosticism).* Religious doubt was by no means new in Western civilization, but the scientific revolution gave it new vigor and appeal. Though the number of doubters remained small (and the number of *professed* doubters even smaller), they would continue to challenge traditional faiths.

True, many among the educated did not agree that science and Christianity contradicted each other as the philosophes claimed. Newton himself, for example, was all his life a believer, who hoped through his discoveries to confirm the wonders of the Almighty. In fact, he divided his energies between scientific pursuits and deep study of the Bible, through which he hoped (among other things) to achieve the traditional Protestant goal of proving that the Catholic Church was a perversion of true Christianity.

As for the churches and synagogues, they continued to be the main influence on the way of life of most people in Europe. Indeed, the age of the Enlightenment was also a great age of religious "revival." In different faiths, beloved leaders of what amounted to religious mass movements arose, who by their preaching stirred up the fervor of many thousands of men and women. In Protestant England, for example, there was the Methodist minister John Wesley; in Catholic Italy, the Redemptorist father and later saint Alfonso Liguori; among the Jews of Poland, the Hasidic rabbi Israel ben Eliezer. All three had in common the ability to interpret the traditional beliefs of their respective religions in deeply personal and moving ways that made sense to ordinary believers. All of them, moreover, had a permanent effect on their respective faiths, through organizations of their followers who have continued their work down to the present.

Nevertheless, as proofs of the Newtonian system continued to accumulate, religious leaders had no choice but to make their peace with the results of scientific discovery. At the level of *basic belief,* they rejected the notion of the philosophes that the new view of the universe made Christianity harder to believe in. But at the level of *social and political thought,* many religious leaders, and educated believers in general, could more or less accept such Enlightenment ideas as religious toleration, more widespread education, or the use of scientific knowledge to improve the condition of the human race. It was through adaptations of this kind that the ideas of the Enlightenment spread beyond the relatively small circles of the philosophes, to become part of the general climate of opinion among educated people in eighteenth-century Europe.

THE VIEW OF HUMAN SOCIETY

If God played an inactive role (or none at all) in the view of the philosophes, the place and powers of humans were dramatically enlarged. Followers of the tradition of the Renaissance humanists (pp. 373–383), after recovering from the initial shock of Newton's astronomy, saw that humans became more important as God's role declined. Writers began to emphasize the grandeur of reason, which had enabled human beings to unveil the mysteries of the universe. Although humans could not control its movements, they had touched the cosmos with their minds. And they had, at the same time, vastly expanded their power over life on earth. Through science and technology, they could improve their well-being and press nature itself into their service.

Human beings might be viewed as not only stronger but *better*. The philosophes did not deny the existence of evil in human affairs, but they generally blamed it on bad *social institutions*. Nature, as revealed by Newton, is orderly and harmonious. Because of ignorance, however, humans had failed to follow nature's ways and had made customs, laws, sanctions, and beliefs that twisted and shackled the individual. Humans would regain their birthright and exhibit their true character when the chains of unreason were broken.

This growing optimism about human prospects had its roots in the Renaissance, but it was strengthened by the new science. The doctrine of Original Sin appeared out of place in the new cosmos, and the observed laws of motion showed no built-in movement in the direction of evil. Within the boundaries of human freedom, it seemed likely that individuals would choose good rather than bad—so long as they followed nature and reason. Some of the philosophes took an extreme position: as knowledge advanced, they held, individuals would become increasingly capable of good, and when at last they reached complete harmony with nature they would be judged perfect. Thus, they concluded, humans are not only good but *perfectible*.

No doctrine of the eighteenth century proved more controversial than this doctrine of human perfectibility. It runs counter to traditional Christian teaching and is hard to reconcile with much of history. The ablest thinkers among the philosophes did not accept such an extreme view, but they joined with others in working for social improvement. They became tireless *reformers*, aiming to remake social institutions according to the lights of reason. The "humanitarian" movement, as an organized force, was in large measure a product of eighteenth-century thought. Voltaire in France (pp. 483–484) and the Marquis de Beccaria in Italy, for example, worked for more effective ways of dealing with crime and punishment. The reformers focused attention, too, on helping the poor, the orphaned, the enslaved, and the sick; in these efforts they were often supported by traditional Christians acting in the spirit of holy charity. The philosophes worked, above all, for broad freedom of expression, tolerance, and a cosmopolitan outlook.

Faith in Nature and Reason

The humanitarian and ethical goals of the Enlightenment were similar to those of Christianity, and the "rational" criteria of goodness came, in fact, from the Judeo-Christian tradition. But the core of the new cosmology was alien to established religion. Whereas the latter evolved out of centuries of human experience, the philosophy of the Enlightenment sprang from the newly found method and vision of science. The essential differences may be summed up this way: Christianity rests its faith in the power of God as known through *revelation;* the Enlightenment puts its trust in nature as understood through *reason.* The supreme goal of one is *heaven* (spiritual bliss after death); the goal of the other is *progress* (physical happiness in life on earth).

To the ancient Greeks, as well as to the Christians, nature had been an uncertain force, more likely to be hostile than friendly. To the thinkers of the Enlightenment, nature had virtually replaced God and had been shown to be regular and knowable. They believed that the secrets of nature could be discovered and applied usefully to ordinary affairs—the farmer, for example, could make the soil more productive by observing and following physical laws. They believed, too, that legislators and judges could provide justice by applying moral and social "laws" to human relations. This confusion of *moral principles* with *physical laws* was to lead to bitter disappointments.

The eighteenth-century "cult of nature" was an outgrowth of excessive enthusiasm. Respect for the harmonious motions of the heavenly bodies led some philosophers to an unscientific, sentimental attitude toward *all* objects in nature. Alexander Pope (p. 532) attributed to nature a grand intelligence and purpose:

> All Nature is but art, unknown to thee;
> All chance, direction which thou canst not see;
> All discord, harmony not understood;
> All partial evil, universal good.

Most eighteenth-century intellectuals, however, kept their eye on the central idea: the extension of useful knowledge through the exercise of reason. Perhaps the most exciting discovery of the age was that nature behaves in a reasoned, even mathematical, manner; therefore its workings correspond to *human logic.* From this the philosophes concluded that reason is the key to nature's secrets and powers and is the proper means of judging and regulating human affairs.

An acceptable model for explaining the working of the mind was supplied by the Englishman John Locke (pp. 502–503). Though interested in science, Locke followed the guide of common sense rather than a strict methodology. He studied medicine, economics, political theory, and philosophy, and he associated with many of the leading political figures of his country. Perhaps because of his familiarity with practical affairs, his writings were readily received by the educated public, and several generations of hardheaded revolutionaries found reassuring arguments in his political writings. His ideas about the nature of human knowledge were especially persuasive, for he rested his case on the ordinary sense experience of his readers. Locke may not have been profound, and he was certainly not scientific. Nevertheless, his writings swept away many ancient beliefs and showed what the "new" reason could do when it was applied to questions about human beings and society.

In his *Essay Concerning Human Understanding* (1690), Locke stated that all knowledge comes from *experience*. This was in line with Bacon's empiricism (p. 468) and challenged long-established convictions that knowledge is *inborn* or *revealed*. Descartes, for instance, held that some ideas are implanted by God, while Socrates and Plato had taught that all knowledge is inborn. According to Christian doctrine, truth is revealed by God.

Locke's theory, however, rested on a very simple model of the mind, whose functioning depended on no concealed or supernatural elements. The mind at birth, said Locke, may be likened to "white paper, void of all characters, without any ideas." The ideas that come to be written on this paper come from but one source: *experience*. By this Locke meant not only immediate sense perceptions (sensation), but the operations of the mind in sorting and arranging those perceptions (reflection). Thus, the intelligent person uses the senses with care and systematically arranges and compares the impressions received through them. These processes are the substance of both reasoning and knowledge, and they enable individuals to understand and control the world about them.

Although Locke's notion of the "thinking machine" was naive (simple), it did call forth further study. Physiologists and psychologists have found that the mind is far more complex than Locke imagined. Still, the Lockean theory proved useful; it suited the eighteenth-century view that people are shaped by their *environment*. According to Locke, ideas are totally dependent on outside stimuli. Hence, if the correct environment is provided, the individual will receive only the "right" ideas. This suggests, in turn, that through the reform of institutions, especially education, rapid improvements can be made in human nature and society.

These beliefs help explain the devotion of eighteenth-century intellectuals to both science and education. To them, ignorance had replaced sin and the devil as the principal enemy. Sinners were to be redeemed not by the grace of God, but by human reason. Research had to be encouraged so that investigators could learn more; education had to be overhauled and extended so that the new knowledge could be carried everywhere. The philosophes threw themselves into these endeavors with the enthusiasm of missionaries. They felt that education should be for adults as well as for children. As propagandists of "truth," they took to writing pamphlets, books, and encyclopedias. (The most notable encyclopedist was the brilliant French editor and critic Denis Diderot.) The world would never be quite the same again; the belief in science and education became a feature of the modern world. In the United States, founded at the peak of the Enlightenment, that belief has remained an article of national faith (though it is being questioned today more than ever before).

The Vision of Progress

The extreme apostles of reason had no doubt that they were on the path to paradise on earth. No Christian heaven existed in their philosophy, but they found its counterpart in their vision of *progress*—a vision they expected to fulfill within a few generations.

Progress, as these philosophes understood the term, was a new idea in history. The ancients had been more "realistic" in this respect, for they believed that life on earth would always be hard and uncertain. If they wished to think of something better than their own lives, they had looked *backward* rather than forward—to an age of heroes or a Garden of Eden. Christianity had taught that sinful mortals must live in this world as "pilgrims" awaiting perfection in the *world to come*. Even the humanists of the Renaissance, though their estimate of human capacity was higher than that of the ancients, did not believe in the certainty of progress. Erasmus saw folly without end, and Montaigne sought the consolation of books (pp. 382, 400). Perhaps their attachment to the classics confirmed such scholars in their pessimism.

But seventeenth-century science at last broke the spell of antiquity. Scientists began to point out how much more they knew than the ancients. They felt moved to say what was plainly true: it was the Greeks and Romans who were "children" in time; and it was the most recent generations, those who had the advantage of ac-cumulated experience, who were in fact the "ancients." Science thus dissolved the myth of classical superiority in knowledge and, with its new tools, pointed the way toward a grander future.

The Marquis de Condorcet made the most eloquent statement of this un-bounded faith in progress. A well-educated nobleman trained in mathematics and science, Condorcet served as secretary of the French Academy of Science. He is es-pecially remembered for his *Progress of the Human Mind*, written, ironically, during a chaotic year of the French Revolution (1794). Though an active reformer, Con-dorcet had broken with the more radical leaders of the revolution and was then in hiding as a fugitive. But he wrote that his sorrow over temporary injustices and barbarities was overbalanced by his vision of the *future*.

Condorcet's expectation of universal happiness on earth would prove mis-taken, but his writing was nonetheless prophetic. He declared that nothing could stop the advance of knowledge and power "as long as the earth occupies its present place in the system of the universe, and as long as the general laws of this sys-tem produce neither a general cataclysm nor such changes as will deprive the human race of its present faculties and its present resources." He forecast that rapid technological advances would lead to a world in which "everyone will have less work to do, will produce more, and satisfy his wants more fully." He saw the eventual achievement of *equal rights for women*, the *abolition of poverty*, and the ordering of economic affairs so that *every individual*, guided by reason, could enjoy true independence.

Condorcet proposed a *social security system* and suggested that population growth would ultimately have to be checked through *birth control*. He also pre-dicted an *end to colonialism and warfare*, declaring that wars would "rank with assas-sinations as freakish atrocities, humiliating and vile in the eyes of nature." His vigorous optimism, characteristic of the eighteenth-century philosophes, marked the high point in the rise of secular values and human self-confidence that had be-gun in Europe after 1400 (pp. 373–374).

POLITICAL RESPONSE TO THE NEW PHILOSOPHY: ENLIGHTENED DESPOTISM

The Enlightenment is an outstanding example of how philosophical ideas conceived by writers and intellectuals can have an overwhelming impact on practical affairs. In the long run, the philosophes helped to bring about massive changes in Western politics, government, and society. The philosophes' emphasis on reason and education, and on perfectibility and progress, naturally led them to judge the social and political institutions of their own time. Did these institutions, they asked, contribute to the moral, intellectual, and material progress of the human race? Needless to say, they mostly condemned what they found.

Only one major European country met with some degree of approval from the philosophes. This was Britain, whose seventeenth-century revolution (pp. 498–503) had produced a government and social system that, at least in some respects, met their standards. On the basis of the British experience, Enlightenment thinkers developed ideas about government and the social order that in turn had a major impact on the eighteenth-century revolutions in America and France, as well as subsequent revolutionary changes in Europe and elsewhere. (These theories are discussed further in chapter 11, pp. 504–509, 510–521.) But Enlightenment ideals influenced not only revolutionary opponents of the existing order. The same ideals also influenced the bureaucrats, nobles, and absolute monarchs who dominated most countries of eighteenth-century Europe. Many members of this elite became dissatisfied with the very social and political order they ruled, producing a reform within the system that later historians called "enlightened despotism."

The most famous enlightened despots were among the rulers of central and eastern Europe: Frederick II of Prussia, Maria Theresa and Joseph II of Austria, and Catherine II of Russia (pp. 459–461). All of these sought, to a greater or lesser extent, to put into practice enlightened reforms such as religious toleration, improvements in the condition of agriculture and the peasantry, and wider access to education. The high point of enlightened despotism was the reign of Joseph II in Austria. In ten years of whirlwind reform between 1780 and 1790, Joseph introduced changes so drastic as to amount almost to a peaceful revolution. Among other things, the emperor, himself a Catholic, granted religious freedom to his Protestant, Orthodox, and Jewish subjects; dissolved hundreds of Catholic monasteries, with much of their funds going to education; and gave the serfs freedom to marry and leave their manors without the consent of the lords (though other features of serfdom, notably labor service, survived until 1848—p. 544).

Partly, the reason for reforms such as these was that, like so many others among the educated elite, the rulers themselves could not escape the influence of the philosophes. Some, like Frederick II and Catherine II, became Deists who made no secret of their contempt for Christian belief; others, like Joseph II, were Christian in their basic beliefs, but eagerly accepted enlightened social and political ideas (pp. 475–476). Either way, to this new generation of absolute monarchs it seemed absurd to say, as Louis XIV had done, "I am the state." Instead, Frederick II spoke for all of them when he described himself, more modestly, as "the state's first servant."

Naturally, in adopting enlightened ideas, the rulers were thinking also of their own power. No less than earlier monarchs, they were enthusiastic makers of war. It did not escape them that a reformed state—with well-fed, well-educated, and productive citizens, with believers in different faiths living peaceably and tolerantly side by side, and with the nobles acting as real social leaders rather than as pampered courtiers—would probably win any war it fought with an unreformed state. And as the "first servants" of such a reformed state, the enlightened despots did not intend to give up even the smallest fragment of their absolute power. On the contrary, they expected to be more truly in control of their dominions than the divine right rulers of traditional absolute monarchies.

Like all efforts at reforming a system from within, enlightened despotism only worked so long as it did not go too far and too fast. Joseph II, the most radical of the despots, ended with his government paralyzed by the opposition of the nobles; those who did not meet such opposition, like Frederick II and Catherine II, left many of their countries' traditional institutions unchanged. Still, it was the enlightened despots who first put some of the ideas of the philosophes into practice, and thereby began to undermine the surviving elements of the social and political order that had emerged in early medieval Europe (chapter 5).

THE RATIONAL SPIRIT IN LITERATURE AND ART

The new ideas in science and philosophy had a marked effect on the literature of the seventeenth and eighteenth centuries. The leading cultural fashion was "classicism," which was an extension of Renaissance ideals—given fresh force by the new stress on logic and universal laws. Bernard Fontenelle, who preceded Condorcet as secretary of the Academy of Science, called attention to the significance of mathematical principles for literature:

> The geometrical spirit is not so tied to geometry that it cannot be detached from it and transported to other branches of knowledge. A work of morals or politics or criticism, perhaps even of eloquence, would be better (other things being equal) if it were done in the style of a geometer. The order, clarity, precision, and exactitude which have been apparent in good books for some time might well have their source in this geometric spirit.

Condorcet insisted that all expression must accept "the yoke of those universal rules of reason and nature which ought to be their guide." The endeavor of writers and artists to apply such rules led to the curbing of the extreme individuality that had developed during the late Renaissance and baroque periods (pp. 398–399, 439–443).

The leaders of classicism sought, through the use of reason, to construct a view of humanity that would be *universally* valid. They also sought to perfect exact *forms* of expression, based on ancient models, and to give to modern languages the precision and charm of classical tongues. Rejecting the force of current usage in determining what is "correct," they looked instead to recognized judges of style and taste. Nicolas Boileau (in France) and Alexander Pope (in England) were respected critics whose opinions were taken as literary *law*. Each wanted to be the Newton of his art.

The advocates of classical standards favored the founding of national academies to promote and enforce those standards. This idea appealed to the monarchs of the period—Louis XIII, for example, created the Académie Française in 1635. Because patronage flowed chiefly from the court and its dependent aristocracy, most writers now felt compelled to observe the official rules of style and taste. The Académie succeeded in imposing classical standards on French writers for more than a century.

CLASSICISM: RACINE, POPE

As we saw earlier in this chapter, France was the center of European power and culture during the seventeenth century (pp. 455–456). And in France classicism had its strongest roots, inspiring one of the richest periods in French literature. In addition to philosophical writers like Descartes and Pascal, there were outstanding individuals in every branch of letters. Chief among them was Jean Racine, France's greatest dramatic poet and a leading promoter of classicism.

Educated by a Catholic religious order, Racine received thorough training in Greek and Latin as well as in theology. His middle-class family wanted him to become a priest, but an urge to write poetry took him to Paris in 1663. When a poem written to Louis XIV brought him to the attention of the king, Racine's literary career was begun. He received a post at the court the following year and was elected to the Académie Française in 1673.

The plots of Racine's tragedies were drawn from classical themes and invariably centered on a single moral issue. Like other plays of the period, his were intellectual in nature, with long speeches and little action on stage. He relied on the spoken word to reveal character and passion under stress. The simplicity, precision, and dignity of his poetry brought Voltaire's comment: "Beautiful, sublime, wonderful."

Classicism was expressed in another literary form by Alexander Pope. In *An Essay on Criticism* (1711) he set down his guidelines for critics and, later, in *An Essay on Man*, he put forward in verse a *rationalistic* view of the universe. Pope, an English Catholic by birth, but strongly influenced by Deism (pp. 474–475), tried to reconcile the discoveries of science with the idea of a benevolent God. He stressed the elements of order in nature, which had been confirmed by the mathematics of Newton. But, while admitting the power of reason, he urged his readers to restrain their curiosity and pride: God's works are ultimately beyond understanding; it is best to accept one's limited place in the scheme of things and to believe that "Whatever is, is Right."

Pope's *Essay on Man* is classical in form as well as substance. It consists of hundreds of rhyming couplets, many of which are cleverly turned and well-remembered:

> Know then thyself, presume not God to scan;
> The proper study of mankind is man.

> Hope springs eternal in the human breast;
> Man never is, but always to be blest.

The work as a whole illustrates the strengths and weaknesses of *didactic* verse (poetry with a "message")—and the classic *form*. Strict form has a power and beauty in itself; at the same time, it may limit the development of ideas and feelings.

SATIRE: VOLTAIRE

Literature in the eighteenth century, responding to the Enlightenment, reached out to an ever-widening public. The classicists, like Pope and Racine, had written mainly for the royal court and a small group of educated readers. The philosophes, however, were less interested in the refinement of literature than in the circulation of new ideas. With literacy on the rise, they found that men and women of all classes, but especially the bourgeois, wanted to be informed. A group of writers appeared whose chief aim was to digest important ideas and put them in readable form for "the public." Along with encyclopedias, dictionaries, and surveys of knowledge, there was a rapid spread of newspapers and magazines.

The most successful and famous of the new writers was Voltaire; he was, in fact, one of the first individuals to make a fortune by his pen alone. The son of a Parisian lawyer, he was schooled by Jesuits, who evidently sharpened his talent for argumentation. Though he was formally trained in law in his homeland, his real education began in England. In trouble in France because he had insulted a nobleman, Voltaire accepted exile across the Channel in 1726. Through private study and conversation he quickly absorbed the ideas of English philosophy and politics.

When Voltaire returned to France, he began to write all sorts of works—plays, histories, poems, scientific surveys, and philosophical essays. The best known and most widely read of his more than a hundred books is the satirical novel *Candide* (1759), which reflects his reasoned outlook, his irony, and his strong convictions. The story is a swift-moving, rollicking caricature of an idea popularized by Pope— that "this is the best of all possible worlds." The "hero," Candide, is an innocent young man who has been brought up to believe that *everything is for the best*. In the course of incredible misadventures he learns differently. At the story's end, Candide and his companions are living on a small farm trying to shut out the stupidities and indecencies of the world. One of them concludes that the only way to do this is to "lose oneself" in some form of satisfying work. "It's the only way to make life endurable."

In the course of the novel, Voltaire struck out with rapier (and bludgeon) at many targets: the bigotry and hypocrisy of organized religion, the atrocities of war, the "inhumanity of man to man." He expressed contempt for arbitrary authority and disgust with ignorance and prejudice. Though a man of the Enlightenment, he criticized many of the new ideas as well: he ridiculed "pseudo" reason, which spins out unsupportable theories and seeks to find "cause" and "effect" in every event; scoffed at the nature cult; and turned the dream of "progress" into a nightmare.

Yet Voltaire had faith in the method of science and the power of reason. He stood courageously for freedom of expression; he admired simple honesty, moderation, humaneness, and tolerance. "Tolerance," he wrote in his *Philosophical Dictionary* (1764), "is the natural attribute of humanity. We are all formed of weakness and error; let us pardon reciprocally each other's folly. That is the first law of nature. It is clear that the individual who persecutes a man, his brother, because he is not of the same opinion, is a monster." If Voltaire sometimes grew bitter, it was because the world seemed so full of what he hated and so empty of what he loved. Like Erasmus, he was no revolutionist, but he and his fellow philosophes nevertheless helped prepare the ground for revolution.

THE ARCHITECTURE OF REASON: WREN, JEFFERSON

The Enlightenment was only partly reflected in the visual arts. On the continent, the style of baroque architecture (pp. 439–443) carried over into the eighteenth century and was gradually modified into the lighter, more delicate style of "rococo" (shell-like). Both styles were elaborate and elegant, suited to the pomp of monarchs and aristocrats. By 1750, however, the *classical* spirit in the other arts led architects back to the simplicity of Roman and Greek models.

In England, the baroque had been more restrained, and the return to classicism came earlier there than on the continent. The most influential architect of the time was Christopher Wren. The Great Fire of London (1666) gave him a

10-2   Christopher Wren. St. Paul's Cathedral, London. 1675–1710.

10-3   James Gibbs. St. Martin's-in-the-Fields, London. 1726. (Engraving drawn by Thomas Shepherd, engraved by H. W. Bond.)

unique opportunity; as the king's principal architect, he was charged with replanning the city and rebuilding St. Paul's Cathedral. As might be expected, Wren had to accept many compromises, and his master plan for London was never realized. He did, however, succeed in having many of the city's churches constructed according to his designs.

Wren's triumph was St. Paul's (*Fig. 10-2*), completed in 1710. The clergy had wanted a tall Gothic building (like Chartres Cathedral—*Fig. II-1*, p. 200), but he won approval for a plan that was essentially classical. Wren was influenced by Michelangelo's plan for St. Peter's and by later Italian architects, but he shunned the curving lines and extravagance of the baroque. He desired a simple though impressive structure crowned by a great dome. In order to satisfy the clergy, he placed tall bell towers above his classical façade and a tall "lantern" on top of the dome. The result was something of a hybrid, though Wren strove to preserve the basic harmony of the plan.

In his designs for parish churches Wren again came into conflict with his clients. The churchmen wanted tall Gothic spires, symbolic of Christian striving. Wren wanted simple, classical structures. The problem of combining the vertical thrust of the Gothic with the horizontal line of the classical was formidable, but somehow he managed to solve it. A well-preserved church of Wren's style and generation is James Gibbs' St. Martin's-in-the-Fields (*Fig. 10-3*). This church and others like it became models for churches in both England and America.

Subsequently, the trend was toward a strict classicism. The preferred manual of taste was now a book by the Renaissance architect Andrea Palladio, who had

10-4   Maison Carrée. Nîmes, France, c. 20 B.C.

10-5   Thomas Jefferson. State Capitol, Richmond, Virginia. 1785.

methodically measured ancient ruins. The "Palladian manner," with its Roman-style porches, rotundas (circular halls), and domes, became the standard for eighteenth-century England. Noblemen who built villas in this style believed that their homes were a reflection of an age of reason—the reason of Newton and Pope. In the second half of the century, admiration for ancient architecture was further stimulated by the excavation of the Roman cities of Pompeii and Herculaneum (at the foot of Mount Vesuvius). The beauty and grace revealed in those ancient buildings had a powerful effect upon the houses, furnishings, and dress of the well-to-do.

Thomas Jefferson was one of the many intellectuals who became enamored of the classical style. On a visit to France in the 1780s he saw the ancient Roman temple, the "Maison Carrée" *(Fig. 10-4)*, in the provincial town of Nîmes. He reported that he gazed at it for hours at a time, "like a lover at his mistress." When Jefferson returned to his home, he designed numerous public and private buildings, thus popularizing the classical style in America. His plan for the Virginia state capitol at Richmond *(Fig. 10-5)* was inspired by the Maison Carrée, and his designs for the Rotunda of the University of Virginia and his home at Monticello were patterned after the Roman Pantheon *(Figs. 3-4, p. 142 and 3-5, p. 143)*. The public architecture of Washington, D.C., has borne the impress of Jefferson and the classical revival. Officials of the new nation were proud to demonstrate visually their enthusiasm for the Enlightenment and its ideals of reason and order.

The leaders of the French Revolution also favored Roman models. And the revolutionary heir, Napoleon (pp. 517–521), continued to support the style for personal reasons: he thought it fitting to his role as a "modern Caesar," and he wished to distinguish his own monuments from the baroque structures of the French kings who had preceded him in power. Classicism thereby carried over to the nineteenth century. It was followed by a Gothic revival (pp. 537–538), which was an expression of the nineteenth-century *reaction* against the ideals of the Enlightenment.

ACADEMY PAINTING: PORTRAITS OF ARISTOCRATIC ELEGANCE

Painting, of all the arts, was least affected by the radical changes in science and philosophy. In the seventeenth century classical rules had continued to govern; during the eighteenth century the rules became less rigid. The painters of France, supported largely by royal and aristocratic patronage, were serving a doomed social order. But their works show no sign of an impending calamity and are marked by unique charm, repose, and grace.

The Belgian master Antoine Watteau was the finest representative of the eighteenth-century style known as *rococo*. He came to Paris in 1715 and went to work on various projects for the nobility. As a designer of interior decorations for courtly festivals and pageants, Watteau caught the spirit of refined ease and gallantry associated with the aristocratic ideal. He began to create oil paintings of picnics in the woods, music parties, and mythical scenes peopled by graceful ladies and gentlemen in lustrous silks and satins *(Color Plate B6)*. But these are not *lifelike* portrayals. They arise out of a dream world, where ugliness is absent and beauty touches all.

10-6   Jean-Honoré Fragonard. *The Meeting*, 1771–1773. Oil on canvas, 10'5" × 8'. Frick Collection, New York.

Watteau worked, like his fellow artists in France, under the watchful eye of the Academy of Painting. Yet his paintings have an unmistakable individuality—with an air of melancholy. Destined to die in his thirties of tuberculosis, Watteau seems to have sensed the fleeting character of life and beauty.

More sensual and lighthearted (but no more realistic) were the paintings of François Boucher and his contemporary, Jean-Honoré Fragonard (*Fig. 10-6*). These artists painted mythical subjects and the frivolities of the nobility in a delicate and delightful manner. Their works, corresponding to the aims and taste of their patrons, had no important function other than playful entertainment.

Painting in England was more sober and solid. The leading figure there was Joshua Reynolds, who became the first president of the Royal Academy of Art (1768). Reynolds is best known for his portraits of the wealthy and for his support

10-7 Sir Joshua Reynolds. *Duchess of Hamilton*. The Trustees of the Lady Lever Art Gallery, Port Sunlight, Cheshire, England.

of traditional "laws" of painting. "I would chiefly recommend," he told the Academy, "that an implicit obedience to the Rules of Art, as established by the practice of the great Masters, should be exacted from the young students." He regarded the Italian Renaissance, rather than ancient Greece or Rome, as the "classic" source for the rules of painting. But he agreed with the classicists that there existed *universal* standards of taste and excellence.

The English upper classes were willing to pay a good price to have their portraits painted in the grand manner. Reynolds felt that historical or mythological subjects offered a greater challenge to his intellect, but he made his fortune by painting the rich. With high skill in texture and composition, he created hundreds of flattering portraits. His *Duchess of Hamilton (Fig. 10-7)* is typical of Reynolds' "classical" style.

THE CLASSICAL AGE OF MUSIC

The seventeenth and eighteenth centuries, taken together, constitute the classical age of European music; during that formative period most of our modern instruments and forms of composition were established. If, however, we use the term "classical" in a narrower sense—meaning the musical *style* corresponding to the style of classical literature and architecture—we find that it applies to the *eighteenth* century only. The music of that century, as we shall see, echoed the general accent on order, balance, and restraint. Seventeenth-century music, on the other hand, is usually called "baroque," because its variety and power corresponded to similar elements in baroque art and architecture (pp. 436–443).

Music in Western Civilization

Music has always been a vital part of the life and expression of Western culture. If we have given it slight attention in our account of ancient and medieval civilizations, it is because we have so little information about the musical instruments and compositions of those times. Almost all the music and instruments we hear today go back no further than the Renaissance. Yet ancient and medieval peoples believed that music had important powers, and they used it for both sacred and secular purposes.

In prehistoric cultures music was regarded primarily as a vehicle of *magic*. Singing and playing on a variety of simple instruments were intended to win supernatural assistance for the individual or the tribe. Certain types of music were thought to lend strength in battle; others promoted fertility; still others preserved health or drove away sickness. With the rise of early civilizations, music began to be viewed also as a medium of pleasure and moral uplift. The further development of music as an art "for its own sake" ranks, in fact, as one of the prime achievements of the human spirit.

Though we possess only a few fragments of ancient Greek music, we know that music held a high place in the Greek scale of values. Belief in its power is symbolized by the ancient myth of Orpheus; his playing on the lyre (harp) tamed wild animals and even secured the rescue of his wife, Eurydice, from the underworld. Music was customarily used also to heal sick bodies and minds and was thought to influence the development of character and temperament. Thus, we find that the study of music was fundamental to Greek education. Aristotle stressed the psychological impact of various combinations of harmony and rhythm: some depressed the emotions, some inspired enthusiasm, while others produced a moderate mood.

Greek music, like that of the Orient, was primarily vocal, as might be expected of the Greeks, who were a highly verbal people. (Plato considered melody and rhythm useless, except as accompaniment for *words*.) Instrumental music was therefore neglected, and singing was confined to a simple tune (*mono*phony) with no harmonizing chords. The monophonic pattern is still characteristic of music outside Western civilization, but complex melodic forms (*poly*phony) began to appear in the West around A.D. 1000.

Most Greeks were amateur musicians, but there were professional singers and players as well. Wandering poets recited or sang their tales to the accompaniment of the lyre (pp. 86–87). The only other standard instrument was the pipes, which usually consisted of two slender tubes joined at the player's mouth. Its sound, scholars believe, was something like that of the modern oboe. Playing and singing were indispensable to Greek religious and civic processions, and they were vital parts of the drama, that high achievement of Hellenic art and intellect. The actors chanted their poetic lines, and the chorus sang and danced solemnly according to set steps and patterns (p. 87).

We know little about the music of ancient Italy, except that the Romans readily adopted Greek forms. We know, too, that they contributed a family of instruments, the military horns. Later, the Roman papacy was responsible for passing on a portion of the musical heritage of antiquity to western Europe. Pope Gregory the Great, the leading figure in shaping the medieval Church, collected and organized Christian sacred music in the sixth century.

This music had originated in a variety of oriental sources, chiefly Hebrew. Exclusively vocal, it was used only in liturgical services (the Mass) and canonical prayers (the Offices), and it was sung by the priest, the choir, or the congregation. It consisted of a monophonic chant, or plainsong. The music collected by Gregory or attributed to him is known as the Gregorian chant. For centuries it has been the principal sacred music of the Roman Catholic Church.

We have reason to believe that secular as well as religious music was popular during the sixth century, but most of it seems to have disappeared in the disorders of the early Middle Ages. There was a cultural recovery, however, from the tenth century onward. Poems and songs were presented by wandering scholars, who called themselves Goliards (p. 303). Still later came the troubadours, who composed and sang love songs and romances of chivalry (pp. 304–305). They, too, used only the monophonic form with simple accompaniment.

Polyphony ("part" singing) had its beginnings in the tenth century. This more complex form demanded a superior means of *musical notation*, and during the twelfth and thirteenth centuries the basis was laid for the modern system, with its staff, time signature, and syllables. Meanwhile, new instruments were appearing. Most important were the clavichord and the harpsichord, the forerunners of the piano. The pipe organ, which was commonly used to accompany sacred music, underwent successive improvements.

During the Renaissance, polyphony reached its full development in both sacred and secular music. It was applied to scriptural texts, Masses, and to dramas of the Lord's Passion. The most popular songs were "madrigals," which consisted of secular poems put into "part" singing. Instrumental music (written mainly for dances) also gained favor. The recorder, a wooden relative of the flute, was introduced at this time, while the most common stringed instrument was the lute, similar to a mandolin. Most instruments of the Renaissance are no longer in general use, although we sometimes hear performances on re-created instruments of the period. More often we hear this music adapted to modern instruments.

BIRTH OF THE "MODERN" STYLE: MONTEVERDI, HANDEL, BACH

The transformation of music to its "modern" form began rather late in the Renaissance and reached full force during the baroque era of the seventeenth century. So sweeping were their innovations that the baroque composers believed they were bringing about a musical revolution. In fact, they referred to the Renaissance manner as the "old style" (in Italian, *stile antico*) and to their own as the "modern style" (*stile moderno*).

In contrast to the even-tempered, complex themes of traditional polyphony, baroque compositions were marked by a heavier stress on a dominant melody. Elaborate harmonic chords and dramatic effects were also characteristic, and, in order to create a wider range of tonal effects, larger numbers and types of instruments were used: flutes, oboes, trumpets, and bassoons, as well as violas, violins, and the harpsichord. Composers now began to write instrumental music for *listening*, not just for dancing. Reflecting the growing social role of the bourgeois, concerts were held in public halls as well as in the private courts of royalty and nobility. This was a secular age, and secular music now became as important as sacred music.

Perhaps the most important cultural development of the time was the appearance of a new art form: the opera. This "music drama," consisting of expressive speech heightened by melody and rhythm, originated in Italy. Its chief creator was Claudio Monteverdi, who had spent the earlier years of his life writing madrigals and Masses but who in middle age turned enthusiastically to the modern style. The most appealing of his operas, *Orfeo (Orpheus)*, was first performed in 1607. Exhibiting most of the elements of modern opera, it contained the first operatic overture (musical introduction) and a number of instrumental passages to heighten dramatic action. Monteverdi, who was also a singer, viol player, and conductor, supported the operatic action with an effective combination of instruments. His ensemble (musical group) was close to that of the modern orchestra.

Opera, however, did not find a ready acceptance outside Italy. Nearly a century passed before the new art form spread north of the Alps, thanks partly to the work of George Frideric Handel (born 1685). Of German origin, Handel spent much of his youth in Italy before settling in England. Admired by the king and aristocracy who acted as his patrons—and beloved also by the growing English middle classes who attended his performances—Handel was enormously successful in his adopted country, and died a wealthy man. Endlessly prolific and versatile, Handel could express in music almost any situation and emotion. These ranged from the sensual passion that marks many of his operas, through the magnificence of his works for royal occasions such as the *Water Music*, to the religious grandeur of his sacred music, notably the oratorio *Messiah*.

Meanwhile, another prolific German composer was writing in every form except opera. Johann Sebastian Bach (also born in 1685) is a giant of the baroque period and one of the great musicians of all time. A devout Lutheran, he composed profound and inspiring scores for religious texts (cantatas and oratorios), Masses, and Passions. Bach was equally talented in secular music, creating superb pieces (chamber music) for performance by small groups at aristocratic courts. He is notable for the power and grandeur of his expression and for his mastery of polyphonic themes.

THE CLASSICAL SPIRIT: HAYDN, MOZART

The death of Bach in 1750 marked the end of the baroque and the beginning of yet another style of musical expression. As in the visual arts, a reaction had set in against the elaborateness and the complexity of seventeenth-century music. The Enlightenment valued rationality, clarity, and restraint; in France, the Academy of Music attempted to impose these qualities in a manner similar to that of the Academy of Painting. Melodies and rhythms were simplified, and form rather than content was stressed. Music, the classicists believed, should not be disturbing but should express balance and repose through perfect craftsmanship. The compositions of this era, which were mainly secular, were designed for enjoyable listening. They appealed as much to the intellect as to the heart.

Not surprisingly, instrumental music was more highly regarded than singing. The sections of the modern orchestra were well established during the eighteenth century, when the first important symphonies were written. Most popular, however, was music intended for *chamber* performances, normally given in small halls. The string quartet was the leading new musical form; the violin was the chief ensemble instrument, and the piano was the foremost keyboard instrument.

Among the most gifted of all the classical composers were Franz Joseph Haydn and Wolfgang Amadeus Mozart, both Austrians. Haydn, the lighthearted Viennese composer, brought the chamber and symphonic forms to a high point of perfection and in doing so created works of enduring appeal. Mozart, a child prodigy, was composing serious works before the age of five. Though he died in poverty in 1791, at the age of thirty-five, he created an astonishing number of magnificent compositions.

Mozart was himself a superb harpsichordist and pianist and wrote many pieces for keyboard instruments. He was a master of all types of composition, however, and displayed the clarity and grace of classicism at its best. But his ultimate triumph was in opera, where his understanding of human character combined with his gift for melody to produce immortal works. Among his most popular operas today are *Don Giovanni*, *The Marriage of Figaro*, and *The Magic Flute*. Though he was truly a man of the eighteenth century, trained in classicism, Mozart transcended both the style and the age.

CHAPTER II

❍❍❍

THE REVOLUTIONS OF LIBERALISM AND NATIONALISM

Overview

The seventeenth and eighteenth centuries—the era of absolute monarchy and aristocratic privilege, of the baroque and classicism, of science and enlightenment—were also an era of *revolutions*. Beginning in seventeenth-century England and eighteenth-century North America and France, the revolutions continued into the first half of the nineteenth century and brought about another great shift in Western civilization.

The revolutions were themselves a response to shifts in civilization that had been underway since the late Middle Ages, which had led to political, social, and economic divisions in many countries. The increase in central government power *within* states often provoked resistance on the part of wealthy and educated people whose interests and authority were threatened—English "country gentlemen," American merchants, or French aristocrats, for instance. The ever-intensifying conflicts *among* states, and the ever-growing armies, navies, and taxes, led to conflicts between rulers and ruled, or between different social groups, over who was to bear the ever-increasing burden—American colonists or the British government; tax-exempt French nobles or the peasants who worked their lands. These discontents among both the elite and the masses made even powerful governments liable to collapse. Meanwhile, the Reformation and the Enlightenment widened divisions over ultimate beliefs and values and inspired opposing parties with idealistic fury—Catholics against Protestants, philosophes against Catholics, different kinds of Protestants or philosophes against each other. Once governments collapsed, the political, social, and ideological tensions reinforced each other and often led to many years of strife as well as endless changes of government: radical dictatorships that tried to build a new heaven and a new earth; military strongmen who used the army to try to enforce their own vision of a new order and win general acceptance by foreign conquest; or counterrevolutionary regimes that staged would-be restorations of the old order.

In the long run, however, out of the turmoil of revolution in different countries there emerged a new way of structuring societies and governments. In place of the traditional order that had developed fifteen hundred years earlier out of the merging of Greek and Roman civilization and the warrior societies of barbarian Europe (chapter 5) there appeared a new order based on two closely related principles: those of *liberalism* and *nationalism*.

Liberalism embodied the forces that had been rising since the late Middle Ages—those of capitalism, materialism, secularism, and individualism. Its ideals were connected in one way or another with these forces: it stood for *freedom* and *equality*, and just as importantly, for *prosperity* and *efficiency*. By these standards, liberals believed, absolute monarchy, aristocratic and Church privilege, and radical revolutionary dictatorship all stood equally condemned. Instead, liberalism put its faith in *representative institutions:* lawmaking and tax-granting bodies that would enable the citizens (through their elected representatives) to control the actions of governments, to provide governments with the resources they needed to operate effectively, and in general to participate in ruling themselves.

Most supporters of liberalism were to be found among the *bourgeois*—or, as this sector of society came to be called in the nineteenth century, the *middle class.* The middle class consisted of businesspeople, property owners, lawyers, and officials who distrusted the uneducated masses as much as they resented the privileged aristocracy. Hence liberalism was not originally democratic. But liberals firmly believed in freedom, equality, and widespread education, and gradually they opened the door for citizens of all classes, and ultimately women as well as men, to elect (or be elected as) representatives to the lawmaking and tax-granting bodies. In this way, modern democratic government came into existence—or, as it is often called, *liberal democracy.*

The rise of *nationalism* was partly an outcome of Europe's long-standing ethnic diversity, and partly an accompaniment to the rise of liberalism. Ever since the end of the Dark Ages, Europe had been divided among many ethnic groups, each having its own history, customs, and culture, and usually also its own language, territory, and pride in its *nationhood* (pp. 247, 304–307, 398–404). But except in some countries of western Europe, the boundaries of *states*—that is, populations and territories under sovereign governments—were not the same as those of *nations*—that is, self-aware ethnic and cultural groups. The Germans and Italians lived under many small independent rulers, and in the empires of eastern Europe—Austria, Russia, and Turkey—one imperial nation ruled over many subject nations.

To most people up until the eighteenth century, this had seemed a perfectly natural order of things, but from that time onward opinions began to change—mainly as a result of the rise of liberalism. Revolutionary leaders acted in the name of the "people" of England, or of the American colonies, or of France. As a result, the English, Americans, and French came to see themselves not as subjects of kings (even if they kept their monarchies) but as self-governing "nations." The ideal of the self-governing nation then spread to large but divided nations like the Germans, to whom it offered equality with other large nations like the French; and to smaller nations living under imperial rule like the Poles or Greeks, to whom it held out the hope of developing their national lives and cultures in freedom from foreign interference. By the middle of the nineteenth century, the *nation-state* came to seem the embodiment of liberal ideals of freedom and equality, whereas multinational states, or nations divided among many rulers, came to seem unnatural and unfair.

In the seventeenth century and for most of the eighteenth century, the shift to the liberal and nationalist order was very gradual. Britain's rulers emerged from the English Revolution of the seventeenth century as "limited" or "constitutional" monarchs, subject to constant legislative oversight, but they were still effective hereditary kings backed by a powerful class of landowning nobles and country gentlemen. Enlightenment thinkers developed theories according to which society was an arrangement among individuals to secure life, liberty, and property; rulers were agents of society who could be resisted if they overstepped their limits; and checks and balances between different branches of government were necessary to protect the liberty of the people. In the late eighteenth century the American Revolution and Constitution put these ideas into effect in a more far-reaching way than ever before, but America was an ocean away from Europe. Meanwhile, in the seventeenth century absolute monarchy became the normal system of government on the mainland of Europe, and in the eighteenth century many "enlightened despots" felt secure enough to initiate reforms such as religious toleration or widespread education, confident that these changes would not undermine their absolute power (pp. 480–481).

At the end of the eighteenth century, however, the French Revolution brought radical and violent change to the European mainland, and spread it to wherever the French armies marched. Even after France was defeated, sympathizers with the aims and ideals of the revolution in every European country refused to accept that the defeat was permanent, and now that kings and nobles across Europe had experienced the full scale of the revolutionary threat, in the first half of the nineteenth century they sought to meet it with repression and force. Once again, it seemed, as in the time of the Reformation, the entire continent was in the grip of a universal conflict, in which everyone must choose sides.

It was after the French Revolution that the words "liberalism" and "nationalism" first began to be used to describe political movements that stood for clearly defined ideas. Liberalism evolved out of the work of western European thinkers who believed that in spite of revolutionary turmoil, the experience of England, the American colonies, and France held promise of a basic

improvement in human affairs. In central and eastern Europe, reforms introduced by the French conquerors, as well as the struggle against French occupation, had given many nations a brief glimpse of freedom and unity, and
liberal-minded thinkers now began to proclaim the ideal of a world of united
and self-governing nations. On the other side of the ideological divide,
thinkers appeared who had become disillusioned with revolutionary turmoil
and had turned against the ideas of reason and progress. Such thinkers took
up older ideas about the *limits* on the ability of humans (or governments) to
change themselves and the world. They refined these ideas into yet another
general school of thought, which also became a powerful political movement, broadly known as *conservatism*.

Thinkers of all these types were influenced by a wider cultural trend,
which brought about a fundamental shift in the *arts* as well as ideas from the
late eighteenth century onward: that of *romanticism*. The romantic movement began as a rebellion against some aspects of the thought and art of the
Enlightenment: it valued *emotion* and *imagination* above reason, *community*
above individualism, and *spontaneity* above established rules. Poets and novelists, painters and musicians celebrated such themes as the movement and
drama of nature, the passions and torments of strong and sensitive souls, the
horrors of war, or the fleeting joys of youth. They looked for cultural inspiration not only to Greece and Rome, but wherever they could find the values
they admired: to medieval tales of chivalry and enchantment, to the barbarian myths and epics of the Dark Ages, to the music and dancing of peasants
and gypsies, or to Gothic architecture. Artists and thinkers influenced by romanticism were found on both sides of the ideological struggle, depending on
whether they saw the Enlightenment or counterrevolutionary repression as
the greater threat to untamed human fancy and feeling. In this way, romanticism lent additional intensity to the passion with which the struggle was
fought.

Eventually, it was the liberal and national forces that prevailed. In western Europe, the new forces were too powerful to be resisted for long. By
shortly after the middle of the nineteenth century, Britain had evolved
peacefully into a democratic constitutional monarchy, and after several aftershocks of revolution, France had become a democratic republic. In central
and eastern Europe, the rulers had held on to power through international
waves of revolution in 1830 and 1848. But in order to make sure of their subjects' loyalty—and so as to strengthen themselves in their ongoing rivalries
with each other—they had made far-reaching changes in their countries' social and political order. They had at last abolished the ancient institution of
serfdom throughout their territories. In Germany, Italy, and Austria they had
introduced parliamentary institutions. The kings of Prussia and the northern
Italian state of Piedmont had taken the lead in the national unification of
Germany and Italy. And the tsars of multinational Russia were busy encouraging nationalist revolts by Slav and Orthodox subjects of multinational
Turkey.

Convinced believers in the new order were sure that liberal equality, freedom, and prosperity would bring harmony to society, while national unity and self-government brought peaceful diversity to the world. But there were others—both conservatives and even many liberals and nationalists—who were not so sure. Liberal freedom and efficiency might stir up class conflict by benefiting some and leaving others behind. National self-government might generate ethnic rivalries and hatreds. And the modernized states of the nineteenth century, in return for the freedom, equality, and national self-government that they granted their citizens, were able to extract from them greater wartime sacrifices of blood and treasure than absolute monarchies had ever done. Would the liberal and national order live up to the hopes of its believers, or would it bring social, ethnic, and international conflict on a scale never seen before?

THE ENGLISH REVOLUTION: PARLIAMENTARY SUPREMACY AND THE BILL OF RIGHTS

The English Revolution of the seventeenth century arose from a mixture of political, social, and religious tensions. In the wake of the Reformation (pp. 425–430), religious issues continued uppermost in many minds; and, as most of the king's opponents were of Puritan (Calvinist) leanings, the term "Puritan" was attached to the revolution. This revolution clearly was more than a struggle for liberalism, but it shared many of the aims of later liberal revolutions in America and France. Equally important, John Locke's *justification* of the English Revolution contributed to liberal ideology everywhere.

CHALLENGE TO THE DIVINE RIGHT OF KINGS: THE CIVIL WAR AND CROMWELL

Why did absolutism fall into disfavor in England after having been strongly supported since the time of Henry VII (p. 352)? One reason seems to be that the middle class and other commoners had backed the monarch in his efforts to end the near anarchy of feudalism, but once order had been established they were eager to reduce his authority. Tudor despotism died with Elizabeth I in 1603. She was succeeded by her nearest relative, James I of the Stuart family, who was already king of Scotland. (England and Scotland remained separate kingdoms, though ruled by one and the same monarch, down to 1708, when they merged to form the "United Kingdom" of Britain.) James upheld the royal tradition of *divine right* (p. 365), but he was not an Elizabeth or a Henry: he failed to win the personal following they had enjoyed, and Parliament (p. 351) refused to agree to his demands. The House of Commons consisted of elected representatives of the gentry (small to

1485		1603	1642	1660	1714
House of Tudor		House of Stuart	Civil War and Cromwell	House of Stuart Restored	

medium rural landholders) and of middle-class townsmen. Most of them were Puritan Dissenters, and they had no affection for the highly structured Church of England (pp. 428–430). Moreover, they disapproved of James' foreign policies and his extravagance. When he asked them to approve new taxes to support his projects, they stubbornly refused. And so James governed without Parliament during most of his reign.

James' son, Charles I, fared worse. His insistence on his divine right to govern won little response from Parliament. Unable to make Parliament do his bidding on new taxes, he resorted to forced "loans" and to increases of established taxes. Resentment toward Charles was aggravated by what the House of Commons considered his violation of English constitutional traditions that went back to the Magna Carta of 1215 (p. 256). When Charles summoned a Parliament in 1640, after a decade of ruling without one, the stage was set for an open clash between the king and his opponents.

The Long Parliament (as it was later called) proceeded to enact measures against the king's ministers and against the king's exercise of illegal power. When, in 1642, Charles tried to arrest the parliamentary leaders, the House of Commons answered by raising a citizens' army for its own protection. Charles, with a minority of the Commons and most of the House of Lords, then withdrew to Oxford; the rest of the Commons held London and prepared for war.

The loyalties of the English people during the struggle followed no fixed lines of social class or religious affiliation. In the main, however, Charles was supported by the great nobles, the high clergy of the Anglican Church, and the Roman Catholics. Parliament was backed by the bourgeois, by most of the gentry, and by Puritan Dissenters from the Anglican Church. In strictly political terms, the Civil War was a showdown between two rival power groups and two theories of government. The king and his hereditary lords were defending their privileges and the idea of absolute *monarchy*; Parliament, representing the smaller landholders and businessmen, was fighting for rule by a broadened *aristocracy*.

In the test of arms, the parliamentary forces kept control of the chief cities and seaports and enjoyed the support of the navy. On land, their campaigns were fought by a "new model" army, which had been organized by Oliver Cromwell—a landowner, a militant Puritan, and a member of Parliament. The first *citizen army* to be recruited in the era of revolutions, this force consisted chiefly of volunteer yeomen (independent farmers), who disliked royal absolutism and the established Church. Showing Puritan zeal and discipline, Cromwell's army decisively defeated Charles' forces in 1646.

But the victorious coalition could not agree on what to do next. Cromwell and his army fell out with the majority of Parliament over questions of religion and the future of the king. Calvinism replaced Anglicanism as the state religion for a

11-1   King Charles I of England on trial (1649). This contemporary engraving shows Charles (seated at center, with his back to the viewer) facing his judges, with the public (behind him and in the galleries) looking on—a position that no king had ever been in before.

few years, but in 1649 a limited sort of *religious toleration* was adopted. Leadership of the revolution fell more and more upon Cromwell himself. At last he decided that Charles must be executed, on the grounds that he was untrustworthy and attracted "ungodly" persons to his cause. When Parliament balked, Cromwell drove out the members who opposed him. The surviving "Rump" Parliament of some sixty members put the king on trial *(Fig. 11-1)* and had him executed in 1649. It then declared the title and office of king abolished and proclaimed England a *republic* (the "Commonwealth").

The beheading of Charles was a psychological shock to most of the English, who still believed (with Shakespeare) that "divinity doth hedge a king." The execution was the work of a determined minority, and the majority of the nation's subjects recoiled from the deed. With the revolutionaries divided among themselves, Cromwell found that he could maintain orderly government only through strong personal rule backed by the army. He sought to institutionalize his control through several written constitutions, including one that called his government a "Protectorate." But, no matter what the name or outward form, Cromwell ruled in fact as a military despot.

THE RESTORATION OF THE MONARCHY AND THE GLORIOUS REVOLUTION

The Protector (Cromwell) conducted foreign affairs to the general satisfaction of his subjects, and he advanced the interests of the business class by encouraging trade and shipping. But this was not the kind of state that supporters of the Puritan Revolution had wanted. The English learned, as the people of other nations would learn again and again, that revolutions can take unexpected courses; they can be bloody and chaotic—often forcing, at last, a choice by the people between *disorder* and *despotism*.

Sentiment in England swung steadily toward a restoration of the Stuart monarchy (and a "free" Parliament). Shortly after Cromwell's death in 1658, a new Parliament assembled—the first in twenty years to have been freely elected. One of its early acts was to invite the dead king's son, an exile in France, to return as Charles II. He was cheered on his arrival in 1660 by an emotional show of loyalty on the part of his subjects, and the nightmare of regicide (king-killing) and Puritan tyranny faded into the English past. The Restoration, an era of relaxed tensions and enlarged individual freedom, had begun.

Parliament did not intend, of course, to restore divine right. It made clear to Charles that his was to be a *constitutional* government, based on the traditional rights of the crown, Parliament, and the people. Although the Anglican Church became once again the established church, it no longer upheld political absolutism. Bloody revolution and Cromwellism may have been viewed as mistakes, but few desired to turn back the clock to 1600.

Charles II accepted all this on the surface, although he was suspected of having private reservations. Whatever his inner convictions, he could not forget the shadow of exile or the block; hence, he avoided extreme policies. The same cannot be said for his younger brother, who succeeded him as James II. A convert to Roman Catholicism, James raised the fear that "popery" might return to England. Moreover, he antagonized both the Anglican clergy and major factions of Parliament, justifying his unpopular acts by claiming the king was "above the law."

Although his critics were exasperated by James' behavior, they expected that matters would improve after his death. The "heir presumptive" (probable) was his Protestant daughter Mary, the wife of William III of Holland. But in 1688 a son was born to the middle-aged English king, who had him baptized a Catholic. Now faced with the prospect of continued political reaction and "Romanization," the leaders of the Parliament secretly invited William to land military forces in England. After William's landing, James found himself without support and quickly sailed for France. Parliament, alleging that James had "abdicated," then declared the throne vacant and offered it to William and Mary. Thus was the Glorious Revolution of 1688 carried out—glorious because it was decisive and bloodless.

Determined to keep the new rulers in check, Parliament in 1689 passed the Bill of Rights, which declared parliamentary supremacy over the crown and spelled out English civil liberties. This historic measure completed the revolution that had started in 1642. It stated that the king could suspend laws, raise armies, and levy taxes *only* with the consent of Parliament; it also provided for frequent meetings of the lawmakers and unlimited debate within their houses. The Bill of Rights also guaranteed every citizen the right to petition the monarch, to keep arms, and to enjoy "due process of law" (trial by jury and freedom from arbitrary arrest and cruel or unusual punishment). This was a restatement of the guarantees in the Magna Carta (p. 256), but they were now expressed in more specific language.

The triumph of Parliament in 1689 was important for two main reasons. It put an end to absolutism and established a governing aristocracy (of property-owners); at the same time, it strengthened the exercise of individual freedoms for all. The wider enjoyment of civil rights led, eventually, to a demand for wider sharing of political power as well (p. 542). Thus, the Glorious Revolution prepared the way for true *representative government* in England.

LOCKE'S JUSTIFICATION OF REVOLUTION

A by-product of the English upheaval was John Locke's political theory, which would have a profound influence on future revolutions. Locke, as we have seen (pp. 477–478), was in touch with the scientific, philosophic, and political ideas of his day. He approved of Parliament's fight against absolutism and felt that both the Puritan Revolution and the Glorious Revolution were justifiable. In 1690, in order to satisfy his conscience and that of other English citizens—and in order to defend the parliamentary settlement—he published *Two Treatises on Government*. The first treatise (study) rejected the theory of divine right, while the second defended the right of rebellion. Though Locke's political ideas were not original, his second treatise became an ideological handbook for liberal revolutionists everywhere.

Locke believed that the English Civil War could be properly understood and judged only in the broadest context of human society and nature. Like his older contemporary, Thomas Hobbes (pp. 462–463), Locke saw the state in a purely secular light and denied that it had been founded by God. Both insisted that the miserable condition of people in the "state of nature" had given rise to an agreement to establish civil government. Both also shared an *atomistic* view of society, regarding it as a collection of self-serving individuals. Starting from these common beliefs, Hobbes and Locke each attempted to set forth universal rules of political behavior and morals.

But there was an important difference between some of their assumptions. Hobbes reasoned that human aggressive tendencies had made life unbearable under "natural" conditions; hence, he argued, individuals must have turned over *all* their rights to the state as a means of securing order. This being so, people are bound to obey the absolute dictates of their ruler. Revolution, therefore, constitutes a breach of contract as well as a return to chaos.

Locke accepted the theory of "social contract," but he disagreed with Hobbes about its *terms*. He held that all people possess certain "natural rights," just as physical objects possess certain natural properties (mass, density, shape, and so forth). Individuals had *retained* most of their natural rights and powers and had agreed (in the contract) to transfer only *one* power to society: the power to preserve their life, liberty, and property. A society, said Locke, holds this power as long as the society lasts, but it delegates the use of this power to political agents. Should any agent (such as a king) push beyond set limits, the society is free, legally and morally, to *resist*. Who should decide whether a ruler's action is, in fact, a step *beyond* the set limits? *"The people shall judge,"* Locke replied, using as an analogy the relation of a private person to a trustee or deputy. And if, in face of this judgment, a ruler refuses to yield, the people have the ultimate right to resort to *force* — to "appeal to Heaven."

Thus, by building on the ancient Roman ideas of "natural rights" and "natural law" (pp. 139–140), on the seventeenth-century style of reasoning, and on appeals to common sense, Locke constructed a "universal" political theory. Though it rested neither on scientific facts nor on actual historical events, it served as a "myth" (fiction) to justify the acts of the parliamentary side in England's civil war. It justified not only acts of rebellion but even the execution of a king. And Locke's atomistic view of society suited the rising spirit of *individualism*. In the next two centuries of liberal revolution, it is clear how the Lockean "myth" proved useful in the large, historical sense. It was heartily embraced by Thomas Jefferson and other liberal leaders as a "self-evident," absolute truth.

A French Enlightenment thinker, somewhat later than Locke, would also exert an important influence on liberal political thought of the following period. He was the Baron de Montesquieu. A distinguished aristocrat, actively involved in political affairs of the nobility, he was deeply concerned about the dangers of any form of *despotism*. In his famous work, *The Spirit of the Laws* (1748), he argued that there is no single form of government suitable to all times and places. But he insisted that some arrangement of *separation of powers* is essential, in every situation, as a guard against tyranny. Montesquieu thought of England as a model of this principle — with its division of authority among king, lords, and commons, and the *separation* of legislative, executive, and judicial functions of government. These ideas had direct impact on the writing of the United States Constitution (p. 508).

THE AMERICAN REVOLUTION
AND CONSTITUTION

Although he wrote the Declaration of Independence nearly a century after Locke's treatise appeared, Thomas Jefferson formed a direct intellectual link between the English and American revolutions. Jefferson expressed many of the liberal ideas of Locke and the Enlightenment and gave them wider circulation. Liberalism, however, was but one element of the American Revolution of 1776. That rebellion also brought about the first expulsion of a European colonial power, replaced monarchical government with a *republic,* and established the principle and practice of popular sovereignty (democracy). As a result of these achievements, the American Revolution served as a hope and model for later revolutions around the world.

The American Colonies and Their Aspirations

The overseas expansion of Europe had brought English settlers to the North American continent in the seventeenth century. Many were "nonconforming" Christians, seeking freedom from the strictures of the established Anglican Church (pp. 428–430, 499). Most of them, after driving back the Native Americans and carving homesteads from the wilderness, inhabited the thirteen colonies of the seaboard between Nova Scotia and Florida. By 1750, the white population of these colonies (including emigrants from the continent as well as Britain) amounted to about two million. Viewed from London, they made up but one part of a far-flung empire; some thirty chartered colonies and companies, in America and Asia, were then controlled by the king and Parliament. (The total number of Britain's subjects was approximately fifteen million at the time.)

The colonies were considered valuable chiefly for economic reasons—as a source of raw materials and as a market for exports. But the costs to the mother country for defense and administration probably equaled or exceeded the commercial returns. After 1750, therefore, Parliament tightened up the regulation of trade and the collection of taxes. Until this time the colonists had paid little more than the local taxes enacted by their colonial legislatures. They had achieved this "immunity" by means of wholesale smuggling and disregard of the British Navigation Acts. At the same time, they showed little desire to provide for their own military defense. The Americans thereby gained a reputation in England for lawlessness, and Parliament began to suspect that the Americans were unworthy of trust and incapable of self-government.

Not surprisingly, the colonists resented British efforts to collect existing taxes or to impose new ones. This was especially true after 1763, when the close of the Seven Years' War (known in the colonies as the French and Indian War) brought England victory over France. With French power on the North American continent broken, there was no longer a serious foreign threat to the thirteen colonies. Feeling more secure than before, the Americans grew even more defiant toward their absentee rulers.

Parliament cast about for some kind of tax that the colonists would pay, but the objections were so violent that most were repealed soon after their enactment. One exception was a tax on imports of *tea;* Parliament refused to repeal this one, mainly to emphasize its *right* to tax British subjects everywhere. But the Americans refused to admit that right. "No taxation without representation!" became the rallying cry of colonial protest.

English leaders argued in vain that the colonies enjoyed "virtual" representation, since members of Parliament, in theory, represented not individual electoral districts, but national and imperial interests as a whole. Thus, although many English towns, cities, and individuals had no elected representatives in Parliament, it was held that their interests were nonetheless represented there. The argument, though accepted in England at the time, did not impress the Americans. In their own colonial governments, legislators represented *particular* districts. This view of representation was firmly rooted in the American experience, and it now suited the economic interest of the colonists.

The squabble over taxation was only one evidence of the rising antagonism. Actions and counteractions led to a firming up of positions and a heightening of emotions. Though a minority remained loyal to the British flag and British law, most colonists were moving toward the point of no return. They saw themselves as heirs of the Glorious Revolution of 1688 and the British king and Parliament as *tyrants*, who went beyond their legal limits.

The Americans at first sought redress of their grievances, but gradually they began to think of seizing control of their own destiny. The urban middle class took the lead, and soon other groups began to sense that they, too, would be better off under self-rule. They realized that British *mercantilism* (p. 456) would check their own economic development and that, under colonialism, their general well-being would always be subordinated to imperial aims. Thomas Paine, a shrewd revolutionary propagandist, described the situation in a geographical perspective. Using the language of the Enlightenment, he declared that America's subjection to England was "contrary to reason." He went on:

> There is something absurd in supposing a continent to be perpetually governed by an island. In no instance has nature made the satellite larger than its primary planet; and as England and America, with respect to each other, reverse the common order of nature, it is evident that they belong to different systems. England to Europe; America to itself.

Paine did much to advance the cause of rebellion in America. Later he aided the radicals in France and England, thus becoming the first international revolutionist of modern times.

WAR AND THE DECLARATION OF INDEPENDENCE

By 1774, the colonists had begun to commit acts of violence and sabotage (notably the Boston "Tea Party"), and the British responded with tough measures. Parliament passed what Americans called the Intolerable Acts, which closed the port of

Boston and virtually canceled the charter of Massachusetts. The British may have thought that this hard-line policy would bring the colonists to their senses (or to their knees), but it had just the opposite effect. County assemblies were called together in Massachusetts to protest; one of them declared that no one should obey any part of the acts, which it described as "attempts of a wicked administration to enslave America." Shortly thereafter, representatives from all the colonies assembled at a Continental Congress in Philadelphia. There they drew up a statement of grievances and formed an association to cut off all trade with Britain. The conflict of words had given way to "direct action."

When the British governor of Massachusetts ordered its legislature dissolved, the legislators defiantly met again and proceeded to raise a defense force of "Minutemen." This step was, of course, illegal; it brought into existence a condition of armed rebellion. Conciliatory measures were now proposed in Parliament, but it was too late. The first clash of arms occurred in April 1775, when British troops set out from Boston to destroy a reported supply of rebel weapons stored near Concord. They accomplished their mission but suffered heavy losses to sharpshooters on their return march. The war for independence was on.

The Continental Congress reassembled shortly after the skirmish in Massachusetts. The Minutemen around Boston were enlisted as the core of a Continental Army and George Washington, a distinguished officer of the Virginia colonial militia, was appointed its commanding general. The war dragged on for six years. Britain, though a leading European power, was hampered by long lines of communication, uneven generalship, and troubles in other parts of its empire. The colonials suffered from the internal differences that normally divide revolutionists, and the Continental Congress was unable to provide enough troops, supplies, or money. Although the rebels fought bravely and endured severe hardships, they could hardly have won without the aid of foreign powers.

The French monarchy, eager to even the score with Britain after the humiliation of 1763 (p. 504), decided to aid the rebels. From the beginning, the French had sent officers and arms to the Americans, whose first significant victory, at Saratoga, was won chiefly with French weapons. Impressed by the American success in that battle, the French became formal allies and declared war on Britain. Spain and Holland followed, swinging the European balance in the Americans' favor. The surrender of the encircled troops of Lord Cornwallis at Yorktown (Virginia) in 1781, which ended the British military effort, was forced by a French fleet controlling the waters off shore. Two years later, by the Treaty of Paris, the United States of America won recognition as a sovereign territory stretching from the Atlantic to the Mississippi River.

The independence of the new government, as well as its bid for allies, had been formally proclaimed in 1776. In fact, the most memorable achievement of the Continental Congress was its adoption of the Declaration of Independence. Drafted by Jefferson, it aimed to justify the resort to force against Britain and to win support *abroad* as well as at home. It is significant that the preamble gives this reason for publishing the document: "a decent respect to the opinions of mankind. . . ." In 1776 (as today) the influence of foreign opinion on the outcome of a struggle" for independence could not be ignored.

The Declaration of Independence is a masterpiece of revolutionary literature fitted to the American cause. Jefferson omitted any mention of the colonists' reluctance to pay their share of defense costs; overlooked the long story of smuggling, civil disobedience, and provocative acts; and gave no hint at all of the deeper motives of the rebel leaders. He knew that Parliament had been supreme in England since 1689 (p. 502), yet he shrewdly focused his charges of wrongdoing upon the *king*. He did so because the king, in an era of absolute monarchs, could more readily be painted as a tyrant.

The ringing paragraph that links the American Revolution with "universal truths" is a paraphrase of Locke, but Jefferson's version is marked by greater simplicity, clarity, and power. Jefferson declares:

> We hold these truths to be self-evident: That all men are created equal; that they are endowed by their Creator with certain unalienable Rights; that among these are Life, Liberty, and the pursuit of Happiness.—That to secure these rights, Governments are instituted among Men, deriving their just powers from the consent of the governed,—That whenever any Form of Government becomes destructive of these ends, it is the Right of the People to alter or abolish it. . . .

In these few lines, Jefferson sets forth a view of humanity, government, and revolution that remains an inspiration to believers in human dignity, liberal principles, and progressive social change.

THE CONSTITUTION OF THE UNITED STATES

The Americans emerged from their war of independence with relatively few scars. Serious divisions had appeared within the colonies, but they were moderate compared with those of revolutions elsewhere. The fact that the enemy was an *absentee* ruler served as a unifying force among Americans of all classes. Even so, there was a minority of die-hard "loyalists" (loyal to Britain) who opposed the "patriots" (revolutionists). Subjected to confiscation of their property and rough treatment by the majority, some sixty thousand fled to Canada. Their departure eased the internal conflict in the colonies, and most of the émigrés (refugees) did not return to stir up trouble. (Canadian colonists remained loyal to Britain.)

After independence, the most pressing need of the former colonies was to agree on a plan for self-government. Each new state drew up a written constitution for itself, but there was disagreement over what form the *union* of the states should take. The "states' rights" feeling, arising from the experiences of the separate colonies, was very much alive. Many citizens preferred complete independence for their states but grudgingly accepted the idea of a loose union, as provided by the Articles of Confederation. When the Confederation proved unable to meet the common needs of commerce and defense, the states sent delegates to Philadelphia (1787) to revise the Articles. Instead, they drafted a new constitution aimed at forming a closer union.

The federal Constitution, approved after bitter debate in the thirteen states, was the earliest *written* constitution of a major country—and is the oldest still in use. The very act of Americans in framing their own basic law fired the imagination of European intellectuals. Here was Locke's "social contract" made real! Here also was a reasoned statement of the new doctrine of *popular sovereignty* (rule by the *people*). Starting with a clean political slate, the Americans rejected the notion of any privileged persons or bodies. The foreword identifies the sole source of civil authority in its opening words: "We, the people . . . do ordain and establish this Constitution for the United States of America."

The new document also launched a successful experiment in *federalism*, in which individuals hold citizenship both in their state and in the nation. The authors of the Constitution tried to strike a balance between powers delegated to the central government and those reserved to the states. With changing conditions, the balance has had to be readjusted through constitutional interpretation or amendment. Thus, a peculiar tension was built into American politics in 1787, with results not wholly satisfactory to anyone. Nevertheless, federalism stands as a noble endeavor to harmonize the requirements of centralized planning and power with the desire for local control.

The Constitution was, above all, a charter of eighteenth-century liberalism. It followed Jefferson's maxim, "That government is best which governs *least*." Fearing possible tyranny by one person or one body, the framers put their trust in a system of "checks and balances." The best protection against the human urge to power, they thought, is to establish *separate* political authorities and to leave them in jealous competition. Thus, the states were to keep a watchful eye on the *national* power; and within all government units a division of executive, legislative, and judicial powers was established. These particular provisions reflected the influence of the French philosopher of the Enlightenment, the Baron de Montesquieu, as expressed in *The Spirit of the Laws* (p. 503).

Although the Constitution provides defenses against the invasion of individual rights, fears of an overly strong central government continued to be voiced. And so, at the insistence of many citizens, the Bill of Rights was added to the Constitution in 1791. Comprising the first ten amendments, it clarifies and and extends the principles of the English Bill of Rights (p. 502). Strongly supported by church leaders, freedom of worship and freedom from an established church head the list. Every person is also guaranteed freedom of expression, petition, and assembly; the right to keep and bear arms; security of person and home; and due process of law. (These principles have been recognized as the basis for "human rights" demands around the globe in the twentieth century.)

By and large, the liberal principles embodied in the Constitution proved well suited to the self-reliant temper of the American people and to the conditions of life during the republic's first hundred years. With no strong enemies on their borders, and with vast resources to be exploited, Americans were free to exercise their inventiveness and talents. The federal power survived secession and civil war during the ordeal of the 1860s. But great forces were not needed for external defense, for eliminating counterrevolutionary elements, or for restraint of *private* powers. Not until the end of the nineteenth century—with the closing of the frontier, the swelling of population, and the rise of giant industry—did conditions develop that were less suitable to limited government.

THE GROWTH OF AMERICAN DEMOCRACY

The desire of the "founding fathers" to maintain checks and balances was frustrated, from the beginning, by the growth of political parties. This development opened the door to "excessive" power by the people, something the founders had feared. They wished to avoid the tyranny of either one person or many. A majority party, however, by securing control of the various branches of government, could rise to a position of virtual dominance. An early example of the effect of parties was their undoing of the constitutional provision for electing the president. The Constitution calls for the indirect election of the chief executive through a *college* of electors, who are presumably independent. In the first vote for a president, the electors gave unanimous support to George Washington, the hero of the Revolutionary War. But afterwards, the *parties* began to nominate *lists* of electors to be chosen by the voters in each state, and the winning list was expected to vote as a unit for its party's candidate.

The opening up of the country and the exploitation of its resources brought a steady expansion of government activities in the United States. This trend stimulated parties and the spirit and practice of democracy. The relation between *liberalism* and *democracy* requires close examination. After the successful challenge to divine-right monarchy in the seventeenth century, the idea of liberalism had been joined to that of majority rule. Locke and Jefferson both believed that, *within the limits assigned to a liberal government*, the individual must submit to the *majority*. But there remained a persistent tension between liberal and democratic principles. What if the majority seeks to do something that the individual regards as a violation of "unalienable" *individual* rights? On this question, the strict liberal took the side of the individual, while the democrat supported the decision of the majority.

United States history shows, in fact, a progressive narrowing of individual rights and a corresponding growth in the power of the majority. Alexis de Tocqueville, a French observer of American institutions, identified this shift as early as the 1830s. In America, he reported, the *people* truly govern. Public opinion is king; its power applies not only to political decisions but to personal convictions and behavior. Tocqueville saw American democracy as the wave of the future and predicted (correctly) that it would soon extend to Europe and the rest of the world. Though impressed by the vigor and promise of America, he feared that the passion for equality and democracy would at last stifle individual liberty. His prophecy has not been altogether fulfilled, but the role of democratic government has grown enormously, and the Jeffersonian liberal state has long since passed from the scene.

THE FRENCH REVOLUTION: "LIBERTY, EQUALITY, AND FRATERNITY"

The American Revolution helped to spark the French Revolution of 1789, which proved to be the most violent and far-reaching of all the liberal upheavals. Not only did the French Revolution advance liberal ideals; it brought drastic changes in the legal, social, and economic order of France, the largest and most populous country in western Europe. The struggle was intensified by the passionate opposition of privileged groups at home and by the intervention of foreign powers. Even more than the English or American revolutions, it was a watershed in the flow of Western history. As Tocqueville later wrote, "The French Revolution had no territory of its own; indeed, its effect was to efface, in a way, all older frontiers. It brought men together, divided them, in spite of law, traditions, character, and language—turning enemies sometimes into compatriots and kinsmen into strangers. . . ." Not until the Russian Revolution of 1917 was an uprising to have such an impact on the Western world.

THE BOURBON MONARCHY AND THE OLD ORDER

Living as we do in an age of revolutions, we have a special need to understand the nature of social revolts. Scholarly research on the French Revolution, which has been studied more intensively than any other, tells us a great deal about the "anatomy of revolution." What were the main causes, phases, and consequences of the movement that began in 1789?

First, let us survey the background of the rebellion. The splendor of the Bourbon monarchy had dimmed with the passing of Louis XIV, though his heirs upheld the grand style at Versailles (pp. 442–443). While preserving its claim to divine right absolutism, the monarchy grew increasingly ineffective during the eighteenth century. Louis XV was a capable but pleasure-loving ruler, and his grandson, Louis XVI, was well-meaning but indecisive. Humiliating military defeats and the loss of the French overseas empire undermined royal prestige, while wars, extravagance, and insufficient revenues brought the monarchy to the edge of bankruptcy. Louis XVI tried to carry through reforms on the lines of enlightened despotism (pp. 480–481). And his queen, Marie Antoinette, under the influence of the eighteenth-century "cult of nature" (pp. 476–477), had a rustic village built near the lavish palace of Versailles, where on sunny days, she and her ladies frolicked as milkmaids. But when it came to serious changes in taxation and administration, the king was frustrated by the privileged classes, who refused to accept their fair share of the tax burden. Though still capable of occasional action, the monarchy could not exert the absolute authority it claimed. Disclosure of its weakness led to mounting criticism of the government and encouraged the hopes of dissatisfied classes.

The landed aristocrats sought to regain historic rights that had been stripped away by the crown in preceding centuries. Their resurgent spirit expressed itself through the provincial *parlements* (judicial tribunals), which in 1763 vigorously protested attempts by the king to raise property assessments. The Parlement of Paris went further: it referred to the existence of the "fundamental laws" of France and declared that no decree of the monarch was valid until it had been approved by the Parlement. Thus, the Parlement virtually proclaimed itself the "supreme court" of France. The members of this haughty tribunal (and of the provincial parlements) were drawn from noble families and so reflected the desire of the aristocracy to modify royal absolutism in the direction of constitutional government (as in Britain). In short, the nobles hoped to regain some of the powers they had enjoyed in the Middle Ages (pp. 212–213, 242–244).

Other social classes sided with the aristocracy in its challenge to absolutism, feeling that some advantage would fall to them from a reduction in royal authority. The French bourgeois were especially eager to advance their social and political status. Growing in wealth and education, and sensitive to the winds of change, they longed for higher prestige and more active participation in the affairs of state. Through enlarged political influence, they also hoped to do away with the obstructions of mercantilism (p. 456) and reap the fruits of a freer economy.

The peasants, who made up by far the largest part of the population, were little concerned with prestige or politics. Their lot was a hard one, often marked by famine and disease. What they wanted was more land, freedom from ancient dues and services to the nobles, and relief from unfair tax collections. The years 1787 and 1788 were especially harsh for most peasants (and urban laborers). In their despair, they felt that *any* change in the existing order might result in some good. Ordinarily slow to act, they now showed themselves ready to play their part in bringing about change.

THE OVERTHROW OF THE KING AND THE NOBLES

Though a "revolutionary situation" existed in France in the 1780s, it took a special chain of circumstances to set off the revolution. Having failed to get the revenues he wanted by means of existing laws, Louis XVI was compelled at last to seek additional taxing authority. According to tradition, such authority could be granted only by the Estates-General (pp. 349–350). This body, representing the three major *estates* (classes) of France, had not met since 1614. The king's call for the election of delegates in 1788 created a stir of expectation, for if the monarch wanted new taxes he would have to offer something in return to the assembled delegates.

As planning for the meeting went ahead at the royal palace of Versailles, a split opened between the nobles and the bourgeois. The latter were legally commoners—members of the Third Estate. They resented this medieval classification, which lumped them with laborers and peasants; but, as leaders of the most numerous class, they sought greater power for themselves in the Estates-General. They demanded of the government that the Third Estate be allowed to send as many delegates to Versailles as the two privileged estates (clergy and nobility) combined, and they insisted that votes be taken by count of individuals in the *total* body of delegates. They won the first demand, but the Parlement of Paris, to which the voting issue was referred, ruled in favor of the traditional method—*one* vote for each *estate*. It became apparent even before the Estates-General met in the summer of 1789 that rivalry and suspicion between the estates would complicate their dealings with the king.

After the session opened, matters soon came to a head. Unable to persuade the two higher estates to sit and vote with them as one body, the representatives of the Third Estate (most of whom were lawyers) decided to "walk out" of the Estates-General. Stating that they were the only true representatives of the people, they then declared themselves to be the "National Assembly" of France. This proclamation (June 17) was the first act of illegality, for it rested on no actual law. A crisis of decision was thereby thrust upon the king.

Louis, forced to choose sides between the nobility and the bourgeois, sided with the nobility. His initial response was to lock the meeting hall of the building where the Third Estate had been sitting. But the action failed; the Third Estate found another meeting place at an indoor tennis court nearby. There the members swore the "Tennis Court Oath," pledging not to return home until they had drafted a *new constitution* for France. Within a few days the National Assembly was joined by many priests from the First Estate and by some of the nobles. Having failed to persuade the rebels to back down, Louis next tried to intimidate them by a show of force. Toward the end of June, he called some twenty thousand soldiers to Versailles.

The National Assembly was rescued by the people of nearby Paris. As order began to break down throughout the country, people everywhere began to arm themselves for defense against the king's forces. The excitement in Paris, fed by rumors of troop movements, rose higher and higher. Crowds began to roam the streets in search of weapons, and on July 14 they demanded arms from the Bastille. Though the old fortress was no longer of military importance, it was a hated symbol of despotism. When its commander refused to turn over arms, the mob attempted to push its way in. After an exchange of gunfire, in which about a hundred of the crowd were killed, the commander agreed to surrender. Then the mob rushed in, killed members of the small garrison (including its commander), cut off their heads, and carried them on spear points through the city streets.

Thoroughly alarmed, and doubting that his troops would fire on the people, Louis quickly sent his forces away from Versailles. He played for time by pretending to yield to the demands of the Paris mob and the Third Estate. The king recognized a self-appointed citizens' committee as the new city government of Paris and directed the representatives of the privileged estates to sit in the National Assembly. Thus, the revolutionary movement was saved for the time being and was strengthened by a new and powerful influence—the Parisian populace (*Fig. 11-2*).

Violence broke out in the countryside as well. By late July it was rumored that the landlords were collecting hired ruffians to attack the peasants. While many of the nobles were away at the capital, the peasants seized the initiative. During the "Great Fear" of late summer they vandalized the manor houses of the nobles and destroyed the hated records of their required payments and services.

As the king had appeased the Paris populace, the National Assembly now tried to quiet the peasants. Many of the bourgeois, as well as the nobles, held landed

11-2   Women of Paris march on Versailles (1789). This contemporary print shows women
from the city on their way to the king to protest the high price of bread. They are es-
corted by soldiers loyal to the Revolution, and are themselves armed with pikes and a
cannon. Compare with *Fig. 13-2*, p. 627.

estates. Frightened by the disorders in the country, they realized that they would
have to take drastic action in order to save their families and properties. At a single night session (August 4), the National Assembly removed all special privileges
in landed property. Liberal noblemen led the way by surrendering their historic
rights to peasant fees and labor, hunting on farmland, tax exemptions and
advantages, and special courts of law for the nobility. A final decree, approved
overwhelmingly, declared that "feudalism is abolished." Thus, a drastic overturn in
property rights was the first major reform of the National Assembly. The chief
losers were, of course, the nobles; the beneficiaries were the peasants, who now had
a substantial interest in defending the revolution.

Now the National Assembly could turn to its original task: the framing of a
new constitution. Although this effort was to prove trying and divisive, there was
wide agreement on the major liberal principles. Those principles were summarized
in the most influential document of the liberal revolutions: the Declaration of the
Rights of Man and the Citizen. Drafted as a preface to the constitution, it served as
a guide to the new order.

The Declaration was the French counterpart of the English and American
bills of rights. It went beyond them, however, in setting forth specific principles of
government. After stating the "natural, inalienable, and sacred rights of man," it
defined the *duties* of individuals in a society. "Every citizen summoned or seized
according to law ought to obey instantly," but law must be an expression of the
"general will." *All* citizens have the right to participate in the making of law, and
its administration must be the same for all. (This statement, however, was not

generally understood to include women—in spite of some feminist demands at the time.) "The source of sovereignty is essentially in the nation," the Declaration continues; "no body, no individual can exercise authority that does not proceed from it in plain terms."

This emphasis on the "general will" reflected in large measure the influence of the French-Swiss philosopher Jean-Jacques Rousseau. It is ironic that the Declaration, so clearly the product of Enlightenment *rationalism*, also bears the imprint of this *romanticist*. Rousseau had died in 1778, eleven years before the revolution. But his political ideas had stimulated the rebels of his own day and lived on in his writings. Rousseau's *The Social Contract* dealt with the same question of rights and authority that had been treated in differing ways by Hobbes and Locke (pp. 462–463, 502–503). Though his explanations were often unclear, Rousseau claimed that the general will is the sovereign power in organized society.

Upon examination, the "will" of Rousseau turns out to be a vague, mystical notion, bound to "moral principles" and the "welfare of the whole society." The chief difficulty lies in discovering how, in practice, the general will is to be found. His interpreters have set forth three broad possibilities—each connected with a different form of government: the general will can be identified with the *decision of a majority* (democracy); it can be "revealed" by a charismatic *individual* (dictatorship); or it can be determined by a chosen *elite* (one-party rule). Thus, the National Assembly, Napoleon, and the modern authoritarian party could each speak in the name of the "general will" of the people.

Rousseau's ideas were raised against all political institutions that rested on a divine or historical right rather than on the general will. His arguments gave philosophical support to the French Revolution and served to justify the National Assembly's claim to sovereign authority. The planners of the new constitution accepted it as their duty to create a framework of government that would respond to and express the general will of France. But from the beginning there was sharp disagreement on how the framework should be built. Some wanted the new government modeled after that of England, with an upper and lower house and a king with executive and veto powers. Others, fearing that this arrangement would give undue power to the nobility, wanted a single legislative chamber and a figurehead king.

The rising distrust of Louis XVI shifted the balance toward the single-chamber (unicameral) plan. The leaders of the National Assembly were properly suspicious of the monarch's loyalty to the revolution; his brother, the Count of Artois, had already fled the country, along with many noblemen. These émigrés proceeded to urge foreign powers to intervene in France, and Louis himself hesitated to accept either the Declaration of Rights or the Assembly's decrees abolishing feudalism. Demonstrating their doubts about Louis, crowds marched from Paris to the Versailles palace in October of 1789 and compelled him and his queen to move to the city (the palace of the Tuileries).

Moderates in the National Assembly, sensing the coming violence, began to draw back from the revolution. This put increasing power in the hands of radical factions, of whom the most influential were members of the Jacobin Society.

(The "Jacobin" name came from that of a former convent in Paris in which the society met.) Founded in 1789, this society soon had local chapters throughout France. By 1793 it had nearly half a million members and had become virtually a government within the revolutionary government. Serving as propagandists and administrators, the Jacobins were a prototype (model) for the revolutionary parties of the twentieth century.

The constitution completed in 1791 provided for a unicameral legislature and a suspensive veto for the king. (He could only *delay*, not prevent, legislation.) At the same time the well-to-do members of the National Assembly managed to limit the right to vote. Moreover, candidates for the "electoral college," which was to name the legislators and administrative officials, had to be male citizens of substantial property. (Only fifty thousand men qualified as candidates in the first elections.) The reason given for these restrictive provisions was that the great majority of the people were uneducated; the *effect* was to hand control to the wealthy families of the country.

Louis XVI, who was named the titular ("official") head of the new government, had sealed his fate earlier in 1791 by attempting to escape from France. Captured near the northeast frontier and brought back to Paris in humiliation, he thus destroyed any serious hopes for a successful constitutional monarchy. Soon this government foundered, the king was deposed, and a new assembly was called (1792) to draft another constitution. (In the election of these delegates, *all* adult males were permitted to vote.) The new body, named the National Convention, met and proclaimed the (first) French Republic. The Convention governed France during troubled years of reform and war and completed its work in 1795 by approving a constitution for the Republic.

FOREIGN WAR AND INTERNAL DISORDER

Reaction abroad deeply affected the course of the revolution. Whereas outside intervention had assured the success of the American Revolution (p. 506), it had destructive consequences for the French. It stimulated extremism and internal splits within the revolution, and it helped to bring about panic, dictatorship, and, ultimately, military defeat. The conflict between revolutionary France and the rest of Europe broke out in 1792. Some individuals outside France sympathized with the aims and deeds of the revolution, but the most influential groups—the royal and privileged ones—had become increasingly alarmed. Their feeling was strengthened by blood ties with the captive Bourbon king and by warnings from the émigrés. Over a hundred thousand aristocrats had left France, including more than half of the officers of the army; but they hoped to return one day to recover their lost positions and lands.

Foreign sentiment had led to a military threat in the Declaration of Pillnitz (August 1791). In this document, Leopold II of Austria, the Holy Roman emperor, stated that if the other European powers would join him he would use force to restore the Bourbon rulers to their full rights. Busy with matters in Austria, the emperor did not really wish to send troops to France, but his declaration encouraged the émigrés and alarmed the French leaders. It also helped the hand of those in France who wished to *internationalize* the revolution—who believed that the reforms could not be made secure in France unless they were also carried abroad.

The more aggressive revolutionists now pressed for an offensive against the reactionary powers of Europe. They pictured their armies carrying the banner of "liberation" into neighboring lands and uniting with native radicals to overthrow established governments. The desire for military action gained support also from those who believed that war would restore *unity* to France and from those who stood to lose should royalist armies invade the country. The government accordingly declared war on Austria in April 1792, thereby launching a period of continental revolution and war that lasted for twenty-three years.

At first the war went against the French, producing panic and disorder in Paris and the provinces. In the autumn a mob rushed the royal palace of the Tuileries and massacred the king's Swiss Guard. Later a band of enthusiastic army recruits invaded the Paris jails and seized a thousand or more prisoners who had been rounded up as suspected sympathizers with the aristocracy. After mock trials these unfortunates were put to death. The winds of violence, released by the revolution and whipped by nationalist hysteria, now swept across France. When the National Convention first met in September 1792, it faced the immediate problems of dealing with the king, restoring law and order, and conducting the war.

Louis' trial for treason opened a major split between the moderates and the radicals. The leaders of the Convention were all radical Jacobins (pp. 514–515), but they were divided into factions reflecting a broad range of philosophy, interest, and temperament. Louis was voted guilty by unanimous decision, but the order of execution was passed by only a narrow margin. The majority of the Convention members thereby marked themselves as regicides (king-killers); the others were thereafter regarded as halfhearted, even *counter*revolutionary. The seeds of mutual distrust and hostility were thus sown within the revolution, and the rival leaders proceeded to devour one another. The guiding spirit of the Convention, the radical Maximilien Robespierre, ruled over the near anarchy of 1793 and 1794. (Violent uprisings, chiefly in the west and southeast, erupted out of opposition to the Convention's radical measures and the growing concentration of power in Paris.) Revolutionary trial courts were set up around the country to limit lynchings and to stifle local rebellions. Probably as many as forty thousand fell to the guillotines, usually on charges of treason (aiding the country's enemies) or sedition (rebellion against authority). Thousands more perished during the uprisings in the provinces.

As foreign peril declined, internal hysteria declined with it. The National Convention, having declared war on Britain, Holland, and Spain (as well as Austria), approved the drafting of all able-bodied men. (This measure proved to be a fateful precedent for the mass armies of the future.) The French draftees, fired by revolutionary spirit, soon showed themselves more than a match for their enemies. By June 1794, they had turned the tide of battle and were overrunning the Low Countries. Within weeks the foes of Robespierre (both left and right) put an end to his political domination. He was *outlawed* by vote of the Convention and, with many of his associates, was executed.

Rule of Napoleon I

1789		1795	1799			1814
Revolutionary Governments		Directory	Consulate		First Empire	

1804

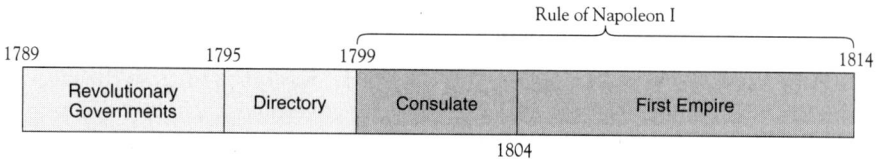

The fall of Robespierre marked the end of the "Terror" and the return to power of the moderates. It was the moderates, chiefly representatives of the well-to-do, who secured the Convention's final approval of the republican constitution of 1795. The government so established (known as the *Directory*) restricted political participation to men of substantial wealth, even fewer in number than those who had held power under the constitution of 1791.

The triumphant bourgeois could well be satisfied with the trend of the revolution, despite its excessive violence and bloodshed. Their liberal principles and their leading political position were guaranteed by the new constitution. Feudal property rights, titles of nobility, and special privileges had been swept away; and the chaotic character of traditional administration had been replaced by self-governing cities and "departments"—units about the size of American counties. Freedom of enterprise had been advanced by the abolition of craft guilds and labor organizations and by the scrapping of the mercantilist regulations of the late monarchy.

The clergy, on the other hand, had seen its wealth and influence sharply reduced. In 1790 monastic orders had been suppressed, and the properties of the Church had been confiscated as a means of financing the revolution. In addition, the clergy had been placed under a Civil Constitution, with *elected* priests and bishops and with salaries paid by the state. These measures provoked not only the anger of most clerics but widespread popular opposition, particularly among women. The clergy, along with surviving members of the nobility, became a continuing source of *counterrevolutionary* activity.

NAPOLEON AND THE REVOLUTIONARY EMPIRE

The bourgeois men of property failed, as they had in 1792, to meet the challenges of national political responsibility. The government of the Directory lacked effective leadership; many sincere reformers had either dropped out of public affairs or had been destroyed in the rivalry of factions. The politicians who remained were largely men of narrow vision and self-interest.

The popular spirit had shifted, too. High hopes had been turned into disappointment, animosity, and bloodshed. Economic conditions had worsened for the poor; families had been torn apart; and mothers, especially, bore a heavier burden of securing food and shelter for their children. Emotionally exhausted by five years of fevered excitement, many citizens fell into a mood of indifference or cynicism. Political officeholders not only failed to inspire but showed themselves lazy, corrupt, and incapable of solving the nation's problems. Challenged from the right by reviving *royalist* sentiment and from the left by the still impoverished urban work-ers, the Directory clung to power only with the aid of the military.

A brilliant young general, Napoleon Bonaparte, was quick to grasp the facts of the political situation. He had first defended the government in 1795 against at-tacks by royalist mobs. (Afterward he boasted that he had dispersed them with a "whiff of grapeshot.") Two years later his troops were called on to enforce illegal measures that had been taken by the Directory, and in 1799 he plotted with some of its leaders to take over the state by a sudden seizure (*coup d'état*). The conspira-tors believed that only a strong government headed by a general could hold off royalism, establish internal order, and defeat France's foreign enemies. Napoleon proclaimed himself "First Consul," a title borrowed from the ancient Roman Re-public (p. 113); later, after receiving a national vote of approval, he proclaimed himself *emperor* (1804). With warm public support, he ruled for fifteen years as a virtual dictator.

Napoleon had made his reputation as a general, but he was more than a sol-dier; he possessed a keen and wide-ranging intellect. Born on the Mediterranean island of Corsica in 1769, only a year after its annexation to France, he had be-come a fervent French nationalist. Though he distinguished himself as an officer of artillery, he would no doubt have remained in the junior grades had it not been for the revolution. But the flight of many aristocratic officers opened the grades above him, and the far-ranging wars of the republic offered him uncommon opportuni-ties. (He once dreamed of conquering Egypt and India.) Owing his rapid advance-ment to the overthrow of the Bourbon monarchy, he heartily declared himself a "son of the revolution."

Napoleon was a master of politics and cunning, but there is no reason to doubt the sincerity of his professed devotion to revolutionary goals. He despised inherited and artificial privilege and was impatient with the inefficiency of the former gov-ernment. He favored *equality of opportunity*, with careers (like his own) open to tal-ent. Interpreting its meaning in his way, he readily embraced the revolutionary slogan of "Liberty, Equality, and Fraternity."

Napoleon was a child of the Enlightenment as well as of the revolution—a skeptic, a rationalist, and a believer in progress. There was a strain of mysticism in him, too, an ever-present faith in himself as a "man of destiny." Viewing himself as above ordinary people, he felt free from ordinary morality. He was the intellectual and moral heir of Caesar, Machiavelli, and Voltaire. With a firm sense of drama and history, he built an image of himself as the creator of a *new* Pax Romana—a *Pax Francica* (French Peace). This image, in turn, was to be transformed into a living myth.

The new master of France had no use for either the old aristocracy or the new democracy. Though his various constitutions gave voting rights to all adult males, the voters elected only lists of candidates, from which his government named the legislators and officials. Napoleon saw to it that only men loyal to him and to his purposes were appointed and advanced in office. The democratic "front" gave satisfaction to the populace and honor to his favorites, but Napoleon himself was the real power. Scornful of the democratic interpreters of

Rousseau (p. 514), Napoleon presented *himself* as the spokesman of the general will of France.

It is inaccurate to conclude that Napoleon snuffed out democracy in France, for it had never existed there before. The great majority of the people—illiterate and uneducated—had enjoyed no political power under either the monarchy or the republic. Napoleon's overthrow of the Directory meant that a non-noble but propertied aristocracy had been displaced by an enlightened despot (pp. 480–481). Declaring a general political amnesty, he invited back to France all the émigrés who were willing to work faithfully for their homeland. He called to his service men of widely varying backgrounds (from royalist to regicide) who would cooperate in consolidating the new order. By and large, every class gained from his statecraft, but his chief helpers and beneficiaries were the bourgeois.

His first task was to secure domestic peace and order. He arranged to have his opponents silenced by means of selective deportations, "exposure" of alleged plots, and the efficient work of his secret police. Catholic disaffection, springing from the earlier measures which had been taken against the Church, was dissolved by a dramatic concordat (agreement) with Pius VII in 1801. In this agreement, Napoleon formally accepted the fact that the Roman Catholic faith was the principal religion of the French, abandoning the attempt of the previous revolutionaries to replace traditional religion with a state-sponsored Deism (pp. 474–475) or "cult of reason." Church seminaries were reopened, and public religious processions were again permitted. Priests who had submitted to the revolutionary Civil Constitution were left to papal discipline, while those who had remained loyal to Rome were recognized as legitimate.

The pope, in return, accepted the new status of Catholicism in France. He dropped Rome's claims to confiscated church property and gave to the French government the right to nominate bishops. He tried, but failed, to eliminate the toleration of all faiths that had been secured by the revolutionary regimes. Although the settlement was criticized by some on both sides of the dispute, it established a peace between state and church in France that lasted for over a century.

Napoleon, privately a nonbeliever, recognized the importance of religion to the people and appreciated the advantage of having the Church on the side of the state. But he would not allow it to be the primary force in the shaping of citizens. The state, through its *own* schools, had to provide for the education and patriotic instruction of the young. He approved the earlier closing of Church schools by the National Convention and put into effect its comprehensive plans for a national educational system. By 1808 his subordinates had completed the structure of state-supported primary and secondary schools as well as public institutions of higher learning. The entire system, supervised from Paris, remains the basis of French education to this day.

Napoleon also carried through the plans of revolutionary leaders for reorganizing French law and administration. His appointed commissions cut through the centuries-old accumulation of rules and regulations and brought to completion the Napoleonic Code. This collection of laws and principles relating to persons and property was the product of a gigantic labor of sorting, eliminating, and condensing. The Code would become the new basis of law in major parts of Europe (and America) and is comparable to the ancient Roman codes that inspired it (p. 140). In later years Napoleon regarded the Code as his most durable accomplishment. While in exile he wrote, "My true glory is not in having won forty battles; Waterloo has effaced the memory of so many victories. What nothing can efface, what will live eternally, is my civil code."

Under Napoleon, the modern techniques of administering a centralized state took shape. The historic provinces of France, the local courts and offices, the administration of justice—all had been swept away by the revolution. Salaried officials ("prefects") responsible to the central government now presided over the cities and "departments" (p. 517). The reform of public administration extended to taxation, expenditure, and money and banking; the day of the *bureaucrat* was at hand and, with it, the equality of citizens before the law. All these changes, along with a grand design for public works, were in keeping with the rationalism (*logical thinking*) of the Enlightenment and with bourgeois ideas of efficiency.

But if Napoleon brought peace, order, and prosperity at home, he caused turmoil abroad. At the very outset of the revolution a sharp tension had developed between France and the rest of Europe. Any revolution, if it is a true revolution, creates such tension, for it is a threat to *established* social systems. The privileged classes of Europe, as we have seen, reacted in fear to the events of 1789; the French leaders, in turn, expected to be attacked. In the warfare that followed, the armies of the revolution extended the frontiers of France to the Rhine River and to central Italy, but the outcome of the struggle was still undecided when Bonaparte took over in 1799.

His first move in foreign affairs was to break the Second Coalition of powers (Britain, Russia, Austria, Portugal, and Naples), which had come together against France. By swift military moves and skillful diplomacy, he had achieved this goal by 1802. For the first time in a decade there was peace between France and its neighbors. But it proved to be only an uneasy truce.

Napoleon, in a position of strength, might have dug in on his advanced lines. The French state now held more territory than the Bourbon kings had dreamed of, and Napoleon pushed its control even farther by bringing Holland, Switzerland, and portions of Italy and Germany under his influence. He could have chosen a defensive military posture, against which his enemies might have struck in vain. But the momentum of the revolution, joined to his own driving ambition, worked against such a strategy. As the heir to what he believed to be *universal* ideals, Napoleon felt he had to *expand* the new order. His political and military moves led to another break with Britain, renewal of the war, and a Third Coalition against France.

Defense of the revolution merged, in Napoleon's mind, with personal and imperial glory, and he began to dream of dominating all of Europe. His genius and the confusion of his enemies brought him near to his goal. But the stubborn defiance of the British and their control of the seas, exhausting warfare against popular uprisings in Spain and Portugal, plus the vast manpower and distances of Russia, brought about his downfall.

A critical defeat for Napoleon was the bloody naval battle off Cape Trafalgar (1805), near the Atlantic entrance to the Mediterranean Sea. Ships of the British admiral, Lord Horatio Nelson, destroyed the French and allied fleets after Nelson himself was killed in battle. Compelled by this loss to abandon plans for invading Britain, Napoleon then tried to bring down the island nation through an economic *blockade*—ordering all ports on the continent closed against British exports. The British took countermeasures, however, and his "Continental System" proved a failure by 1810.

Napoleon's second failure was in Spain, which he invaded in 1807. His troops easily crushed the regular Spanish army, but the people of that country and neighboring Portugal continued to resist the French, using the methods of what they called the *guerrilla*, or "little war." Their tactics were those of ambush, surprise, and retreat before superior forces, and they were backed by the British with money, supplies, and an expeditionary force of regulars. As a result, the guerrillas held down tens of thousands of troops that Napoleon badly needed elsewhere.

Frustrated in the west, Napoleon turned eastward in a land attack on Russia in 1812. This proved to be his fatal blunder. His "Grand Army" of French and allied troops was annihilated (after initial victories) by the terrible winter, disease (typhus), and the stamina of the Russian guerrillas, using similar tactics to those of Spain and Portugal. Napoleon fought more battles after his disastrous retreat from Moscow, but his chance for final success was buried in the Russian snows.

After abdicating as emperor in 1814, Napoleon was banished to the Mediterranean island of Elba. Escaping a short while later, he raised a new army in a foolish gamble against the odds of power. On the battlefield of Waterloo (in modern Belgium) his last minutes as a maker of history ran out. But Napoleon had planted the seeds of a new order in Europe, and the continent would never again be the same.

THE CONSERVATIVE REACTION

While Napoleon was making his dash from Elba in the spring of 1815, the victorious powers were assembled at the glittering Congress of Vienna. Here the crowned heads of Europe and their chief ministers were trying to restore the continent to what it had been before the revolutionary disturbance. They were chilled by the news that the Corsican was once more at large. For the aristocrats of Europe viewed Napoleon not as a liberator, but as a vulgar upstart, a destroyer of the culture they were privileged to enjoy. A sigh of relief passed through Vienna when, after Waterloo, "that madman" was again shipped away—this time to the far-off isle of St. Helena, in the South Atlantic Ocean.

METTERNICH AND THE "CONCERT OF EUROPE"

Although there were many signers of the settlement of 1815, the management of the treaty was in the hands of the four major powers that had brought about

Napoleon's defeat: Britain, Russia, Prussia, and Austria. Prince Klemens von Metternich, the chief minister of Austria, was the leading spirit of the conference. An aristocrat of distinguished family, he had been a career diplomat in the service of the Habsburg dynasty (pp. 352–353). He had demonstrated his shrewdness when Napoleon was at the height of power (1810) by arranging a marriage between the conqueror and Maria Louisa, daughter of the Austrian emperor. (At the same moment, though Austria was formally at peace, Metternich was working secretly for a new alliance against France.) Then, after Napoleon's disastrous defeat in Russia, Metternich threw Austria's weight against him. Though beaten many times by the French, Austria thus came out of the wars in a victor's role; and Metternich, to clinch the advantage, persuaded the allies to hold the peace congress in Vienna, the Austrian capital.

Metternich's cunning was matched by that of the clever Prince Talleyrand. Talleyrand was loyal only to himself and to France. He had served as a bishop under Louis XVI, as a statesman of the revolution, and as Napoleon's foreign minister. When it appeared that the French emperor was overreaching himself, Talleyrand offered secret aid to Napoleon's enemies abroad, thereby preparing a place for himself in the postwar government. When the emperor fell, Talleyrand urged the victors to restore the Bourbon rulers in France; this, he explained, would follow the principle of "legitimacy" (legality). He hoped, by applying that principle, to hold for France the territories it had possessed before the revolution.

The allies accepted the principles of *legitimacy* and *restoration*. The royal succession of France fell to the eldest surviving brother of the executed king, who assumed the title of Louis XVIII. (The late monarch's young son, who had died in 1795, was considered by the royalists as Louis XVII.) The restored monarch, having lived as an émigré in England, was brought back to Paris in 1814 by courtesy of the victors and at once rewarded Talleyrand by appointing him foreign minister.

At Vienna, Talleyrand played skillfully on the differences among the four principal victors, thus giving France, the defeated nation, a role in the settlement. The chief concerns of the conference were to restore, so far as practicable, the legitimate holdings of all titled rulers and the European balance of power. That balance, which had been established by the Peace of Westphalia *(map, p. 454)*, had aimed to secure the independence of European states by preventing one or more of them from gaining too much power. In the course of the Vienna conference, for example, Talleyrand joined Metternich and Lord Castlereagh (of Britain) in a secret pledge to go to war should Prussia and Russia carry through their joint plans for expansion in central Europe. When word of the agreement leaked out, a compromise plan was proposed and accepted.

The Congress of Vienna by no means restored the borders of Europe exactly as they had been before 1789; it proved territorial *compensations* for those states that had contributed the most to toppling Napoleon. Russia, for example, was allowed to take Finland from Sweden, and Sweden was awarded Norway in exchange. (Norway regained its independence in 1905.) The redrawn map of Europe *(map, p. 523)* was to remain in effect, save for minor alterations, for half a century. The most unstable boundaries proved to be those in central Europe. There, Napoleon

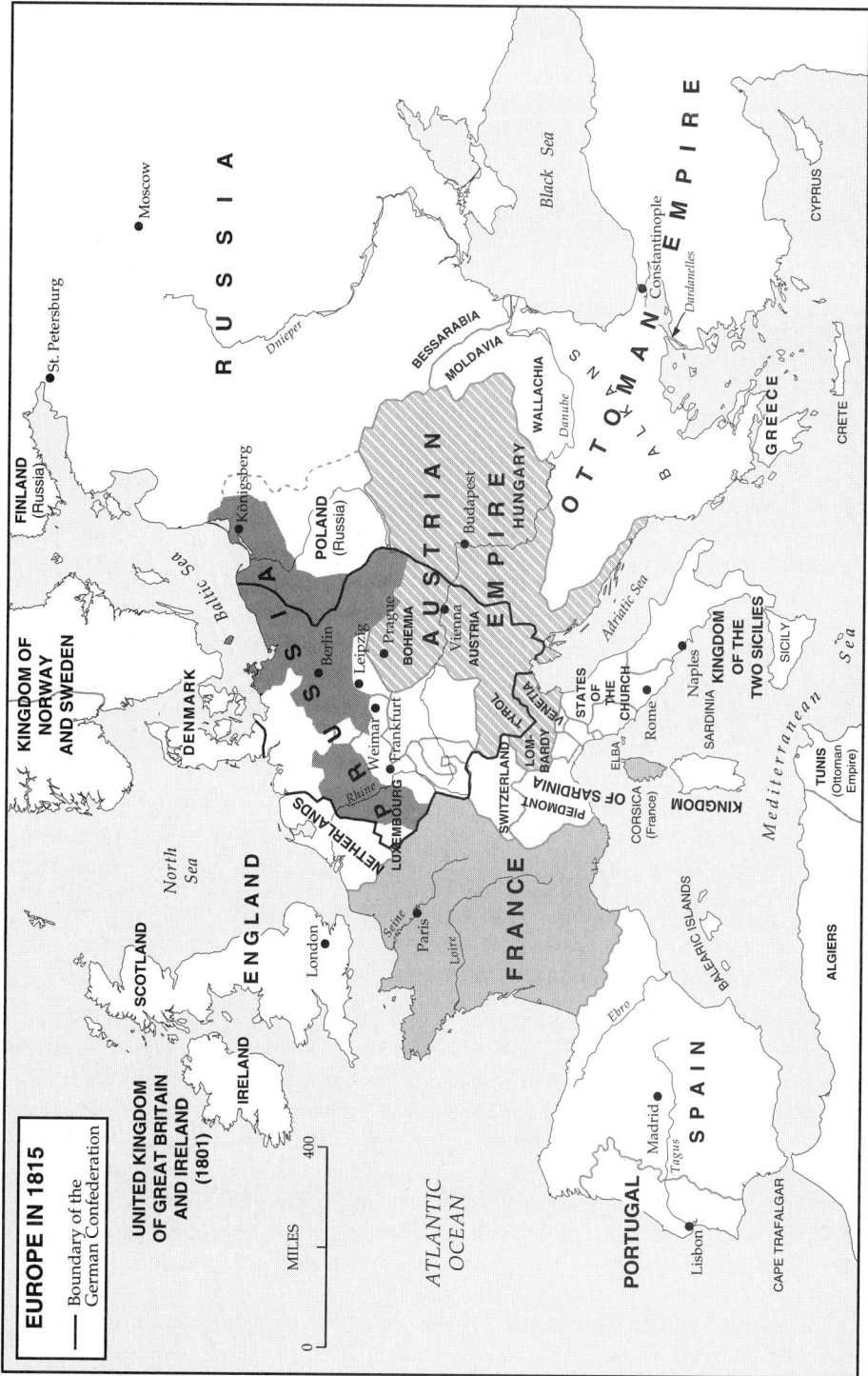

EUROPE IN 1815

— Boundary of the
German Confederation

UNITED KINGDOM
OF GREAT BRITAIN
AND IRELAND
(1801)

MILES

0   400

ATLANTIC
OCEAN

PORTUGAL

SPAIN

Madrid

Lisbon

Tagus

Ebro

CAPE TRAFALGAR

BALEARIC ISLANDS

ALGIERS

Mediterranean   Sea

TUNIS
(Ottoman
Empire)

SARDINIA

CORSICA
(France)

KINGDOM
OF
SARDINIA

PIEDMONT

ELBA

Rome

STATES
OF
THE
CHURCH

Naples

KINGDOM
OF THE
TWO SICILIES

SICILY

VENETIA

LOM-
BARDY

Adriatic Sea

SWITZERLAND

TYROL

FRANCE

Paris

Seine

Loire

Rhine

NETHERLANDS

LUXEMBOURG

Frankfurt

Weimar

BOHEMIA

Prague

AUSTRIA

Vienna

Leipzig

Berlin

P R U S S I A

Königsberg

DENMARK

North
Sea

London

ENGLAND

SCOTLAND

IRELAND

KINGDOM OF
NORWAY
AND SWEDEN

FINLAND
(Russia)

St. Petersburg

Baltic Sea

POLAND
(Russia)

Budapest

HUNGARY

A U S T R I A N   E M P I R E

BESSARABIA

MOLDAVIA

WALLACHIA

Danube

Dnieper

R U S S I A

Moscow

Black Sea

O T T O M A N   E M P I R E

Constantinople

Dardanelles

B A L K A N S

GREECE

CRETE

CYPRUS

had given the final blow to the Holy Roman Empire in 1806 and had merged many of the smaller German states into a league of minor kingdoms (Confederation of the Rhine). The Congress kept this general arrangement, which was joined by Austria and Prussia and renamed the German Confederation. Subject mainly to Austrian control, this grouping forestalled for the moment Prussian desires for dominance in Germany.

Metternich was realistic enough to know that he could not completely undo the effects of the French Revolution. In France, the restored King Louis felt it necessary to grant a constitution that made the country a *limited* monarchy. The legal, administrative, clerical, and educational reforms of the revolution were retained. And beyond the borders of France the ideas of liberalism could not be altogether erased. Still less could Metternich prevent the rising sentiment of *nationalism*, which had been strengthened by the revolution's stress on "fraternity" and by Napoleon. The people of Germany and Italy, especially, were impressed by the power and accomplishments of the French nation-in-arms and by the psychological lift that accompanied national solidarity. Their hatred for the conquerors (which followed their initial admiration of the French as liberators) also stimulated their own sense of cultural identity. All across Europe, patriotic societies arose to champion the cause of national unity and independence.

But, for the time being, liberal and nationalistic movements were kept down. The privileged classes and the rulers of states with mixed nationalities saw them as threats to their interests. They agreed at Vienna to guard closely against them. Metternich arranged a "Concert of Europe" (in actuality, a Quadruple Alliance of Austria, Prussia, Russia, and Britain) that would use diplomacy and force against moves to change boundaries or social systems. Accordingly, several conferences ("congresses") of those states under Metternich's guidance, were called to meet threats to the established order. This "Metternich System" thus provided a type of collective security for the nations of Europe. It worked well for a while (until the middle of the nineteenth century), preserving order and forcing both liberal and national movements underground.

The Rejection of Revolution and Rationalism: Burke

Opposition to liberal ideas found wide support among ordinary people, as well as intellectuals. A longstanding division within Western culture had been deepened by the Enlightenment and widened by the Revolution. For generations afterward, those who stressed science and reason, equality and democracy, stood in opposition to those who stressed tradition and sentiment, aristocracy and authority. While some people straddled this broad division, most felt a sense of identification with one side or the other. Throughout the nineteenth century both sides appeared to make advances. The liberals succeeded in changing political, economic, and social institutions, and the conservatives made their influence felt in philosophy, the arts, and the general mood of Europe.

During the period immediately following 1815 the conservatives enjoyed a resurgence on all fronts. This was natural enough, for Napoleon, who personified the triumph of the revolution, had fallen. Victory had passed to the defenders of privilege and the old order, and the *ideals* of the Enlightenment had been dimmed by the *realities* of revolution, politics, and war. Many who had sympathized with the ideals now recoiled from the bloody cost of attempting to put them into practice.

One of the ablest spokesmen of the *conservative* point of view was the thinker and statesman Edmund Burke. As a British observer of French affairs, he had been one of the first to become alarmed by the events of the revolution. Opposing from the beginning the underlying principles of the revolution, he had feared that those ideas might win favor in his homeland. His *Reflections on the Revolution in France* appeared in 1790 and has remained to this day an important statement of conservative principles.

Burke's first point of attack was the doctrine of natural rights, which John Locke (p. 503) and the revolutionary leaders had used to justify their actions. David Hume, a skeptical Scottish philosopher, had already demolished the proofs for natural law in *A Treatise of Human Nature* (1740). Though Burke agreed that one might speak of natural rights in an *abstract* sense, he insisted that this had no bearing on the actual distribution of authority in a civil society. The liberties of the English people, wrote Burke, were those that had been slowly forged in the fire of history; he saw them as part of a specified "inheritance," handed down from generation to generation. And that inheritance was by no means equal for all. The king, the lords, and every other group within the English social body had the right to enjoy the particular privileges and liberties passed on to it from "a long line of ancestors." Burke thus expressed his belief in aristocracy and attacked efforts made in the name of equality to interfere with "legitimate" privilege.

Burke warned against undue reliance on human reason. He felt that each person's private stock of reason is pitifully small and therefore a poor guide to action. He much preferred the wisdom deposited in the "general bank and capital of nations and ages"—by which he meant *tradition*. It is arrogant for reform-minded thinkers, said Burke, to try to reconstruct institutions out of their own minds; such "progress" as might result from their efforts would prove a cruel disappointment. It is far better, he concluded, for people to follow the "prejudices" (established convictions) that bind them to tried and tested institutions.

Burke reserved his bitterest scorn for the Lockean-Jeffersonian belief in the right and benefit of revolution. Denouncing the social *atomism* of both Hobbes and Locke (p. 503), he thought of individuals as parts of a larger organism—*society*. He saw the state as a divine creation, binding past, present, and future generations. He referred to it as a *partnership* embracing all human purposes and not to be broken by individual human wills.

The state, being sacred, must be looked upon with awe and reverence. It should not be "hacked to pieces" by would-be innovators; such recklessness can lead only to anarchy. And, Burke felt, the absence of firm social control is "ten thousand times worse" than the blindest and most stubborn government. A devout Anglican, he held to the doctrine of Original Sin and rejected the Enlightenment faith in human goodness and progress. Only by strict social discipline, he believed, is the individual made decent and civilized. And once restraints are broken, people fall back to beastlike behavior. Thus, Burke argued, revolution leads to an intolerable chaos, which can be ended only by some form of despotism.

Burke did not think, however, that institutions should remain frozen. His view of society as an *organism* led him to think in biological terms. Thus, useless growths should be cut off and new shoots and branches allowed to develop. He was, therefore, a *flexible* conservative. He even stated that conditions in a given society might become such that a resort to revolution would be permissible. But it should never be a *calculated* action. Mystically (and dangerously) he declared that the justification for revolution must be "the first and supreme necessity only, a necessity that is not chosen, but chooses, a necessity paramount to deliberation, that admits no discussion, and demands no evidence. . . ." In other words, he placed his ultimate reliance on *intuition* (*inner* conviction), thus giving his approval to *irrational* social action.

Although Burke struck his critics as contradictory, hypocritical, and dangerous, he gave a classic expression of conservative thought, scoring hits on key points in liberal doctrine. Other writers soon joined in the assault. The English clergyman Thomas Malthus attacked the idea of human perfectibility, which had been put forward by some eighteenth-century writers (pp. 478–479). Noting the general misery of the poor, Malthus found the explanation in the pressure of population growth. Because of the sexual urge, said Malthus in *An Essay on the Principle of Population* (1798), people tend to increase faster than food supplies. Population growth is held down mainly by the "positive checks" of starvation, disease, and war. Seeing no way out of this condition (save the unlikely prospect of sexual restraint), Malthus predicted continued suffering for the human race. And without a favorable balance between food and people, the material foundation for happiness (and perfectibility) is missing. Malthus thus called attention to one of the root problems facing the modern world.

A New Philosophical Synthesis: Kant, Hegel

The conservative reaction was also strong on the European continent, where the intellectuals of the Enlightenment were held responsible for the unhappy events of revolution and war. After 1815 liberal writers and critics were regarded with official hostility and general suspicion. The frequent persecution of authors and the suppression of their works were products of the haunting fear of new social upheavals. Defenders of the restored order concluded also that the weakening of religious faith had eased the way to social subversion. They therefore encouraged the revival of religious fervor that had arisen as a reaction to the secularism of the Enlightenment and the revolution. The Roman Catholic Church, traditionally conservative, played a leading role in this renewal of piety, morality, and respect for authority.

European philosophy was affected even more deeply than religion by the reaction against eighteenth-century thought. A German professor, Immanuel Kant, was a key figure in the shift from the outlook of the Enlightenment to that of the nineteenth century. Born in East Prussia, he spanned in his long lifetime

(1724–1804) the confident period of science and rationalism as well as the aftermath of disenchantment. His keen, analytical mind, coupled with a profound moral and religious sense, gave his philosophy its special shape.

Deeply impressed by the achievements of Newtonian science (pp. 469–471), Kant retained much of the rationalist spirit and methodology. However, he set limits on its use and marked off areas of knowledge where religion and moral conviction applied. It was Hume's skepticism (p. 525) that first awakened Kant to the limitations of reason and observation as means of knowing. Hume had argued that science has no way of *proving* causal relationships; it can only note that a certain event is *preceded* by another. This relationship in time and space may be witnessed over and over again; yet the idea of *causation* remains a suggestion of the mind, not a proven fact.

Kant carried the point further, asserting that even "perceived objects" are in large measure a reflection of the mind. Locke had previously stated that knowledge comes chiefly from sensation—the result of external stimuli striking our sensory mechanism and registering upon our consciousness. But Kant was critical of this simple explanation. He insisted that our minds, *independent of experience,* establish certain internal structures, which impose their patterns on our perceptions. For example, we have the concept of "time"—which cannot be perceived and is therefore mental rather than experiential. Yet this concept, along with many others, controls and puts in order all our observations.

From this Kant concluded that scientific knowledge, though highly useful, is not knowledge of the "real" world but a creation of the human mind, drawn from bits of observation. While science thus provides a restricted means of knowing about material things, it cannot even ask the questions that go *beyond* material things. On such issues as the existence of God, immortality of the soul, and moral responsibility, science is mute. In these vital matters, Kant declared in his *Critique of Pure Reason* (1781), the individual must rely chiefly on *conscience* and *intuition.* Such teachings found ready response in Germany, where the Enlightenment (*Aufklärung*) had been comparatively weak. Cultural traditions there were more favorable to romantic hopes, mysticism, and faith.

Following Kant's lead, German philosophy in the nineteenth century reached its fullest development in the work of another professor—Georg Wilhelm Friedrich Hegel, an energetic and imaginative man who helped make the University of Berlin a center of philosophic activity. In response to the doubts and contradictions current among serious thinkers, he attempted nothing less than a complete reconstruction of formal thought. He sought a new methodological approach that would enable him to reconcile opposing philosophic tendencies and bring them into a unified system. He found that approach in the *historical method.*

Hegel steeped himself in the study of history, convinced that true understanding of any subject—whether politics, art, or religion—can be found only through examining its historical development. (This idea came to be known as "historicism.") He saw the general history of an age as more than a collection of events; politics, art, and religion are related parts of a cultural *whole*—guided by a unifying

Reason, or Spirit (*Zeitgeist*). The scholar must employ a talent for synthesis as well as analysis in order to bring historical truth to light. This truth, claimed Hegel, is the fulfillment in time of a divine and logical *Idea*.

The Idea may be invisible to most individuals—before it takes shape as historical *happening*. Hegel illustrates this point by declaring: "Great revolutions which strike the eye at a glance [like the French Revolution] must have been preceded by a quiet and secret revolution in the *Spirit* of the age (*Zeitgeist*), a revolution not visible to every eye. . . . It is a lack of acquaintance with this spiritual revolution which makes the resulting changes astonishing."

Hegel's thought is related to Greek philosophical theories during the classical age (pp. 82–85). The Christian philosopher Augustine had also seen history as the unfolding of divine will (pp. 192–193). Hegel's special contribution was his development of the notion of *dialectic* in history. Like Augustine, he saw the continual struggle between opposing forces as the dynamic (power) behind events. But he defined those forces as opposing *ideas*, which become ever more inclusive at successive stages of the struggle. The dominant idea at any given stage he defined as the *thesis*, which (because it is imperfect and incomplete) calls forth a negative or opposing idea—its *antithesis*. In the conflict between the two, neither is entirely destroyed; the opposing elements are reconciled and absorbed into a higher idea, the *synthesis*. (This "Hegelian triad" was a *model* of the dialectical process—not always perfectly fulfilled in the flow of history.)

As an example of his theory, Hegel suggested that the idea of oriental *despotism* had been opposed by the Greco-Roman idea of limited freedom (*aristocracy*); both were being superseded by the German-Christian idea of *universal freedom* under monarchy. His concept of freedom was an *ordered* freedom governed by law. Hegel in this sense glorified the *state* and taught that it was approaching perfection in the Prussian monarchy of his day (pp. 457–458). Though discarding the eighteenth-century concept of progress and reform as naive, he regarded the dialectic of history as leading surely to a freer and happier condition for humanity. (This condition would not include equality for women, whom he regarded as, by nature, inferior to men.)

Since Hegel saw the development of *ideas* as the guiding force and the underlying reality of history, he is usually classified (like Plato) as a philosophical *idealist*—as distinguished from a *materialist*. "Whatever is rational is real, and whatever is real is rational." But he did not deny material existence; he merely subordinated it to the superior reality of ideas and logic. Human reason, in the eighteenth-century sense, he discounted, putting in its place the Reason of history. Hegel insisted that history provides its own solutions to problems that even the wisest of thinkers can understand only dimly.

The human individual, so precious to the philosophes (pp. 472, 479), was reduced by Hegel to a relatively minor role in history. Great leaders, he thought—in fact, all people—are instruments of the *dialectic*. Individuals, acting upon their own purposes and passions, can nevertheless accomplish notable deeds; political genius consists in identifying oneself with a *developing* idea. In this way he would explain the greatness of a Caesar, a Jefferson, or a Napoleon.

Although Hegel stressed the role of logic in historical development, he was at the same time both religious and mystical. He was not a practicing Christian, but he viewed religious doctrines and rituals as natural expressions of the total life of an age. (He saw *Christian* teachings as agreeing with his own philosophy.) Hegel's thought was indeed a blend of many elements that had previously been regarded as contradictory. It assigned value, on the one hand, to science, reason, and individual freedom—and, on the other hand, to faith, intuition, and authority. As might be expected, this comprehensive philosophy had a broad appeal: Hegel's books provided stimulus and support for a wide range of ideas. After his death (1831), his disciples branched off in many directions.

THE ROMANTIC SPIRIT IN LITERATURE, ART, AND MUSIC

The reaction against the Enlightenment showed itself not only in philosophy but also in the arts, where it was to take on the name of "romanticism." The romantic movement included an extraordinary variety of creative expressions in the life and work of individual artists, some of whom were political and social conservatives, while others were supporters of liberalism.

APPEAL TO THE HEART: ROUSSEAU

The pioneer of romanticism was Jean-Jacques Rousseau, whose impact on the French Revolution we have already mentioned (p. 514). Though he lived during the Enlightenment, Rousseau's career was in part a revolt against the dominant thought of his age. His style and values became increasingly popular after his death, causing him to be known later as the "father of romanticism."

A man of little formal education or personal discipline, Rousseau had reacted spontaneously against the eighteenth-century emphasis on reason and science. Through a stormy career, which we know largely through his own *Confessions*, he found time to write hundreds of letters, as well as essays and books. His attacks on rationalism struck home not because he wrote from deep knowledge, but because of the power of his language and his appeal to *inner* experience. He wrote, he said, from the heart (and to the heart). Science, he declared, gives knowledge to people that they are better off without. The only knowledge worth having is knowledge of virtue (moral goodness)—and for this, science is not needed. The principles of virtue are "engraved on every heart."

The appeal of Rousseau was due chiefly to his intense sentimentalism. Readers who were unmoved by the theories of science and philosophy responded warmly to his emotional outpourings. In his novel *The New Héloïse* (1761), the hero is madly in love with one of his pupils, but she must marry another. The two frustrated souls experience many temptations and torments that end only after the death of the heroine. The theme of passion and suffering, of morbid self-examination, became a mark of romantic prose and poetry in the nineteenth century.

Another theme of *The New Héloïse* is Rousseau's criticism of sophisticated society and his glorification of nature. The hero of the novel seeks relief from his anguish by wandering through a wilderness. This provides the author with an opportunity to fashion eloquent word pictures of lakes, mountains, and flowers, which inspired such romantic nature poets as William Wordsworth. Rousseau's romantic worship of wildlife also inspired the "back to nature" movement of the nineteenth and twentieth centuries, with its love of hiking and camping as ways of bringing one nearer to earth, rocks, and scenery unspoiled by human beings.

Rousseau's individualism and his rejection of imposed patterns of behavior are best expressed in his famous *Émile* (1762). This is not really a story but an account of a proposed type of education for life. From infancy to manhood, the fictional Émile is cared for and taught in a manner contrary to the educational practices of the eighteenth century. Rather than forcing the boy into a succession of studies corresponding to the "knowledge" of the day, his teacher encourages Émile to *learn for himself*. When the need or desire strikes him, the youngster asks for instruction in reading and writing and in nature studies. Meanwhile, he lives a spare, simple, athletic life in the country. The teacher refrains from punishing his pupil for destructive acts, confident that such errors will be corrected through the boy's own experience of consequent loss. There are no naturally bad boys; real vices are learned from "civilized" elders.

Rousseau held that girls as well as boys deserved a sound education. But it must be suited to the female role in life, which he sharply distinguished from the male role. In *Émile*, he states that girls should be taught only what they will need as women, that is:

> To please men, be useful to them, and make themselves loved and respected by them; to educate them when they are young, care for them when grown, counsel and console them, and make life agreeable and sweet to them. . . . The search for abstract and speculative truths, principles, and scientific laws is beyond the capacity of women; all their studies therefore ought to be of a practical sort.

There is much of Rabelais (pp. 398–399) in Rousseau's ideas about educational methods, but Rousseau wrote seriously rather than playfully. His *permissiveness* appealed to romantic individualists and impressed a number of educational reformers. Rousseau's religious sentiments, too, influenced succeeding generations. His was a romantic brand of Deism, rejecting theology and sacred books. As taught to Émile (at the appropriate time), this religion consisted of a simple faith in God and immortality. All that needs to be known about the deity and his commandments, wrote Rousseau, can be found in one's heart and in the study of *nature*.

POETS OF NATURE AND HUMANITY: WORDSWORTH, GOETHE

Rousseau's insistence on the divinity and beauty of nature was echoed by the lyric poets of the nineteenth century, especially in England. Lyric poetry, as a literary form, traces back to ancient Greece—to Solon and Sappho (pp. 87–88). It was a perfect means of expression for the romantic writers, who desired to tell others of their innermost feelings and visions. William Wordsworth was one of the early romantics; his most moving verses deal with the excitement and meaning of wild nature. Schoolchildren of many generations have recited:

> I wandered lonely as a cloud
> That floats on high o'er vales and hills,
> When all at once I saw a crowd,
> A host, of golden daffodils.

But Wordsworth sensed something beyond the colors and movements of a landscape. His perceptions of nature opened the way to moral and spiritual insights. As he confessed in his "Lines Composed a Few Miles above Tintern Abbey" (1798):

> . . . Therefore am I still
> A lover of the meadows and the woods,
> And mountains; and of all that we behold
> From this green earth; of all the mighty world
> Of eye, and ear, — both what they half create,
> And what perceive; well pleased to recognise
> In nature and the language of the sense,
> The anchor of my purest thoughts, the nurse,
> The guide, the guardian of my heart, and soul
> Of all my moral being.

Wordsworth shared Rousseau's contempt for formal learning as well as his passion for nature. In "The Tables Turned," Wordsworth wrote:

> Books! 'tis a dull and endless strife:
> Come, hear the woodland linnet,
> How sweet his music! on my life,
> There's more of wisdom in it.

●   ●   ●

> One impulse from a vernal wood
> May teach you more of man,
> Of moral evil and of good,
> Than all the sages can.

> Sweet is the lore which Nature brings;
> Our meddling intellect
> Misshapes the beauteous forms of things —
> We murder to dissect.

Enough of Science and of Art;
Close up those barren leaves;
Come forth, and bring with you a heart
That watches and receives.

Beauty, youth, and rebellion were common themes of three other poets—
Keats, Byron, and Shelley—each of whom died young. John Keats saluted the ancient Greek ideal of beauty in a poem honoring a painted vase ("Ode on a Grecian
Urn," 1820). Addressing this classical work of art, Keats concludes with these
words:

When old age shall this generation waste,
    Thou shalt remain, in midst of other woe
Than ours, a friend to man, to whom thou say'st,
    "Beauty is truth, truth beauty,"—that is all
    Ye know on earth, and all ye need to know.

Lord Byron (George Noel Gordon) lived a turbulent life of passion and adventure, corresponding to the romantic quality of his writings. He died in 1824 at the
age of thirty-six while taking part in the Greek war for independence from the
Turks (p. 540). His famous poem, *Don Juan*, includes a stanza (Canto IV:12) that
explains Byron's admiration for youth and his contempt for life "after thirty":

"Whom the gods love die young" was said of yore,
    And many deaths do they escape by this:
The death of friends, and that which slays even more—
    The death of friendship, love, youth, all that is,
Except mere breath; and since the silent shore
    Awaits at last even those who longest miss
The old archer's shafts, perhaps the early grave
Which men weep over may be meant to save.

Byron's young friend, Percy Bysshe Shelley, also lived an unconventional
life—devoted to the cause of unrestricted personal freedom. Expelled from Oxford
University because of his open profession of atheism (pp. 474–475), Shelley continued to rebel against all forms of authority. He spent his last years in Italy, where
he composed his most eloquent poems. In one of these ("Hellas," 1822), he ends
by expressing anguish over the human sufferings of the past and hope that a better
world may be dawning (signaled by the Greek war for independence):

Oh, cease! must hate and death return?
    Cease! must men kill and die?
Cease! drain not to its dregs the urn
    Of bitter prophecy.
The world is weary of the past,
Oh, might it die or rest at last!

Shortly after writing this poem, at age thirty, Shelley was drowned while sailing in the Mediterranean Sea.

Shelley's young wife, Mary Wollstonecraft Shelley, survived him. She, too, was a romantic writer, and an active feminist. (Her mother, Mary Wollstonecraft, had written A *Vindication of the Rights of Woman* in 1792 as an answer to the sexist views of Jean-Jacques Rousseau.) Mary Shelley's best-known book is *Frankenstein*, the story of a medical student who creates and brings to life a manlike monster. Her work cut a bold pattern, borrowed by countless authors afterward in the making of "horror" stories, plays, and films.

Though romantic writers sometimes focused on themes of horror, mystery, and death, they more often wrote about broader human experiences. One of the most popular prose writers in Britain was Sir Walter Scott, whose works made him a Scottish national hero. He created the *historical novel*, choosing the Middle Ages or the turbulent border country between Scotland and England as the setting for many of his books. Novels such as *Waverley* (1814) and *Ivanhoe* (1820) show the drama, color, and imagination that marked his best romances.

In Germany the leading literary figure was Johann Wolfgang von Goethe. Born in the middle of the eighteenth century, he grew up during the Enlightenment and lived on into the age of romanticism. Goethe came from a well-to-do family of lawyers and administrators; his "conversion" to romanticism took place while he was studying law at Strasbourg. He later became a member of the court of Saxe-Weimar, a small German duchy. He remained for most of his life in Weimar, the capital of the duchy, where the duke's generosity allowed him freedom to study, travel, and write.

Goethe's interests embraced the whole range of the arts and sciences, in keeping with the Renaissance ideal of *virtù* (p. 374). A man of high intelligence and feeling, he wrote beyond the limitations of most romantic authors. But his personal life was notably romantic—a series of passionate love affairs, many of which he described in his writing. Goethe's lyric poetry reflects his fascination with love, nature, and death. In prose, the most striking expression of his youthful romanticism is *The Sorrows of Young Werther* (1774), which describes the extravagant sufferings of a forlorn hero tortured by frustrated passion.

Faust, a dramatic poem on which Goethe worked during most of his long life, parallels the conflicts and growth that took place in his personal development. Part One, published in 1808, retells the Renaissance legend of a learned professor, Doctor Faust, who bargained his soul to the devil in return for youth and power. (This portion was put to music by several romantic composers.) Part Two, which was not published until after the author's death in 1832, carries Faust on a kind of philosophical excursion in search of man's ultimate purpose and way to happiness. The soul of the hero, in Goethe's poem, is saved at last because he loves God and humanity and tries, in spite of errors, to serve both. Goethe's Faust is a literary model of "modern" man—the individual who seeks to understand and experience the lowest and the highest, and to harmonize sensual and spiritual urges.

The romantic spirit in literature brought forth an impressive response from Russian writers. As a result of Russia's turning toward the West (pp. 459–460), eighteenth-century Russian literature had been largely imitative of the French. In the nineteenth century, however, it developed its own character. Alexander Pushkin (who died in 1837) was the first Russian writer to command serious attention in western Europe, with his romantic poems, plays, and short stories. In his homeland, he is still revered both as a writer of genius whose own short life was filled with romantic passion and adventure, and as the forefather of modern Russian literature in general. The grand tradition of the Russian novel was started by Nicolai Gogol. His *Taras Bulba* (1835) tells of adventures and conflicts among the high-spirited Cossacks, those warrior-horsemen who fought the Tartar enemies of Russia (p. 459). But the finest Russian novelists came later in the century—Fyodor Dostoevsky and Leo Tolstoy. Both were concerned primarily with the inner life and struggles of the individual, while describing at the same time the color and detail of Russian life. The best known of their works are Tolstoy's epic historical novel, *War and Peace* (1868), and Dostoevsky's profound *The Brothers Karamazov* (1880).

Rebellion and Romance in Painting

The early-nineteenth-century reaction against rationalism in philosophy and literature was paralleled in the visual arts by a reaction against the classicism of the preceding century (pp. 484–489). In France, the main target of the artistic revolt was the classical style that had been established by Jacques-Louis David. David had turned away from the elegant, frivolous works admired by the aristocracy and had sought inspiration in ancient Roman and Greek sculptures. The classical revival in French painting may be said to have begun with the exhibition in 1785 of his heroic painting of Roman heroes in the *Oath of the Horatii (Fig. 11-3)*; it became the official style of the French Revolution.

David, a middle-class man who sympathized with the radical political reforms of the period, was elected to the National Convention (p. 516) and helped abolish the royal Academy of Painting. The leaders of the revolution regarded art primarily as an instrument of *propaganda*; they destroyed the academy because it upheld aristocratic traditions. In its place they established the École des Beaux-Arts (School of Fine Arts), which adopted the classical style and sought to impose it on all French painters.

David reached the height of his influence later, under Napoleon. As "First Painter of the Empire," he made portraits of the new caesar, supervised the national galleries, arranged imperial ceremonies, and saw to the licensing of artists who wished to exhibit their works. After Napoleon's fall, David was ordered into exile, and the Academy of Painting was restored. But David's classicism remained the official style in France for a century afterward.

Romantic painters everywhere revolted against classicism, against official styles of any sort, and against academic rules of painting. One of the earliest rebels

11-3 Jacques-Louis David. *Oath of the Horatii*. Oil on canvas, approx. 11' × 14'. Louvre, Paris.

was Francisco Goya, a Spanish contemporary of David. Heir to the rich legacy of Spanish painting of the baroque period (pp. 436–443), Goya preferred it to the restraints of classicism. However, he did not paint in the traditional aristocratic manner, which aimed to ornament or glorify. His portraits of Spanish royalty and nobility are proofs of his extraordinary honesty and powers of observation.

Goya's active social conscience also made him sensitive to the tyranny, civil strife, and poverty that he saw on every hand in his native land. (Hundreds of his etchings reveal the cruelty and desperation of the times.) In his painting *The Third of May, 1808 (Color Plate C1)*, he presented an execution scene in the streets of Madrid; Napoleon's soldiers had been attacked by civilians the day before and are here making their reprisal. Goya chose to dramatize the horror of war and the human capacity for brutality—a side of war that David had preferred to ignore. Though he became more bitter as he grew older, he preserved his artistic independence to the end.

The romantic style achieved its fullest expression in France during the generation after Napoleon's downfall. Its most brilliant exponent was Eugène Delacroix. After a classical education, he decided to become a painter and began his training in Paris, which now eclipsed Rome as the art center of Europe. He became almost at once an enthusiastic convert to the new style. "If by Romanticism is meant the free expression of my personal feelings, my aloofness from the standardized types of paintings prescribed by the Schools, and my dislike of academic formulas," he wrote later, "I must confess that not only am I a Romantic but that I already was one at the age of fifteen!"

Through the strength of his personality and talent Delacroix made the new style dominant in France, even though it was opposed by the academy critics. He was an excellent draftsman, but he disregarded formal rules of drawing and achieved his effects mainly through the use of color. He believed that imagination was more important to an artist than knowledge, and he sought above all to inject excitement and movement into his works. As did Goya, he often played down detail in the interest of sharp focus and strong impact.

Delacroix first gained public attention in 1822 through the showing of his *Dante and Vergil in Hell.* This scene, illustrating a passage from Dante (p. 307), shows a group of tormented individuals writhing in the dark waters of the river Styx (in hell). Friendly critics saw in this work suggestions of the figures of Michelangelo and the colors of Rubens, the opposites of classical serenity. In his historical painting, the *Entrance of the Crusaders into Constantinople (Color Plate C2),* Delacroix raises the emotions of the viewer by contrasting the triumphant invaders with their crouching victims (see Fourth Crusade— pp. 312–313). Responding to the romantic taste for the exotic (foreign), Delacroix once traveled to Algiers, in Africa. Some of his most popular works, paintings of lion hunts and of the Muslim court and concubines, grew out of that experience.

The love of nature, which was a central feature of romanticism, was best expressed in painting by the English artists J. M. W. Turner and John Constable. Turner's paintings are visionary rather than realistic. A superb colorist, he gave his landscapes and seascapes a sense of grandeur and mystery. He often used a sentimental subject for his canvases, as in *The Fighting Téméraire (Color Plate C3),* painted in 1839. English patriots were stirred by this picture of the ghostly *Téméraire,* a sailing ship of Lord Nelson's battle fleet (p. 521), being towed away for destruction. It is led to its inglorious fate by a squat black tug, symbol of the triumph of steam over sail, iron over timber, efficiency over beauty. Turner showed the ship against a sweep of sky and sea. The time, symbolically, is sunset and a reddish light is cast on the water. Turner's imaginative treatment of nature proved extremely popular; he sold hundreds of paintings and etchings and built up a fortune during his lifetime.

Constable, Turner's contemporary, approached nature in a different manner. His love of the English countryside was akin to that of his good friend the poet Wordsworth; but he studied nature with the eye of a scientist, and, though he finished his canvases indoors, he worked from oil sketches prepared in the open. His paintings were so strikingly different from the commonplace studio landscapes of the period that they created a sensation at first showing. When *The Hay Wain (Color Plate C4)* was exhibited in Paris in 1821, French painters were astonished by its truth to nature, and many set out to imitate Constable's technique.

Constable referred to Turner's works as "airy visions, painted with tinted steam," while he based his own painting on "observable facts." He wanted nature to speak for itself, without artificial effects. Limiting his subject matter almost entirely to rural scenes, he painted rich canvases—with people and animals (as in *The Hay Wain*) fitting into a scheme clearly designed for human satisfaction. The atmosphere of Constable's paintings is often set by his treatment of the sky, which he believed was "the key note, the standard scale, and the chief organ of sentiment."

THE GOTHIC REVIVAL IN ARCHITECTURE

In the nineteenth century, architectural style became more and more a matter of *individual* taste or fancy. This was a time of vast activity in construction, especially in the industrial cities; most of the older buildings still standing in Europe today were erected during the nineteenth century. They represent a confusing variety of styles springing from several architectural *revivals*. The architect sometimes aimed at a "pure" style, sometimes at a mixed one, and sometimes at an original design. But by mid-century certain "associations" had developed: banks and government buildings, for instance, were usually built in the Greek or Roman manner; churches and colleges, in the Gothic. There were, of course, notable exceptions to the rule, and all buildings, regardless of their design, suffered a general decline in workmanship.

Of the various styles, the Gothic is most often associated with romanticism. The Gothic *revival* first appeared in England before the French Revolution, as a reaction to the classical Palladian style (pp. 485–487). Horace Walpole, a writer and the son of a noted statesman, wanted to make his country house distinctive from other aristocratic houses. Feeling a romantic attachment to the medieval past, he decided to remodel the house in the manner of a Gothic castle. The result was anything but "pure" Gothic, despite the addition of spires and towers. As with many such attempts, Walpole's creation turned out to be a curious mixture.

The romantic movement, after the turn of the century, gave new force to the Gothic revival. The outstanding example of this period is the Houses of Parliament (*Fig. 11-4*). When the old building burned down in 1834, the lawmakers, remembering that English liberties and Parliament itself traced back to the thirteenth century, decided to rebuild it in the medieval style. At about the same time, across the North Sea in Germany, numerous "medieval" castles began to appear. All over Europe and America the Gothic revival proved popular.

11-4   Charles Barry and Augustus Pugin. Houses of Parliament, London. Designed 1835.

ROMANTICISM IN MUSIC: BEETHOVEN, WAGNER

The eighteenth-century classical style in music, as we have seen (p. 493), stressed order, grace, and clarity; the nineteenth century cast off restraint and released the emotional power of music. The classical style did not disappear altogether, but it was submerged in the tide of romanticism. Ludwig van Beethoven, born in Bonn, Germany, in 1770, bridged both styles. His early works are similar to those of Haydn and Mozart, and he followed established compositional forms throughout most of his life. But he responded to the romantic spirit, and his later works are marked by heightened drama, suspense, and brilliant climaxes. Unlike some romantic composers, Beethoven never lost control of his musical themes; his works throb with energy but are contained within an orderly pattern. For this reason, he is sometimes called a "classical romantic."

Compositions in the romantic style were usually written for the concert hall, rather than for the small chamber or drawing room. They called for more volume and range of sound; Beethoven's orchestra was nearly twice the size of Haydn's. Although few new instruments were introduced, the number of strings, winds, and percussion instruments was enlarged. The symphony became the most popular form, but pieces for solo performance also found favor. Melodies were highly expressive and original; harmonies were rich and often dissonant; and rhythms were subject to sudden or subtle changes.

Leading composers in the romantic style were an Austrian, Franz Schubert; a Pole, Frédéric Chopin; a Frenchman, Hector Berlioz; and a Russian, Peter Ilich Tchaikovsky. (The latter's Piano Concerto no. 1 in B-flat Minor is perhaps the most brilliant work of its kind ever composed.) Much of the serious music performed today—in the concert hall, on the air, and on records, discs, and tapes—is by romantic composers. The high point of romanticism, however, appeared not in the symphony hall but in the opera house. Richard Wagner, born in Leipzig, Germany, in 1813, created a new concept of opera—or music-drama, as he preferred to call it. Wagner personified the deepest yearnings of the romantic spirit. Above all, he stressed the idea of the *unity* of thought and feeling and believed that this unity should be reflected in all art forms. He had contempt for art as mere entertainment or spectacle—"effects without cause." His new kind of opera, which was modeled on the performances of Greek tragedy (pp. 88–89), joined poetry, music, scenery, and action into one unified whole.

Wagner's "Ring cycle," a sequence of operas drawn from Germanic legend, best illustrates his idea of form. Here the drama—which is concerned with the curse of gold and the lust for power—is central. Voices and orchestra combine to carry forward the powerful themes; instead of writing separate speeches, arias, choruses, and accompaniments, Wagner created an "endless melody" out of all the musical elements. His music is rich and complex, full of passion and suspense, wholly romantic.

Italian opera, it should be added, remained close to the tradition established by Monteverdi (p. 492). But it, too, reflected the new stress on emotion and the enlarged capabilities of the orchestra. Giuseppe Verdi, Wagner's artistic rival, is probably the most successful of operatic composers; his spectacular *Aïda* has been performed more often than any other opera. Verdi chose plots that focused upon the most elemental human feelings and set them to thrilling vocal music. A political activist, he also used stories in his operas that inspired the rising desire for liberty and nationhood in Italy (pp. 546–547).

THE SPREAD OF LIBERAL DEMOCRACY AND NATIONALISM

The defeat of revolutionary France, and the conservative reaction that followed, slowed the momentum of liberal and national revolution; but in the long run they could not reverse it. The forces making for change were too strong to contain. These included the resentment of the middle classes against absolutism and privilege, continued deprivation among the urban poor, the growing discontent of eastern European serfs, and the appeal of liberal romantic ideas to educated young people of all classes. On the other side, the conservative rulers and nobles, divided by traditional power rivalries and inclined to waver between repression and reform as the best way of preventing renewed violent revolution, were not so united and

1804		1814		1830		1848	1852		1870
First Empire (Napoleon I)		Bourbon Restoration		July Monarchy (Louis-Philippe)		Second Republic		Second Empire (Napoleon III)	

determined as they seemed. Down to 1871, the nineteenth century saw the gradual crumbling of conservative resistance and the emergence of a new Europe, dominated by the hopes and ideals—and the ambitions and rivalries—of liberalism and nationalism.

THE REVOLUTIONS OF 1830 AND 1848

The struggles for liberal democracy and national unity and independence followed a general pattern in Europe during the nineteenth century. In the first decade after the Congress of Vienna, most of the uprisings were quickly suppressed (as in Naples, Spain, and Russia). Revolutionary successes were achieved only in Greece (against the Ottoman Turks—pp. 327–329) and overseas, where the Spanish and Portuguese colonies in Latin America gained their independence by 1825. Waves of revolution continued to break across Europe, however—notably in 1830 and 1848. The most significant victory for the liberal forces came in France in 1830.

Even with the restoration of the Bourbon king, Louis XVIII, in 1814, France had preserved the principal reforms introduced by the revolution and Napoleon. Louis reigned as a constitutional monarch, with a legislature that represented the restored nobility and well-to-do members of the business class. Though the limited voting rights displeased the majority of citizens, the arrangement was close to what the moderate bourgeois had sought in 1789. It was threatened in 1824, however, when Louis was succeeded by his brother (the Count of Artois)—Charles X.

Charles had been an enemy of the revolution, a leader of the émigrés who had urged other European nobles and princes to attack revolutionary France (p. 514). After becoming king, he and his reactionary friends moved to turn back the clock. They sought to require the government to make annual payments to former nobles whose lands had been confiscated during the revolution. They also wanted to bring back the old feudal law of *primogeniture* (exclusive inheritance of an estate by the firstborn son), and they favored a return of clerical influence in education and politics. Charles himself, proud and stubborn, was contemptuous of the popular criticism his measures caused. When the elective Chamber of Deputies refused, in 1830, to bend to his will, he violated the constitution that had been issued by Louis XVIII. By decree, Charles dissolved the Chamber, censored the press, and changed voting rights to strengthen the power of the former nobles.

Paris responded to this revival of absolutism by throwing up barricades in the streets. The "July Revolution" lasted only a few days, for the troops and police refused to fire on the populace. Charles, who had no desire to share the fate of Louis XVI, promptly abdicated and left for England. The rebels now found themselves divided on what to do next. The workmen, students, and intellectuals who had hoisted the revolutionary *tricolor* (flag) at the city hall, in place of the Bourbon *fleur-de-lis*, demanded that the monarchy give way to a republic. The bourgeois politicians, however, opposed such a change, feeling that their interests would be safer under a constitutional monarchy. All they wanted was a different kind of king, one who would serve their purposes. The politicians found such a man in Prince Louis-Philippe, who, though a member of the Bourbon family, had fought on the side of the revolution in 1789. They persuaded the aged and respected national hero, the Marquis de Lafayette, to support Louis-Philippe. This helped to make the "left-wing" Bourbon prince acceptable to those who wanted a republic.

The reign of Louis-Philippe brought a modest extension of liberal and democratic practices. Though the number of voters was still only a small fraction of the total citizenry, it was double what it had been before. The chief significance of the July Revolution was that it decisively ended the threat of counterrevolution in France and shattered the principle of legitimacy, hallowed at Vienna in 1815 — Louis-Philippe became king upon the *invitation* of an elected Chamber of Deputies. The French thus struck a blow against the "Metternich System" (p. 522), and their success encouraged liberals and patriots elsewhere.

The first uprising outside France occurred in the Belgian Netherlands. This territory, for centuries under either Austrian or Spanish control, had been joined to the independent Dutch Netherlands by decision of the Congress of Vienna. Metternich and his colleagues had hoped that a united Netherlands would serve as a barrier to the French, whose rulers had frequently sent armies northward toward the Rhine River. But there were deep-seated problems in the cultural relations between Dutch and Belgians. The Dutch were mainly Protestant, while the Belgians were mainly Catholic; and the French-speaking population of southern Belgium (Walloons) resented the required use of the Dutch language in most areas. Discontent with the Dutch king, William I, led to street riots in Brussels shortly after the July uprising in France. At first the Belgian leaders demanded only local self-rule. But when William took up arms against them they declared for complete independence.

Metternich and his allies in central Europe would have moved against this eruption of nationalism in the Low Countries had they not been occupied with threats nearer home. With French and British backing, the Belgians managed to hold off the Dutch king. Finally, in 1831, an international conference in London provided for an independent Belgium, with a German prince (Leopold of Saxe-Coburg) as constitutional monarch. In 1839, King William also recognized the new state, and its independence and neutrality were guaranteed by the major European powers.

Polish patriots, meanwhile, had tried and failed to establish the independence of their homeland (p. 457). After long diplomatic "trading" among the powers at the Congress of Vienna (pp. 521–524), Poland had been given over to Russian control as a separate kingdom — under the personal rule of Tsar Alexander I. Early in 1831 the Polish Diet (assembly) of nobles rejected Alexander's successor Nicholas I as their king; Nicholas sent a large army and crushed the brave but divided Polish forces. Revolutionary stirrings also arose in 1830 in various parts of

Germany, Italy, Spain, and Portugal. In almost every case, they were put down by force, as they had been in Poland. But the widespread agitations demonstrated that liberal nationalist forces were rising throughout Europe, kept in check only by political repression and military measures.

In Britain, where substantial change could be brought about through legislation, liberal ideas and practices made a striking advance. Even during the 1820s, Parliament moved away from a mercantilist economy toward free international trade. It also gave to Catholics and dissenting Protestants political rights equal to those of Anglicans. But the most significant single act was the Reform Bill of 1832, which altered the voting franchise and the system of representation in the House of Commons. In response to shifts in the English population, this bill assigned seats to the growing urban centers of the North and the Midlands at the expense of districts in the South.

The individual right to vote remained tied to property ownership, but more lenient requirements almost doubled the number of eligible voters (men only)—to nearly one million. The new voters were chiefly of the middle class; the Reform Bill raised its share of power in the Commons to roughly that of the landed gentry (pp. 498–499). It also opened the door to further liberal and democratic reforms during the ensuing decades, including extension of the vote to women. ("Cabinet" government, responsible to the Parliamentary majority, had been established a century earlier by Robert Walpole, Britain's first "prime minister.") Although the British achieved this transformation without revolution or civil war, at critical moments the use (and threat) of violence was no doubt decisive. In 1832, for example, the Reform Bill was driven through Parliament under the pressure of street demonstrations and signs of possible insurrection.

Some of these pressures came from the English "Radicals" of the time, who wanted to go far beyond the liberals in overhauling British society and politics. The Radicals—chiefly from the working class, with some of the new industrialists like Robert Owen (p. 569)—were both philosophical and action-minded. Inspired by such older writers as the American Tom Paine (p. 505) and their own countryman Jeremy Bentham (p. 545), they demanded radical changes in voting laws, Parliament, courts, prisons, the Anglican Church, and the privileges of the lords. Many of these changes were brought about later in England. But for the time being, in 1832, the controlling powers in Parliament showed enough skill to permit *mild* reforms rather than face the risk of rebellion.

On the continent the strongholds of privilege proved more unbending. Rather than submit to change or attempt to guide its course, the conservatives generally sought to *repress* it. Liberal and nationalist discontent continued to build up, however, and another series of explosions came in 1848. In France, Louis-Philippe, the "citizen-king," had become exceedingly unpopular. Voting rights remained limited to a small fraction of citizens, and many of the bourgeois, as well as working people, became increasingly discontented. The critics of the government fell into two groups: the radicals, who wanted to discard the monarchy and establish a republic with *universal* voting rights, and the liberals, who wanted only a limited extension of voting rights. Had Louis-Philippe yielded to the liberals, he could have gained broader support and kept his crown. But he stubbornly rejected *any* constitutional change, and in February 1848 the streets of Paris bristled once again with barricades.

In a virtual repetition of the events of 1830, the royal troops refused to march against the people, and the king sensibly sailed for England. The victors were again split between monarchists and republicans, but this time the disagreement developed into deeper civil conflict. The republican leaders of Paris were concerned about *social* as well as political reforms. They spoke for the growing number of workers, many of them unemployed, who had been drawn into the industrial centers. The victims of low income, insecurity, and poor working conditions, these "proletarians" were generally anticapitalist and antibourgeois.

In 1848 the republicans overcame monarchist opposition and forced the proclamation of a *republic*. They then arranged for the election, by a universal male vote, of a Constituent Assembly to frame a new basic law for France. The Assembly, which met in May, no doubt represented the sentiment of the nation as a whole (outside Paris). It favored democratic political changes but no substantial social or economic reforms. This view was assailed by the aroused workers of the city, most of whom wanted the government to establish industrial workshops as a means of providing employment.

Fearing that the majority of the Assembly would reject their demands, groups of workers attacked it and yet again the barricades went up. This time, however, the result was very different. An ugly class war started in Paris, and some ten thousand were killed or wounded in several days of bloody street fighting. The regular army, called upon to defend the Assembly, crushed the revolt and thereby raised the bitterness of most of the urban workers. They concluded that the army had been used to defend the "exploitation" of laborers by the capitalist class. The bourgeois, for their part, were shaken by the threat of social revolution.

After those bloody "June Days," the Constituent Assembly drafted a new constitution that provided for a legislature and a president with strong powers. It decided to call for the president's election at once, even though the final work on the constitution had not been completed. Of the four well-known candidates who entered the contest, the victory went to the one who promised the most to both sides in the civil struggle. Prince Louis Napoleon Bonaparte, a nephew of the famous Corsican, represented himself as standing for both social *order* and social *change*. Playing upon his family name, he swamped his rivals and became president of the Second Republic in December 1848. Three years later, he brought about the dissolution of the legislature and had himself elected for a new term of ten years. In 1852 this shrewd politician proclaimed the Second Empire, taking the title of Napoleon III. (His cousin, the son and direct heir of Napoleon I, had died in 1832.)

The cycle of revolution and counterrevolution also took place beyond the borders of France. In central Europe liberal demands were mixed with nationalist hopes. Revolutionists rushed into the streets in a dozen capitals, proclaiming political rights and calling for the unity and independence of their own national groups. Monarchs and ruling classes were at first frightened by these demonstrations and generally responded by offering concessions or new constitutions. But the protesting movements lacked the internal cohesion and the organized force needed to hold their gains. When it became clear that they could be stopped by military action, the authorities recovered their poise, withdrew their concessions, and put down the rebels with troops and police. In the course of these uprisings, peasants who were still *serfs* won their freedom, but liberal reforms and progress toward national self-determination were checked.

Nevertheless, the movements of 1848 had significant consequences. The Austrian Empire felt the greatest shock, a warning of things to come. Until 1848 Prince Metternich (p. 522) had remained the outstanding leader of "legitimacy" and conservatism. Yet a liberal uprising in Vienna so unnerved him that he hurriedly resigned as imperial chancellor and departed for London. The flight of Metternich brought joy and hope to the advocates of change everywhere. These feelings were premature, however, for within two years imperial troops had suppressed the disturbances in the Habsburg domains, and Metternich could return to his beloved Vienna to write his memoirs. But he was no longer in power, and the Metternich System was broken.

Nationalist aspirations, though frustrated, were intensified throughout central Europe. Hungarians, Czechs, Italians, Serbs, Croats, and Romanians became more dissatisfied within the Austrian Empire. Many Germans, meanwhile, were looking toward the creation of a large united German state. The various German territories (including Austria proper) sent delegates to Frankfurt in 1848, with the aim of setting up a German federal union. This Frankfurt Assembly could not reach agreement, however, on the type of constitution for such a union. Upset by the political reaction that had set in by 1849, this assembly produced no solid results. Nationalist sentiment had nonetheless been stirred, and within a generation a united Germany would be created by the more "realistic" methods of diplomacy and war (pp. 547–550).

THE LIBERAL IDEAL: MILL

The immediate aims and actions of the liberal and nationalist movements were in keeping with their maturing ideologies. The liberal demands were for extension of voting rights, free expression, guarantees of legal protections, and constitutional checks on government power; the nationalist demands were for the political union and independence of distinct cultural groups. Neither set of aims can be fully understood without a knowledge of its underlying system of thought.

Nineteenth-century liberal thought was the outcome of a trend that had started in the Renaissance, or even as far back as the late Middle Ages. It was represented in succeeding stages by men like Erasmus, Locke, Rabelais, and Jefferson (pp. 380–383, 398–399, 502–503, 506–507). Central to the thinking of these men was their stress on human personality and its free development. This idea could be realized, they believed, only through each individual's exercise of personal *freedom*. The nature of freedom and the proper conditions for its use had been outlined before the French Revolution; after Napoleon, those views had to be modified considerably.

Nineteenth-century liberals were bitterly aware that something had gone wrong with the revolution—"Liberty, Equality, and Fraternity" had led to bloodshed and dictatorship—but they clung to the same basic beliefs, while studying the mistakes that had been made. They became more respectful of *history* than earlier liberals had been, observing that human rationality is not sufficient to overcome, in a short time, the lasting power of old institutions and habits of thought. They were also more wary of *popular* tyranny, concluding that the will of the majority can be as wrong and oppressive as that of a despot. Many liberals emphasized, finally, that freedom must be guided by morality if it is not to go astray. Thus, the nineteenth-century liberals held that a *tempered* doctrine of liberty is the best means to individual happiness and the fulfillment of human potential.

On the continent, liberal voices were generally overpowered by those of the conservatives and romantics. In England, however, they remained vigorous, and liberal speeches and writings accompanied the advance of political reforms. John Stuart Mill was the foremost spokesman of nineteenth-century liberalism. His conceptions of personal freedom, precisely and eloquently expressed, have had a persistent appeal to those everywhere who admire the ideal of liberty.

Mill was a follower of Jeremy Bentham, the founder of a philosophy called "utilitarianism." According to Bentham, who took an *atomistic* view of human society (p. 503), the most acceptable way of evaluating social institutions is to measure their total *utility* (usefulness) to all the affected individuals—looking to "the greatest good of the greatest number." Mill defended this view, explaining that the measurement of the "greatest good" must take into account *qualitative* differences in human satisfactions. He believed that the highest satisfactions can be reached only under conditions of personal freedom, and he set out to specify those conditions and work for their achievement. Mill's carefully reasoned *On Liberty* (1859) remains the classic statement of the historic liberal view of individual rights in relation to society.

The book accepts Aristotle's conviction that the purpose of human life is the harmonious development of one's abilities (pp. 85–86). This purpose, declared Mill, requires two conditions: "freedom, and a variety of situations." He would give to each individual, therefore, the utmost freedom in relation to society and the state. (Like John Locke, he distinguished between freedom and *license*, for the latter means interference with someone else's freedom.) Each person's freedom he regarded as *sacred*—"the only purpose for which power can be rightfully exercised over any member of a civilized community, against his will, is to prevent harm to others." Mill justified this position not by resorting to the outmoded doctrine of "natural rights" or the "social contract" (p. 503), but on the *utilitarian* ground that freedom is essential to the greater happiness of the individual and the species.

He included females as well as males in his philosophical judgments. His partner in writing *On Liberty* and other major works was a woman, Harriet Taylor. A close intellectual associate for many years, she at last became his wife. Mill, unlike other writers of the nineteenth century, viewed women as equal to men in intelligence. He helped found the first woman's suffrage society in England in 1867 and published, soon after, *The Subjection of Women*, a persuasive statement of the case for female political rights.

Mill abhorred the drift toward large bureaucracies and cultural conformity. The state itself, he insisted, is worth no more than the individuals who make it up: "a State which dwarfs its men, in order that they may be more docile instruments in its hands even for beneficial purposes, will find that with small men no great thing can really be accomplished. . . ." It is by cultivating individual *differences*, concluded Mill, that human beings become noble and enrich social life. As people become more valuable to themselves, they are capable of being more valuable to others. Each person thus "strengthens the tie which binds every individual to the race, by making the race infinitely better to belong to."

He opposed increases in public services by government, even when done for the benefit of individuals. He preferred that citizens and groups act on their own initiative to forestall the "deadening hand" of centralized power and uniformity. But his first concern was the preservation, at any cost, of liberty of *thought* and *discussion*. This, he thought, is crucial to the health of the individual and society. He denied the right of any government, popular or despotic, to interfere with free expression: "If all mankind minus one were of one opinion, and only one person were of the contrary opinion, mankind would be no more justified in silencing that one person, than he, if he had the power, would be justified in silencing mankind." The evil of forbidding the expression of an opinion is more than the injury to an individual, Mill asserted: it hurts the human race, and it hurts those who dissent from the opinion more than those who hold it. "If the opinion is right, they are deprived of the opportunity of exchanging error for truth; if wrong, they lose, what is almost as great a benefit, the clearer and livelier impression of truth, produced by its collision with error."

The Nationalist Ideal: Mazzini

While many people, especially in England and France, applauded Mill's sentiments, others subordinated individual freedom to nationalism. In Italy and Germany, still "geographical expressions" rather than national states, the desire for national unity and prestige overshadowed all other aims. Freedom, like every good thing, was seen to be rooted in the *nation*. Unlike Mill, who took Britain's power for granted, the nationalists on the continent did not glorify the individual, "free" of interference by the state; they regarded the building of a powerful state as the necessary means to full nationhood and individual realization. Hence, in Germany and Italy the moving ideology was national liberalism (or liberal nationalism). Its special form and tone, in the first half of the century, were expressed by the Italian patriot Giuseppe Mazzini. Though inspired by the humanitarian and egalitarian ideals of the Enlightenment, Mazzini was caught up in the romantic and nationalist passion of his own generation. In him, the "religion of liberty" became the "religion of the fatherland."

The nationalist ideal, as described by Mazzini, was linked to a sentimental concern for all humanity. Mazzini described his feeling in a series of essays, *The Duties of Man*, written at midcentury and directed to the Italian working class. "You are men," Mazzini told his readers, "before you are citizens or fathers." The "law of life" requires that individuals embrace the whole human family in their love, confessing their faith in the unity and brotherhood of all peoples. But the lone individual, declared Mazzini, is powerless to work for the benefit of all: "The individual is too weak, and Humanity too vast." Effective action requires fraternal cooperation among individuals who can work together—those of a common language and culture—in other words, a nation. Starting with this line of reasoning, Mazzini went on to glorify the nation as divinely created for serving *humanity*. But many of his readers, then and later, became so attentive to the glory of the nation that they forgot his teaching of a prior duty to humanity.

Mazzini saw the independent nation as a promoter of individual liberty and equality: "A Country is a fellowship of free and equal men. . . . The law must express the general aspiration, promote the good of all, respond to a beat of the nation's heart." But, in fact, the push for national strength through unity often reduced freedom, especially when freedom involved dissent from national objectives. Nationalism could readily become *statism*, as it did north of the Alps. The historian Heinrich von Treitschke, writing later in the century, declared that the individual's *first* duty is *obedience to the state*. This influential professor at the University of Berlin gave academic and philosophical respectability to the German drive for discipline, unification, and dominance.

THE ACHIEVEMENT OF NATIONAL UNIFICATION: BISMARCK

The unsuccessful liberal-nationalist uprisings of 1830 and 1848 had failed because of inadequate organization and power. It is significant that the eloquent Mazzini, who labored tirelessly to rid Italy of foreign occupation, spent most of his years as a revolutionary exile. But his patriotic propaganda paved the way for the diplomatic and military successes of others, notably Count Camillo di Cavour and Giuseppe Garibaldi. Though his liberal ideals were far from realized, Mazzini lived to see the achievement of a united Italy in 1870.

But in Germany the practical means to national unification were most forcefully demonstrated, and the consequences for Europe and the world were most profound. After the disappointment of 1848, German nationalists looked for more effective means of bringing their dreams to fulfillment. One of them, Count Otto von Bismarck, was sure he knew the way. Born into an aristocratic landowning family, he rose to power as a high official of the Prussian kingdom. In the tradition of Frederick the Great (p. 458), Bismarck admired autocracy and militarism. He had despised the liberal leaders of 1848 and had urged the Prussian king to use the army to restore order and civil obedience. (Many German liberals later supported Bismarck, however, because his methods proved effective in building national power.)

1806	1815		1862	1866	1871	1890
Napoleon's Confederation of the Rhine	Metternich's German Confederation (including Austria)		Years of Unification			Bismarck Chancellor of Germany

Bismarck Chancellor
of Prussia

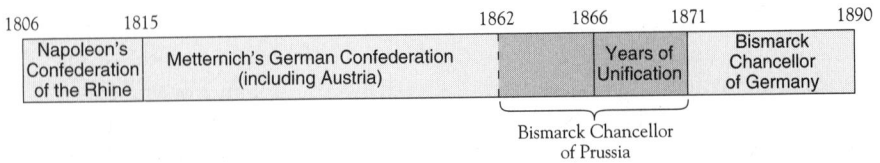

He set out, after 1848, to make Prussia the dominant German power. His desire was both to glorify Prussia and to unify Germany. He was convinced that the German princelings would never join together through their own efforts, and he had only contempt for what the "people" might accomplish. The important decisions and acts had to be taken, he thought, by the ruler and ministers of the leading German state, Prussia. "Not by speeches and majority votes," declared Bismarck, "are the great questions of the day decided—that was the mistake of 1848 and 1849—but by blood and iron." Acting upon this conviction, he proved to be Europe's master of the art of "power politics."

Appointed chief minister to the Prussian king in 1862, Bismarck determined to remove, by diplomacy and war, whatever stood in the way of German unification. Austria was clearly the chief obstacle, for Metternich had managed to establish and maintain Austrian dominance in central Europe, and he and his successors looked with distaste and fear upon the ambitions of Prussia. Prussia cooperated with Austria in a military campaign to take the duchies of Schleswig and Holstein from Danish control, but the two powers quarreled over the division of their conquests. In 1866 the argument turned into armed conflict, and Prussian troops invaded Austria and its allied German states. European diplomats were impressed by the efficiency of the Prussian military machine, which Bismarck had created at heavy expense. After the conclusion of the Seven Weeks' War, defeated Austria gave up all influence over northern Germany to Prussia. Metternich's German Confederation (pp. 523–524) was abolished, and Bismarck raised in its place the North German Confederation, under the presidency of the king of Prussia. This new political grouping had a firm economic foundation, for Prussia had previously led the way in establishing a customs union (Zollverein) that equalized tariffs among the states that joined it. The union included most of the German states outside Austria.

It was now France's turn to be uneasy, for the French, like the Austrians, had traditionally opposed a strong and united Germany. Aggressive factions in both Prussia and France viewed a military showdown as inevitable; diplomatic maneuvering and reciprocal insults led, in 1870, to a declaration of war by France. The whirlwind Franco-Prussian War was another brilliant success for the Prussian armies, resulting in the death of one empire and the birth of another. Napoleon III, humiliated by defeat and capture, lost his throne, and in 1871 William I of Prussia was proclaimed the emperor (Kaiser) of a united Germany. (William was a descendant of the Hohenzollern dynasty, which had come to rule Prussia by the eighteenth century, p. 458.) Four south German states, which had remained aloof from the North German Confederation, took their places in the proud new empire

Color Plate C1   Francisco Goya, *The Third of May, 1808, at Madrid: The Shootings on Principe Pio Mountain,* c. 1814. Oil on canvas, 8′9″ × 13′4″. Museo del Prado, Madrid.

Color Plate C2   Eugène Delacroix, *Entrance of the Crusaders into Constantinople,* c. 1841. Oil on canvas, 13′4″ × 16′2″. Louvre, Paris.

Color Plate C3 Joseph Mallord William Turner, *The Fighting Téméraire*. Oil on canvas, 36″ × 48″. National Gallery, London.

Color Plate C4 John Constable, *The Hay Wain*, c. 1821. Oil on canvas, 51″ × 78″. National Gallery, London.

Color Plate C5   Claude Monet, *Impression: Sunrise, 1872*. Oil on canvas, 19″ × 25″. Musée Marmottan, Paris.

Color Plate C6   Paul Cézanne, *Still Life*, c. 1865. Oil on canvas, 26″ × 33″. National Gallery of Art, Washington, D.C.

Color Plate C7   Vincent van Gogh, *Cornfield with Crows, 1890.* Oil on canvas, 20″ × 41″.
National Museum Vincent van Gogh, Amsterdam.

Color Plate C8   Jackson Pollock, *Lavender Mist: Number 1, 1950.* Oil, enamel, and aluminum on
canvas, 87″ × 118″. National Gallery of Art, Washington, D.C.

EUROPE IN 1871

(*map*, p. 549). Bismarck, now the *imperial* chancellor, had achieved the central ambitions of his career: Prussia was supreme in Germany, and Germany was supreme
in Europe.

During the Franco-Prussian War, Napoleon III (p. 543) recalled his troops
from Rome, where they had been protecting the territory and political independence of the pope. (Rome was all that was left of the States of the Church—
p. 341.) The French withdrawal permitted the newly created kingdom of Italy to
send in forces and annex Rome, thereby completing national unification in 1870.
Italy and Germany, both of which had been divided for centuries, now became independent members of the European state system. This would be the central fact of
international relations during the years to follow. The greater power, Germany,
which had achieved unity and strength by the methods of authority, discipline, and
militarism, was determined to win its "place in the sun" after its late arrival as a
state. The successful revolutions of national unification were thus a prelude to European and global struggle, climaxed by the First and Second World Wars.

CHAPTER 12

❂ ❂ ❂

THE IMPACT OF THE MACHINE

Overview

A ll through the nineteenth century, movements aimed at social change, political reform, and national unification and self-government rose and fell throughout Europe. But there was another force behind the nineteenth-century changes that operated unceasingly, and indeed accelerated through the century and down to the present day: the *technological* revolution and the accompanying development of *machines*. The social, political, and national movements had parallels in the past, but the acceleration of technology was without precedent. It set Europe and other regions across the world on an irreversible course, as nineteenth-century observers already recognized when they started calling it the "Industrial Revolution." In fact, the Industrial Revolution would prove comparable, in its impact on human culture, to the Agricultural Revolution of the New Stone Age (pp. 12–17).

Technology—that is, the use of artificial devices and processes as an aid to activity in every field—is as old as the human race. From the earliest times, history and prehistory have been full of world-changing inventions: stone tools and the use of fire; plant cultivation, woven cloth, bricks, and bread; wheeled vehicles, metalworking, and plows; printing presses and firearms (pp. 9–10, 12–14, 335–339). It was not the use of technology as such that proved revolutionary in the nineteenth century, but rather the *rate* and *scope* of its development. Before 1800, most of the world's agriculture, industry, and transport relied on human and animal muscles. After 1800, these activities were increasingly carried on by power-producing and power-using machinery—and over time, the technological drive has grown ever stronger. Today, the use of machines has passed beyond the abundant provision of goods and services; machines are extending and replacing human functions of every sort. Technology and the scientific knowledge that undergirds it have given to modern societies a power for good and evil that is unique in human history.

Just as the Agricultural Revolution began in certain favored regions such as the Middle East, so the Industrial Revolution began in one country, Britain, where conditions were ripe. Eighteenth-century Britain had benefited from earlier shifts in Western civilization to become exceptionally wealthy, free, and dominant in worldwide trade, so that it had both the ability and the incentive for technical innovation. By 1800, business owners in one industry, cotton textiles, were already making cloth in unprecedented quantities with production machinery powered by steam engines. By 1850, mechanization had spread to many other industries, and Britain was a land of factories and railroads where more than half the population lived in towns and cities—the world's first industrial society.

Around that date, the Industrial Revolution—again, like the Agricultural Revolution before it—began to spread beyond its place of origin, as other countries across Europe and the world adapted British innovations to their own circumstances and became leaders of innovation themselves. Also from the middle of the nineteenth century, the Industrial Revolution made its fateful alliance with science. Throughout history, technical innovation had been mainly a matter of good ideas, trial and error, and rules of thumb. Now, however, "applied" scientists began systematically exploiting the discoveries of "pure" scientists to produce an endless stream of new products and processes. Once firmly hitched to the accelerating scientific juggernaut, the Industrial Revolution became a permanent feature of the modern world, constantly progressing, and constantly spreading. By 1900, the revolution had reached western and central Europe, North America, and Japan; and the number of industrialized countries was destined to go on growing throughout the twentieth century.

The speedup of technology brought with it massive economic and social change. Large-scale capitalism, up to now confined mainly to trade and banking, came to rule the entire economies of industrial countries. A new type of capitalist business organization came into existence—the big privately owned corporation, which alone could raise the vast amounts of money and manage the vast scale of operations needed by railroads, steelworks, electricity systems, and other such new undertakings of the Industrial Revolution. Workers crowded into cities to supply the vast labor forces needed by the new undertakings, migrating from farms to factories and offices—both within countries, over frontiers, and even across oceans to wherever they hoped for a better life than in their native countrysides. Once arrived, many workers organized themselves into labor unions, to bargain with employers and lobby with governments so as to make sure that some of the increased wealth they were producing came back to them in the form of satisfactory working and living conditions.

Along with economic and social change there also came political change. Labor unions came to be linked with political parties, which sought political power and the right to vote for the workers they represented. Governments, worried that the armies of laborers encamped in the towns might rise in revolution, and seeing the big corporations as possible rivals for power, moved from forbidding to tolerating labor unions, and from noninterference in industry to labor legislation. Thinkers and politicians, whether liberal, conservative, or radical, tried to understand the changes that were going on around them, and to foretell where they would lead. In so doing, the thinkers and politicians created the basic concepts that would guide the main political movements of the twentieth century—from Marxism, which would become the guiding ideology of the socialist and communist movements, to various forms of Christian social thought, which would help conservatism to continue as a powerful force even after the traditional world of kings and nobles passed away.

Meanwhile, the growth of scientific knowledge was not only pulling the Industrial Revolution onward, but also bringing about additional revolutions of its own. The progress of science, which in the eighteenth century had still been gradual, now became a broad advance on many fronts: chemistry; electricity and magnetism; cell biology, bacteriology, and genetics; and the investigation of the fundamental nature of matter, energy, space, and time. The pace of science's advance, and the unprecedented understanding of the natural world that it provided, were a revolution in themselves—again, one that has continued down to the present day. Impressed by the overwhelming success of this revolution, investigators in other fields began to imitate its methods. "Social sciences" like sociology and economics, and "human sciences" like anthropology and psychology sprang up, which applied measurement, observation, and experiment more or less systematically to society, culture, and human nature itself.

But the greatest single revolution in ideas and beliefs to come out of nineteenth-century science was that of Darwinism. In the strictly scientific field, Charles Darwin's theory of evolution of species was an idea whose time had come. It solved all kinds of problems raised by earlier efforts to distinguish between different species, as well as by the discoveries of extinct species and of the immense age of the earth. But evolution also had implications far beyond science, since it seemed to remove God's guiding hand from yet another vast area of the natural world—the creation of living things, including human beings—and to replace God's hand with ceaseless and ruthless competition. For this reason, Darwinism appalled many religious believers, and led to a new phase of conflict in the relationship of theology and science. On the other hand, the idea of the "struggle for existence" gave comfort to capitalists, nationalists, imperialists, and revolutionaries—everyone who felt that the course of human affairs was going their way, who realized (or hoped) that others would suffer as a result of their success, and who wanted to feel that science had proved this to be in tune with nature. As a result, Social Darwinism, as this way of thinking was called, fed into many political ideologies of the twentieth century, all the way from communism to fascism.

The overwhelming nineteenth-century changes also had their effect on literature and the arts. From about the middle of the century, the exotic and emotional themes and styles of romanticism began to seem less exciting, and the pull of the medieval, the classical, and even the Christian past began to weaken. Instead, to a greater extent than in previous eras, writers and artists found their themes in the life and objects of their own times: a destitute boy growing up in a workhouse, or a middle-class woman awakening to the meaninglessness of her life of pleasing her husband; weary passengers in an overcrowded railroad car, or an arrangement of fruit, a water carafe, and a liquor bottle on a table. To depict these themes, new and contrasting styles evolved. The Realists treated their subjects in full and accurate detail, often accompanied by fierce denunciation of social evils; the Impressionists, on the other hand, deliberately stripped detail to the bare minimum and carefully avoided social comment, so as to leave the most hauntingly evocative "impression" of the scenes they portrayed. Because the Realists and Impressionists rejected so much that had traditionally seemed essential to the beauty and nobility of art, they were controversial. But they lived in an age that in any case was breaking with its own past amid dispute and conflict—a pattern that from now on became normal in the arts, too, as the West approached the great cultural divide of the twentieth century.

THE INDUSTRIAL REVOLUTION

The Industrial Revolution was unplanned. Perhaps the most remarkable thing about it was that it ever happened. True, many of the developments that had transformed Europe and the rest of the world from the late Middle Ages onward had also prepared the way for the Industrial Revolution. The rise of capitalism had created a class of merchants and manufacturers who were willing to take risks, as well as new forms of business organization that were adaptable to the needs of large industrial enterprises (p. 369). In the technical field, waterwheels had accustomed manufacturers to using stronger sources of power than human or animal muscles; printing had set a precedent for complex mass-production operations; and clocks had provided an example of accurately functioning automatic machines (pp. 265–266, 337–339). The Scientific Revolution had aroused the expectation that scientific discovery would result in practical benefits (p. 472). And the growth of colonial empires had brought much of the world's trade to the countries of western Europe, giving them the wealth to invest in new technology and worldwide markets for their resulting products (pp. 368–369).

But the turning of an agrarian society into an industrial one is not something that comes about easily or "naturally." It is, in fact, an extraordinary development, and there is reason to believe that industrialization came when and where it did only because of an unusual set of circumstances. Those circumstances included a social system and entrepreneurial skills that could convert the *potential* of technology into the *actuality* of large-scale production.

The Agrarian Transformation

It was in England that the Industrial Revolution began; from there the pattern of change spread to the European continent and to the Americas. Preceding and accompanying the Industrial Revolution were significant changes in agriculture. In the course of the eighteenth century, English landlords had substantially increased their holdings and revenues by speeding up the practice of *land enclosure*, which had been going on since the end of the Middle Ages. Under the old manorial regime, the lord's tenants had enjoyed access to the common lands of pasture, meadow, and wood lot (pp. 259–260). By successive parliamentary acts of enclosure, these lands were gradually removed from common use and were *rented* to individuals to farm. Over the same period the "open fields" of cultivated strips were also switched into single plots and fenced in for individual use. In this process of redistribution, the landlords usually gained additional land, while tenants often found that they could no longer make a living.

Although the redistribution brought hardship to thousands of farm families, it put large tracts of land under more efficient management. Whereas the typical small farmer clung to old-fashioned ways, the more ambitious landlords were willing to experiment with improved methods. They tried new farming tools and fertilizers, planted soil-renewing crops, and developed scientific breeding of livestock. The result was a substantial rise in output. This revolution in agriculture also created a pool of displaced farmworkers, both men and women, who desperately sought employment. Some hired themselves out to successful farm operators; others turned to spinning or weaving. They were ready to go wherever they could earn better wages.

At about the same time British traders were discovering profitable new markets. By 1750 Britain had built up a globe-circling empire supported by a large navy and merchant fleet (p. 365). Rich profits awaited those who could increase their exports. Woolens merchants, whose business was well established, were in a favored position to do so; all they needed was a larger production of woolen cloth. There was a brisk demand for cotton goods, too. If English cottons could be made competitive in price with goods produced in the Orient, quick fortunes could be made in the cotton-textile trade.

The Mechanization of Industry and Transportation

A series of inventions gave the textile merchants what they were looking for and led to the general mechanization of industry in England. The first breakthrough, about 1760, was a hand-powered, multispindled spinning wheel (jenny). Soon afterward came Richard Arkwright's water-powered spinning "frame," which spun stronger threads than the jenny. Advances in spinning were soon matched by the development of powered weaving looms. At first designed for use in the cotton industry, these inventions were eventually (from the 1830s onward) adapted to woolen production as well.

12-1   The opening of the world's first railroad using steam locomotives, the eight-mile Stockton and Darlington Railway (1825), as depicted in a contemporary engraving.

The logic of events led next to the building of factories. Spinning and weaving under the domestic system (p. 331) were to persist for many years, but the new machines were not well suited to household use. They were a substantial capital investment; therefore, they had to be operated around the clock. Moreover, they required a source of *power*, which at first was supplied by the traditional waterwheels (p. 265); thus, factories could only be built on the banks of swift-running streams. For these reasons, and for reasons of maintenance and supervision, power machines were set up in special establishments. Arkwright launched the first spinning mill in the 1770s, and within a few years he was employing hundreds of workers, who attended thousands of spindles. Other entrepreneurs soon followed his example.

The greatest boost to the building of factories came from the development of efficient steam engines, which could be built to be more powerful than waterwheels, and were not confined to riverbanks. The steam engine was initially developed by Thomas Newcomen about 1700 in response to a problem in coal mining: the tunnels, always liable to fill with underground water, were being dug too deep for the water to be drained from them by animal-powered pumps as in the past. Newcomen, though no scientist himself, knew about seventeenth-century discoveries concerning the behavior of water when heated and cooled, and used his knowledge to build a machine that would do the job. In this way, the steam engine was the first modern technical device to owe its existence to the progress of science. Later in the eighteenth century, James Watt and other practical inventors made important improvements on Newcomen's machine, greatly increasing its power and harnessing it to turn a wheel. As a result, the steam engine eventually became the chief source of power in the factories and was adapted to both water and land transportation. The "age of railways" began in 1825, when the steam locomotive pioneer George Stephenson opened a stretch of line between the coal mining town of Darlington and the harbor of Stockton, eight miles away, from which the coal went by sea to London (*Fig. 12-1*). Five years later, Stephenson linked two much more important centers—Manchester, the headquarters of the industrialized cotton industry, and Liverpool, the seaport through which Manchester imported raw cotton from the United States and exported finished textiles to customers in every continent. Within twenty years, steam trains were running between all the principal cities of Britain. With its cities linked by steam transportation, with its mechanized cotton industry, and its coal mines deep beneath the earth, Britain now provided the pattern for future industrialization around the world.

Development of a "Permanent" Industrial Revolution

At the middle of the nineteenth century, Britain's industrial productivity and technical progress were unique. But it did not keep this position for long. In the second half of the nineteenth century, with astonishing speed, the Industrial Revolution spread to other countries of western Europe, North America, and the Far East.

In these regions, there were many countries possessing more or less the same features that had enabled Britain to pioneer the Industrial Revolution. They, too, had resources of coal and iron ore. They, too, had middle-class businessmen who were eager to build factories, and landless country-dwellers who were eager to earn wages in them. Even landowning nobles wanted to farm their land more efficiently and profit from the coal and iron ore that might lie beneath it. National monarchs, for their part, struggling to keep what they could of their political power, were well aware that industrial wealth and advanced weapons could only make them stronger. In addition, the progress of science, on which continued technical advancement came to depend (pp. 576–579), was international. In the second half of the nineteenth century, other countries besides Britain joined in the push for technical invention.

By the end of the nineteenth century, Britain was one among a global spread of industrial countries, and not even the most advanced or productive. In Europe, that position had been taken by Germany, while other countries such as France, Belgium, Italy, and Austria-Hungary were also important industrial producers. In the Far East, the ancient empire of Japan, responding to the threat of U.S. and European imperialistic control, was well on the way to becoming a modern industrial country (p. 609). But the most advanced and productive of all the industrial countries, thanks to its vast natural resources, its hardworking population (swelled by immigration), its scientific progress, and its technical know-how, was the United States.

Industrialization not only *spread* from country to country, it also *progressed*. That is, more and more traditional products came to be manufactured by the new methods, and more and more new products and manufacturing processes were invented. The main reason for this was that the machine itself, and the science and technology from which it sprang, were progressing at an accelerated rate. With the rapid increase in scientific knowledge in the nineteenth century (pp. 576–579), more and more industrial firms recognized the connection between "pure" and "applied" science, and sought to exploit it. Practical engineers and backyard tinkerers could still make significant breakthroughs, but more and more inventors were professionally qualified scientists. Indeed, invention itself became an organized activity, as industrial companies (and governments) began to invest large sums in *research and development*. Purposefully conducted and linked to the seemingly limitless progress of pure science, the surge of technological progress continued beyond the nineteenth century, down to the present day. The Industrial Revolution that began in eighteenth-century Britain has continued without interruption ever since.

The new age of "permanent" Industrial Revolution linked to science began shortly after the middle of the nineteenth century. It was inaugurated by the development of new processes in the iron industry—mostly arising from better understanding of the chemistry of metallic ores—that enabled iron to be rapidly and cheaply transformed into a stronger form of the metal, *steel*. By the end of the century, steel had largely replaced iron for rails, bridges, shipbuilding, and other types of construction where superior strength is required. Meanwhile, advances in the physics of heat, gas, electricity, and magnetism led to revolutionary inventions in the field of power production and distribution (pp. 576–577). A new and far more powerful form of steam engine, the turbine, was coupled with generators that turned steam power into electrical energy, so as to make electric light and power.

At the end of the nineteenth century, steam and electrical power were joined by the internal combustion (gasoline or diesel) engine. Fueled by previously untapped petroleum resources—which could be located thanks to the rapidly developing science of geology (p. 580)—the new type of engine brought about yet more revolutions in transportation. Small, light, and yet powerful, it made possible the twentieth-century development of both automobiles and aircraft. With petroleum available in vast amounts to supply the needs of motorists and pilots, chemists also found ways to produce from it an endless variety of textiles and plastics. Other twentieth-century scientists, building on basic discoveries in physics from the late nineteenth century onward, created a whole range of electronic devices that have transformed the transmission and processing of information: radio, television, recording devices, and computers.

Each of these and many other inventions of the last hundred and fifty years has amounted to a revolution in itself. Whole industries—such as steel, oil, plastics, electronics, automobiles, and aircraft—have sprung from nothing to produce and sell these inventions. Usually in not more than twenty or thirty years after the initial invention, each new industry has developed its giant corporations, its massive production plants, and its labor force of hundreds of thousands. As for the *consumers* of these new inventions—the motorists and television viewers, the owners of washing machines and refrigerators, and the users of countless more trivial devices—their way of life has been utterly transformed. Taken together, the new inventions have profoundly altered traditional views of the world, attitudes toward work and leisure, and personal and social habits.

This "permanent" worldwide industrial revolution has been far from painless. It has led to massive changes, usually accompanied by conflict and hardship, in the way businesses are organized and run, and in the patterns of work and life of ordinary people. It has given rise to radical ideologies that have promised relief from the evils of capitalism and industrialization, but in practice have often brought their own forms of mass suffering. It has altered the balance of power in the world, giving dominance to the advanced and productive nations, subjecting nonindustrial ones to imperialistic control, and providing the weapons to fight wars more terrible than any in history. Much of this and the following chapters is concerned with exploring these aspects of the impact of the machine.

THE BUSINESS CORPORATION AND CAPITALIST EXPANSION

As industrial operations grew in number and size, entrepreneurs had to raise capital from sources other than their own profits. Up to midcentury the single proprietorship and the partnership were the principal forms of business organization, but after that time those forms proved less and less able to raise the amounts of risk capital needed. Large undertakings, calling for heavy initial investment in buildings and equipment, required the pooling of money from hundreds of thousands of individuals. The apparatus that business leaders developed for raising and controlling such funds was called the *limited company* in England, the *corporation* in the United States. Its forerunner, the joint-stock company, had first appeared in the seventeenth century as a means of financing commercial and mining ventures.

The Structure and Control of the Corporation

The distinctive feature of the corporation (or limited company) is the financial protection it gives its stockholders. The earlier joint-stock company (p. 369) had sold transferable shares and had served as a means of risk-sharing, but the stock owners collectively had been liable for the debts of the enterprise. The corporation, on the other hand, is a clever *legal invention*, a fictitious "person" created by law. It is authorized to hold property, borrow money, and sue and be sued—without direct involvement of the stockholders. Should the assets of the corporate "person" be lost, the stockholders would lose only the value of their shares of stocks.

"Limited liability" is of crucial importance, since it permits individuals far removed from the control of a business to invest money in its stock without the risk of losing *other* property that they hold. They delegate direction of the firm's operations to a small body, the board of directors, who are elected (usually routinely) by an annual vote of the stockholders. The board, in turn, chooses the executive officers of the firm. So long as the managerial group—the directors and the executives—produces profits for the stockholders, it normally remains in control.

As corporations grew in size (especially after 1900), and as stockholders became increasingly numerous, more and more power went to the managers. The historic link between property *ownership* and property *control* was radically altered by the giant corporations of the twentieth century—a process that has been aptly called the "managerial revolution."

The modern large corporation, whose development was a direct response to the massive use of machines, has become the main functioning unit of Western capitalism. Because these enterprises affect the lives of people everywhere, it is worth examining how they function. The typical large corporation is *multinational*, conducting operations around the globe. It is owned by thousands of stockholders, whose primary concern is to receive regular dividends or an increase in the value of their stock. It employs thousands or hundreds of thousands of people, provides commodities for millions, and pays taxes to national, state, and local governments. The corporation's assets may run into billions of dollars; its gross income may exceed the revenue of many states and nations. Yet this vast economic empire is *controlled* by a small group of corporate managers and professional experts. Their decisions, made within the limits of law, finance, and consumer acceptance, determine the flow of investment, research, and development—and thereby influence the tastes and habits of the public. In the latter decades of the twentieth century, some modifications of this managerial power have been made, with a view of improving the "bottom line" of the business. Thus, employees of some corporations have been invited to participate in operational decisions—and are "motivated" through company stockholding and profit-sharing plans. But the sheer size and structure of the typical large corporation impose strict limits on the scope of such provisions.

The Global Reach of Capitalism

The large corporations, from the very beginning, usually had important *foreign* interests. They sometimes sought to eliminate competition in world markets through private agreements (cartels), and, by extending their investments abroad, they controlled the rate of economic growth in many lands. Industrial capitalism thus became a global force, with money and business seeking the best rates of return, and with an international elite of owners, managers, bankers, and promoters. The push of industrialization was a major factor, along with liberalism and nationalism, in shaping Europe and the world in the nineteenth and twentieth centuries.

Risk capital was especially drawn to "backward" countries by the promise of extraordinary profits. Labor was cheap there, the demand for capital was high, and in some cases rich resources were awaiting exploitation. Overseas investments also aided the creation of an *interdependent* global economy—geared to the interests of the industrial ("advanced") countries. Thus, European capital built railways in Africa that brought out raw materials to be manufactured in Europe and sold in markets around the world.

The industrialists of Great Britain had the jump on those of other nations. By 1914, British private investments overseas amounted to more than $18 billion. French capitalists were next, with some $7 billion. These figures are a fair index of the two nations' comparative penetration and influence in the "backward" continents. (United States capitalists had only $3 billion in foreign investments by 1914; by 1970 the figure was close to $150 billion.)

As early as 1900, some thoughtful observers began to ask whether the concentration and expansion of economic power could go on without seriously disturbing political relations within and among nations. The corporate leaders knew well enough that their wealth was guiding politics both at home and abroad. They saw nothing wrong in this; in fact, they felt their political influence was essential to the full development of the world's resources. Encouraged by the doctrines of economic liberalism, they believed they could serve humanity best by the unrestricted pursuit of profit.

ECONOMIC LIBERALISM: THEORY AND PRACTICE

Such political and economic views were quite different from the doctrine of mercantilism, which was widely accepted up to the end of the eighteenth century. Mercantilism held that economic activities should be used to strengthen the state and that the state, in turn, should guide industry and commerce (p. 456). The Scotsman Adam Smith had been the most effective critic of mercantilism during the eighteenth century. His classic *The Wealth of Nations* (1776) attacked the system and called for a new order of "liberal" economics. Basing his ideas on Hobbes' atomistic view of society (p. 503) and the widely held idea of natural law, he argued that there exists a "natural" economy geared to *human selfishness*. People, if left free to follow their own nature and interests (laissez-faire), will be led by an "invisible hand" to promote the economic welfare of *all*.

Smith's writing had reflected the general optimism of the Enlightenment, but later theorists—the developers of "classical" economics—presented a darker outlook as far as the working class was concerned. One such theorist was David Ricardo, a financier who had made his fortune in England during the Napoleonic Wars. In his *Principles of Political Economy and Taxation* (1817), he set forth the main "laws" governing economic affairs, such as the "law of supply and demand." He is best remembered, perhaps, for his "Iron Law of Wages." Ricardo declared that in a *free-market economy* with a plentiful supply of labor, wages must remain close to the level needed for *bare subsistence* of the workers. More than that would allow more of the workers' children to survive; this would increase the supply, which in turn would *lower* the "natural" price (wages). On the other hand, should wages fall so low that some workers died off, the supply of labor would then decrease, which would *raise* wages back to the subsistence level.

One can see why the teachings of "free-market" economists gave a feeling of hopelessness to wage earners. But the "dismal science" (economics) did not dishearten the captains of trade and industry. On the contrary, it furnished them with respectable and compelling "reasons" for keeping wages down, for seeking profit when and where they could, and for working toward the elimination of un-wanted government "interference." They proved generally successful in striking down controls that were not to their liking and in promoting government action that *favored* their interests. Toward the end of the nineteenth century and on into the twentieth, the latter practice became increasingly common, as economic and political realities moved further away from the models of Adam Smith. His doc-trines nonetheless persisted—as a kind of mythology—to be called up or ignored, according to the interests of particular industries.

THE REACTION OF LABOR AND GOVERNMENT

"To every force, there is an equal and opposing force." Those familiar with this Third Law of Motion (of Isaac Newton) should have expected that bigness in busi-ness would call into being an opposing force (or forces). And, indeed, by the turn of the century Big Business was being confronted by Big Labor and Big Govern-ment. The "autonomous" (self-directed) individual found independent actions ever more limited by huge "autonomous" *organizations*.

THE APPEARANCE OF TRADE UNIONS

There is no doubt that in the long run industrialization raised standards of living and lightened the burden of manual labor. But the transfer of production to fac-tories from family farms and workshops weakened the traditional *family* unit, for it took away one of its foremost functions. Work henceforth became associated, rather, with *class*. Further, working conditions in the early factories were danger-ous and oppressive, hours were long, and wages were low. The factory owners beat down the workers' protests and plowed profits back into more efficient ma-chines. The capital accumulation and investment of the nineteenth century were thus drawn from the unhappy laborers, whose only choice was to work or starve.

The conditions typical of the early factories gave rise to bitter discontent. In some respects conditions were little worse than those under the "domestic system" of production (p. 331). But the factory system, by bringing large numbers of work-ers together, made workers more aware of their common plight and gave them a sense of what their *united* power might be. Alone, the laborer was at the mercy of a large-scale employer. With a surplus of hungry workers seeking jobs, an em-ployer could run a factory without the help of any single wage-hand. Wage-hands, however, often had no place to turn should they lose their jobs. In the early part of the nineteenth century, therefore, there was no bargaining over wages and hours; they were set by the employer, and the worker could either take them or leave them.

Collective action for the purpose of bargaining with employers or influencing legislation offered some promise of relief to the laborers. They discovered, however, that whenever they tried to organize, the odds were against them. Local "trade clubs" had existed in England before the Industrial Revolution, but only in a few skills (printing, tailoring, weaving) and only in certain communities. When artisans tried to organize on a wider basis, their combinations were broken up by the joint action of employers and the government. Generally viewed by the courts as "conspiracies," trade unions had been prohibited in both France and England by 1800. Governments feared that they might lead to riots or uprisings; employers feared that they might lead to higher costs. Later legislation in England (1825) allowed unions to exist but closely limited their activities.

Workers themselves were far from unanimous in their support of unions, partly because of the harsh punishments given by employers to those suspected of belonging to such organizations. The charges of conspiracy were no doubt another discouraging factor. Nevertheless, by the middle of the nineteenth century steps had been taken in England to organize some skilled workers on a nationwide basis. The cotton spinners, for example, began to gain recognition for their associations and to develop modern collective-bargaining procedures (supported by the power of strikes). Many legal battles still had to be fought and won by British labor unions, but by 1900 two million workers (skilled and unskilled) had been organized into effective bargaining associations. A similar pattern of struggle—legal, economic, and political—followed in the United States and in other industrial countries.

THE TREND TOWARD STATE INTERVENTION

Many workers looked to *legislation* as a means of remedying certain evils of industrialism. Some believed that legislation was a helpful addition to direct economic action by unions; others thought legislation, eventually, might make direct action unnecessary. In England, the laboring classes themselves had virtually no political power until after midcentury; even before that, however, other social groups succeeded in bringing about some needed reforms through legislation. Most disinterested observers had come to agree that protective measures by the state (contrary to the doctrines of economic liberalism) were essential to the health and safety of the nation.

Reform legislation was initiated by the Tory party, which represented primarily the interests of the landed aristocracy. Since the landowners did not usually have large investments in industry, they could best afford to promote humane treatment of factory workers. Numerous intellectuals and humanitarians, without respect to party, also supported the Tory proposals. And it is only fair to add that some of the industrialists themselves, after accumulating their fortunes, supported reforms. Factory owners as a group, however, bitterly fought all proposed limitations on their freedom to conduct their enterprises as they saw fit.

A series of parliamentary acts, beginning in 1833, removed the worst conditions in British industry. Employers were forbidden to hire children under nine years of age, and the labor of those under eighteen was restricted to nine hours a

12-2   This picture of a young boy hauling coal along a tunnel in a mine comes from an official report to the British Parliament in 1842. Though the working classes had little political power in Britain at the time, depictions like these influenced middle- and upper-class politicians to pass labor legislation.

day. Women and children were excluded from mine labor *(Fig. 12-2)*, and better hours and safety devices were required in the mines. Government inspectors were hired to ensure that the regulations were observed. After wage-earners themselves gained the right to vote (in 1867), additional measures were enacted for their protection and welfare.

On the continent of Europe, France and Belgium began to catch up to the English in industrial growth. Napoleon III established the Second Empire in 1852 with the active support of the French bourgeois (p. 517). He took effective measures to promote agriculture, manufacturing, and commerce. The popular emperor also showed sympathy toward the industrial working class, legalizing labor unions in 1864 and providing many social welfare institutions. Workers benefited further from his grand public works projects, among them the rebuilding of Paris into a splendid city of broad boulevards and impressive public squares.

Germany was several decades behind England in industrial growth; but in the latter part of the century it took the lead in social legislation. Conditions in mines and factories were similar to those in England and France, and laws regulating job safety, age of employment, and hours of labor were passed in due course. Labor unions, intellectuals, and religious groups helped bring about these reforms. After Bismarck became imperial German chancellor in 1871 (pp. 548–549), he used social legislation as a means of improving the nation's health, ensuring his own popularity, and increasing the loyalty of citizens to the new German Empire. The crowning regulatory measure was the Industrial Code of 1891, which guaranteed uniform protection to workers (with respect to hours and conditions) throughout the nation. Equally significant were later laws providing for sickness and accident insurance and old-age pensions for workers. The Social Insurance Code of 1911 became a model for other industrialized countries.

In adopting measures of this nature, the United States was at least a generation behind western Europe — though in another field of government intervention America was ahead. Giant industries developed rapidly after the Civil War; by 1890 mergers, trusts, and other forms of business combination were eliminating competitors and making huge profits. Many liberals, labor leaders, populists, and small entrepreneurs became alarmed by the growing concentration of economic power. They demanded legislation to check the expansion of monopolies and to keep enterprise "competitive and free."

Thus, in the name of liberalism, the power of the American government was called up as a *counterforce* to Big Business. The Sherman Antitrust Act of 1890 declared illegal "every contract, combination, or conspiracy in restraint of interstate commerce." The passage of this law was only the starting point of a long and tough contest in which government has sought to protect the public against the excesses of private economic powers; it was looked upon, however, by those powers as an encroachment upon *their* freedom. A further interference with wealth concentration was the enactment by the federal government of a *graduated income tax* in 1913.

URBANIZATION AND STANDARDIZATION OF SOCIETY

Personal freedom for millions of people was reduced by their crowding into large cities. This had been foreseen by the classic liberal Thomas Jefferson, who had written in 1800, "I view great cities as pestilential to the morals, the health, and the liberties of man." Population congestion calls forth regulation as a means of organizing essential services and protecting citizens from the trespasses of their neighbors. Although the move from farm to town had begun in the high Middle Ages as a response to the revival of commerce (p. 263), for centuries the flow was insignificant. It was the Industrial Revolution, along with a sudden rise in population — and in eastern Europe the belated end of serfdom, giving the peasants freedom to move and change their occupations (pp. 461, 544, 553) — that brought about the rapid expansion of European cities.

Population figures before 1800 are only estimates, but it is evident that the number of people in Europe had risen very slowly until that time. The nineteenth century saw a startling increase, however. From 1800 to 1914 the population of western Europe grew from about 150 million to nearly 450 million — an increase greater than that of the preceding *ten* centuries (p. 262). (The total figure would have been still higher except for *mass emigration* — the largest movement of people in history. The big wave began to roll after 1870. From that year until 1914, over twenty-six million Europeans left their homes for the New World, more than half of them for the United States.) The extraordinary increase in population cannot be explained by a change in birthrates, for these remained fairly stable. The lowering of the *death* rate was the decisive factor, and this resulted from numerous causes. Chief among them were increased food production (aided by agricultural improvements), planting of more nutritious crops (the potato and Indian corn), decline of infanticide, advances in sanitation, and control of epidemics. In addition, the Industrial Revolution provided more purchasing power in the manufacturing countries, and that power was used to import more food from overseas.

By 1910, Germany, with fifty-eight million, had the largest population of any western European nation. Britain was next, with forty-two million; then France, with forty-one million; and Italy, with thirty-six million. The most striking growth, everywhere, was taking place in the cities. At the start of the Industrial Revolution there were only four English cities of over fifty thousand inhabitants. By 1850 there were thirty-one, and half the population of Britain was living in cities—a proportion unprecedented in European history. Manchester, in the cotton-manufacturing region, was the largest and best known of the new industrial communities. Formerly a market town of twenty-five thousand, it had grown to half a million by 1850. Its civic officials, like those of other urban centers, lacked the authority and organization they needed to meet the city's needs.

The nineteenth-century growth of cities led to a momentous change in the way of life of the western peoples. For thousands of years since the Agricultural Revolution (pp. 12–17), the average man or woman had lived on the land, either as a smallholding peasant or as an agricultural laborer. As late as the year 1800, in most European countries eighty to ninety percent of the population was occupied in agriculture, with only ten to twenty percent gaining a living from industry or commerce. By the late twentieth century, the proportion was exactly reversed. In western Europe and the United States, less than ten percent of the population worked in agriculture, and much of the rest of the world was moving in the same direction.

The "backwash" from industrialization and the swift overflow of people from towns and farms overturned deep-set patterns of family and community life that traced back to the Middle Ages and even earlier. The end result in the countryside, as one observer concluded, was "the death of tradition itself."

As it brought an end to the traditional way of life, the factory carried the Western peoples from a world in which they were surrounded and dominated by nature to one that was more of their own making. And the new environment was ugly. The cities lacked sewers and paving. Housing for workers was cramped, rickety, and drab. Into the crowded, soot-blackened tenements poured the refugees from rural poverty—strangers in their own land. The chronic urban maladies of alienation, disease, and crime have persisted into the twentieth century.

Cities, in time, also brought much that was positive: better education, medical care, theaters, libraries, and merchandise from all over the earth. Even these advantages, however, were shared unequally, and poor people felt even more deprived in the presence of commodities they could not afford. Moreover, they seldom found the satisfaction in their daily labor that had brought meaning to the life of the craftsman in earlier times. The factory system reduced workers to the attending of machines and subjected them to its rigid discipline. Narrowing specialization of tasks chained them to deadening, repetitive motions. Workers, like the machine and all its parts, became standardized, replaceable cogs in a production line that turned out standardized, replaceable things.

Alongside the factory, there grew up another institution that shaped the lives of millions of people from the late nineteenth century onward: the office. Big business and big government needed office workers and other "white-collar" employees even more than they needed factory workers. In pay and standards of living, white-collar employees (including increasing numbers of women) did not differ much from ordinary "blue-collar" workers, but since they did not do heavy or dirty manual labor, they considered themselves more respectable. Together with self-employed small business owners and storekeepers, they formed the "lower middle class" as opposed to the "working class."

Mass production and maximum profits required not only *standardized commodities* but *mass demand*. In order to keep capital and plant capacity working at their full potential, advertising was developed to force-feed natural desires. Organized "buy" appeals supported and expanded the media of mass communication— overcoming local resistance and tending to make the demand for goods uniform and universal. As the twentieth century proceeded, the individual came to be viewed increasingly as a *consumer* of goods, a permanent target of the commercial persuaders. Daily choices (whether conscious or not) would be governed to a mounting degree by enticing propaganda.

When technology was applied to the art of salesmanship as well as to production, it weakened many time-honored habits and customs. Mass culture thus came into being, essentially as we know it today—plastic, commercialized, and conformist. Though it included numerous and varied subcultures, it held to one constant value: concern for *material* things. The materialism and secularism of the West, on the rise since the Renaissance (pp. 334–335, 374), had reached new heights by the beginning of the twentieth century. The westerners' acquisitive character had always opened them to the lure of worldly goods. The machine now enabled them to produce wealth beyond their dreams, and the new salesmanship ensured that those dreams would never cease.

THE DEVELOPMENT OF SOCIALIST THOUGHT AND ACTION

The impact of the machine provoked a wide range of intellectual responses. Ever since the Industrial Revolution, people have been struggling with the vast problems and the vast promise of technology. In alternating moods of gloom, bewilderment, and hope, they have sought to understand where the machine is leading them and how to adapt it to human ends. Since the machine was identified in the nineteenth century with the system of industrial capitalism, that system became the focus of analysis and criticism.

The first reactions were to the factories themselves. Beyond the low wages, the oppressive working conditions, and the wretched housing was the misery caused by *unemployment*. Operating, in the main, according to "natural economic laws," nineteenth-century capitalism was a dynamic, unstable mechanism. Good times (booms) alternated with bad times (depressions), and the economic crises appeared to grow worse and worse. Wage earners, whose daily bread depended on their pay envelopes, were hardest hit when the factories laid off workers. Under the doctrines of economic liberalism, they were bound to suffer for as long as the system endured.

We saw earlier in this chapter that many workers turned to unions and social legislation to protect themselves and their families. But some workers and intellectuals became convinced that reform within the system was insufficient. Reacting to the social reality of *nineteenth-century capitalism,* they believed that the only hope for a better economic life and a just society lay in a radical change of the *system itself.* Most of these critics, though their ideas ranged across a broad spectrum, may be classified generally as *socialists.*

UTOPIAN SOCIALISM

Among the socialist thinkers of the nineteenth century the major division was between "utopians" and Marxists. The former belonged to a tradition reaching back as far as Plato (pp. 83–85). Their general approach was to turn from the evils apparent in the existing order and to seek in their imagination something closer to their ideal of life and society. Some of these thinkers were influenced by the *Utopia* of Sir Thomas More, written in the sixteenth century (pp. 401–402). Sir Thomas despised the grasping landlords and entrepreneurs of his day; for his imaginary island of Utopia (literally, "no place") he envisioned a *planned* society of common ownership, tolerance, and equality.

In France, the utopians pursued two distinct lines of thought. Count Henri de Saint-Simon proposed a reorganization of society from the top, with state ownership of the means of production, and control by a national board of scientists, engineers, and industrialists (technocrats). The purpose of industry would be *production* rather than *profit,* and workers and managers would be rewarded according to individual merit. In his chief work, *The New Christianity* (1825), Saint-Simon stressed philanthropic motives: "The whole of society ought to strive toward the amelioration of the moral and physical existence of the poorest class; society ought to organize itself in the way best adapted for attaining this end." Saint-Simon's writings drew the sympathetic attention of numerous European intellectuals. His disciples in France, some of whom became leaders in politics, were among the first modern advocates of a nationally planned society.

Charles Fourier, a younger contemporary of Saint-Simon, took a different approach. Resisting the idea of centralized economic control, he favored the creation of thousands of small production units, which he called "phalanxes." Limited in size to four hundred families, each phalanx would contain a residential hotel, school, market, health service, and other public facilities—in addition to its own farms and manufacturing plants. All these were to be *community* property, and the rule governing labor and distribution would be: "*From* each according to his *ability; to* each according to his *needs.*" (The Marxists were later to adopt this slogan.)

Surplus production would be exchanged for other goods by barter among the phalanxes; within each plant, workers would change jobs often, in order to reduce the monotony of performing repetitive tasks.

Fourier anticipated many of the problems of industrialism and believed that the free association of cooperative producers was the soundest way of meeting them. His ideas attracted numerous followers, and a few isolated phalanxes were actually established in America—notably Brook Farm, near Boston. Each phalanx had its own internal problems, and each was doomed to failure. Success for Fourier's plan would have required the development of an *extensive system* of phalanxes, and there was scarcely a chance that this could have come into being.

The efforts of Robert Owen, an industrialist and utopian planner, failed for the same basic reason. A successful cotton mill owner in New Lanark, Scotland, Owen was distressed by the poverty, ignorance, and immorality of his employees. He determined to change matters and succeeded in setting up a model factory and community in New Lanark. He was not satisfied, however, with his own *local* reforms and sought to reform the whole industrial order.

Owen observed that the factory system had not freed workers—it had enslaved them. Under laissez-faire, their condition remained at a miserable level. Morals had fallen along with material standards of living, and the traditional ties of compassion between master and servant were missing in the new industrial order. Owen had fair success in promoting remedial factory legislation, but this served only to check the worst abuses. After failing to persuade factory owners to follow his example at New Lanark, he proposed that the poor be organized into cooperative, self-sufficient villages.

Owen's plan won commendation in the British press and in Parliament, but nothing more. Abandoning his appeals to the leaders of government and industry, he next turned to the working people themselves. Out of his efforts grew several producers' cooperatives, including one overseas—at New Harmony, Indiana. Founded in 1824, this venture (like the others) lasted only a few years. Owen nonetheless left his mark on public thought and on the struggle to lighten the harshness of industrialism. But it took another, more rigorous thinker to produce a tougher brand of socialism that would meet the capitalist system head on.

SCIENTIFIC SOCIALISM: THE SYNTHESIS OF MARX

Karl Marx brushed aside "utopian" ideas as sentimental and unrealistic; in this he shared the opinion of most of the capitalists of his time. Marx's study of history told him that events are shaped by underlying *economic* developments, rather than by idealistic reformers, and he believed that these developments were leading toward the collapse of capitalism. Therefore, he insisted, the proper task of workers and intellectuals is to *understand* the trend of history and to *participate* in its forward movement. While accepting some of the observations and principles of Owen and Fourier, he felt that their appeals distracted people from the "correct" course of thought and action.

It was in this sense that Marx and his followers regarded his own doctrine as "scientific." Marx set forth certain theories and sought to prove them by the evidence of history. He was not primarily an inventor of ideas; his achievement was a grand *synthesis*. Materialist, rationalist, libertarian, and revolutionist, Marx was an heir of the Enlightenment—who drew upon the leading scientific, economic, and philosophic ideas of the nineteenth century. But, reflecting also the romantic spirit of his age, Marx's teachings contain strong elements of faith and feeling as well as of reason and science.

Born in the Rhineland (Germany), of a middle-class Jewish family, the youthful Karl attended the universities of Bonn and Berlin. His father (a Lutheran convert) was a lawyer, and the son began to prepare for the same profession. Soon, however, Karl became attracted to the study of history and philosophy and would have liked to qualify himself for a professorship. But he feared that his Jewish identity and his liberal political views would block his chances of winning a university appointment, for this was the period of the conservative reaction in Germany. Caught up by the revolutionary stirrings of the 1840s, he turned instead to journalism and pamphleteering.

With his lifelong friend and partner, Friedrich Engels, Marx organized revolutionary groups and wrote *The Communist Manifesto* of 1848. After participating in the insurrections of that year in the Rhineland, he escaped to London, where he remained for the rest of his life. He was one of the first critics to stress the *international* character of working-class movements—thus placing himself in opposition to the mounting spirit of nationalism in Europe (pp. 546–550). From London, Marx continued his association with revolutionary movements in various countries, helping to found the First (socialist) International in 1864. And he spent long hours in the British Museum studying history and economics.

The most famous product of his labors, *Das Kapital (Capital)*, appeared in part before his death and was completed by Engels. It consisted chiefly of theory and analysis and is closely related to the writings of the "classical" liberal economists (pp. 561–562). While Marx scorned their ignorance of history, he respected their understanding of the dynamics of nineteenth-century capitalism. Working largely from their stated "laws" and principles, he concluded that all economic *value* is produced by *human labor* and that the capitalist unjustly takes over a portion of this value. The system, he claimed, promises nothing but misery to the laborers and contains *contradictions* that ensure its own destruction. But Marx's economic conclusions were perhaps the least original, least proven, and least important of his ideas. His enormous influence would come from the fact that he was able to join his criticism of capitalism with a revolutionary program based on a *unified view* of history, politics, and morals.

The philosopher Hegel gave Marx the key to his general view. History is an unceasing process, said Hegel, governed at any moment by the struggle between a dominant idea and its opposing idea (pp. 527–529). This was a relatively simple explanation that made order and purpose out of the bewildering tangle of events. Marx was excited by Hegel's *dialectic* principle, but he had no use for the notion that *ideas* are the prime forces in history. After much study and reflection, he concluded that the "mode of production" (economic structure) is the main determining force in a given society; its *opposing* force arises from technological changes that are no longer suitable to the established economic structure. In Marx's own words:

> In the social production which men carry on they enter into indefinite relations that are indispensable and independent of their will; these relations of production correspond to a definite stage of development of the material powers of production. The sum total of these relations of production constitutes the economic structure of society — the real foundation, on which rise legal and political superstructures and to which correspond definite forms of social consciousness. The mode of production in material life determines the general character of the social, political, and spiritual processes of life. It is not the consciousness of men that determines their existence, but, on the contrary, their social existence determines their consciousness.

Thus did Marx "turn Hegel upside down." The flow of history and the growth of ideas and institutions, Marx thought, are all shaped by changes in the mode of production. And this evolution had passed through four principal stages: "the Asiatic, the ancient, the feudal, and the modern bourgeois methods of production."

Engels later sought to modify the rigidity of Marx's economic determinism (sometimes called "historical materialism"). What he meant, explained Engels, was that the economic factor is "the strongest, most elemental, and most decisive." But to admit the influence of *various* factors is to weaken the claim of *economic* determinism. Even non-Marxist historians agree that the system of production is *one* important factor among the "determinants" of a given culture.

Marx saw the "class struggle" as part of historical materialism — a view that had special significance because it related to the actual struggles of working people in the nineteenth century. Each mode of production, he said, serves a particular "ruling" class, which takes advantage of its opposing "exploited" class. The ancient world had its masters and slaves; the feudal age, its nobles and serfs; the capitalist age, its bourgeois and *proletarians*. (This last word, derived from the Latin name for *propertyless* citizens of ancient Rome, was applied by Marx to the swelling number of industrial wage-hands.) Marx believed that the ruling class of each age provides laws and institutions to guarantee its continued exploitation of the opposing class. The state itself thus becomes a mechanism of *suppression*. The executive of the nineteenth-century capitalist state, he declared, was "a committee for managing the common affairs of the whole bourgeoisie" (the bourgeois *class*).

Social revolutions occur, according to Marx, when a new mode of production — taking shape within the framework of the old — bursts the bonds of established laws and relationships. The agents of the revolution are the "new" class, which, in time, becomes the ruling class. Thus, he argued, the bourgeoisie had promoted the *liberal* revolutions, thereby paving the way for a new economic order — and for a new ruling class (itself). But the hour had struck for the bourgeoisie, as it had earlier for the European nobility. The potential of expanding technology could not be realized within the structure of private capitalism; and the capitalist system of production, hit by increasingly severe depressions, was stumbling toward its end. In accordance with the dialectic principle, the old system had already brought into existence the class that would overthrow it and build a new order upon the ruins. This class, the proletariat, was being drawn into the industrial centers in ever larger numbers. All it needed in order to help history along was Marxist instruction and organization.

Though Marx had bitter feelings toward the bourgeoisie and regarded its exploitation of the proletariat as the most brutal in history, he felt that it had played, in preceding centuries, a constructive and progressive role. This was in keeping with his (and Hegel's) view of history as moving irresistibly toward higher and higher goals of human fulfillment. Marx also approved the liberal revolutions, whose results were chiefly *political*. The freedoms gained were of primary benefit to the entrepreneurial class, but they also increased the opportunities of the lower class to work for *social* revolution. Political freedom was meaningless to the hungry and the homeless, thought Marx, but it was a step toward achieving a new order of production that could provide a decent living for all—and liberate the worker from humiliation and servitude. Only after those changes had been brought about could individuals realize their full potential, the goal Marx desired for *everyone*.

Marx predicted that the mounting clashes between the proletariat and the bourgeoisie would lead to the triumph of the working class. This victory would bring an end to the historic class struggle, for all individuals would then be included in *one* body of workers. Dismantling the old social order and taking over the means of production would be carried out under a temporary "dictatorship of the proletariat." This would be followed, in turn, by an intermediate period of democratic "socialism," during which individuals would "work according to their ability and receive according to their output." Socialism would lead eventually to pure "communism."

Once *communism* had been reached, the state would "wither away," Marx believed, because without a class struggle there would be no reason for the existence of a state. Thus would come into being, for the first time in civilized history, "true" liberty for all. In the vaguely outlined communist society, voluntary associations would plan and carry out production; individuals would work according to their *abilities* and receive according to their *needs*; private persuasion and restraint would replace police, prisons, and war.

Close observers of human nature, from Aristotle and Augustine through Montaigne, Hobbes, and Voltaire, would no doubt have felt that this sketch of an earthly paradise is highly unrealistic. Even if we grant a measure of scientific truth to Marx's analysis of the past, his vision of the future was a romantic one—as demonstrated by failures of Marxist societies in the last decade of the twentieth century. If accepted at all, it had to be accepted on *faith*. Indeed, the followers of Marx found in his doctrines a *kind* of religion; they called it the *religion of man*.

Their "god," the prime mover, was "historical materialism," and Marx its prophet. There were Marxist equivalents of apostles and saints—as well as despised heretics. The sacred books were his writings, defended by "dialectical" theologians. The Church was the Party, and true believers had to have unquestioning faith in its gospel and its works. The Marxist heaven was their idealized society to come.

c. 1800	1848	1889	1914
Utopian Socialism	Development and Spread of Orthodox Marxism	Revisionist Marxism Dominant	

First International
(1864–1872)

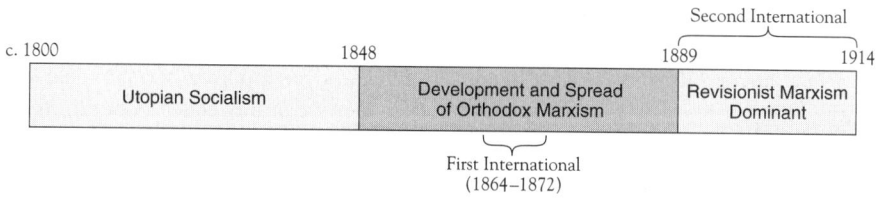

This analogy with traditional Christianity, or Islam, each with its authoritative doctrines, is given here to suggest the emotional quality of Marxism—and to stress the fact that it presented a *total* view of the past, present, and future of human society. This is a crucial point to grasp if we are to understand the attraction of Marxism for over a century and a half. At a time when the foundations of "old-fashioned" religion and liberalism were being challenged, Marx created a new worldview of the facts, theories, and hopes of the *industrial age*. Its promise appealed to the working class, but it appealed also to many intellectuals who felt alienated from industrialism and were looking for some kind of total reorientation. Partial critiques and actions based on a mix of traditional values (as in utopianism) left such people unsatisfied. Marxism offered a unified view and psychological substitute for traditional religion.

The Interpreters of Marx: Revolutionary and Evolutionary

The Marxist "truth," however, has been open to differing interpretations. Had capitalism faltered and collapsed during the nineteenth century, as Marx himself expected, the division among his followers might have been less profound. But the established order proved much tougher, much more adaptable, than he had expected. Reform laws and unions strengthened capitalism (as did Marxist criticism), improved the distribution of purchasing power, and bettered the conditions of the workers. The rich were getting richer, as Marx had predicted, but the poor (at least in the West) were *not* getting poorer. And in the United States, the young giant of capitalism, no strong revolutionary feeling or class-consciousness appeared among the wage earners.

How did the Marxists deal with this indefinite postponement of the day of revolution? Marx had considered two possible paths to the overthrow of capitalism: one by legal means, the other by force. He did not exclude either, and he recognized the power that an extension of voting rights might hold out to the working class. But he leaned toward the view that the ruling class was unlikely to surrender its property under democratic processes and that a resort to violence must ultimately be expected.

After Marx's death (in 1883), the capitalist states showed no signs of tottering, and most socialist workers tended to make their peace with the existing system. True, a small group of Marxists stuck by the "hard" line, scorning "legalism" and "gradualism." But the larger group recognized that such a stand would not appeal to the bulk of workers. They stated frankly that Marxist doctrine would have to be *revised* if it was to continue as a major force.

The "revisionists" mapped a much longer (and different) road to the ideal society. They stressed democracy, parliamentary methods, and class cooperation as means of achieving further reforms. Eduard Bernstein, a German socialist, was the leading advocate for this view. (The "Fabian" socialists of England, though non-Marxist, held a similar position.) The broad term "social democratic" can be applied to most of the labor parties in European politics after 1890; they represented the "evolutionary" wing among the heirs of Marx. The "revolutionary" wing remained significant only in eastern Europe, where the absence of effective representative government prevented change by peaceful, legal methods. It was there, in a relatively backward country, Russia, that the revolutionary Marxists would achieve the first great victory of socialism (pp. 624–634).

A different sort of attack upon the established order of the nineteenth century took the form of *anarchism*. This view holds that any use of *authority*—economic, religious, or political—is an unjustified interference with the individual. Believing that human beings are basically *good*, the anarchists claim that voluntary, harmonious relationships could be achieved among individuals if the power of the *state* were removed. Some, like the Russian writer Leo Tolstoy (p. 534) and the American essayist, Henry David Thoreau, were anarchists only in a philosophical sense; they firmly opposed the use of violence as a means of realizing their ideas. But others pursued what they considered to be the direct and necessary route to the abolition of government: assassination of government officials, terrorism, and insurrection. Though these anarchist ideas were first expressed in western Europe, it was Mikhail Bakunin, a Russian nobleman, who exerted the largest influence. Bakunin died in 1876; his followers succeeded in killing (among others) Tsar Alexander II of Russia, President Sadi Carnot of France, King Humbert I of Italy, and President William McKinley of the United States. Such acts of *terror* horrified the powerful everywhere, but failed to produce an effective movement for social change or for the abolition of state power. (Nevertheless, these acts were forerunners of terrorist killings in the twentieth century—pp. 692–693.)

THE CHRISTIAN RESPONSE

It was unthinkable that the established churches of the West could ignore the impact of industrial capitalism *or* the Marxist (and anarchist) attack upon it. While the one appeared destructive of certain Christian values and virtues, the other appealed openly to class-hatred and violence. Both unrestricted (*laissez-faire*) capitalism and Marxist materialism were roundly condemned, at last, by the most powerful spokesman of Western Christendom, the pope. In 1891, Leo XIII addressed his bishops through a formal letter (encyclical) entitled *Rerum Novarum (Of New Things)*. In this carefully drawn, comprehensive statement, he set forth the position of his Church on the relations between capital and labor.

The pope's immediate concern, as expressed in his letter, was for the "misery and wretchedness which press so heavily at this moment on the large majority of the very poor." The workers, he went on, "have been given over, isolated and defenseless, to the callousness of employers and the greed of unrestrained competition." Going still further, he declared that "a small number of very rich men have been able to lay upon the masses of the poor a yoke little better than slavery itself."

But the socialist remedy, the pontiff declared, called for the destruction of private property. Such action would be unjust to the present lawful owners of property and would deprive workers of the main object of their labors. He also rejected the socialist idea of equalizing wealth—as being "against nature." The overriding mistake of the Marxists, however, was their feeling that social classes must be mutually hostile, "that rich and poor are intended by nature to live at war with one another." On the contrary, stated Pope Leo, "it is ordained by nature that these two classes should exist in harmony . . . capital cannot do without labor, nor labor without capital."

Quoting freely from his favorite philosopher, Thomas Aquinas (p. 301), who was known for his efforts to harmonize conflicting positions, the pope urged a Christian "middle course." Moderation and cooperation should guide the common affairs of employers and employees. Working people must give honest work and never injure the owners or their property; the owners must never make excessive demands on their employees' labor or pay them less than the needs of their families require. For the purpose of mutual help and wage-bargaining, workers should be allowed to form unions; and if workers find themselves too weak to defend their rightful interests, the government must intervene with *protective legislation*. At the same time, however, the government must preserve absolutely the *sanctity of private property*.

The *Rerum Novarum* was significant not so much for its originality as for its authority. Approved by succeeding popes, including John Paul II (pp. 730–731), it served as a rallying point for individuals (Catholic and non-Catholic) who were perplexed or frightened by the social crisis. The message gave little comfort to aggressive entrepreneurs on the political right, or to angry critics of capitalism on the left. But it offered a guide for moderates who wished to see the rewards of labor improved while avoiding industrial violence. It also prompted the founding of new Catholic trade unions and Catholic political parties in most of the countries of Europe. These organizations have exercised notable influence, continuing to the present day. Finally, *Rerum Novarum* pointed the way, morally and philosophically, to the democratic "welfare states" of the twentieth century (pp. 642–645).

Because of its organizational structure, it was possible and logical for the Roman Catholic Church to present a unified response to the disturbing economic changes of the nineteenth century. The response by Protestant churches, on the other hand, reflected their historical divisions into numerous national and denominational groups. In the wake of scientific findings and rising secularism in the Western world, Christian (and Jewish) believers were already torn between "modernists," who accepted the new science, and "fundamentalists," who rejected it and adhered to the "higher truth" of the literal Bible. Now, with respect to the impact of industrialization, another serious split was developing. Most Protestant preachers and congregations remained essentially conservative on economic issues, but an activist minority began to speak out for increased *social consciousness*, measures to assist the poor, and greater "economic justice."

In England and America, the Anglican Church played a prominent role in these efforts, often called the "Social Gospel." And, aside from the well-known churches, a new evangelical movement, the Salvation Army, was founded in 1865 by William Booth. He began this campaign in England, but it soon became a visible international operation. The "army" sent its "soldiers" (male and female) onto the city streets seeking to "save souls," but also to collect contributions for helping the needy with food, clothing, and shelter. This unique organization and the many other carriers of the "Social Gospel" would continue their humanitarian work into and through the twentieth century.

THE ACCELERATING PROGRESS OF SCIENCE

Accompanying the technological progress, social changes, and class conflicts of the nineteenth century were great leaps in pure science. The scientific revolution of the seventeenth century had lost none of its force: the organization of science became even wider and better supported. As more and more trained minds were focused on the riddles of nature, their combined efforts and findings rose at a rapid rate.

Physical scientists continued to build on the foundations of Galileo, Newton, and Boyle (pp. 466–471). One of the most important subjects of their investigations was energy. Experimenters proved the equivalence of *heat* and *energy* and formulated two basic laws of thermodynamics. The First Law states that the total energy (or heat) in the universe remains constant, though it is continually changing its form. The Second Law states that energy systems tend toward degradation (heat, for example, flows from a hotter body to a colder one); hence, the amount of *useful* energy is diminishing in the universe. These generalizations, supplementing the Newtonian laws of motion (pp. 469–471), gave fresh understanding to physicists, chemists, astronomers—even philosophers.

In addition, major theoretical discoveries were made, with far-reaching practical applications, about *electricity*, *magnetism*, and *light*. Newton had observed that when sunlight passes through a prism it spreads into a band of colors or *spectrum*—red at one end and indigo (dark blue) at the other. Scientists of the nineteenth century discovered that each chemical substance, when heated to incandescence (strongly enough to emit light), yields a spectrum distinct from every other. Spectrum analysis was developed as a tool for chemists—and for astronomers in studying sources of light in space (pp. 716–717). In addition, researchers made progress in identifying the actual nature of light, as a series of vibrations or *waves:* in the spectrum, red is longer wavelength light, and indigo is light of shorter wavelength.

These results, in turn, were linked with new findings about the nature of electricity and magnetism. Ever since the Renaissance, researchers had been investigating these two forces, and had gradually come to suspect that they were in some way closely related. Finally, about the middle of the nineteenth century, Michael Faraday proved that this was so, and devised many ingenious experiments by which he used magnetism to produce electric currents and vice versa; in others he used electricity in one coil of wire to cause a flow of current in another, with which it was not connected. Out of these experiments, inventors soon developed electrical generators and motors, and Alexander Graham Bell devised the first telephone; thus the modern electrical and communications industries were born.

Meanwhile, in 1861, a brilliant Scottish physicist, James Clerk Maxwell, used Faraday's results to produce an exact mathematical description of the behavior of electricity and magnetism. Remarkably, Maxwell's laws for the behavior of electricity and magnetism turned out to be exactly the same as those already discovered for the behavior of light. Evidently, all three were simply different forms of one and the same phenomenon—*electromagnetism.* True, only light was visible to the human eye, but invisible electromagnetism, too, must be able to travel in wavelike form with no obvious pathway to conduct it.

This hypothesis was confirmed about 1887 by Heinrich Hertz, the first to generate invisible electromagnetic waves and receive them in a separate device, not connected by wires to the originating equipment. Not long afterward, in 1895, W. K. Roentgen discovered electromagnetic waves of extremely short wavelength that could travel through objects that appeared solid to the human eye, and leave a picture of their internal structure on a photographic plate: he called these X-rays. Hertz's achievement pointed the way to Guglielmo Marconi's development of "wireless" transmitters and all that followed in the field of radio communications; and Roentgen's discovery proved immensely valuable to technology and medicine.

The nineteenth century also witnessed many discoveries in chemistry and the theory of matter. The ancient Greek Democritus (p. 80) had theorized that matter was reducible to invisible, indivisible particles or *atoms.* John Dalton, a British schoolteacher, accepted this general notion but found, early in the nineteenth century, that each chemical element was composed of atoms of different weights. Scientists later assumed the existence of *molecules*—combinations of atoms of the same or different elements. Most material substances, they concluded, other than those pure chemical elements in which the atoms do not combine with each other, are made up of molecules. In the nineteenth and early twentieth centuries, much chemical research was devoted to the analysis of molecules and the synthesis (artificial creation) of new ones, with astonishing results: basic understanding of the way in which atoms combine to form molecules; the invention of new dyestuffs, explosives, drugs, and the earliest plastics; the identification of many substances found in living tissue; and the analysis of what turned out to be enormously large molecules, with many hundreds or even thousands of atoms, that made up these substances.

All these advances took place within the understanding of the workings of nature that had developed on the basis of Newton's discoveries (pp. 469–471); but further developments starting shortly before 1900 began to correct or modify this "classical physics" in various ways. Toward the end of the nineteenth century it was discovered that certain chemical elements, such as uranium, emitted rays, so to speak, "of their own accord" (without being heated, electrified, or otherwise stimulated)—a phenomenon that the Polish scientist Marie Curie, who was mainly responsible for identifying the elements concerned, called "radioactivity." Subsequent research showed that radioactive and other types of rays in fact consisted of streams of tiny *particles*, which were evidently smaller than the atoms out of which the emitting substances must be composed. Clearly, for this to happen, something must be going on *within the atoms*, which must themselves be built up of still smaller particles. By studying various forms of radioactivity, Ernest Rutherford and Niels Bohr introduced their *model* of the atom (about 1910), which they saw as a miniature solar system, containing a nucleus of one or more *protons* with encircling *electrons*—and like the solar system, consisting mainly of empty space. Later research would show the atom to be even more complex than Rutherford or Bohr at first believed (pp. 718–720), but their concept was the starting point for modern atomic physics.

In this way, one of the main assumptions of classical physics, the solidity of objects, began to dissolve. At the same time, the German physicist Albert Einstein attacked some other major classical assumptions—those that concerned mass, energy, space, and time. In his special theory of relativity, announced in 1905 and later extended to a general theory, Einstein recognized that Newtonian physics "worked" well enough for ordinary purposes; but he believed that it did not truly describe the universe of nature and that it could lead to hopeless errors in *cosmic* calculations. Newton and his followers had conceived of space and motion as *absolute*. They assumed the existence of an "ether," a kind of immovable substance that fills the universal void (empty space). All changes in positions of objects, they thought, could be measured absolutely by reference to this ether. But experiments in the late nineteenth century proved that no such substance exists, thus destroying any fixed basis for reference.

Einstein met this puzzlement with a radically different approach. Matter and motion are not absolutes, he declared, but are *relative*. They can be measured only from a given point or system in time and space. (What is the velocity of a fly buzzing about inside a speeding aircraft?) Einstein believed, further, that objects have a *space-time* dimension that affects their length, breadth, and thickness. Bodies moving toward or away from a given point have shifting proportions of length and mass with respect to that point. The alterations are not noticeable in ordinary motions, but they become significant as bodies approach the speed of light. The speed of light is the one *constant* he found in the universe; it remains the same for *all* physical systems. Though Einstein's theory, expressed in mathematical equations, was incomprehensible to the average person, it exploded many of the fundamental assumptions of scientists. One especially important practical application grew out of another Einstein equation ($E = mc^2$)—explaining the relation between *energy* and *matter*: E (Energy, in metric units called ergs) equals m (mass in grams) times c^2 (the speed of light squared, in centimeters per second). This now-famous equation led to the development of the atomic bomb during the Second World War (pp. 657–658).

Alongside these spectacular advances in physical science, the nineteenth century was just as much the century of biological and medical progress. Drawing upon seventeenth-century descriptions of cellular structure in plants, Theodor Schwann developed the cell theory to explain *organic (living)* matter. It was realized by about 1835 that all living things consist of tiny cells, whose health and growth determine the physical fate of the total organism, and a special branch of biology (cytology) was established for the study of *cells*. Embryology and bacteriology also became specialized fields of inquiry.

Bacteriology, an outgrowth of the germ theory of disease, opened for examination the world of microorganisms. These tiny forms of life had been seen through the primitive microscopes of the seventeenth century, but little attention was given to them until after 1850. It was a French chemist, Louis Pasteur, who first theorized that bacteria (germs) were the cause of many deadly illnesses. Physicians knew of the existence of bacteria but thought them the result, rather than the cause, of disease. After years of ridicule, Pasteur at last had the opportunity to demonstrate the correctness of his theory and the practice of preventive inoculation (vaccination). His first successful test was against an epidemic of anthrax disease in sheep.

Once the germ theory was accepted, it led quickly to the identification, treatment, and prevention of countless bacteriological and viral diseases, as well as to antiseptic procedures in surgery and improvements in public hygiene and sanitation. No other development in science can match the importance of the germ theory in its effect on the world's *death* rate—and the consequent upward curve of human population. The mass killers—bubonic plague, typhus, smallpox, and cholera—were at last subject to human control. (In the twentieth century an ancient crippler of children, poliomyelitis, would also be conquered, and improved vaccines and antibodies would aid the general fight against all germ-caused illnesses.)

Medicine was not the only area where the growth of scientific knowledge had an impact beyond the lecture halls and laboratories. It was chiefly the progress of pure science that drove forward the Industrial Revolution after the middle of the nineteenth century (p. 558). Science, further, provided a *model* for other branches of thought and investigation, or at least was called upon to make their views and theories more believable. Marxists, for example, and social thinkers of other persuasions, claimed that their methods and results were "scientific"; so, also, did some psychologists dealing with human feelings and behavior (pp. 569, 584–585). Moreover, due especially to the work of Charles Darwin, science once again called into question traditional ideas on the place of humanity in the universe and its relationship to God.

THE CHALLENGE OF DARWIN'S
THEORY OF EVOLUTION

The discoveries about *bacteria* raised no serious controversy after Pasteur's classic proofs. But the emerging theory about the *origin of human beings* caused bitter disputes that continue more than a century afterward.

NEW PERSPECTIVES IN HUMAN BIOLOGY

The work of Charles Darwin may be compared with that of Isaac Newton, who lived two centuries earlier. As Newton completed the overturn of ancient ideas about the physical universe and its governing principles, so Darwin completed a revolution of thought with respect to the earth's *creatures*—the human species, in particular. Scientific opinion, until about 1850, had supported the idea of the *fixed nature* of each species, within a "Great Chain of Being." A Swedish botanist, Carolus Linnaeus, was in part responsible for the persistence of this idea. His work as a classifier (in the 1730s) helped to develop the notion that all creatures had been placed in a neat and permanent overall scheme. Linnaeus assumed, and most of his readers believed, that all members of a particular species could be traced back, without change, to an original pair formed at the time of Creation (the "Creationist" theory).

Before the nineteenth century there had been insufficient evidence either to prove or to disprove this theory. But by 1850 discoveries in comparative anatomy, embryology, and geology were pointing toward one inescapable conclusion. Even before Darwin published *On the Origin of Species by Means of Natural Selection* in 1859, the theory of *change* in species had been accepted by a number of naturalists and philosophers. Darwin focused his life's work on that theory and established it securely on the basis of his observations, collected data, and reasoned explanations.

Though the evolutionary theory raised many thorny problems, it won acceptance because it better suited known facts than did the competing "Creationist" theory. According to Darwin, all forms of life are descended from a few original creatures. Each individual (and the species of which it is a part) has come into existence as the result of an unbroken competitive struggle. Continuing slight variations in physical qualities give an advantage to some creatures over others; the losers in the struggle die out, while the winners pass on, through heredity, their distinctive qualities ("survival of the fittest").

Without the concept of "geologic" time, Darwin could not have convinced even himself, for the process of "natural selection" required a sweep of centuries beyond human imagination—to produce, in tiny steps, the kind of changes that carried upward from plankton to mammals. But Charles Lyell, an English geologist, had opened the door to Darwin's theory. Prior to the appearance of Lyell's *Principles of Geology* in 1830, most educated individuals believed that the earth's history had been relatively short and that the earth's surface had undergone sudden and drastic changes ("catastrophism"). Lyell helped to reverse this view, holding that geologic change had been slow and gradual and that the earth's age ran into hundreds of *millions* of years.

Second only to Lyell in direct influence on Darwin was Thomas Malthus, whose *An Essay on the Principle of Population* (p. 526) offered a key to the process of natural selection. Malthus pointed out that reproduction in animals advances at a rate that outstrips the supply of food. Hence, the fate of all nature's creatures is one of struggle for survival. This point was crucial to Darwin's doctrine, for without the elimination of some individuals and the *survival* of others, there would be no *selection* among the variant creatures.

The least satisfactory portion of Darwin's theory concerns the mechanism by which "survival" characteristics are transmitted to succeeding generations. He believed this to be essentially a matter of passing along to offspring the *physical characteristics* of superior *individuals*. But even in Darwin's time, research by the Austrian botanist Gregor Mendel was already laying the basis for a different explanation of heredity. By lengthy experiments with successive generations of plants and careful analysis of the results, Mendel was able to show, among other things, that a plant could carry what he called "hereditary factors" for particular characteristics even if it did not possess those characteristics itself: thus, a short plant could carry the "factor" for tallness. Later researchers in the new science of genetics used Mendel's results to correct Darwin's understanding of heredity in a way that actually strengthened the theory of evolution as a whole. Evolution, they said, depended not so much on the physical characteristics of individuals as on an entire species' supply of "hereditary factors," or, as they came to be called, *genes*. Only *widespread* mutations (changes) in *gene supply* could make a change in the species.

Early in the twentieth century, the new theory of genes was linked up with the results of research into the cells, of which all living things are composed. Nineteenth-century cytologists (cell researchers—p. 578) had discovered that both the *growth* of living things, and also their *reproduction* (the generation of new living things by existing ones) take place by means of *cell division* (the splitting of one cell into two). They had also discovered that when a cell divides, thread-like structures form within it called *chromosomes*, which are transferred by various processes into the new cells. In 1911, the American geneticist Thomas H. Morgan suggested that Mendel's genes are tiny physical entities that are somehow strung out along the chromosomes—thereby moving from cell to cell in both growth and reproduction, so as to determine and regulate the physical characteristics of new organisms. This insight not only further filled in the picture of evolution; out of it, the twentieth-century science of molecular biology would eventually be born (pp. 720–721).

Darwinism in Philosophy and Social Thought

Whatever may have been Darwin's limitations and his debts to other scientists, he fully deserves the acclaim that has been his. He combined a stirring new vision of living creatures with the courage to publish and defend his ideas. What others had

MR. BERGH TO THE RESCUE.

THE DEFRAUDED GORILLA. "That *Man* wants to claim my Pedigree. He says he is one of my Descendants."
Mr. BERGH. "Now, Mr. DARWIN, how could you insult him so?"

12-3   Of all Darwin's ideas, the hardest for people to accept was the claim that humans had not been directly created by God in his own image, but had evolved from lower animals. It was a notion that inspired both indignation and—as in this contemporary cartoon by the American Thomas Nast—mockery.

hinted at or backed away from, Darwin at last expressed openly and honestly. Although his theory brought criticism from all sections of the community, by the close of the century it had become generally accepted among educated people.

At first the more severe attacks came from religious thinkers and devout Christians. Though some Darwinists argued that the divine hand can (and does) work its will through evolution, critics of the theory preferred to think that humans had been fashioned *directly* in God's image. The Copernican theory had dwarfed the importance of the earth in the heavens (pp. 465–466); the Darwinian theory now reduced the importance of human beings by associating them with animal evolution (*Fig. 12-3*). Moreover, it contradicted the literal reading of the Book of Genesis. It is small wonder that many Christians were shaken by what appeared to be another blow to their faith and pride.

On the other hand, there were philosophers, statesmen, industrialists, and theologians who welcomed the doctrine and sought to extend it beyond the

biological field. Herbert Spencer, a brilliant and self-educated advocate of evolution, was one of those most excited by Darwin's writings. It was he who stressed
Darwin's phrase "survival of the fittest" to describe the governing principle in nature, and, more significantly, Spencer asserted that the principle applies not only
to physical creatures and galaxies but to human institutions, customs, and ideas
as well. All of these, he reasoned, have their cycle of origin, growth, competition, decay, and extinction. Thus, there can be no "absolutes" of religious or
moral truth; there is only the *passing* truth of those ideas that have evolved, and
that have (so far) *survived*.

These convictions, however, did not drive Spencer to mechanism or atheism
(pp. 473, 475). As did some church leaders of his day, he adapted his faith in God
to the new facts of science. Behind these facts, he believed, there must exist a
supernatural power—one that humans cannot fully know. He believed, however,
that moral standards can be established on the basis of what we *do* know. Spencer
put forward a "science" of ethics based on the principles of natural evolution:
moral acts are those that contribute to human adaptation and progress. Moral perfection will be reached, he concluded, by "the completely adapted man in the
completely evolved society."

Spencer's philosophy of morals did not pass unchallenged in the nineteenth
century. If morality is geared to the evolutionary processes of nature, what becomes
of one's own moral responsibility and freedom? What has science to do with ethics?
Even if Darwinism explained the development of the moral sense, it could not lay
down a particular code of behavior. A further objection was that nature itself had
been shown by Darwin to be ruthlessly *amoral* (lacking in moral concern). How,
then, could nature serve as a foundation for morals?

The "tooth-and-claw" nature of organic evidence does indeed present nature
in a mixed light. Some saw magnificence in it; Darwin himself found it thrilling:

> Thus, from the war of nature, from famine and death, the most exalted object
> which we are capable of conceiving, namely the production of the higher animals,
> directly follows. There is grandeur in this view of life . . . from so simple a begin-
> ning endless forms most beautiful and wonderful have been, and are being
> evolved.

But this creation so admired by Darwin had been achieved through monstrous
waste and universal conflict. The sweet Mother Nature of the romantic poets
(pp. 530–534) had revealed another and terrible face.

It soon became clear that Darwinism could be interpreted and applied in conflicting ways. All could agree on one central point: the idea of a static world, of
fixed relations and values, had been overthrown and replaced by the idea of continuous change and struggle. But how people should think and act in relation to
the struggle, especially human struggle, was a question that drew profoundly different answers.

Philosophers of Hegel's school viewed Darwin's theory as a confirmation of the
dialectical idea in history (p. 528). Among theologians, Calvinists most often

found support for their teachings in Darwinism, for their doctrine of human salvation by *election* is paralleled, in nature, by the survival of the few and the destruction of the many (pp. 420–421). As one Calvinist teacher put it, Darwinism is to science what Calvinism is to theology: it serves as a foe of sentimentalism and optimism and as a check on the reign of law and trust in reason.

The implications of Darwinism for social action had far-reaching consequences. After reading *On the Origin of Species*, Karl Marx declared that it furnished a "basis in natural science for the class struggle in history." He hoped that it would bring support to his revolutionary appeals. Marx gave Darwin a copy of *Das Kapital*, but it is doubtful whether the scientist read it. While Darwin sought to avoid controversy outside his own field of biological study, he rejected the notion that his theory was connected with socialism. He was, rather, inclined to agree with the classical economists of his time, who saw the social struggle as a "natural" expression of human competition. Like them, he opposed interference with the system of laissez-faire, no matter what the motives might be. As his friend Herbert Spencer explained, "The poverty of the incapable, the distresses that come upon the imprudent, the starvation of the idle, and those shoulderings aside of the weak by the strong, which leave so many 'in shallows and miseries,' are the decree of a large far-seeing benevolence."

The American billionaire, John D. Rockefeller, once used an attractive metaphor to explain how natural selection worked to the advantage of all. The man who had built Standard Oil into a giant monopoly by beating out his competitors compared his work with the breeding of a lovely flower. The American Beauty rose, with its splendor and fragrance, could not have been produced, Rockefeller told a Sunday School audience, except by sacrificing the buds that grew up around it. In the same way, the development of a large business is "merely survival of the fittest . . . merely the working-out of a law of nature and a law of God."

Rockefeller and other titans of industry were unashamed promoters of what was later called *Social* Darwinism. Essentially, it approved a no-holds-barred struggle of "all against all," in the manner of the jungle. And the idea readily passed from one of battle among individuals to one of battle among races and nations. Darwin's theory strengthened the convictions of slave owners, racists, militarists, and extreme nationalists. Many individuals, including some respected philosophers, glorified *war* as a "pruning" hook for improving the health of humanity. "Making war is not only a biological law," declared a famous general, "but a moral obligation, and, as such, an indispensable factor in civilization."

DEVELOPMENT OF THE SOCIAL SCIENCES

The nineteenth century saw the prestige of science rising to its apex. Generals, industrialists, statesmen, theologians, and philosophers sought to ally themselves with scientific doctrines. And social researchers of various sorts tried to model their methods of inquiry upon those of mathematics, physics, or biology—and, in the process, to establish new branches of "social knowledge" that might draw the kind of respect paid to natural science.

One of these individuals, the Frenchman Auguste Comte, was the first to use the term "sociology" as a term for the "science of society." A disciple of Saint-Simon (p. 568), Comte was a lifelong reformer. He shared with Saint-Simon the view that society is best managed by "experts," but he believed that the experts needed a more reliable body of knowledge about people and their social relations than was at hand. Scorning "knowledge for its own sake" and narrow academic specialization, Comte believed that learning should serve *human needs*, and he felt that all studies should be directed to that purpose.

He believed that the most useful knowledge is the sort that rests upon empirical evidence (pp. 379–380)—"positive" knowledge, he called it—which was to be found in his day only in the natural sciences. But empirical methods can and must, he insisted, be extended to "social" science; human conduct is neither random nor altogether unpredictable, and it can be "quantified," analyzed, and classified. From the resulting social "laws," the proposed managers of society would be able to draw guidance for social regulation and planning.

Comte died in 1857, before he could complete his ambitious studies directed toward reconstructing knowledge *and* society. (Before breathing his last, he is said to have sighed, "What an irreparable loss!") But the foundations of sociology had been laid, and they were extended by the energetic Herbert Spencer (pp. 581–583). At about the same time a companion discipline, anthropology, came into being. This word means, literally, the "study of man," but the study has focused on physical evolution, prehistoric cultures, and *comparative* social institutions.

While anthropology analyzed and classified the broad patterns of social conduct, observed over time and geographical space, a new discipline, psychology, concentrated on individual human actions. In 1872 Wilhelm Wundt established the first laboratory (in Leipzig, Germany) for the observation and testing of human and animal subjects. A Russian, Ivan Pavlov, soon afterward gained worldwide notice by his remarkable experiments with dogs. He discovered the "conditioned reflex," a principle that could (and would) be extended to humans.

By 1900 psychology was moving in several directions. Followers of Pavlov's experiments developed a view called "behaviorism." Believing that human thoughts and actions can be understood on a purely *physiological* basis, they dismissed as meaningless such concepts as "mind" and "soul." They studied the various systems of the body—nervous, glandular, muscular—and the mechanisms of "stimulus" and "response," and *measured* them. From the accumulation of such data the behaviorists hoped to develop "positive" knowledge of human nature. (Within a century of Pavlov's experiments, the American psychologist B. F. Skinner concluded that the time had arrived to construct a workable "technology of behavior." His *Beyond Freedom and Dignity*, published in 1971, proposed systematic management of human actions within the framework of a *planned society*.) Most theologians, philosophers, and humanists found such ideas distasteful. They argued that a person's true being is spiritual rather than physical—or, if only physical, that it is far more complex than the behaviorists imagined.

Other investigators, meanwhile, were trying to penetrate the dark *interior* of the individual by means of *psychoanalysis*. The Austrian physician Sigmund Freud was a bold leader in this effort to investigate the subconscious and unconscious depths underlying thought and action. His methods were neither quantitative nor statistical but rather, clinical. Each human subject was examined, by means of free discussion and dream recollection, for clues to the inner self. (The broader philosophical and social significance of Freud's thought will be developed in chapter 15—pp. 725–726).

Freud's one-time associate, the Swiss psychologist Carl G. Jung, also stressed the importance of the unconscious as a major part of "psychic wholeness." Jung believed that each individual, as a result of biological evolution, possesses a "collective" unconscious in *addition* to a "personal" unconscious. The "collective" contains those emotion-filled instincts and images connected with long-past experiences of the *species*. Jung called such images "archetypes"—such as the "Great-Mother" figure, the Hero, the Sage, the Betrayer, the Savior-God, and other types that appear widely in popular myths and religions. In keeping with this view, he held that "great" works of art and literature are seen as great because they portray such figures—projected from the collective unconscious of their creators.

We have reviewed the emergence of new branches of "social" knowledge in the nineteenth century, along with the startling advances in the natural sciences. The older branches of learning dealing with human relations were also influenced by the trends of the times. Political economy, which traced back at least to Adam Smith and the eighteenth century, reached its "classical" development in the nineteenth century in the formulation of economic "laws" (pp. 561–562). Later in that century, economists established a "scientific" vocabulary, statistical techniques, and instruments of *prediction*.

History, one of the most ancient studies concerned with human affairs, also flourished in the nineteenth century. Much of the writing, though marked by careful research and literary merit, was essentially romantic and nationalistic. The effort to apply *scientific methodology* centered in Germany, where Leopold von Ranke started the "objective" school of historical writing. He announced that he and his students would describe the past as it "actually happened." Sentiment and national bias were to be set aside, and historical documents were to be collected and interpreted in a rigorously critical fashion. Near the end of the century the "scientific" approach was carried by historians from German to American universities.

Ranke wrote some excellent histories, and his insistence on correct method was wholesome. He did not convince all historians, however, that it is possible to reconstruct a *single* true picture of what "actually happened." Serious philosophical and practical objections have been raised against his assumptions, and most twentieth-century historians have concluded that the account of individuals and societies can never be told with anything like the precision of natural science. There are indeed "lessons" of history, but they are interpreted in different ways by different writers. For example, a prominent group of twentieth-century French authors (the "school" founded by Fernand Braudel) holds that events in history can be presented properly only in their *total context*—including climate, geography, and cultural heritage—a method referred to as "structuralism." Still others ("deconstructionists") argue that words in any source document are but *words* and can never truly equate with *reality*. At any rate, the fact is that the Muse of history, Clio (p. 86), has never felt altogether at ease among the social *sciences*. She is more at home with the *humanistic* disciplines, especially philosophy, literature, and the arts.

LITERATURE AND ART IN THE MACHINE AGE

Writers and painters responded sharply to the changes in civilization triggered by science and the machine. They developed, by the middle of the nineteenth century, new goals and forms that would eclipse romanticism in European literature and art (pp. 529–539).

EXPRESSIONS OF SOCIAL CHANGE: DICKENS, IBSEN, SHAW

The new trend in literature was known as "Realism." It started in France with Honoré de Balzac, who began writing successful novels late in the 1820s. (His collected works were later published as *The Human Comedy*.) Balzac placed under close examination men and women of all stations in society. A keen observer, he set the style of insightful reporting of human strengths and weaknesses that marked French literature for the rest of the century.

In England, Realism spotlighted the social effects of the Industrial Revolution. Charles Dickens, one of the most popular authors of the era, called the attention of his readers to the cruelties and hardships of the urban working class. In the generally light-hearted *Pickwick Papers* (1836), he nevertheless exposed the grim debtors' prisons; in *Oliver Twist* he revealed the horror of the English workhouses (places of forced labor for the poor). Though his many novels range widely over human themes and problems, they have a strong note of *social protest;* the world of Dickens' characters is not far from Karl Marx's view of a warped capitalist society. Dickens' books contributed, no doubt, to the reform legislation of the nineteenth century (pp. 563–564).

The continental writer who addressed himself most directly to the problems of his day was a Norwegian, Henrik Ibsen. Though he is today recognized as one of the prime molders of modern dramatic form and technique, his reputation at first rested on the social content of his dramas. The son of a once-prosperous businessman, Ibsen grew up with contempt toward his own society, especially the new bourgeois. In *Pillars of Society* (1877) he revealed the corruption and hypocrisy he had observed among "established" Norwegian families. His next plays dealt with such issues as female emancipation (*A Doll's House*) and the conflict between commercial interests and personal honesty (*An Enemy of the People*). Not surprisingly, these works brought hostile reactions from the middle-class audiences. In his later plays, Ibsen gave up his challenges to the social system and created memorable portraits of *individuals* (*Hedda Gabler*).

c. 1800	c. 1830	c. 1860	c. 1890	c. 1905
Romanticism	Realism	Impressionism	Post-Impressionism	

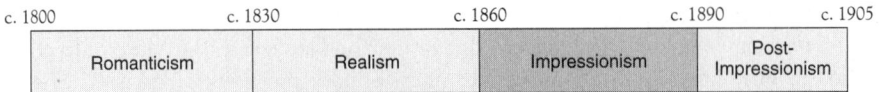

George Bernard Shaw, a brilliant Irish author, was among Ibsen's admirers. He appreciated the intelligence and purpose that Ibsen had brought to the nineteenth-century theater, and he turned his own pen to the cause of social criticism. To Shaw, nothing was sacred; he even faulted Shakespeare for lacking a social message for his own time. One of the most prolific of writers, Shaw composed nearly fifty plays during the course of his long life. Virtually every one of them contains both satire and "message"; his characters, accordingly, tend to be two-dimensional, serving mainly as bearers of intellectual argument.

The relation of literature to social questions during the latter part of the nineteenth century is underlined by the fact that Shaw was a self-taught economist and one of the founders of English socialism. "In all my plays," he once said, "my economic studies have played as important a part as a knowledge of anatomy does in the works of Michelangelo." The drama that first attracted public attention was his *Widowers' Houses* (1892), a condemnation of slum landlordism. This was followed by *Mrs. Warren's Profession*, showing the economic roots of modern prostitution, and *Arms and the Man*, satirizing the military profession. Later dramas dealt with such matters as poverty, war, religious faith, and eugenics (human genetic improvement). By 1915 Shaw's fame was known around the globe, and in 1925 he was awarded the prestigious Nobel Prize in literature.

THE RESPONSE OF THE ARTIST: MONET, CÉZANNE, VAN GOGH

In the arts, social protest was expressed in the works of only a few individuals. Most prominent among them were two French artists of the Realist school: Gustave Courbet and Honoré Daumier. Both rebelled against the romantic tradition, sympathized with the poor, and felt that art should correspond to social facts. While Courbet stressed the simple and truthful representation of nature, Daumier pictured the poverty and despair of the working class. He is best known, perhaps, for his thousands of lithographs (prints) caricaturing all levels of French society; they complement the *word* pictures of his contemporary, Balzac, in revealing the "human comedy." One of Daumier's masterpieces in oil, *The Third-Class Carriage*, reveals his ability to paint, with sincerity and compassion, the ordinary people of his time *(Fig. 12-4)*. He experienced in his own life the miseries recorded in his art—he died a pauper in 1879.

Daumier's artistic techniques, particularly the "unfinished" effect of his canvases, continued beyond his death. They influenced the style of "Impressionism," the most important development in nineteenth-century painting. The Impressionists, however, had nothing to do (as artists) with social satire or protest. They tended to be strictly *formal*, wishing to record images with optical accuracy and without concern for any kind of message.

12-4   Honoré Daumier. *The Third-Class Carriage*, c. 1862. Oil on canvas, 26″ × 36″. Metropolitan Museum of Art, New York.

The whole trend of painting after 1870 was toward "art for art's sake." This indicated, perhaps, an even deeper sense of alienation than that which inspired the Social Realism of Daumier. Rather than trying to speak for the downtrodden or to change society, most artists now turned their backs on society, seeking escape into a *separate* world of art, where painters could impose whatever rules they desired upon elements of their own creation.

Claude Monet represented most fully the aims and achievements of Impressionism. He desired to record physical appearances immediately as he saw them. In order to do this faithfully, he disciplined himself to suppress his prior *knowledge* of the shape and detail of things—a break with traditional painting. Fascinated by the change in appearances resulting from alterations in light, Monet insisted on working in the *open air*, putting his visual impressions to canvas in rapid strokes, almost as though he were making a sketch. As the eye, in glancing, sees only a few objects clearly, he deliberately left major areas of his pictures blurred or "unfinished."

This absence of clear detail in Monet's work at first called forth the scorn of critics. In 1874, in an exhibit with other painters of the new style, he showed a picture of a harbor seen through morning mists. He called it *Impression: Sunrise* (*Color Plate C5*). From this title, an unfriendly observer coined the term "Impressionists" as a label for these artists. In time, critics and public alike grew to appreciate the special aims of this kind of painting. Some of the Impressionists associated their techniques with the methods of scientific observation. Most, however, simply yielded to the delight of producing their riches of color and tone. Among such painters were, notably, Auguste Renoir in France, and Mary Cassatt in the United States. Renoir was admired especially for his voluptuous nudes, Cassatt for her charming portraits of young children with their mothers.

The ultimate success and popularity of the Impressionists gave all artists a fresh sense of freedom and power. Any chosen combination of forms and colors might now be considered a legitimate work of art. Gone were the rules that had required "dignified" or "worthy" subjects, "correct drawing," "rules of perspective," and "balanced composition."

Impressionism itself, however, was a beginning, not an end. Toward the close of the nineteenth century there came new stirrings in art—largely reactions to Impressionism. Paul Cézanne, who came to Paris in 1861, had adopted many of the techniques of the new style. He objected, however, to what he regarded as the airy, temporary quality of Impressionist paintings; he longed to combine the brilliance of their coloring with more *substantial* forms.

As may be seen in his *Still Life (Color Plate C6)*, one of hundreds of such studies that Cézanne painted, he tried to develop *solidity* in his works. As a means of furthering this aim, he slightly shifted eye levels in looking at the various objects in the painting, thus creating several angles of view on a single canvas. He also *distorted* the natural shapes of objects and avoided symmetrical lines. These techniques make his paintings a source of continuing interest and pleasure.

While Cézanne sought to rearrange nature into what he considered a more satisfying balance of light and form, a younger artist, Vincent van Gogh, had different objectives. Like Cézanne, van Gogh learned the special brush techniques of the Impressionists. But he was not really interested in the outward appearances of things; he wanted to express his own *deep feelings* about nature and life. Van Gogh was thus the pioneer of the modern school of "Expressionist" painters.

Extraordinary spiritual and mental stress marked van Gogh's brief life. The son of a Protestant minister, he had experienced in his youth an urgent though unfulfilled missionary impulse. In later years he sensed a divine creative force within nature and all forms of life; he sought to show this force in his paintings. His works were the products of an emotional frenzy that passed into periods of mental illness. Finally, when he found himself no longer able to paint, he took his own life (1890).

But in the years before his death, especially during a final stay at Arles, he produced a series of remarkable canvases. Stimulated by the sun-drenched countryside of southern France, he painted it with fevered excitement, applying color with greater vigor and freedom than had any painter before. He did not try to imitate the hues of nature; the colors represented his feelings. Yellow, his favorite color, was his means of expressing the ever-present love of God. Blue, pale violet, and green expressed rest or sleep. A striking example of van Gogh's last works is *Cornfield with Crows (Color Plate C7)*, finished just before his death. It presents "vast stretches of corn under troubled skies," expressing, as he wrote, "sadness and the extreme of loneliness." Such was the final response of a great and sensitive talent in the closing years of the nineteenth century.

Expressionism took a somewhat different turn in Germany. An exemplar there, Käthe Kollwitz, focused more upon human subjects than upon nature. She chose, most often, to portray the emotional life of women—their joys and sorrows—in their numerous roles, occupations, and endeavors. And, instead of using the paintbrush, she usually worked in the *print* media (woodcuts, etchings, lithographs), as well as in sculpture.

V-1 Fireworks explode and a laser beam shoots upward at Giza, Egypt, on January 1, 2000, to celebrate the new millennium; behind them loom the pyramids of King Menkaure (see *Fig. 1-5*, p. 35) and two of his queens. Symbolic of the endurance of civilization, the forty-five-hundred-year-old monuments of the pharaohs look down upon a celebration of modernity; symptomatic of the international reach of Western civilization, a date in the Western time reckoning is marked by a predominantly Muslim country.

PART FIVE

THE WEST IN THE
CONTEMPORARY WORLD

1850–2000

	POLITICAL, SOCIAL, AND ECONOMIC DEVELOPMENTS	RELIGION, SCIENCE, AND PHILOSOPHY	HISTORY AND LITERATURE	ARCHITECTURE, ART, AND MUSIC
1850	Growth of nationalism French Second Empire: Napoleon III German unification and empire: Bismarck Rise of corporate big business Rise of labor unions Urbanization of Western society Exploration of Africa The new imperialism Triple Alliance	Kierkegaard Mill Spencer Maxwell Pasteur "Social Gospel" Leo XIII Nietzsche Freud Jung Einstein Planck	Ranke Ibsen Dostoevsky Tolstoy Shaw	Courbet Daumier Impressionism: Monet Renoir Cassatt Cézanne Expressionism: van Gogh Kollwitz Verdi
1900	British Empire at full extent Russo–Japanese War Triple Entente First World War League of Nations Russian Revolution: communism Lenin Stalin Rise of fascism and nazism: Mussolini Hitler Franco The Great Depression (1930–1940) Roosevelt and New Deal Second World War and Holocaust Atomic bomb: "unlimited" warfare United Nations	Pavlov Rutherford, Bohr, Curie Barth Heisenberg Hubble Existentialism Tillich	Joyce O'Neill Wharton Proust Eliot Woolf Orwell Beckett A. Miller	Schönberg Stravinsky Organic style: Wright, "Falling Water" International style: Gropius Bauhaus Mies van der Rohe Seagram Building le Corbusier Kandinsky Picasso

	POLITICAL, SOCIAL, AND ECONOMIC DEVELOPMENTS	RELIGION, SCIENCE, AND PHILOSOPHY	HISTORY AND LITERATURE	ARCHITECTURE, ART, AND MUSIC

1950	The Cold War (U.S. and U.S.S.R.)
	End of colonialism:
	  Gandhi
	  Kenyatta
	  Mao
	Indochina War (Vietnam):
	  Ho Chi Minh
	European Economic Community
	National liberation movements:
	  Castro
	  Allende
	Israeli-Arab wars:
	  Sadat
	  Begin
	Student movement and youth culture
		World Council of Churches
		Crick, Watson
		"Liberation Theology"
		Graham
		John XXII
		Second Vatican Council
		Paul VI
		New sexuality
		Revival of hedonism
		Gell-Mann
		Man on moon: Armstrong
			Braudel
			Sartre
			Huxley
			Frost
			Mailer
			Pasternak
			Solzhenitsyn
				Pollock
				Moore
				Calder, *La Grande Vitesse*
				Niemeyer, Cathedral
				Saarinen
				Pei
				Porter
				Gershwin
				Armstrong
				Ellington
				Lerner

1970	Emergence of "Third World"
	Struggle against racism:
	  King
	  Jackson
	  Malcolm X
	Women's movement:
	  Beauvoir
	  Frieden
	  Steinem
	World population and resources crisis
	Resurgence of Japanese power
	
	U.S.-China renewal: Nixon
	East-West détente
	Conservative reaction
			Updike
			Heller
			Márquez
			Borges
				Lowe
				Presley
				Lennon
				Jackson

1975	Iranian revolution: Khomeini International terrorism	John Paul II		

	POLITICAL, SOCIAL, AND ECONOMIC DEVELOPMENTS	RELIGION, SCIENCE, AND PHILOSOPHY	HISTORY AND LITERATURE	ARCHITECTURE, ART, AND MUSIC
1980	Cold War renewal: nuclear arms race Thatcher, Reagan "revolutions"	Islamic revival Christian "fundamentalism"		
1985	Gorbachev revolution	Pentecostals Space probes of solar system		

1990	End of Cold War
	U.S.S.R. dissolved
	Persian Gulf War: Iraq versus the U.N.
	Clinton
	Apartheid ended: Mandela
	General Agreement on Tariffs and Trade
	Yugoslavia civil war
	Palestinian negotiations:
	    Rabin
	    Arafat
		Internet
		Genetic engineering		

2000	Palestinian-Israeli conflict Kostunica Bush			

CHAPTER 13

● ● ●

IMPERIALISM, WORLD WAR, AND
THE RISE OF COLLECTIVISM

Overview

As spectacular as were the nineteenth-century shifts in Western civilization, by the end of that century they had hardly begun to make their full impact felt. Science and technology, capitalism and urbanization, liberalism and nationalism, and artistic and cultural experiment were forces that had almost limitless potential for change, and these forces could not be confined to Western civilization's European homeland but were bound to take effect throughout the world. The result was a growing break with the past, not just of Western civilization but of the human race as a whole, that went on throughout the twentieth century and is still going on in the twenty-first century. The break is taking place amid an explosion of invention and discovery and of new ways of thinking and feeling. It has brought repeated breakdowns of seemingly stable social and political orders and the erosion of ancient beliefs, values, and patterns of behavior. And it has been accompanied by the deliberate infliction of suffering on the largest scale ever seen in the history of the human race.

This worldwide break with the past is the subject of the final chapters of this book. In this chapter, we will see how the break began with three closely related developments of the late nineteenth and early twentieth centuries: the spread of Western influence across the world as a result of imperialism; the collapse of the global order resulting from imperialism in and after the First World War; and the rise of competing economic and political systems following that war.

By the second half of the nineteenth century, industrial, social, and political change had opened up a gap between a small group of more or less "advanced" countries—mostly European, but also including the United States and Japan—and the rest of the world. The advanced countries had powerful motives of economic interest, national self-esteem, and mutual competition that led them into empire building, and they swiftly divided up the world among themselves. The ancient civilizations and cultures of Africa and Asia that had so far not felt the full force of Western influence, and even the Latin American countries with their regional version of Western civilization—by 1914, nearly all were directly ruled or indirectly controlled by the imperialist countries. A new and permanent world order, it seemed, was coming into existence—a world not unlike the Roman Empire but on a vastly larger scale, with a single dominant civilization, and local cultures and civilizations that in time would give way to the dominant one.

But the new world order of the early twentieth century was not so stable as it seemed—largely because the dominant Western civilization could not overcome its ancient tradition of internal competition and strife. Imperialism itself was highly competitive, breeding conflicts and resentments between imperialist countries that were more or less satisfied with their shares of worldwide power and those that felt they had been short-changed. Within Europe itself, the ascent of nationalism had brought not harmony but conflict. New nation-states reached not just for unification and self-government but for territory and power, arousing the jealousy and suspicion of older states. Eastern European nations fought wars of independence against the multinational empires to which they belonged, notably the Balkan nations against Turkey—and if successful, they immediately began disputing among themselves over border territories and populations, thus opening the way to rival influences from the major powers. Once-absolute monarchs throughout central and eastern Europe who could no longer govern without the support of parliaments and public opinion cast themselves in the role of leaders in promoting national self-assertion and military power.

Gradually, a pattern emerged among these rivalries that pitted Britain, France, and Russia against Europe's strongest, yet most insecure and dissatisfied power, Germany, and its ally Austria-Hungary. The two sides formed opposing military alliances, with the intention not of fighting but of deterring war, and statesmen at the time liked to think of the European alliance system as a pillar of the Western-dominated world order. But the alliances also created a deadly danger: if deterrence failed and any two countries went to war, the other alliance members would have little alternative but to join in. Any local conflict was almost certain to become a general European war.

That was what happened in 1914, when the Balkan rivalries of Austria-Hungary and Russia led those two countries to war. The fighting could not even be confined to the members of the rival alliances. Countries near and far joined in, hoping to benefit, or feeling that their interests and ideals would be threatened by the victory of one side or the other— Italy, Japan, and eventually the United States on the side of Britain, France, and Russia (the "Allies"), and Turkey on the side of Germany and Austria (the "Central Powers"). In this way, the European war turned into a world war. But most of the fighting was done in Europe, where the

progress of arms technology—coupled with the ability of liberal and national states to mobilize their citizens for years of bloodletting—made the
war the most devastating in history up to that time.

At first sight, the outcome of the First World War seemed likely to lead
to a new and more stable version of the prewar world order. The main winners were the three countries where the liberal and national changes had
gone farthest, and which had the largest shares of worldwide imperial power:
Britain, France, and the United States. The main losers were Russia, defeated by the Central Powers in 1917, and the Central Powers themselves,
defeated by the remaining Allies in 1918. The hereditary monarchies that
had led Russia and the Central Powers to defeat were all overthrown;
throughout much of Eastern Europe, nation-states replaced the multinational
empires of Russia, Austria-Hungary, and Turkey. A new international organization, the League of Nations, backed by the power of the war-winning countries, was planned to ensure the stability of the worldwide order and bring
troublemakers to heel without the need for alliances. Now, it seemed, was
the moment for liberal democracy and national self-government to bring
harmony within and among the countries of the world.

But during the 1920s, it soon became clear that the world order had not
been stabilized, but fatally weakened by the First World War. Of the victorious countries on which the world order depended, Britain and France had
suffered huge loss of life and economic resources, and the United States returned to its traditional isolation from European power politics. As for the
losers in the First World War, Germany was harshly treated in defeat, and
Russia fell under Communist rule. Neither country was willing to accommo-
date itself to a world order contrived by the victors. Nor were two other
countries that had been on the winning side but had failed to get as much
territory and power as they had hoped—Italy and Japan. In addition, the
sight of the imperial powers at war, and calling upon their subject nations to
shed their blood for democracy and national self-government, had shaken
Asia, Africa, and Latin America out of their passive acceptance of imperial
domination. Finally, the worldwide capitalist economic system that under-
pinned the world order had been disrupted by the war, and instead of recovering, in 1929 it plunged into a desperate crisis of depression and unemployment.

Accordingly, in the 1920s and 1930s three different alternatives to the
existing world order gained ground: those of communism and fascism, which
intended to destroy and rebuild the world order in different ways; and that of
the democratic welfare state, which was intended to uphold the existing
world order by reforming it. All three alternatives shared a general tendency
toward *collectivism*—that is, more or less restriction of individual choice and
freedom in the collective interests of society. But in other respects, they were
profoundly different ways of organizing societies and the world as a whole.

Communism inherited its basic principles from the nineteenth-century
Marxist movement, and it was also heir to a broader tradition of radical dictatorship that had been forged in earlier European revolutions. It stood for

the revolutionary overthrow of the entire existing world order. Capitalism, imperialism, national and class conflict, religion (which helped uphold these evils), and liberal democracy (which helped disguise them) would all disappear. Instead, the wealth made possible by technology would be shared justly and equally, to produce complete social and international harmony. Having seized power in relatively backward Russia in the turmoil that followed defeat in 1917, the Bolsheviks (the unofficial name of the Russian Communists) soon put off the goal of *worldwide* revolution in favor of consolidating the revolution in their own country. Their dictatorship held on to a great deal of Russia's prewar empire under the new name of the Soviet Union, took over control of the economy, and set about industrializing the country on a vast scale by means of *centralized economic planning*. In pursuit of these goals the Bolsheviks used coercion and bloodshed on a far larger scale than any earlier revolutionary dictatorship, both to crush opposition and to settle internal differences. Even so, their vision of social and international harmony, their proclaimed sympathy with the victims of imperialism, and the example they set of economic development and full employment gave them widespread appeal, and Communist parties that accepted Soviet leadership appeared across the world.

Fascism was a much less clearly defined movement than communism, and existed in many different varieties—all of which, however, were different mixtures of the same basic ideas and feelings. One of these was nationalism in its most competitive and assertive form, reinforced by Social Darwinist ideas of the "struggle for existence" between nations and races, and often linked with vicious anti-Semitism. Another motivating force behind fascism was the fear and resentment of the middle classes following the First World War, who saw themselves caught between the opposing menaces of failing capitalism and rising communism. Yet another source of fascism's appeal was widespread contempt for both the monarchs and nobles, and the parliamentary politicians, who had led their countries into the bloodshed of the First World War—yet failed to achieve the goals of assertive nationalism. Instead of these leaders, fascists yearned for a "Leader" with a capital "L": a man of brutal authority and power, who would embody the collective might of the nation and its collective anger at its enemies without and within, and who would not plead for support but give orders and be obeyed.

All these forces were strongest in countries that had lost the war or not gained as much from it as they hoped—above all, Germany, Italy, and Japan. By 1939 all three had overthrown the liberal democratic political system so far as it existed in their countries, and Germany and Italy were under the rule of the longed-for dictatorial Leaders. All three countries had restructured their economies in ways that were claimed to eliminate conflict between management and workers, and in actual fact established joint economic control by capitalists and government bureaucrats. Furthermore, all three were building up their armed forces, and since they had a common interest in undoing the results of the First World War, they constituted a major threat to the existing world order.

Meanwhile, in Britain, France, and the United States, victory had more or less satisfied the need for national self-assertion, and liberal democracy had passed the acid test of war. But there was one area where the existing order badly needed shoring up: the economic system. Unregulated capitalism was clearly failing to deliver the economic security and high standard of living that voters in industrial societies expected. Accordingly, in the 1920s and 1930s the voters shifted their support to parties and leaders that promised in one way or another to change the workings of capitalism. Labor movements, and political parties linked to them, began to be more powerful in politics than ever before. Governments began to intervene in the economy far more than before — above all to set up economic "safety nets" in the form of unemployment, medical, and retirement insurance plans. The basic features of capitalism — private ownership of most of the economy, and competitive business practices — remained untouched. Democracy was actually extended, most notably by the admission of women to the political process as voters. Intertwined with capitalism and democracy, however, there was now the collectivist institution of the welfare state.

But the failing economic system was only one of the problems that faced the major winners of the First World War in upholding their world order. There were also the fascist and communist rival countries, and the increasingly assertive nations and peoples living under imperial domination. The world was about to enter an era of conflicts, "hot" and "cold," between rival global orders, and of changing relations between imperial powers and the nations they controlled, that was to endure throughout most of the twentieth century.

~

IMPERIALISM AND EUROPE'S WORLD DOMINION

The expansion of Western civilization, which made lasting marks on a large portion of the earth, began at the close of the Middle Ages (pp. 354–370). Overseas exploration and colonization proceeded steadily from the sixteenth century into the eighteenth and then, about 1750, slowed down for a time. For more than a century thereafter, Europeans were busy at home with their liberal-nationalist revolutions and the Industrial Revolution (chapters 11 and 12). As a result, however, the countries that underwent these revolutions built up a much wider margin of political, military, and technological supremacy over the rest of the world than ever before. Thus, when overseas expansion resumed after 1870, a small group of advanced countries soon came to dominate the entire world.

Nineteenth-century overseas expansion differed in important ways from earlier colonial efforts. The countries that took part were no longer exclusively

European, but included two non-European nations that had undergone similar political and industrial changes—the United States and Japan. The forms of overseas expansion included not only simple conquest, but also more indirect penetration and domination. Moreover, just as the imperialist countries had undergone changes, so also the *motives* for expansion (pp. 355–357) had changed. Alongside the desire of the clergy to spread the Christian gospel, there appeared the nonreligious belief in racial superiority; more powerful than the desire of monarchs for dynastic power and glory was that of whole peoples for nationalistic self-assertion; and the desire of the merchants for gold was replaced by that of industrialists for raw materials and markets, and of bankers for investment outlets.

Because of these differences, the overseas expansion of the nineteenth and early twentieth centuries is usually called the "new" imperialism. But the new imperialism had one thing in common with the old: its *competitive* nature. The imperialist countries were not collaborators but rivals, and their rivalries played a major part in bringing about the world wars of the twentieth century.

Imperialism itself is as old as history. Broadly defined, it means *control* by one group of people over other groups beyond its borders. It takes a wide range of forms, from outright occupation and enslavement to the exercise of hidden and subtle influence. Imperialistic adventures fill the accounts of our most ancient writers—Homer, Herodotus, and Thucydides (pp. 86, 91–92). The most successful imperialists of ancient times were the Romans; the *Pax Romana*, though based on conquest, brought order and prosperity to the Mediterranean world for several centuries (pp. 126–132).

Imperialism, no matter what its form, may be divided into two types. Roman imperialism was on balance *beneficent*. It brought peace and relative prosperity to its conquered peoples; it did not deliberately try to alter their cultures and civilizations; and it gave their wealthy upper classes full participation in the empire's government. A second type is clearly *exploitative*: as with Cortez in Mexico, it aims primarily at using the resources and peoples of other lands for the benefit of the conquerors, and often also at changing their cultures, beliefs, and values—usually in the name of one or other monotheistic religion (pp. 361–365).

MOTIVES FOR NINETEENTH-CENTURY EXPANSIONISM

The imperialism of the late nineteenth century was *exploitative*; its impact (intended and unintended) was shattering. What was it that moved Europeans to strike out across the seas and force themselves and their technology upon the peoples of Asia and Africa? The economic motive, arising from the growth of industrial capitalism, was certainly powerful. We saw in the preceding chapter how surplus profits found their way to "backward" countries (pp. 560–561). The urge to secure raw materials, markets, and investments gave a mighty push to overseas penetration.

J. A. Hobson, an English socialist, wrote an influential analysis of the economic causes of expansionism. His book *Imperialism* (1902) attacked the system of overseas exploitation as "a depraved choice of national life, imposed by self-seeking interests." Hobson suggested that the system had grown out of the maldistribution of profits from industry. Since wage-earners lacked the purchasing power to buy all they produced, manufacturers had to go abroad to sell part of their output and invest their profits. He claimed that colonial administration and defense were costly and dangerous, and that economic problems could be better solved by providing higher wages and better social services at home. By these means the home market would be expanded, and capitalists would have better opportunities to invest their funds there. In effect, Hobson was urging a change in policy that would bring British capitalism closer to humanistic aims.

Vladimir Lenin took a different tack. As a Marxist (pp. 569–574), he did not think it possible for "reformers" like Hobson to alter the preordained course of capitalism. He accepted Hobson's analysis of imperialism, but he viewed imperialism as the inevitable last stage of capitalism. In *Imperialism, the Highest Stage of Capitalism* (1916), Lenin declared that profits flowed overseas because they produced a higher rate of return there. And only in a colony, under formal political control, did investments yield their maximum return. Colonies had extended the life of capitalism by bringing into existence *new proletariats*. But now that the globe had been parceled out, the capitalist states were being driven by their economic systems to wage wars against one another. These, he predicted, would be followed by proletarian revolutions, the establishment of socialist states, and the death of imperialism. Although Lenin's argument is inadequate, its partial confirmation by events and its acceptance by communist leaders throughout the world made it enormously influential.

The economic motive, no matter how interpreted, was only one of the forces behind imperialism. Probably more important was the drive for national power and prestige. European nationalism had come of age by 1870, as we saw in chapter 11 (pp. 547–550). Germany, proud and militant, now set out to find its "place in the sun." It is no accident that the renewed scramble for colonies began at about the time that Germany and Italy became unified nations. The pride and effort that go into achieving self-determination for a nation (nationalism) can lead easily to the desire to control other nations and peoples (imperialism).

The balance of power in Europe itself seems to have stabilized after 1870, and the field of conflict shifted overseas. The armed forces of the rival nations sought strategic fueling stations, military bases, and sources of raw materials. They also looked to colonies for new reservoirs of combat troops. But, above all, many Europeans came to regard overseas possessions as the measure and substance of national power and glory.

Now intellectuals began to speak and write of their nation's "civilizing mission." Along with the soldiers and merchants came hundreds of Christian missionaries, responding to the challenge of bringing the Gospel to heathen lands. In addition, many members of the upper and middle classes sought careers in the overseas services. Ordinary citizens, as well, thrilled to phrases like "advance of the flag," the "white man's burden," and "manifest destiny." Men, women, and children of all classes studied the new global maps showing their nation's overseas possessions in distinctive colors. The vocal minorities that protested against

c. 1860	1871		1914	1918
Unification of Italy and of Germany		Era of the New Imperialism		First World War

imperialism on practical or moral grounds were swept aside as "small-minded" or *unpatriotic*.

METHODS OF PENETRATION AND EXPLOITATION

Imperialism did not always mean colonies; control could be informal as well as formal. In fact, many economic and political experts preferred informal control, because it was cheaper and enabled a nation to avoid many risks and responsibilities. Prior to 1870, the British, with their shipping and financial responsibilities, had proved especially skillful in securing economic privileges abroad. But informal and formal relations were woven together into a single fabric of empire: trade with informal control if practicable, trade with *rule* when necessary. The United States pursued a similar strategy in the Western Hemisphere, where it was the dominant power. Though it annexed Puerto Rico and secured special constitutional privileges in Cuba (1898), the United States controlled the rest of the Caribbean republics through economic influence ("dollar diplomacy"), aided when necessary by the Marines.

When rival states began to challenge British economic privileges in particular areas, Britain responded by seeking exclusive arrangements. Thus, after 1870 its Foreign Office sought treaty rights, "spheres of interest," and colonies. Germany and Italy, as well as the older European nation-states, joined in the sweepstakes. All employed various methods for gaining a foothold or an advantage and backed up their efforts by the threat or use of military force. The "underdeveloped" or declining countries of Asia and Africa found themselves helpless before this combined onslaught. Even more than in the case of earlier confrontations between Europe and the non-Western world (pp. 365, 368), the Europeans held the advantages of aggressive purpose, superior organization, and advanced technology.

The assault on Africa began in earnest after 1870. In earlier centuries of trade and exploration, Europeans had had extensive contacts with many coastal peoples of Africa, in which they had dealt with African states and tribal chiefdoms pretty much on equal terms (p. 367). But the interior of Africa, south of the Sahara desert, had remained virtually unknown to the Western world, and was therefore thought of by Europeans as the "Dark Continent."

As we know today, Africa, the second largest continent on earth, has a wide variety of climates and geography: deserts, prairies, farmlands, jungles, mountains, lakes, and mighty rivers. Its inhabitants in 1870 were of many ethnic stocks, speaking hundreds of languages and dialects, and worshiping countless gods and spirits. Some were farmers, some were herdsmen or hunters, and some lived mainly by trade (gold and ivory).

As a consequence of persisting tribal differences and geographical obstacles, the Africans had never achieved a *unified* culture or political organization—though prosperous cities and regional empires had arisen, with splendid arts and crafts, poetry, and music. Probably the chief hindrance to the development of sub-Saharan cultures was their relative *isolation* from the rest of the world (except for limited contact with Muslim and Christian raiders, traders, and missionaries). With only elementary technology, no written languages of their own, and no science, the various tribes and kingdoms had remained within the limits of their traditional cultures.

The conditions of Africa and the slight knowledge of it by outsiders restricted the avenues for penetration and conquest. Nineteenth-century ventures, nevertheless, showed the Western capacity for investigation, missionary activity, and greed for wealth. David Livingstone was the first white person to explore substantial areas of the interior. (Earlier expeditions had been turned back by tropical diseases, to which whites had proved susceptible.) Livingstone, a Scottish physician and missionary, survived some thirty years among the Africans, doing medical and religious work; during that time he had traveled the upper courses of the great rivers. When he was reported in Europe and America as being "lost" in the jungles, a New York newspaper sent a reporter to find him—as a journalistic stunt. Henry Stanley "found" the good doctor in 1871, decided to conduct further travels of his own, and later publicized his adventures in a book called *Through the Dark Continent.* More important, Stanley saw the possibilities of extracting wealth from central Africa. He succeeded at last in interesting King Leopold II of Belgium in his promotional plans.

Belgium, a small country that had gained independence only a generation before (p. 541), had no overseas possessions. Leopold's venture was entirely *private*—in keeping with the individualistic, buccaneering spirit of the times. He formed a company, with himself as president, and sent Stanley and other agents into the Congo region. Taking the view that the African interior was open for sale to the white race, Leopold acquired "possession" of an enormous area by making "treaties" with hundreds of tribal chieftains. (The treaties were usually "signed" after the Belgians handed over trifling gifts to the native leaders.) He thus created a "Congo Free State" under his personal rule—recognized as legal by the major powers in 1885. The Congo boundaries enclosed an area equal to that of the United States east of the Mississippi River.

Although Leopold claimed scientific and humanitarian purposes for his venture, his prime purpose was personal gain. His eye was fixed on the booming industrial demand for rubber: the Congo had rubber trees and a large supply of native laborers. But the natives were infected by tropical diseases and proved unresponsive to European work incentives; they could be forced to work only by the harshest methods.

Leopold's agents used up the trees and natives of the Congo without restraint. But, though the annual value of its rubber exports reached $10 million by 1908, Leopold did not make operations there self-sustaining. He used much of the income for personal extravagance and borrowed huge sums from the Belgian

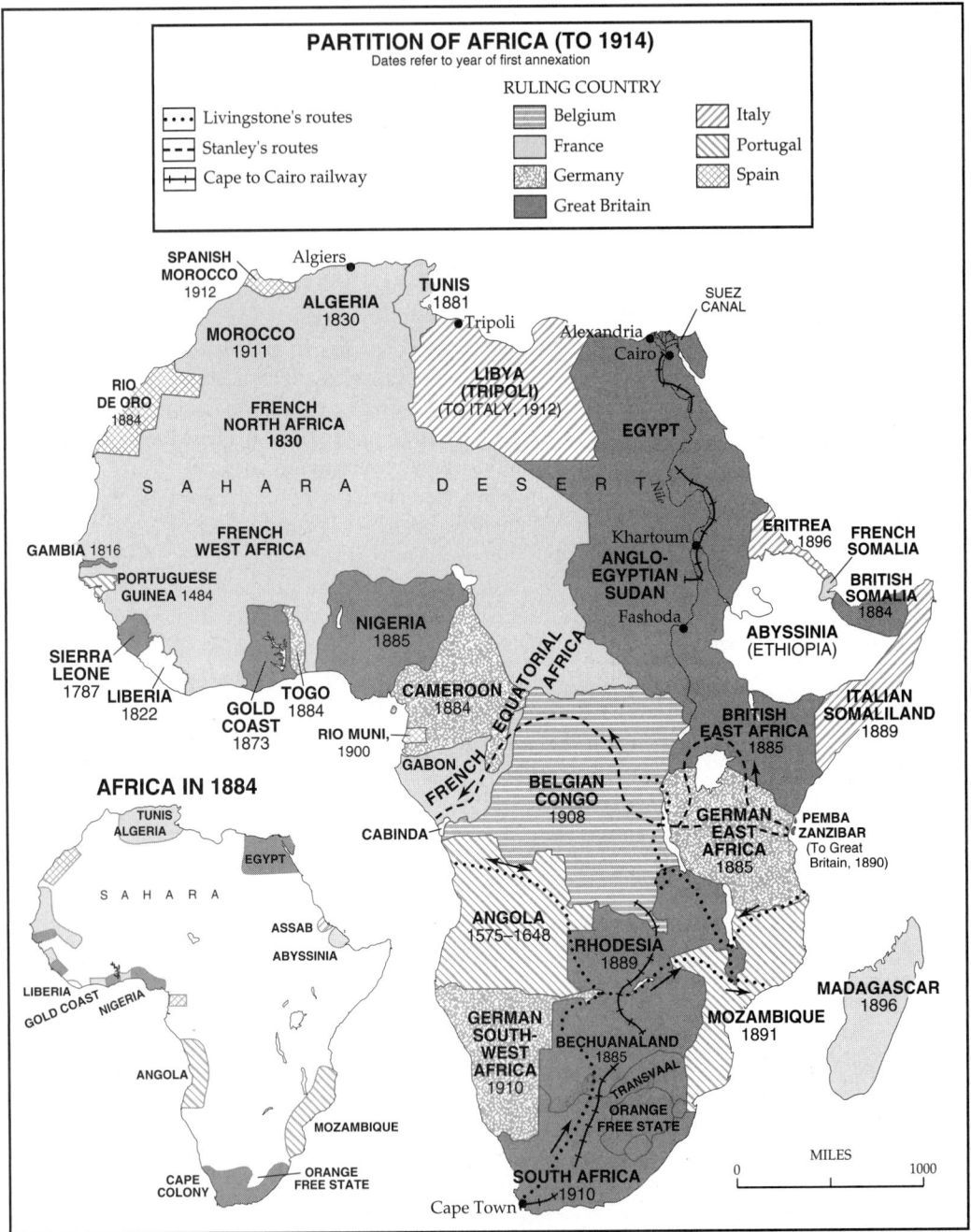

PARTITION OF AFRICA (TO 1914)

Dates refer to year of first annexation

····· Livingstone's routes
- - - Stanley's routes
├┼┤ Cape to Cairo railway

RULING COUNTRY

Belgium
France
Germany
Great Britain
Italy
Portugal
Spain

SPANISH MOROCCO 1912
Algiers
ALGERIA 1830
TUNIS 1881
Tripoli
SUEZ CANAL
MOROCCO 1911
LIBYA (TRIPOLI) (TO ITALY, 1912)
Alexandria
Cairo
RIO DE ORO 1884
FRENCH NORTH AFRICA 1830
EGYPT
S A H A R A   D E S E R T
Nile
GAMBIA 1816
FRENCH WEST AFRICA
Khartoum
ANGLO-EGYPTIAN SUDAN
ERITREA 1896
FRENCH SOMALIA
PORTUGUESE GUINEA 1484
Fashoda
BRITISH SOMALIA 1884
SIERRA LEONE 1787
NIGERIA 1885
ABYSSINIA (ETHIOPIA)
LIBERIA 1822
GOLD COAST 1873
TOGO 1884
CAMEROON 1884
FRENCH EQUATORIAL AFRICA
BRITISH EAST AFRICA 1885
ITALIAN SOMALILAND 1889
RIO MUNI, 1900
GABON
BELGIAN CONGO 1908
GERMAN EAST AFRICA 1885
PEMBA ZANZIBAR (To Great Britain, 1890)

AFRICA IN 1884

TUNIS
ALGERIA
EGYPT
CABINDA
S A H A R A
ASSAB
ABYSSINIA
ANGOLA 1575–1648
RHODESIA 1889
MADAGASCAR 1896
LIBERIA
GOLD COAST
NIGERIA
GERMAN SOUTH-WEST AFRICA 1910
BECHUANALAND 1885
MOZAMBIQUE 1891
ANGOLA
TRANSVAAL
MOZAMBIQUE
ORANGE FREE STATE
SOUTH AFRICA 1910
CAPE COLONY
ORANGE FREE STATE
Cape Town

MILES
0   1000

government. In return, he mortgaged the Free State to the government, which took it over at his death. As the *Belgian* Congo, the region received somewhat better treatment, but it remained a shocking example of human and resource exploitation.

Leopold's taking of the Congo attracted the attention of other European states to the prizes of Africa. A conference was called in 1885 to give some order to the carving up of the remainder of the continent. Certain ground rules were agreed upon: a nation with possessions on the coast had prior right to the related hinterlands; but, in order for a claim to any territory to be recognized, it must be supported by the presence of administrators and soldiers. The conference agreement was thus a signal to all competitors to move in with civilian and military forces. Within twenty-five years Africa had been completely staked out by the Europeans (*map*, p. 606).

The methods employed were similar to those used by Leopold's agents. White men trekked into the interior in search of tribal chiefs who would sign treaties. The chiefs seldom understood what the treaties meant or had the authority to transfer property rights, but the whites acted as if they did. These "rights" were then transferred to some European government, and a colony was thereby established. The only serious difficulties arose when rival nations secured overlapping grants in the same region. Such problems were usually referred to the European capitals for settlement.

In Asia the situation was different. There were no "dark" or "unoccupied" zones. China, for example, was a historic empire, well mapped and administered. Chinese civilization, like that of India, traced back to 3000 B.C. A developed culture, including a written language, an agrarian economy, feudal political relationships, and superb arts and crafts had become established by 1000 B.C. For many centuries the Chinese lacked a strong central government. This was achieved at last in the third century B.C. and led to a lengthy period of rule by the Han dynasty—200 B.C. to A.D. 200—about the same period as Roman rule in the West. The country afterward fell under continued pressure from nomads dwelling north of China's Great Wall. These barbarians repeatedly attacked (and sometimes ruled) China—as they attacked the Middle East, India, and Europe (pp. 54–55, 158, 206, 327–328, 355, 459). But China absorbed the invaders and pressed steadily forward with its brilliant and unbroken civilization. The excellence of Chinese practical and fine arts, scholarship, philosophy, and literature made a lasting impression on all of east Asia (including Japan).

China, however, did not match the scientific and technological advances of the West after 1500. Thus, when the Europeans eventually decided to penetrate the Chinese "wall" of isolation from foreigners, they possessed superior military equipment and made effective use of it. What the Europeans wanted initially were trading privileges. They coveted the luxury goods of China (silks, precious stones, porcelain), and they wanted to secure them in exchange for their factory-made products. Unfortunately, the Chinese did not want such articles. The one item they would buy in substantial quantities was the narcotic drug opium, grown in India and sold by British merchants. When the Chinese government tried to check its importation, Britain started hostilities. (This was the so-called Opium War.)

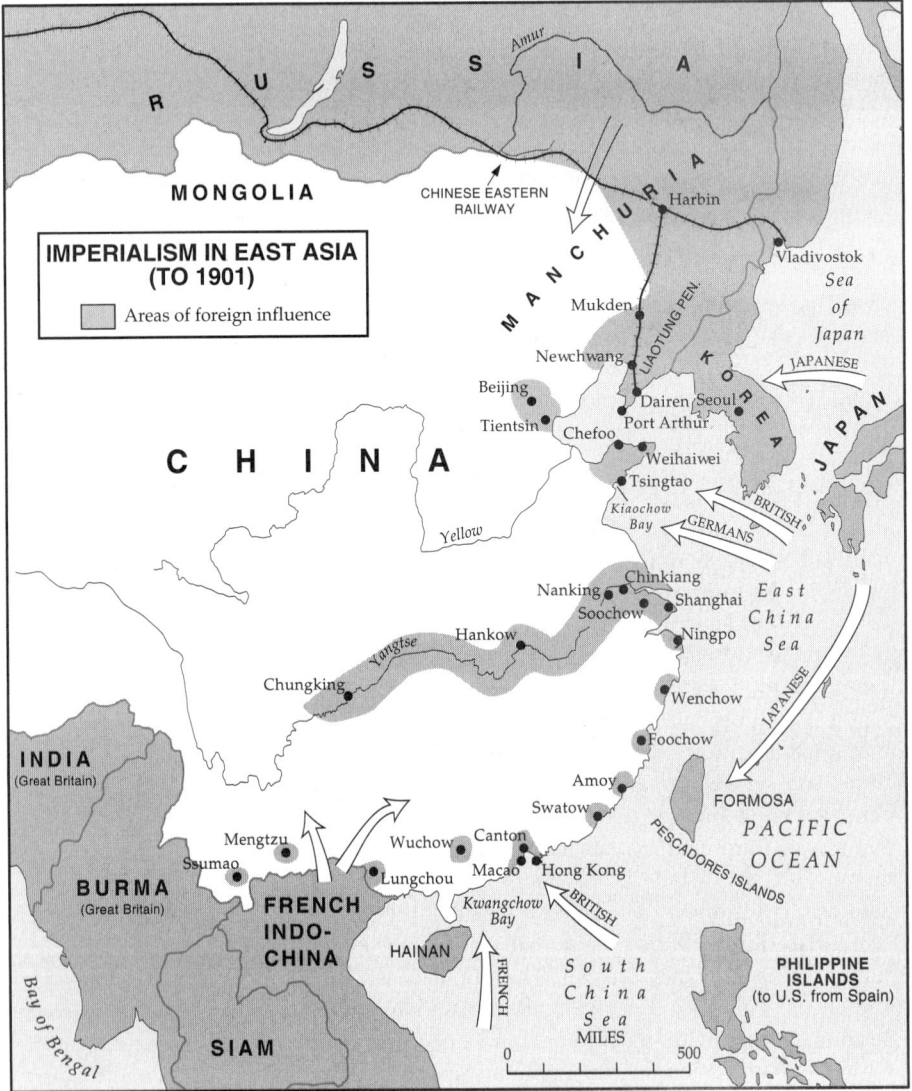

IMPERIALISM IN EAST ASIA (TO 1901)

Areas of foreign influence

The treaty forced upon China at the end of the Opium War (1842) was the first of countless impositions on that country. According to the treaty's terms, the opium trade was to be resumed without further interference. In addition, Britain demanded and won possession of the strategic Chinese city of Hong Kong. Within the next few decades other countries made their own demands. Under the "treaty system" a dozen Chinese port cities were opened to European traders (map, shown above), and in each port city the leading European powers were allowed to establish their own settlements, free from Chinese authority. European nationals, under further agreements, were allowed to travel inside China, subject only to the laws of their *own* homelands. The Chinese government was deprived of control over its external commerce; the European powers required that no tariff of more than five percent be placed on imports and that the tariffs be collected by Europeans. A good portion of this revenue was then siphoned off as "war indemnities" to the invaders. Small wonder that the Chinese felt growing resentment toward the "foreign devils"!

No matter what technique the Europeans used to impose their control, the results were disastrous to native institutions and morale. Although most Westerners are seldom aware of the effect of their technology when it is brought into traditional cultures, historians generally agree that modern industrial civilization has been one of the most disturbing cultural forces ever known. It breaks down and transforms premachine social organization, habits of life, and ways of thought. In this sense, the damage brought by imperialism resulted as much from "culture shock" as from the economic exploitation of "backward" peoples.

China suffered the full consequences of economic and social dislocation. Before the British broke in, there had existed a kind of balance between farming and handicrafts. A merchant class had prospered in the cities, and there were some large-scale workshops. China had a lively export trade in silks and porcelains, and its skilled craftsmen had been kept busy. But the entry of low-priced manufactured goods in the nineteenth century upset the entire structure. And, by building factories in the free ports and using the cheapest labor, the Europeans further undermined Chinese handicrafts and demoralized the regular workforce. Quick fortunes were made from these enterprises by foreign traders and manufacturers, but the cost to the Chinese people was beyond measure.

The Japanese were more fortunate. Though they had long admired and accepted Chinese ways, their conservative leaders feared the influence of Western ideas on their tightly organized, traditional society. After unhappy experiences with Portuguese and Dutch traders, the Japanese had closed their ports to foreign vessels in the seventeenth century. They did not reopen them until 1854. It was then that the American Commodore Matthew Perry, by threatening naval bombardment, persuaded the ruling power to negotiate a commercial treaty. The Japanese soon yielded to the idea that they must accept industrialization if they were to survive in the modern world. But they were determined to develop it *themselves*, without disruptive interference by foreigners. They jealously guarded control over their finances and tariffs, and in an extraordinary national effort they modernized their economy and armed forces. By 1890, they were thus able to meet the Westerners on even terms. (Asians, generally, learned a lesson from the Japanese example. Today most Asian leaders prefer to build their own national economies, in accordance with the character and needs of their societies.)

The Partitions of Asia and Africa

The concessions of trade and treaty ports by China failed to satisfy imperialist appetites, and the major powers continued to jockey for advantage. The Russians began, about 1850, to develop their long-neglected Siberian possessions (p. 459), founding the city of Vladivostok (Ruler of the East) on the Pacific Ocean. Then they turned their attention to Manchuria and Korea, both of which had close historical ties to China. The Japanese, also infected by expansionism, shortly revealed that they had plans of their own in this area. They drew China into war over clashing rights in Korea in 1894, and their western-style army won easily. China was compelled to cede to Japan the large island of Formosa (also called Taiwan), as well as its claims to Korea (*map*, p. 608).

The Europeans were astonished by this demonstration of Japanese will and strength. Now that it appeared that China might fall prey to greedy neighbors, they decided to protect their interests by seizing control of whatever territories they could. The Germans, French, Russians, and British pressured the Chinese government to give them vital coastal zones, in addition to their settlements in the "treaty ports." Only suspicions and disputes among the great powers saved the rest of China from complete partitioning at this time.

The intervention of the United States, which had become a Pacific power in 1898 when it took the Philippine Islands from Spain, had only a minor effect on the situation. The Americans feared that their commerce with China would be cut off if the foreign interests already there succeeded in spreading their territorial holdings. The secretary of state, John Hay, therefore pushed vigorously (in 1899) for the acceptance of an "Open Door" policy in China, which would guarantee the "territorial integrity" of the country against further losses and extend to *all nations equally* the commercial privileges that had been won from the Chinese government.

Britain supported the Open Door policy, for it promised to block the threat of more annexations by China's neighbors. The other powers viewed it coolly, however, for they hoped to pounce upon portions of the faltering empire. Ignoring the Open Door principle, Japan determined to tighten and extend its grasp. In both Korea and Manchuria, Japan faced the Russian imperialists. After failing to negotiate an agreement for two separate "spheres of influence," and fearing further Russian advances, the Japanese decided to settle the issue by force.

Japan opened hostilities in 1904 with a surprise naval attack on the Russian fleet and base at Port Arthur, in China, declaring war a few days *afterward*. This strike was a glaring violation of international law (repeated by the Japanese some forty years later in their sneak attack on American forces at Pearl Harbor— p. 656). The tsarist government never recovered from this opening blow and was roundly beaten on sea and land (in Manchuria) during the Russo-Japanese War. As a result, Russian expansion in this area was checked, and Japan strengthened its special rights in Korea and Manchuria, as well as in Port Arthur. Japan also gained enormous international prestige for having humbled the (supposedly) mighty Russian Empire.

Meanwhile, the rest of Asia had been gobbled up. The French, over the years, had taken control of large areas of southeast Asia; they combined them in 1887 to form French Indochina (*map*, p. 608). The British had begun to plant settlements in India back in the seventeenth century; in the nineteenth century the crown assumed direct control of the Indian government and extended its grip to Burma and Malaya. The Dutch widened their earlier holdings in the East Indies (p. 364), while Persia and Afghanistan were split into British and Russian spheres of influence (1907). Russia also established a "protectorate" over Mongolia in 1913.

As for Africa, the entire continent had been partitioned by 1914. France held most of the bulge of west Africa, which was largely desert; the British held the richest lands, running from South Africa in the south to Egypt in the north. The main possessions on the southern and eastern coasts, and in the central region, were those of Portugal, Germany, Italy, and Belgium (*map*, p. 606).

At last this era of fabulous conquest came to an end. The "new" imperialism had added five million square miles to the British Empire. (In 1900 Queen Victoria ruled nearly four hundred million subjects, with overseas territory *forty times larger* than the home island.) French possessions had expanded by almost as much; substantial though lesser areas had been acquired by Germany, Russia, Belgium, Portugal, and Italy. And Japan and the United States had joined the list of imperial powers.

The moral issue aside, imperialism brought some advantages to colonial peoples. It pushed them abruptly into the mainstream of world development. Roads, railways, sanitation, hospitals, and schools were introduced, while tribal wars and gross physical abuses, where practiced, were stopped. Most significant, "modernization" was brought to the colonial territories—though it could have come in a less coercive fashion. But all these benefits must be measured against the physical and psychic blows inflicted by imperialism upon the subject peoples. It left them with a lasting sense of confusion, defeat, and degradation.

In 1914 Europe stood at its peak of power and arrogance. But its outward thrust had intensified the forces that were pushing the Western nations toward war among themselves. Europeans claimed to look after the problem of "backward" peoples, but they proved unable to solve their own. Europe was about to explode in a frightful conflagration, leading to the collapse, soon after, of their colonial empires.

THE FIRST WORLD WAR AND THE DECLINE OF EUROPE

The two "world wars," one starting in 1914 and the other in 1939, are closely linked. Both were products of the international political system created and legitimized by the European powers. The First War ended not with a stable peace, but with a truce; the Second War was its nightmarish sequel. It was 1914, rather than 1939, that was the major turning point of modern history.

Yet on the eve of 1914 there were few who could see what the future held. The trend of surface events had indeed been deceptive. Europe had been spared a *general* war for one hundred years—since the downfall of Napoleon (p. 364). The advance of science, liberal institutions, and material well-being was indisputable. The years before 1914 were a time of expansiveness and optimism, with the promise of the

Enlightenment (pp. 478–479) apparently nearing fulfillment. Given another half-century of peace, Europe might have made the *liberal order* secure.

As we look back, however, it seems evident that such an outcome was unlikely. The existing peace was shaky; and, even without war, it seems doubtful that the liberal order could have endured. For there was another, gloomier side of the European picture. Technology had created forces that were dissolving the foundations of traditional liberalism, and imperialism had opened wounds, both in Europe and overseas, that continued to fester. There was, too, a rising romantic mood, irrational and illiberal, associated with mystical ideas of racial purity and national "soul." But Europe's fatal flaw was excessive *nationalism*—especially when it became connected with militarism and military alliances among the great powers.

NATIONALISM, MILITARISM, AND THE ALLIANCE SYSTEM

By the close of the nineteenth century the nationalist ideal of Mazzini (pp. 546–547) had hardened into a self-centered and self-destroying passion. Its characteristics were the same in every Western land: the people of each nation believed in their own superiority, sovereignty, and special mission in the world. They saw the advancement of national power and glory as the supreme aim of all of its citizens.

Nationalism, the "religion of the fatherland," was, in fact, the true faith of most Europeans at the turn of the century. Each nation viewed itself as the chosen instrument of God; its founders and heroes were its apostles and martyrs; its political charters were revered as holy texts. The flag was the sacred symbol of each nation, and pledging allegiance to the flag—and visiting historic shrines—were honored rituals.

This patriotic enthusiasm fell hard on certain ethnic minorities within states—groups suspected of having less than *total* loyalty to the larger community. Most Jews, for instance, were seldom accepted as "full" citizens of the states where they resided. Reacting to this feeling, some Jews began to think of securing a national state of their own; this fitted in with an age-old yearning following the Jewish "Diaspora" of ancient times (p. 167). A "World Zionist Organization" was founded in 1897 by an Austrian journalist, Theodor Herzl. It sought to create a Jewish *nation* in Palestine; "Zion" is the name of the hill that had once been the site of King Solomon's temple and palace (p. 166). Herzl and his successors appealed to world leaders to support their cause—leading, in time (1948), to the creation of the state of Israel (p. 670).

The armed forces of each European nation became the principal embodiment of its sovereign spirit and honor. They served, at the same time, as the ultimate means of pursuing national aims; both pride and interest, therefore, moved public officials and citizens to respect and strengthen the army and navy. Bismarck, building on the military tradition of Frederick the Great (p. 458), had pursued this policy in Prussia. His forces had impressed the rest of Europe as they paved the way to the creation of the German Empire in 1871 (pp. 547–550).

The other powers had worked to catch up militarily as rapidly as possible; all ex-cept Britain adopted universal male conscription and military training. Competi-tion in weaponry accompanied the rise of huge standing armies; by the end of the century, Europe had become a bristling camp. Nationalism and militarism were thus fatefully joined.

Stated simply, militarism is the belief that preparation for war provides sound moral training and the best safeguard of peace and the national interest. Militarists scorn diplomacy except when it is used as an expression of force. They aim, there-fore, to build ever stronger military power—greater, if possible, than that of any likely combination of enemies. "Peace through strength" is their slogan. But strength is *relative*, and each of the major nations wants to be the *strongest*. When the European peoples embraced militarism in the nineteenth century, they took off on an unrestricted *arms race*. All were caught up in it; for though a nation might never hope to win such a race, it dared not fall behind.

Unwilling or unable to agree upon principles for peaceful coexistence, the European powers were left to the deadly consequences of their own nation-alisms. For in relations *between* states there was no enforceable law comparable to that which existed *within* states. Because each sovereign power recognized no au-thority superior to itself, the ultimate resort was to go to war. The situation then, as now, has been correctly called *international anarchy*. There is only one funda-mental difference today: the weapons of war have become infinitely more destructive.

Metternich's "Concert of Europe" (p. 524) had been an attempt to deal with the problem of international anarchy by harmonizing the interests of the great powers. But this idea, basically at odds with nationalism, was doomed from the start. During the course of the nineteenth century, a few farseeing individuals tried earnestly to modify the sovereignty principle, strengthen international law, and es-tablish international courts of justice. Peace conferences were called, notably those at The Hague (in the Netherlands) in 1899 and 1907. Representatives of twenty-six nations, assembled at The Hague, tried and failed to agree on a proposal for *arms control*, but they did conclude several treaties on the "law of war" and the "rules of warfare." They pledged not to use poison gas or other weapons that were considered especially inhumane or indiscriminate. They also created an inter-national court of *arbitration*, to which countries might submit their disputes. Moreover, numerous "peace societies" were formed in various parts of Europe and America during the prewar period.

These efforts were forerunners of more substantial moves toward replacing an-archy with international order. But the responsible leaders of that era did not take them seriously. Those leaders believed that the only path to security, beyond keep-ing their own nation strong, was to enter into *alliances* with "friendly" powers. Thus, nationalism and militarism led to the alliance system of the late nineteenth century. Like the arms race, the alliances were competitive, and they added strength only in *relative* terms. The European states did not find safety from war in either arms or alliances. The pursuit of both served only to make the war fires hot-ter and more widespread when they flared up.

The Road to War

Though most of Europe's leaders, even as late as 1914, declared that war was *unthinkable*, we can see now that war was built into the existing international system. The pronouncements of the statesmen of that time are strong evidence of the human tendency to indulge in wishful thinking—to cling to comforting *myths* rather than face disturbing *realities*. Some said war would not happen because it was "too expensive," or "too frightful," or "too irrational." But we know now that those characteristics of war do not prevent it. The research of countless scholars on the origins of the First World War shows how international anarchy leads, in fact, to international war.

Until 1914, there had been grounds for optimism about keeping the peace in the fact that a number of international crises had been settled without resort to arms. But the pressures for war were cumulative, and the right type of crisis at the right time was virtually certain to strike the igniting spark. Many countries were working at cross-purposes internationally; Germany, however, held the chief initiative. Its triumphal unification in 1871 made it the dominant power on the continent. The eyes of European diplomats were fixed on the Germans, watching what they would do and how far they would go. The acts of other powers were closely related to German actions.

It was Bismarck (p. 547) who started peacetime alliances, as a means of maintaining Germany's new dominance in Europe. His motives were no doubt defensive; he feared that the French, stung by their defeat in the Franco-Prussian War (1870), would seek revenge. And so he arranged an alliance with another vanquished rival, Austria-Hungary, in 1879. Italy joined this pact a few years afterward, making it the Triple Alliance (*map*, p. 615).

The isolation of France, shrewdly arranged by Bismarck, was broken soon after he fell from office in 1890. His fall was due in part to the ambitions of the new German emperor (*Kaiser*), William II, who replaced Bismarck's cautious, *continental* policy with a policy that would propel Germany into its "rightful" place as a *world* power. The emperor's policy was an open challenge to Britain, whom Bismarck had sought to keep neutral in European affairs. Britain responded by developing closer relations with France.

Britain's island security and world position had depended for over a century on its superiority on the seas. But the new German ruler, convinced of the importance of sea power to overseas commerce, colonies, and national prestige, was determined to have a great navy as well as the world's finest army. Beginning in 1898, Germany began to lay out huge expenditures for a fleet of warships. Britain, alarmed, reacted with still larger sums, insisting on the principle that its navy remain the equal of any other *two*. And, though traditionally committed to "splendid isolation" from European "entanglements," the British now began to consider European alliances to counter the rising power of Germany (*map*, p. 615). (Britain had already signed an alliance with Japan in 1902.)

The French, meanwhile, had not forgotten 1870, and they, too, were seeking military partners. They looked first to the power on Germany's eastern border. Russia—autocratic and conservative—was ideologically and socially in sharpest

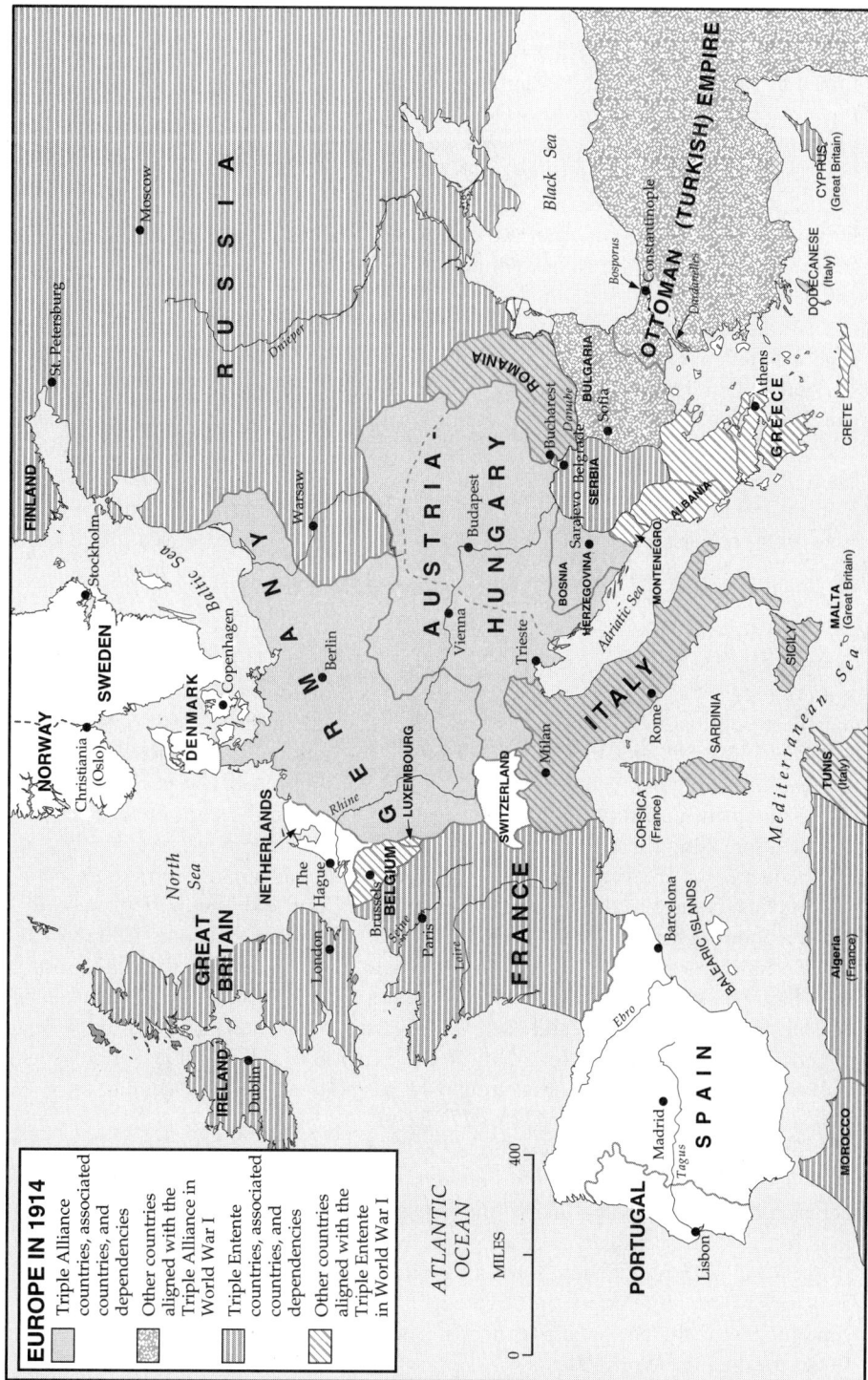

EUROPE IN 1914

Triple Alliance countries, associated countries, and dependencies

Other countries aligned with the Triple Alliance in World War I

Triple Entente countries, associated countries, and dependencies

Other countries aligned with the Triple Entente in World War I contrast to liberal and progressive France. But internal differences between states do not necessarily stand in the way of common goals in foreign policy. Already linked to each other by substantial French loans to the extravagant tsarist regime, the two countries entered into a Dual Alliance in 1894. This action confronted Germany with the threat that Bismarck had most feared — the possibility of a two-front war. From that time until 1914, the governments of Europe studied the military, diplomatic, and economic moves of the various powers with a view toward measuring their effects on the two opposing alliances. Any development that might decisively shift the balance of power between them could set off immediate and general war.

Britain found itself swinging ever closer to France and Russia. The French *revanchists* (revenge-seekers) accepted British advances in Africa that they had earlier opposed, and persuaded Russian diplomats to settle longstanding disputes with the British in the Middle East. For their part, the British were growing more worried with each "tough" move by the Kaiser. They made no formal military commitments, but after 1907 there existed a "close understanding" *(entente)* between Britain, France, and Russia. British and French military officers began to carry on joint staff conversations. The Dual Alliance was thus extended into a Triple Entente. That "understanding" was to grow firmer as trouble erupted in the Balkan peninsula (southeastern Europe — *map*, p. 615).

The Balkans and the narrow waterways (straits) of the Dardanelles and Bosporus had long been objects of great-power interest. The Ottoman Turks, in spite of losses of territory from the seventeenth century onward, continued to hold much of southeastern Europe, as well as the Middle East, until after 1815 (pp. 327–329, 458, 460). But the Balkan subject nationalities mostly differed in language, religion, and general culture from the Muslim rulers, and in the first half of the nineteenth century the Balkans began to respond to the spirit of nationalism that was spreading through all of Europe. The Greeks, for example, had won their independence in 1829 (p. 540), and the Romanians, Bulgarians, and others were waiting for a chance to throw off the Turkish yoke. But the Balkan nations were divided among themselves. Most were of Slavic ethnic origin, but some belonged to other ethnic groups that had lived in the Balkans for longer than the Slavs; most were Eastern Orthodox Christians, but some were Roman Catholic or had become Muslim under Turkish rule; and each was eager to claim the largest possible share of territory and population for itself, at the expense of fellow subject nations as well as the Turks. (For the background of religious and ethnic conflict in the Balkans, see pp. 218–219, 246, 325, 327–329.)

This was a situation that was bound to lead to interference by the great powers. Depending on the course of their rivalries, individual great powers wavered between trying to prop up Turkey, "the sick man of Europe," and supporting the efforts of this or that Balkan nation to gain independence or to assert itself against rival Balkan nations. The result was a seemingly endless round of Balkan uprisings, atrocities, wars, conferences, and treaties. It was this grasping of the great powers, combined with the nationalist ferment in southeastern Europe, that furnished the tinder for the First World War.

The Russians had three objectives in the area: to liberate their fellow Slavs and Orthodox Christians, to win control of the Black Sea coasts, and to secure a warm water outlet for themselves at the straits. The tsar nearly achieved these objectives in 1878, when he invaded the Turkish Empire and crushed its forces. But Austria and Britain demanded, upon threat of war, that the Russians reduce their peace demands. At the ensuing Berlin Conference, presided over by Bismarck acting as an "honest broker," Russia gained only a few harbors and border territories. But Romania, Serbia, and Montenegro were recognized as independent states, and Bulgaria secured self-rule under the Turkish sultan (ruler).

The alarmed sultan now tried to check the decay of Turkish strength by inviting German experts to reform his army and finances. He tried, at the same time, to play off the great powers against one another. But he had to pay a price: in return for their continuing diplomatic aid against Russia, he permitted the British to occupy Cyprus and the Austrians to administer the provinces of Bosnia and Herzegovina (*map*, p. 615). Egypt, nominally part of the sultan's empire, was occupied by the British in 1882 as part of their colonial schemes in Africa. The island of Crete broke free from Turkey in 1896 and became part of Greece; in 1908 Austria-Hungary formally *annexed* Bosnia and Herzegovina (took them over as part of its own territory). Finally, in 1912 Serbia, Montenegro, Bulgaria, and Greece invaded and liberated most of what remained of European Turkey—and immediately went to war among themselves over the division of territory and population. Another international conference gave independence to the last of the Turkish-ruled Balkan nations, mostly Muslim Albania. (Those Albanians who lived in the territory of Kosovo, however, came under Serbian rule, as in medieval times it had been mainly inhabited by Serbs, and was still regarded by them as sacred national territory—p. 328). By now, almost nothing was left of the dying Ottoman Empire's European territories; its Middle Eastern territories (mostly inhabited by Arabs) would be lost in the treaty ending the First World War (p. 621).

The conflicts of the Balkans reflected the deadly clash of opposing national aims. Russia, as we have seen, wanted to make the Black Sea an Orthodox and Slavic lake by controlling its outlet (the straits) at Constantinople. But Britain considered Russia's southward push a threat to its own "line of empire," which ran through the Mediterranean to India, and therefore sought to keep Russia bottled up in the Black Sea. Austria-Hungary, and Germany, too, had aims in the Balkans. Austria, which wanted to expand trade and influence in the region, resented growing Russian prestige there. And the Germans were building a Berlin-to-Baghdad railway, to open up the Middle East and India to German economic and political penetration. This ambitious project required understandings with the Balkan states through which the railway passed, as well as the Turkish sultan. Britain, Russia, and France regarded the German enterprise as a source of unwelcome aid to the Turkish Empire and an invasion into their own spheres of interest.

The most serious and irrepressible conflicts, however, were between some of the Balkan nations and the empire of Austria-Hungary. The Habsburg emperor ruled an empire consisting of a dozen different nationalities, which stretched from central Europe to the Balkans. In the Balkans the empire included several "South

Slav" nationalities—Catholic Croats, Muslim Bosnians, and Orthodox Serbs—who were closely related to or actually identical with what were now independent Balkan nations living farther east in the Balkans—above all, the Serbs. The leaders of Serbia had an ambitious sense of national mission and wanted to unite all the South Slavs—including those who lived in Austria-Hungary—into a single independent state. As a first step, the leaders of the "Greater Serbia" movement began agitation and subversion in Bosnia and Herzegovina, where Serbs, Croats, and Muslim Bosnians lived side by side, in an effort to win over the allegiance of these fellow Slavs and bring about their liberation from Austria.

The statesmen in Vienna were understandably worried. A Serbian success would pull important territories away from the Austrian Empire. Still more dangerous was the force that such a success would set in motion. The Magyars (Hungarians) had already gained self-rule within the empire (in 1867), but the Czechs, Slovaks, Poles, and other nationalities were still treated as subordinate peoples. They, too, were aroused by nationalist feelings and were eager to split the Habsburg domain into independent national states. The explosive situation also affected the alliance system, on which the general peace of Europe seemed to hang. If Austria-Hungary were to break apart, the Triple Alliance would be decisively weakened. Germany, the senior partner of the alliance, therefore kept in anxious touch with Vienna. On the opposing side, the Russians did all they could to *encourage* the Serbs to seek independence.

The Serbian nationalists, knowing that their country was militarily weaker than the Austrian Empire, resorted to *terror* to further their "holy" cause. Their efforts reached a climax in the streets of Sarajevo, Bosnia, in June 1914. A young terrorist assassinated the Archduke Francis Ferdinand (heir to the Austrian throne) and his wife. World leaders were shocked by the murders, and the Austrian government decided to use the occasion for a showdown with Serbia. Believing that the Serbian government was involved in the assassination plot, the Austrians sent a harsh *ultimatum* (a demand, backed by threat of action if not agreed to). The Serbs accepted in substance all but one of the requirements. But the Austrians rejected their response as unsatisfactory, broke off diplomatic relations, mobilized their army, and declared war on Serbia. The small Slavic nation, having received reassurances from Russia, also mobilized.

The responsibilities of the great powers in the face of this grave threat to European peace are difficult to assess. Germany, for reasons already suggested, had advised Austria to move ahead. Russia, having made a commitment to the Serbs, felt it could not back down. France, determined to preserve its alliance with Russia, urged its partner to be firm and to avoid any compromise that might cause a "loss of prestige" for the Triple Entente.

The decisive step in widening the war was the tsar's order to mobilize the Russian army. A week or more was needed before an army could be made ready for battle, and German leaders decided that they could not stand by while Russian mobilization went ahead. They sent a telegram demanding that the Russians halt their call-up within twelve hours. Failing to receive a positive reply, the Germans declared war on Russia on August 1, 1914. As Paris ordered mobilization, Berlin declared war on France as well. The catastrophe that "nobody wanted" had at last come about.

Though Britain had made no public pledge to aid France, its ministers had privately promised to help if the French were attacked by Germany. Parliament put aside any reluctance it might have had to make good this promise when the Germans, according to their war plan, invaded Belgium. Britain, as one of the guarantors of Belgian neutrality and security (p. 541), now had a legal basis for action. Parliament declared war on Germany on August 4. Japan, Britain's treaty partner in the Pacific, soon entered on the side of the "Allies," while the Turks, renewing their struggle with Russia, joined the "Central Powers" (Austria and Germany). Italy, a member of the Triple Alliance, did not enter the war at once, taking the position that its military obligation to its partners (Germany and Austria) was binding only if they were *attacked*. Italy remained neutral until 1915, when secret promises of extensive territorial rewards won it over to the Allied side. Many smaller nations were gradually drawn into the war (at least formally), but they did not influence its outcome.

THE COURSE AND CONSEQUENCES OF THE WAR

The strategy of the First World War was basically simple. The Allies, with control of the seas, were sure of winning a *long* war of attrition. The Central Powers aimed for a quick, decisive victory based on superior military technique and forces already in place. They also enjoyed the advantage of interior lines of communication, which meant that they could concentrate their troops swiftly on chosen fronts. The Germans, wishing to avoid dividing their army between west and east, had planned to strike an overwhelming first blow against France and then turn against the Russian forces, which would be slower in mobilizing. In executing their plan, the German generals did not hesitate to sweep through tiny Belgium, violating the treaty guaranteeing Belgium's neutrality. The treaty, explained the Germans, was but a "scrap of paper"; the invasion was a matter of "military necessity."

The German attack, which aimed to roll up the French army in a grand wheeling movement, stalled at the Marne River, near Paris. After the first few weeks, the battle on the western front changed from one of movement to one of *fixed positions*. Now the advantage shifted to those who were on the defensive. Trench warfare, with its barbed wire, machine guns, artillery barrages, and bayonet charges, became a routine of slaughter for the next four years (*Fig. 13-1*). Some new types of weapons were tried, aimed at breaking the military stalemate there: tanks by Britain, poison gas by Germany, and aircraft by both sides. These weapons failed to change the course of the conflict, but two of them—tanks and aircraft— would develop into decisive forces during the *Second* World War (pp. 655–657).

On the eastern front the Germans quickly gained the upper hand. The soldiers of the tsar, brave but poorly supplied, suffered disastrous losses and were practically out of the war by 1917. This military loss to the Allies was more than balanced, however, by the entrance of the United States on their side in 1917. Americans had been generally sympathetic with the British and French from the start of the

13-1   Trench warfare in the First World War. Allied soldiers hold a forward position, consisting of trenches to protect them against German fire. The soldier at left stands next to a machine gun; behind him are water-filled shell holes, the work of the other main killer weapon of the war, heavy artillery. Water and gunfire between them have turned the landscape to mud. Beyond the soldiers stretches "No Man's Land"; somewhere on the other side are the Germans, living in exactly the same circumstances.

war, though there was a pro-German ethnic minority in the country. There was also a stubborn antiwar movement that demanded that the United States remain *neutral*. But, in the end, opposition to joining the conflict was overcome by a combination of forces: the American government, fearing the strategic consequences of a German victory, pushed for intervention on the side of the Allies; and the public, alarmed by reports of German atrocities and the sinking by German submarines of commercial vessels, rallied to support the government. By bringing in fresh troops and equipment, and by pledging the resources of their continent, the Americans ensured ultimate victory for the Allies. Bowing to the inevitable, the Germans at last responded favorably to President Woodrow Wilson's offer of a moderate settlement, on Allied terms—a "peace without victory" (p. 652). In November 1918 they agreed to lay down their arms.

At the peace conference, which met at Versailles and other suburbs of Paris, separate treaties were arranged with each of the Central Powers. None of the defeated nations was given any effective voice in the settlements; it turned out to be a victor's peace after all. France, Britain, and the United States laid down the conditions, which were severe. (Had the Central Powers won, the conditions would probably have been even more severe—against the Allies. Evidence for this lies in the drastic terms imposed by Germany in its separate peace with Russia a year earlier—p. 628.) Delegates from the Central Powers protested bitterly, but they were compelled to accept under threat that the war would be renewed. In a vengeful stroke, the French required the Germans to sign their treaty in the Hall of Mirrors at Versailles (*Color Plate B7*), where in 1871 Bismarck had proclaimed the German Empire.

The most objectionable part of the Versailles Treaty, from the German point of view, was the "war guilt" clause—which stated that Germany and its partners accepted responsibility for *all* loss and damage caused by the war. The Germans did not feel that they alone were to blame, and the historical facts indicate that other powers shared the responsibility. The guilt clause no doubt reflected popular sentiment in the Allied countries, which had been fed strong propaganda by their wartime governments. It was put into the treaty to justify huge damage claims by the victors. Only small amounts of these claims were ever collected, but the "war guilt" clause aroused among Germans a violent and lasting hatred of the treaty (p. 639).

Under the territorial provisions, Germany lost the provinces of Alsace and Lorraine (which had been taken from France in 1871), its overseas colonies, and valuable lands on its eastern frontiers. Germany also had to surrender most of its merchant shipping and to dismantle its armed forces. The treaties with the other defeated powers (1919–1920) provided for the remaking of the map of central and eastern Europe, for now three empires (the Russian, Austrian, and Turkish) were in partial or total dissolution (*map*, p. 622). The guiding principle in drawing the new frontiers was Woodrow Wilson's principle of "self-determination" for nationalities. Seven new national states came into being. In northeastern Europe there were Finland and the Baltic states of Estonia, Latvia, and Lithuania. In central Europe there were Poland and Czechoslovakia (where there lived two closely related Slav nations, the Czechs and Slovaks). In the Balkans, there was Yugoslavia, whose name meant "land of the South Slavs," and which fulfilled the dream of the Serb nationalists who had started it all at Sarajevo. Within Yugoslavia's borders, there lived not only Orthodox Serbs, but also Catholic Croats and Slovenes, Muslim Bosnians and Albanians, and others. Austria and Hungary were separated and reduced to small landlocked states. All that remained of the Turkish (Ottoman) Empire was the Republic of Turkey, limited to Asia Minor and a small area in Europe that included Constantinople (renamed Istanbul in 1930).

Despite the general application of national self-determination, the problem of national conflict continued to plague Europe. The diverse nationalities were so intermixed that no state boundary could be drawn that did not leave a national minority on the "wrong" side. Since the boundaries were drawn by the victors, these minorities usually came from nations that had lost the war: the new nation-states of central Europe and the Balkans were full of aggrieved minorities of Germans, Hungarians, and Turks. And in Yugoslavia and Czechoslovakia, nations that were ethnically related but divided by history and religion had endless opportunities for conflict within their "joint" nation-states.

NORWAY

SWEDEN

FINLAND

Oslo

Stockholm

Helsinki

Leningrad
(St. Petersburg,
Petrograd)

*North
Sea*

Baltic Sea

ESTONIA

LATVIA

LITHUANIA

UNION OF SOVIET
SOCIALIST
REPUBLICS

DENMARK

Copenhagen

Memel

The
Hague

NETHERLANDS

Danzig

EAST
PRUSSIA

POLISH
CORRIDOR

Berlin

Posen

Warsaw

Kiev

G
E
R
M
A
N
Y

Rhine

POLAND

Brussels

BELGIUM

LUXEMBOURG

Prague

GALICIA

UKRAINE

Paris

Versailles

CZECHOSLOVAKIA

ALSACE-
LORRAINE

Vienna

Munich

Budapest

BESSARABIA

Prut

Berne

SWITZERLAND

AUSTRIA

HUNGARY

ROMANIA

*Black
Sea*

S.
TYROL

ISTRIA

FRANCE

Milan

Fiume

YUGOSLAVIA

Bucharest

B
A
L
K
A
N
S

I
T
A
L
Y

Sarajevo

Belgrade

Danube

BULGARIA

Sofia

Constantinople

Adriatic Sea

ALBANIA

*Bosporus
Dardanelles*

Rome

Naples

GREECE

*Aegean
Sea*

TURKEY

Athens

Mediterranean   Sea

PEACE SETTLEMENTS
IN EUROPE (1919)

TERRITORY LOST BY:

Germany   Austria-Hungary

Bulgaria   Russia

MILES

0   300

The deeper consequences of the war went far beyond the treaties and the breaking and making of states. The war had brought a catastrophic loss of lives and treasure. Of the more than sixty million men mobilized, some nine million were killed. Total civilian deaths, direct and indirect, amounted to more than thirty million; economic costs ran into *trillions* of dollars.

France was the hardest hit. During the first year of war French soldiers defended their homeland with a reckless courage, due as much to the foolhardy tactics of the generals as to the bravery of the men. French military theorists before 1914 were committed to the doctrine of the offensive: "Attack"—always and everywhere. With disastrous results for the French, this doctrine was put to test at a time when offensive techniques were decisively inferior to defensive techniques. In the first sixteen months of fighting, France lost three-quarters of a million men—half its total losses in the war. Such casualties were unprecedented. During the first traumatic year nearly one family out of two received the dreaded message announcing the death of a loved one in action. As the struggle wore on, a sense of doom and despair spread across embattled France.

After 1916, a year in which the British suffered the highest losses in any single offensive (at the river Somme), all the combatants realized that such wholesale squandering of lives was futile. Yet the daily slaughter went on to the end, resulting in the destruction of half a generation of young men. The spirit of Europe, especially of its surviving aristocracy, was broken. The youth who lived through the war, and wondered why, regarded themselves as the "lost" generation. The old beliefs and slogans had for them become mockeries; traditional morals, manners, and standards seemed, at best, irrelevant.

Men and morals were not the only casualties of the war. The *liberal order,* which in 1914 had appeared firm, was badly damaged. France and England, the leading liberal states, were crippled. In addition to their irreplaceable losses in manpower, their world positions had been shaken. In prosecuting the war, both nations had found it necessary to sell off a large portion of their overseas investments. Moreover, the spectacle of Europe at war with itself stripped away the awe with which colonial peoples had viewed their conquerors. The Western powers had given them reason to hope that they might one day send the imperialists packing.

The loss of physical and psychological power by the liberal states was equaled by the injury to their professed ideas and institutions. Liberalism was rooted in the Enlightenment, with its optimistic faith in humanity, reason, nature, and progress. But this faith had been crushed in the agony and futility of the war. Could liberalism survive after its supporting faith had collapsed? Disenchanted Europeans were unsure. Some drifted into skepticism (doubting all), cynicism (scorning all), or nihilism (rejecting all). Other Europeans were drawn toward socialism or toward a new and more violent strain of nationalism.

The war had undermined specific liberal institutions as well. This was most evident in the economic sphere, where "free enterprise" had been jealously guarded during the nineteenth century. Every nation at war was forced to clamp controls on business; just as the draft on manpower was compulsory, so was the call on economic resources. Raw materials, exports and imports, banking, wages, prices—all had been regulated in the pursuit of victory. Laissez-faire principles (p. 561) had been ignored "for the duration," and this experience of government planning and direction continued into the future. The war had also disrupted the intricate mechanism of international trade, and a chain of financial dislocations after 1918 marked the end of historic laissez-faire. It would be demonstrated time and again that private enterprise, both domestic and international, was not always "self-regulating" in the public interest. To maintain employment and save business from mass failures, Western governments would be called upon to take action.

The World War was fought, declared President Wilson, to make the world "safe for democracy." As he looked at Europe from Versailles in 1919, he might well have thought that the goal was now within reach. Prussian militarism had been defeated, long-standing empires had been reduced to ruins, and proud monarchies had been toppled. Democracy (as well as nationalism) appeared triumphant. Yet Wilson and others of liberal-democratic convictions were to suffer bitter disappointment. For most of the new democracies were only superficially democratic, and the older democracies were soon to lose their once-liberal character. Moreover, the shock and aftershock of the war were to open the doors of revolution in several countries. From the underground of the nineteenth century sprang the promoters of new social orders—people who were radically opposed, in theory as well as in practice, to both liberalism and bourgeois democracy.

COMMUNIST COLLECTIVISM: THE RUSSIAN REVOLUTION

The most comprehensive term applicable to the entire range of antiliberal ideologies and systems is "collectivism." Collectivism opposes historic liberalism (individualism) most directly on the issue of the amount of personal freedom in society. The liberal idea favors *maximum freedom for each individual* from any kind of restraint. Each person is to be "let alone"—to do whatever pleases that person (without injuring the freedom and rights of others). The collectivist idea, on the other hand, favors active *social planning and direction*—to promote the "general welfare" of all members of the society. In pursuit of this idea, collectivist systems restrict some freedoms of individuals and leave many areas of decision making to large organizations—above all, to *government*. (In their extreme form, collectivist systems are properly called *totalitarian*.) Collectivist organizations and governments may be controlled in various ways—from autocratic to democratic—but, no matter what the form of control may be, the individual is bound by decisions of others in many spheres of life. We should distinguish the collectivist state from the political absolutisms of the past, in which both the intentions of the rulers and their means of control were relatively limited. In fact, we can fully comprehend modern collectivism only in the context of the scientific, technological, and social conditions of the *twentieth* century.

Collectivist systems have shown a wide variety, arising from their differing values, ideologies, principles of action, and historical settings. They have come into being through one or the other of two modes of development: *revolution* or *evolution*. The former mode has appeared in countries where peaceful change had been blocked and where experience in liberal democracy had been slight, while the latter mode grew directly out of liberal democracy and with little or no violence. Most collectivist developments had this much in common: they were active responses to the failures of historic liberalism and to the chronic troubles of industrial society.

Russia before the Revolution

Strangely, the first collectivist state was established in a country where modern forces had scarcely started to develop. Autocratic Russia was a century or more behind the changes that had swept over western Europe. In 1917, the position of the Romanov dynasty was not far different from what it had been more than two centuries earlier under Catherine the Great (pp. 459–461). It resembled, in its pretensions and ignorance, the Bourbon monarchy of France in 1789 (pp. 510–511).

Russia had created a vast empire of many distinct nationalities, stretching eastward from central Europe to the Pacific Ocean (pp. 458–459, 609–610, 632). East of the Ural Mountains, the sparse population consisted of various Asiatic peoples, some of whom were seminomads. In European Russia (which then included Poland and the Baltic lands), the population was settled and dense; in 1900 it totaled about one hundred million. More than eighty percent of these people were peasants, and most of them had only recently been freed from serfdom (1861). They held more than half the arable land of the country, either as individual owners or through their village organization (*mir*), and they had gained limited political rights. Nevertheless, they remained largely illiterate and were regarded by the landed aristocracy (less than ten percent of the population) as an inferior caste. Over all was the heavy hand of the Russian Orthodox Church, which resisted Western ideas and supported the tsar's "divine" rule of Holy Russia and its empire.

Western influences had nevertheless reached into Russia. The late nineteenth century saw the rise of a new social element, the *intelligentsia*, made up of educated members of the aristocracy and the small urban middle class. Though the intelligentsia usually identified themselves with Slavic traditions, they were familiar with Western books and ideas. Writers like Tolstoy and Dostoevsky were members of this group (p. 534). Their popularity in the West reflected a growing common ground of culture. Russia also produced musical composers, philosophers, and poets, as well as some outstanding mathematicians and scientists.

The Industrial Revolution served as the chief spearhead of Westernization. After 1880, with the help of outside funds, the capitalist pattern of economic growth began to take shape in Russia. Substantial investments went into factories, mines, and railroads, and Russia became active in the world trading system. Capitalist development, however, was still limited in comparison with that of England or Germany. Industrial wage earners made up only a small fraction of the total labor force in 1914, and their working conditions resembled those in England fifty years earlier. The capitalist class was very small and had to share the economic field with numerous state-owned enterprises.

Though in theory an absolute monarch, Nicholas II was troubled by a wide range of domestic criticism and opposition. Around 1900 the rising business and professional class, in combination with liberal landowners, had formed a political party known as the Constitutional Democrats. Eager to follow the example of western Europe, they wanted to convert Russia's autocracy into a liberal, constitutional government. At about the same time two radical parties were founded—the Social Revolutionaries and the Social Democrats. The former, drawn mainly from the intelligentsia, was an agrarian party; its goals were to give more land to the peasants and to strengthen the functions of the *mir*. The Social Democrats were a Marxist group, also chiefly intellectuals. They viewed the peasants as hopelessly backward and believed that social change would have to follow Marxist theory— that is, the continuing growth of capitalism followed by the rise (and triumph) of an urban proletariat.

In 1905 a large body of protesting workers had gathered in front of the tsar's Winter Palace in St. Petersburg and had been fired on by troops. This "Bloody Sunday" set off insurrections across the country that were supported and used in various ways by the opposition parties. As a means of restoring order, the tsar promised a constitution and civil liberties and agreed, further, to the creation of an elected legislative body (Duma). Thus, by 1914 some concessions had been made to demands for political and economic reforms, but discontent still rumbled among most classes of the population. Only by means of a hated secret police was the tsar able to keep down the opposition. Even so, some revolutionaries resorted to *terrorism*, and no public official was safe from assassination. The grandfather of Tsar Nicholas (Alexander II) had been killed by a bomb, and Nicholas' prime minister was shot dead in 1911.

THE COLLAPSE OF THE TSARIST REGIME AND THE TRIUMPH OF LENIN

Russia's military disasters in the First World War, following defeat in the Russo-Japanese War (p. 610), opened the way to revolution: they laid bare the inadequacy of the tsarist administration and heaped disgrace upon it. Soldiers and sailors, poorly supplied and hungry, at last refused to continue the hopeless fight against the Germans. In March 1917 food riots and strikes in Petrograd (formerly St. Petersburg) led to mutinies among the garrisons of the capital (*Fig. 13-2*). The tsar, then at the front, abdicated upon the advice of his generals; thus the Romanov dynasty ended, and Russia became a *republic*. A provisional government, composed chiefly of the reformist leaders in the Duma, now assumed power. This government was challenged, however, by the Petrograd Soviet of Workers' and Soldiers' Deputies, a body representing the radical parties. The country's future now hinged upon the struggle for power between the provisional government and the Soviet.

In April, Vladimir Lenin arrived in Petrograd. The son of a middle-class civil official, Lenin had enjoyed a comfortable childhood. But at the age of sixteen, after

13-2 Women in Petrograd demonstrate against high bread prices—the first street protest that led to the fall of the tsarist government in Russia in March 1917. The women know they are not alone—the banner says: "Comrade workers and soldiers, support our demands!" In fact, workers were already on strike, and soldiers refused orders to disperse the protesters. Compare with *Fig. 11-2*, p. 513.

the execution of his elder brother for alleged participation in a terrorist plot, he had thrown himself into opposition to the tsarist regime (1886). Depending on friends for his livelihood, he made revolution his life career. Lenin spent most of his years in exile—first in Siberia and later in western Europe.

   An early convert to Marxism, Lenin worked to make the Russian Social Democratic party a disciplined revolutionary organization. The "revisionist" wing of the party (pp. 573–574) appeared to outnumber Lenin's faction, but at a meeting in 1903 he temporarily secured majority backing for the radical position. His followers thenceforth called themselves Bolsheviks, from the Russian word meaning "majority"; their reformist rivals came to be known as Mensheviks (minority). In 1912 the Bolsheviks broke away completely from the Social Democratic ranks and formed an independent revolutionary party. They changed their name to "Communist" in 1918.

During most of the war Lenin promoted international Marxist activities from Switzerland. His return to Petrograd in 1917 was aided by the Germans, who hoped that his activities there would help to overthrow the new government and take Russia out of the war—which is what Lenin succeeded in doing. First, however, he had to take power from the provisional government, which was making an earnest effort to restore internal order and uphold Russia's obligation to its allies to continue fighting the Germans. But conditions grew steadily more desperate in the country. Though Russia's economy had not developed to the point at which a proletarian revolution in the Marxist pattern could be expected, Lenin became convinced that the war had opened a *shortcut* to socialism. He saw that the bulk of the Russian people wanted three things above all: *peace, land,* and *food.* The provisional government, headed after July by Alexander Kerensky, a Social Revolutionary, had failed to satisfy these longings.

Lenin's road to power was through the Petrograd Soviet. Local soviets (councils) had first appeared during the insurrection of 1905; these "spontaneous" bodies had supposedly spoken for the peasants, city workers, and soldiers. Similar councils were formed in the crisis of 1917, and the Petrograd Soviet began to act as a "shadow" government. Though the Bolsheviks were a minority within the Soviet when Lenin arrived, he saw that the Soviet could be a key agency for seizing control of the state. He cleverly outmaneuvered his opponents (the Mensheviks and the Social Revolutionaries), and his repeated promises of peace and land won growing popular support for the Bolsheviks. In October 1917 Lenin's faction won the upper hand in the Soviet and elected Lenin's close ally, Leon Trotsky, chairman. As Kerensky's power slipped and as soldiers once more began to desert their units, Lenin decided to move against the provisional government.

The seizure of power (on November 7) was carefully planned and swiftly executed. With the support of the Petrograd military garrison, a revolutionary force occupied the telephone exchanges, power plants, and railway stations of the capital. The cruiser *Aurora*, stationed on the Neva River (fronting the Winter Palace) trained its guns on the building and fired the signal for the main attack. Kerensky found no troops to defend his government; he escaped, and the rest of his ministers fled or were captured.

On the afternoon of the *coup*, according to plan, Lenin arranged a meeting in Petrograd of delegates from soviets in other parts of the country. This "all-Russian" congress, controlled by the Bolsheviks, declared the provisional government at an end and claimed full authority. It approved decrees for an immediate peace with Germany and for the distribution of land to the peasants. (Under the terms of the subsequent peace treaty [1918] the Soviets agreed to surrender control of Finland, the Ukraine, much of Poland, and the Baltic territories of Lithuania, Latvia, and Estonia—all historically parts of the former Russian Empire.) The congress also elected a Council of People's Commissars (Deputies) to conduct the government, with Lenin at its head. These formalities could not conceal the fact that a small group, shrewdly and boldly led, had moved into the confused situation and had taken command. Thus was established the world's first communist state under the first "dictatorship of the proletariat." Could such a government, facing enormous internal and external problems, keep itself in power? Its only organs of administration were the Communist party, the soviets, and the Council of Commissars. The commissars established a secret police and authorized the recruiting of a Red Army. The military commissar, Trotsky, was to be its builder and leader.

One of the early tests of the new government came with the arrival in Petrograd (January 1918) of delegates to a national Constituent Assembly. This body had been authorized months before by the provisional (reformist) government and was to write a liberal constitution for the country. The delegates had been chosen in a general election in which thirty-six million citizens voted, and a majority of them belonged to Kerensky's Social Revolutionary party. But Lenin refused to surrender power to the "malignant bourgeoisie" and sent a company of Soviet sailors to stop the meetings of the Assembly.

A more severe challenge soon followed. Former tsarist generals organized and led counterrevolutionary forces ("Whites") in several regions of the country. They were joined by property owners, reactionaries, liberals, and anti-Bolshevik revolutionaries. In addition, the western Allies sent military units to aid the Whites against the Reds; the Allies were trying to keep Russia in the war and wanted to help destroy communism. But after two years of frightful civil war, marked by the use of terror on both sides, the hardened Communists emerged victorious. (Their ruthlessness, developed during this early period of their struggle for survival, established a pattern of behavior that led, ultimately, to the massive atrocities of Stalin.)

The Red triumph owed much to the extraordinary will of Lenin and to the military and organizing genius of Trotsky. And it owed something to the confusion and splits among the counterrevolutionary groups and their association with *foreign* powers. But, in the last analysis, it owed most to the attitude of the common people. Many of the commoners, to be sure, opposed the new regime. But the majority feared that a White victory would probably lead to the withdrawal of land from the peasants and to a restoration of the old order of autocracy, caste, and privilege. Though they also feared the Communists, they preferred them to the reactionaries. And popular support, in the fluid, guerrilla-type struggle, proved decisive. After 1920, with the bloody ordeal over, Lenin and his party sought to bring order out of chaos.

BUILDING A SOCIALIST SOCIETY

The task of pulling together a battle-torn country (formerly the multinational empire of the tsars), and at the same time overhauling its social structure, was staggering. The violence of civil strife had brought more distress than had the war against the Central Powers. During the fight with the counterrevolutionaries the government had resorted to temporary measures—later called "war communism." These included the drafting of workers into labor teams and forced deliveries of food from the peasants, in order to relieve hunger in the cities. Lenin was eager to start building socialism, but economic conditions were still so bad in 1921 that his plans had to be postponed.

1917	1924	1928	1953
Lenin	Trotsky versus Stalin	Stalin	

Food was the primary problem; drought had made matters worse, and famine now stalked large areas of the country. Something had to be done quickly to spur the efforts of farmers and to encourage them to market their produce. The New Economic Policy (NEP) aimed at doing just that. Launched in 1921, it removed restrictions on the ways in which land could be held and operated. (The peasants now possessed *all* the farmland; in accord with the Soviet land-distribution decree of 1917, the peasants of each community had divided the properties of the landed aristocracy among themselves.) Now they were permitted to hire laborers and to sell or lease land as they saw fit. Forced food deliveries were stopped, and the growers could market as they wished. The NEP was also extended to industry and commerce. While the state kept its grip on public utilities and other large industries (which had been nationalized in 1918), it encouraged private entrepreneurs to undertake new business ventures.

This temporary return to capitalistic methods brought about substantial recovery of production. But it fell short of the hopes and promises of the Communists. By 1928, output was at about the same level as it had been in 1913, and the momentum of the New Economic Policy seemed to slacken. Meanwhile, in 1924, the revered Lenin had died, and his former colleagues were maneuvering to take his place. Trotsky was the best known and probably the most talented. He, better than anyone else, expressed the impatience of the party with respect to economic development. In 1926 he openly criticized the NEP, complaining in particular about the new bourgeois and the richer landowners (kulaks). He called for the *collectivization* (government takeover) of agriculture, vigorous expansion of heavy industry, and a master plan for balanced and rapid economic growth.

Trotsky, who also urged the promotion of Marxist revolution in countries beyond Russia, could not gain the support of the majority of the party. Joseph Stalin, who held the post of party secretary, had quietly and skillfully built a following for himself as Lenin's heir. He appealed to those who wanted to concentrate on the revolution inside Russia, to those who looked inward rather than to the world. The party congress expelled Trotsky in 1927; he was first sent to Siberia and then deported. During his years of exile he attacked the Stalinist leadership as a perversion of Marxist ideals and tried to develop the "true" international revolutionary movement. Branded a communist heretic ("deviationist"), Trotsky was assassinated in Mexico in 1940 — probably by agents of Stalin.

With Trotsky and other rivals out of the way, Stalin in 1928 commenced the building of "socialism in one country." He announced the party's first Five-Year Plan, which concentrated on the collectivization of farming and the accelerated development of industry. State-controlled planning proved to be the most significant communist contribution to modern economics (though it came to be widely discredited in the late 1980s and 1990s). It was the fulfillment of an idea that had been worked out by Marx's partner, Friedrich Engels (p. 570), many decades before. Engels had noted that planning was indispensable to the efficient operation of individual factories and industries. The logical and ultimate goal, he thought, was the creation of a unified and complete *national* plan, embracing all parts of the economy. Since planning from above necessarily limits individual freedom of decision and action, it is clearly a *collectivist* idea.

Stalin's first plan ran into near-ruinous resistance. His officials scoured the countryside, joining private farms into large collectives of one thousand or more acres each. Strictly speaking, the farmers of each collective, as a "cooperative" unit, retained possession of the land, but individual farmers no longer controlled any portion of land as their *own*. The poorer peasants usually submitted to these forced measures, but the richer farmers, the kulaks, who possessed many acres, animals, and capital improvements, fought collectivization bitterly.

The government at last decided to coerce the resisting landowners and brutally removed, as a class, some two million kulaks and their families. Most were shipped off to labor camps in Siberia; others were forced into obedience; and many were killed. Some of them, in a final act of defiance and sabotage, destroyed their animals and implements before yielding. The heavy losses, and government manipulation of the surviving supplies, brought renewed famines in the early 1930s. Nevertheless, the collective-farm program was driven through; Stalin pursued it as a means of effecting complete state control over the rural population and of increasing agricultural efficiency and output. He believed that the collectives could make better use of machinery and scientific methods than could the single-owner farm. However, there was a loss of *personal incentive* in this system. (In the late 1980s, the government recognized this and began to permit limited production for market by individual farmers.)

Stalin's farm policy aroused sharp protests within the ruling bodies of the Communist party. His most notable critic was Nikolai Bukharin, a veteran activist and theoretician, who was a long-time associate of both Lenin and Stalin. Bukharin condemned the use of force against the peasants; he supported a flexible economic policy—based on persuasion, compromise, and *gradual* development.

But Stalin outmaneuvered his opponents. In 1930 Bukharin was shunted out of party influence and, later, was denounced as an "enemy of the revolution." Following a rigged "show" trial, he was sentenced to be shot in 1938. Had Bukharin and his allies succeeded in stopping Stalin, the course of Soviet history might have been quite different. (Bukharin's political reputation was gradually "rehabilitated" by Communist leaders over the years following Stalin's death in 1953. One of these leaders was the reformer, Mikhail Gorbachev, whose own pragmatic views were close to Bukharin's.)

While the painful and destructive events were taking place in the countryside, positive advances were being made in industry. The *rate of growth* in the decade of the 1930s surpassed that of any Western nation during that ten-year period. Much of the new development was located east of the Urals, in central Asia, where it altered the life and culture of a vast region. It was the combination of socialist planning and state exploitation of labor that made rapid modernization possible—and

without the aid of foreign capital; this example captured the attention of other underdeveloped countries around the world. The industrial successes, of course, were
trumpeted to Russian workers and peasants, who developed a fierce pride in Soviet
material accomplishments. They found deep satisfaction in the feeling that "backward Russia" was at last catching up, scientifically and industrially, with the West.
Access to education and the arts was also extended, and most Soviet children enjoyed greater opportunities than their parents had.

The price of all this, in addition to the early years of bloodshed, losses of
property, and severe hardships, was the domination of life by the Communist
party and government (*totalitarianism*). The Orthodox Church was stripped of its
property and influence; other traditional faiths were barely tolerated. (Marxism
became, in effect, the state religion.) There was no free press, free speech, free
unions, or freedom of assembly. Political power remained a monopoly of the
party, which was supported by the feared secret police. Dissenters, under Stalin,
were put down or destroyed by systematic terror: "show" trials, purges, labor
camps, and mass executions. In these respects, the political atmosphere resembled that under the tsars. But the new government was more efficient, used
modern tools of control, and succeeded in deadening virtually every nerve of
resistance. (Years after Stalin's passing in 1953, the full scope and nature of this
repression were illuminated by Aleksandr Solzhenitsyn, a gifted Russian writer.
His massive *Gulag Archipelago* [1974] reveals not only the island-like chain of inhuman labor camps and prisons, but the entire apparatus for suppressing internal
dissent.)

The major political institutions of the new state had been formed before
Lenin's death. According to the constitution of 1923, the Union of Soviet Socialist Republics (U.S.S.R.) was a federal, democratic state. The former Russian
Empire had embraced some fifty nationalities, and the Communists debated the
question of how to deal with them. They wanted to preserve native languages and
customs while guarding against *separatist* tendencies. Lenin decided on the *federal*
principle (borrowed from the United States) as the most suitable answer. Each major nationality became a republic (or a self-governing region within a republic). By
1940 there were sixteen republics; by far the largest was the Russian, which contained over half the U.S.S.R.'s total population of two hundred million. The
Ukrainian Republic (retaken by the Reds during the Civil War) had about half as
many inhabitants as the Russian Republic, and the White Russian (Byelorussian),
about one-tenth. Most of the other republics were relatively small, with from one
to six million inhabitants each.

Each republic had its own administration for its internal affairs. The highest
body in the federal structure was the Supreme Soviet, which was composed of two
chambers: a Council of Nationalities, having equal numbers of deputies from each
republic, and a Council of Union, having numbers proportionate to the population
of each republic. The Supreme Soviet enacted national legislation. However, this
body met for only a short time each year, when it elected a Presidium of some
thirty members, to which its functions were delegated. The Supreme Soviet also
chose the Council of People's Commissars, whose members served as the executive

heads of the federal government. (The Soviet capital was moved in 1924 from Petrograd—renamed Leningrad—to Moscow.)

The controlling power of the U.S.S.R. lay in the Communist party rather than in the agencies of the state. It was not a party in the liberal-democratic sense, but a disciplined organization whose self-appointed mission was to run the country. Accordingly, the constitution of 1923 authorized it to carry out this special role. Thus, while one did not have to be a party member to vote or run for office in the Soviet Union, party representatives determined whose names would be placed on the election ballot. Within the party itself, organization and authority followed the principle of "democratic centralism": officers and delegates to higher bodies were elected at several levels—from the level of the smallest party "cell," to intermediate bodies, to the All-Union Party Congress, which normally met every other year. Though the Congress was recognized as the highest party authority, actual control resided in its Central Committee, to which the Congress delegated its power. After the time of Lenin, power tended to go more and more to the top. And, once policy was decided upon there, it was the duty of every Communist to work for its fulfillment. Without the party organization and its carefully selected and trained membership, the Soviet state could not have transformed, as it did, a country that covers one-sixth of the land surface of the earth. On the other hand, this monopoly of power by a single party—with its stultifying bureaucracy and lack of accountability—would prove incapable, in the long run, of satisfying the desires of the subject peoples.

INTERNATIONAL COMMUNISM

Although the Bolsheviks succeeded in "building socialism in one country," they were less successful in spreading socialism abroad. As Marxists, they believed in and worked for *world* revolution (as Trotsky had urged), but they made little headway in that direction. Marx himself had given to socialism its international character, regarding national states as narrow creations of the bourgeoisie. In 1864 he had organized the First (socialist) International. During the rest of the nineteenth century, however, the international socialist movement proved weak. It was troubled by internal differences—ideological and personal—and, ultimately, by rival patriotisms. A Second International foundered in 1914. An association of the socialist parties of many nations, it fell to pieces with the start of the First World War. A minority stuck to their convictions and refused to support their war governments, but most "reformist" socialists supported the "patriotic fronts" of their homelands.

Lenin, who had predicted the war as a natural outcome of capitalist imperialism, scorned the reformist parties as bourgeois. In 1919 he invited left-wing socialists throughout Europe to join the Soviet Communist party in forming a *Third* International. This, Lenin declared, would be a "pure" successor to Marx's original organization. Free of the reformist socialists, it pledged itself to worldwide revolution and the dictatorship of the proletariat.

Left-wing socialists of other countries, impressed by Lenin's stand and by the Russian Revolution itself, readily accepted radical leadership. During the 1920s, the methods of the Soviet party were adopted by the new association. Tight organization, centralized control, and the name "Communist" were imposed on the international body and on each of its national parties. As a result, sharp hostility arose between rival groups of Marxists outside the Soviet Union. The reformist socialists viewed with horror the violence used by the Communists, especially under Stalin, and despised the intolerance of party leaders toward members with different views.

Having alienated the large majority of Marxists outside the Soviet Union, the Third International (known as the Comintern) had little chance of success. It was the reformist (democratic) socialists, strengthened by their break with revolutionary Marxism, who made impressive gains in the Western nations. After the failure of several communist-led uprisings immediately following the War, the reformists helped advance collectivism by legal and democratic means in France, Germany, Scandinavia, and Britain. Despite the predictions of Marx and Lenin, proletarian revolution was clearly not coming soon in the industrial countries of the West.

Meanwhile, communist parties, with Moscow's support and direction, were at work, usually underground, in fifty or more countries. (In most of the European democracies there were large and legal Communist parties, but they were generally excluded from governing power.) Though all of these failed during the 1920s and 1930s to bring about successful revolutions, they served as arms of propaganda and espionage for the U.S.S.R. The principal international influence of communism came not through the activities of the Comintern, but through the fact that the Soviet Union *existed* as a world power. Collectivists of all shades could point to it as a concrete alternative to liberalism and capitalism. Though they objected to many characteristics of the Soviet Union, they could use it as a working example of state planning and cooperative social principles.

FASCIST COLLECTIVISM: THE REVOLUTIONS IN ITALY AND GERMANY

The fear of communism helped push several European nations into revolutionary collectivism of another sort. In Italy and Germany, the fascist revolutions sprang from two conditions: a social crisis that arose in the wake of the First World War and the inadequacy of liberal-democratic government. (Wherever governments effectively met their problems, they were able to resist subversion.) Moreover, the revolutions in Italy and Germany were propelled by violent nationalisms growing out of the frustrations of the war. Whereas the communists focused on *class* and interclass struggle, the fascists stressed the *nation* and international struggle.

There is another significant difference between the two kinds of collectivist revolution. The communist uprisings in Europe had been anticipated in the decades of Marxist organization, propaganda, and threats of action. (Bolshevism was unwelcome but not unexpected.) Fascism, on the other hand, came as a surprise. As an explicit doctrine, it had no ideological founders, no authoritative books, and no forces in evidence before 1918.

Its explosive appearance can now be understood as a breaking out of strong ideas and passions, some open to view and some hidden, that were opposed to liberalism, democracy, and rationalism. Though revolutionary, fascism had a broad appeal to privileged groups as well as to ordinary people. Its militant nationalism aroused all patriots, and its support of class interests (including those of the military) satisfied individuals of property and power. This appeal of fascism to national spirit and class power makes it a persisting (though veiled) threat to capitalist democracies everywhere. Fascism, we should remember, was destroyed in its major strongholds only by *external military force* (in the Second World War); should severe internal crises strike again in the industrialized countries, existing governments will no doubt find fascism (under whatever *name*) a serious threat. The relative ease with which such movements can take over a nation was *demonstrated* in the historical example of Italy.

FASCISM IN ITALY: MUSSOLINI

Italy after 1918 provided a favorable setting for the rise of fascism. Its parliamentary institutions, less than fifty years old, had never won much loyalty or enthusiasm from the people. Even before the war Italians often complained of graft and inefficiency in government, and the Italian legislature seemed incapable of dealing with the acute economic challenges of the 1920s. The majority of citizens, suffering from postwar inflation and unemployment, were disillusioned with the nineteenth-century ideas of liberty, reason, and progress. Moreover, they were bitterly disappointed over Italy's role in the war. Though they finished on the side of the victors, their armies had experienced hardships, losses, and humiliating defeats. And at war's end the Allies gave Italy only a portion of what they had promised as a reward for Italy's entering the conflict on the Allied side (p. 619).

Many voters turned to the socialists in the hope that they would do something about the worsening economic situation. The elections of 1919 gave the Socialist party one-third of the seats in the national Chamber of Deputies; with the Catholic Popular party, the Socialists might have developed a constructive program for the country. Mutual distrust between Catholics and Marxists made such cooperation impossible, however, and the socialist trade unions began to take direct action. In 1920 unionists occupied a number of factories and tried unsuccessfully to operate them. The workers soon withdrew, but their action had given the propertied classes a fright. In the following year the Socialist party split over the question of whether or not to join the Communist Third International (the Comintern—p. 634), thus losing what chance it might have had of becoming a dominant political force. It was on this scene of confusion, discontent, and fear of communism that Benito Mussolini presented himself as the national savior.

A shrewd propagandist and politician, Mussolini might be regarded as the Lenin of the Italian revolution. But, unlike the Russian hero, he did not find it necessary (as we shall see) to seize power by military force. Born into a socialist family, the son of a blacksmith, Mussolini was a man of the laboring class. He went to school to become a teacher but turned to journalism and radical agitation. In

1912 he secured the position of editor of the Socialist party newspaper in Milan, and he gained a reputation as a dynamic radical leader. As a Marxist, he had initially opposed war and had escaped military conscription by going to Switzerland; but in October 1914 he reversed himself by urging Italian entry into the war against Germany. For this he was expelled from the party and from his newspaper. Thereupon he founded a journal of his own, which he used to publicize his new convictions and to advance his political career.

Mussolini served in the war as a corporal until he was injured in an accident in 1917. Resuming the editorship of his paper, he tried to stir popular support for the flagging war effort. He turned wholly against socialism after the Russian Revolution, growing more and more militant and nationalistic. He opposed the floundering parliamentary government of his own country; the legislature, he declared, was a collection of special interests and selfish individuals who lacked the desire and the ability to serve the national interest. Mussolini, like many other veterans of the war, became attracted to violence as a way of life and as a means of securing change. He started organizing his followers into paramilitary black-shirted units (*fasci di combattimento*—hence the name *fascist*). These units took it upon themselves to take part in street fighting with socialists and others they disliked, to smash opposing party and newspaper offices, and to assassinate some of the opposing leaders. The Blackshirts thus came to be regarded as the fighting arm of the new social movement.

Mussolini next organized his forces into a fascist political party, even though he had only contempt for the parliamentary party system. In the national election of 1921 he and his followers won thirty-five seats in the Chamber of Deputies. As their leader, Mussolini made fiery nationalist appeals and attacks on socialism. He began to gain widespread support, especially from the shopkeepers and white-collar class, but from the rich as well. Young people were strongly attracted by the uniforms, parades, mass rallies, and calls for *action*. During 1922 his Blackshirts drove the legally elected socialist governments from control of Italy's northern industrial cities, and later that year a huge Fascist assembly in Naples called for a march on Rome.

The constitutional king of Italy, Victor Emmanuel III, was now faced with the prospect of black-shirted bullies converging upon his capital. His prime minister, unable to secure an effective legislative majority, urged him to declare martial law. But the king decided to do otherwise; he invited Mussolini to come from Milan and form a new administration. The Fascists, camped near Rome, marched on the city while Mussolini arrived by railway car to take over the government.

The new leader, who preferred his party title of *Duce* (leader), was not long in consolidating his position. The Chamber of Deputies, which had surrendered to the Blackshirt threat without a fight, quickly voted Mussolini dictatorial power for one year. During that time he altered the election law to allow the party that received the most votes (even though less than a majority) to take *two-thirds* of the seats in the chamber. A Fascist victory was thus assured (again, by "legal" means), and in the election of 1924 the party won about seventy percent of the total national vote. Despite its unclear aims and its fondness for violence, the party

1860	1870		March on Rome 1922	1943
Period of Unification		Constitutional Monarchy	Mussolini (Fascism)	

received the support of many moderates who hoped that they could exercise a restraining influence on the Duce. Within a few years he had eliminated almost all opposition and had established a fascist state.

The collapse of Italian democracy was clearly due to its own failures, but Mussolini's triumph resulted from a variety of factors. Critical among them was the backing of the army and the great industrialists of the country. Mussolini did not have to create a new army (as did Lenin), though his Blackshirts became a permanent military body. The regular army came readily to his side. Many of its high officers had had fascist sympathies from the beginning, and the Duce's glorification of militarism and his extravagant support of the army gained their active loyalty.

The industrial leaders, for their part, had been uncertain about Mussolini at first. They approved his smashing of the Socialist party and the unions, but they were worried about his intentions toward business. In 1925 the associated industrialists signed an agreement with the Duce. In return for their support of the Fascists, the industrialists were given a recognized position in the government, with the authority to regulate the nation's industrial affairs. The major employers in agriculture and commerce were later given similar authority. Together with hand-picked labor and professional bodies, these regulatory groups made up what Mussolini called the "corporate" state. In theory this state represented a harmonizing of all the economic and social interests in the country. In fact the corporate state was an instrument of the dictator, through which he permitted the leading capitalists to administer the nation's economic affairs.

Mussolini completed his structure of power by negotiating an alliance with the pope. Ever since the move for national unification had begun, in the middle of the nineteenth century, state and church in Italy had been in opposition (pp. 341, 350). After lengthy and difficult discussions, Mussolini and Pius XI signed the Lateran Treaty and Concordat of 1929. By their terms, the pope gained sovereignty over the area of Vatican City, which includes St. Peter's Basilica and its immediate environs. The Church also secured state financial aid and a special position in the educational system. In return, Pius gave his weighty support, and that of the Italian clergy and laity, to the Fascist state. Mussolini was himself an atheist, but, like Napoleon before him (p. 519), he sealed his position as dictator by a bargain with the Church. Afterwards, not surprisingly, he violated the terms of the Concordat as he saw fit.

Though Fascism stressed action and was anti-intellectual in tone and character, it nevertheless developed a distinctive ideology. In the beginning, as Mussolini himself admitted, it was largely a negative movement: *against* liberalism, democracy, rationalism, socialism, and pacifism. This negative feeling flowed from Mussolini's personal experience and that of countless other Europeans during and after the war. They had been cast adrift, let down by failed hopes of progress and happiness. Faceless in a mass society, they also felt *alienated* from *themselves*. The Fascists found an answer to this emptiness by arousing extreme nationalism. One could get an emotional lift by forgetting one's problems as a person and by giving oneself to something larger and grander—the nation. Mussolini and his associates developed this idea into the myth of the "organic state."

The Fascists asserted that the state is a *living entity*, above the individuals who compose it. Yet, though personal liberty in Italy was under the control of state authority, they held that the individual's power was enlarged through association with the body of citizens. This view contrasted sharply with liberal and Marxist ideas about the individual and the state (pp. 544–546, 572). "The state," declared Mussolini, "is a spiritual and moral fact in itself. . . ." It encompasses every sphere of life (totalitarianism); the state alone can "provide a solution to the dramatic contradictions of capitalism." And, as a living organism, the state must *expand* in order to express its vitality. This meant a continuous and disciplined *will to power*, which requires unity within the nation, militarism, imperialism, and war.

The fascist myth rejected the liberal reliance on reason and replaced it with a mystical faith. Stridently anti-intellectual, it held that the "new order" would spring from the conviction of the "heart." Fascists therefore looked upon intellectuals in general as outmoded and suspicious characters, unduly concerned with their private mental fancies. Yet most Italian intellectuals willingly cooperated with the Fascists, thus confirming Mussolini's view that they were lacking in honesty and courage. The few who opposed the government were either silenced or forced into exile—the Fascist secret police struck down any active opposition.

Most ordinary Italians accepted Fascism with enthusiasm. The individual, who formerly felt alone and unneeded, enjoyed a new sense of "belonging"; this feeling of personal identification and participation was deepened by the paternalistic measures of the government and by various other means. Many types of workers wore distinctive uniforms, and mass rituals were staged in the great public squares of Rome and other cities. By 1930, Fascism appeared to have gained the firm support of most of the Italian people, as well as the admiration of many conservatives abroad.

The political institutions of Italy underwent a steady evolution under Mussolini. The corporate associations, which guided economic affairs, gradually became the basis for political representation in the national legislative body. But the true power in all fields was the Fascist party, headed by the Duce. The party resembled, in many ways, the Communist party of the Soviet Union (p. 633). It was the only legal party; it consisted of only a fraction of the total citizenry; and its members were carefully drawn from the ranks of select youth organizations. Corresponding to the Communist Central Committee was the Grand Council of Fascism. Its members generally held high offices in the government in addition to their party positions; this connection, too, paralleled the interlocking of party and state officials that existed in the Soviet system.

Fascist ideology frankly supported rule by an elite (the "chosen" best). While Marxists taught that the state and its officeholders would gradually disappear after the abolition of capitalism (p. 572), the Fascists believed in *permanent* rule by their "natural" leaders. These would be individuals of rare intuitive power, capable of rising above self-interest and of sensing the character and desires of the nation. Their superiority, the Fascists declared, came chiefly from *action* rather than thought: it was basic that the leaders would have fought for the fatherland, taken part in the Fascist revolution, and helped to build the "new order."

THE NAZI COMPOUND OF FASCISM AND RACISM: HITLER

Just as the ideas of communism carried beyond the borders of the U.S.S.R., so the fascist philosophy spread quickly across Europe—and the world. It won a substantial following in Austria, Portugal, Spain, and Argentina; but its world-shaking triumph was in Germany. Here fascism as a doctrine fused with deeper and older forces in the German tradition; here the fierce words of elitism and imperialism turned into deeds of conquest and genocide (race-murder).

Germany's humiliation at Versailles (pp. 620–621), coupled with severe economic problems after the war, prepared the ground for Adolf Hitler and his National Socialists (Nazis). The Germans adopted a democratic constitution in 1919, but its success was unlikely from the start. The new government was inexperienced, it suffered from the usual stresses and divisions within liberal states, and it was associated with the crushing military defeat. (In the closing days of the war, the German generals had shrewdly withdrawn and left the country's surrender to a liberal civilian government hastily appointed by the Kaiser.) Unlike the parliamentary regime in Italy, the German Republic did not collapse in the years immediately after the war. But it failed to win the full allegiance of the people, and in little more than a decade it fell under the weight of its unsolved problems.

One of its problems was Adolf Hitler, who had been born of middle-class parents in a small Austrian town. Early in life he had become an ardent German nationalist, and, though he spent some of his formative years in Vienna, he found its cosmopolitan atmosphere especially distasteful. A moody drifter, he did not find a place for himself until the outbreak of the First World War. When he enlisted in the German army, Hitler experienced the comradeship and discipline of military life and exulted in his service to his adopted fatherland.

In 1919, embittered by the war's outcome, he went to Munich, capital of the south German state of Bavaria. Large numbers of unemployed veterans and political dissidents had congregated there. Hitler joined a budding group that called itself the National Socialist German Workers' party and soon became its leader (*Fuehrer*). This new role provided an outlet for Hitler's deep-seated animosities and ambitions. He attracted to the National Socialist banner others who shared his intense nationalistic feeling and hatred for Jews. Among his supporters were Hermann Goering, a swaggering pilot-hero; Dr. Josef Goebbels, a university-trained journalist; and General Erich Ludendorff, an arch-conservative and one of Germany's chief military commanders during the First World War.

Hitler threw himself fully into the life of politics and national "regeneration." Though he had but limited formal education, he had an intuitive grasp of the

1871		1918	1933	1945
Hohenzollern Empire (Reich)			Democratic Republic	Hitler Third Reich

concerns that were disturbing his fellow Germans, especially the middle class. (Among their concerns were deep anxieties about the decline of "culture," the threat of social revolution, and the mixing of the races.) And, like Mussolini, he had a gift for rousing speech-making. The early 1920s were a time of restlessness and disorder in Germany; street clashes and rioting were commonplace. In 1923 Hitler led an attempted coup (Putsch) against the Bavarian state government. It was stopped in the streets of Munich by police fire, and the Nazi party seemed to have been crushed by the government reprisals. Hitler was imprisoned for nearly a year, during which time he wrote Mein Kampf (My Struggle), the statement of his life and beliefs. Upon his release from prison, he refounded the party. For a while it made little headway, but financial contributions, mainly from the middle class, enabled Hitler to purchase newspapers and periodicals through which he could spread Nazi propaganda.

The international economic crisis of 1930, a product of the dislocations stemming from the World War, gave the German revolutionary parties their great opportunity. Rising numbers of unemployed men were looking desperately for work. Many of them found "jobs" as brown-shirted Nazi storm troopers, similar to Mussolini's Blackshirts (p. 636). The party gained electoral strength steadily during the years of economic hardship. And when at one point it ran out of funds, some powerful industrialists came to the rescue. In January 1933 Hitler received from them a promise to pay the wages of his storm troopers and the party's debts. German business leaders, generally, preferred the familiar conservative politicians to Hitler. But in this time of crisis, they turned to the Nazis as a "bulwark against communism"—and to ensure themselves against the possibility of a Nazi victory in the elections.

A few weeks later, backed by conservative politicians and generals, Hitler succeeded in pressuring the aged president of the Republic, Paul von Hindenburg, to appoint him head of the national government (chancellor). The Nazis had the largest number of elected delegates in the legislature (Reichstag), but they still did not have a majority. However, after the Reichstag building was mysteriously burned, Hitler enforced a suspension of constitutional guarantees. He banned the Communist party and had its leaders imprisoned; the Social Democrats were the only opposition party left. The Nazis, with the support of other conservative parties, then passed the Enabling Act of March 1933—giving the government power to rule by decree for a four-year period. Hitler next replaced the flag of the Republic with the Nazi swastika (the "crooked cross") and declared the beginning of the "Third" Reich (Empire)—successor to the medieval and Hohenzollern German empires (pp. 244, 550).

Soon afterward Hitler outlawed all parties save his own, duplicating the Fascist example; by mid-1933 his political opponents were either in jail or in exile. A year later, after Hindenburg's death, he assumed the office of president in addition to that of chancellor. This act was ratified in a vote of overwhelming approval by the German electorate. Thus, the mad Austrian became the sole ruler of one of the most educated and civilized nations of the world. He proceeded, with the cooperation of the army and leading industrialists, to marshal the country's manpower and resources. Hitler's aim was to make Germany the most powerful nation in Europe and, ultimately, the world.

Nazism had much in common with Italian fascism. Both rested on the myth of the "organic state," the importance of struggle and will, the glorification of militarism, insistence on authority and discipline, rule by an elite, and a mystical faith in the leader. But in Germany there were added elements of violent racism, neoromanticism, and nihilism. The first two were largely out of the nineteenth century; the last was mainly an outgrowth of the war and took the form, essentially, of a mindless lust for power.

For the Jews of Europe the Nazi racial theories led toward *genocide*. During the Middle Ages the Jews had suffered from the religious prejudices of Christians (pp. 190–191, 313–314), and persecutions and segregation had persisted up to the time of the French Revolution. In the course of the nineteenth century the liberal philosophy of equal civil rights for all had liberated Jews from the ghetto in some parts of Europe. However, the decline of discrimination on *religious* grounds was counterbalanced by the rise of new theories of *racial* differences. Some writers in France, England, and Germany began to assert the supremacy of Nordic "races" over others—especially over the "Semitic" and "Negroid."

Hitler and his associates, resentful of resurgent Jewish social and cultural influence in postwar Germany, embraced these racial ideas and made them a central part of their program. They became vicious anti-Semites, portraying the Jew as a seducing, bloodsucking fiend who longed to pollute Nordic "purity." The Nazis, in the name of racial "science," thus revived the dark and primitive Jew-hatred of the Middle Ages (pp. 313–314). Building on that passion, they enacted discriminatory legislation, outlawed marriage and sexual relations between Jews and citizens of "German blood," forced Jews to wear a humiliating badge, burned their synagogues, and laid plans for the systematic annihilation of the Jewish people (Hitler's "final solution"—the inhuman death camps of the Holocaust). Like the Fascists, the Nazis had contempt for reason and intellectuals. Hitler saluted the "simple and honest" values of the German peasantry and declared that those values were the foundation of Nazi goals. Yet under Hitler the country became increasingly industrialized and urbanized. Cleverly, the Nazis covered up the disturbing reality of technological change by encouraging popular belief in the myths of rustic purity and racial superiority. Millions became converts to the Nazi faith during the 1930s. It suited the traditional romantic yearnings of most Germans, offered a total view of life in place of fragmentation and alienation, and appealed strongly to national and racial pride. Finally, it released the urge to violence. Nazism led, by successive steps, not only to the murder of Jews and political opponents, but to the wider catastrophes of the Second World War.

Although Hitler roused powerful support for his measures within Germany, some individuals and groups struggled to resist him. The Roman Catholic hierarchy criticized many of the Nazi policies, but the Church, generally, looked to its own survival first and was able to secure its functioning while enduring an uneasy relationship with the state. (For his part, Pope Pius XII, in Rome, kept a discreet silence with respect to the systematic destruction of the Jews; his silence was interpreted by the Nazis as a tacit approval of their actions. Pius believed, however, that moral condemnation of the Nazis by the pope would only make the situation *worse* for both Jews and Catholics in Germany.)

Less fortunate were the German Protestant churches, which Hitler determined to organize into a supporting force for his party. Most of them yielded to the relentless threats and pressure, but some individuals refused; they formed a separate "Confessing Church," which openly opposed the Nazi power. They failed to stop Hitler and paid the high price of conscience: their chief leader, the Lutheran pastor, Martin Niemöller, was arrested in 1937 and remained in a concentration camp until liberated by the Allies at the end of the War. Also arrested, imprisoned, and executed (in 1945)—was the distinguished theologian, Dietrich Bonhoeffer, among many others.

DEMOCRATIC COLLECTIVISM: EVOLUTION OF THE WELFARE STATES

While collectivist societies built on totalitarian lines were taking shape in Germany, Italy, and the U.S.S.R., the shift from liberalism went forward in a different manner in the still-democratic countries of the West. In the Scandinavian lands, France, Great Britain, and the United States, the major prewar social institutions appeared to hold firm. But none was secure from the disturbances that followed the war or from the ceaseless march of science and technology.

In response to these forces, democratic governments intervened more and more in matters formerly considered to be "private." And as their functions expanded, governments left behind some of the principles and practices of historic liberalism. They created, without full-scale planning, forms of *democratic collectivism*. Some observers called this "social democracy" or "creeping socialism"; but a more fitting term is the capitalist "welfare state."

A European Example: Britain

Events in Britain after the war illustrate the evolution of a welfare state. This country had been identified, more than any other, with the historic liberal spirit and principles. John Locke and John Stuart Mill were among many English men and women who had developed and promoted liberal ideas both at home and abroad (pp. 502–503, 544–547). Britain in the nineteenth century had stood as the chief stronghold of capitalism and free trade; furthermore, its people enjoyed an extraordinary tradition of stability. Prior to 1914 one would hardly have expected this nation to move toward any form of collectivism.

Yet, as we have seen, even before the war the British had traveled a substantial distance away from liberalism (p. 563). Trade unions had become a distinct force between individual workers and their employers; Parliament had passed numerous laws regulating industrial conditions. By 1914 the foundations had been laid also for compulsory national insurance, which protected workers against the costs of accident, sickness, unemployment, and old age. The revenues to support such programs were to be drawn in large measure from progressive income taxes.

The First World War brought new problems that demanded further action by the government. During the war itself, additional regulations were viewed as a matter of necessity; that experience made it easier for the British to accept growing state intervention in the postwar period. England had suffered severe losses of manpower and wealth during the struggle against Germany, and its most pressing problem at war's end was to recover its financial and trading position in the world. British investments overseas had been largely sold off, and many British markets had been taken over by American and Japanese firms.

It is a fact that Britain must "export or die," and both public officials and industrialists tried to improve the nation's competitive position. One obstacle to the effort was Britain's aging industrial plants. Another was organized labor: the unions, accustomed to high wages during the war, would not agree to lower wages afterward. For these principal reasons Britain failed to regain the lost markets, and after 1921 the country fell into a chronic depression that lasted until the Second World War. Unemployment and poverty became a way of life for several million Britishers.

Organized labor grew into a powerful force in British *politics* during the 1920s. The unions, in combination with moderate socialists, had formed the Labour party in 1892. By 1924 it had the largest number of seats in Parliament and stood as a challenge to the dominant Conservative party. Labor discovered, however, that its exercise of political power did not guarantee a better standard of living for workers or a solution to the country's economic problems. The domestic policies of Labour governments did not, in fact, depart sharply from those of Conservative governments. Both parties agreed that they could not rely on "automatic" economic forces to produce business recovery. The protection and advancement of the public well-being required continuing and widening intervention by the state.

As the British depression grew deeper during the early 1930s, laws were passed that ended the traditional policy of free trade. Tariffs were enacted to guard the home market against imports, especially from the United States. (This action was explained as a countermeasure against high tariffs in America.) The government also went off the "gold standard" (in 1931) and devalued its money (the pound) in terms of other currencies. The latter step was taken as a means of aiding British exports, but its effect was shortly undone by corresponding devaluations of other currencies in capitals around the world. When key industries, like coal, proved unable to compete, they were voted subsidies by Parliament. Extensive plans were also laid by the government for the general development of British industry and agriculture.

Democratic governments on the continent were forced to adopt measures similar to those in Britain. Sweden was the most successful example (aided by its having remained neutral in the two world wars). Its dominant Socialist party blended private capitalism with economic planning and social legislation—a "Middle Way" between laissez-faire capitalism and socialism. Sweden imposes steep income and inheritance taxes on its citizens. But its strong economy and "cradle-to-grave" security programs sustain a *general standard of living* that is perhaps the highest in the world.

THE AMERICAN EXPERIENCE: ROOSEVELT

The United States, as a consequence of the First World War, became the strongest capitalist country. During the 1920s the nation pulled away from its military adventure overseas and from the domestic controls imposed during the mobilization for war. It was the decade of "normalcy," a word coined by the amiable and easygoing President Warren Harding. Though laissez-faire was more myth than reality, the power of big business and finance was seldom checked by the governing Republican party.

Normalcy, however, soon proved anything but normal, and the government of the United States, during the 1930s, was pushed into the kind of intervention that had become common in other Western democracies. The economic boom of the postwar years had brought temporary prosperity to the nation, but the boom was driven by artificial and unstable forces. In the spectacular stock-market Crash of 1929, many of the inflated values were wiped out within a few hours. More serious, the Crash signaled the coming of the Great Depression—a long and bitter experience for millions of Americans. During that time they discovered the underlying shortcomings of the "free-market" economy.

President Herbert Hoover, the Republican leader, was in office when the Crash occurred. A competent administrator and a well-meaning humanitarian, Hoover never understood that a system and an era had ended. Although he approved limited government measures to assist certain financial institutions and railroads, he held stubbornly to the view that business in general would recover by itself. (The restrictive fiscal and monetary policies of his administration actually dampened the prospects of business.) While Hoover was telling a worried public, repeatedly, that recovery was "around the corner," production and employment skidded downward. They struck bottom during the winter of 1932–1933. By then, physical production had fallen nearly forty percent from the 1929 level; wages were down by the same proportion; farm income was reduced to half. Construction had nearly ceased, and about fifteen million people were out of work.

Depressions were by no means a new experience in capitalist countries (p. 567). The ups and downs of the "business cycle" had been carefully studied, if little understood. This depression, however, was the worst in history, and there was reason to believe that "normal" recovery forces were unlikely to prove effective. This was due to several factors: the rigid price and wage structures, rapid technological advances in industry (which displaced workers), and the near-hopeless situation of farmers, who were producing for a depressed and uncontrollable world market. Given enough time, some kind of balance in the economy would no doubt have come about through "natural" forces. But the economy had grown so complex and interdependent that these forces would have been too slow. So many individuals and families would have been crushed in the process that the strain on the social system could have proved intolerable.

In the presidential election of 1932 the American people turned to Franklin D. Roosevelt, who promised that he would *act* in this crisis—that he would lead the federal government in an attack on the depression as if it were an attack on a physical enemy. The temper of the country was such that, had he not promised to act, more radical leaders might well have gained a mass following. After an overwhelming electoral victory for his Democratic party, Roosevelt began the first hundred days of his "New Deal" program. This program marked a shift from the traditional policy of limited governmental interference to one of acceptance by the government of responsibility for the "general welfare."

The New Deal was new only to a degree, since it built on the ideas and policies of earlier American "progressives" as well as the wartime experience of industrial mobilization (p. 624). But Roosevelt realized that the challenges were now far greater and that they demanded a new boldness. He proposed remedies in a frankly experimental fashion, with no developed ideology. The New Deal was not anticapitalist; on the contrary, it aimed at *preserving* and *strengthening* the capitalist system. Recognizing the *interdependence* of social and economic forces, the New Dealers turned their attention to all aspects of national life: finance, agriculture, industry, labor, foreign trade, natural resources, public works, education, and personal security.

Roosevelt classified his measures under the headings of relief, recovery, and reform. Those measures were too numerous and extensive to specify them all here. Among the most important and enduring were legislative provisions for the Social Security system, bank deposit insurance, regulation of the securities exchanges, stabilization of agricultural production, direct relief for needy citizens ("welfare"), guarantees for labor collective bargaining, and natural resources conservation. The New Deal programs did not cure all of the nation's ills, but most of them *worked*, at least to a degree; and they placed the federal government in a new and generally accepted role in the social and economic life of the country. Though Roosevelt, a well-to-do landowner, was attacked by some of his opponents as a "traitor to his class," he saw himself, simply, as a popularly elected president making necessary reforms in light of new economic realities.

The democratic welfare state, in America as in Europe, did not lose sight of the individual person. In a technological, mass society, it aimed to do what was needed for the protection and well-being of the majority of individuals. In many respects, Western men and women have had less economic freedom in the twentieth century than they had in the nineteenth. On the other hand, the greater wealth and economic security resulting from advances in technology and social organization have offered them expanded areas of freedom in their *personal* lives. These areas include education, leisure and travel, the arts, books and magazines, entertainment, and material consumption.

CHAPTER 14

● ● ●

GLOBAL TRANSFORMATION:
DAWN OF A NEW AGE

Overview

With this and the following chapter, we come to the last of the many periods, eras, and ages into which history is divided—the "contemporary" period, which coincides with the lifetimes of older, but not exceptionally aged people who are still alive today. In itself, a lifetime does not make a historical period. For that, a particular span of years has to mark off a definite stage in the development of human activities and experiences over time. But it so happens that today's elderly people have, in fact, lived through an important stage in the worldwide break with the past that the last several generations have all experienced (and which the next several generations will probably experience as well).

In the social, economic, and political fields with which this chapter deals, this particular stage has been one in which the existing world order, dominated by democratic and capitalist countries, has survived the challenge of the would-be alternative world orders of fascism and communism, as well as the collapse of the nineteenth-century worldwide empires. The main reason for this outcome is that the leading democratic-capitalist countries of the twentieth century—Britain, France, and the United States at the opening of the century, and later the United States alone—were the ones that had gained the most from earlier shifts in Western civilization. From the liberal and national revolutions, the scientific and industrial revolutions, and nineteenth-century imperialism they inherited a combination of governmental effectiveness and individual freedom, economic efficiency and technological superiority, military power and worldwide resources, which enabled them to overcome all challenges and changes.

As victors in the First World War, Britain, France, and the United States had already hoped to build a world order after the war that reflected

14-1   Adolf Hitler is seen here in an unusually joyful mood. He has good reason to be happy. The date is June 1940, and his aides have just brought him the news of France's acceptance of German cease-fire terms. Germany has not only conquered France but also become the dominant power on the mainland of Europe.

their values and interests, but they were weary of fighting and divided among themselves. The leading fascist nations, on the other hand—Germany, Italy, and Japan—were strongly motivated by anger and hate-filled ideologies, and were themselves highly advanced in science, technology, and industry, even though they could not match the worldwide resources of the democracies. As a result, the fascist countries were able to sweep aside the treaties that had ended the First World War, defy the collective security arrangements of the League of Nations, and "win" the first stages of the Second World War. Of their two main opponents, France was defeated and occupied (*Fig. 14-1*), and Britain stayed in the fight but was not strong enough on its own to roll back the early fascist gains.

For a few short years, especially in Europe, fascism was put into practice on an international scale, and proved itself the most sinister and destructive of systems that ever governed a sizable part of the world. Its features included ruthless exploitation of the occupied countries, the forced labor of millions of prisoners of war and civilian workers, and the extermination of most of the Jews of Europe. But the fascist countries' ideology of brutality and force made them reckless, and they got involved in war with the Soviet Union and the United States. It was the superior combined resources of these countries and Britain that enabled them eventually to crush the fascist challenge.

At the end of the war in 1945, just as in 1918, a united group of victor countries seemed about to dominate the world. Once again, with the backing of the victors a worldwide international "alliance" was formed—the United Nations, which was supposed to resolve conflicts peaceably or end them quickly by the joint use of force by the most powerful countries. But in fact, a new phase of conflict was about to begin—this time between the democratic-capitalist countries and communism.

On the side of democracy and capitalism, the main force upholding the world order was the overwhelming power of one country—the United States. Most other countries on both the winning and the losing sides in the Second World War were so weakened by the war that their conflicting ambitions for regional and worldwide dominance no longer made sense. Instead, they were willing to group themselves as junior partners around the United States—a status that the linking of many countries of Europe into the European Union has done little to change. In this way, there came into being an intercontinental grouping of one "superpower" and a dozen other advanced, prosperous, and stable countries that has been the single most powerful influence on world affairs ever since.

The democratic-capitalist grouping has been far more than just a military alliance. It has also created many international trade and financial institutions, which have so far enabled the democratic-capitalist countries to regulate the worldwide economy in their interests, and to avoid another world economic crisis of the kind that made fascism and communism seem attractive between the two world wars. The same international arrangements have also provided a framework for multinational corporations to operate on a worldwide scale, regardless of national borders. In the long run, this economic and financial *globalization* may make nation-states obsolete, but so far it has bolstered the worldwide dominance of the democratic-capitalist countries. The same countries have also combined democracy and capitalism with welfare state "safety nets." In every democratic-capitalist country there have been endless debates among political parties over how wide to stretch the safety net, but all parties are agreed in principle that the net must be there. This has not prevented the democratic-capitalist countries from suffering massive social problems of poverty, crime, drugs, and racial conflict, but so far at least, these problems have not threatened the stability of the general social and political order. Thus, by pooling some of their government power, giving multinational corporations a fair amount of freedom from government control, and spending heavily on both social welfare and armaments, the democratic-capitalist countries have maintained their worldwide power—and they have successfully held off the challenge of communism.

The rise of communism itself to the status of a possible alternative world order was another result of the Second World War. The Soviet Union, the world's only communist country at the outbreak of the war, came through to victory in spite of terrible bloodshed and destruction; and, as it recovered, its vast size and state-controlled economy enabled it to compete with the United States in military strength. Furthermore, the defeat of Germany and

Japan enabled communism to spread well beyond the Soviet Union's borders, to Eastern Europe and much of the Far East, above all China. The Chinese communists soon rejected the leadership of the Soviet party and even competed with it for leadership of the worldwide communist movement. But the Soviet Union was able to fend off the Chinese challenge as well as to quell by force occasional efforts by the "satellite" countries of Eastern Europe to shake off its control. In this way, communism emerged as a second grouping of countries under the leadership of a superpower.

The rivalry between the two groupings that began soon after the Second World War might in turn have led them into a Third World War, if it had not been for a new factor, which was far more effective in deterring full-scale war than any alliance system or international organization—the existence of nuclear weapons. Under the shadow of nuclear war, the two sides settled for something less than all-out military conflict. They built up world-threatening armaments against each other that they intended never to use. They fought "limited" or "proxy" wars in regions of mutual rivalry across the world such as Korea, Vietnam, Central America, and Afghanistan, which caused millions of civilian and military casualties without basically changing the balance of power. They competed in offering military and economic aid to the poorer countries of the world, in the hope that these countries would look to democracy and capitalism, or to communism, as the right path to industrialization and prosperity. This was the pattern of the long-enduring worldwide rivalry that came to be known, not long after it began, as the Cold War.

From the start it was clear that the democratic-capitalist countries were far wealthier and stronger than the communist countries. But from the 1940s to about the 1970s, the state-planned communist economies grew faster than those of many capitalist countries, the communist dictatorships learned to dominate their societies without actual bloodshed, the Soviet armed forces grew to match those of the United States, and once in a while, one or another country "went communist." It seemed conceivable that communism might either win the Cold War, or at least settle down as a permanent rival world order alongside that of democratic capitalism.

But as the 1970s turned into the 1980s, it became clear that communism would never catch up with the democratic-capitalist countries. The dictatorships and state-run economies were too rigid to satisfy consumer wants and needs, or to adapt to the freewheeling revolution in information technology that was transforming the capitalist economies. The production figures stagnated, living standards dropped, and the burden of the armed forces became ever more difficult to bear. As the failures of the system grew harder to disguise, the hold of the dictatorships on their societies began to weaken. The desire for democratic freedom grew, and religious believers and national minorities began to stir from their passivity.

Eventually leaders took over in communism's superpower, the Soviet Union itself, who tried to save the system by reforming it. They relaxed state controls on the economy, permitted freedom of information and discussion, and eagerly pursued *détente* (relaxation of tensions and disarmament) with the democratic-capitalist countries. But the reforms soon spun out of control, and instead of merely moderating their power, the Soviet reformers saw it shrivel to nothing. First the Eastern European countries broke away, and then the Soviet Union peacefully disintegrated. China remained under one-party communist rule, but had already begun restructuring its economy even more radically than the Soviet reformers had planned to do. Although China was far from democratic, it was no longer committed to the traditional ideology of communism. By the early 1990s, the communist would-be world order had faded away, and the ex-communist countries were mostly facing massive problems of adjustment to democracy and capitalism that are still going on today.

Besides the rivalry of the democratic-capitalist and communist systems, the other great change in the world order to come out of the Second World War was *decolonization*—the end of the intercontinental empires that had grown up in the nineteenth century.

Just as in the First World War, the subject peoples of these empires had shed their blood for the imperialist countries, and expected the promises of postwar democracy and national self-government to apply to them too—and this time, the worldwide balance of power was in their favor. Many of the imperialist countries had been either defeated or weakened in the Second World War. At first, they sometimes resisted the demands of their subject peoples, but their empires soon came to seem no longer a source of strength and prosperity but an economic and military burden. As for the superpowers, though they both had their own imperialist traditions, they opposed the practice of imperialism by anyone else. From the late 1940s to the 1960s, the worldwide empires vanished even more swiftly than they had arisen a hundred years before.

Like the democratic-capitalist countries and the communist ones, the decolonized nations, as well as many Latin American countries that had been under less direct imperialistic control, wanted to build a world order that would reflect *their* interests and values. They hoped to form a grouping of "nonaligned" nations—the "Third World," as it came to be called—that would stand apart from the democratic-capitalist and communist groupings (the "First World" and "Second World" respectively). The Third World countries hoped to preserve their non-Western (or Latin American) traditions of civilization and their hard-won national independence, while building democratic nation-states and wealthy, government-controlled industrial economies. But in actual fact, political instability, ineffective economic planning, and internal ethnic, religious, and tribal conflicts kept many Third World countries dependent on their former imperial rulers or on the United States: having broken the chains of imperialism, they found themselves caught in the web of *neocolonialism*.

In the effort to escape this dependence, some countries came under communist rule, notably Cuba and Vietnam—but that simply brought them into dependence on the Soviet Union. In the Muslim world, Islamic fundamentalists sought to rebuild the economic and social order on the basis of strictly interpreted Muslim beliefs and values—but so far, Islamic fundamentalism has not been able to create a new order, independent of the democratic-capitalist countries, for the Muslim world as a whole. In fact, those non-Western or Latin American countries that have been most successful in escaping neocolonial dependence are those that have accepted both capitalism and democracy—such as India, South Korea, or Brazil. And the most revered leaders of movements for national independence, racial equality, and the relief of sickness and poverty in both the Third and First World countries—such as Mahatma Gandhi, Martin Luther King Jr., and Nelson Mandela—have generally fought for democracy and at least felt able to live with capitalism. If ever a truly harmonious world order develops, such people as these will undoubtedly be, so to speak, its "patron saints."

But such a world order has yet to appear. Rather, at the beginning of the twenty-first century the world is in some ways back to where it was after the First World War, with the democratic-capitalist countries victorious over all comers, and hoping to remake the world in accordance with their own values and interests. In the next historical period—the one that will be "contemporary" for today's college students and their children—this endeavor will run its course.

So soon after the collapse of communism, it is still too early to predict what will come of the endeavor. Will ethnic, religious, and international rivalries be contained, and will economies be able to grow without exhausting the world's resources and destroying its environment, so that democratic freedom and capitalist prosperity will be genuinely shared among the nations? Will there be a far less benign world order, with a fierce "struggle for existence" among nations, ethnic groups, religions, and economic competitors, and the "fittest" countries—whichever they may be—holding down the rest by economic power, technical supremacy, and military force? Or a lifetime from now, will remnants of the human race be desperately struggling to survive in the aftermath of environmental disaster or nuclear war? No one knows, but what does seem likely is that if any kind of stable and decent world exists late in the twenty-first century, its political and economic structures will be to a large extent those that have developed within Western civilization.

In the second half of the twentieth century, it became customary to refer to the democratic-capitalist countries as "the West," and we still use the term in this sense today. But "the West" does not just include the countries of Western civilization's European homeland and its colonized territories of North America. Non-Western Japan, having recovered from defeat to become one of the most successful of democratic-capitalist countries, also counts as part of "the West." And in fact, the one-party dictatorships and state-run economies of "the East"—as the communist countries used to be called—were based on the Western ideology of Marxism.

Likewise in the future, it is probable that many non-Western countries will adopt democratic-capitalist structures, and that even if they do not, the ways in which they organize themselves will be patterned on one or other model that has developed within Western civilization. This pervasiveness of Western ways of running countries and doing business will not necessarily mean that the dominance of the present-day "West" will be long-lasting. That may happen, but it does not have to. One of the main themes of Western history is the way in which nations learn from other nations, improve on what they learn, and end by outstripping their "teachers." It is possible to imagine a future world of diverse civilizations, all of which will have adapted their traditional ways to those of Western civilization, while "the West" itself will have lost its dominance and no longer be in the forefront of change. That, perhaps, would be Western civilization's ultimate worldwide triumph.

THE SECOND WORLD WAR AND ITS CONSEQUENCES

When President Woodrow Wilson led the United States into the First World War in 1917, he declared that it was a "war to end war." When that conflict ended, Wilson began a determined effort to make his promise come true. He urged the Allies to put into effect the peace proposals that had persuaded the Germans to quit the war (p. 620)—his widely publicized "Fourteen Points." These included the goals of "open" diplomacy (no more *secret* treaties), freedom of the seas, arms reductions, removal of trade barriers, and political "self-determination" (independence) for peoples everywhere.

The fourteenth and crowning point was Wilson's proposal for a "general association of nations," to guarantee their independence and boundaries. And with a view to ensure that this association be established, Wilson traveled to Paris after the war and took part personally in the peace conferences. At his insistence, the plan for a League of Nations was written into the Treaty of Versailles in 1919 (p. 621).

THE FAILURE OF THE LEAGUE OF NATIONS

Most of the European diplomats at Paris, still *nationalists* to the core, had little enthusiasm for the League. They approved it largely to please Wilson, who, in return, made concessions to them on the other provisions of the treaty. To Wilson, the League was the saving feature of a treaty that in many respects seemed harsh and unjust to the defeated peoples. He believed that the League, once established, could correct such injustices and lay the foundation for a *warless world*—an emerging idea, which now had substantial popular support. Ironically, the Treaty of

Versailles, including the League plan, was later ratified by all the Allied governments *except* the United States. Its defeat in the Senate was due to a combination of factors: persisting nationalism, disillusionment with the late "crusade" in Europe, Wilson's refusal to accept amendments to the treaty, and the constitutional requirement of a *two-thirds* affirmative vote for ratification. (A simple *majority* did vote for the treaty.)

Whatever chance the League may have had to fulfill its high purpose was crippled by America's failure to join it. Both Germany and the Soviet Union were excluded from membership for a number of years, so the organization was far from being universal. Nevertheless, it had some strong supporters, and it carried on in the hope that the United States would one day become a member. During the economic boom of the 1920s, however, most Americans became absorbed in making money and showed a lessening interest in the problems of the world. The later miseries of the Great Depression turned them even more inward. By 1933, the United States was clearly committed to an *independent* course in foreign affairs.

The League performed many useful international functions, including the conduct of plebiscites (popular votes) in disputed territories, returning prisoners of war to their homelands, and providing aid to refugees. Through its commissions, it also arranged for the exchange of scientific and cultural information and the collection of social and economic statistics. Its sponsorship of disarmament conferences proved completely fruitless, for the participating nations viewed proposals for arms reduction as another arena for the continuing *power struggle*.

The primary purpose of the League, as planned by Wilson, was to *prevent war*. The treaty required that member states submit their disputes to arbitration (decision by an impartial umpire) and, if that failed, to the Council of the League. The Council, which consisted of representatives of the principal countries, could, by unanimous vote only, call for economic or military actions ("sanctions") by member states against any aggressor state. The principle underlying this provision was that of "collective security." This was a simple idea, one that Wilson fervently believed in. It held that if *all* "peace-loving" countries acted together (collectively) against *any* violator of the peace, the violator would be overwhelmingly defeated. Potential aggressors, once convinced that collective action against them was a certainty, would not start acts of conquest.

Collective security might have worked if the leading powers (including the United States) had put an overriding priority on stopping aggressors. Unfortunately, the idea was never taken seriously in the major capitals. In and out of the League, each nation continued to pursue its own particular aims and refused to act except when its own immediate interest seemed to be threatened. Furthermore, a number of powers (notably Japan, Italy, and Germany) were conspiring to support one another's seizure of territory. The balance between countries wishing to preserve territorial boundaries and those prepared to use force to break them proved to be too nearly equal for the collective-security idea to succeed.

Japan was the first country to test the will of the League's members. In 1931 Japanese soldiers occupied Manchuria, driving out the legal Chinese authorities. Responding to China's appeal, the League sent an investigating commission to

Manchuria; in 1932 the commission concluded that Japan was guilty of aggression and recommended appropriate action. But the Council of the League could not agree on sanctions. Britain, with extensive interests in the Far East, was reluctant to offend the Japanese, who had a powerful Pacific fleet. Unable to secure a guarantee of assistance from the United States should sanctions lead to war with Japan, the British decided that *nothing* should be done. And Britain was the most influential member of the League and its Council.

The exultant militarists in Tokyo, having successfully defied the League, strengthened their grip on Japanese politics and prepared for more ambitious conquests in China, and beyond. Had the League and the United States joined in placing sanctions on Japan, that island nation would have been compelled to back down. Instead, the League's failure encouraged aggressors in both Asia and Europe. Little more than a decade after the First World War, the Wilsonian hope for collective security lay shattered. The great powers were already on the road to the Second World War.

FASCIST CONQUESTS AND DEFEAT

Benito Mussolini viewed the League's failure with special satisfaction. In keeping with the fascist ideology of militarism and imperialism, he was seeking to expand Italian control in Africa (*map*, p. 606). During the 1920s he had attempted by negotiation to gain a foothold in the ancient empire of Ethiopia. But the Ethiopian emperor, Haile Selassie, had stubbornly refused. Mussolini, after observing the impotence of the League, decided to move by force of arms.

Selassie's tribesmen, armed with primitive weapons, could not hold out against the artillery and aerial bombardment of the Italians. Within a year Ethiopia was beaten and annexed to Italy (1936). In this affair Britain had been more deeply aroused than in the case of Manchuria; it had persuaded the Council of the League to call for economic sanctions against Italy, the declared aggressor. The measure was only partially effective, however, and Mussolini continued to receive needed supplies from Germany. Italy resigned from the League; Japan and Germany had already pulled out.

By now it was becoming clear that these three nations were linked in a plan for wide-ranging conquest. The "Rome-Berlin Axis," joining the two fascist states of Europe, was formalized in 1936. In the following year the militaristic and profascist government of Japan joined Germany and Italy in signing an Anti-Comintern (Anti-Communist) Pact. The pact was intended, supposedly, to check the spread of communism; actually, it was a general defensive-offensive military alliance. And the strongest member of the alliance, Germany, was preparing to strike. In 1935 Adolf Hitler had announced his decision, in defiance of the Treaty of Versailles, to rearm Germany. His army and air force were growing steadily in strength. Though he moved cautiously at first, Hitler continued to violate the 1919 peace settlement. His troops crossed into Austria in 1938, and the Fuehrer announced the absorption of that state into the new German Empire (the Third Reich—p. 640).

A year earlier, Hitler had extended his influence southward by intervening in the Spanish Civil War. He supported an army rebellion, led by General Francisco Franco, against the newly established Republic of Spain. The government—which had been elected by a "Popular Front" of democratic, socialist, and communist parties—appealed to the Soviet Union for help against the rebels, and the war soon became a bloody theater for the ideological struggle between Left and Right in Europe. It also proved to be a testing ground for new weapons and tactics of war. Hitler and Mussolini sent equipment, troops, and pilots in decisive numbers to Franco (now called *Caudillo*, leader). The war ended in 1939 with total victory for the fascists. With the support of the Spanish Church, Franco established a tough, repressive government that was to endure until his death in 1975. He added Spain to the armed camp of Germany and Italy.

Britain and France by now were thoroughly alarmed, but popular antiwar sentiment and political incompetence kept them from responding effectively to the fascist threat. The Soviet Union seemed to be the only power that could check Hitler. France had concluded a defensive alliance with the Soviets in 1935, but the agreement proved short-lived.

One reason for the collapse of the Franco-Soviet alliance was the failure of France and Britain to honor their treaty obligations to defend Czechoslovakia. (The Soviets also had an agreement to aid the Czechs—but only if the French acted with them.) At Munich, in September 1938, the two Western powers, ignoring Soviet concerns, agreed to Hitler's demand for a portion of Czech territory. (Six months later the Nazis took over the rest of Czechoslovakia.) Joseph Stalin's suspicions of the Western powers were strengthened by their act of "appeasement." The Soviet dictator feared (rightly) that some British diplomats were secretly hoping that Hitler would smash eastward into the Soviet Ukraine, thus locking in mortal combat the two great land powers of Europe. Such a struggle could serve the British interest by reducing or eliminating one or both of the Nazi and Soviet threats. Stalin now chose to remove the threat of an invasion of his country by working out a deal with Hitler: the Nazi-Soviet Nonaggression Pact of 1939 came as a shock to British and French diplomats. It provided, in return for mutual pledges of nonaggression (and territorial promises to the Soviet Union), that Stalin would not interfere with Hitler's next territorial grab in Europe.

The ink was hardly dry on the pact when the Nazis, without warning, pounced on Poland on September 1, 1939. In a desperate effort to deter or contain Hitler, the British and French had given "last-minute" pledges of assistance to the Poles. This time they stood by their word and declared war on Germany. The Second World War was under way. Poland was crushed militarily within a month as the Germans displayed new tactics of mobile warfare. Swift tank formations, supported by aircraft and paratroops, paralyzed and surrounded the Polish troops. So successful were these tactics that the Germans appeared to be invincible. (Soviet troops, meanwhile, by prior agreement with the Nazis, moved into the eastern portion of Poland. To create a further "defensive buffer," on the Baltic Sea, the U.S.S.R. also occupied and annexed the newly independent states of Estonia, Latvia, and Lithuania—p. 621; *map*, p. 622).

In 1940 Holland, Belgium, and France fell before the German *Blitzkrieg* (lightning war) and Italy formally joined the conflict. Hitler, ignoring his nonaggression pact with Stalin, savagely attacked the Soviet Union in June 1941. In Russia and elsewhere in eastern Europe the Germans not only sought swift military victories, they launched a ruthless program of exterminating all Jews and a portion of the Slavic peoples, whom they regarded as racially inferior *(Untermenschen)*. Six months after the German attack on Russia, the Japanese, pursuing their own conquests in Asia, struck the United States Pacific fleet at Pearl Harbor, Hawaii. (This daring and devastating assault by carrier-based bombers came without warning—while Japanese diplomats were "negotiating" in Washington.) By 1942 all the major powers were involved in the war by land, sea, and air.

The fascist forces, having seized the initiative, scored astonishing gains in the early period of fighting. They secured control of most of continental Europe and much of North Africa, while Britain held out defiantly against Nazi bombers and threats of invasion. In Asia, Japanese forces had occupied large areas of China before 1941. They now launched spectacular moves—winning mastery of the western Pacific Ocean and its islands, and conquering the British colonies of Burma and Malaya, French Indochina, the Dutch East Indies, and the American-controlled Philippine Islands (pp. 610–611).

The population and resources of the Allies were vastly superior, however, and in the end they achieved unconditional victory. By mid-1943 they were counterattacking; thereafter, the Axis powers were generally on the defensive, both in the Pacific and in Europe. On "D-Day" (June 6, 1944) Allied combined forces based in Britain, under command of American General Dwight D. Eisenhower, executed a massive landing on the defended beaches of Normandy. Once on the Continent, they moved cautiously but relentlessly toward Berlin, while their Russian allies advanced from the east. The Germans surrendered in May 1945, thus ending the conflict in Europe.

Soviet armies and United States air power proved to be among the decisive factors in the final outcome of the six-year war. The Nazis, after their surprise attack on Russia, had penetrated deep into the country and had nearly toppled the regime. But they were stopped at last, just short of Moscow, having suffered heavy losses. At this point the Russians turned to the *offensive*, at Stalingrad (now Volgograd—*map*, p. 659). In the largest single battle in history, they surrounded and destroyed twenty-two Nazi divisions—numbering some three hundred thousand soldiers.

Meanwhile, in the war in the *air*, the Americans had first pursued a tactic called "strategic" bombing; it aimed to destroy key transport and production facilities whose elimination would cripple the enemy's war machine. This type of bombing, which depended upon "pinpoint" accuracy and which spared the civilian population, was only partially successful, however. In the last year of the war (1944–1945), the Americans switched to the British method of bombing: massed attacks upon enemy cities—contrary to traditional "rules of warfare" (pp. 453, 613). (The Allies were not the first to bomb cities, but when they did so, they bombed on an unprecedented scale.) Fire raids on Hamburg and Dresden were

14-2   Hiroshima after the explosion of a single atomic bomb in 1945. By the standards of nuclear weapons fifty years later, the weapon that wreaked this destruction was puny.

among the deepest horrors of the war against Germany. And in the Pacific theater, American forces had "island-hopped" to bases within aerial range of the Japanese home islands before the end of 1944. The enemy's population centers and their air defenses were now open to unlimited attacks from the sky. By mid-1945, virtually every Japanese city had been reduced to ashes by giant bombers (B-29s).

This new kind of "unlimited" warfare was most dramatically demonstrated by the dropping of the world's first *atomic* bombs on Hiroshima and Nagasaki (*Fig. 14-2*), cities that the Americans had spared from earlier bombings so that they could better measure the destructive power of the new weapons. The public justification for using atomic bombs against these defenseless cities was that this "shock" action was necessary to bring a quick end to the war—and thereby save millions of lives that would otherwise have been lost in a military invasion of Japan.

Recent historical evidence throws serious doubt upon that public explanation. Japan, in fact, was ready to surrender *before* the bombs were dropped and *without* an invasion. The Soviets were poised to attack the remaining Japanese forces in Manchuria. Peace could indeed have come even sooner than it did if the Americans had not held back from negotiations while awaiting completion of their secret atomic tests. Emperor Hirohito, with his nation near collapse from prolonged air bombardment and naval blockade, had been seeking desperately for a dignified way out of the war. Washington knew this, for it had broken the Japanese communication codes. But President Harry Truman (who had been in office only a few months) had become convinced by some of his most trusted advisers that dropping the atomic bombs would strengthen the *strategic position* of the United States *after* the war—against a perceived threat from the Soviet Union. Upon learning that the tests had been successful (in late July 1945), Truman ordered the Air Force to hit the preselected target cities as soon as the new bombs could be delivered.

Each of the two weapons (small in power by present-day standards) incinerated tens of thousands of men, women, and children. These superscientific devices for mass killing assured the quick and "total" victory of the Allies. (Germany had already surrendered.) More significantly, they also confirmed a radical shift in the nature of all-out warfare: from attacking opposing *armed forces* to destroying *whole populations*.

The Emergence of New Power Balances and the Cold War

The human toll in the Second World War exceeded that of any previous conflict. Of the more than one hundred million persons mobilized for military service, some seventeen million were killed. Civilian deaths, direct and indirect, amounted to more than forty million; among these were six million Jews, victims of the Nazi Holocaust (p. 656). The political consequences of the war were decisive: Japan was stripped of imperial sovereignty and placed under American military occupation, Italy lost its possessions in Africa, Germany was divided, and fascism was destroyed in all the defeated countries. The states of Western Europe, which a generation before had dominated global affairs, had now fallen to the rank of secondary powers. The Soviet Union, though it had suffered enormous losses and damage from the Nazi invasion, extended its control in both Asia and Europe *(map, p. 659)*. The United States, untouched at home by the ravages of battle, emerged as the dominant military and economic power of the globe. This "post–Second World War era" would last for about forty years—until the late 1980s.

President Franklin Roosevelt, who had been the principal leader of the victorious alliance until his death in April 1945, anticipated the new distribution of power. During the war he had joined in top-level ("summit") conferences with the British prime minister, Winston Churchill, and with the Russian dictator, Joseph Stalin. The "Big Three," by working together despite grave differences, succeeded in defeating their common enemies. Roosevelt hoped that when the war was over the major powers could continue to cooperate for peace as they had for victory. The key to this accomplishment, he thought, was American-Soviet understanding.

It was in part to develop such understanding and cooperation that Roosevelt proposed a new international organization, the United Nations. Its general outlines were approved by the Big Three at the Yalta Conference (1945), and the organization came into being some months later, after Roosevelt's death in 1945.

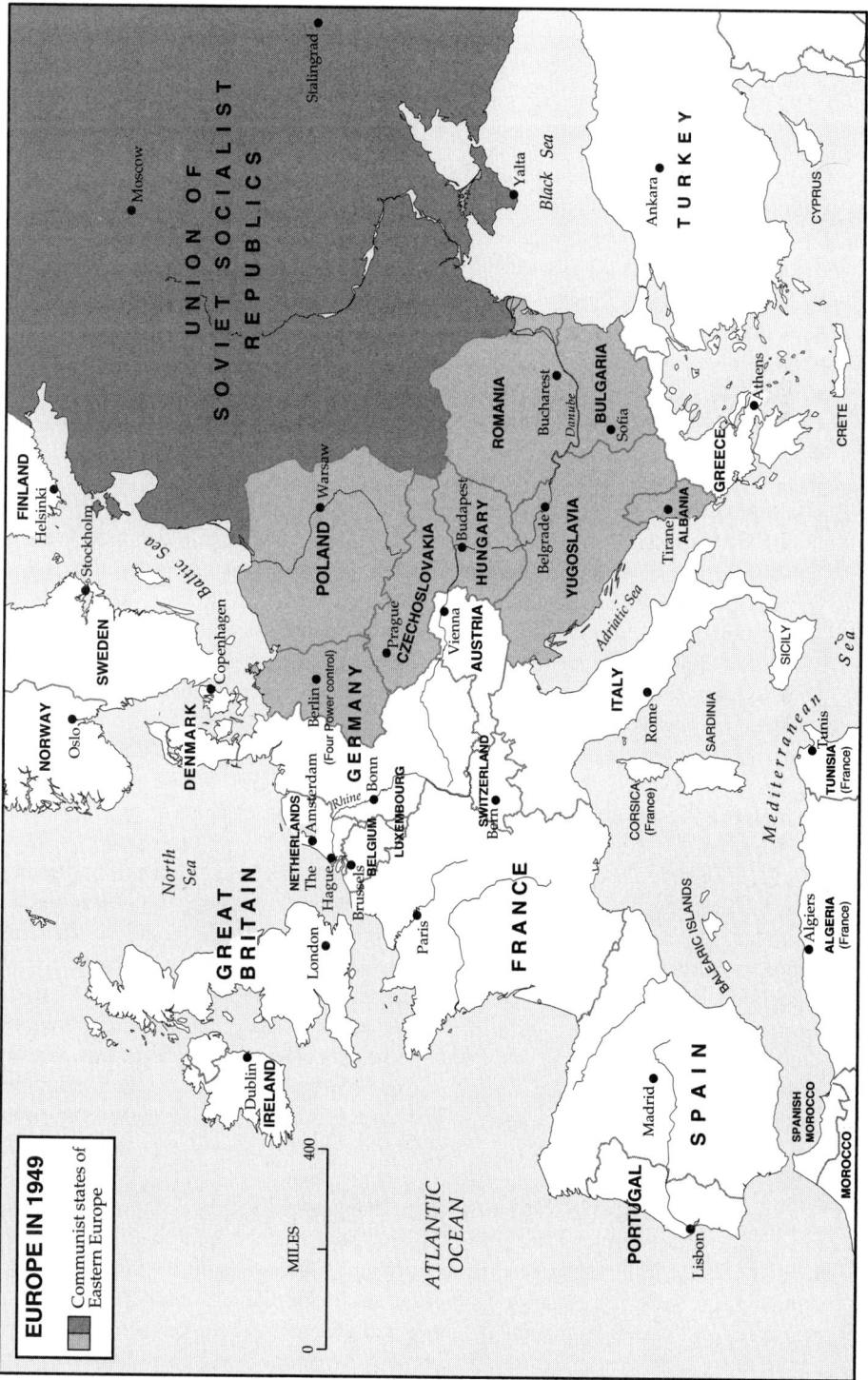

EUROPE IN 1949

Communist states of Eastern Europe

UNION OF SOVIET SOCIALIST REPUBLICS

Stalingrad

Moscow

Yalta

Black Sea

TURKEY

Ankara

CYPRUS

FINLAND

Helsinki

SWEDEN

Stockholm

Baltic Sea

NORWAY

Oslo

DENMARK

Copenhagen

POLAND

Warsaw

CZECHOSLOVAKIA

Prague

GERMANY

Berlin (Four Power control)

Bonn

Amsterdam

Rhine

NETHERLANDS

The Hague

Brussels

BELGIUM

LUXEMBOURG

AUSTRIA

Vienna

SWITZERLAND

Bern

HUNGARY

Budapest

Belgrade

YUGOSLAVIA

ROMANIA

Bucharest

Danube

BULGARIA

Sofia

Tirane

ALBANIA

GREECE

Athens

Adriatic Sea

ITALY

Rome

SARDINIA

CORSICA (France)

SICILY

CRETE

Mediterranean Sea

TUNISIA (France)

Tunis

Algiers

ALGERIA (France)

GREAT BRITAIN

London

Paris

FRANCE

North Sea

IRELAND

Dublin

ATLANTIC OCEAN

BALEARIC ISLANDS

SPAIN

Madrid

PORTUGAL

Lisbon

SPANISH MOROCCO

MOROCCO

MILES

0   400

1914	1918		1939	1945	
First World War		League of Nations	Second World War		United Nations

In planning it, Roosevelt had sought to avoid what he regarded as the visionary and rigid aims of his predecessor, Woodrow Wilson.

Although the United Nations was similar in structure to the disbanded League of Nations, it was not based on the failed principle of collective security (p. 653). Nor was it viewed as a world government or anything approaching it. The organization, thought Roosevelt, might be a *step* in that direction, but its immediate function was to serve as an instrument that would enable the two "superpowers" (the U.S. and the U.S.S.R.) to maintain world order. This was a practical, short-range objective that might have been achieved had Roosevelt lived a while longer.

Within a few months of the president's death, a chill descended on East-West relations; as this chill deepened into the "Cold War," hopes for cooperation evaporated. The reasons for the deterioration in relations have been sharply debated by diplomats and scholars. On the Soviet side there was fear and suspicion of the Western powers, tracing back to their intervention in Russia after the Bolshevik (Communist) Revolution (p. 629). During the struggle against Hitler, the Soviet leaders had developed a cautious trust in Roosevelt, but they had little faith in the word or intentions of Churchill. Shortly after Roosevelt died, Churchill had proposed to the new American president, Harry Truman, that prior agreements about Allied military occupation zones in Germany be ignored by the Western powers. Truman turned down that proposal, but later (1949) joined with the British in merging the Western occupation zones into an *independent German state* (the Federal Republic).

As it became clear that the United States had decided to restore and rearm western Germany, contrary to the wartime understandings, Stalin showed more determination than ever to keep under communist control the countries that his troops had "liberated." The Soviet zone in eastern Germany became the German Democratic Republic, one of eight "satellite" states erected in Eastern Europe (*map*, p. 659). Soon afterwards, Churchill declared that Stalin had lowered an "Iron Curtain" between East and West. (What became the most infamous portion of this barrier was the "Berlin Wall," built in 1961 by the GDR to stem the outflow of its citizens to the more prosperous Federal Republic. Its physical destruction in 1989 would signal the end of the Iron Curtain and the Cold War—see *Fig. 14-4*, p. 705.)

On the Western side there persisted a deep-seated fear of communist expansion. This fear also traced back to 1917, but now it was heightened by the presence of Soviet military power in central and eastern Europe. Churchill and Truman protested vainly against Stalin's failure to provide free elections (as he had promised) in Poland, Romania, Bulgaria, and Hungary. Their concern rose when communist-led guerrilla fighters threatened the Western-supported government of Greece in 1947. President Truman responded vigorously by sending military and economic aid to Athens. More important, he declared a general American policy of communist "containment," which pledged military assistance to *any* regime threatened by "armed minorities or by outside pressure." In support of this policy, he undertook a multibillion-dollar program of aid for economic recovery and integration in Western Europe (the "Marshall Plan," named for his secretary of state). In 1949 Truman concluded a twelve-nation military alliance (the North Atlantic Treaty Organization—NATO) for unified defense against the presumed Soviet threat. This treaty was later supplemented, for defense of areas outside Europe, with alliances in the Middle East (the Central Treaty Organization—CENTO) and in southeast Asia (SEATO). Huge arms expenditures by the United States, corresponding to these expanding overseas commitments, would lead to creation of the most powerful military strike forces ever assembled. The Soviets responded predictably with a military buildup of their own and formation of a military alliance to counter NATO. Consisting of the communist states of Eastern Europe (except Yugoslavia), it came to be known as the "Warsaw Pact" (1955).

The American nuclear monopoly was the most decisive single fact in world politics immediately after the war. It caused deep worries in Moscow, where leaders feared that some American generals might gain backing for a "preventive" war against the U.S.S.R. (Such a proposal was, in fact, vigorously advanced before the National Security Council, the president's top military advisory body after 1947.) Soviet scientists worked feverishly to build a bomb of their own as a counter to the American weapon. This they succeeded in doing in 1949, much to the surprise of scientists and military leaders in the United States.

It soon became evident that the Russians, aided by secret information supplied by their agents in the West, were a match for the Americans in advanced technical undertakings. When the United States exploded its first *hydrogen* (fusion) device in 1952, the government revealed that the energy released was *hundreds* of times greater than that of the Hiroshima (fission) bomb. Within a year the Soviets announced the explosion of their own hydrogen bomb, and in 1957 they became first in space by rocketing *sputnik* (a small satellite) into orbit around the earth. In a real sense, these Soviet demonstrations lent a degree of stability to the international situation. With each side in the Cold War capable of destroying the other (with aircraft or intercontinental missiles), a new kind of balance was struck—a "balance of terror."

RETURN TO INTERNATIONAL ANARCHY

No balance, however, could last for long, because the power alignments and the nature of power itself were continually changing. The *bipolar* world of American and Soviet power began to dissolve soon after it appeared. Stalin died in 1953, and his place was taken by Nikita Khrushchev. The new leader uncovered the massive crimes committed by Stalin, and initiated a policy of internal relaxation and "peaceful coexistence" among nations. Marshal Tito of Yugoslavia, though a communist, took actions that were increasingly independent of Moscow. After an anti-Soviet uprising in Hungary in 1956, all the satellite states displayed somewhat greater freedom of action.

The limits of such freedom, however, were driven home to the Czechs in 1968 by a Soviet-led military suppression of "too much" liberalization in that unhappy land. Leonid Brezhnev, who had succeeded Khrushchev, later declared that his country had the right to intervene in any country of Eastern Europe where "socialism" was threatened. This declaration was labeled in the West as the "Brezhnev Doctrine," and it revealed the primary fear of Soviet military strategists. They were convinced that the defection of the satellite states, most of which were historically anti-Russian, would deprive the Soviet Union of its "defensive buffer" against the West, and swing the world balance of power against it. Awareness of these Soviet views caused Western leaders to worry when Polish labor unions (the "Solidarity" movement, led by Lech Walesa) challenged communist authorities in the 1980s. They feared that, as a final resort, the Soviets would use troops to hold Poland rather than risk the ultimate danger of a strengthened Europe, backed by American nuclear weapons, facing directly upon the borders of the Soviet Union. (As it turned out, the Polish government was able to repress Solidarity, temporarily, by placing the country under martial law. But the unions, with the support of the Polish Catholic Church, eventually brought down the communist government; and Walesa, in 1990, would become the first democratically elected president of the new Poland.)

Most weighty of the changes within other communist lands was the growing power of China (which faced the southern and eastern borders of the Soviet Union—*map*, p. 666). In 1949, Mao Zedong had led his revolutionary forces to victory over Chiang Kai-shek's Nationalists, bringing the most populous country on earth under the Red banner. (Chiang transported his retreating army from the mainland to the nearby island province of Taiwan, which had been returned by its Japanese conquerors in 1945. There he established a rival "Republic of China," with its capital at Taipei and a claim to authority over the whole nation.) After a period of dependency on Soviet aid, the Communist Chinese (the "People's Republic") began to regard Mao as the principal ideologist of Marxism and Beijing as the true capital of proletarian revolution. By 1962, a bitter split had opened between the two communist giants. Mao accused the Soviets of ideological "revisionism" (backsliding toward capitalism) and collaboration with the United States; Brezhnev replied with charges of Chinese defection from the "socialist camp." The harsh verbal exchanges during the 1960s were accompanied by military clashes along their common frontiers in central Asia.

Soviet concern over the growing power of China grew stronger during the 1970s when the United States reversed its policy toward the People's Republic. John Foster Dulles, the American secretary of state under President Dwight D. Eisenhower, had previously sought to *contain* the communist regime through diplomatic and economic strangulation. But, as other nations recognized and opened commerce with China, it became apparent that the Dulles policy had failed. President Richard M. Nixon, a longtime opponent of communism, made

1921	1928		1945	1949		1976	1997
China United by Nationalists	Nationalists Nominally in Control		Civil War	China under Communism and Mao Zedong		Deng Xiaoping	Jiang Zemin

Japanese Incursions
(1931–1945)

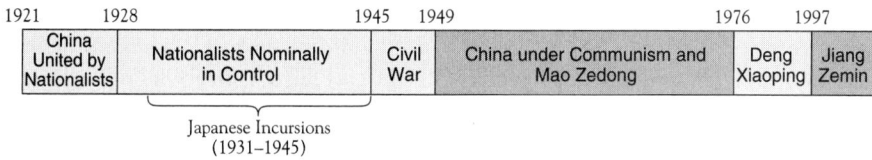

the practical decision to abandon the American policy and come to terms with the People's Republic. Guided by his national security adviser (later secretary of state), Henry A. Kissinger, Nixon made a dramatic visit to Beijing in 1972. Diplomatic missions were soon afterward established in the two capitals, and "friendship" replaced hostility.

The Chinese aim was clear: to neutralize the American threat as a means of improving their position with respect to the Soviets. By pursuing at the same time a policy of relaxation toward the Soviets, Nixon and Kissinger thus initiated a *triangular* power relationship among the three rival nations. President Jimmy Carter strengthened the China ties by extending formal recognition in 1979. By then the dominant leader in the People's Republic was Deng Xiaoping, who rose to power after Mao's death in 1976.

Deng actively sought American help for his country's technological advancement, and China became more outward-looking than before. He also moved to "liberalize" China's economy, and he dissolved the large farm "collectives" of the Mao era, returning land ownership to individual farm families. (Eighty percent of the people of China live on or near farms.) In the following years, Deng *decentralized* the management of the vast state-owned industrial enterprises, permitting greater flexibility and individual initiative. The result of these policy innovations was impressive. By the 1990s, China's economy was showing the fastest *rate of growth* of any major nation and was receiving substantial amounts of investment from abroad. In political matters, however, Deng allowed only a slight relaxation; he effectively put down a swelling "democracy movement" in 1989, which was centered in the universities and chief cities of the country. China continues to be criticized by international agencies for alleged "human rights" violations. Nevertheless, it strengthened its economic position when in 1999, under a new leader, Jiang Zemin, it made steps toward admission to the World Trade Organization (p. 694).

The new relationships with China following Nixon's and Carter's actions disturbed diplomatic links around the globe. It became clearer than ever that earlier assumptions and alignments of the Cold War were being substantially modified. Communism, once seen by the West as a "monolithic" (single) force, had become a loose alliance of states that gave priority to their *national* identities and interests. As nationalism proved stronger than liberalism in the nineteenth century, so it countered communism in the twentieth.

The Atlantic alliance (NATO) was similarly transformed, due in large measure to the swift recovery of Western Europe. The recovery, made possible by large American loans, was linked to the creation in 1957 of the European Economic

Community (EEC)—the "Common Market." It consisted initially of six countries: France, West Germany, Belgium, the Netherlands, Luxembourg, and Italy. In 1973 Britain, Ireland, and Denmark joined the EEC, which sought to draw the separate European economies into a single trading area. (Greece was added in 1981; Spain and Portugal in 1986.) Tariffs and trade restrictions were steadily reduced within the Community, and a common set of tariffs was adopted for imports from outside the Market. Free movement of capital and labor across Community frontiers was assured, and commissions were appointed to coordinate national plans for investment and development.

The consequences were dramatic: during the 1960s and 1970s Europe experienced the most rapid economic advance in its history, and the rising standards of living were shared in some degree by all classes of the population. Food and housing were better than before the war; travel became more widespread; and class lines were blurred by increasing social mobility. This prosperity also had its effects on internal politics and ideology: the radical, "proletarian" parties of Western Europe turned away from the Soviet political model and worked out their own platforms of "democratic" Marxism (Eurocommunism).

While the Western European nations now accepted lesser roles in global affairs, they felt a mounting urge to reassert their traditional character and independence. France in particular, under the guidance of President Charles de Gaulle, enjoyed a cultural as well as an economic resurgence. French leaders desired to reduce or eliminate the strong influence that American politicians, generals, and business representatives had exerted in Europe after the Second World War, and de Gaulle acted openly against the dominant role of the United States in NATO. By 1963 he had established, independently, a French nuclear strike force, and in 1966 he ordered United States military forces and bases out of France. Though somewhat softened, de Gaulle's policies were carried on by his political successors in Paris, including the socialists, François Mitterrand and Lionel Jospin.

A contributing factor in Europe's mounting spirit of independence was a lessening of the earlier fear of the Soviet Union. The American-Soviet "balance of terror" cast a protective cloak over Europe, and Kremlin policy after Stalin's death gave no indication of a desire for military adventure on the Continent. Britain, whose scientists shared atomic secrets with the United States during the Second World War, developed its own nuclear force in the late 1950s. The later spread of atomic weapons to France and to China (1965) further contributed to the equalizing of military strength and the consequent diminution of single-power influence. Responding to this new situation, the chancellor of the German Federal Republic, Willy Brandt, sought to turn off the Cold War on the Continent. In 1970 he undertook successful talks in Moscow, accepting for his prospering country the postwar political boundaries of Central and Eastern Europe. Brandt's initiative marked a dramatic step toward an easing of tensions ("détente") between once-hostile groups of states. It was capped in 1975 by a "summit" meeting at Helsinki, Finland, where heads of thirty-five countries (including the United States) signed a pact for European "security and cooperation."

The Helsinki agreement, pledging the signatories to assure "human rights" for their own citizens, gave formal support to East-West détente. European political leaders, like Helmut Schmidt of West Germany and Valéry Giscard d'Estaing of France, saw no alternative to détente in their dealings with the Soviet Union. But the continuation of eased relations proved shaky at best. This was due in part to alleged violations of human rights and to military moves by Russia outside Europe, notably in Afghanistan (p. 682), and in part to revival of the Cold War spirit in America. While Leonid Brezhnev alarmed the West in the 1970s by a rapid buildup to achieve nuclear "parity" with the United States, President Ronald Reagan alarmed the Russians in the 1980s with evident determination to regain American nuclear "superiority" (p. 665).

With or without the Cold War, existing treaty organizations and alliances (like NATO and the Warsaw Pact) grew less solid than in the earlier postwar period. The United Nations remained a forum of political discussion and debate, but it appeared unable to *act* as a "collective" power. The international scene during the 1980s and 1990s was marked by growing national independence, a wide variety of sociopolitical systems, and numerous insecure governments. There was no evidence of a trend toward a *unitary* world or even a world "police force." Each nation desired to go its own way, without interference in its internal affairs by any outside power. This development, encouraging in one way, appeared nevertheless to be a return to the kind of international anarchy that prevailed before the First World War (p. 613).

THE SWEEP OF NATIONALISM AND MODERNIZATION

The trend toward collectivism, through either revolution or evolution (pp. 624–645), was accelerated during and after the Second World War. Total war, as waged by the main combatants, called for the total organization of the human and nonhuman resources of each country. When the fighting stopped, some of these controls were relaxed in the democratic welfare states. But collectivist patterns persisted elsewhere. The most dramatic expansion of collectivism, revolutionary style, occurred in Asia, when communism, after long and devastating wars, triumphed on the mainland of China in 1949 (pp. 662–663).

THE RESURGENCE OF JAPANESE POWER

Korea, adjacent to China and formerly a Japanese possession (p. 610), was given divided "independence" by the victors of the Second World War. The northern half was turned into a communist state under Soviet guidance; the southern half, under American guidance, was organized as a "democratic-capitalist" state. Each area was ruled by a dictatorial strongman dependent on one of the superpowers.

In 1950, North Korean troops, with Soviet arms, crossed the dividing thirty-eighth parallel (of latitude—*map*, p. 666), thus starting a bitter civil war. The

RUSSIA

Sea of Okhotsk

KAZAKHSTAN
1991

MONGOLIA

NORTH
KOREA
1948

UZBEKISTAN
1991

KYRGYZSTAN
1991

Sea of Japan

TAJIKISTAN
1991

CHINA

JAPAN

AFGHANISTAN

NEPAL BHUTAN
1947   1947

*East
China Sea* SOUTH
KOREA
1948

*Pacific
Ocean*

PAKISTAN
1947

INDIA
1947

LAOS   VIETNAM
1953   1953

TAIWAN
1945

BANGLADESH
1971

MYANMAR
(Burma)
1948

HONG KONG
1997

MACAO
1999

Philippine Sea

Arabian Sea

Bay of Bengal THAILAND

*South
China
Sea*

PHILIPPINES
1946

SRI LANKA
1948

KAMPUCHEA
1953

MALAYSIA
1963

Indian Ocean

SINGAPORE
1965

INDONESIA
1947

PAPUA
NEW GUINEA
1975

E. TIMOR
1999

Coral Sea

ASIA IN 2000
Dates refer to year of independence

AUSTRALIA

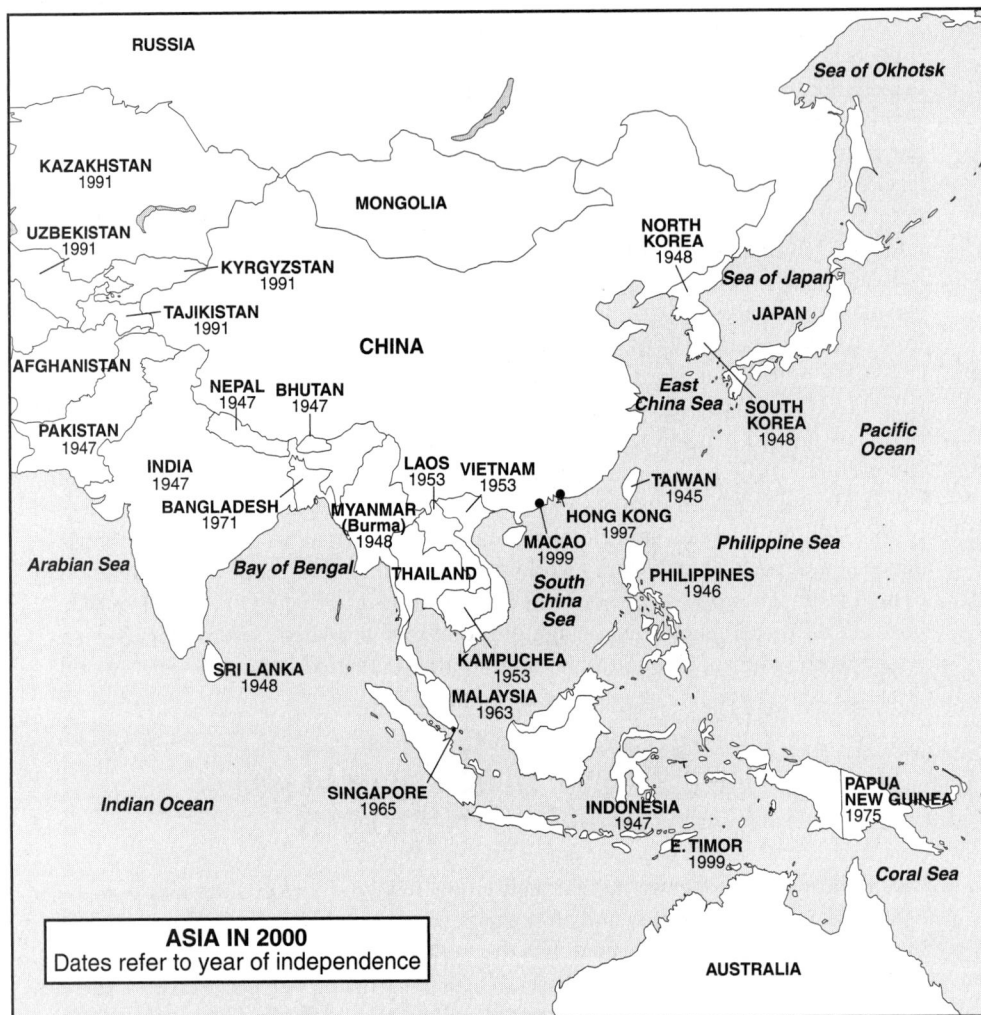

government in the south was saved only by swift United States military intervention, directed by General Douglas MacArthur, hero of the late war in the Pacific and Supreme Commander for the occupation of Japan. (MacArthur acted, legally, as head of a United Nations "police force," authorized by the Security Council upon motion by the United States. In fact this "police action" was mainly an American operation.) After hard fighting, a cease-fire was arranged in 1951, but two more years of drawn-out negotiations passed before a final truce was signed. Korea, bloodied and devastated, remained divided at the thirty-eighth parallel. Each half, with substantial foreign assistance, quickly achieved reconstruction, however. Though still under authoritarian rule, South Korea became a model of westernization and economic prosperity in the 1970s and 1980s.

Like much of the rest of Asia and Africa, Korea was caught up in the world-wide confrontation between opposing social systems and power balances. Japan, defeated in the Second World War, proved more fortunate than its former victims in that war. Under the umbrella of American arms, a newly democratized Japan made astonishing technological and economic advances. By 1970, this disciplined, creative nation (of one hundred million people) had surpassed its huge neighbor, China, in gross national product (GNP) and ranked *third* in the *world*.

Japan was bound by its peace treaty and new constitution to a nonmilitary foreign policy. However, its strong *economy* made Japan the leading power of east Asia and the western Pacific. In the 1980s and 1990s most experts agreed that this area (including China) had the brightest economic prospects of any part of the world. Borrowing Japan's industrial and commercial methods, numerous smaller states joined the Pacific boom: South Korea, Taiwan (Formosa), Hong Kong, Singapore, Malaysia, and Thailand all achieved high rates of economic growth.

The reasons for this success seem clear: business leaders worked closely with each other and their governments; they vigorously promoted new factories and advanced technology; they pursued intensive market research and efficient management—and enjoyed, generally, the competitive advantage of low labor costs and low taxes. As a result, aggressive Asian entrepreneurs, led by Japan, attracted foreign capital and undersold most other manufacturers around the world.

The consequences for the older industrialized countries have been dramatic since 1980. Millions of jobs were taken away, and the United States has run up huge trading debts to Asian nations, especially Japan. They, in turn, have used their trade surpluses to purchase billions of dollars' worth of American stocks and bonds, real estate, banks, and other businesses. There was, however, a serious interruption in 1999. Due to financial mismanagement, several of the Asian countries fell into sharp recession, from which, in the year 2000, they are gradually recovering.

In most countries outside of the Pacific area, traditional institutions changed more slowly. In Africa and the rest of Asia, colonialism was repudiated wherever it existed and was replaced, usually, by some type of independent collectivist regime. This shift was closely tied to the rising spirit of nationalism there and the spreading passion for modernization.

THE LIQUIDATION OF COLONIALISM

Even before the end of the Second World War, nationalist leaders in the various colonies were planning for independence. As we saw in chapter 13, the impact of European intruders on native cultures had been shattering (p. 609). Within a few decades after 1870, millions of people and millions of square miles had fallen under Western control. The conquered peoples had reacted in awe, confusion, and hatred, but they were pretty well convinced that the whites could not be driven out.

The Second World War, even more than the First, changed their feelings of apathy and despair. Though the British and French made free use of colonial troops and resources during the war, native leaders were mightily impressed by the defeats

| 1763 | 1857 | 1947 | 1971 |

| India Controlled by British East India Company | Direct Rule by British Government | Independent India and Pakistan |

Bangladesh
Breaks Away from
Pakistan

that the Western powers suffered. Between 1945 and 1960 most of the peoples of Asia and Africa gained their independence. The spurt to freedom outran the hopes of native leaders and the fears of the colonial powers. Men like Mahatma Gandhi (India), Achmed Sukarno (Indonesia), and Kwame Nkrumah (Ghana) found that the force of nationalism in their countries, once unleashed, was irresistible. The swiftness of European colonial takeovers was more than matched by the swiftness of colonial undoing.

For their part, Western political leaders sought to salvage what they could from the colonial wreckage. The British took the most realistic and enlightened view. For many decades the various portions of the British Empire had been evolving into a "British Commonwealth of Nations." Self-governing countries, like Canada and Australia, were sovereign states, but linked in friendship and cooperation with Britain. (The governing party in Australia forecast, in 1995, its complete separation from the British Crown by the end of the century.) Recognizing that they could no longer play the role of masters, Britain's leaders sought to change once-subject peoples into friendly allies. They hoped thereby to keep a measure of political influence around the globe and to benefit from established ties of commerce and culture. In keeping with such aims, the British offered leadership training to selected individuals of the colonies. These individuals, usually educated in Britain, aided in the transition of their homelands to independence and Commonwealth association.

The freeing of India from British rule was the largest single step in the ending of colonialism. The subcontinent, with its (then) four hundred million people, had been granted limited self-rule before the Second World War. This had not satisfied Indian nationalists, however, and at the war's end they insisted on full independence. The chief obstacle arose from the demand by Muslim leaders in India for a state separate from the Hindu majority. At last, in the hope of avoiding widespread violence, the last British viceroy, Lord Louis Mountbatten, agreed (1947) to partition the colony into two independent states. The larger, mainly Hindu portion of the subcontinent took the name of India; the smaller, mainly Muslim portion was called Pakistan (map, p. 666). Both, by their own action, became members of the British Commonwealth. Unfortunately, the violence that Mountbatten had hoped to avoid took place. Thousands of Muslims and Hindus, dissatisfied with the terms of the division, launched reciprocal atrocities and expulsions.

The new state of Pakistan originally consisted of two territories, east and west, separated by nearly a thousand miles. In 1971 the eastern territory rebelled against the central government, which was located in the west. After months of fighting, the rebels established an independent state, Bangladesh. This poor, war-torn land thereafter depended on aid from India and other outside powers. The remaining state of Pakistan encountered stubborn difficulties in achieving stability. After some ten years of military rule, a civilian government—headed by a woman, Benazir Bhutto—was voted into power. In 1990, under allegations of incompetence and corruption, her party suffered defeat at the polls—and a return to political influence by the military. Since then, the country has swung back and forth between civilian and military rule. A recurring problem, under either administration, has been relations with neighboring India. Both claim all or a portion of Kashmir, an area bordering the two nations. Military clashes have erupted, and an arms race, including nuclear weapons, has placed all of east Asia in jeopardy.

India, for its part, has also faced mounting economic and political problems. In 1975 the Indian prime minister, Indira Gandhi, suspended constitutional guarantees and tightened her personal control over the country. Shortly afterward, the voters reacted by defeating the prime minister and her Congress party in parliamentary elections. But the opposition groups soon fell apart, and in 1980 Gandhi and her party were swept back into power.

A few years later, the country suffered a severe shock—as a result of fighting between government forces and Sikh separatists in Punjab state (northern India). The Sikhs are a reform sect of Hinduism. Militants among them, members of Indira's bodyguard, shot her dead as an act of revenge for earlier government killings. Her son, Rajiv Gandhi, was elected to take her place as prime minister in 1984. He raised fresh hopes for national reconciliation. But tension and violence persisted, and Rajiv was voted out of power five years later by a coalition of opposition parties, to be assassinated in his turn in 1991.

Since then, India has seen a steady growth in religious and ethnic tensions. In addition to the troubles in the Punjab, the country has been torn by clashes between traditional Hindu castes and between Muslim and Hindu religious zealots. The political power of Hindu religious parties has steadily increased, and following elections in 1998 they took over the government. In addition, the country's total population continues to soar. Now reckoned at nearly *one billion* people, the number is expected to overtake the population of China by the middle of the twenty-first century. But in spite of all its troubles, the country has become a regional economic and military power, comparable in strength to China, the Hindu parties have been more moderate in government than in opposition, and a rising middle class has sustained steady growth in the economy.

Britain's postcolonial policy toward the Indian subcontinent was applied also to Ceylon (now Sri Lanka), Burma (now Myanmar), and Malaya. In Africa, too, the British took steps to prepare their colonies for independence. Acting swiftly, they ended their previous treaty rights in Egypt in 1954 and granted freedom to the Gold Coast (Ghana) in 1957, and to Nigeria in 1960. Within a brief span most of Britain's other African territories became independent members of the Commonwealth (*maps*, pp. 606, 674).

An exception was Kenya, in east Africa, where the white minority resisted black participation in the government. After a rebellion by blacks, involving "Mau Mau" terrorists, Britain in 1963 granted independence to Kenya under the leadership of Jomo Kenyatta. A true national hero, Kenyatta launched the first African experiment in multiracial government. In southern Africa, a longer and still more bitter racial fight took place. An all-white government, headed by Ian Smith, proclaimed Rhodesia independent in 1965. Britain reacted with economic sanctions against Rhodesia, and some blacks formed bands of armed resistance. It was not until 1980 that the British succeeded in bringing all parties to agree on a new constitution and free elections. The black majority chose a former guerrilla chief, Robert Mugabe, as the new leader, and they changed the name of the country to Zimbabwe (an ancient capital of the region). By 1990, only one of Britain's former colonies remained under white rule: the Republic of South Africa (pp. 682–683).

In Palestine, the British had taken political control from the dissolving Turkish Empire at the close of the First World War (p. 621). After the Second World War, however, Britain was prepared to give up authority there. One reason was the growing friction between the long-established Arab residents (Palestinians) and the recently arrived Jews, who sought to establish in Palestine a "national home" for their people. "Zionism" as an organized movement had appeared in Europe at the turn of the century (p. 612). It was seen by many Jews as the only permanent solution to their age-old problem of repeated persecution and discrimination in Christian states. During the First World War, the British cabinet had responded to Zionist appeals by promising support for a national home in Palestine (the Balfour Declaration of 1917). Following the Nazi extermination of an estimated six million Jews a generation later, the need for a place of refuge seemed even more desperate; thousands of Jews (chiefly from central and eastern Europe) made their twentieth-century exodus to the "Promised Land." There they were joined by large numbers of Sephardic Jews, who had settled years before in Arab countries, and who came now as refugees.

The Arabs of Palestine (and elsewhere) saw this migration as a new form of Western imperialism. They believed the Jews, with their (mostly) European ways, to be an expansionist colony on the Arab shore. Violence broke out between Jewish and Arab armed factions in 1946; there were also *terrorist* acts, by both sides, against the British. Two years later Britain withdrew, and the United Nations voted for an independent Palestine, divided into two separate states. The Arabs, refusing to accept this division, tried unsuccessfully to overthrow the new state of Israel. Israel gained recognition from most non-Arab nations, however, and quickly established itself as an economic and military power in the Middle East.

In the years immediately after independence, Israel defended its existence against continuing Arab pressures and threats. Its most impressive demonstration of strength was in the "Six-Day War" of June 1967. In a lightning attack, Israel smashed a larger surrounding force of Arabs (mainly Egyptians). They wrested several Arab territories, including Gaza and the West Bank of the Jordan River, from the Palestinians, and the Golan Heights from the Syrians (*map*, p. 671). But the Arabs continued to refuse to recognize Israel and its occupation of their territories. They acquired new arms from the Soviet Union, which desired to expand its own influence in the Middle East. In the United Nations, the Arab states won passage

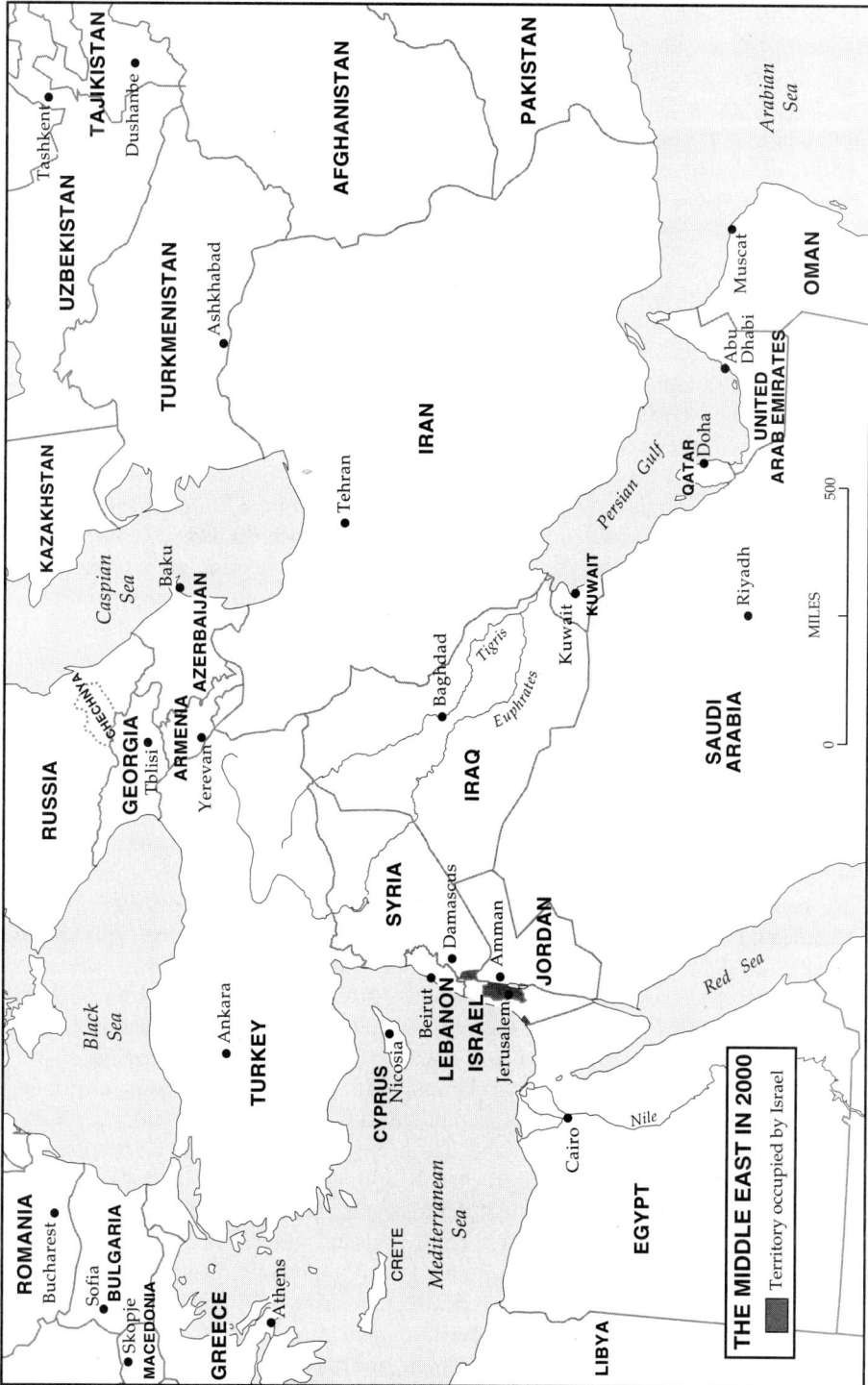

THE MIDDLE EAST IN 2000

Territory occupied by Israel

ROMANIA
Bucharest

BULGARIA
Sofia

MACEDONIA
Skopje

GREECE
Athens

CRETE

Mediterranean
Sea

Black
Sea

Ankara

TURKEY

CYPRUS
Nicosia

LEBANON
Beirut

ISRAEL
Jerusalem

EGYPT

Nile

Cairo

LIBYA

Red Sea

RUSSIA

CHECHNYA

GEORGIA
Tblisi

ARMENIA
Yerevan

AZERBAIJAN
Baku

Caspian
Sea

KAZAKHSTAN

UZBEKISTAN

Tashkent

TAJIKISTAN

Dushambe

TURKMENISTAN

Ashkhabad

AFGHANISTAN

PAKISTAN

IRAN

Tehran

SYRIA
Damascus

JORDAN
Amman

IRAQ

Baghdad

Tigris

Euphrates

Kuwait

KUWAIT

SAUDI
ARABIA

Riyadh

Persian Gulf

QATAR
Doha

Abu
Dhabi

UNITED
ARAB EMIRATES

Muscat

OMAN

Arabian
Sea

MILES

0   500

of Security Council resolutions calling for Israeli withdrawal from the conquered lands in exchange for a settled peace. The Israelis, however, held on to the occupied territories; and the Egyptians and Syrians, after six years of waiting, opened a surprise attack in October 1973. Israeli forces, hastily reinforced by weapons from the United States, recovered from heavy initial losses and turned to the offensive. With the United States and Russia poised to enter the war, each to protect its client states, the United Nations stepped in and secured acceptance of a cease-fire.

The Middle East War of 1973 thus ended in a draw, but it appeared that Israel could not continue indefinitely to withstand Arab pressure to give up the conquered lands—including a place for the resettlement of Palestinian refugees from Israel. (Israel's population was less than one-thirtieth the population of the opposing Arab countries.) Pressure against the Jewish state mounted when the Arab oil-exporting states imposed, as a war measure, an embargo on shipments to all nations supporting the cause of Israel. Since the industrialized countries were critically dependent on oil, they pressed Israel to come to an agreement with the Arabs. Egypt, meanwhile, shifted from its reliance on the Soviet Union to a close relationship with the United States. It now realized that only the United States (by withholding its massive aid to Israel) was in a position to influence the Israeli course of action. Henry Kissinger, the American secretary of state, became an intermediary among the contesting parties in 1974, but his "step-by-step" diplomacy did not bring a peaceful settlement to the Middle East.

Anwar Sadat, the Egyptian president, next attracted world attention in 1977 by a surprise flight from Cairo to Jerusalem. With his nation desperate for peace, he proposed a permanent settlement to Menachem Begin, the Israeli prime minister. Begin responded favorably, and in 1978 the terms were painstakingly worked out at a series of "summit meetings" in Washington (Camp David), chaired by President Jimmy Carter. The Arab states (Libya, Syria, Jordan, Iraq, and Saudi Arabia) viewed Sadat's negotiations as a "separate peace" with a common enemy, and they furiously denounced the Camp David agreements. Nevertheless, the understandings between Israel and Egypt were largely fulfilled. The most controversial issue—a homeland for the Palestinians—remained to be settled. Sadat himself was killed by Muslim fanatics in 1981; Hosni Mubarak succeeded him as president.

As we have seen, the general policy of the British after the Second World War was to grant political independence to their colonial territories. In contrast, the French attempted to bring their colonies into *closer* political association. They offered them membership in a "French Union," which integrated overseas territories with continental France. This approach proved a failure; it appealed only to a limited number of colonial subjects who had been educated in French schools and who had come to respect and admire French culture. Moreover, Charles de Gaulle, who led the "Free French" movement during the Second World War, had promised the colonies that assisted him a free choice of status after peace was won. They chose independence, though most of them joined the French Community, a short-lived association that resembled the British Commonwealth. Regardless of their political choice, the former French territories in Africa have continued to rely heavily upon French military aid, investment, and trade.

In two areas—Algeria and Indochina—the French resorted to war in a vain attempt to hold political power. After brutal fighting and heavy losses, they were at last compelled to withdraw from both. Algeria became independent in 1962. Portions of Indochina—Laos and Cambodia—secured their independence from France in 1954, but the remainder—Vietnam—was temporarily divided by an international conference and soon fell into a prolonged and bloody civil struggle. Its agonies were worsened when the United States intervened to forestall an expected communist victory in the southern half of the country (pp. 676–678). The northern half, with its capital at Hanoi, was already under communist control.

The smaller colonial nations—the Netherlands, Belgium, and Portugal— tried to regain or hold on to their colonies after the Second World War. The Dutch, who had lost their rich holdings in the East Indies to Japanese forces in 1942, sought to reestablish their control. But they were compelled in 1949 to recognize the newly formed state of Indonesia, with a population of nearly a hundred million. Belgium made little preparation for the transition of its African Congo to independence, but in 1960 the rising tide of nationalism forced the Belgians to agree to freedom—without adequate preparation. The result was temporary chaos, followed by the formation of an independent state of Zaire under military rule (*map*, p. 674).

The Portuguese were determined to keep their grip on the vast African territories of Angola and Mozambique, which they continued to view as part of Portugal. The native resistance forces, however, through guerrilla tactics, at last broke the will of the colonial masters. Portuguese commanders in the field, observing the futility of their own military efforts, brought about a turnover in the imperial home government in Lisbon. The new Portuguese government, veering toward the political Left, granted independence to both these territories in 1975.

In Mozambique, where the resistance movement remained unified, the turn to independence went ahead on schedule. But in Angola the Portuguese withdrawal was followed by a civil war among three competing parties; this struggle was complicated by intervention from outside powers (South Africa, Zaire, the United States, the Soviet Union, and Cuba). By the spring of 1976 the "Popular Movement" party, backed by the Soviet Union and Cuba, gained control in most of Angola. South Africa, however, did not accept the new government and supported "UNITA" guerrillas in Angola; thus, the civil war dragged on. An "official" peace was at last negotiated in 1991, but sporadic fighting has persisted. In neighboring Namibia, formerly a German colony, South Africa continued an illegal occupation until 1990. An international agreement in that year provided for independence and free elections in Namibia.

All the new nations faced severe problems, for political independence did not automatically bring them prosperity and happiness. It became the responsibility of their new leaders to deal with the grave challenges of hunger, disease, ignorance, and *tribal* conflicts. They found, too, that they were seldom free of external influences. They were still bound to the economic structures developed earlier by the colonial powers; to a large extent their countries continued to serve the purpose of foreign capital ("neocolonialism").

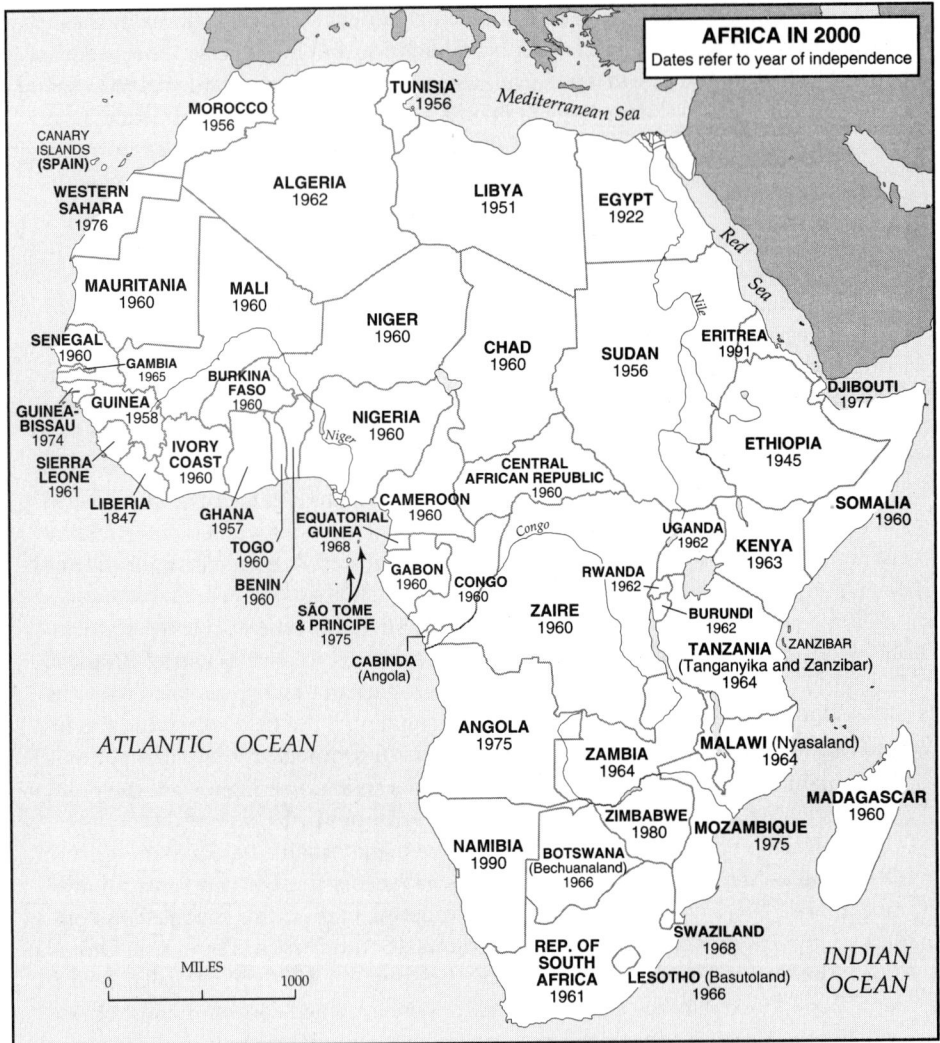

AFRICA IN 2000
Dates refer to year of independence

RISING MATERIAL EXPECTATIONS AND THE "LIBERATION" MOVEMENTS

It was under these difficulties that the new leaders sought to satisfy their peoples' "revolution of rising expectations." Even as their own pride had been stirred earlier by the pride of their conquerors, the former colonials were now dazzled by Western affluence and technological mastery. Though glad to see the foreigners depart, they were impatient to learn their ways and enjoy their material advantages.

What, specifically, did the new nations desire? Their goals often seemed contradictory, for they desired to keep their cultural identity while adapting Western ideas and techniques to their own patterns of life. They did not often succeed; in the encounter between the old and the new, the old was usually destroyed. The ancient social structures of Asia and Africa proved no more capable than those of Europe of withstanding the impact of technology.

The emerging countries wished first of all to gain *economic* independence, for political sovereignty was hollow so long as foreigners ran the economy. In most instances there was only one practicable means of transferring control: *nationalization*. Foreign owners, supported by their home governments, naturally resisted such measures.

Nationalization went forward at a different pace in each developing country. In China, the communist revolution quickly took over all major sectors of the economy. Elsewhere, most of the new governments practiced some degree of socialism, though a number continued to protect established business interests, both foreign and domestic.

An example of the problems and achievements of nationalization was Cuba, where political independence from Spain (achieved in 1898) did not lead to economic independence either before or after the Second World War. The United States, which had driven the Spaniards from the island, had kept a heavy hand in Cuban affairs. From 1933 through 1959 it exerted its influence chiefly through one man, a former army sergeant—Fulgencio Batista. With or without elections, he remained the real force in most of the Cuban governments of that period. Batista was a friend and client of Washington and had kept Cuba open to American capital investment. But in 1959 Fidel Castro led a revolutionary movement that ousted the hated dictator. One of Castro's first acts in power was to *nationalize* the country's agriculture and industry, both of which had been owned in substantial part by Americans. Cuba thus became an authoritarian model of "national liberation" from a foreign-controlled political and economic establishment.

The underlying aim of Castro's movement, as of similar efforts to uproot the remains of colonialism, was to put the resources of the country at the disposal of its own people. But Castro and the other leaders were well aware that continued independence and the effective use of resources depended on health care and improved education; universal literacy was essential if their purposes were to be understood and their programs successfully carried out. They stressed technical education in particular, so that the young men and women of each new nation could operate the complicated machines that promised a better future. Ignorance was associated with the miseries and humiliations of the colonial era; "backwardness" had to be overcome at all costs. But the new leaders discovered that the cost of education was high indeed and that resources were usually unequal to requirements. The result, often, was popular disappointment and frustration. In Cuba, for example, many thousands fled their homeland to seek a freer and more comfortable life in the United States (usually in south Florida—only ninety miles distant).

In carrying his program forward, Castro faced not only grave internal handicaps but an external enemy as well: the United States. Despite public professions of the right of all peoples to *self*-determination, the American government (both Democratic and Republican) took a hostile attitude toward social revolutions—on the ground that they violated "human rights" and that they were or might become "communist." In keeping with this policy the United States has maintained a *trade embargo* against Cuba, and President John F. Kennedy in 1961 approved the "Bay of Pigs" invasion, guided unsuccessfully by the Central Intelligence Agency. (The CIA subsequently plotted for the assassination of Castro.)

Kennedy's successor, the Democrat Lyndon B. Johnson, sent troops into the Dominican Republic in 1965 for similar reasons; he further announced the "Johnson Doctrine"—that the United States would feel free to intervene in *any* country of the Western hemisphere that appeared threatened by communism. President Richard M. Nixon, a Republican, pursued the same general policy after his election in 1968; but his "Nixon Doctrine" proposed a shift in *means* for areas *outside* the hemisphere. Native troops (with American arms) would be expected to do their own ground fighting against rebel "communist" forces there. If United States combat assistance was needed, it normally would be limited to air and sea units. President Gerald Ford, Nixon's appointed successor, confirmed this strategy in 1975. The next president, Jimmy Carter, followed a more restrained policy of intervention; but Ronald Reagan, who became chief executive in 1981, ordered stronger action and a buildup of American military forces overseas (pp. 697–699).

VIETNAM

Vietnam (*map*, p. 666) proved to be the key testing ground for American opposition to national-liberation movements. This was especially the case because in Vietnam the United States met a firm determination on the part of the Soviet Union and China to *support* the movement led by their ally, the nationalist (and communist) Ho Chi Minh. (The communist powers generally aided revolutionary movements everywhere—for their own ideological and political purposes.) What had begun in 1946 as a Vietnamese revolt against French colonial rule turned into a desperate civil war between North and South (p. 673). As part of his global anticommunist policy, John Foster Dulles, President Eisenhower's secretary of state, had provided substantial economic and military assistance to the French. After the French pulled out in 1954, Dulles persuaded Eisenhower to send military "advisers" to help the American-sponsored regime in Saigon, the chief city of the southern portion of Vietnam. Eisenhower's successor, President Kennedy, went further: he authorized United States special forces ("Green Berets") to conduct *sabotage* operations against communist-held northern Vietnam, whose capital was Hanoi. But it was the next president, Lyndon Johnson, who decided on a major escalation of American combat forces in 1965.

Johnson sent hundreds of thousands of troops to South Vietnam to aid the Saigon army; they were supported by hundreds of warships and thousands of aircraft, which also ranged northward to pour bombs on "enemy" installations. By the end of the war the total tonnage dropped by the United States in Indochina amounted to more than *three times* the tonnage dropped by the United States in all areas during the Second World War. It became clear by 1968, however, that the communist forces, supplied by the Soviet Union and China, would not give up— and that the American voters were becoming increasingly opposed to the continuing slaughter. American war deaths already exceeded forty thousand; Vietnamese deaths were estimated at more than a million; dollar costs had risen to hundreds of billions. (It was these huge expenditures and borrowings that opened the door to runaway price inflation and federal debt in the 1970s.) President Johnson at last stopped the military escalation and announced that he would not run for re-election.

Although Johnson did not run in 1968, his party's candidate (Hubert Humphrey) was defeated at the polls; the victor, Richard Nixon, was elected on a platform that included a "secret plan" for peace in Vietnam. The plan, as revealed during the Nixon years, called for the "Vietnamization" of the struggle and the gradual withdrawal of American combat forces. The plan also called for carrying the war into neighboring Cambodia and Laos as a means of "facilitating" United States withdrawal from Vietnam.

By 1971, it became apparent that what the Nixon administration desired was a "Korean-type" solution (p. 666) — by which limited United States units would remain in the South indefinitely as guarantors against a takeover by the Vietnamese National Liberation Front. (The Front consisted of guerrillas in the South, opposed to the Saigon government and closely linked to the northern communist forces.) But Nixon's critics in Congress called for *total* withdrawal of American forces from Vietnam and the rest of Indochina. The war had become a central issue of domestic politics in the United States. By the summer of 1971 the "antiwar" movement had displayed growing strength — in persistent acts of protest and mass marches on Washington and other cities.

Nixon, mindful of the approaching presidential election of 1972, sent his security adviser, Henry Kissinger, to conduct peace talks with the North Vietnamese. Kissinger found that there were irreconcilable differences in political objectives between the North and the South. Just before the election, he nonetheless claimed that he had negotiated "peace" in Vietnam and the withdrawal of all American troops "with honor." Most voters chose to believe that the Nixon-Kissinger "magic" had ended the fighting for good and cast their ballots heavily for the president.

The following year, 1973, brought a time of reckoning and revelation for Nixon and the American people. The communist forces of Vietnam, convinced that South Vietnam would never permit the political compromises suggested in the Kissinger agreement, resumed hostilities. With most American forces now withdrawn, the Saigon armies began to give ground. The climax of the war came suddenly in 1975, when all of South Vietnam was swiftly taken over by "liberation" troops. (The victors quickly *renamed* Saigon, the former southern capital, calling it "Ho Chi Minh City.") Since then, the leaders in the North have tried, painfully, to consolidate the two sections of the country, repair the enormous damages left by the war, and develop a workable *national* economy. During the 1980s and 1990s considerable foreign investment came in. The United States, following the lead of other nations, at last extended full diplomatic recognition to the Hanoi regime in 1995.

A disastrous sequel to the Vietnam War unfolded in Cambodia (since renamed Kampuchea). Caught in the drawn-out Indochina battle, Cambodia fell to the Khmer Rouge, an extreme Marxist group that had fought for years as guerrillas against various governments in Phnom Penh (the capital). Its leader, Pol Pot, sealed off the country in 1976 (save for contacts with China) and proceeded to transform the nation by force into a collectivized agrarian society. People were uprooted from the cities and compelled to clear new lands or work on irrigation projects and farms. As a result of these shocking dislocations and accompanying repression, malnutrition, and disease, several million Kampucheans perished.

In 1978 this near-genocidal government was overturned by Cambodian rebels and Vietnamese troops, though the Khmer Rouge (and other groups) fought on as guerrillas. The Vietnamese, unpopular in Cambodia, subsequently withdrew, and the United Nations intervened to attempt to settle the political and military situation but could not prevent further prolonged fighting. During the periods of chaos, thousands of refugees fled Kampuchea, as well as other parts of Indochina, by both land and sea (the desperate "boat people"). Finally the United Nations succeeded, in 1993, in establishing a democratic government in Phnom Penh headed by a respected constitutional monarch, the former ruler Norodom Sihanouk. At first, the Khmer Rouge refused to participate, but in 1996 a large group came over to the government. Since then the country has been largely free of civil war, though the democratic legitimacy of the present prime minister Samdech Hung Sen, who staged rigged elections in 1998, is questionable.

While Nixon's Vietnam operation was falling into ruin in 1973 his position at home was also collapsing. Starting in that same year, a Senate committee of inquiry, the "Watergate Committee," looked into charges of White House involvement in a political burglary at the Watergate apartment complex in Washington. It also investigated illegal financial contributions, misuse of government agencies, campaign "dirty tricks," and obstruction of justice. The charges were proved true, with decisive information coming from secret White House audiotapes the president had ordered made of conversations in his office. Facing impeachment by an aroused Congress, Nixon abruptly resigned from his high position—the first such action by an American president. Shortly before that historic happening, his vice-president, Spiro Agnew, had resigned to avoid prosecution for bribery and tax charges. Thus, the "law and order" administration, overwhelmingly reelected in 1972, fell in disgrace in 1974. Gerald Ford, previously appointed by Nixon to replace Agnew as vice president, then moved up to the presidency. One of his first public acts was to proclaim a complete pardon of Nixon for any and all crimes that he might have committed in office. (Nixon's subordinates in the Watergate affair, however, were brought to trial and most were convicted.)

The disaster in Vietnam and the shocking disclosures in Washington drew American and world attention away from efforts by some "developing" nations to achieve modernization. A promising start in that direction had been made in a small country of Latin America—Chile. One of the few truly democratic states in the Western hemisphere, Chile was a test case for seeing if radical social change could be brought about through peaceful, democratic methods. Salvador Allende, an avowed Marxist, was elected president in 1970 by regular constitutional procedures. He had the direct support, however, of only a *plurality* of the voters, not a *majority*. While in office, Allende sought authority for sweeping landholding reforms and for state ownership of banks and basic industries; with equal vigor, he defended democratic methods, legality, and civil liberties. The president's conservative opponents made full use of the press, their control of the Chilean Congress, and their economic power to block Allende's legislative program and his efforts to increase national production. Faced with staggering inflation, internal unrest, and secret intervention by the American CIA, Allende had reached an impasse by 1973. Then, as some observers had predicted, his generals and admirals struck against his democratic government in a bloody military coup. Allende, holding to his principles to the end, stayed at his desk in the presidential palace; there he was gunned down by the rebel soldiers.

The new military government, headed by General Augusto Pinochet, proceeded to destroy its opponents by relentless harassment, torture, and executions. It was promptly recognized by the United States government, which later admitted having spent millions of dollars to "destabilize" (make unworkable) the Allende democracy. With the aid of American loans and financial advisers, Pinochet set out to establish a laissez-faire economy within the bounds of his anticommunist dictatorship. The Chilean economy was thus stabilized, though it later stagnated. After repeated popular protests against the military dictatorship, a citizens' *referendum* at last restored the substance of Chilean democracy in 1999. As for Pinochet himself, he was arrested and held in 1998, while in Britain for medical treatment. The Spanish government had charged him with war crimes committed against Spanish citizens residing in Chile under his regime. It demanded *extradition* from Britain of the former general for trial in Spain. Eventually the British returned him to Chile on the grounds that he was too sick to stand trial, but the Chilean Congress stripped him of his immunity from prosecution as a senator—the first move to putting him on trial at home.

Elsewhere in Latin America, most countries remained under the control of the wealthy, the Catholic Church, and the military—even when democratic *forms* of government were adopted. Though liberalism had been the declared ideal of the first independent states of Latin America (p. 540), the twentieth century brought chiefly dictatorships and repression. However, while the higher clergy continued generally to defend the established social order, many parish priests began to preach, toward the end of the century, a new "liberation theology"; this aimed to improve the conditions of the poor. Catholic power as a whole was diminished by the rapid spread of evangelical Protestant faiths in the area. In any case, it was economic *modernization* that became the principal goal of the Latin nations, and with it came the impact of foreign capital. American business was the major outside influence, buttressed by the CIA.

In the 1970s there was a determined effort to break away from "Yankee imperialism." Mexico, for example, attempted with some success to conduct a foreign policy free of American influence. In Brazil, tough military rulers, while making use of foreign investment, pursued a generally independent course of "directed" economic growth. (This program ultimately failed and led to unmanageable inflation, foreign debt, and overthrow of the regime.) In the Caribbean area, tiny

Panama in 1978 regained control of its Canal Zone, which had been occupied by United States forces in 1903. (The handover did not take place until 1999.) The treaty of transfer, submitted to the Senate by President Jimmy Carter, was ratified over furious objections by some senators. And in 1990, United States power was once again asserted in Panama when a later president, George Bush, sent an invasion force to topple its dictatorial "strongman," Manuel Noriega.

In nearby Nicaragua, in 1979, the "Sandinista National Liberation Front" brought down the regime of the corrupt Somoza family, longtime American clients. The Sandinistas, headed by Daniel Ortega, quickly installed a socialist government, and this time, in spite of ideological reservations, President Carter responded with cautious friendship and assistance. However, his successor, Ronald Reagan, reversed this position in 1981 (p. 698).

IRAN

Of all the "liberation" movements of recent years, the one that most disturbed the great powers was in the troubled Middle East—in oil-rich Iran (map, p. 671). Called Persia until its change of name in 1935, this strategically located country has long been fought over by imperial states, especially Russia and Britain. After the Second World War, Iran turned to America as a counterweight against Soviet pressure from the north; in 1947 the United States sent military and economic advisers to Iran as part of a joint plan for the country's development. Its ruler, Reza Shah Pahlavi, was strongly supported by the Americans, whose primary interest was in the Iranian oil fields.

All went smoothly for the American (and British) oil companies until 1951, when the Iranian Parliament, headed by Premier Muhammad Mossadeq, nationalized the petroleum industry. Within two years the American president, Dwight Eisenhower, decided that Mossadeq must be turned out. Shah Pahlavi accordingly dismissed Mossadeq, but the populace rioted and forced the shah to flee the country. Then the American CIA, giving out large sums of money and military supplies, engineered a counteraction that drove Mossadeq from office and brought back the shah. Pahlavi's new premier at once negotiated a petroleum agreement favorable to the American oil companies.

Shah Pahlavi made full use of American aid and his government's oil revenues. He lavished funds on his armed forces and started a program of rapid modernization and industrialization. The oil prosperity was shared by many members of the Iranian middle class, but most of the benefits were channeled to a privileged few. The poor remained poor, their plight worsened by high inflation resulting from the swift influx of oil money. Public resentment rose in the 1970s against the shah's personal extravagance, foreign (especially American) influence, and the corrosive impact of Western secular ways on traditional Muslim culture. Numerous groups and parties became involved; but religious leaders (the *mullahs* and *ayatollahs*) were the principal promoters of the swelling protest. These leaders called for a fairer economic order as well as a return to religious fundamentalism. The protest continued to grow, in spite of harsh measures by the shah's security forces, which had been trained in part by American police experts.

In 1979 the pent-up pressures exploded against the shah. Riots and street demonstrations mounted in anger and violence. Thousands were imprisoned, tortured, or killed by the military during this period, but at last the shah's soldiers refused to shoot at their rebelling fellow Iranians. Though his American support continued, the monarch was compelled to flee for his life; and the Ayatollah Khomeini, who had been guiding the revolt from his exile near Paris, returned in triumph to the capital (Tehran).

Once the revolutionaries were in power, they moved to establish a theocratic (church-controlled) "Islamic Republic of Iran." The new Revolutionary Council tracked down hundreds of the shah's military and civilian officials, put them on trial, and executed them. At the same time it enforced strict Muslim rules and punishments respecting dress and behavior, especially for women. In November 1979, when the hated shah was received in New York City (for medical treatment), Iranian militants protested by seizing the American embassy in Tehran and taking the staff hostage. In return for their release, the militants demanded return of the shah (for trial), recovery of the enormous wealth he had transferred abroad, and an end to American interference in Iran's affairs.

The public reaction in the United States was one of surprise and anger. (President Carter had been previously warned of the possible seizure of the embassy and staff.) Some people called for a military response, but the president's concern for the lives of the hostages overruled the desire to resort to force. Carter did react with tough economic steps: he froze Iranian assets in the United States (worth many billions) and cut off all trade with Iran, including imports of oil. He also appealed to the United Nations and his European allies to take diplomatic and economic actions against these flagrant violators of international law. (Embassies have always been considered part of a nation's territory abroad.) But the Iranians did not yield. They remained in the grip of nationalistic excitement, hatred for the American government, and religious fanaticism. It was not until 1981, after a failed rescue mission by the Americans, that they finally released the hostages. They did so in exchange for the unfreezing of Iranian assets and a pledge of noninterference in Iranian affairs.

The "loss" of Iran was a heavy blow to American prestige and interests. The shah had been regarded as America's "policeman" in the Middle East, providing security for investments there as well as military bases for "monitoring" the U.S.S.R. (Iran's northern border runs parallel to the former Soviet boundary lines.) After the shah's overthrow, the Carter administration feared that the oil fields of the entire Middle East, needed by the American economy, were endangered. Carter saw the possibility of Iranian-style revolutions spreading to nearby oil states, and the possibility of a Soviet march southward into a weakened Iran. He responded by increasing the number of American warships in the Persian Gulf and by starting up a "Rapid Deployment Force" for use in the Middle East.

The Soviets, for their part, feared that the revolutionary Islamic tide might flow from Iran to a neighboring Muslim country, Afghanistan—or even to the millions of Muslims who lived in the southern republics of the U.S.S.R. It was this concern, in part, that moved the Soviets to send troops into Afghanistan late in 1979 to install a pro-Soviet regime. This move, in turn, caused a negative reaction in the United States and Europe, jeopardizing the frail détente with Russia (pp. 664–665). Thus, the liberation movement in Iran not only brought upheavals within that country, but had serious effects beyond its borders. It also brought war to Iran from neighboring Iraq in 1980. This conflict further split the Islamic world and continued to run its bloody course until peace between these two countries was concluded in 1990 (*map*, p. 671). Because of Iran's suspected support of *international terrorism*, the United States placed a trade embargo on that nation.

In the late 1990s, there were signs of a reaction within Iranian society against extreme fundamentalism. The relatively moderate Mohammad Khatami was elected president in 1997, and since then a struggle has been underway between "liberal" and "conservative" groups: in 1997 there were riots in Tehran by students favoring democracy and liberalization. Iranian and American officials have made mildly conciliatory statements, though the trade embargo remains in place. Elsewhere, Islamic fundamentalism remains a powerful force. It played a role in the conflicts in Bosnia and Chechnya (pp. 708, 709) and most notably in Afghanistan. Soviet troops were withdrawn from that country in 1988, and after years of civil war the fundamentalist Taliban ("students of religion") movement came to power in 1996. The new regime imposed the strictest version of Islamic law yet seen, including prohibitions on women working outside the home, and provided a base of operations for the suspected terrorist organizer Osama bin Laden which the United States attacked with missiles in 1998 following an attack on its embassy in Kenya (p. 693). The Taliban regime has been ostracized by most of the world, and has had unfriendly relations even with Iran.

THE STRUGGLE AGAINST RACISM

Western colonialism had been laced with racist feeling; the fight against colonialism—and the liberation movement—were marked by *rejection* of racism. (There were, of course, some outbursts of "reverse" racism. The memory of exploitation of dark-skinned peoples by whites did not vanish with the departure of the colonial masters.) In the new black-controlled states of Africa, whites seldom displayed the racial arrogance of earlier times, though some still held feelings of superiority and contempt toward black citizens.

However, in the one remaining white-controlled state of sub-Saharan Africa (the Republic of South Africa), racism continued to flourish. Attitudes were changing even there, but the system of *apartheid* (enforced racial separation) remained in effect. In the 1980s pressure began to mount against it. The chief white political leader, P. W. Botha, tried to reduce this pressure by offering limited reforms within the system; but he stuck to his pledge to keep black communities *separate* from whites and to keep *white control* over national policies. Botha's successor as prime minister, Frederik de Klerk, moved further in 1990 and 1991—bringing about *repeal* of the laws that established apartheid. He also extended recognition to the African National Congress (ANC), the principal black organization seeking equality, and released from prison Nelson Mandela, its charismatic leader.

World opinion supported the blacks, who make up about seventy-five percent of the total population of forty-five million. They were still denied basic civil rights and decent pay for their work. In fact, the South African labor system, for blacks, was thought to be worse than "old-fashioned" *slavery* (abolished in most parts of the world more than a century earlier). Growing unrest in the black communities led to countless protest marches, clashes with police, and hundreds of deaths and imprisonments.

In addition to Mandela, another outstanding black leader is the eloquent Anglican archbishop of Capetown, Desmond Tutu. Within South Africa his protests inspired other sympathetic clergy to speak out for an end to apartheid in both law and practice. Outside of his country, Tutu gained the world's attention in 1984 when awarded the Nobel Prize for Peace. This recognition strengthened his efforts to persuade foreign governments to enact trade and financial sanctions against South Africa. Nation after nation responded, and the white-controlled economy suffered serious damage.

The eventual result of these rising pressures was to convince many members of the ruling National party to "face the inevitable." Accordingly, they agreed in 1993 to confer with representatives of some twenty other political parties to draft a *new constitution* for South Africa. It provides for an elected National Assembly, which chooses a president of the nation. The constitution guarantees full political rights for all citizens, regardless of color, and *forbids discrimination* of any kind based on race, gender, sexual orientation, age, or physical disability. The constitution was given force when approved, quickly, by the existing white-only Parliament.

In the election for the new National Assembly, held on schedule in 1994, the African National Congress, as expected, won the overwhelming majority of seats. The Assembly then elected Nelson Mandela as the first president of the now multiracial government. His appointed cabinet consisted of representatives from the various parties, including, notably, Frederik de Klerk, the National party leader who had opened the door to the historic changes in South African politics and society. (Both he and Mandela were awarded jointly the Nobel Prize for Peace in 1993.)

The victorious President Mandela and the ANC faced towering problems. Chronic hostility remained between the races, and Mandela therefore made *conciliation* his first priority. In spite of his efforts, a militant white minority continued to agitate for a return to apartheid. And within the black population a divisive struggle went on. Tribal Zulus, who enjoyed a special autonomous status in Natal province under the former regime, resisted control by the new central government. Thousands of deaths resulted from clashes between Zulus, led by their chief, Mangosutho Buthelezi, and supporters of the ANC.

Yet the most urgent challenge for Mandela and his successor Thabo Mbeki (elected president in 1999) lay in the economic sphere. Millions of blacks have high expectations for better conditions of life, now that their race controls the government. One significant accomplishment was passage by the National Assembly in 1994 of the "Land Restitution Act." It provides that lands arbitrarily taken from blacks under the old apartheid laws can now be legally reclaimed by the dispossessed. But unemployment is still at more than thirty percent, and much needs to be done for housing, education, and health care for blacks. Racism has been tamed in South Africa, but huge difficulties remain there.

The fight against racism has not been limited to South Africa or to other former colonies. In the United States racism has a long and dismal history—going back to the early European settlers in New England and Virginia. It was directed first against the Native Americans, whom they called "Indians" and whom they viewed as *savages* and *pagans*. From the seventeenth century onward, the tribes were pushed constantly westward; they were nearly annihilated over the years and their culture destroyed. As a leading American scholar concluded, "The U.S. Indian policy is the classic example of racial, cultural, and religious bigotry." It was not until the administration of President Franklin Roosevelt that the Indian policy was reversed (1934). The new policy aimed at *respecting* and *protecting* the cultures of the surviving Native Americans (nearly two million individuals)—though other serious problems affecting their welfare have persisted.

Racism has been directed also toward other minority peoples in the United States. These include Hispanic Americans (Latinos) and Asian Americans—both of whom are rapidly growing in numbers. But the most visible victims are African Americans, who have played a special role throughout United States history. A notable effort to combat this racism took place in the post–World War era. Some black leaders declared then that their community (over twenty-five million) remained, in effect, a colony within the larger nation. Their ancestors, indeed, had been brought to America from the slave markets of Africa (pp. 337–338), and their history, for some three hundred years, had been one of exploitation and unequal treatment. The end of legal slavery in 1865 left African Americans still in a very inferior condition; this condition included the not infrequent *lynchings* of black men accused of serious crimes against whites. It was not until after the middle of the *twentieth* century that African Americans began to approach equality with whites in civil, political, social, and economic affairs.

In spite of their subjection and disadvantages, blacks in America contributed creatively to the sciences, literature, art, and music of the nation and the world. Their aspirations were lifted in 1954 by a landmark decision of the Supreme Court of the United States. This decision put an end to the earlier principle of "separate but equal" education for black children and called for progressive *integration* of the races in public-supported schools and colleges. The decision was bitterly resisted by whites in many communities, but by 1970 the new *principle* appeared to have been widely accepted. (Actually, the tradition of the "neighborhood school" and resistance to "busing for racial balance" kept schools substantially segregated in spite of the ruling.) Black leaders also worked harder than ever to end "Jim Crowism" (separate seating in transportation and public-service facilities) and to place more blacks on voter registration rolls. These efforts, backed by sit-ins, boycotts, mass demonstrations, and civil disobedience, proved largely successful during the 1960s.

In the forefront of the drive were aggressive legal actions guided by the National Association for the Advancement of Colored People (NAACP) and the leadership of the Baptist minister Dr. Martin Luther King Jr. (He has since been honored by an act of Congress designating his birthday as a national holiday each year.)

King stood squarely for full integration of the races, equal opportunity, and nonviolence (pp. 738–739). In the late 1960s, however, some of the younger members of the black community began to fall away from his leadership. Blacks still endured poor food and housing, especially in the urban ghettos, and unequal opportunity for jobs, health care, and schooling. Some concluded that more forceful methods were needed to persuade the white power structure that more must be done for blacks. Among them was the eloquent Malcolm X (Malcolm Little), whose *Autobiography* (1967) gained a wide readership. Also contributing to this view were works by talented African-American novelists, notably Richard Wright's *Native Son* (1940). Cries arose for "black power," militancy, and violence. The police became a particular target of hatred; in the eyes of most blacks, they patrolled black neighborhoods like soldiers of an occupying army. Clashes with the police sometimes erupted into ugly riots, burnings, and lootings—such as those in Watts, California (1965), and in Detroit and Washington (1967).

The assassination of Martin Luther King Jr. in 1968 was a shocking and demoralizing blow to the black movement. It had the effect of pushing the movement further toward militancy—toward more radical leaders. This shift was clearly reflected in James Baldwin's provocative novel, *No Name in the Streets*, written after King's death and published in 1972. It was reflected also in the growing numbers of black converts to Islam; these converts were motivated, in part, by dissatisfaction with their situation in a society dominated by white Christians. A "white backlash," meanwhile, heightened racist feelings and sharpened the "law and order" issue in the country. Police forces were enlarged and more heavily armed; they sought out militants (like the Black Panthers), kept them under surveillance, raided their headquarters, and often brought court charges against their leaders.

In the 1970s and 1980s, violence and threats of violence diminished, but racial tension remained high. Within the African-American community itself, division grew between those who favored continued efforts toward integration and a small minority who favored racial *separation* as a goal. In any event, blacks who were "successful" displayed a stronger spirit of pride, independence, and energy than ever before. This spirit showed itself in virtually all the arts and professions— most visibly, perhaps, in the advance of black athletes in competitive sports.

The business recession of 1981 through 1983 bore most heavily on nonwhites, especially the young. In spite of "affirmative action" programs designed to employ more minorities in industry and public service, the unemployment rate for African Americans rose substantially. Cutbacks in government spending, which began at all levels in 1981, reduced the number of public jobs and decreased financial aid for the poor. This trend was boosted in 1995 by deficit-cutting measures of the Congress (p. 700). In the same year, a further blow to the opportunities of blacks and other minorities (and women) was struck by a nationwide backlash against affirmative action. The *white majority* of the country (especially *males*) resented these programs as *"reverse* discrimination" and supported moves to repeal them. If successful, these actions will diminish still more the opportunities for education, jobs, and advancement for most nonwhites and women.

As a matter of fact, economic "entrapment" has brought more frustration to poor blacks than what remains of racial discrimination. African Americans still make up a disproportionate number of the nation's "underclass." Living mainly in the ghettos, these individuals suffer from severe handicaps—financial, social, educational, and psychological. Thus, while watching their traditional menial and unskilled jobs become fewer, they usually find the "better," middle-class jobs beyond their reach. The Reverend Jesse Jackson has become the most consistent and outspoken leader, nationally, in calling attention to this frustration. Another (more controversial) figure is the Minister Louis Farrakhan, leader of the "Nation of Islam." In 1995 he successfully called upon African Americans from all over the country to join in a "Million Man March" on the Capitol in Washington. In the same year a potential presidential candidate emerged in the person of General Colin L. Powell (retired). An African American and a hero of the Gulf War of 1992 (p. 710), he was seen as a political moderate and enjoyed wide popular favor but he announced that he would not run for any public office in the elections of 1996. In 2000, however, he was chosen as secretary of state in the cabinet of George W. Bush. At the local level, African Americans have gained some help through the election of mayors of their race in the large cities—notably, Detroit, Los Angeles, Philadelphia, Atlanta, and Washington, D.C.

ECONOMIC REASSESSMENT AND THE "THREE WORLDS"

American public attention to world affairs during the 1970s and 1980s was largely absorbed by the troubles in Vietnam and the Middle East. For at least a generation, however, some experts had been warning of broader and deeper dangers: world population is rising to insupportable levels and the limited resources of the planet are running short. In the late 1940s one expert, the Swedish-American food scientist Georg Borgstrom, had undertaken a broad examination of the world's life-support systems and their interrelationships. He reported his findings in a trilogy of books, commencing in 1965 with *The Hungry Planet*. Borgstrom was joined by growing numbers of scientists and other experts who were now looking with alarm at the prospects of humanity. The "ghost of Malthus" (p. 526), once forgotten, has reappeared.

THE INTERLOCKING CRISES OF POPULATION, RESOURCES, AND POLLUTION

Advances in science and technology, as we have seen (p. 531), were primarily responsible for sweeping changes in social conditions. After 1800, the decrease in death rates, flowing chiefly from improvements in food production and medical practices, led to a sharp rise in the number of people in the world (p. 576). The rate of increase grew even steeper in the twentieth century; the numbers being added to the world's population each year were greater than ever before. In the decade of the 1980s, the cumulative *increase* amounted to more than one billion people—bringing the total to more than five billion in 1990. By the year 2000 the total reached *six* billion.

The fact is that the food supply is not keeping up with population growth. The poor two-thirds of the globe (Asia, Latin America, Africa), where numbers are rising the fastest, *already* suffer from malnutrition and periodic famines. The "Green Revolution," which introduced better grain seeds during the 1970s, lifted yields somewhat, but the increases were limited by inadequate supplies of water and fertilizer. Overconsumption in the rich one-third of the globe has intensified the feeding problem. The average American or European, for instance, consumes many times more calories and proteins than the average Asian or African. A primary explanation of these dietary differences lies in the fact that the Europeans, with their historic command of the oceans and their conquests in the New World, secured control centuries ago of immense resources outside their own countries (pp. 365–370). After 1850 some seventy million Europeans emigrated to the New World; they and their descendants thus relieved the pressure on Europe's food supply by putting to use the vast, fertile lands of North and South America and Australia.

Other resources have also come up short. In spite of the efforts of scientists and technologists, the earth's supply of water, minerals, and fossil fuels remains *finite*. Residents of the industrialized countries were shocked into an awareness of this reality by the unexpected Arab oil embargo of 1973 (p. 672). Suddenly the wheels of factories and automobiles slowed. For the first time in their lives, many consumers in the West became aware of the extended and intricate resource network on which their lifestyle rested.

Even after the embargo was lifted, the fourfold increase in oil prices indicated the true value of a substance that previously had been bought cheaply and squandered recklessly. The dramatic price hikes by the Organization of Petroleum Exporting Countries (OPEC) upset the importing nations, the flow of international monetary payments, and the world balance of economic power. Experts could see that all production based on the use of energy would cost more in the years ahead. Though temporary gluts in oil production would bring prices down at times, the long-run prospect for prices of *all* nonrenewable resources is *upward*.

Atomic energy, produced by nuclear reactors, has been urged as a replacement for fossil fuels (oil and coal). Here is another illustration of the predicament of modern technologists: while the reactors help fill energy needs, they create *new* problems such as operational safety, radioactive wastes, and the possible misuse by terrorists of the plutonium produced (p. 693). The world was sharply alerted to such dangers by the reactor disaster at Chernobyl, in the U.S.S.R., in 1986 *(Fig. 14-3)*. And dozens of other nuclear plants around the globe could be similar disasters "waiting to happen."

14-3   Reactor at the Chernobyl power station, U.S.S.R. (present-day Ukraine), the day after an explosion in 1986. The wreckage shows the violence of the blast; radioactive steam is still spewing into the atmosphere.

Beyond these special problems is the general threat of environmental pollution caused by rising energy consumption, industrial wastes, and the use of chemicals. (These dangers were highlighted in 1985 by the accidental release of a deadly gas from an American plant in Bhopal, India. Thousands of people were killed by this gas in a matter of hours or days.) Degradation of the earth's air and water, as well as overheating of the earth's atmosphere, seems inevitable as the upward trend in energy use continues. The exploration of the world's seabeds and the exploitation of outer space might provide solutions to some of these problems in the long run, but neither activity promises much aid for earthlings in the foreseeable future. Many scientists believe, therefore, that the survival of the species demands a leveling off in total population and a *reduction* in energy and resource consumption. Some public recognition of these facts took place in the 1970s and 1980s, but more *action* is needed as the century ends.

A notable advance in this direction was the outcome of the United Nations World Population Conference (held every ten years) that convened in Cairo in 1994. The final Conference Declaration, approved in spite of strong protests by the papacy and delegates from many Muslim countries, called upon *all* nations to make available the means of birth control and general health services to women. (World population in 1994 was 5.7 billion. This plan, if followed, would lower the projected population by the year 2015 from 8 billion to 7.3 billion.)

ECONOMIC AND POLITICAL DIVISIONS

With the world seen as a finite, interdependent whole, many traditional ideas and hopes have been challenged. Narrow nationalism, in particular, has become outmoded. The nation-state can no longer assure either security or sustenance to its citizens. Accordingly, men and women in many countries find themselves more and more alienated from their "central" government, which they see as too big and remote to command their allegiance, but not big enough to guarantee their safety. Hence, there is talk of "devolution" in Britain (the proposed transfer of certain powers from London to the Scots and the Welsh). Northern Ireland (Ulster) is a special case. There were long years of conflict between "Republicans," who wanted it joined with the Irish republic, and "Unionists" who insisted that it remain under Britain. Critical negotiations, mediated by the former United States senator, George Mitchell, eventually reached compromises (1999). A local Ulster Council, representing equally the two sides, was given authority to govern, and has so far survived one temporary breakdown over the issue of "decommissioning" of weapons used in the conflict.

Separatism has proved a powerful force also in Spain, India, and other countries. Canada has been the scene of outright demands for independence ("sovereignty") from the federal state. The mainly French-speaking province of Quebec, viewing itself as a "distinct culture" within a predominantly English-speaking Canada, has sought separation through successive popular referenda. In October 1995, the "No" vote defeated the "Yes" vote for independence by a slim margin, but separation sentiment was boosted by the closeness of the outcome—and remains a divisive force in Quebec and in the rest of Canada. All these moves toward greater local control have a sentimental and practical appeal, but moves in the opposite direction—toward units of organization *larger* than the nation-state—continue to be driven by economic and security requirements.

Nations have begun to group themselves into common-purpose blocs: the Organization of Petroleum Exporting Countries (OPEC), the European Union (p. 694), and the Organization of African Unity (OAU). And the tendency is toward still larger groupings. In the 1980s virtually all of the approximately one hundred fifty nation-states belonged to one of "Three Worlds." As seen by observers in the West (and in the Soviet Union), the *First* World consisted of the industrialized, noncommunist states, led by the United States; the *Second* World consisted of the communist states, headed by the Soviet Union; the *Third* World included the rest—the developing states—located mainly in Asia, Africa, and Latin America, whose peoples were, for the most part, nonwhite and poor. (Though the category of the *Second* World appears to have dissolved with the breakup of the communist bloc, the distinction between First and Third Worlds remains valid.)

Within the Third World there is a further division based on unequal resources. A minority of the Third World countries, which possess rich oil reserves, enjoy large revenues and the potential for rapid development; but the majority, which have few natural resources, are very poor and have little expectation of development. These countries, since 1980, have become burdened with huge foreign debts (to the "developed" world); and in Africa, millions of people have suffered hunger and starvation, due mainly to droughts, lack of money for importing food, and (often) internal military conflicts.

The central issue in relationships between the poor of the Third World and their economic betters has to do with food and other necessities for existence. In order to reach at least survivable standards of living, the poor ("have-not") countries are asking for creation of a "new international economic order" based on fairness and sharing rather than on power and inequality. They want control, for their own benefit, of whatever resources and natural advantages they may possess. And they demand changes in the "terms of trade": the relation between prices received for their exports and prices paid for their imports.

For their part, the satisfied ("have") countries now accept the fact of global interdependence, but they insist on being the ones to decide what "adjustments" are to be made. The "North-South dialogue" of the 1970s and 1980s (between the rich and the poor nations) produced little help for development of the Third World. The poor countries, partly because of their own mistakes in economic planning and execution, were *worse off* in the 1990s than they were in the 1970s. And the present global economic situation gives little prospect of improvement: while the rich of the world, in general, are growing *richer*, the poor are becoming *poorer*. Some corrective action was taken, however, in 1999 — when major creditor countries took steps to "forgive" some of the foreign debts of the poor countries.

A troubling side-effect of the contrasting living standards among nations is the steep rise in the number of *immigrants* to the better-off states. Many of these people are refugees from political repression, "ethnic cleansing," or social chaos (as in Rwanda, Somalia, and the former Yugoslavia). A United Nations study reports the alarming increase in refugees: their count in 1973 was 2.5 million; within twenty years, in 1993, it was *nineteen* million. But the number is swelled by millions more who migrate for the simple reason of poverty in their homelands. Private humanitarian aid agencies are unable to meet the needs, and governments are being strained to deal with them.

Most of the industrialized countries are facing the inflow — Germany, France, Britain, the United States, and others. Immigration, legal and illegal, has become a daunting problem — especially for housing, education, and medical care. The resulting financial cost, jobs competition, and social frictions with the newcomers are disturbing the *established* residents and producing worrisome consequences. Anti-foreign and racist sentiments are mounting, and in some of the affected nations (France, Germany), extremist right-wing political parties are exploiting the situation to their advantage.

THE NUCLEAR ARMS RACE AND TERRORISM

The "Three Worlds" of the 1980s were frequently at odds with one another. And the relative distribution of strength, both military and economic, was what usually determined the outcome of disputes. Arab oil (more than Arab votes in the United Nations) brought to the Third World whatever influence it has gained in global affairs. Recognition of the importance of *power* speeded the race for weaponry, both nuclear and "conventional." The superpowers, notwithstanding their existing "overkill" capabilities and their lip service to "arms control," spent hundreds of *billions* of dollars annually in a technological struggle for "superiority." This contest struck many observers as futile and wasteful, for military power is only *relative;* as each side matched the escalation of the other, neither gained in security or influence.

The most dangerous and costly contest was in *nuclear* arms. The race had started in 1945 with the dropping of the first atomic bomb on Japan (p. 657). This action by the Americans let the world know of their *ability* and *will* to use these "ultimate" weapons when they saw fit. The Soviets responded by building nuclear bombs of their own (p. 661); during the 1950s the race went onward for more efficient warheads (explosive charges)—and for faster and more accurate means of delivery. In this race the Americans generally kept ahead, both in technological advances and in numbers of deliverable warheads.

Though many types of weapons were designed—for such purposes as short-range ("tactical") use against armies and for use at sea against submarines—the most critical area of competition was in long-range ("strategic") weapons that could reach the *homeland* of the other superpower. The Soviets put most warheads of this type into land-based missiles, placed in underground "silos." The United States put most of theirs in nuclear-powered submarines, as well as in land-based missiles and bombers.

No matter what the differences in numbers and locations, it was clear by 1970 that each side had more than enough warheads to wipe out the population of the other side. So why did both sides continue to spend billions for *still more?* The answer is that each side sought a "breakthrough," by technological advance or sheer numbers, that would give it "superiority" over the other side. Essentially, this means gaining a "first-strike" capacity: that is, the ability to destroy enough of the opponent's nuclear weapons (in a surprise attack) so that the opponent's retaliatory ("second") strike would cause only limited losses to the attacker. The nation that gained first-strike capacity would thus have "superiority"—and with it, supposedly, the final "say" in disputes with the other superpower. That is why each side *wanted* the advantage—and, even more important, why it could not permit the *other* side to gain it.

As it became obvious that neither side would be permitted to win superiority by adding *more* offensive weapons (because the other side would add more also), nuclear war planners turned to *defensive* weapons as a way to gain the advantage. If one side had a "near-perfect" defense against enemy warheads, while the other did not, the first side would then have gained the desired "first-strike" capacity. So, a race began about 1970 to build "antiballistic missile" defenses (ABM).

It was shortly realized, however, that this simply added *another* threatening and expensive side to the arms race—one that, again, neither side could win, nor yet afford to lose. In 1972 President Richard Nixon and the Soviet leader, Leonid Brezhnev (p. 662), signed a treaty limiting the building of ABM systems. This agreement was followed by further efforts to achieve "arms control" (limitations or reductions) of *offensive* weapons. A promising advance was achieved in 1979 when a Strategic Arms Limitation Treaty (SALT) was signed by Brezhnev and a new president, Jimmy Carter (p. 663). However, the Senate of the United States failed to ratify the treaty, and the race in offensive weapons remained open.

Britain, France, and China were also producing nuclear arms (p. 664). They did so chiefly for national prestige; a nation, to be considered a *first-class* power, now had to belong to the "nuclear club." But none of these nations was in the same "league" as the superpowers. Their relatively small supply could hardly give them a first-strike capacity, and they viewed their weapons only as a "last resort"—to be held as a "deterrent" threat against any nation that might plan to attack them. In addition, Israel possessed nuclear weapons, and in 1998 India and Pakistan conducted series of nuclear tests to demonstrate their capabilities against each other. Iraq and North Korea were trying to acquire such weapons, and many more countries had the capacity to build them if they chose. This "proliferation" (spread) raised the risk of a "small" nuclear catastrophe somewhere, which might also ignite a *total* catastrophe should the major nuclear powers become involved.

Most other countries, however, did not desire, nor could they afford, to "go nuclear." They contented themselves with a buildup of other types of arms, whose power and accuracy were also growing remarkably. The poor countries found that they could not compete very well even on that level; this explains in large part the attraction of *terrorism* as a type of armed force. (Terrorism means the use of violence to achieve the aims of states or groups within states. These aims cover a broad range, including certain national goals, social revolution, expulsion of foreign influences, or revenge for injuries to ethnic pride and interests. By waging "mini-war" and thereby creating an atmosphere of *fear*, the terrorists hope to compel targeted governments or other groups to give in to their demands.) "Senseless" violence, such as bombing, sabotage, and hijacking, is cruel and indiscriminate (as are most other forms of warfare)—and usually ineffective. But in a world ruled by *force*, terror is often viewed as the only weapon left to those who lack "regular" military forces.

The widespread use of terror by armed gangs—of both the Left and the Right—has been an extremely nagging worry of government leaders from the 1970s up until the present. In addition to using standard police methods for countering violence, some officials have been developing highly sophisticated devices for dealing with kidnappers, hijackers, and assassins. But terrorist threats and actions persist—and have even escalated. This danger struck home to Americans in 1993 when a car-bomb hit the one-hundred-story World Trade Center in New York City, an action evidently carried out by anti-American Muslim extremists.

Only two years later there followed a more devastating attack on the Federal Building in Oklahoma City. That disaster was apparently the work of home-grown terrorists who view their own government as an oppressive, intolerable "tyranny." The Oklahoma shock spurred Congress to propose additional laws to combat terrorist threats within the country, including the threat of private military units that call themselves "militias." The threat of organized Islamic terrorism resurfaced when U.S. installations in Saudi Arabia were bombed in 1995 and 1996, and the U.S. embassy in Kenya was destroyed in 1998. All these attacks seemed to be the work of a well-organized network financed and led from Afghanistan by a wealthy extremist of Saudi origin, Osama bin Laden. A still more frightening menace arises from the transfer of nuclear technology, equipment, and fuels to desperate Third World countries. Plutonium, diverted from power reactors into nuclear explosive devices, could become a nightmarish means of international blackmail.

END OF THE POSTWAR (COLD WAR) ERA

In the late 1980s an unexpected *change* began in the internal and external relations of many countries of the world—especially those in the European communist bloc. This change had *roots* in the past that were not clearly perceived by outside observers, but that rose suddenly to the surface as the last decade of the twentieth century opened (1990). A new order was clearly in the making— affecting millions of individuals in both East and West. Its most important feature, no doubt, was the abrupt turn away from the "Cold War" toward a new era of *cooperation* among the leading world powers. In order to understand the nature and prospects of this new era, we must review the chief developments of the decade preceding this "historical surprise."

Political and Economic Changes in the West: Thatcher, Reagan, Clinton

In Western Europe, the 1980s and 1990s saw continuing movement away from old-fashioned nationalism (pp. 612–613) to the idea of a "common European homeland." Progress in this direction took place mainly in the economic field; it had started as far back as 1957 with the creation of the European Economic Community (pp. 663–664). The purpose was to create a prosperous "free trade" zone, comparable in market size to the United States. Twelve countries had joined by 1991 (and four more later), and in that year they approved important further steps: plans for a *common currency* and for *common social and labor policies*. (The new currency, called the "Euro," came into being in 1998.) Going beyond economic matters, they also agreed to work toward *common defense* and *foreign policies*. (Some observers have expressed doubts that these plans will actually be realized.) In the following year the EEC found agreement with seven other nations belonging to a parallel economic organization, the "European Free Trade Association" (EFTA). Together, they extended their joint common market to embrace virtually all of Western

Europe within a free trade zone. And in 1994 the EEC indicated its continued move toward closer *political* association by changing its name to "European Union." (Only Britain "opted out" of some of the EU agreements.)

The push for freer international commerce reached beyond Europe. Across the Atlantic, the United States led the way to creation of the "North American Free Trade Agreement" (NAFTA). Approved in 1993, it includes the United States, Canada, and Mexico and anticipates the later addition of the other countries of the Western hemisphere. More sweeping still was the 1993 revision of the *global* "General Agreement on Tariffs and Trade" (GATT). This updated pact was signed by 117 nations (out of 184, total) after years of hard bargaining by the major trading powers. It requires sharp cuts (over time) in tariffs and other barriers to trade in goods and services around the world. It also establishes, for the first time, an authorized agency for settling trade disputes among the signatory countries: the World Trade Organization (WTO). The resulting "open markets" have been vigorously sought by the giant multinational corporations (pp. 559–561), growing ever larger. On the other hand, critics of the pact argue strongly that GATT causes massive *disemployment* and removes domestic market protections from the less powerful home-based enterprises—especially in the poor "developing" states (pp. 689–690). A massive street protest by some American workers against the operations of the WTO took place at its 1999 meeting in Seattle.

The Western European states have been principal beneficiaries of the worldwide moves to freer trade—and of their own closer political association. During the 1980s and 1990s these developments were accompanied by a swing to conservative domestic policies. (One notable exception was France, where the socialist François Mitterrand held the presidency until 1995, when he was replaced by the conservative, Jacques Chirac.) The *conservative movement* was primarily a reaction against the *liberal* policies that had generally prevailed in the West from 1933 until about 1980. The terms "liberal" and "liberalism," of course, no longer meant what they had meant in the eighteenth and nineteenth centuries. In that earlier time liberalism had been equated with *individualism* and with the revolt against hereditary privilege and absolute monarchy (pp. 494–498). In the twentieth century, liberalism still stood for individual rights (civil liberties) and openness to social reform, but came to be most strongly identified with "social democracy" and the "welfare state" (pp. 642–645). The social and moral changes that accompanied the welfare state also came to be linked with liberalism.

Although the conservative reaction to these changes proceeded unevenly in most countries of the West, it took decisive form in Britain and the United States. Margaret Thatcher was chosen as leader by Britain's Conservative party in 1979, and she led her party to victory in Parliament during the ensuing decade. With large majorities in the elected House of Commons, she was able to enact sweeping reforms. Many government-owned enterprises were sold off to private corporations; the educational system was overhauled at all levels—and with reduced expenditure; the power of trade unions was curbed; and taxation policies shifted ever more to favor the rich. While these changes were not altogether pleasing to many British voters, Thatcher gained and held power largely because of splits within the opposition Labour party. By 1990, her public support had fallen sharply; she was re-placed as party leader and prime minister by John Major, a member of her cabinet.

The Conservatives continued to hold their majority in the House of Com-mons until the required general elections of 1997. A reunited Labour party then won decisive control of Parliament and elected Tony Blair as prime minister. Blair successfully pursued liberal policies into the year 2000. Among his measures were a historic action removing *hereditary* peers from membership in the House of Lords, a privilege they had held for some eight hundred years. The House of Lords will also be reconstituted, to provide for more elective elements.

In the United States the conservatives did not achieve a full grip on the federal government. This was due to the constitutional provision for "checks and balances"—which *distributes* authority among the legislative, executive, and judi-cial branches. However, with Ronald Reagan as their leader and president, the conservatives made a deep impression upon public thinking and acting in the 1980s. Their ascendancy in national politics had been demonstrated even before that time—by the election and reelection of Richard Nixon to the presidency (1968, 1972). But his second term was undermined by the ugly "Watergate" affair (p. 678), and it took several years thereafter for the conservatives to regroup and rally around their emerging chief spokesman, Ronald Reagan.

By 1980, conservative opinion-makers were also setting the national mood. Writers and television commentators like William Buckley and George Will were displacing, in the public view, well-known liberals like Arthur Schlesinger and John Kenneth Galbraith. The conservatives, like the liberals, had a considerable range of interpreters. But the central thrust of the movement was becoming quite clear. Their common wish was to *conserve*—actually, to *restore* and keep American institutions and lifestyles as they were thought to have been around 1930 (or even earlier). They therefore objected to many of the features of the welfare state (intro-duced in 1933 by Franklin Roosevelt's "New Deal"—p. 645) and to some of the social and ethical changes that had come about during the period of liberal control (pp. 731–739). *Opposition* was thus a principal part of the conservative program—opposition to the expanding functions of government (business regulation, "wel-fare" services, deficit spending, high taxes), and opposition to social "permissive-ness"—feminism, abortion, pornography, and busing to improve racial balance in the public schools.

The *affirmative* aims of American conservatives included a more nationalistic foreign policy, military "superiority" over the Soviet Union, restoring laissez-faire economic policies, strengthening "law and order," rejuvenating the traditional family and morals, and returning to religious "fundamentals" (p. 575). This latter concern reflected a widespread demand for prayers in public schools and massive responses to television preachers. Best known among them is the Reverend Billy Graham, who for some sixty years addressed hundreds of thousands in America and around the world—urging them to "commit to Jesus as their Savior." At the same time, many new religious sects appeared, notably the Pentecostals, who exhibit the Holy Spirit by "speaking in tongues," and the "Charismatics," who are witnesses to miraculous healings.

Thus, while membership and attendance in Christian churches were dwindling in Europe, the total numbers in the United States rose significantly. And these numbers, allied with the conservative movement, have exercised a strong influence on electoral polities in the country. (The religious upsurge is not unique to this country or to Christianity; it parallels developments in Hindu India and the Islamic nations, notably in the Middle East—pp. 680–682.) All are responses, in large part, to the widespread sense of personal *alienation* from the multiple changes that have taken place in the twentieth-century world.

The issues between conservatives and liberals found clear focus in the elections of both 1980 and 1984. The Republican party, which had stood in opposition to most of the reforms of the New Deal, remained the political stronghold of conservatism. The Democratic party, beginning with the New Deal, had become identified with liberalism. The Republicans won the presidency for Ronald Reagan in 1980, as well as control over the United States Senate. At the same time, five leading liberal senators were defeated, including George McGovern, the Democratic presidential candidate of 1972. The election results signaled that conservatives had gained the balance of power in the nation—politically, psychologically, and philosophically.

When Ronald Reagan took office in 1981, he was determined to lead a "second American revolution." He put himself at the head of the powerful forces that already supported conservative ideas, and he appealed to large numbers of voters, in both parties, who were antitax, anti-union, anticommunist, and antigovernment. President Franklin Roosevelt, the "father" of America's welfare state (p. 645), had viewed government as a *positive* agency for solving the nation's problems and aiding its citizens. President Reagan, rejecting that view, declared that "government is not the solution; it is the problem."

The main direction of Reagan's first term was in keeping with that declaration. He sought to cut back on federal services and regulations—and in so doing, to reduce taxes. The primary accomplishment of his first year in office was to carry through Congress a sharp reduction in tax rates on personal incomes. While the reduction was "across the board"—twenty-five percent—the largest *amounts* of money were saved by the wealthiest individuals.

The chief result of the Reagan tax cut—for the country—was that federal tax *revenues* fell far below what the government was spending. This put heavy pressure on Congress to make up for the loss in income by reducing spending. In response, Congress did make cuts in social programs, including those for the "truly" needy; but Reagan insisted, at the same time, on large *increases* in military spending. As a result, the federal budget could not be balanced, and the huge annual deficits (money shortages) had to be made up through extravagant government *borrowing*, much of it from foreign investors.

When Reagan came to power in 1981, the *accumulated federal debt* stood at about $1 trillion—after some *fifty* years of moderate increase. In the *eight* years of the Reagan administration, the debt tripled to nearly $3 trillion. The substantial economic growth of those years was due chiefly to the stimulus of this borrowed money. But it left the country with a mountain of government debt (in addition to an unprecedented level of private debts). Payments of *interest alone* on the federal debt were estimated at $250 billion for the fiscal year 1991—a sum equal to the appropriation that year for the entire Department of Defense.

Reagan and his advisers downplayed the deficit problem; he promised that his "low tax" policy would eventually correct it. But his Republican successor, elected in 1988, fell heir to the *reality*—as the debt soared ever higher. President George Bush, yielding at last to the views of financial experts around the world, decided (in 1990) to face up to making substantial cuts in the annual deficit. But success in accomplishing this proved to be minimal; the American people, accustomed to living beyond their incomes, were prepared to punish any politicians who voted for higher taxes. Thus, the burden of debt upon the economy—and essential public services—remains a continuing legacy of the Reagan years.

In addition to reducing tax rates, Reagan pushed for *deregulation* of the economy. This was favored by the business community but contributed to some serious negative results. Lax supervision of the savings and loan industry, for example, was a factor in permitting gross mismanagement and fraud there. And since the Congress had guaranteed depositors' savings accounts, the *losses* to *taxpayers* would run into hundreds of billions of dollars. Reagan sought also to eliminate numerous federal agencies that had been established to safeguard the public (like the Environmental Protection Agency). In most cases he was unable to gain congressional approval for abolishing them, but he often succeeded in cutting their funds—and in choosing agency heads who would limit their effectiveness. But his most lasting impact was upon the *courts* of the land. During his eight years in office, Reagan was able to name hundreds of federal judges, most of whom shared his conservative political and social views—and whose lifetime tenure on the bench will run many years beyond the time of their appointment.

Aside from domestic affairs, Reagan sought a "revolution" in the nation's military and foreign policies. He wanted, first of all, to "rearm" America—with more and better weapons, both "conventional" and nuclear. By 1980 the nuclear arms race with the Soviet Union had come to a standoff (pp. 691–692). The superpowers had reached rough equality ("parity") in offensive power. But Reagan and his conservative advisers were not satisfied with "parity."

When he became president, he began steps to regain nuclear "superiority"— which the United States had enjoyed right after the Second World War (p. 661). He believed this could be done through a massive buildup of arms: annual military spending *doubled* from $150 billion for the year 1981 to about $300 billion in 1985—and continued to increase thereafter. The Soviets, though sorely pressed financially, matched the buildup, and the strategic standoff persisted.

With the effort to gain superiority through *offensive* weapons at a dead end, Reagan next proposed (1983) to build a *defensive* system against intercontinental nuclear missiles. This was a return to an earlier idea in the arms race, which had been rejected by both sides in 1972 (the ABM treaty—p. 692). But advances in technology—lasers, computers, space mirrors—had led some weapon scientists to advise the president that another try should be made.

In response, Reagan agreed to give up the "stability" of the existing nuclear balance and seek to construct a *space*-based system—one that could give the United States a "first-strike" capacity (p. 691). Reagan called his plan (estimated to cost hundreds of billions) the "Strategic Defense Initiative," but it was quickly tagged "Star Wars" by the news media. The Soviets, predictably, protested this new turn in the arms race and tried to raise world opinion against it. They saw it as "destabilizing" and declared that they could not reduce their offensive arsenal if "Star Wars" went ahead. Hence, the hopes of many observers for some *reduction* in nuclear weapons appeared to be dashed by Reagan's "Defense Initiative."

The Star Wars issue was one of the main subjects discussed at the Geneva "summit" meeting (November 1985) between Reagan and a new Soviet leader, Mikhail Gorbachev. This was Reagan's first meeting with a top official of the U.S.S.R., and its purpose was to reduce tension between the two superpowers. During his early years in office, Reagan had turned the previous relation of "détente" (p. 684) into one of hostility. His words and actions had been partly a response to Soviet moves around the world (in Ethiopia, Poland, and Afghanistan); but they reflected, chiefly, his intense anticommunism—going back to his earliest years in politics. As president, he aimed, through a military buildup, to deal with the Soviets from a "position of strength"—which meant *superior* strength. He believed that this policy would stop communist "expansionism"—and, by overstraining the Soviet economy, would lead to the undermining of the "evil empire."

However, at the 1985 summit, responding to concessions and fresh initiatives from Gorbachev, Reagan displayed a definite shift in his tone and words to the Soviets. This shift was welcomed by America's European allies and by people everywhere who feared war between the superpowers. It proved to be a critical turning point, built upon later by both leaders, toward slowing down the arms race and ending the Cold War. (The "Defense Initiative" was shelved.)

On other international fronts, Reagan improved relations with China, the NATO alliance, and anticommunist governments everywhere (including Japan, South Africa, and Chile). In Latin America, he held to a hard line against communists. When the Caribbean island of Grenada fell into a political crisis under its Marxist leaders (1982), he sent United States military forces to occupy the island and install a prodemocratic government there. Though contrary to international law and the United Nations charter, these actions were welcomed by most Grenadans—and cheered by a majority in the United States.

Reagan also defied international law in moves against the Central American republic of Nicaragua.[1] Although at first denying it, he later admitted that his goal was to help overthrow the established Marxist government there. Reagan steadily raised pressure on Nicaragua (p. 680) with hints of an American invasion and with direct aid to rebel guerrillas (the "Contras"). The president justified these actions by charging that the Cubans and Soviets were building bases in Nicaragua that threatened the United States. Eventually, the suffering Nicaraguan people voted

---

[1] The International Court of Justice, at The Hague, so ruled (by 12–3 vote) in June 1986.

for peace — by defeating the Sandinista party (p. 680) in a free election. A democratic coalition, headed by Violeta Chamorro, came to power in 1990.

In another part of the world, the Philippine Islands, Reagan continued American support for the dictatorial rule of President Ferdinand Marcos. (Reagan's main concern there was to keep United States lease-rights to important military bases in the Philippines.) However, there was a growing Filipino opposition to the corrupt Marcos government — an opposition led, finally, by the courageous Corazon Aquino, widow of an assassinated popular leader. Following a national election in February 1986, the "people's movement," joined by some high military officers, brought about Marcos' removal from office. American forces rescued the tyrant from his capital, Manila, and flew him to the United States. At the same time, the newly elected President Aquino, having agreed to respect the existing military leases, gained official recognition from Washington.

Reagan's deepest frustrations were in the troubled Middle East (pp. 670–672). In 1982 America's ally, Israel, invaded the neighboring country of Lebanon. Its forces cleared out anti-Israeli guerrilla units of the "Palestine Liberation Organization" (PLO) that were based there. But in doing so, they killed thousands of Lebanese civilians and caused heavy damage to towns and cities by bombings. During the Israeli occupation, Reagan ordered American marines to the capital, Beirut, and sent a fleet of warships to remain offshore in the Mediterranean Sea.

These American ("peacekeeping") forces were seen by most Lebanese and other Arabs as military support for the Israeli effort to set up a client (dependent) government in Lebanon. During the battles around Beirut (between pro- and anti-Israeli militias), the marine barracks were a target of snipers; and one night (in 1983) a "terrorist" drove a truck full of explosives into the main barracks building. More than 240 marines died in their beds in one of the worst disasters in Marine Corps history.

The president accepted responsibility for the losses and declared that such terrorist acts would not force the United States to run out on its "commitments." Within a few months, however, American ground and naval forces were pulled out of Lebanon. (The neighboring Arab state of Syria then became the dominant influence there — map, p. 671.) Israeli troops withdrew gradually; after 1985 they occupied only a small "security" strip north of Israel's border, which they eventually evacuated in the course of peace negotiations with Syria in 2000.

After Reagan left office in 1989, the Israelis faced a new uprising (the "intifada") by Palestinians in the occupied territories (p. 670). Yet the demands of the Palestinians for a "homeland" were stubbornly resisted until 1993. In that year a crucial agreement was at last concluded. The Israeli government of Yitzhak Rabin officially recognized the Palestinian Liberation Organization (PLO), headed by Yassir Arafat, as the sole representative of the Palestinian people. It also granted limited Palestinian self-rule in Gaza and the city of Jericho, on the West Bank, and further negotiations in 1995 expanded the area of self-rule and provided for withdrawal of occupation forces (map, p. 671). This agreement was followed by an Israeli peace pact with neighboring Jordan. Notwithstanding persistent episodes of violence, it appeared that the "peace process," mediated by the United States, would eventually bring peace and self-determination to the entire region. For their historic endeavors, Rabin and Arafat shared the Nobel Prize for Peace in 1994. Tragically, in the following year, Rabin was assassinated by an Israeli opponent of the peace process. Elected in his place was Benjamin Netanyahu, a "hard-liner" who pursued a different course from Rabin. However, within a few years of continuing frustrations, Ehud Barak came to power in Israel, and the peace process with the Palestinians and Syria was resumed. Sometimes the process seemed to be moving ahead faster on one "track" than the other, but by the end of 2000 it had ground to a halt on both tracks. The Syrian track was stalled by disagreement and then the death of Syrian President Hafiz Assad following many years of power. On the Palestinian track, the parties at first seemed more willing to compromise, but intensive negotiations, leading to face-to-face meetings of Arafat, Barak, and Clinton in the United States, only revealed the depth of the remaining disagreement, above all over the status of Jerusalem and its holy sites. The result was an outbreak of fierce fighting between Palestinians and the Israeli army, which lasted for many weeks and at the end of the year still showed no signs of dying down.

Shortly after his intervention in Lebanon, President Reagan prepared for his reelection bid (1984). Widespread support for his conservative policies contributed to his successful campaign, but much of his support came from the president's *personal appeal*: his good looks, humor, and confident public assurances. Other conservative candidates, generally, did not fare as well as he did at the polls. In subsequent congressional elections, Republicans lost control of the Senate to the Democrats. With Democrats controlling *both* houses of Congress (after 1986), a legislative gridlock developed in the confrontation between conservatives and liberals. George Bush sustained the conservative position by keeping the presidency in Republican hands in the election of 1988, but proved unsuccessful in trying to bring about a majority for his party in either the Senate or House of Representatives. In 1992 the swing of the political pendulum was completed when President Bush lost the White House to the Democratic candidate, Bill Clinton.

The new president, with his party retaining its majorities in Congress, declared an end to political gridlock and initiated a number of liberal-oriented measures. These included legislation for crime and gun control, family-leave for employees, direct loans to students, an increase in the minimum wage for workers, and tax changes that aid low-income earners. He also secured a budget that reduced the federal deficit in *gradual* steps, to avoid negative impact upon the economy. In fact, the Clinton years saw the longest period of sustained economic stability and prosperity in the twentieth century. These successes contrasted with Clinton's inability to achieve another goal: passage of his proposal for a comprehensive reform of the nation's health-care system. In spite of his strenuous efforts, the plan was blocked in Congress because of its complexity and cost, powerful resistance by health-care providers and insurers, and legislative tactics by members of the opposing political party.

In any case, the political swing to the liberals proved very short as Republicans won control of *both chambers* in the mid-term congressional elections of 1994. Led by the new Speaker of the House, Rep. Newt Gingrich, the Republicans launched a "revolutionary" legislative effort aimed at rolling back many reforms of the Democratic New Deal (p. 645) and reducing the size of the federal government. They achieved some immediate victories, but their efforts were weakened after sustaining some loss of seats in the elections of 1996 and 1998. They still held their majorities, however, and confronted Clinton (reelected in 1996) with the now familiar gridlock between the two parties. For his part, the president was stymied in his hopes for better successes in protecting the environment and for providing better medical care for more Americans.

Unfortunately for Clinton (and the nation), the substantial achievements he did make were overshadowed by his sexual misbehavior in the White House. This was brought to light by Kenneth Starr, an "independent counsel" appointed under a new law to look into possible crimes in the administration. Starr charged the president with having had improper relations with a young intern (Monica Lewinsky) assigned to the White House, and then seeking illegally to cover up the truth. Clinton confessed to having "misled" the public about the relationship, but declared that his mistake should not require his resignation from office.

The Republicans in Congress, however, were determined to use the charges as a basis for Clinton's removal by *impeachment*. The House of Representatives, in a clearly partisan action, voted two specific articles of impeachment against him. The issue absorbed public and media attention for many months. At last, on trial by the Senate in February 1999, Clinton was acquitted of all charges—for lack of the two-thirds vote required for *conviction* on the charges. (Subsequently, the "Independent Counsel" law was allowed by Congress to expire.) Clinton remained in office, and gridlock with Congress remained as well.

The results of the elections of 2000 did not seem likely to change this. The Senate was evenly divided between Republicans and Democrats, and the Republicans held on to a majority in the House that was too narrow to give them secure control. The struggle for the presidency was between Albert Gore, Clinton's close policy partner as vice president, and George W. Bush, a moderate Republican and son of the president whom Clinton had defeated in 1992. The campaign ended in a bizarre dispute over an extremely close election result in a single state. Although Gore won a slender majority of the national popular vote, he and Bush both needed to win Florida to gain a majority in the Electoral College, the body that actually chooses the president. Although the initial count put Bush ahead in Florida, his lead was well within an unusually wide "margin of error" created by technical problems with voting machines. After several weeks of recounts and legal wrangling, the election was finally decided by the United States Supreme Court, which ordered the recounts stopped at a moment when Bush was still ahead though likely to lose his lead if the recounts went on. The United States Supreme Court's decision brought upon the court widespread accusations of political bias from Democrats—just as the recounts themselves, and earlier decisions of lower courts permitting them to continue, had brought the same accusations from Republicans. Gore and the Democrats nevertheless accepted the result and rallied behind Bush as president, while Bush for his part promised cooperation across party line. But it was not certain that he would be able to overcome the habit of political feuding that had grown up in Washington, aggravated as it now was by the even balances of power in the Congress, and by the resentments left over from the contest for the presidency.

The Revolutions in Eastern Europe: Gorbachev, Yeltsin

While conservative reforms were gradually taking shape in Western Europe and America during the 1980s, the Eastern (communist) bloc showed little change on its *surface*—until the end of the decade. Then that region commenced to *explode* in radical changes—political, social, economic, and cultural.

For some seventy years (since the Russian Revolution of 1917) the Communist party grip on the Soviet Union had appeared to be unbreakable. So, too, appeared its forty-year grip on the "satellite" countries of East Germany, Poland, Czechoslovakia, Romania, Hungary, and Bulgaria. There had been some outspoken dissidents, like Aleksandr Solzhenitsyn (pp. 632, 741), but it seemed that the instruments of control and repression were so systematic and powerful that no *major* change could erupt from below. Yet the "historical surprise" of the century suddenly dawned upon those lands.

Although largely unknown to foreign observers, serious doubts about the viability of the communist system had begun to grow among some of the higher officials of the Soviet party even before 1980. As far back as the 1930s, Nikolai Bukharin had criticized the Stalinist regime and had called for greater flexibility in the economy (p. 631). And after Stalin's death (1953), Nikita Khrushchev, as party chief, introduced some measures of relaxation (pp. 661–662). Such views and actions, however, were not sustained by the party as a whole.

It was not until a generation after Khruschev that disenchantment with the system became a rising force. More and more party members (as well as ordinary citizens) were concluding that the long-time promises of communism—and centralized economic control—were not being fulfilled. They viewed with envy the rising prosperity of the capitalist West; they became convinced that *changes had to be made* to rescue their faltering economy. In 1985 the central committee of the party chose Mikhail Gorbachev as their agent of change. He moved quickly in two directions: what he called *glasnost*—the "opening up" (democratization) of Soviet society; and *perestroika*—the "restructuring" of the economy. Similar efforts were also being made at this time in other states within the Soviet orbit.

With respect to foreign affairs, Gorbachev urged "new thinking"—for his own and other countries. (He supported his words with action by pulling Soviet troops out of Afghanistan in 1988—p. 682.) The Cold War and its confrontational policies had proved enormously wasteful "dead ends." A new era of *cooperation* in addressing the *real problems* of the planet was called for. These goals, articulated and vigorously pursued by Gorbachev, were the main factors that precipitated the revolutions of Eastern Europe—still in progress. Worldwide recognition of his historic role was symbolized by the awarding to Gorbachev of the Nobel Prize for Peace in 1990.

The progress of change within the Soviet Union itself was uneven. Gorbachev had powerful domestic critics on both "left" and "right" (those who wanted to *move faster* and those who tried to *hold back* reforms). Nevertheless, swift action was taken to implement glasnost. Thousands of political prisoners were released, and free expression and free assembly were permitted. Perhaps the most significant constitutional reform was the abolition of the Communist party's *monopoly* on political power (p. 633). New elections took place throughout the U.S.S.R., with rival nonparty groups vying for office.

Gorbachev's principal frustrations lay in the area of perestroika—the restructuring of the economy. Some individuals wanted to move as quickly as possible from the existing system of centralized control to a full-fledged "market economy." Others believed such a rapid move would be too disruptive and painful to workers and consumers; they favored a "go-slow" approach. Gorbachev, walking the tightrope, proposed a plan combining features from both sides. In October 1990 his compromise was approved by the newly elected Soviet Parliament—and he was authorized, as president, to set it in motion by executive decree.

But Gorbachev's economic plan proved to be too little and too late. (Ironically, it served only to identify him, in Soviet eyes, with the collapse of the U.S.S.R.) The underlying causes of the system's failure were numerous: critical mistakes, over the years, by the central planning establishment, lack of provision for individual incentive and initiative, gross neglect of ecological considerations, and overall political and social rigidity. Beyond these intrinsic causes was, perhaps, the most decisive single cause—the waging of the Cold War with the United States and its NATO allies (pp. 660–661). Diversion of resources and manpower from peaceful production to pursuit of the extravagant arms race severely strained the American economy and left it with a huge burden of debt; but the arms race brought to the "enemy" Soviets what Washington had sought: the *fatal crippling* of their economic system (pp. 691–692, 697–698).

The worsening economic situation was aggravated by the dissolving of the ties that had held the Soviet Union together. Gorbachev's general policy of repudiating the use of *military force* to keep the country unified opened the door to long pent-up desires for independence from the multinational state. The Baltic republics (p. 655) were the first to declare their own individual *sovereignty*. The Russian Republic, the largest by far (p. 662), quickly followed, along with the Ukraine, Georgia, Azerbaijan, and most of the other republics. How could a multinational economic plan work if the now sovereign states each took off upon their *own* plans? This dilemma was highlighted in the case of the Russian Republic. Boris Yeltsin, a former Communist turned radical reformer, was elected president of that new republic in 1991. He declared, with the support of the republic's parliament, that Russia would press toward a market economy by a much faster route than Gorbachev had envisioned.

The momentous happenings of August 1991 gave added force to Yeltsin's plan. The political "right," backed by the secret police (KGB), ranking army officers, and Communist party conservatives, launched a coup against Gorbachev (still, officially, the president of the U.S.S.R.) and the *reformers* in the Russian Parliament. But the coup lasted only seventy-two hours as thousands of Muscovites filled the streets to defend their parliament—and the deployed army units were pulled back. Opinion elsewhere in the country, and in the world, strongly condemned this effort to overthrow the legal order. The failed coup thus damaged the reactionaries—and gave decisive impetus to the supporters of democracy, market economy, and independence for the constituent republics. Within days, the reformers in the Parliament initiated far-reaching measures: to deprive the Communist party of any effective role in government; alter drastically the functions of the secret police; loosen controls over the media; and ensure that the armed forces were kept under the command of loyal officers. The way was also cleared for achievement of complete independence by the individual republics—whose elected leaders would now be free to negotiate their relations with one another and with foreign countries.

Shortly after these actions, the governing organs of the U.S.S.R. ceased to exist. In early December 1991 the presidents of three of the new republics—Russia, Ukraine, and Belarus (formerly Byelorussia)—met together and announced the creation of a substitute version of the Union, which they called the "Commonwealth of Independent States" (CIS). This association was quickly joined by most of the other new republics. Modeled after the idea of the British Commonwealth of Nations (p. 668), the CIS functioned as an international organization with limited powers, though many of its members have since taken steps for economic cooperation, and in 1997 Russia and Belarus agreed on a "union" with a common currency and citizenship, though still remaining separate and independent states. In addition, the three presidents agreed on a declaration that the Russian Republic was to be accepted as the principal inheritor of the assets and obligations of the Soviet Union—including, especially, control over its nuclear missiles and its commitments to reduce their numbers. This declaration was welcomed by the United States and the European Economic Community.

On Christmas Day 1991, Mikhail Gorbachev, responding to these events, officially resigned his now-empty office as president of the now-dissolved multinational state. Gorbachev had aimed to "reform" communism and to maintain the unity of its political domain. But in the country's critical "time of troubles" he was swept aside by the swelling popular demand for *radical economic change* and *national self-determination*.

The unraveling of the Soviet Union was paralleled by the breaking away of the "satellite" countries of Eastern Europe (*map*, p. 706). They had been held as "allies" of the U.S.S.R. through the Warsaw Pact of 1955 (p. 661). At that time, the Soviet leaders viewed them as a needed "buffer"—to help protect their war-ravaged homeland from any future attack by a resurgent Germany and the West. The economies of these states had suffered from the same growing paralysis that the Soviets were enduring. Once Gorbachev signaled that force would no

14-4   An East German policeman reaches down from the Berlin Wall for a rose offered by a West German woman, November 1989. The Cold War has ended, Germany is about to be reunited, and communism itself will soon pass away.

longer be used to hold them in tow, popular movements exploded against their communist regimes (all the more despised because they were *imposed* by a *foreign power*). Thus, democratic revolutions (mostly nonviolent) followed in 1989 and 1990 in Poland, East Germany *(Fig 14-4)*, Hungary, Romania, Bulgaria, and Czechoslovakia. (The latter country was *divided* in 1993, by joint consent, into the Czech Republic and Slovakia.) Though Yugoslavia had not been part of the Warsaw Pact, that country took a similar course of democratization, *separation* into its component republics—and *civil war*. All of these states, like the former Soviet republics, have also had to manage the complicated transition to a new kind of *economy*: from state-owned enterprises and central planning to "privatization" and production for the "free market."

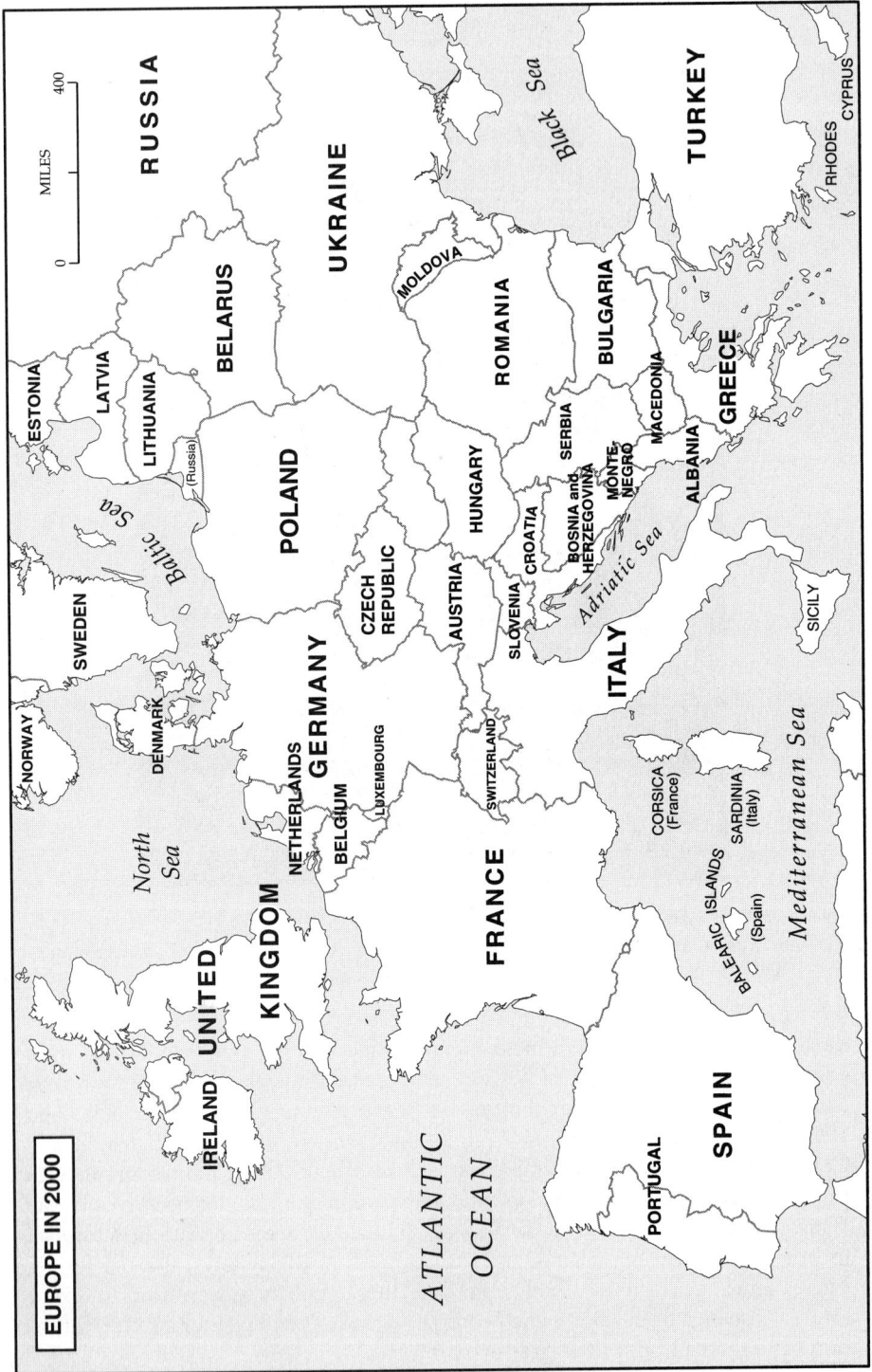

EUROPE IN 2000

New Dangers and New Opportunities of the 1990s

These dramatic developments were important and challenging to the citizens of those individual countries. They raised challenges as well in the broader arena of European and world affairs. The wholesale overthrow of a major, once-dynamic ideology (Marxism) had repercussions far beyond Eastern Europe. The coming apart of one of the two superpowers also had an unsettling impact upon international diplomacy and the global balance of power. And a special effect followed from the reunification of Germany, which occurred in October 1990. This was a direct result of the anticommunist revolutions and was adroitly managed by Helmut Kohl, chancellor of the Federal Republic (West Germany). Though apparently inevitable, the merger raised old fears—memories of what a united Germany did to Europe in two world wars of the twentieth century. Leaders in Europe and the United States hoped to keep that nation in bounds, through placing it in a co-operating role within some sort of federated Europe (pp. 693–694).

In the first ten years of the reunified German state, this policy seemed to be working—largely because it was what the majority of Germans wanted for themselves. The new government of Gerhard Schröder, elected in 1998, faced major problems of integrating eastern Germany, reviving an economy that seemed to have lost a good deal of its momentum, and assimilating millions of immigrant "guest workers." But the new government consistently followed Kohl's policy of working within NATO and the European Union, while maintaining good relations with Russia.

Meanwhile, from Germany's eastern borders all the way to the Pacific, two dozen countries were coping with the after-effects of the collapse of communist dictatorships and state-owned economies, and there was far less assurance of the ultimate shape (or shapes) of the postcommunist regimes (*map*, p. 706). The westernmost countries of the region, Poland, the Czech Republic, Hungary, and Slovenia seemed to be making a harsh but successful transition to Western-style democracy and capitalism—with the former Communist parties often transformed into moderate leftist parties and working alongside more conservative forces to make the transition work. Farther east were countries whose peoples and leaders mostly seemed eager to move in the same direction, but where the difficulties of economic adjustment were much worse—Slovakia, Romania, Bulgaria, and Ukraine. Then there were countries fringing Russia in Europe, the Caucasus, and Central Asia (*maps*, pp. 666, 671), where poverty and corruption were endemic, and former Communist party bosses had in many cases made successful transitions to become nationalist dictators.

Finally there was Russia itself, where Boris Yeltsin, the victor over both the Communist conservatives and the Communist reformers in 1991, presided over almost a decade of national misfortune and humiliation. True, there seemed to be general acceptance (even within the still powerful Communist party) that traditional communism was dead and would never be resurrected; and a rough-and-tumble version of democratic politics seemed to have won legitimacy. But ten years after the end of the Soviet Union, most Russians lived in poverty and squalor far worse than those of communism; privatization had led not to the modernization of industry and the economy, but to the plundering of the country's assets by wealthy tycoons and gangsters; the government could not collect taxes, the armed forces were in decay, and the space program, once the pride of the Soviet Union, was kept going only by United States subsidies. Yeltsin's handpicked successor, Vladimir Putin (elected president in 2000), promised to strengthen the state, rein in the tycoons and gangsters, and restore Russia's standard of living and pride in itself. But turning Russia into a prosperous and powerful modern country was a vast and still unaccomplished task, and for the moment the country remained in a state of resentful dependence on its former capitalist rivals.

Furthermore, with the erosion of an effective controlling power within the Soviet Union and across Eastern Europe, there loomed the possibility of regional and local forces pulling apart the fabric of civilized order. Rising ethnic and national feelings, repressed for several generations, often burst into destructive and hardly controllable conflicts, above all in Chechnya and Yuogoslavia.

Chechnya, a territory within Russia whose Muslim population had a long history of resistance to rule from Moscow, moved in 1995 to achieve complete *independence*. This proved to be a severe test for Yeltsin, already beset with pressing economic problems and mounting political opposition. He decided to use force to put down the secession, and a bitter war ensued between Russian and Chechen troops in which the Russians suffered many setbacks and eventually withdrew, leaving Chechnya apparently set for eventual independence. But Islamic fundamentalist forces in Chechnya provoked Moscow with raids on neighboring territories and terrorist bombings, and the conflict resumed in 1999. This time the Russians reoccupied the territory with savage bombardments and systematic destruction, but were left with an apparently unwinnable guerrilla war on their hands.

Meanwhile, the breakup of Yugoslavia led to disastrous consequences in the Balkan area. Ever since the barbarian invasions of the early Middle Ages, the Balkans have been a region of many small nations. Since that time, these nations came to be divided in religion, first as a result of the split between the Roman Catholic and Eastern Orthodox churches, and then as a result of conquest and widespread conversion by the Muslim Turks. As the Balkan nations regained their independence in the nineteenth and early twentieth centuries, they were further divided by rival nationalisms and great power intervention. As a result, many of them committed cruel atrocities against each other in both world wars. (For details of this historical background, see pp. 218–219, 246, 325, 327–329, 616–618, 621.) Yugoslavia, the largest Balkan country, was organized as a *federated* state, consisting of six republics, by Marshal Tito after the Second World War (pp. 661–662); Tito permitted the various nations in the republics wide cultural freedom while holding them on a short leash in most other respects, so that they lived together more or less peaceably.

In 1991 most of the republics declared their independence, and at that point their hostilities exploded. The principal inheritor of the former federal state and its army was the republic of Serbia, which (together with the republic of

Montenegro) declared the formation of a "new" federated Yugoslavia in 1992. The president was Slobodan Milosevic, a former Communist leader who had reinvented himself as an extreme nationalist. The Serbs are of the Eastern Orthodox faith. They promptly gave encouragement and military aid to fellow Serbs, living in neighboring Bosnia-Herzegovina (alongside Roman Catholic Croats and Muslim Bosnians—pp. 246, 328), as well as in Roman Catholic Croatia, in order to help "free" them from those republics. (This action appeared to be a revival of the "Greater Serbia" movement that precipitated the First World War in 1914— p. 618.) Military struggles erupted throughout the area. Serbs most of all, but also Croats and Bosnians, attacked the other groups, forcing them out of the areas they lived in ("ethnic cleansing") and occupying these areas with their own people. At last, however, an American initiative succeeded in bringing the warring parties to a general peace agreement, and its implementation by NATO military forces commenced in December 1995. In 2000, the various nations of Bosnia and Herzegovina were living uneasily together within a republic held together by NATO troops and civilian administrators, in the same way that Yugoslavia was once held together by Tito's communist regime.

The Serbs struck again in 1999—against their own province of Kosovo, most of whose population consisted of ethnic Albanians of Muslim faith (pp. 219, 325, 328), seeking to regain the *autonomy* they had enjoyed while Tito had ruled Yugoslavia. Some local Serbs joined military units from Belgrade (the Serb capital) to drive the Albanians out of their province. The world community was shocked by this ruthless example of ethnic cleansing. While the United Nations failed to *act* (a Russian veto in its Security Council would have prevented this action), the members of the North Atlantic Treaty Organization (NATO—p. 661) agreed that the Serbian crimes must be stopped and the refugees allowed to return. When Milosevic refused this demand, air forces (mainly American) attacked the Serb army and targets inside Serbia until he gave in. Most Muslims returned to their smashed homes, and some fled to other countries. Once again, NATO troops and administrators moved in and normal life was gradually restored for most of the Albanian population; the Serb minority mostly moved out, under pressure from Albanians thirsting for revenge.

In Serbia itself, this renewed disaster finally led to the ouster of Milosevic. He was defeated in a bid to win reelection as president against opposition forces led by Vojislav Kostunica, and when he tried to hold on to power in spite of the elections, he was finally forced out by massive street demonstrations. Kostunica's victory was welcomed by the NATO countries, and it probably meant the end of Serb efforts to unite their entire ethnic group within a single nation-state. But it did not seem to bring the goals of national reconciliation and viable self-government in Bosnia and Kosovo any closer.

As a result of these events in the Balkans, hundreds of thousands died or became refugees. Unfortunately, since these conflicts were seen as *civil war*, rather than acts of aggression by one *country* against another, the United Nations (and individual countries, like the United States) did not find a proper principle for pursuing effective intervention. And the United Nations itself has been critically strained by faltering financial support from its member states. By 1995, delinquent pledges of payment amounted to some *four billion* dollars, and in the year 2000, the United States still owed the largest amount.

Over and against the painful struggle in the Balkans and the prospect of widening international anarchy elsewhere, there lies an alternative possibility of better understanding and *cooperation* among peoples. The unifying moves in Western Europe, economic and political, have already been indicated in this chapter (p. 663–664, 694). And with the Cold War properly buried, the United States and the "successor states" to the Soviet Union *could* combine their strengths and work together toward solving many of the critical problems facing this planet.

One of those problems is *war* itself. In September 1991, with an unprecedented show of unity and determination, the United States led a coalition of powers within the United Nations (including the U.S.S.R.) to declare and enforce a total *trade embargo* against an aggressor state, Iraq (*map*, p. 672). When, after five months of trial, this measure appeared insufficient to compel Saddam Hussein, the Iraqi leader, to withdraw his army from neighboring oil-rich Kuwait, the UN Security Council authorized the coalition powers to resort to military action (January 1992). These forces, headed by the United States, quickly and decisively routed the Iraqis (Operation "Desert Storm"). Iraq remains under United Nations trade sanctions because of its alleged development of weapons of mass destruction.

This successful demonstration of *collective action* in turning back aggression raised hopes for developing effective means for providing global security. President Bush hailed the new level of international cooperation as the beginning of a "New World Order" (NWO). Converting this promise into reality will prove to be a formidable task; one has only to recall the fate of similar aspirations of two earlier presidents: Woodrow Wilson (pp. 652–653) and Franklin Roosevelt (pp. 658–660).

Shortly after the achievement in Kuwait, the United Nations (as we have seen) experienced painful frustrations in dealing with the ethnic conflicts in former Yugoslavia—as well as civil war in Somalia, tribal massacres in Rwanda (*map*, p. 674), and numerous disturbances elsewhere. More positive was the United Nations' action in the Caribbean. President Clinton, with United Nations approval, sent American-led joint forces to Haiti that removed its repressive military regime and restored to office the democratically elected government of Jean-Bertrand Aristide.

Another example of successful cooperation, in a different field, was the agreement between the Americans and the Russians sharply to *reduce* their stockpiles of nuclear weapons, and for each side to end targeting the other side's cities. Progress appeared also in a worldwide move to ban all nuclear weapons *tests*. This move, however, received a severe setback late in 1995, when the United States Senate voted *against* ratification of the Comprehensive Nuclear Test Ban Treaty (CTBT). Without America, by far the greatest nuclear power, agreeing to stop testing, other nations feel obliged even more to go ahead with *more* testing of their own. Thus, the likelihood of *proliferation* (p. 692) and additional weapons of mass destruction has increased—with their awful menace to civilization.

CHAPTER 15

● ● ●

THE REVOLUTION IN WESTERN CULTURE

Overview

The twentieth-century global transformation was not limited to political, social, and economic matters. Decisive changes also came about in science and technology, philosophy and religion, personal values and behavior, and the creative arts. Changes in these fields do not usually take place in lockstep with those in politics, economics, and society, and this chapter covers many developments that began rather earlier than those dealt with in chapter 14. All the same, changes in all areas of human activity and experience are interconnected. The "contemporary" era, extended backward to about the beginning of the twentieth century, has been a decisive stage in a break with the past that is taking place in thought, knowledge, culture, and values as well as in other fields.

In the sciences, the period has been one when knowledge of the material universe has expanded with extraordinary speed. Today, humanity is reaching toward ultimate understanding of what the pioneers of the Scientific Revolution called the "macrocosm"—the origins and nature of the universe as a whole and the medium of space and time in which it exists—as well as of the "microcosm"—the almost infinitely tiny yet unimaginably complex "worlds" that make up both living and nonliving matter. And the expansion of scientific knowledge has in turn led to an extraordinary growth in the human race's technological capacities for good and evil.

The onrush of science and technology has also had a powerful influence on thought, culture, and values in general—an influence that, like science and technology themselves, has been double-edged. Science has provided ever deeper insight into nature, but it has also made the human race seem unimportant and unexceptional as part of the universe, and made whatever ultimate reality lies beyond the universe seem more distant than ever. Technology has provided plenty, comfort, and safety on a scale that earlier generations would have considered miraculous, as well as bringing into existence new and exciting forms of art and culture. Yet it has also brought into being the gas chambers, the threat of environmental disaster, and the hydrogen bomb, as well as the possibility of controlling and manipulating not only the natural world but also human beings themselves. Thus, science and technology have reinforced two age-old—and opposing—tendencies in humanity's understanding of itself and the universe: on the one hand, self-confidence and the consciousness of power; and on the other, pessimism, perplexity, and fear.

The effect has been especially strong on philosophy and religion, precisely because it is these that have traditionally provided the human race with guidance as to what to believe about itself and the universe. In philosophy, thinkers have given up creating "systems"—total and harmonious explanations of everything that exists inside and outside the human mind. Instead, some philosophers have restricted themselves to studying and refining the basic *methods* of philosophy, while others look for ways of holding on to individual human dignity and freedom in a universe that seems to them indifferent and ultimately unknowable, and in societies that they see as materialistic and conformist.

For Christianity, with its central role in the culture, power structure, and daily life of Western civilization over the last fifteen hundred years, the onrush of science and technology is only part of a wider problem of responding to the shifts in civilization that have been under way since the Renaissance. Should Christianity adapt to these shifts, or hold out against them?

In contemporary times, this has not been an "either-or" choice, but rather a question of where to draw the line, and different Christian schools of thought see it in different places. In response to the rise of the scientific view of humanity and the universe, for example, the so-called "fundamentalists" (mostly Protestants) resist this view where it contradicts the Bible—above all, in the area of creation and the origin of human and animal species. "Orthodox" theologians, both Protestant and Catholic, accept the complete picture of the universe drawn by modern science, but try to make a "leap of faith" past the universe of science to the one almighty God who exists beyond it and has given the human race a unique place in it. And "liberal" Protestant thinkers regard the traditional beliefs of Christianity as no more than compelling myths, which are nevertheless worth retelling and reenacting because they express humanity's need for and hope of some kind of "higher" reality.

Likewise, many Christian churches have also responded to the contemporary shifts in Western civilization by staking a claim to be, so to speak, the "keepers of the conscience" of the wealthy and powerful democratic-capitalist countries. Regardless of religious differences, most of the churches are to be found on the side of reining in materialism and consumerism, extending the welfare state safety net, helping the Third World countries, and promoting racial equality as well as tolerance and "pluralism" in general. On the other hand, there has probably been more blood shed between Christian and Muslim religious groups, and between different Christian religious groups, in the twentieth century than at any time since the Crusades and the Reformation.

Besides these changes in science, technology, and religion, the contemporary era has witnessed the beginnings of yet another historic transformation. Following several centuries of political, social, economic, and cultural shifts, Western civilization is now undergoing shifts in values concerning sexual behavior and family life, and in the distribution of status and power between men and women.

Many of the other shifts in Western civilization have contributed to these changes. Industrialization replaced the household with the factory and the office as the main places of work for women as well as men, and the progress of medicine drastically lowered infant mortality, as well as making contraception reliable. As a result, the division of labor and social roles between women and men that seems to have existed since Neolithic times (pp. 15–16) began to break down. Meanwhile, the eighteenth- and nineteenth-century liberal belief in freedom, equality, and individualism, and the twentieth-century ideals of diversity and pluralism, spread from public life to influence values concerning personal behavior and the relations of men and women. Under the influence of these forces, sexual values and gender relations first began to shift in the late nineteenth and early twentieth centuries, and not long after the middle of the twentieth century, the shift in values concerning sexuality and gender relations began to gather speed. As with so many other contemporary changes in civilization, it was the democratic-capitalist countries that took the lead. The turning point came in the 1960s, with the rise of the international "youth culture" or "counterculture," whose values had a decisive influence on society in general.

The counterculture was in part a protest against all that was most threatening to human survival, individuality, and freedom in a changing civilization—such as nuclear weapons, environmental pollution, consumerism, conformity, and racial discrimination. The protest was especially widespread among college students. In and around the colleges of North America and Western Europe, there grew up the nonconforming, "alternative" society of the counterculture, in which traditional sexual values and gender roles were rejected in the name of individuality and freedom. Yet the alternative society never broke away from the mainstream one, and it did not have to. The mainstream society's values had already shifted far from the traditional ones, and it was ready to listen to the counterculture's message.

The result was a whole series of fast-moving changes that are still underway in most Western countries today. Women entered the workforce in larger numbers than ever before—with the expectation of staying at work throughout their lives, and doing so on equal terms with men. Single mothers, once regarded as "fallen women" or at best as unfortunate victims of divorce, agitated for themselves and their children to be looked upon as families like any other. Homosexuals, once members of a secret and illegal subculture, formed organized interest groups within democratic politics. Abortion became legal, and teenagers were taught methods of contraception as early as middle school. The law, which had once punished homosexuality and favored families with one male breadwinner, now (in many places) banned various forms of discrimination against working women and gays.

Like all far-reaching social changes, these changes both aroused resistance and created new problems. There were heated disputes over what kind of rules and conventions should henceforth govern sexual behavior and relationships, how children were to enjoy a secure and stable family life, and how far the law should be used to uphold the new values. It was not at all certain that Western civilization's sexual and gender shifts would spread to the rest of the world as overwhelmingly as so many other Western changes had done. Even so, it did seem as if in matters of sexual values and gender relations, Western civilization had entered on a path from which there was no turning back.

Contemporary changes in the creative arts have been as drastic as those in the fields of thought, knowledge, beliefs, and values, and have often taken place in interaction with changes in these other fields. But the only trends of the era that have actually been affirmed or celebrated by the most admired artists have been those of *experimentation* and sexual liberation. Otherwise, art has been, so to speak, in opposition, championing the individual against the blind forces of the universe and society; or it has withdrawn from direct depiction of society and the external world into exploring the *subjective consciousness* of individuals, especially the artists themselves.

Thus, the styles and techniques of literature and drama have moved far from the Realism and Impressionism of the nineteenth century—largely because neither of these styles seems adequate to express the inner life or describe the outer experiences of people in contemporary times. Instead, events in fiction are described not in normal storytelling fashion, by a narrator outside the story, but as they are remembered or perceived by characters inside the story. The normal sequences of time (one event after another) and causation (one event causing another) are broken up. And fantastic and impossible things happen as part of ordinary daily life. Similar trends in the visual arts have gone even farther. Early in the twentieth century, Cubism still depicted conventional subjects such as nudes and still lifes, but it reduced them to abstract geometrical forms that were hardly recognizable. By the middle of the century, Abstract Expressionist artists no longer depicted objects or scenes that existed outside their paintings, Instead, they produced abstract designs that expressed their own inner consciousness, or emerged directly from their subconsciousness.

In addition to these changes, the arts, like every human activity, have felt the transforming impact of contemporary technology. For technology to have an effect on art is nothing new. A Greek bronze statue, a Gothic cathedral, or a violin are as much products of technical innovation as a skyscraper or a television set. But because the contemporary onrush of technology has been so overwhelming, its impact on the arts has been more spectacular than ever before. It is technology that has made it possible for talented architects to design buildings that combine bigness with clean-cut elegance or fantastic, gravity-defying shapes—and for untalented architects to spread dehumanized dreariness around the world's cities on an unprecedented scale. And it is technology that has devised a whole new range of artistic media—photography, film, and the countless present-day forms of electronic recording and broadcasting. By doing so, technology has not only influenced creative art in the traditional sense, but has brought into being a whole new branch of the arts—*mass entertainment.*

Mass entertainment certainly overlaps with both "high" art and older forms of "popular" art, but all the same its appearance is the single greatest cultural change of the contemporary era. The age of mass entertainment began in the nineteenth century, when rising literacy rates and technical innovations in printing made it possible to sell books and magazines by the hundreds of thousands. But it was twentieth-century technology that made mass entertainment central in the lives of individuals and societies. Today, children spend more time watching television than in any other activity, except sleeping; baseball stars and cycling champions, depending on their public and private behavior, become role models for millions or people whom millions love to hate; the sudden deaths of celebrities inspire worldwide outpourings of grief; candidates for high office in democratic countries pay court to talk show hosts in between pummeling each other with attack commercials; and the celebration of a new millennium in a time reckoning of Western and Christian origin is an intercontinental media event for Western and non-Western civilizations alike (*Fig. V-1*, p. 592).

People often shake their heads over the present-day dominance of mass entertainment, but no one can escape it. In the "global village" of the twenty-first century, it plays the same role that gossip among neighbors, Sunday churchgoing or its non-Christian equivalents, and the feasts and celebrations of the traditional farming year play in real villages that still survive from earlier times. Mass entertainment is a glue that holds a changing world together, as civilization breaks with its past and moves toward whatever destiny the future holds.

⌒

THE ONRUSH OF SCIENCE AND TECHNOLOGY

The accelerating nineteenth-century progress of science (pp. 576–579) turned in the twentieth century into a headlong rush of discovery that left no aspect of nature unexplored. The distribution of galaxies across the endless reaches of space, the movement of continents across the face of the earth, the ages of prehistoric artifacts and human remains, the "language" in which bees communicate with each other in the hive—over an astonishingly wide range of matters that until recently were completely mysterious, science can now provide systematic knowledge and explanations.

From the lonely activity of a few researchers, moreover, science has become a large-scale social undertaking, employing tens of thousands of highly trained people and supported by massive state subsidies (though these are only a small fraction of total government budgets). Scientists used to boast of doing experiments "with string and sealing wax," but much scientific equipment has become spectacularly huge and complex. The United States recently devoted two space shuttle missions to placing the Hubble telescope in orbit and then repairing it, so that astronomers could get pictures of distant features of the universe unobscured by the earth's atmosphere. Likewise, fourteen European nations pooled their resources to build the Large Electron-Positron Collider near Geneva, Switzerland—a machine that hurls subatomic particles at each other over a distance of more than fifty miles, so that physicists can produce collisions violent enough to break the particles down into their still more basic constituents. And in some ways, the pursuit of scientific knowledge has become the single most highly respected of human endeavors. Of all the ways in which the present-day world honors individuals as benefactors of humanity, perhaps the most prestigious are the Nobel Prizes, established by the Swedish industrialist Alfred Nobel in 1904. Of the six prizes annually awarded, one each is given for literature, economics, and peace, and the other *three* (physics, physiology and medicine, and chemistry) are all given for science.

The reason for this high valuation of science is not only that science has unlocked so many secrets of nature. It also has to do with the fact that the explosion of scientific knowledge has transformed every other aspect of human life on this planet: politics and warfare, industry and the economy, social life and culture. Most of the matters dealt with in this and the preceding chapter, from the atom bomb to the "pill," and from the "Green Revolution" in agriculture to the revolution in politics produced by television, would never have happened without the onrush of science, towing technology in its wake at vastly accelerated speed.

Penetrating the Secrets of the Physical Universe

Among the countless twentieth-century achievements of science, perhaps the most significant—both as discoveries in themselves and in their consequences for human life and thought—are those that have taken humanity to the outermost edges of the universe, and to the innermost structure of both nonliving matter and living organisms.

In astronomy, the twentieth century has seen the "discovery of a new cosmos" comparable to that which took place in the sixteenth and seventeenth centuries (pp. 464–471). These advances in cosmology (understanding of the workings of the universe) are partly the result of other scientific and technical discoveries, which have enabled astronomers to see ever farther into space. Already in the nineteenth century, spectrum analysis (p. 576) of the light emitted by stars showed that they are made of the same basic elements known on earth; comparison with geological estimates of the earth's age also indicated that the stars must somehow have the capacity to "burn" hot and bright for billions of years. From about 1900 on, huge new telescopes revealed that stars are clustered throughout space in galaxies similar to that called our Milky Way, the two-hundred-billion aggregation of stars in which the sun was already known to be located. Further, spectrum analysis of the galaxies themselves indicated that they are mostly moving away from one another at vast speed. In the 1920s, the American astronomer Edwin Hubble made the fundamental discovery on which the new cosmology rests: that the farther apart galaxies are, the faster they seem to move away from each other. This was clinching proof that the totality of galaxies—that is, the universe itself—must be expanding.

This, in turn, led astronomers to a scientific theory about the probable origin of the universe—one as imaginative and ingenious as any earlier creation myth or philosophical speculation (pp. 22–23, 27, 80, 474–475). If the universe has been growing larger over time, it seemed to follow that there must have been a moment in the past—most likely about fifteen billion years ago—when it was infinitely small; and if the galaxies are still today hurtling away from each other, then the reason must be that "in the beginning," the original tiny universe exploded outward with unimaginable violence. In the 1960s, confirmation of this theory was provided by a new type of observing device, radio telescopes, which detect radio signals emitted by stars and other objects in space. It turned out that the entire universe is saturated with radio signals, all of the same very short wavelength, that have no source in any individual object—the remains, it is believed, of the mighty outburst of electromagnetic radiation (pp. 576–577) given off by the original "big bang."

To explain these discoveries, and for guidance in searching for such things in the first place, astronomers turned to the concepts of Einstein's theory of relativity (p. 578). Only the large-scale conversion of matter into energy, as proposed by Einstein, could provide a "fuel" powerful enough to keep the stars "burning" for billions of years at a time. Only the concept of space and time, matter and energy, being related to one another allowed astronomers to conceive of how all four could originally have been packed into a tiny point, and then have expanded outward into a universe that grows without having an actual boundary, but where space and time simply "curve" back on themselves. This new view of the universe did not invalidate the view developed by Copernicus and Kepler, Galileo and Newton, as their view had invalidated that of Aristotle and Ptolemy (pp. 464–465). But it became clear that what the sixteenth- and seventeenth-century giants had discovered was only the "tip of the iceberg." Their twentieth-century successors were exploring the full outlines of the whole awesome structure of mass and energy extending through time and space.

Alongside the astronomers' search for the origins of the universe, there also proceeded the quest of the physicists for the inner secrets of the atom. What drove this quest forward were questions raised by the early twentieth-century discovery of Rutherford and Bohr (pp. 577–578), that the atom is not a basic unit of matter, but itself a tiny *structure* or *system*, with its own constituent parts. What exactly are these constituent parts, or *subatomic particles?* What forces keep them in balance with each other to form a stable system, and what kind of imbalances can cause the system to change? How do the atoms of different chemical elements differ in their inner structure, how do atoms join their structures to form molecules, and what kind of changes within the atom produce such things as radioactivity or light? What is the best way of describing the particles and forces at work in the atom, and how can such tiny entities be detected and measured? In the course of the twentieth century, atomic physicists have come a long way toward answering many of these questions.

As with the astronomers, the physicists needed theories—both to guide them as to what to look for inside the atom, and to explain what they found there. These theories were mostly devised between 1900 and 1930. What they said was that just as on the ultra-large scale of the universe as a whole, so in the ultra-small world of the atom, the "classical" (p. 577) scientific concepts that seem to do well enough for the vast range of "middle-sized" items, such as falling apples or planets in their orbits, do not apply. Thus, to make sense of the world of the atom, it turned out to be necessary to think of many subatomic particles sometimes as tiny pieces of matter orbiting within the atom, and sometimes as tiny packets of energy, lapping wavelike around it. Likewise, forms of energy that might be emitted by the atom, such as light, which it had become customary to think of as traveling in waves, now came to be regarded also as streams of tiny particle-like packets of energy, or *quanta*. Major contributors to these new concepts were Einstein—the most universal of scientific theorists since Newton—together with Max Planck and Erwin Schrödinger.

It was also necessary to define most carefully what it was, within the world of the atom, that was to be observed, and how this could be done. In the 1920s, Werner Heisenberg announced a new basic concept of physics: the principle of *uncertainty*, which states that it is impossible to observe at the same time both the position and the motion of a subatomic particle. (The reason is that the particle is so tiny that there is no way of observing it without significantly changing either its position or its motion.) Many physicists, including Einstein, feared that the uncertainty principle would make the internal workings of the atom unknowable, but this turned out not to be so. True, physicists had to give up hope of ever "looking" at an *individual* atom as Galileo had looked at Jupiter and its moons (p. 467), exactly measuring the behavior of all its parts, and thereby exactly predicting how they would work as a system. Still, physicists could theorize on the basis of *large numbers of atoms*, so as to predict what the *"average atom"* would most likely do— rather as a market-research company can never know for certain what brand of breakfast cereal an individual consumer will buy, but given data about many consumers, can predict with very high probability which brand the average consumer will purchase. And even if subatomic particles could not be directly observed *inside* the atom, they could be knocked *out of* atoms by powerful beams of rays or streams of other particles; their probable paths could be indirectly tracked and measured once they had been released in this way; and from this data it was possible, by complex calculations, to "read back" to conditions within the atom. Thus, an array of increasingly powerful "atom-smashing" and later "particle-smashing" devices has made atomic physics one of the most spectacular and expensive branches of science.

With the help of concepts and devices such as these, physicists were able to perceive how the atom works to produce many features of the physical world as we know it. Thus, by the 1930s, it was known that the differences among chemical elements are due to the different numbers of various subatomic particles among the atoms that make up the elements; that atoms combine to form molecules, whether of the same or of different elements, by sharing their outermost constituent particles; and that phenomena such as radioactivity, electricity, and light are the result of the emission of particles by atoms, of the flow of particles among them, and the change of position of particles within them. This theoretical knowledge had far-reaching practical consequences. Thus, it was the understanding of the flow of electrons among atoms in certain types of solid materials—the "semiconductors"—that made possible the miniaturization of electronic components, enabling complex devices like televisions and computers to become cheap, compact, and hence widespread.

As for the actual workings of the atom as a system in itself, from the 1930s onward, the original model devised by Rutherford and Bohr, of a proton-filled nucleus with electrons orbiting around it (p. 578), grew increasingly complex. New atom- and particle-smashing devices revealed ever more subatomic particles that theoretical physicists then had to incorporate into the model; or the theorists themselves, in order to account for discrepancies in the model, would think up new particles, or new forces acting on the particles, for which the atom- and particle-smashing devices would sooner or later provide actual evidence.

Some of the most significant discoveries made in this way concerned the structure and behavior of the atomic nucleus. This turned out to consist of two kinds of particles, protons and *neutrons*, clamped together by the action of a hitherto unsuspected force, the "strong interaction"—which itself was carried by the ceaseless exchange among neutrons and protons of yet another particle, the *meson*. Nevertheless, in 1938, Enrico Fermi succeeded in breaking apart some of the relatively large clumps of particles that formed the nuclei of uranium atoms. About ten years later it became clear that the relatively small clumps of particles that formed the nuclei of hydrogen atoms could be forced together, to create larger nuclei. Either way, these processes of *nuclear fission* and *nuclear fusion* involved the conversion of tiny amounts of mass into vast amounts of energy (according to Einstein's principles—p. 578). Furthermore, they released neutrons that would hit the nuclei of neighboring atoms and start the same processes there, initiating *chain reactions* of enormous power. These discoveries led to the atom and hydrogen bombs (pp. 657–658, 661), which make use of *uncontrolled* fission and fusion chain reactions, respectively; and to the use of *controlled* fission in nuclear power stations (p. 687). Scientists still hope to learn how to control fusion reactions, so as to fulfill the dream of cheap, plentiful, and nonpolluting energy.

Recently, the complex picture of particles and forces at work in the atom has been simplified in various ways. In the 1960s, physicists began to suspect that many of the newly discovered particles could be regarded as differing combinations of no more than three still tinier entities—*quarks*, as these perhaps truly basic constituents of matter were christened by one of those mainly responsible for the idea, the American, Murray Gell-Mann. Another American, Steven Weinberg, together with a Pakistani, Abdus Salam (atomic physics long ago ceased to be confined to citizens of the Western countries) showed that two of the forces at work within the atom, electromagnetism and the "weak interaction" among particles outside the nucleus, were in fact one and the same *electroweak* force.

Atomic physicists hope that discoveries such as these are stepping stones toward a "Grand Unified Theory," which in the not too distant future may show that all the various forms of matter and energy in the universe are all manifestations of a very few basic particles and perhaps only a single force. If this is in fact achieved, at least some physicists believe, it will mark the end of a stage in the Western quest for rational understanding of the physical "nature of things" that began in ancient Greece more than twenty-five hundred years ago (pp. 80–81).

DISCOVERING THE MAKEUP OF LIVING ORGANISMS

Similar progress toward what seems like an ultimate explanation of one of the main features of the natural world has been made by scientists investigating the basic structure of *living organisms*, and the ways in which they reproduce and grow. Already in the nineteenth and early twentieth centuries, there had been many advances in this field (pp. 578–579, 580–581). Biologists had found that organisms are built up of cells, and that growth and reproduction take place by means of *cell division*. They had observed that when a cell divides, its central structure, the *nucleus*, dissolves, and threadlike *chromosomes* form, which divide and are then shared between the two new cells. Geneticists had come to believe that characteristics are transmitted from one organism to another by means of *genes*, and that the genes are somehow present in the chromosomes. Chemists had found that cells are made up of some of the same elements, formed in the same way into molecules (although far bigger and more complex) as nonliving matter. They had identified many of the resulting substances, which seemed to be basic building blocks of life—*proteins* and their constituent *amino acids*, as well as two other substances of unknown function within the cell: *ribonucleic* and *deoxyribonucleic* acid (RNA and DNA).

Later twentieth-century researchers assembled these scattered pieces of evidence, and followed where they pointed—and more and more, the researchers found that they were led to the mysterious substances RNA and DNA. By the 1940s, it was known that the molecules of both consist of extremely lengthy strands built up of four basic units or *nucleotides*, the order of which continually varies along the strands. RNA was found mainly outside the nucleus of the cell, and DNA mainly within it—except during cell division, when the nucleus dissolves and the DNA moves to the chromosomes. Experiments with bacteria (p. 579) showed that a bacterial variety with a rough-coated exterior could be *altered* to have a smooth exterior, when "fed" with DNA from a closely related, smooth-coated variety. It seemed, then, that somehow, within its molecular structure, DNA carried the genes, and had the ability to transfer them from one cell to another. But how did it do this?

In 1953, an Englishman, Francis Crick, and an American, James D. Watson, opened the way to answering this question with their famous "double-helix" model of the DNA molecule. It consists, they said, not of one but of two identical strands, interconnected along their lengths and twisted around each other. In the course of cell division, the two strands break apart and untwist, so that each can carry its genes into a new cell. Then, as each strand settles down within the newly formed nucleus, by chemical combination with surrounding substances it produces for itself a new "partner" strand. Thus, these two, in turn, can separate when the time comes, thereby transferring their genes to yet further cells.

On the basis of this insight, *molecular biologists* have been able to build up as full a picture of the inner workings of the living cell as physicists have done with the atom. All of the following are now fairly well understood: the way in which DNA strands sometimes replicate themselves in the slightly different form of RNA; how RNA, in turn, moves outside the nucleus and then combines with surrounding substances to produce different amino acids and proteins; the actual "genetic code"—the different sequences of nucleotides within DNA and RNA that produce different amino acids; and details of the ways in which these processes are speeded, blocked, or altered, so as to foster or discourage cell growth, or to produce different kinds of cells and hence, different living organisms.

THE ADVENT OF HIGH TECHNOLOGY

Ever since the link between science and technology was forged in the nineteenth century, the human race has lived in a state of "permanent" industrial revolution (pp. 557–559). But in the twentieth century, this revolution accelerated as science reached the point of unlocking truly cosmic powers, and technology found ways of harnessing these powers for use (and abuse) by society. The result, from about the middle of the century onward, was an explosion of new types of machines, processes, materials, medicines, and weapons that seemed so marvelous (or so threatening) that as a group they came to be called "high technology."

Of course, the rise of high technology was not the result of scientific advance alone. To translate "pure" scientific knowledge into usable technology takes "applied" scientists and engineers obsessed with technical problems, and corporation executives hungry to stake the biggest claim in new and profitable markets; in the second half of the twentieth century more than in earlier times, it also often took generals and admirals bent on victory in wars or arms races. The fact that the United States had plenty of all three types, as well as massive resources for investment and a massive home market for new products, helped make it, more than any other country, the homeland of high technology.

That, for example, is why the United States led the world in the single most spectacular field of high technology, computers. It was advances in the "pure" mathematical field of information theory that made computers possible, and discoveries in the "pure" science of semiconductor physics that made them cheap and small enough to be everywhere. Generals and admirals, wanting to win the Second World War and then the Cold War, spent the money to "jump-start" many computer technologies at a time when they seemed too risky and unprofitable for private companies. In the 1940s, the United States Defense Department sponsored the first-ever computer in hopes of speeding up the production of mathematical data needed for heavy artillery; in the 1950s, it invested in computer-controlled machine tools that would accurately make complex parts for state-of-the-art warplanes; in the 1960s and 1970s, its scientists developed ways of linking military and government research computers into "interactive networks" that would be so decentralized that not even a hydrogen bomb hit could totally knock them out. And once all these basic technologies had been proved, the engineers and corporation executives moved in. The results were mainframes and desktops, automated factories and "smart" photocopiers, the Internet and the World Wide Web.

At the end of the twentieth century, another, very much older field of technology had been pulled forward by pure science to the point where it was producing just as spectacular results as computers—that of biotechnology. For thousands of years humans have manipulated living things, or products derived from living things, by such processes as selective breeding, cooking, brewing, and distilling. What turned biotechnology into "high technology" was the rise of new methods and processes derived from "pure" biochemical understanding of the living cell as a chemical "factory." In the 1970s an American molecular biologist, Paul Berg, managed to "cut" DNA strands and recombine the pieces in a different order, thereby altering also the order of their nucleotides to produce new types of genes. Many different types of *recombinant DNA* were developed, which could be implanted in the DNA of bacteria to alter their genetic makeup. In this way new strains of bacteria could be created, with the "hereditary" capacity to produce biological substances useful to humans—for example, insulin, an essential medicine for people with diabetes. The result, in the 1980s and 1990s, was the growth of a whole new industry of *genetic engineering.*

In this new industry, "pure" and "applied" science were hard to tell apart, and by the time it arose, the arms race was past its peak. As a result, "pure" scientists were often directly involved in genetic engineering, while generals and admirals played little part in sponsoring it; their place was taken by civilian bureaucrats eager to get a return on government funding for pure science, and by college presidents dreaming of patent royalties from discoveries made by their biochemistry departments. In any case, genetic engineering became a massive industry as computers had before, and early in the twenty-first century it passed an important milestone. In the 1990s, scientists came to realize that for this new industry to reach its full potential, it would be necessary be able to identify the location of the genes in the DNA molecules of various species, ranging from bacteria to mice, that were commonly used in genetic engineering—and also, most ambitiously, of humans themselves. Without this information, genetic engineers were like readers in a library with many stacks, tens of thousands of books, and no catalogue or floor plan. The completion in 2000 of the human "genome mapping" project meant that the catalogue and floor plan were now available to anyone who needed them, though most of the books themselves were still unopened.

THE CHALLENGE TO CONTEMPORARY CULTURE AND BELIEFS

In all these and many other ways, the onrush of discovery brought humanity to previously unsuspected realms of knowledge, while its technological applications transformed daily life. In addition, the rise of science to become the predominant intellectual enterprise of the human race could not fail to affect many other fields of thought and culture—and very often, the result was unsettling.

Partly this was because science (precisely because it was so successful at explaining the material universe) left many other matters all the more mysterious. Human beings, it seemed, could be explained as complex assemblages of molecules that interacted in just the same way as those that made up plastics and dyestuffs. Where, in such an explanation, did such things as consciousness and free will fit in? The universe, physicists hoped, would soon be explained as the outcome of the interactions of a few grandly simple forces and particles. Where, in this explanation, did a creating and intervening God fit in? Earlier mythologies, theologies, and philosophical systems had generally contrived to link the material universe, human consciousness, and religious faith into a single whole; but science, by its very success in explaining the *first* of these things, seemed to shoulder the other two aside.

Moreover, the procedures of science, with its theories that were constantly modified or discarded in the light of new knowledge, and its principles of uncertainty and relativity that explained phenomena in terms of probabilities and the viewpoint of observers, seemed to go against traditional philosophical, religious, and artistic ideals of truth. Even if the physicists realized their dream of a Grand Unified Theory, the total insight into the material universe that it would provide gave little promise of having much to do with the age-old human quest for "ultimate" or "absolute" reality.

Likewise, the achievements of technology were in many ways double-edged. On the one hand, technology enormously increased human freedom and power; on the other, it raised the question whether creatures so used to being at the mercy of each other and the universe as humans could live with all this freedom and power. At the beginning of the twenty-first century, the World Wide Web seemed a kind of symbol of the new freedom—an enormous marketplace where everyone was equal, and where even an ancient and prestigious institution like the British monarchy was just another "vendor," offering its wares of information, entertainment, and products to the passing surfer (*Fig. 15-1*). But the surfer's path from Web site to Web site could be tracked keystroke by keystroke by anyone who had the expertise and equipment to do so, just as the genetic "destiny" of individuals could be tracked nucleotide by nucleotide. Thus, technology also offered the possibility of an ant heap society where individuals were controlled and manipulated—as well, of course, as the threat of environmental disaster or nuclear extinction. In some ways, it made the individual seem even more than before at the mercy of vast impersonal forces in society and the universe.

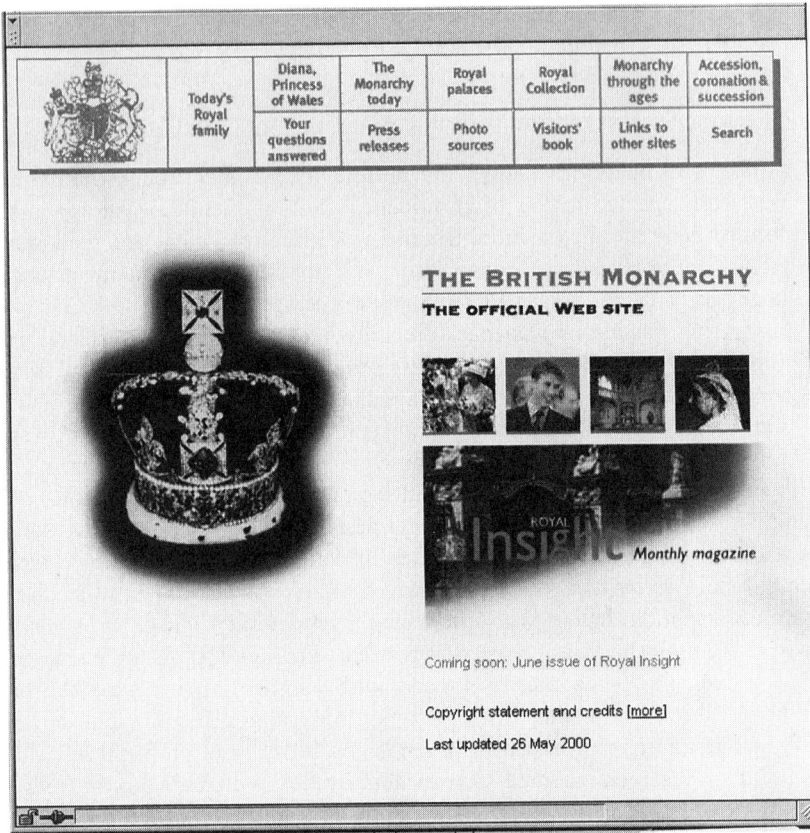

	Today's Royal family	Diana, Princess of Wales	The Monarchy today	Royal palaces	Royal Collection	Monarchy through the ages	Accession, coronation & succession
		Your questions answered	Press releases	Photo sources	Visitors' book	Links to other sites	Search

THE BRITISH MONARCHY

THE OFFICIAL WEB SITE

ROYAL Insight *Monthly magazine*

Coming soon: June issue of Royal Insight

Copyright statement and credits [more]

Last updated 26 May 2000

15-1   The British monarchy's Web site. Even this thousand-year-old traditional institution cannot do without the easy access to the world of mass information and entertainment provided by the Internet.

Of course, many other forces have been at work in the cultural life of the twentieth century besides the onrush of science and technology. But there is no doubt that, alongside the traumatic happenings of this century, science and technology have had a great deal to do with several differing trends in modern culture. Many writers, artists, and architects have glorified scientific and technical mastery in their work; others have abandoned the external world to science and technology, and retreated into an inner world of human consciousness, usually imagined as irrational and subjective; still others have imagined the individual as alone in an indifferent or hostile society or universe. Some philosophers have tried to imitate scientific method, with its gradual approach to limited truth through provisional theories; others have developed the idea of the lonely individual struggling against vast natural and social forces. And many religious thinkers have challenged the idea that science provides the only knowable kind of truth, and continue to proclaim an absolute spiritual truth beyond the material truth of science.

RECONSTRUCTION IN WESTERN PHILOSOPHY AND RELIGION

One of the areas most affected by the onrush of science was philosophy. Many philosophers, impressed by Einstein's *relativity* theory and Heisenberg's *uncertainty* principle (pp. 578, 718) virtually gave up efforts to explain objective "reality." They generally agreed that no such explanation is possible. The two most influential schools of philosophy in the twentieth century were those of the "linguistic analysts" and the "existentialists." The former held that nothing significant could be said about "being in general"; they focused attention, therefore, on limited intellectual problems, especially the applications of symbolic (mathematical) logic. The existentialists (pp. 727–728) insisted that our very humanity prevents us from seeing things *in themselves*.

As in all times of change and upheaval, inherited beliefs and ways died hard. The *idea of progress*, born of the Enlightenment, still persisted—especially in the United States. As we saw in chapter 13, "old-fashioned" *liberalism* in Europe had become discredited by 1919 (p. 623–624); and the void was filled, in part, by Marxism, fascism, or extreme nationalism.

Some disillusioned Westerners turned, or returned, to traditional Christian doctrines. The crimes and horrors of world wars and revolutions heightened their awareness of "evil" and man's "sinful nature"; and their quest for truth beyond the findings of science led them to the centuries-old intellectual system of Christian theology. In response, certain religious leaders—notably, the American Reinhold Niebuhr—rekindled Augustinian teachings (pp. 191–193) and called for a resurgence of orthodoxy and ritualism. Some philosophers, beginning about 1970, went still further, rejecting the Western rationalist heritage altogether. In particular, they saw "Modernism," grounded in the Enlightenment vision of the world (pp. 472–479), as a failure. This approach, called "Postmodernism," found expression in a variety of ways in philosophy, literature, and the arts (p. 752). Their view stresses the principles of uncertainty, pluralism, and experimentation in all fields of knowledge and action.

The Implications of Depth Psychology: Freud

The source of the twentieth-century challenge lay as much in the new psychology as in the new physics: John Locke's simplistic view of the mind (pp. 477–478) was as completely superseded as Newton's mechanics. The major figure of modern psychology was Sigmund Freud, to whom we referred in chapter 12 as a pioneer in the discipline (p. 585). Freud was a practicing physician whose initial interest was in curing the mental ailments of his patients. In the course of his clinical work, however, he discovered aspects of the human mind and personality that had long lain hidden. Freud published his significant *The Interpretation of Dreams* in 1900, but his broader impact on thought was not felt until after the First World War.

Although Freudian psychology has been disputed and amended (especially his views on female sexuality), much of its substance gained acceptance. Freud held that human beings are not rational machines, consciously directing their appetites and will. On the contrary, reason plays a relatively minor and subordinate role in most people, for the conscious life and its expression are but a covering of the "real" person. Beneath the surface are unconscious and subconscious drives, which are the chief engines of motivation; these include the desire for sexual gratification, love, power, and even death. In addition, behavior is influenced by *physiological* responses and acquired attitudes.

Society, Freud wrote in *Civilization and Its Discontents* (1930), compels individuals to *repress* many of their "natural" desires. In a highly organized civilization, these repressions take a heavy toll from the individual; yet without some repression civilization would be impossible. The "normal" person accepts the damage without breaking down, but the neurotic (or psychotic) person cannot do so. The Freudian view of the individual in relationship to society posed a sharp challenge to traditional morals, religion, and politics. All those had rested on a base of supposed rationality and conscious control. According to the new view, those traditions were not geared to psychological reality and might therefore be dangerously false. Freud believed that human personality would suffer even under "enlightened" social codes of behavior, because there exists an inescapable conflict between personal drives and the social order. Hence, "perfectionist" social dreams can never be fulfilled, and the goal of complete individual happiness is a tormenting mirage.

Rejection of Traditional Systems and Values: Nietzsche, Kierkegaard, Sartre

Friedrich Nietzsche, a German philosopher who died in 1900, lived in Freud's time and shared many of his views on human nature. And the impact of both men was most strongly felt in the *twentieth* century. Nietzsche's influence was perhaps wider than Freud's, for he challenged not only the traditional view of human nature but the entire institutional and ideological heritage of the West. When he said, "God is dead," he meant not only the God of the Judeo-Christian faith but the whole range of philosophic *absolutes*, from Plato down to his own day. Because all Western values had been linked to those ultimate "eternal" values, they crashed to earth with "God's death." Facing the void alone, thought Nietzsche, people value but one goal: *power*. Thus would he explain the ceaseless drive for power by individuals and nations.

Nietzsche's most revealing work is his most poetic, *Thus Spake Zarathustra* (1884). In it he allowed his unconscious self to speak freely, without regard to logical organization. The book is a flowing stream of images, symbols, and visions, some of which have not yet been fully understood. In *Zarathustra* and other works, notably *Beyond Good and Evil*, Nietzsche considered the various conditions of human beings and their relation to the universe. He was one of the first thinkers to stress the *absurdity* of human existence: the inability of our reason to comprehend our surroundings—though we are born to try.

All existing systems, whether based on reason or revelation, appeared false to Nietzsche. He focused his attack on the bourgeois civilization of the late nineteenth century: on science, industrialism, democracy, and Christianity. As an untamed *individualist*, he rejected theism (belief in God as Creator and Ruler), mechanism, and any other idea that would deny human *freedom*. What he hated most was the reduction of people to narrowly specialized creatures and their subjection to a Christian ("slave") morality. Nietzsche presented these particular ideas most fully in *The Genealogy of Morals*, published in 1887. He longed for a return to the heroic Greek idea of the "whole man"; this goal could be achieved only by the overthrow of current values and the permitting of determined individuals ("supermen") to recover their wholeness through disciplined struggle and sacrifice. Nietzsche left unanswered many questions as to how these aims could be accomplished. His importance lay primarily in his bold challenge to "sacred" beliefs and in his shrill protest against the smothering of the individual by the "herd."

A thinker of different temperament was Søren Kierkegaard, a Danish theologian-philosopher. Though he was born a generation earlier than Nietzsche, the influence of both was felt at about the same time. Writing from widely separated points of view, they were the forerunners of twentieth-century "existentialism." It was, in fact, Kierkegaard who gave special meaning to the word "existence" (though his works were scarcely read until after the First World War). He defined "existence" as a unique attribute of human beings. They alone exist "outside" nature, possessing the power to *think* about the universe and to *choose* what they will believe and how they will act. This very freedom, thought Kierkegaard, gives individuals both responsibility and anxiety *(angst)*. They must suffer anxiety, for they can never be certain about the consequences of their own free choice.

Kierkegaard, like Nietzsche, attacked the rationalism and determinism of Hegel's philosophy (pp. 527–529). He branded as ridiculous the generalization that the world is rational and that it represents the unfolding of a divine plan. How can any person, a particular part of an uncompleted scheme, know what the completed form will be? If the world *is* a system, only God can know it! It follows, therefore, that people cannot presume that they occupy a specific place in a known scheme of things. One must act, rather, from day to day, as best one can, always *unsure* of the consequences.

Kierkegaard had a profound influence on Christian theologians, but his writings appealed also to individuals of agnostic or atheistic leanings—especially, modern "existentialists." These people were impressed by Kierkegaard's assertion of the individual's nakedness and loneliness in the universe—"condemned to be free." They saw the individual increasingly depersonalized and alienated by the forces of modern society: huge economic organizations, mechanization, bureaucratization, and the high level of abstraction encountered in most phases of living. Following this observation, the existentialists sought to awaken in each person a sense of individuality and the possibility of an "authentic" life.

Jean-Paul Sartre, more than any other writer, brought the existentialist view to the educated public (through *Nausea, No Exit,* and other works). Sartre, partly through his own experience in the French Resistance against the Nazis, came to believe that personal commitment and action are essential to genuine living. He felt this especially during the war, in his daily decision-making and risk-taking. He proved to himself that, even in extreme situations, the individual possesses the *irreducible liberty* of saying "no" to overpowering force. Such a force, Sartre inferred, might be an occupying army—or it might be the conformist cultures in which most of us live (p. 567). The freedom to say "no," even to "disaffiliate" oneself from the system, is the individual's ultimate defense against being swallowed up as a *person*.

Sartre himself in later years severely modified his wartime view of the *degree* of individual freedom. He conceded (as a Marxist) the powerful grip of social conditioning—yet insisted that each individual nevertheless has the ability (and the *responsibility*) to "make something out of what is made of him." Sartre's idea of limited freedom contrasted with the optimistic, rational liberalism of the Enlightenment (pp. 578–579). It was closer to the "tragic view" of the ancient Greek poets and dramatists, who likewise saw pain and absurdity in the human condition, yet held that one remains *responsible* for what one is and does within an established order (pp. 89–91).

REVISION OF CHRISTIAN THEOLOGY: BARTH, TILLICH

The blow to "systems" and "absolutes" in philosophy was paralleled by a rethinking of Christian doctrines. We have seen that Kierkegaard opened the way to philosophic existentialism; he was the pioneer also of profound *theological* changes. A deeply committed Christian, Kierkegaard insisted that rational proofs for the existence of God, promoted by some liberal theologians, were irrelevant. The logic of Aristotle, Aquinas, or Descartes (pp. 468–469) left him unconvinced. In order to become a Christian, asserted Kierkegaard, one must make an inward choice: *a leap into faith*. All other human choices, he insisted, are secondary to that *one*. And that choice must be made without knowledge of whether it will lead to salvation or damnation. Thus, a *true* Christian lives in a kind of despair. (Kierkegaard attacked most modern churches for enjoying and preaching a "comfortable" but counterfeit Christianity—"the *opposite* of what is in the New Testament.")

The leading theologians of the twentieth century advanced, in their own ways, this fundamental view of Kierkegaard's. While respecting the value of reason in connection with scientific and practical affairs, they insisted that it cannot answer the questions of "ultimate concern." Karl Barth, an influential Swiss Protestant theologian, stressed human dependence on God, but concluded that there is no *straight line* from the mind of humans to God: "What we say breaks apart constantly . . . producing paradoxes which are held together in seeming unity only by agile and arduous running to and fro on our part." Rather than preaching that there are compelling reasons for believing in God, religious thinkers like Barth would say: "This community of faith invites you to share in its venture of trust and commitment."

In addition to seeing religious faith as a matter of trust instead of something "objectively" proved, many theologians of the twentieth century sought to reconstruct the ancient symbols and myths. They believed that the traditional Christian *image* of God and the universe had crumbled under the bombardment of scientific findings and historical scholarship. The "vision of reality" expressed in the Bible no longer served as a believable frame of reference for many educated people. They were convinced that if Christianity was to endure as a meaningful teaching, it would have to create images that fitted with scientific knowledge.

To some religious thinkers, this was another way of saying "God is dead." For the German-American theologian Paul Tillich, the phrase meant simply that the ancient image of God had passed into history. This did not mean that Christianity was obsolete, but that it had to find, as it had found in the past, new forms to carry its message to the living. The idea of a Supreme Being—"out there," or "up there"—is not an essential part of Christian truth. Tillich dissented from Barth's view that God lives *outside* humankind; he insisted that God is not a special *part* of creation, but, rather, Ultimate Reality itself. Modern men and women, Tillich suggested in his *Shaking of the Foundations* (1948), must look for God as the *ground of all being*, as the *depth* and *center* of their culture and their lives.

THE MOVEMENT TOWARD UNITY: POPE JOHN XXIII

Though the Protestant churches were more absorbed than the Roman Catholic Church in theological reappraisal, all the major branches of Christianity gave serious attention to closer relations with one another. The period following the Second World War, especially, was marked by a lessening of interfaith hostility and a growing sense of Christian *oneness*. This was due in part to the consciousness that all churches were being challenged, as never before, by secularism in general and Marxism in particular. Religious leaders could see that many people were turning toward agnosticism (no belief) and that a more united front would strengthen the appeal and power of Christianity.

On the Protestant side, an important step was taken in 1948 when the World Council of Churches was formally established at Geneva, Switzerland. One of its primary purposes was to bring some two hundred separate denominations into closer association. It included in its supporting membership most Protestant churches, Anglicans, and Eastern Orthodox groups (pp. 182–184, 406). The Roman Catholic Church held aloof at first but later opened formal relations between the Vatican and Geneva.

The election by the College of Cardinals (p. 280) of Pope John XXIII, in 1958, gave a decisive boost to the movement toward unity. As leader of the largest organized body of Christians, John was in a position to aid greatly, and he did so with the full force of his warm personality. Though he did not abandon the papal claim to being the "one shepherd" of the Christian flock, John broke down centuries-old barriers to communication with Protestants. At the same time he started a sweeping program for *aggiornamento* (bringing the Roman Church up to date). This included a fresh attitude of humility and affection toward the "separated brethren" (no longer "heretics")—and toward "men of good will" beyond the fold (no longer "atheists"). John opened windows and let fresh air into the Vatican, while introducing a new era of hopeful dialogue between the Roman Church and all other Christian groups.

The most complete expression of Pope John's thought and feeling was his encyclical *Pacem in Terris (Peace on Earth)*, issued in 1963. This document, an extraordinary appeal to reason and humane sentiments, called for the harmonious *coexistence* of all faiths and social systems. John's work for peace, both religious and secular, was carried on after his death by Pope Paul VI and the reforming Second Vatican Council (1963–1965). Paul dramatized the new responsiveness of the papacy by breaking its historic confinement to Rome and making visits to such places as the Holy Land, India, Latin America, and the United Nations headquarters in New York. Paul secured friendlier relations with the Eastern Orthodox churches and renounced the traditional Christian hostility toward Jews. On issues of Catholic faith and morals he remained a conservative. His immediate successor (in 1978) was the reputedly liberal John Paul I, but he died unexpectedly within months of becoming pope. In his place the College of Cardinals elected a conservative pontiff, in the mold of Paul VI.

POPE JOHN PAUL II: RENEWAL OF CATHOLIC TRADITIONALISM

The new pope, who took the name of John Paul II, was the first non-Italian elected to the office in over four hundred years. Formerly the archbishop of Cracow, in Poland, he was a learned and appealing figure—known especially for his resistance to the Communist government there. During his long reign as pope, John Paul urged the clergy to uphold *traditional roles and rules*, and he reinforced his advice by appointing bishops of established conservative views. A notable result of this policy occurred in Brazil, the world's largest Catholic country. The leading archbishop there, who had endorsed "liberation theology" (p. 679), was replaced in his position in 1995 by a conservative archbishop—one strongly opposed to social reform in Brazil.

John Paul disappointed many liberal Catholics who were looking for some sign of *change* on such pressing issues as clerical celibacy, the use of contraceptives, and admission of women to the priesthood. On the latter issue, the Anglican Church in Britain and the United States broke with centuries of tradition and ordained women as priests (1993); but the pope remained firmly opposed to the change for the Roman Church.

Though insisting that the Catholic clergy must not hold any *political office*, the pope traveled widely around the world and spoke freely on political issues. He consistently urged national leaders to avoid war, and he approved an important "pastoral letter" of the Catholic bishops of the United States condemning nuclear weapons. Their letter, *The Challenge of Peace*, was sent out in 1983 as a "teaching" of the Church. It opposed *any* "first use" of nuclear arms (p. 691), and it appealed for immediate international agreements to end their testing and production.

John Paul attacked what he called the modern "culture of death," including abortion, "mercy killing," and capital punishment. With respect to relations with other Christian churches, the pope followed the path of Paul VI, pursuing closer ties with the Orthodox churches. In 1995 he hosted a historic meeting at the Vatican with Bartholomew, patriarch of Constantinople (Istanbul), generally recognized as the ranking patriarch of Eastern Orthodoxy. They sought to strengthen their own positions of Church leadership and to work together toward checking the growing influence of Protestantism and secularism. A divisive issue, however, was an ongoing dispute over zones of Christian religious activity. Following the fall of communism, Roman Catholic bishops and missionaries entered the historically Orthodox lands of the former Soviet Union—an intrusion much resented by the patriarchs of those countries.

John Paul established a unique legacy of his reign in March 2000. During the course of the liturgy of the Sunday Mass in St. Peter's Basilica, the seventy-nine-year-old pope offered the most sweeping apology for past sins "by children of the Church" ever publicly expressed. As the new millennium opened, he asked God's *forgiveness* for errors made during the preceding *two thousand years*. He declared that this "purification of memory" was essential as the Church moves forward with its evangelical mission. Though not specifying individual events, he placed them in seven categories: general sins; sins in the service of truth; sins against Christian unity; against the Jews; against respect for love, peace, and cultures; against the dignity of women and minorities; and against human rights.

THE SHIFTING WAYS OF SOCIETY

Religious and philosophical teachings and problems, no matter what their character, did little to alter the continuing *social* revolution in the West. *Technology* was the chief engine of this revolution but psychologists, educators, and advertisers accelerated the rate of change.

THE NEW SEXUALITY

The most visible, and perhaps the most profound, of these changes were new sexual attitudes and practices (the "sexual revolution"). Sex has been a demanding concern in all societies: how to value sex and how to deny, repress, or channel it. Sex can be regarded as any or all of the following: an instinctive impulse, a source of pleasure, the means of creating children, an expression of physical love, the bond of faithfulness in marriage, a sign of gender, and a personal property. Social and moral codes of behavior aim to contain and balance the multiple functions of both male and female sexuality.

During the nineteenth century, while scientific and technological innovations were altering the economy and society in the West (pp. 559–567), religious and civic leaders made a determined effort to prevent changes in traditional sexual mores. Thus, during the "Victorian Age" (1840–1900), a cloak of puritan morality obscured the realities of sexual behavior. It was Sigmund Freud who, by reporting his clinical observations, showed that *sexual repression* could cause psychic illness (p. 726). Freud, by bringing sexuality into the open, revealed it as a normal and powerful force in human behavior.

As the twentieth century progressed, other physicians, psychologists, and educators began to reexamine the human organism and its needs. They challenged all types of authoritarian controls over individuals—not only in sexual matters but in personal behavior as a whole. Traditional taboos began to fall, especially after the two world wars; the age of "permissiveness" and "self-fulfillment" was at hand. With moral, social, and legal restraints loosened, men and women gave freer rein to their instincts for self-gratification. In 1960, scientific medicine gave a liberating boost to worry-free sex: a new means of birth control, the "pill," made sex easy and safe. (In the 1980s, however, the appearance of the AIDS disease—p. 737— brought fresh worries to the sexual scene.)

The sexual revolution was quickly exploited by profit-seeking publishers, theatrical producers, broadcasters, and filmmakers. Sex manuals flourished; no one any longer had to be ignorant. Magazines and books catered to the newly released desire for titillation, and the walls of literary censorship were leveled in nearly every Western nation (p. 742). Pornography, hard and soft, became readily available— in both verbal and pictorial forms. The "ultimate" in pictorial pornography seems to have been reached in X-rated videotapes designed for home use.

Among the sexually provocative magazines, the most respectable and successful in the United States is *Playboy*, first issued in 1953. Its self-made publisher, Hugh Hefner, also built a thriving entertainment business around his magazine— geared to the theme of guilt-free sensual enjoyment. His *Playboy* "philosophy" is a modern form of historic hedonism (p. 82).

The new hedonism reaches, of course, beyond the frontiers of sexuality. Huge industries have been built around the popular hunger for every sort of pleasure. Given good health and sufficient income, people in the West today enjoy limitless opportunities for personal gratification. There is, unfortunately, another and darker side of the pleasures of freedom. This is best exemplified by the widespread consumption of illegal drugs throughout the Western world. The drug problem is now recognized as a serious threat to the health of millions of individuals—and to the functioning of every technological society. It also feeds a related problem: *organized crime*. Although enormous human and financial resources have been marshaled to fight against both drugs and crime, the battle seems far from won. A leading cause of this failure is the stress placed on *personal freedom* within most democratic countries. Though unlawful acts are supposed to be beyond its permitted "limits," the *dynamic* of freedom tends to counter the efforts of law *enforcement*. Thus, many activities ("evils") that "good citizens" deplore—such as drugs, crime, and pornography—are closely linked to freedom itself.

THE YOUTH CULTURE

The changing ways of Western society have had their main effect on men and women born after the Second World War. Their fathers and mothers were, as a rule, too rooted in older ways to alter their own views or behavior. But the immediate postwar generation in most Western countries grew up within a radically different culture. Especially for the middle classes, the postwar period was a time of widespread affluence and leisure. The dominant materialistic morality placed high value on competitiveness, achievement, and "success." As pointed out by the existentialists (pp. 727–728), it was an era of bureaucracy, depersonalization, manipulation, and social "adjustment." All this, moreover, was seen and heard each day in the "instant" world of radio, television, films, records, and tapes.

While parents expected their children to accept these cultural gifts with appreciation—and many of them did—a substantial minority experienced a disturbing sense of *alienation*. Not having to struggle for a livelihood, as most of their Depression-reared fathers and mothers had done, they found more time to reflect on the surrounding culture and their relation to it. These young people found much to object to. Taking for granted the ability of the "system" to satisfy their basic physical needs and pleasures, they saw in its workings a lessening of their personal identity and a great deal of hypocrisy, violence, and injustice.

These perceptions arose at a time when the philosophical and psychological barriers to doubt and idol-breaking had largely dissolved under the influence of thinkers like Freud, Sartre, and Tillich. By the 1960s, many among the postwar generation felt free to move in their own way—toward creating a "counterculture." While uncertain and groping, they appeared to share some central goals: humaneness in personal relations, self-discovery and independence, sexual freedom and equality, simple enjoyments, love of nature and peace. As a badge of these beliefs, the young revolted against adult styles of dress and began to develop styles of their own. The long hair, beards, fatigue jackets, and jeans—so repugnant to older believers in clean-shaven, starch-shirted efficiency and conformity—were symbolic challenges to the established order of values.

By 1970, a new lifestyle was taking shape among many young people across the Western world. It allowed for a wide range of individual differences, but it displayed certain characteristics: an underlying "philosophy," flexibility and informality in family relations, an esoteric ("in") vocabulary, and its own brands of pop music (p. 755). The young tended to be suspicious of governments, corporations, and military organizations. And they often scorned intellectualism in favor of "spontaneous experience."

The freshness of their approach and their willingness to try something new offered promise of creative ideas and remedies where old methods had failed. The parents of this youth, having recovered from their initial shock and disapproval, seemed increasingly to recognize some promise in their children. In the United States, for example, a constitutional amendment was passed in 1971 that lowered the *voting age* from twenty-one to eighteen years.

The youth activity found its focus in colleges and universities; from there it spread, in considerable measure, to the rest of society. Students thus formed a leading part of the larger youth culture, but much of their concern naturally was with the campus environment. Universities had mushroomed after the Second World War. They had become, especially in the United States, vast aggregations of researchers, teachers, and students. They represented hundreds of millions of dollars in capital investment and served as the principal workshops for the production and spread of specialized knowledge. Many students saw their universities as examples of corporate bureaucracy—a huge machine that reduced the individual to a *number*. They perceived the university also as a service center ("multiversity") for the larger society—preparing technicians for business and industry, conducting research for the military establishment, and turning young people into pliable servants of the state. Individual courses and curricular requirements often appeared to them as arbitrary and sterile—lacking in "relevance" to them.

In the 1960s, student discontent was translated into protest—then rebellion—at many educational centers around the world. In the United States, most adults first learned of the crisis through news reports from one of the most distinguished public institutions of learning, the University of California at Berkeley. The "Free Speech Movement" of 1964 sought a larger exercise of student political rights on campus; it also demanded (among other things) that the highly regarded and highly paid professors spend more of their time *teaching students*. Demonstrations, sit-ins, and classroom "strikes" followed in support of these demands.

The protests spread from Berkeley to Columbia, Harvard, MIT, and hundreds of other campuses. "Local" demands often were combined with demands on the nation as a whole: end the war in Vietnam (pp. 676–679), check the power of the "military-industrial complex," stop discrimination against African Americans and other minorities. The student actions were generally led by small numbers of committed radicals, who hoped to bring on a general dislocation and change of the social order. Their immediate demands, however, often had sufficient merit and attractiveness to win the support of "moderate" students as well. When college administrations overreacted, still larger numbers of students joined the action.

Protest fever ran high in 1969 and reached a climax in May 1970, immediately following the United States invasion of Cambodia. In response to student violence at Kent State University (Ohio), National Guardsmen were called in to restore order. During a "clearing maneuver," they shot and killed four students; a few days later, state patrolmen killed two youths in a confrontation at Jackson State College (Mississippi). A severe reaction against the student movement promptly set in. Many Americans were shocked by the killings; others blamed the students for damaging property and thus bringing on the ugly consequences.

After Kent State "the movement" lost much of its force. Most students recoiled from the violent turn it had taken; others became convinced it had reached a dead end; still others thought the "system" had been opened up a bit. Actually, the American student protests of the 1960s seldom achieved great immediate successes. In many instances, however, they gave added force to university self-reform that expanded student rights and benefits.

In Europe, Japan, and Latin America, during these same years, students protested against grossly inadequate facilities and outmoded curricula. They also sought wider power over national affairs. A student revolt in Paris in 1968 very nearly toppled the government of President de Gaulle; strikes and demonstrations had to be forcibly put down in Mexico City and Tokyo. Discontent and protest are by no means novel among university students. But seldom before had protest been linked so closely to the profound alienation of youth from the established culture and order.

In the 1970s college campuses, particularly in the United States, grew peaceful once again. Some observers saw in this a return to the comparative apathy and conformism of the 1950s, but the reality was more complex. Students generally were reacting to the abnormal level of social concern that had marked the preceding decade. They withdrew to more personal concerns: to careers, to greater "inner awareness," to religion, or even to self-centered ways that have been called "narcissistic" (the "me" generation). Students were sobered, too, by the fewer job opportunities, and in the 1980s and 1990s preparing for a "good" *job* became the first concern of a majority of students. But another important reason for their changed attitude and conduct was that most of them now *possessed* the freedoms of lifestyle that previous students had worked for in the sixties.

The Women's Movement

The youth culture, in its core values, was linked to the long tradition of *humanism* in the West (pp. 373–374). And that tradition, in its current expression, supports equality for both young and old—and for both *women* and *men*. It is a cruel yet undeniable historical fact that women have suffered severe deprivation in most civilizations; education and political rights have been withheld from them, and the professions have been generally closed to them. In the United States, after the end of the Civil War (1865), some energetic feminists undertook a long and painful campaign to win equality of opportunity with men. Women gradually moved into jobs in industry, commerce, and education and began to insist on broader legal and political rights. Most notable among their leaders were Elizabeth Cady Stanton and Susan B. Anthony.

Their demand for the right to vote (suffrage) met with strong resistance— from some females as well as males. Opponents charged that the feminine intellect was unable to deal with problems of government and that political equality with men would diminish feminine charm and loosen family ties. But the "suffragettes" pushed on toward their goal. Finally, the politicians responded. Impressed by the contributions of women to the American effort in the First World War, Congress at war's end proposed the Nineteenth Amendment to the Constitution. Eliminating all restrictions on voting based on *sex*, the amendment was ratified by the states in 1920. Since then most other Western nations (and Japan) have extended the suffrage to women, but the female vote, by itself, appeared to make little immediate difference in the course of politics and legislation.

Interest in women's rights in America was subdued for some forty years after approval of the Nineteenth Amendment. But in the 1960s efforts started up again, and by the early 1970s a "women's liberation movement" was in full swing. Social conditions had altered a great deal since 1920: more women were working outside the home, and improved contraceptive devices (as well as more easily obtained abortions) were making it practicable for women to control their traditional role of childbearing.

At first the expanding ideas and goals of feminism were limited to a small number of "emancipated" women; but books, magazines, and the mass media soon aroused the enthusiasm of hundreds of thousands. A key work, *The Second Sex*, by the French author Simone de Beauvoir, called worldwide attention to numerous false assumptions about women. But it was chiefly *The Feminine Mystique*, written by an American, Betty Friedan, and published in 1963, that sparked the popular response. She pointed to the social and psychological pressures that kept women "in the home," the false notions about female sexuality, and the persisting stereotypes of female intellect and behavior. Friedan became a political activist in order to further her cause, founding the National Organization for Women (NOW) in 1966. Another leading activist and author is Gloria Steinem, cofounder of *Ms.* magazine, a popular journal speaking to and for women, especially feminists.

The women's movement—in part organized, in part unorganized—has employed both advocacy and political action. Its leaders demand an end to discrimination in legal rights, education, and jobs. (Moves in 1995 to repeal "affirmative action" programs—pp. 658–686—could lead to the loss of one practical means of correcting gender imbalance in these spheres.) Feminists in the United States achieved initial political success in bringing about the passage in Congress of a proposed "Equal Rights" amendment to the Constitution (ERA); it was submitted to the fifty states for ratification in 1972. Opposition to ERA came from men and women with traditional views, plus some women who feared it might take away from them such existing advantages as exemption from military conscription, protective laws for women in hazardous occupations, and other established legal benefits. The proposed amendment failed (narrowly) to win approval by at least thirty-eight states, as required by the Constitution for adoption. President Ronald Reagan and the Republican party opposed ERA; but the Democratic leaders have supported it, and they reintroduced the amendment in Congress in 1985 and in subsequent years. The ultimate fate of the proposal remains in question.

Feminism embraces a wide spectrum of beliefs about social institutions (like marriage and the family), sexual relations, and lifestyles. But contrary to what is alleged by some critics of the movement, very few feminists desire to *exchange* roles with men. Most of them desire, rather, to open all social roles to *both* sexes. An increasing number of men, for their part, express agreement with this goal and view its achievement as an enrichment of life for themselves as well as for women. In keeping with this growing feeling for sharing, family relations and responsibilities have become more flexible than in earlier times. In fact, the traditional family unit itself is being challenged by variant forms: the one-person household, the childless household, and the single-parent household are rising in numbers.

Probably the most controversial issue affecting American women during the 1980s and 1990s was *abortion*. In most parts of the world abortion is and has been permitted, but in the United States it had been illegal until 1973—though it was in fact widely practiced. In that year, however, the anti-abortion laws of two states, Texas and Georgia, were under challenge in the federal courts—on the grounds that they violated the constitutional protection of a woman's rights. The resulting decision of the Supreme Court, by a 7–2 vote, concluded that no state could prevent a woman from having an abortion during the first six months of her pregnancy. The Texas and Georgia laws were therefore declared invalid, and this principle obviously extended to similar laws in other states as well.

This landmark case (*Roe* v. *Wade*) was hailed by feminists and others as a triumph for a woman's "right to control her own body." But a fierce opposition to the ruling also erupted—from many church groups and individuals who asserted that a fetus is a *person* and therefore abortion is *murder*. They protested actively (under the banner of "pro-life") and were encouraged during the Reagan years to expect changes in the judicial makeup of the Supreme Court. Reagan's conservative appointments to the high bench (p. 697) did bring about a decided shift in its outlook on abortion and other civil rights matters. In a series of cases in 1989 and 1990 the Court reopened the issues raised earlier by *Roe* v. *Wade* and indicated that some state laws relating to abortion could be ruled constitutional. It was even hoped by the anti-abortionists that *Roe* v. *Wade* might be overturned in its entirety. The issue, still controversial, continued to stir bitter debate throughout the nation and has become a critical factor in electoral politics.

Abortion proved to be a prominent issue also at the Fourth United Nations Conference on Women, held in Beijing, China, in 1995. (This influential gathering meets only once every ten years.) Attended by 5,000 delegates from 189 countries, it reflected a worldwide awakening of women to their individual and collective needs. The conference's concluding "Platform for *Action*," approved overwhelmingly, contains a declaration that all women possess the *right* of sexual and reproductive control over their own bodies—as part of the conference stress upon universal human rights. Most of the delegations from Muslim and Roman Catholic states registered their dissents from this particular declaration. However, there was total agreement by *all* delegations on the central thrust of the conference deliberations—demands for the economic and political empowerment of women and their protection from physical violence.

The women's movement, along with growing sexual permissiveness in the West, encouraged the rise of still another social movement—"gay liberation." Homosexuals, historically subject to contempt and abuse, called for the right to live freely according to their own sexual natures. In the 1970s, "gays" (male) and "lesbians" (female) sought changes in laws and institutional practices that would prohibit acts of discrimination against them. Because their aims ran counter to traditional Judeo-Christian moral teachings and ingrained social attitudes, the movement to win public acceptance for sexual diversity encountered fierce hostility. This feeling was intensified in the 1980s by the sudden appearance of a mysterious viral disease that seemed to affect, mainly, homosexual men. Called AIDS (Acquired Immune Deficiency Syndrome), this disease is transmitted through bodily fluids and is usually fatal. In the 1990s, however, the AIDS threat receded in advanced Western societies as drugs to manage the disease were developed, and the general level of tolerance for male and female homosexuality seems to have increased. However, the rise of homosexuals to the status of an organized interest group challenging traditional values and practices has also led to fierce conflicts over such issues as "gays in the military" and hate crime legislation.

BELIEFS IN VIOLENCE AND NONVIOLENCE

The frustrations of youth, women, and other groups outside the "mainstream" gave rise in the 1960s and 1970s to a widespread rejection not only of some institutions but of the accepted ways of *altering* institutions. The liberal-democratic tradition had generally given citizens a healthy respect for "law and order." The principles of "majority rule," "proper channels," and "legitimate authority" had been emphasized by politicians, parents, teachers, and preachers. But in the years of the Vietnam and Middle East wars, some nonconformists began to raise provocative questions: Is it consistent to assert that *individual* or group acts of violence are "senseless" while *governments* spend billions on armaments for the mass killings of "enemy" peoples? Are *laws* necessarily *right*—or are they simply the products of *might?*

The answers to such questions are not self-evident. Some individuals argued that it is the *aim*, rather than the *means*, that is most important in social actions. The use of violence toward a good end, then, would be permissible; its use to defend a bad institution would be condemned. This line of reasoning led to a belief in "acceptable" violence, supported by arguments drawn from the writings of Luther, Jefferson, Marx, Bakunin, and Nietzsche. The belief appealed most directly to the frustrated and despairing person, the adventurous, and the instinctive rebel; its connection with *terrorism* (pp. 692–693) is apparent.

"Idealistic" violence generated its opposite: idealistic *nonviolence*. Nonviolence, whether religious or philosophical, has been for centuries a *way of life* for some men and women (in both the West and East). In the twentieth century this historic practice was modified to serve as the basis for a new method of *social change*. Its advocates were convinced that the use of violence brings on counterviolence, and that even when violence achieves an immediate goal it creates new tensions and problems that perpetuate the chain of inhumane actions and counteractions. The leader of the Indian national independence movement, the deeply religious Hindu, Mahatma Gandhi, saw this truth most clearly and turned to *satyagraha* (militant nonviolence) in order to free his people from British imperialism (p. 668).

Gandhi's ideas impressed the Reverend Martin Luther King Jr. (p. 685). Both Gandhi and King saw nonviolence as the preferred method for all social change. Their idea was by no means one of cowardly "passivity." They urged their followers to strive for social goals through courageous (but nonviolent) action; this often involved acts of *civil disobedience*, which might bring down violence on the "offender." They taught that one must never respond with *hate*; one must try, through feelings of *love*, to win opponents over to a just point of view. Their conviction rests on certain key assumptions: that *everyone* has an inner decency that can be appealed to and that people possess the capacity to live together nonviolently.

The principle of nonviolence, though it lost some support among African Americans in the early 1970s, appeared to gather strength within the youth culture of the time. When, during the Nixon administration, the cycle of force-counterforce-repression appeared to have stalled the protest movement on college campuses (pp. 734–735), some students began to feel that nonviolent methods were the *only* effective way of resisting "the system." These methods include refusal to register for or serve in the armed forces. Between such commitments to nonviolent action, on one side, and resorts to violence, on the other, stand the large majority of youth—and most older citizens as well.

FRESH DIRECTIONS IN LITERATURE AND THE ARTS

Literature and art were parts of the twentieth-century transformation of Western society, thought, faith, and action. We saw in chapter 12 how writers and artists reacted to the impact of machine civilization during the nineteenth century (pp. 585–589). Some mirrored society; some wanted reform; still others turned inward upon themselves. In every age the arts are intimately involved in the life of the times, and as they respond to events they in turn influence events.

THE SEARCH FOR A NEW LANGUAGE OF EXPRESSION: JOYCE, ELIOT

"Contemporary" literature may be thought of, roughly, as that written since the First World War. (We noted in chapter 13 that the year 1914 marked a crucial divide in the course of Western civilization—pp. 623–624.) The decades that followed brought radical innovations in the *forms* of writing; the *content* brought daring new insights into the human condition.

The key element in this literature was its emphasis on *subjectivity*. As in modern psychology, philosophy, and religion, the tendency was away from seeing the individual as an object geared to an orderly and purposeful environment. The new view held that everyone is unique and can be comprehended only through one's *internal* experiences. Authors felt, therefore, that they must assume a position quite different from the traditional one.

Before the First World War, most writers controlled their stories from the *outside*, furnishing dialogue and action for their characters. This technique seldom stressed the subjective life. New-style authors desired to penetrate more deeply the *minds* of their characters, to enter into the characters' private thoughts. The reader, then, also became intimate with their internal experiences. The effect was sometimes accomplished by the "stream-of-consciousness" technique, in which the author puts down words in the way in which ideas appear in the mind; the result is a running jumble of sense and nonsense, a mixture of past, present, and future.

Numerous literary experiments were tried in the endeavor to communicate "inner truth." In many of these, set plots and well-developed characters are missing. The traditional models of dramatic structure are abandoned as artificial. The moment-by-moment, *existential* reality is all. As one modern critic has commented,

> Recent novelists tend to explore rather than arrange or synthesize their materials; often their arrangement is random rather than sequential. In the older tradition, a novel was a formal structure composed of actions and reactions which were

finished by the end of the story, which did have an end. The modern novel often has no such finality.

James Joyce was a pioneer of the new literature. Born in Dublin, Ireland, he abandoned his homeland and his Catholic faith to live on the European continent. He made *himself* the subject of his work, and by examining his own experience he sought to understand the general human problems of his times. In A *Portrait of the Artist as a Young Man* (1916), he drew on the first twenty years of his life.

The hero of Joyce's novel, Stephen Dedalus, struggles with major crises during his youth. In early years he is indoctrinated with religion, and a love affair at sixteen brings on a period of tormented guilt feelings. During his years in college, Stephen at last abandons religion, turns his back on conventional society, and takes up the artistic life. His departure from Ireland is also a symbolic rejection of his cultural heritage and a seeking for goals and forms of his *own* making. The escape does not bring him contentment; it is only the beginning of a lonely and bitter search. In his story Joyce deals hardly at all with action but presents an association of words that flow through consciousness.

In his later works, notably *Ulysses* (1922), Joyce continued to draw from his personal experience. In doing so, he developed further his unusual use of language. In its complexity and obscurity his writing reflects the loneliness and alienation felt by many artists (and others) of the time. He was an inspiration to authors of his own and later generations. Many of them, using a variety of styles, have explored his method of "interior monologue." One of the most successful was the Frenchman, Marcel Proust, famous for his *Remembrance of Things Past* (1913–1927). This seven-volume novel draws upon Proust's detailed recollections of figures in fashionable society that he had known in Paris around the turn of the century.

Another who experimented in similar fashion was Virginia Woolf, a distinguished English literary critic and author. In one of her best novels, *To the Lighthouse* (1927), she followed Joyce's "stream-of-consciousness" technique as a means of revealing the interior complexity of her characters. Woolf also used her writing skills to advance the cause of "equal opportunity" for *women*—for education and careers. Her views are eloquently set forth in a book-length essay, composed in the form of a "lecture" for college girls. She entitled it A *Room of One's Own* (1929), a unique and challenging blend of autobiography and advocacy.

Some leading authors of the times followed traditional methods of writing. The brilliant Englishman, Aldous Huxley, was one of these. He turned his talent to numerous topics; one was the "future" society. In his novel, *Brave New World* (1932), Huxley reveals a "probable" world to come, based on the rapid strides in the physical and social sciences. He sees a *world* state—achieved, at last, as the only means of avoiding suicidal nationalistic warfare. And to eliminate conflicts *within* the society, he sees the planned use of genetic engineering, social conditioning, easy sex, and safe drugs. Efficiency and "happiness" are the goals of this future society—at the cost of losing individuality, dissent, and struggle. Another "anti-utopia" of the period is a gloomier novel by another Englishman, George Orwell's *Nineteen Eighty-Four*. Published in 1949, it is the prophecy of a future society built on *totalitarian* lines, one even more repressive than that of *Brave New*

World. It uses psychological terror, rather than pleasure, as the primary means of social control.

In the Soviet Union, where totalitarianism was a fact, not a prophecy, some great literature appeared in the tradition of Dostoevsky and Tolstoy (p. 534). Notable is Boris Pasternak's *Dr. Zhivago* (1957), an epic historical novel about Russia before, during, and after the Communist revolution, for which Pasternak was awarded the Nobel Prize for Literature. (The novel was also made into a memorable film.) Another giant is Aleksandr Solzhenitsyn, a voice of furious dissent against totalitarianism (pp. 632–633). He first became known for his gripping novel, *One Day in the Life of Ivan Denisovich* (1962). It draws upon the author's experience as a prisoner in a Russian labor camp, and highlights the struggle of one individual to uphold his personal spirit against determined efforts to crush it. Solzhenitsyn won the Nobel Prize for Literature in 1970.

Several writers of Latin America emerged during the twentieth century as world-admired figures. One was Jorge Luis Borges of Argentina, whose works of erudite fantasy (mainly short stories) are intriguing, though above the grasp of many readers. More accessible are the writings of the Colombian, Gabriel García Márquez. His best-known book is *One Hundred Years of Solitude* (1967). In this tale of a single fictional community, he encapsulates the essence of the total Latin American historical experience since the Conquest, including war, corruption, isolation, poverty, love, hope, and disappointment. In accomplishing this feat, the author makes effective use of "magic realism," a literary device employed by a number of recent writers. Supernatural events occur alongside natural events; "flashbacks" from the long past take place as if in the present. Nonetheless, the novel holds together convincingly; García Márquez was awarded the Nobel Prize for Literature in 1982.

In the United States some of the finest prose writing of the century was that of Edith Wharton. Among her numerous works, the best-known are her romantic, ironic novel, *Ethan Frome* (1911), which takes place in rural New England, and *The Age of Innocence* (1920), set in her native New York City. This novel focuses upon the wealthy upper class of society and describes in rich detail its strict code of customs, dress, and manners. Underlying these, Wharton exposes the universal conflict between *peer pressure* to conform and the individual's own aspirations. For this sensitive work, she was awarded the Pulitzer Prize for Fiction in 1921.

Another modern master of prose is John Updike, who also possesses extraordinary social and psychological insights. His *Couples* (1968) reflects the intimate lives of well-to-do suburbanites, with heavy attention to sex; his four-volume series, starting with *Rabbit, Run* (1960), reflects the private lives of middle-class Americans caught up in the "success" ethic. More radical in his reactions to contemporary culture is Joseph Heller. His *Catch 22* (1961) is a hilarious story about some eccentric airmen in the Second World War. *Something Happened* (1974) treats peacetime frustrations in personal affairs and in working for a large business corporation with insight and humor.

The major *poet* of the recent period was the American-born T. S. Eliot, who, like Joyce, became an expatriate. Eliot found his spiritual home in England and deep meaning in the Christian religion. The writings of Eliot, like those of Joyce, are self-searching and rich in symbols and imagery.

Eliot moved to London in 1914 and soon began to write poems and literary criticism. His early works reflect a profound disenchantment with modern civilization, a sense of its emptiness and sterility. "The Love Song of J. Alfred Prufrock" (1917) was followed by other poems in the same mood, notably "Gerontion," "The Waste Land," and "The Hollow Men." These are scholarly works, full of echoes from the literary past. With subtlety and sensitivity, Eliot stripped bare the corruption within Western culture. These "confessional" poems blame the breakdown on the loss of religious spirit; after Eliot's confirmation in the Anglican faith, he began to write more cheerfully about the human condition. If the waters of God's grace have dried up within us, he said, we must discover how to make them flow again. In a bid to reach a wider public, he turned to the theater; his most successful dramatic work, a modern "morality" play, is *Murder in the Cathedral* (1935). Other American poets—who chose to remain in their native land—included the gifted Robert Frost, who gave sympathetic expression to the charms and hopes of America.

Drama, like prose and poetry, came under subjectivist and experimentalist influences. Such notable playwrights as Eugene O'Neill, Tennessee Williams, and Arthur Miller dealt with ancient themes in new ways; they did not hesitate to alter methods of staging, as well as plot, form, and dialogue. The "theater of the absurd" reflected meaninglessness and the failure of human communication. The Irishman Samuel Beckett was perhaps the best known of the "absurdists." In *Waiting for Godot* (1948), his characters find themselves trapped in a nonsense world of neither "logic" nor "decency." Theatrical producers in the late 1960s pressed experimentation still further, including the novelty of having nude characters on stage (notably, *Oh, Calcutta!* and *Hair*).

A trend common to all forms of literature in the last decades was the steady sloughing off of *restraint*. Legal censorship of books and plays diminished in most Western countries, while reader resistance was shattered by rising shocks to traditional sensibilities. Each adult was thought to be the sole and proper judge of what he or she would see or hear. Thus, the once-suppressed writings of authors who dealt frankly with sexual themes, like D. H. Lawrence and Henry Miller, became readily available—as did later works containing sex and violence like those of Norman Mailer, Philip Roth, and Jerzy Kosinski. The Scandinavian countries generally took the lead in relaxing censorship. The Danish parliament, in an unprecedented act of 1969, authorized the printing of *any* sort of literature intended for adults.

The twentieth century brought three entirely *new* means of expression to world culture: the motion picture, radio, and television. Producers of motion pictures drew on most of the established arts, including writing, drama, music, and photography; but what they created was a *unique* art form. As a product of technology, this form seemed perfectly suited to the new era. It was associated with rapid movement and possessed virtually limitless capabilities (not always utilized). From experimental beginnings prior to the First World War, films grew into an immensely popular medium of entertainment. They are truly *international* in character, with writers, directors, and actors coming from many cultures. But the largest single source of filmmaking is in the United States (chiefly, Hollywood). Motion pictures have been generally subject to censorship, but by the 1980s restrictions in most Western countries had become minimal.

Radio broadcasting was developed during the 1920s, offering a flexible and powerful new dimension in the field of communications. It has flourished worldwide, featuring information programs and music of all types. However, radio has been overshadowed since about 1940 by still another new medium: television. In some respects, TV is a *projection* of motion pictures, but it has special capabilities that give it enormous influence on its own. Millions of viewers in Western nations faithfully watch the daily "soaps," talk shows, and "sit-coms"; and most persons now rely mainly upon television for "news" and for watching sports events. This medium has also become a prime carrier for commercial advertising—and has revolutionized the conduct of political campaigns in democratic countries.

THE PRIVATE WORLD OF PAINTERS AND SCULPTORS: PICASSO, MOORE

Artists in the purely *visual* arts, like painting and sculpture, expressed many of the same feelings and ideas that moved the serious novelists and poets of recent times. The artistic protests of the late nineteenth century (pp. 585–589) became a storm of rebellion as the twentieth century proceeded.

15-2 Pablo Picasso. *The Guitarist,* 1903. Oil on panel, 48″ × 32″. The Art Institute of Chicago, Helen Birch Bartlett Memorial Collection.

15-3   Pablo Picasso. *Un violon accroché au mur*, 1913. Oil on canvas, 26″ × 20″. Museum of
Fine Arts, Berne, Switzerland.

Pablo Picasso, a Spaniard who made his home in France, is the giant of modern art. His productive life spanned the major developments in art since Paul
Cézanne and Vincent van Gogh (pp. 588–589). A gifted draftsman, trained at the
Barcelona Academy of Fine Arts, Picasso began painting in a fairly conventional
manner. *The Old Guitarist*, produced in 1903, illustrates his early interest in portraying the poor, the outcast, and the alienated *(Fig. 15-2)*. Through his distortion
of bodily contours and his careful attention to composition, Picasso quickly
achieved mastery of the Expressionist style (p. 589). But he moved restlessly on
through successive experiments (he called them *discoveries*). From Cézanne he took
the idea of building *solidity* into his works, of reducing natural subjects to their
basic "cubes, cones, and cylinders." Picasso thus became a leading exponent of
"Cubism," perhaps the most fruitful movement in painting during the first half
of the twentieth century.

Though it appeared in numerous varieties, Cubist art involved essentially a
breaking down and *reordering* of nature. For example, in Picasso's treatment of a violin *(Fig. 15-3)*, he not only has taken the instrument apart; he shows the parts at
whatever angle and in whatever degree of distortion he desires. More correctly, he
projects onto the canvas his own thoughts and feelings about a violin, about

15-4   Pablo Picasso. *Guernica, 1937.* Oil on canvas, 11'6" × 25'6". Museo del Prado, Madrid.

handling and looking at it. At the same time, he arranges the pictorial elements in an aesthetically pleasing composition. The finished work, then, is Picasso's private, disciplined response to the *idea* of a violin. Like Joyce's literature, Picasso's painting is *radically subjective,* personal, unique: it is not a copy or an imitation of something, but a *special creation* of the artist.

Such inward creations have not been easily understood by the general public. If alienation influenced artists to paint private and secret visions, such paintings only lengthened the distance between them and the public. But informed and sensitive viewers were able to grasp Picasso's intent. They understood, too, that his technique could be more than a visual reduction of objects to geometrical forms; it might also reflect the breaking down of traditional culture and values. The latter possibility is starkly displayed in Picasso's *Guernica (Fig. 15-4),* a commemoration of the bombing of a small town during the Spanish Civil War (1937). The fascist general Francisco Franco (p. 655) had used German bombers in a terror raid against the civilian population. (The attack was a prelude to the mass killings of the Second World War.) Picasso, who was both antifascist and antimilitarist, responded by painting this large canvas (twelve by twenty-six feet) in black, white, and gray. It is a masterful protest—using techniques of Cubism and Expressionism—against the indiscriminate and hideous character of modern war.

Social protest, however, has seldom been the motive of contemporary painters. They were generally absorbed in problems of their craft, especially the problem of form. Since the Second World War the principal trend has been "abstractionism"—work completely divorced from any objective model. A Russian, Vassily Kandinsky, had begun to paint such works as early as 1911. His researches into the psychological properties of color, line, and shape led him to conclude that a "pure" art, not connected with representation, could be developed. This would be *visual* art on its own terms, corresponding to the purely *auditory* art of music.

Though the new idea took various forms, perhaps the most exciting was "Abstract Expressionism." This combined spontaneity with nonobjectivity and was

15-5   Henry Moore. *Recumbent Figure*, 1938. Green stone, 4'6" high. Tate Gallery, London.

most forcefully advanced by an American, Jackson Pollock. Pollock used unorthodox techniques in order to express most fully his vigorous feeling for lines, shapes, and colors. He preferred to begin painting with no pattern in mind, allowing one stroke to lead to another and responding almost subconsciously to his strong inner feelings. He spoke of his designs as *creating themselves*; he did not know what the final appearance would be while he was "still in the painting." In order to achieve desired effects, Pollock sometimes worked from a scaffold—pouring, spraying, and dripping his paints on a large canvas below—often achieving a hauntingly beautiful effect, as in his *Lavender Mist* series (*Color Plate C8*). His techniques were regarded as extreme by some of his fellow artists; others moved beyond him in even freer uses of pigment and plastic materials. These experimental efforts, some sincere and some for sensationalism, created an "art of the absurd."

Less absurd, perhaps, in the public view, was a passing style that attracted considerable attention from the 1960s until about 1990. It was called "Pop Art," and represented somewhat realistically "everyday" objects. This effort was chiefly a reaction to the mass "consumer culture" of the times—a reaction that appeared more negative than positive. But the works, displaying subjects like a soup can, a toilet seat, or the portrait of a pop celebrity (in caricature) succeeded in drawing substantial notice for a period. The best known of these creators of such works was an American, Andy Warhol, formerly a commercial artist. "Pop Art," however, caused no more than a ripple in the broader art movements of the twentieth century.

15-6   Henry Moore. *Nuclear Energy*, 1965–1966. Bronze. 10′ high. University of Chicago, Illinois. Commemorating the first controlled nuclear chain reaction at The University of Chicago.

As in painting, the general trend in sculpture was away from traditional forms of representation. Considered the greatest modern sculptor, the Englishman Henry Moore is comparatively conservative in this respect. Many of his figures, though distorted, do suggest a *subject*. His primary interest, however, lies in the *materials* and *forms*. One of Moore's best-known works is his *Recumbent Figure*, done in 1938 (*Fig. 15-5*). The figure suggests the idea of woman, or femaleness; but it is at the same time a remarkably fashioned *stone* creation. The sculptor, by freeing himself from the requirement to reproduce naturalistic details, can concentrate on curves, texture, and the balance of masses.

In 1967 Moore produced a most unusual work, in cast bronze. His *Nuclear Energy* monument (*Fig. 15-6*) was created to mark the twenty-fifth anniversary of the world's first nuclear (atomic) "chain reaction"—a scientific feat that led to the making of the atomic bomb (p. 719). The sculpture, ten feet tall, is located near the site of the event, on the campus of the University of Chicago. Moore's design cleverly *combines* the shape of an exploding atomic cloud with a human skull.

15-7   Alexander Calder. *La Grande Vitesse*, 1969. Steel plate. Grand Rapids, Michigan.

The American sculptor Alexander Calder also took a novel approach to three-dimensional abstract form. He was the first sculptor to design works that *moved*, called *mobiles*. Typically, Calder linked together components of wire and flat pieces of carved metal and suspended them (usually from a ceiling) in a carefully balanced assembly. He preferred "natural" movement to mechanical means; his mobiles are usually activated by air currents or a slight touch. Thus, space and motion, rather than mass, dominate in his sculptures—transmitting a *kinetic* (moving) sensation to viewers as they watch the ever-changing assembly.

Calder, schooled in mechanical engineering, also found that he could construct *static* forms that transmit a feeling of motion. His *stabiles*, sometimes designed as large outdoor sculptures, project a sense of movement—and they change continually in appearance as the viewer walks around them. A splendid example is the Calder centerpiece for the civic plaza of Grand Rapids, Michigan: *La Grande Vitesse* (Fig. *15-7*). Completed in 1969, it consists of giant, curved steel plates linked together in dynamic (energetic) unity of form.

15-8   Frank Lloyd Wright. "Falling Water" (Kauffman House), Bear Run, Pennsylvania, 1936.

TECHNOLOGY IN ARCHITECTURE: WRIGHT, GROPIUS

Architecture was affected far less than painting and sculpture by the philosophical and psychological currents of recent decades. This was due, no doubt, to the generally *utilitarian* (service) character of architecture. Yet there have been striking innovations, spurred by the availability of new materials of construction. The twentieth century is one of the great ages of architecture.

Contemporary building is notable not only for its unprecedented quantity but for its distinctive *styles* as well. Architecture in the nineteenth century had been a mixture of "revival" styles, none of which came from the spirit or technology of the times (pp. 537–538). During the 1890s a number of designers in Europe and America began to express dissatisfaction with the state of architecture. They pointed to the contradiction in putting up a structure by modern engineering methods and then covering it with a façade (facing) of "historical" ornamentation. They also complained about the mediocre workmanship of the façades, for *craftsmanship* in building declined sharply during the Industrial Revolution.

Frank Lloyd Wright, an American, was the pioneer of a new architecture. He concluded that the machine was here to stay and that the crafts could not be rescued. One should break entirely, he declared, with the forms and decorations of the past. One should try to utilize whatever kind of beauty the machine is capable

15-9   Walter Gropius. Bauhaus, Dessau, Germany, 1926–1927.

of producing and allow *"form* to follow *function."* An authentic (true) style is one that provides the kind of space suited to a particular kind of human activity (work, rest, or play); its beauty will lie in the character of the building materials themselves. Because his structures were designed around the needs and desires of the individuals who occupied them, and because they preserved the natural appearance of the materials, Wright called his style "organic."

Wright began building residences at the turn of the century. In order to maximize the free flow of space inside and to join that space with its natural surroundings, he made effective use of the "cantilever" method of construction. The cantilever, an outgrowth of the post-and-lintel method of the ancient Greeks (p. 92), provides for an *unsupported extension* of the horizontal members. Traditional construction materials, like stone, wood, or cement, can be used only in a limited way as cantilevers. But steel or ferroconcrete (concrete reinforced by steel rods or mesh) can be boldly employed in this method of building.

Wright's "Falling Water" (1936) is a spectacular example of organic architecture using cantilevered elements *(Fig. 15-8).* This home, built over a rustic waterfall, appears to grow out of its surroundings. Inside the house, free space and a sense of contact with nature are maintained. While Wright is especially respected for his designs of private dwellings, he also created impressive structures for public and industrial uses.

Outside the United States, leading architects were deeply impressed by Wright's "functional" ideas. Perhaps the most influential among them was a German, Walter Gropius. He designed his school of art and architecture (the Bauhaus, at Dessau) according to the new principles *(Fig. 15-9).* Though it appears commonplace today, it caused spirited controversy when it was built in 1926. Gropius,

15-10   Mies van der Rohe. Seagram Building, New York, 1958. Ezra Stoller © ESTO.

like Wright, emphasized that attention to function is the first principle of architecture; a good *design* in an object (no matter what it is) ensures its *beauty*. His
Bauhaus became a model of what today is called the "international" style. Especially as applied to large buildings—factories and offices—this style aptly expresses the precision and efficiency of the machine age.

The most brilliant architect in the international style was the German-
American, Ludwig Mies van der Rohe, who held that function alone is not enough
to assure beauty. His stunning skyscrapers please the eye because of their balanced

15-11   Le Corbusier. Notre-Dame du Haut, Ronchamps, France, 1951–1958.

proportions, richness of materials, and painstaking details. His shimmering glass walls hang upon frames of cantilevered steel. Van der Rohe's masterpiece, the Seagram Building in New York *(Fig. 15-10)*, has been appropriately described as "dignified, sumptuous, severe, sophisticated, cool, consummately elegant architecture for the twentieth century and for the ages."

In lesser hands the "glass box" of the international style was often undistinguished and monotonous. In recent years this decline led to a turning away from that mode and a searching for more imaginative, if less efficient, designs (a move sometimes referred to as "Postmodernism", see p. 725). The French-Swiss architect Le Corbusier produced some striking examples of an architecture that appears to *reject* the machine. His mountain chapel near Ronchamps, France, completed in 1955, is startling and mysterious in its sculptured masses *(Fig. 15-11)*. Lacking in symmetry or evident plan, its interior suggests a primitive sacred cave.

Numerous other architects subordinated function to interesting forms; one of them is the Brazilian Oscar Niemeyer, whose glass-crowned cathedral (1961) is among the number of marvelous structures he designed for his country's new capital of Brasilia *(Fig. 15-12)*. Still others applied the freer design principles to utilitarian buildings. Outstanding was the Finnish-American Eero Saarinen. He is best known for his design of *airports*. An airport combines enormously complex movements of people, ground transport, and aircraft. Most world travelers are familiar with Saarinen's TWA Building (1961) at Kennedy International, near New York, and his Dulles International, near Washington, D.C. In the capital itself stands a superb achievement by the Chinese-American architect, I. M. Pei. This building (1978, *Fig. 15-13*) is an intricately designed annex to the National Gallery of Art,

15-12   Oscar Niemeyer. Cathedral, Brasilia, Brazil, c. 1956.

15-13   I. M. Pei. Interior, National Gallery addition, Washington, D.C., 1978.

which was built a generation before. Notable for its skylight illumination of the masterpieces it houses, the structure is prominent among Pei's many creations. Each of these named architects has one thing in common with Wright and the internationalists: they all abandoned the backward-looking imitativeness of the nineteenth century and committed themselves to an architecture that is *modern* in both spirit and materials.

Novel Patterns of Tonality and Rhythm: Schönberg, Stravinsky

The changes that swept through the visual arts around the turn of the century affected music as well. Romanticism continued to dominate concert and operatic performances (pp. 538–539); a leading composer carrying forward this musical style was the Russian, Sergei Rachmaninoff. Other composers, however, began to embrace new aims and methods. Some turned to Impressionism, which was inspired in part by the movement in painting (pp. 588–589). Musical Impressionism, as developed by the Frenchman Claude Debussy, was anticlassical as well as antiromantic. It sought to record the composer's fleeting responses to nature (clouds, sea, moonlight). Departing from traditional patterns of melody, tone scales, and rhythms, Debussy's music has a dreamy, shimmering quality.

As in painting, Impressionism in music was followed by Expressionism. Expressionist composers were not interested in responding to their environment; they sought, rather, to record musically their inmost, even subconscious feelings. (This motive corresponded to the literary subjectivism of Joyce—p. 740.) Viennese composer Arnold Schönberg was one of the earliest Expressionists. Just before the First World War he turned from the large orchestral productions of the nineteenth century and began writing string quartets and other forms of chamber music (p. 493). Abandoning tonality, Schönberg stressed melodic distortion and the chance coincidence of notes—often producing a harsh dissonance. Later in life he adopted a unique tone scale of his own invention. Musically, Schönberg was not unlike van Gogh or Picasso (pp. 590, 744–745) in seeking vigorous and disturbing means of expression.

Contemporary composers, like painters or sculptors, freed themselves from the traditions of their craft and chose whatever musical elements they wished. The result was an unbounded diversity of individual styles. One of the best known and most successful of the moderns was Russian-born Igor Stravinsky. Younger than Schönberg, he, too, worked with established forms before discarding them. He also decided to ignore public tastes (as the painters had done) and to write "abstract" music to suit his own ideas. The chief characteristics of his mature works are stress on polyphony, free use of dissonance, and quickly changing rhythms.

In popular culture the Broadway-type "musical" proved highly successful in the United States and Europe. The leading geniuses of this entertainment medium were three Americans: Frederick Loewe, Alan Jay Lerner, and Cole Porter; their most acclaimed productions included *My Fair Lady*, *Camelot*, and *Kiss Me, Kate*. (These live shows were also adapted for films and sound recordings.)

The most original American contribution to world music, however, was *jazz*. Europeans, who had been creators and exporters of classical compositions for centuries, became eager *importers* of jazz. African rhythms are the foundation of this musical innovation, which flowered chiefly among the talented writers and musicians of black America. But the principal feature is its unending novelty and the improvisations of its interpreters; among the greatest of these were the prolific composer-conductor, "Duke" Ellington, and the trumpet-playing "Ambassador of Jazz," Louis Armstrong. A brilliant white composer, George Gershwin, created a unique blend of jazz rhythms and classical styles. He is best remembered for his piano *Rhapsody in Blue* and the folk opera, *Porgy and Bess* (first performed in 1935). More than any other type of artistic expression, jazz seems to incorporate the spirit of rebellion against traditional forms and restraints. It is plainly an antidote for the tensions and frustration that are a part of contemporary living.

Rock music, which first became popular in the 1960s, has a similar appeal. It grew out of black "rhythm and blues" and white "country" music, but it is a unique form. Rock is directed mainly to young adults; its sensual beat, electronic amplification, and frank lyrics excite audiences around the world. By means of the mass media, it quickly created idols (and legends) like Elvis Presley, John Lennon, and Michael Jackson. The power of rock was further extended in the 1980s through another new art form: music video (MTV).

THE END OF THE BEGINNING: A NEW AGE OF HUMANITY

Music and the arts furnish strong proofs that Western civilization has entered a new age. Some writers use the word "postmodern" to describe it. But that term does not suggest the magnitude of change that has occurred since 1914 in the West (and elsewhere). *The new age marks a break with the past as decisive as that between precivilized and civilized times.* The lessons of the past, though still valuable as guides for the present and future, must be *adapted* to radically altered realities. Humans now stand on the threshold of a different world—one largely of their own making and subject, in substantial measure, to their own control.

THE RADICAL MUTATION IN HUMAN CULTURE

Today, literature, arts, philosophy, and religion show a disconnection from the past in both form and content. Also, varying types of "mixed" economies have largely displaced both laissez-faire capitalism and centrally planned systems. In international relations, the growing self-awareness of non-Western peoples is challenging the domination of the West, while some Western nations are moving toward the lessening of ethnic chauvinism and the development of "ethnic diversity" and "multiculturalism" within their own societies.

Overall, the particular features of individual nations are growing more and more alike. The impact of the global *economy* has already been discussed (pp. 560–561). That fact has promoted an increasingly global *culture*—affecting habits of dress, food, drink, and general lifestyles. Prominent symbols of all this are the omnipresent McDonalds and Coca Cola in towns and cities around the world.

But the distinctiveness of today's civilization arises from more than shifts in patterns and relationships. Totally *new* elements have emerged in human culture. One is *acceleration* itself: changes on every side are moving ahead, it appears, by *geometric* progression. Before a given problem can be identified and addressed, the problem is altered or obscured by new problems. People of no previous era have faced the prospect of living in a cultural *centrifuge*.

The machine, originally a simple tool, is in large part responsible for this bewildering rate of change. The ultimate impact of computers and genetic engineering, as well as countless other developments in technology such as organ transplants, weather management, synthetic chemistry, lasers, and controlled nuclear energy, can hardly be imagined. Perhaps the most fitting symbol of the possibilities of the modern age is that televised instant in 1969, shared by millions of people around the world, when an earthling first set foot on the moon. "That's one small step for a man," declared the astronaut Neil Armstrong, "one giant leap for mankind." No one can predict how far space searches will go or what they may discover; science fiction is fast becoming reality. Meanwhile, notwithstanding the end of the Cold War, the destructive products of science still threaten the very existence of this unique planet. Nuclear, radiological, chemical, and bacteriological weapons have passed the level of overkill—and their use could cripple or destroy most of life on earth.

THE CHALLENGE OF SURVIVAL AND MASTERY: A SUMMARY

The new age thus confronts *Homo sapiens* with a profound challenge: Can humans preserve themselves from self-destruction? Can they use their new powers to create a more satisfying life for themselves? Having overcome nature, humans must now overcome many of their *own* values and institutions. History has been marked by endless competition and warfare, but it now appears that humans must learn to *cooperate* in order to *survive*.

War remains the most immediate but not the sole threat to existence. Exploding population, if unchecked, may outrun the supply of food and other life-supporting elements. The air, water, earth, and sea are falling to levels of sterility and pollution that may prove fatal to human and other forms of life. "Spaceship earth" is flashing red warning signals.

In this perspective, differences over ideologies, faiths, and "national interests" must be viewed in the light of higher considerations. Disagreements and conflicts will doubtless persist, but the overriding priorities are survival and peace. These require, in turn, that concern for the *world* community be placed above traditional concerns about absolute national sovereignty. *Transnational* authorities to regulate population levels, resource development, health services, arms expenditures, education, and research seem indispensable if the poor—and the rich—of the world are to *live*.

Such controls would impose restrictions on the freedoms and privileges of individuals and nations. Westerners, who have used much of the world for their own purposes, may find the prospect uninviting. But they cannot ignore the facts or the challenge. Perhaps they can find a fresh source of satisfaction in the *adventure* of the new age they have created. They cannot, in any event, turn back; Western men and women now share with all peoples the burden of godlike knowledge—and a *common fate*.

RECOMMENDED FURTHER READING

History embraces everything that human beings have said or thought or done—so there is no substitute for the widest possible reading. The most rewarding reading, no doubt, is in the original (primary) writings of the past. Many such writings are cited in this book and can be read as individual works. (Most are available in paperback.) For practical reasons, however, a careful selection of portions of original works may better fit the needs and desires of the majority of students. Several suitable anthologies (collections) are available; especially recommended is the paperbound set prepared to accompany this book: *Classics of Western Thought* (Harcourt, 4 vols.).

In addition to original source materials, many "secondary" works are of great value and interest. The authors of such works attempt to sort out and interpret human experience in the light of later events and differing points of view.

The books recommended in the list that follows are up-to-date, authoritative, and readable secondary works. All of them are currently available—mostly in paperback—and some in inexpensive hardcover editions. The dates given are those of first publication or of the most recent revised edition.

7 THE TRANSFORMATION AND EXPANSION OF EUROPE

DISSOLUTION OF THE MEDIEVAL SYNTHESIS

The best short introduction to all aspects of the transformation and expansion of Europe is E. F. Rice and A. Grafton, *The Foundations of Early Modern Europe* (1994); D. Nicholas, *The Transformation of Europe* (1999), is an excellent detailed survey.

Specifically on late medieval times, J. Huizinga, *The Waning of the Middle Ages* (1927), is a work of subtle insight, dealing with cultural aspects. W. C. Jordan, *The Great Famine* (1996), and D. Herlihy, *The Black Death and the Transformation of the West* (1997), discuss the effects of plague and famine on economy, society, and culture; P. Ziegler, *The Black Death* (1969), and B. W. Tuchman, *A Distant Mirror* (1978) (a more general account), vividly describe the horrors of the fourteenth century. For the effects of disease on human cultures from the earliest times to the present, see W. H. McNeill, *Plagues and Peoples* (1976). R. Hilton, *Bond Men Made Free* (1973), analyzes medieval peasant movements throughout Europe, in particular the English uprising of 1381.

On eastern Europe, R. Milner-Gulland, *The Russians* (1997), is an excellent general account of Russian civilization, stressing the medieval period; R. H. Davison, *Turkey* (1968), includes a brief and readable treatment of the Ottoman expansion.

THE NEW ECONOMY

N. J. G. Pounds, *An Economic History of Medieval Europe* (1994), is a good introduction. E. S. Hunt and J. M. Murray discuss changes in business organization and methods in *A History of Business in Medieval Europe, 1200–1550* (1999); E. S. Hunt, *The Medieval Super-Companies* (1994) vividly describes the rise and fall of the Peruzzi banking firm. J. Le Goff, *Your Money or Your Life* (1998), explores changing religious attitudes to usury in the era of the medieval origins of capitalism.

THE NEW TECHNOLOGY

F. and J. Gies, *Cathedral, Forge, and Waterwheel* (1994), is an excellent nontechnical account of the development of technology throughout the Middle Ages; A. Pacey, *Technology in World Civilization* (1990), discusses the intercontinental flow of technical innovation in the Middle Ages and the rise of the West to technical supremacy. C. M. Cipolla, *Guns, Sails, and Empires* (1965), and D. Cline, *Navigation in the Age of Discovery* (1990), deal with the evolution and impact of seafaring and sea warfare technology. P. Contamine, *War in the Middle Ages* (1984), is a readable standard work that includes treatment of the development of firearms. W. Chappell and R. Bringhurst, *A Short History of the Printed Word* (2000), covers the origins of printing in Europe; L. Febvre, *The Coming of the Book* (1976), is a classic account of printing's cultural and economic impact. D. S. Landes, *Revolution in Time* (1983), includes both technical aspects and discussion of the impact of clocks on civilization.

THE NEW POLITICS

D. Hay and J. Law, *Italy in the Age of the Renaissance, 1380–1530* (1989), and G. Mattingly, *Renaissance Diplomacy* (1955), are good introductions; D. Waley, *The Italian City-Republics* (1988), covers the medieval city-states. For individual city-states, see G. Brucker, *Renaissance Florence* (1969), and F. C. Lane, *Venice: A Maritime Republic* (1973). Q. Skinner, *Machiavelli* (1981), is an authoritative short account.

For the growth of government power outside Italy, see H. Kamen, *Spain, 1469–1714: A Society of Conflict* (1991); D. Potter, *A History of France, 1460–1560: The Emergence of a Nation-State* (1995); G. Elton, *England under the Tudors* (1991); and J. Bérenger, *A History of the Habsburg Empire* (1994).

The impact of changing methods of warfare on government, society, and the economy is dealt with in J. R. Hale, *War and Society in Renaissance Europe* (1985). C. Allmand, *The Hundred Years War* (1988), is a brief account of the war's course and impact. G. Parker, *The Military Revolution: Military Innovation and the Rise of the West: 1500–1800* (1996), gives insight into the long-term impact of changes in warfare on both Western and non-Western civilizations. M. Howard, *War in European History* (1976), is a brief interpretation by a leading scholar that includes treatment of late medieval changes in warfare.

THE NEW GEOGRAPHY

D. J. Boorstin, *The Discoverers* (1983), is a brilliant account of *all* discoveries about the world and humankind. J. L. Abu-Lughod, *Before European Hegemony* (1989), discusses the intercontinental developments in the Old World that led to European exploration and empire building. J. H. Parry, *The Age of Reconnaissance* (1981), describes the beginnings of exploration; a brief biography of the most famous of the explorers is S. E. Morison, *Christopher Columbus, Mariner* (1983).

G. V. Scammell, *The First Imperial Age* (1989), surveys European exploration and worldwide empires up to the early eighteenth century. H. S. Klein, *The Atlantic Slave Trade* (1999), gives an overview of the economic, social, and cultural impact of the trade on Africa, the Americas, and Europe. P. Bakewell, *A History of Latin America: Empires and Sequels* (1997), is an excellent account of the Spanish and Portuguese conquest of the New World and its impact on Latin America down to the twentieth century.

8   THE RENAISSANCE: UPSURGE OF HUMANISM

THE RENAISSANCE VIEW OF HUMAN NATURE

J. Burckhardt, *The Civilization of the Renaissance in Italy* (1860) is a readable masterpiece whose influence on understanding of the Renaissance has lasted down to the present; the best reprint is that of 1990, with an introduction by P. Burke that assesses the validity of Burckhardt's approach. Burke's own *The European Renaissance: Centers and Peripheries* (1998), provides an authoritative present-day interpretation. J. Kraye, ed., *The Cambridge Companion to Renaissance Humanism* (1990), contains brief essays by leading scholars describing the impact of humanism on many fields of thought and art. P. Burke, *The Italian Renaissance: Culture and Society in Italy* (1999), relates culture and art to social and political institutions.

The best short treatment of philosophy in the Renaissance is P. O. Kristeller, *Renaissance Thought* (1961); a longer and more recent account is B. P. Copenhaver and C. P. Schmitt, *Renaissance Philosophy* (1992).

On individual humanists, J. McConica, *Erasmus* (1991), and A. Kenny, *Thomas More* (1983), are good brief accounts, both available in J. McConica et al., *Renaissance Thinkers* (1993).

THE REVOLUTION IN ART

The best introductions to all forms of Renaissance art and architecture throughout Europe are P. and L. Murray, *The Art of the Renaissance* 1963), covering the fourteenth and fifteenth centuries; and L. Murray, *The High Renaissance and Mannerism* (1977), covering the sixteenth century. Specifically on architecture, see P. Murray, *The Architecture of the Italian Renaissance* (1980).

On individual artists, the following books are recommended: G. Gaeta Bertelà, *Donatello* (1998); L. Bellosi, *Giotto* (1982); K. Clark, *Leonardo da Vinci* (1968); L. Murray, *Michelangelo* (1985); F. Pedrocco, *Titian* (1993); and F. Zollner, *Botticelli* (1998).

LITERATURE AND DRAMA

W. A. Coupe, *The Continental Renaissance 1500–1600* (1991), surveys literature in Italy, France, Spain, and Germany. M. J. Heath, *Rabelais* (1996); P. Burke, *Montaigne* (1981); M. Duran, *Cervantes* (19974); and G. Greer, *Shakespeare* (1986), are good short introductions giving cultural and social background.

P. Hyland, *An Introduction to Shakespeare: The Dramatist in His Context* (1996), is an excellent short account of Shakespearean drama, including Elizabethan staging and the theatrical profession. A. Burgess, *Shakespeare* (1970), is a well-illustrated biography by a distinguished present-day man of letters.

9   THE REFORMATION: DIVISION AND REFORM IN THE CHURCH

BACKGROUND OF THE REFORMATION

J. Bossy, *Christianity in the West 1400–1700* (1985), is an excellent brief overview and interpretation of religious change throughout late medieval and early modern times. R. H. Bainton, *The Reformation of the Sixteenth Century* (1952), and O. Chadwick, *The Reformation* (1964), are readable brief accounts by leading scholars; a more recent and detailed treatment is E. Cameron, *The European Reformation* (1991). A. E. McGrath, *Reformation Thought: An Introduction* (1993), is an excellent guide to theological issues, as well as to Protestant and Catholic ideas on society and government. For the general history of the period, see E. F. Rice and A. Grafton, *The Foundations of Early Modern Europe* (1994); and the more detailed account by G. Elton, *Reformation Europe* (1999).

Specifically on the background of the Reformation, F. Oakley, *The Western Church in the Later Middle Ages* (1979), is an excellent survey dealing with all aspects of both Catholic and dissident religion.

THE REVOLT OF LUTHER: "JUSTIFICATION BY FAITH"

R. H. Bainton, *Here I Stand* (1950), is a readable and reliable classic; R. Marius, *Luther* (1974), is a more critical interpretation. W. R. Estep, *The Anabaptist Story: An Introduction to Sixteenth-Century Anabaptism* (1996), is a scholarly and sympathetic survey of the radical Reformation movements.

CALVIN AND THE ELECT: "PREDESTINATION"

W. Bouwsma, *John Calvin: A Sixteenth-Century Portrait* (1988), insightfully depicts Calvin as a man of his time; A. E. McGrath, *A Life of John Calvin: A Study of the*

Shaping of Western Culture (1990), stresses Calvin's thought and its impact. J. T. McNeill, *The History and Character of Calvinism* (1954), is a good short account of Calvinism's theology, church organization, and impact throughout Europe and the New World.

M. Weber, *The Protestant Ethic and the Spirit of Capitalism* (1930), is the classic statement of the relationship between Calvinism and capitalism; the 1998 reprint has an introduction by R. Collins assessing the validity of the Weber thesis. See also the books by Bainton, Chadwick, and Cameron, listed in the first section, and McGrath's book listed here.

Henry VIII and the Church of England

A. G. Dickens, *The English Reformation* (1991), and C. Haigh, *English Reformations: Religion, Politics, and Society under the Tudors* (1993), survey not only the policies of rulers and the activities of religious leaders, but also the response to the Reformation at the grass roots: Dickens stresses popular acceptance of religious change, and Haigh emphasizes popular resistance to it. An excellent brief guide to the much-disputed question of when and how the English people became wholeheartedly Protestant is D. Rosman, *From Catholic to Protestant: Religion and the People in Tudor England* (1996).

The Roman Catholic Response: Reform and Reaffirmation

A. G. Dickens, *The Counter Reformation* (1969), is a good brief introduction to the activities of rulers, religious leaders, and artists, which covers both religious and cultural aspects; M. D. W. Jones, *The Counter Reformation: Religion and Society in Early Modern Europe* (1995), also includes material on the popular response to and acceptance of the Counter Reformation, with source selections. R. Po-chi Hsia, *The World of Catholic Renewal 1540–1770* (1998), discusses the practice and culture of Counter Reformation Catholicism and its differences from the Catholicism of the Middle Ages.

Historical Significance of the Reformation

The books by Bainton and McGrath listed in the first section, as well as C. Lindberg, *The European Reformations* (1996), all include good summaries of the impact of the Reformation on politics, economics, and thought.

Art during the Reformation

The best introduction to Baroque art and architecture is G. Bazin, *Baroque and Rococo* (1964). J. R. Martin, *Baroque* (1977), deals with the distinguishing features of Baroque style. On individual artists, see H. Hibbard, *Bernini* (1965); W. Stechow, *Pieter Brueghel the Elder* (1990); C. White, *Rembrandt* (1984); and C. Scribner, *Rubens* (1989). On the commercial and patronage side of Baroque art, see S. Alpers, *Rembrandt's Enterprise: The Studio and the Market* (1988).

10   SCIENCE AND A NEW COSMOLOGY

NATIONAL AND INTERNATIONAL DEVELOPMENT

H. G. Koenigsberger, *Early Modern Europe 1500–1789* (1987), is an excellent brief overview of the period covered by this chapter; R. Bonney, *The European Dynastic States 1494-1660* (1991), and J. Black, *Eighteenth-Century Europe: 1700–1789* (1990), are more detailed surveys. G. Parker, *The Thirty Years War* (1984), includes social as well as military and political aspects; and his *The Military Revolution: Military Innovation and the Rise of the West: 1500–1800* (1996), deals with the impact of military changes on politics and government.

On individual states, see R. Briggs, *Early Modern France* (1998); S. B. Fay, *The Rise of Brandenburg-Prussia to 1786* (1937); C. Ingrao, *The Habsburg Monarchy 1618–1815* (1994); and C. E. Ziegler, *The History of Russia* (1999). P. Goubert, *Louis XIV and Twenty Million Frenchmen* (1970); G. Ritter, *Frederick the Great* (1968); and M. S. Anderson, *Peter the Great* (1995), are brief and authoritative biographies.

W. M. Spellman, *European Political Thought: 1600–1970* (1998), deals with theories of absolutism. A. Martinich, *Thomas Hobbes* (1997), is a brief account by a leading scholar.

THE SCIENTIFIC REVOLUTION OF THE SEVENTEENTH CENTURY

H. Butterfield, *The Origins of Modern Science: 1300–1800* (1957), and S. Shapin, *The Scientific Revolution* (1996), are brief interpretations; Butterfield voices the "classic" view of the seventeenth-century changes in science, and Shapin explains how far that view is still regarded as valid. A. R. Hall, *The Scientific Revolution 1500–1800: The Formation of the Modern Scientific Attitude* (1962), surveys the specific changes that took place in each field of science; J. R. Jacob, *The Scientific Revolution: Aspirations and Achievements 1500–1700* (1998), is briefer and more recent. T. S. Kuhn, *The Copernican Revolution: Planetary Astronomy in the Development of Western Thought* (1957), describes and interprets the field of science where the most spectacular and decisive changes took place. All these books are nontechnical, though they assume basic scientific knowledge.

THE IMPACT OF SCIENCE ON PHILOSOPHY: THE ENLIGHTENMENT

Two excellent general surveys are N. Hampson, *The Enlightenment* (1968), which considers philosophy against its social and political background; and D. Outram, *The Enlightenment* (1995), which includes discussion of the role of women and non-Western civilizations in Enlightenment thought. On individual thinkers, J. J. Jenkins, *Understanding Locke* (1983), and E. Goodell, *The Noble Philosopher: Condorcet and the Enlightenment* (1994), are good brief biographies; P. S. Woodhouse, *The Empiricists* (1988), has brief essays on Locke and Hume, among others. J. B.

Bury, *The Idea of Progress* (1932), covering one of the main themes of Enlightenment thought, is still well worth reading.

The Rational Spirit in Literature and Art

F. Kermode, *The Classic: Literary Images of Permanence and Change* (1983), explores the concept of classicism in literature, including the eighteenth century. On individual writers, see L. Goldmann, *Racine* (1972); F. Rosslyn, *Pope: A Literary Life* (1990); and H. Mason, *Candide: Optimism Demolished* (1992).

Two excellent introductions to art and architecture are M. Levey, *Rococo to Revolution: Major Trends in Eighteenth-Century Painting* (1966) and J. Summerson, *The Architecture of the Eighteenth Century* (1986). On individual artists and architects, see J. Massengale, *Fragonard* (1993); R. Wendorf, *Sir Joshua Reynolds: The Painter in Society* (1995); and M. Whinney, *Wren* (1971).

The Classical Age of Music

A. Einstein, *A Short History of Music* (1937) (from ancient times to the late nineteenth century); N. Anderson, *Baroque Music: From Monteverdi to Handel* (1994); and J. Rushton, *Classical Music: A Concise History from Gluck to Beethoven* (1986), are excellent introductions by leading scholars. Brief and authoritative biographies of leading composers are D. Arnold, *Monteverdi* (1975); M. Boyd, *Bach* (1983); W. Dean, *The New Grove Handel* (1982); J. P. Larsen, *The New Grove Haydn* (1982); J. Rosselli, *The Life of Mozart* (1998) (stressing his musical creation and career); and P. Gay, *Mozart* (1999) (analyzing his inner personal development). All books listed are nontechnical, apart from occasional musical examples.

11   THE REVOLUTIONS OF LIBERALISM AND NATIONALISM

The English Revolution: Parliamentary Supremacy and the Bill of Rights

On revolutions in general, the following books are recommended: C. Brinton, *The Anatomy oÉ Revolution* (1952), identifies common features of the English, American, French, and Russian revolutions; A. Todd, *Revolutions 1789–1917* (1998), does the same for all European revolutions during that period; and C. Tilly, *European Revolutions, 1492–1992* (1993), traces the course and impact of revolutions throughout modern times.

Specifically on the English Revolution, C. Hill, *The Century of Revolution 1603–1641* (1980), concisely analyzes the seventeenth-century changes in government, economic, religious, and cultural life; M. Kishlansky, *A Monarchy Transformed: Britain 1603–1714* (1997), is a readable and up-to-date survey, tracing both changes in the government and social order and the emergence of the British state. N. Carlin, *The Causes of the English Civil War* (1999), is an excellent summary of the current thinking of historians on the process of revolution in England. On the strengths and weaknesses of two dominant rulers, see C. Haigh, *Elizabeth I* (1998), and P. Gaunt, *Oliver Cromwell* (1996).

Locke's political ideas are discussed in W. M. Spellman, *John Locke* (1997). W. Prest, *Albion Ascendant: English History, 1660–1815* (1997), describes all aspects of the state and society that emerged from the English Revolution.

The American Revolution and Constitution

R. Middleton, *Colonial America* (1996), is a standard survey; J. A. Henretta and G. H. Nobles, *Evolution and Revolution: American Society, 1600–1820* (1987), deals with the social aspect of the emergence of the American nation.

On the period of the Revolution, E. S. Morgan, *The Birth of the Republic, 1763–1789* (1977), is a classic brief account; a more recent introduction is C. Bonwick, *The American Revolution* (1991). R. Horsman, *The New Republic* (2000), describes the government and social order that emerged from the Revolution. N. Risjord, *Thomas Jefferson* (1994), and the classic C. Becker, *The Declaration of Independence* (1922), deal briefly with the ideas of the declaration and its drafter.

The French Revolution: "Liberty, Equality, and Fraternity"

N. Hampson, *A Social History of the French Revolution* (1963) (to 1799), and J. D. Popkin, *A Short History of the French Revolution* (1995) (to 1815 and after), are excellent introductions to events in France; N. Hampson, *The First European Revolution, 1776–1815* (1979), and P. M. Pilbeam, *Themes in Modern European History, 1780–1830* (1995), cover the revolution's impact throughout Europe. W. Doyle, *The Oxford History of the French Revolution* (1999), and M. Broers, *Europe under Napoleon, 1799–1815* (1990), are more detailed accounts. G. Lefebvre, *The Coming of the French Revolution* (1947), is a noted work by an outstanding scholar; W. Doyle, *The Origins of the French Revolution* (1999), is more recent. J. Hardman, *Robespierre* (1999), and G. Ellis, *Napoleon* (1997), are brief biographies of two of the dominating figures of the revolutionary period.

The Conservative Reaction

T. C. W. Blanning, ed., *The Oxford Illustrated History of Modern Europe* (1996), is an up-to-date general introduction to European political, social, and cultural history from the late eighteenth century to the present. E. J. Hobsbawm, *The Age of Revolution, 1789–1848* (1962); R. Gildea, *Barricades and Borders: Europe 1800–1914* (1987); and M. Broers, *Europe after Napoleon: Revolution, Reaction, Romanticism* (1996), include concise accounts of the period of conservative reaction.

R. Nisbet, *Conservatism: Dream and Reality* (1986), is an excellent brief introduction to the main themes of conservative thought and action from the late eighteenth century to the present. On individual thinkers, see R. Kirk, *Edmund Burke: A Genius Reconsidered* (1997); J. V. Price, *David Hume* (1991); R. Scruton, *Kant* (1982); and P. Singer, *Hegel* (1983).

The Romantic Spirit in Literature, Art, and Music

The following introductions to romanticism in all fields of literature, the arts, and thought are recommended: M. Cranston, *The Romantic Movement* (1994) (Europe and the Americas), and S. Pritchett, *The Romantics* (1981) (England). I. Berlin, *The Roots of Romanticism* (1999), is an interpretive essay by a renowned scholar. C. M. Bowra, *The Romantic Imagination* (1949), and N. Frye, *A Study of English Romanticism* (1995), are works of a high order dealing with English literary romanticism. On individual authors, see R. Wokler, *Rousseau* (1995); R. Noyes and J. O. Hayden, *William Wordsworth* (1991); and V. Lange, *The Classical Age of German Literature, 1740–1815* (1982) (Goethe).

D. Irwin, *Neoclassicism* (1997); W. Vaughan, *Romantic Art* (1978); and K. Clark, *The Gothic Revival: An Essay in the History of Taste* (1962), are excellent introductions to the art and architecture of the period. J. Rushton, *Classical Music: A Concise History from Gluck to Beethoven* (1986), and A. Whittall, *Romantic Music: A Concise History from Schubert to Sibelius* (1987), are readable, authoritative, and nontechnical.

The Spread of Liberal Democracy and Nationalism

E. J. Hobsbawm, *The Age of Capital, 1848–1875* (1979), and B. Waller, ed., *Themes in Modern European History, 1830–1890* (1990), are excellent introductions to all aspects of European development in the mid-nineteenth century. The following introductions to liberalism are recommended: L. T. Hobhouse, *Liberalism* (1911) (a classic statement of the British liberal tradition); J. Gray, *Liberalism* (1986) (Britain and the United States); and J. Manent, *An Intellectual History of Liberalism* (1994) (France). J. Dunn, ed., *Democracy: The Unfinished Journey, 508 B.C. to A.D. 1993* (1992), includes essays on nineteenth-century democracy in Europe and America. H. Schulze, *States, Nations, and Nationalism from the Middle Ages to the Present* (1994), is a wide-ranging work on the rise of nationalism and nation-states; L. Kramer, *Nationalism: Political Cultures in Europe and America, 1775–1865* (1998) is a concise account of the era of nationalism's triumph.

P. M. Pilbeam, *The 1830 Revolution in France* (1991); P. N. Stearns, *The Revolutions of 1848* (1974); and R. J. W. Evans and H. Pogge von Strandmann, eds., *The Revolutions in Europe, 1848–1849: From Reform to Reaction* (2000), are concise and readable accounts of the revolutions of the period. On individual countries and leaders, see Eric J. Evans, *Parliamentary Reform, 1770–1918* (1999) (Britain); J.

Breuilly, *The Formation of the First German National State, 1800–1871* (1996);
B. Waller, *Bismarck* (1997): M. Clark, *The Italian Risorgimento* (1998); and H.
Hearder, *Cavour* (1994).

12   THE IMPACT OF THE MACHINE

THE INDUSTRIAL REVOLUTION

P. M. Deane, *The First Industrial Revolution* (1979), is an excellent introduction
to all aspects of the Industrial Revolution in Britain down to the mid-
nineteenth century; K. Morgan, *The Birth of Industrial Britain: Economic Change,
1750–1850* (1999), concisely summarizes recent research. E. J. Hobsbawm,
Industry and Empire: An Economic History of Britain since 1850 (1969), covers industrial Britain's zenith and its subsequent loss of supremacy. D. Landes, *The Un-
bound Prometheus: Technical Change and Industrial Development in Western Europe
from 1850 to the Present* (1969), is a readable standard work; T. Kemp, *Industrialization in Nineteenth-Century Europe* (1969), is a briefer account. W. Licht, *Industrializing America: The Nineteenth Century* (1995), is a concise introduction to
the rise of the world's largest industrial economy. P. N. Stearns, *The Industrial
Revolution in World History* (1993), discusses nineteenth- and twentieth-century
industrialization across the globe.

    D. Cardwell, *The Norton History of Technology* (1994), includes readable and non-
technical treatment of all major technologies of the Industrial Revolution. E. D. Brose,
Technology and Science in the Industrializing Nations, 1500–1914 (1998), is a concise introduction to the relationship of science and technology. A. Pacey, *The Maze of Inge-
nuity: Ideas and Idealism in the Development of Technology* (1992), treats technology as a
form of human creativity that needs both encouragement and restraint.

THE BUSINESS CORPORATION AND CAPITALIST EXPANSION

R. Heilbroner and W. Milberg, *The Making of Economic Society* (1998), is the most
recent edition of a classic introduction to the development of capitalism in modern times. Specifically on the growth of large corporations, M. G. Blackford, *The
Rise of Modern Business in Great Britain, the United States, and Japan* (1998), is a
concise discussion. G. Porter, *The Rise of Big Business, 1860–1910* (1973), deals
with the United States; M. Klein, *The Flowering of the Third America: The Making
of an Organizational Society, 1850–1920* (1993), explores the social and cultural
impact of the rise of American corporations.

    A clear exposition of economic theories from the eighteenth century to the
present is R. L. Heilbroner, *The Worldly Philosophers: The Lives, Times, and Ideas of
the Great Economic Thinkers* (1992). D. D. Raphael, *Smith* (1985), and D. Winch,
Malthus (1987), both available in D. D. Raphael et al., *Three Great Economic
Thinkers: Smith, Malthus, Keynes* (1997), are brief and authoritative.

The Reaction of Labor and Government

J. R. Gillis, *The Development of European Society, 1770–1870* (1983), discusses the changes of the period among all social groups. S. P. Hays, *The Response to Industrialism: 1885–1914* (1995), is the latest edition of a classic short account of political and social change in the industrializing United States.

On the industrial working class and labor movements, D. Geary, *Labour and Socialist Movements in Europe before 1914* (1989), and M. Dubofsky, *Industrialism and the American Worker, 1865–1920* (1985), are up-to-date short introductions.

T. Katsaros, *The Development of the Welfare State in the Western World* (1995), includes discussion of nineteenth-century social legislation in Europe and America. See also such general histories as T. C. W. Blanning, ed., *The Oxford Illustrated History of Modern Europe* (1996); R. Gildea, *Barricades and Borders: Europe 1800–1914* (1987); E. J. Hobsbawm, *The Age of Capital, 1848–1875* (1979); and B. Waller, ed., *Themes in Modern European History, 1830–1890* (1990).

Urbanization and Standardization of Society

The general histories listed in the previous section include up-to-date treatments of social change in the nineteenth century. P. M. Hohenberg and L. H. Lees, *The Making of Urban Europe, 1000–1950* (1995), and Z. L. Miller, *The Urbanization of Modern America: A Brief History* (1977), are good introductions to the rise of cities; W. Rösener, *The Peasantry of Europe* (1994), deals with change in the countryside. M. Livi-Bacci, *A Concise History of World Population* (1992), explains increases in and movements of population.

The Development of Socialist Thought and Action

A. Lindemann, *A History of European Socialism* (1983), is a concise and comprehensive account of Marxist and non-Marxist theories and movements in the nineteenth and the first half of the twentieth centuries. R. Levitas, *The Concept of Utopia* (1990), describes the ideas of Utopian Socialism and the various efforts to put the ideas into practice. G. Lichtheim, *Marxism: An Historical and Critical Study* (1964), discusses Marxist theory from its origins to the rise of Stalinism. I. Berlin, *Karl Marx: His Life and Environment* (1978), is a balanced biography, including treatment of Marx's ideas; P. Singer, *Marx* (1980), is a brief interpretation.

The Accelerating Progress of Science

S. F. Marron, *A History of the Sciences* (1962), is a good nontechnical account, with concise and comprehensive coverage of the physical and life sciences in the eighteenth and nineteenth centuries; S. G. Brush, *The Rise of Modern Science: A Guide to the Second Scientific Revolution, 1800–1950* (1988), is more detailed and includes treatment of experimental psychology and psychoanalysis. For a readable account of the life of Louis Pasteur and his place in the development of medical science, see R. Dubos, *Pasteur and Modern Science* (1988). Einstein's theory of relativity and its influence on the development of physics are briefly and comprehensibly outlined in L. Barnett, *The Universe and Dr. Einstein* (1950).

THE CHALLENGE OF DARWIN'S THEORY OF EVOLUTION

J. W. Burrow, *The Crisis of Reason: European Thought, 1848–1914* (2000), is a concise and authoritative account of all major intellectual trends. Specifically on Darwinism, J. Bowler, *Evolution: The History of an Idea* (1984), is a standard work on evolution as a scientific concept; his *Charles Darwin: The Man and His Influence* (1990), assesses Darwin's place in the development of the concept.

R. Hofstadter, *Social Darwinism in American Thought* (1955), is clear and provocative; P. J. Bowler, *Biology and Social Thought, 1850–1914* (1993), covers Europe as well as America. P. Dickens, *Social Darwinism: Linking Evolutionary Thought to Social Theory* (2000), deals with the implications of evolutionary ideas down to the present.

R. Smith, *The Norton History of the Human Sciences* (1997), is a clear general account of the nineteenth-century rise of sociology, anthropology, and psychology. W. M. Simpson, *European Positivism in the Nineteenth Century: An Essay in Intellectual History* (1963), is a concise and readable standard work; A. R. Standley, *Auguste Comte* (1981), is an excellent brief introduction. M. Wertheimer, *A Brief History of Psychology* (1970), includes treatment of the rise of experimental psychology. A. Storr, *Freud* (1989), is a good brief introduction to the founder of psychoanalysis; an interpretation of his pervasive influence on contemporary culture can be found in P. Rieff, *Freud: The Mind of the Moralist* (1979). D. M. Robinson, *An Intellectual History of Psychology* (1995), relates both experimental psychology and psychoanalysis to their philosophical and scientific background.

LITERATURE AND ART IN THE MACHINE AGE

L. R. Furst, *Realism* (1992), is a collection of statements by nineteenth-century western European Realist authors and of later critical responses, with a useful introduction; on American Realism, see D. Pizer, *Realism and Naturalism in Nineteenth-Century American Literature* (1985). On individual authors, D. Festa McCormick, *Honoré de Balzac* (1979); H. S. Nelson, *Charles Dickens* (1981); S. Ledger, *Henryk Ibsen* (1999); and E. C. Hill, *George Bernard Shaw* (1978), are brief and reliable. G. K. Chesterton, *Criticisms and Appreciations of the Works of Charles Dickens* (1911), and G. B. Shaw, *The Quintessence of Ibsenism* (1913), are brief and enjoyable critical classics.

L. Nochlin, *Realism* (1970), is a concise and readable standard work on the visual arts. B. Thomson, *Impressionism: Origins, Practice, Reception* (2000), and B.

Denvir, *Post-Impressionism* (1992), are reliable introductions. B. Denvir, *The Impressionists at First Hand* (1987), is a short and interesting documentary history. On individual artists, see R. Verdi, *Cézanne* (1992); W. Seitz, *Claude Monet* (1960); and M. McQuillan, *Van Gogh* (1989).

13 IMPERIALISM, WORLD WAR, AND THE RISE OF COLLECTIVISM

IMPERIALISM AND EUROPE'S WORLD DOMINION

M. W. Doyle, *Empires* (1986), compares imperialism through the centuries from Athens and Sparta to the nineteenth-century scramble for Africa. W. J. Mommsen, *Theories of Imperialism* (1980), is a succinct guide to the main interpretations. E. J. Hobsbawm, *The Age of Empire* (1987), is an excellent treatment of European imperialism in general.

B. Davidson, *Africa in History: Themes and Outlines* (1988); C. Schirokauer, *A Brief History of Chinese and Japanese Civilizations* (1989); and P. Bakewell, *A History of Latin America: Empires and Sequels* (1997), give general background on those regions of the world. R. Oliver and A. Atmore, *Africa since 1800* (1994); J. K. Fairbank, *The Great Chinese Revolution: 1800–1985* (1986); and Bakewell's book describe the impact of nineteenth-century imperialism.

On individual imperialist powers, see F. Quinn, *The French Overseas Empires* (2000); W. O. Henderson, *The German Colonial Empire* (1993); T. O. Lloyd, *The British Empire, 1558–1995* (1996); T. Parsons, *The British Imperial Century, 1815–1914: A World History Perspective* (1999); E. R. May, *Imperial Democracy: The Emergence of the United States as a Great Power* (1961); and A. Stephanson, *Manifest Destiny: American Expansionism and the Empire of Right* (1995). The books by Parsons and Stephanson are brief interpretations; the others are readable detailed treatments.

THE FIRST WORLD WAR AND THE DECLINE OF EUROPE

R. Gildea, *Barricades and Borders: Europe 1800–1914* (1987), includes treatment of the political, social, and cultural forces making for war. A. J. P. Taylor, *The Struggle for Mastery in Europe, 1848–1918* (1954), is a readable account of the long-term diplomatic background; L. Lafore, *The Long Fuse: An Interpretation of the Origins of World War I* (1971), is a fascinating story of the diplomatic step-by-step to war. On the Balkans, see S. K. Pavlowitch, *A History of the Balkans, 1804–1945* (1999); on imperialistic conflicts, see E. J. Hobsbawm, *The Age of Empire* (1987).

J. Keegan, *The First World War* (1989), is a first-rate military history; M. Ferro, *The Great War, 1914-1918* (1987), deals with the war as a social and cultural upheaval; S. Robson, *The First World War* (1998), is an up-to-date introduction. The experience of the war is unforgettably conveyed by works of fiction and personal narratives. Among the most memorable of these are E. M. Remarque, *All Quiet on* the *Western Front* (1929) (German); R. Graves, *Goodbye to All That* (1929), and S. Sassoon, *Memoirs of an Infantry Officer* (1930) (British); and C. A. Brannen, *Over There: A Marine in the Great War* (1996) (American). P. Fussell, *The Great War and Modern Memory* (1975) is a general account of the traces left by the war in modern consciousness; the war's wider impact on culture and values is the subject of M. Eksteins, *Rites of Spring: The Great War and the Birth of the Modern Age* (1990).

A. Sharp, *The Versailles Settlement: Peacemaking in Paris, 1919* (1991), is a concise and comprehensive account of the treaties that ended the war.

COMMUNIST COLLECTIVISM: THE RUSSIAN REVOLUTION

J. N. Westwood, *Endurance and Endeavour: Russian History, 1812–1986* (1987), is a detailed and readable standard work dealing with all aspects of nineteenth-century imperial Russia and the Soviet Union. R. Pipes, *Russia under the Old Regime* (1995), and T. H. von Laue, *Why Lenin? Why Stalin? Why Gorbachev?* (1993), are excellent brief accounts of the rise and fall of imperial Russia and the Soviet Union, respectively. P. Waldron, *The End of Imperial Russia, 1855-1917* (1997), concisely describes the political, social, and economic changes that led to the downfall of imperial Russia.

On Marxist ideology in general, see the books listed for chapter 12, "The Development of Socialist Thought and Action." P. Pomper, *The Russian Revolutionary Intelligentsia* (1970), briefly describes the social and cultural roots of the Russian revolutionary tradition, both Marxist and non-Marxist. The best short account of the 1917 Revolution and the consolidation of Bolshevik rule is S. Fitzpatrick, *The Russian Revolution, 1917–1932* (1982); on the Revolution's leader, see B. Williams, *Lenin* (2000).

A. Nove, *Stalinism* (1981); R. G. Wesson, *Lenin's Legacy: The Story of the CPSU* (1978); G. Stern, *The Rise and Decline of International Communism* (1990); and R. J. Hill, *The Soviet Union: Politics, Economics, and Society from Lenin to Gorbachev* (1989), are authoritative introductions to the workings of Stalinism, the Soviet Communist party, the worldwide Communist movement, and the Soviet government, economic, and social system.

FASCIST COLLECTIVISM: THE REVOLUTIONS IN ITALY AND GERMANY

W. Laqueur, *Fascism* (1996), is a good introduction to fascism in the past and present, and its future prospects; M. Neocleous, *Fascism* (1997), is a brief interpretation that seeks to define the basic features of fascist ideology; H. Arendt, *The Origins of Totalitarianism* (1973), deals with the ideological origins of the fascist movements. S. J. Lee, *The European Dictatorships, 1918–1945* (2000), deals with the emergence of dictatorship in Europe between the world wars; R. J. Overy, *The Inter-War Crisis, 1919–1939* (1994), is a brief guide to the political and economic failures that led to the emergence of fascism.

F. Chabod, *A History of Italian Fascism* (1963), is a classic brief account by a distinguished Italian scholar who lived through the period; A. De Grand, *Italian Fascism: Its Origins and Development* (2000), is an up-to-date introduction. J.

Whittam, *Fascist Italy* (1995), concisely describes the workings of the fascist state; D. Mack Smith, *Mussolini* (1983), is a readable biography of the Italian dictator.

On Hitler's methods of gaining and exercising totalitarian power, and his personality and ideology, see E. Jäckel, *Hitler's World View: A Blueprint for Power* (1981), and I. Kershaw, *Hitler* (1991). P. Bookbinder, *Weimar Germany: The Republic of the Reasonable* (1996), and F. McDonough, *Hitler and Nazi Germany* (1999), are good brief accounts of politics and government in Germany before and after the Nazi takeover. R. Bessel, *Life in the Third Reich* (1987), vividly describes the impact of Nazi rule on many aspects of German life and culture.

J. Katz, *From Prejudice to Destruction* (1980), is a reliable general history of anti-Semitism; A. S. Lindemann, *Anti-Semitism* (2000), is a brief interpretation of anti-Semitism as a historical phenomenon; G. L. Mosse, *Toward the Final Solution: A History of European Racism* (1978), analyzes the racist element in anti-Semitism.

DEMOCRATIC COLLECTIVISM: EVOLUTION OF THE WELFARE STATES

C. P. Kindleberger, *Manias, Panics, and Crashes* (1978), is an enjoyable brief interpretation of these features of capitalism by a leading economist; the same author's *The World in Depression, 1929–1939* (1986), is a somewhat more technical account of the worldwide economic crisis; and J. K. Galbraith, *The Great Crash, 1929* (1955), describes the economic collapse in America. M. Beaud, *A History of Capitalism, 1500–1980* (1983), includes brief and nontechnical discussion of the crisis of the 1930s. T. Katsaros, *The Development of the Welfare State in the Western World* (1995), concisely describes the formation of welfare states in Europe and America, and their development down to the present.

P. Clarke, *Hope and Glory: Britain, 1900–1990* (1996), is a readable and up-to-date general history, including coverage of the crisis of the 1930s; specifically on the impact of the crisis and the British response, see K. Laybourn, *Britain on the Breadline: A Social and Political History of Britain between the Wars* (1991).

A classic brief history of the New Deal era is D. Perkins, *The New Age of Franklin Roosevelt, 1932–1945* (1957); R. Edsforth, *The New Deal: America's Response to the Great Depression* (2000), is an up-to-date introduction. W. Leuchtenburg, *Franklin D. Roosevelt and the New Deal, 1932–1940* (1963), and T. H. Greer, *What Roosevelt Thought* (1958), treat the nature of the Roosevelt revolution and its central ideas. E. D. Berkowitz, *America's Welfare State, from FDR to Reagan* (1991), is a useful account. For the development of the welfare state in Scandinavia, see M. Childs, *Sweden's Middle Way on Trial* (1990).

14   GLOBAL TRANSFORMATION: DAWN OF A NEW AGE

THE SECOND WORLD WAR AND ITS CONSEQUENCES

A. P. Adamthwaite, *The Making of the Second World War* (1979), summarizes the events leading to war, as well as scholarly debates over the war's origins, with documents. G. Wright, *The Ordeal of Total War, 1939–1945* (1968), is an excellent introduction to the war in Europe; R. A. C. Parker, *The Second World War: A Short History* (1997), covers all theaters; and for focus on the Russian front, see A. Werth, *Russia at War, 1941–1945* (1964). In C. Wilmot, *The Struggle for Europe* (1971), a critical Australian journalist views the strategy of the war.

The victims of Nazi genocide are the subject of L. Dawidowicz, *The War against the Jews, 1933–1945* (1975); W. Benz, *The Holocaust: A German Historian Examines the Genocide* (1999), is an excellent brief interpretation; and P. Levi, *Survival in Auschwitz: The Nazi Assault on Humanity* (1961), is a vivid and horrifying personal narrative. J. Hersey, *Hiroshima* (1986), gives a moving account of the effects of the first atomic bomb on its victims.

D. S. Painter, *The Cold War: An International History* (1999), is a good brief introduction; S. J. Ball, *The Cold War: An International History, 1947–1991* (1998), is more detailed, and covers the debates over Cold War origins; and R. Pearson, *The Rise and Fall of the Soviet Empire* (1998), deals readably with the "satellite" countries under Soviet domination.

On the postwar recovery of Europe, see W. Laqueur, *Europe in Our Time: A History, 1945–1992* (1992), and G. Ambrosius and W. H. Hubbard, *A Social and Economic History of Twentieth-Century Europe* (1989).

THE SWEEP OF NATIONALISM AND MODERNIZATION

A. D. Smith, *Nations and Nationalism in a Global Era* (1996), assesses the status of nationalism in the present-day world. M. E. Chamberlain, *Decolonization: The Fall of the European Empires* (1985), is a good brief guide, concentrating on the British Empire; F. Ansprenger, *The Dissolution of the Colonial Empires* (1989), has more on other European empires; R. F. Beth, *Decolonization* (1998), is a brief interpretation of the passing of imperialism as a social and cultural development. C. Clapham, *Third World Politics: An Introduction* (1985), briefly describes the patterns of rule that have emerged in Africa, Asia, and Latin America since decolonization.

E. E. Moise, *Modern China: A History* (1986), concisely puts Communist China against its background of traditional Chinese civilization and Western imperialism; A. Lawrance, *China under Communism* (1998), is an excellent introduction to the period of Communist rule; and R. E. Barrett and F. Li, *Modern China* (1999), concentrates on the country's economic and social life. E. Reischauer, *The Japanese Today* (1988), is an excellent study of a people on the rise. F. Fitzgerald, *Fire in the Lake: The Vietnamese and the Americans in Vietnam*, is a moving account by a gifted writer. A frank explanation of the mistakes in prosecuting this war can be found in R. S. McNamara, *In Retrospect: the Tragedy and Lessons of Vietnam* (1995). For the revolution in Iran, see S. Akhavi, *Religion and Politics in Contemporary Iran*; useful also is R. K. Ramazani, ed., *Iran's Revolution*. For Iraq, see S. Al-Khalil, *Republic of Fear* (1989). For the overthrow of apartheid in South Africa, see N. Mandela, *Long Walk to Freedom* (1995); the viewpoint of an African-American militant is articulated in *The Autobiography of Malcolm X* (1965).

Economic Reassessment and the "Three Worlds"

Sound and readable treatments are P. R. Ehrlich, *The Population Explosion* (1990), and G. Myrdal, *The Challenge of World Poverty* (1970). L. Evans, *Feeding the Ten Billion: Plants and Population Growth* (1998) is a nontechnical introduction to the interaction of population and agriculture from the Agricultural Revolution to the twenty-first century. The critical issue of birth control is discussed in G. Hardin, *Living within Limits: Ecology, Economics, and Popular Taboos* (1993). M. and R. D. Friedman, *Free to Choose* (1980), is a popular exposition of monetarism and laissez-faire economics. D. K. Fieldhouse, *The West and the Third World* (1999), discusses the historical background and present state of relations between the two, and assesses the prospects of Third World countries in the global economy. The ferment in portions of the Third World is set forth in F. Fanon, *The Wretched of the Earth* (1966). For the rising terrorist threat, see W. Laqueur, *The Age of Terrorism* (1987).

End of the Postwar (Cold War) Era

W. C. Berman, *America's Right Turn: From Nixon to Clinton* (1998), is a concise and readable account of U.S. politics in the 1970s and 1980s; on neoconservatism, see M. Gerson, *The Neoconservative Vision: From the Cold War to the Culture Wars* (1996). E. J. Evans, *Thatcher and Thatcherism* (1997), examines the British model of conservatism.

On the end of the Cold War and the collapse of communism in the "satellite" countries, see the books by Ball, Painter, and Pearson listed in the section on "The Second World War and Its Consequences." On the Soviet Union, see T. H. von Laue, *Why Lenin? Why Stalin? Why Gorbachev?* (1993), for a good brief account; B. Nahaylo and V. Swoboda, *Soviet Disunion* (1990), for the critical nationalities problem; and M. Galeotti, *Gorbachev and His Revolution* (1997), for the life and policies of the last Soviet leader. A. Zwass, *From Failed Communism to Underdeveloped Capitalism: Transformation of Eastern Europe, the Post-Soviet Union, and China* (1995), describes the uncertain economic future of the post-communist world.

15   THE REVOLUTION IN WESTERN CULTURE

The Onrush of Science and Technology

T. Williams, *Science: A History of Discovery in the Twentieth Century* (1990), covers technology as well as pure science, and is excellently illustrated. J. Abbate, *Inventing the Internet* (1999), and S. Aldridge, *The Thread of Life: The Story of Genes and Genetic Engineering* (1997), are clear and up-to-date accounts. H. Collins and T. Pinch, *The Golem: What You Should Know about Science* (1999), and *The Golem at Large: What You Should Know about Technology* (1998), present case studies of recent scientific and technical achievements that undermine the view that advances in these fields result from an inevitable and infallible process.

Many leading twentieth-century scientists have written accounts for the general reader of their own discoveries and those of their colleagues. Among the most notable of these are J. D. Watson, *The Double Helix* (1968), by one of the discoverers of the structure of DNA; and S. Weinberg, *Dreams of a Final Theory: The Scientist's Search for the Ultimate Laws of Nature* (1992), in which a Nobel prize-winning physicist describes the origins and present status of Grand Unified Theories, as well as their implications for the other sciences, philosophy, and theology.

Reconstruction in Western Philosophy and Religion

R. C. Solomon, *Continental Philosophy since 1750: The Rise and Fall of the Self* (1988), deals with the tradition of thought leading from Hegel to Existentialism and beyond; A. J. Ayer, *Philosophy in the Twentieth Century* (1982), concentrates on the "linguistic analysis" school and its forerunners. P. Roubiczek, *Existentialism: For and Against* (1964), presents two opposing viewpoints; and M. Warnock, *Existentialism* (1996), is an excellent brief introduction to the intellectual background and the thought of the leading Existentialist thinkers.

M. Sarup, *An Introductory Guide to Poststructuralism and Postmodernism* (1993), covers developments since Existentialism in an understandable way; and T. Woods, *Beginning Postmodernism* (1999), is a readable introduction to postmodernism in all fields of philosophy, social thought, art, and mass culture.

Recent developments in Christian thought and action are discussed in a thoughtful treatment for the general reader: in D. L. Edwards, *Christianity: The First Two Thousand Years* (1997).

The Shifting Ways of Society

For the youth culture, T. Roszak, *The Making of a Counter Culture: Reflections on the Technocratic Society and Its Youthful Opposition* (1969), is helpful; J. A. Califano Jr., *The Student Revolution* (1970), is a concise worldwide review of the campus agitations of the 1960s. C. Lasch, *The Culture of Narcissism* (1978), is a provocative statement on contemporary attitudes and values; currents of dissent in Europe are effectively analyzed in H. S. Hughes, *Sophisticated Rebels* (1988). S. de Beauvoir, *The Second Sex* (1952), is the classic modern study of the status of women; up-to-date treatments, including the history of the women's movement, will be found in G. Fraisse and M. Perrot, eds., *Emerging Feminism from Revolution to World War* (1992), and F. Thébaud, ed., *Toward a Cultural Identity in the Twentieth Century* (1994) (vols. 4 and 5 of G. Duby and M. Perrot, eds., *The History of Women in the West*). The concept of nonviolence is explained in depth in E. H. Erikson, *Gandhi's Truth* (1969).

Fresh Directions in Literature and the Arts

On literature, E. Wilson, *Axel's Castle*, is a respected study of imaginative writing, 1870–1930; and P. Faulkner, *Modernism* (1977), is a good introduction to English-speaking literature in the early twentieth century. For the period since 1930, see L. Trilling, *The Liberal Imagination: Essays on Literature and Society* (1950), and I. Howe, *Celebrations and Attacks: Thirty Years of Literary and Cultural Commentary* (1979).

E. Lucie-Smith, *Visual Arts in the Twentieth Century* (1996), is an excellent general account of the various movements and schools in painting, sculpture, photography, and architecture. C. Crouch, *Modernism in Design, Art, and Architecture* (1999), is a brief interpretation of the twentieth century's leading artistic tendency. E. Lucie-Smith, *Movements in Art since 1945* (1984), chronicles the decline and fall of modernism; M. Archer, *Art since 1960* (1997), explains postmodernism. On architecture, W. Gropius, *New Architecture and the Bauhaus* (1935), is a classic work by a pioneer of modernism. D. Ghirardi, *Architecture after Modernism* (1996), is a good introduction to the architecture of the last thirty years; A. L. Huxtable, *The Unreal America: Architecture and Illusion* (1997), is a personal view by a distinguished critic.

For music, S. Bechet, *Treat It Gentle* (1960), illuminates the spirit of jazz; R. J. Gleason, *Celebrating the Duke et al.* (1956), offers readable sketches of the leading jazz heroes. I. Whitcomb, *Rock Odyssey* (1983), is written by a musician of the sixties.

THE END OF THE BEGINNING: A NEW AGE OF HUMANITY

D. Bell, *Coming of Post-Industrial Society* (1973), is a well-grounded effort of social forecasting. A. Toffler, *Future Shock* (1970), considers the psychological impact of rapid social changes. J. Schell, *The Fate of the Earth* (1982), examines the probable consequences for our planet should nuclear war take place.

On economic and cultural globalization, T. L. Friedman, *The Lexus and the Olive Tree: Understanding Globalization* (1999), takes a positive view; R. Heilbroner, *Twenty-First Century Capitalism* (1993), makes more skeptical predictions about the short-term future of the world's dominant economic system; D. Harvey, *The Condition of Postmodernity: An Enquiry into the Origins of Cultural Change* (1989), considers postmodernity as a global economic and political as well as cultural and intellectual development; and S. Amin, *Spectres of Capitalism: A Critique of Current Intellectual Fashions* (1998), is an onslaught on all currently dominant forms of global economy and culture by an unrepentant Marxist. B. R. Barber, *Jihad vs. Mc-World* (1995), analyzes the rising conflict between the capitalist thrust for profit and globalization and the resistant forces of tribalism, nationalism, and traditional provincial or local cultures. E. Zwingle, "Goods Move. People Move," in *National Geographic*, August 1999, pp. 12–35, is an excellent brief summary of the worldwide fusion of styles and ideas.

RECOMMENDED VIDEOCASSETTES

In addition to the recommended books (pp. A-1 to A-19), we have chosen a number of excellent videocassettes that relate to the history of Western civilization. Many tapes have recently been produced, and are helpful visual supplements to printed historical works.

The videocassettes (VHS) listed below are arranged according to the major divisions of our textbook. Within each of the five sections, they follow a general *topical* and *chronological* order. Where the title is not self-explanatory, it is followed, in brackets, by a brief clue. The *length* of each tape is shown in minutes.

Many of the listed tapes are available on loan from college instructional media centers and libraries, or from public libraries. (If a particular tape is not on hand, the facility sometimes may order it for use, upon faculty or student request.)

The Coming of Modern Times: 1300–1650

The Ottoman Empire. 20 min.; *Florence: Cradle of the Renaissance.* 30 min.; *Age of Leonardo and Raphael.* 30 min.; *Michelangelo.* 35 min.; *Vatican City.* 30 min.; *Return to Glory: Michelangelo Revealed* [Sistine Chapel]. 52 min.; *Shakespeare and the Globe.* 31 min.; *Olivier's Hamlet.* 155 min.

The Changing West: 1600–1850

Daily Life at the Court of Versailles. 60 min.; *Music at the Court of Louis XIV.* 53 min.; *The Industrial Revolution* [technology in eighteenth-century England]. 23 min.; *The Immigrant Experience: The Long, Long Journey.* 28 min.; *Vincent: A Dutchman* [van Gogh]. 25 min.; *Goya: His Life and Art.* 44 min.; *Road to Modern Art.* 30 min.; *Monet—Legacy of Light.* 28 min.; *Vienna* [Music of Mozart and Schubert]. 60 min.

The West in the Contemporary World: 1850–2000

Sorrow—The Nazi Legacy [Holocaust]. 33 min.; *Hiroshima: The Legacy.* 30 min.; *Martin Luther King: An Amazing Grace.* 60 min.; *Picasso: The Man and His Work* [2 parts]. 90 min.; *The Architecture of Frank Lloyd Wright.* 75 min.; *Robert Frost: A First Acquaintance.* 53 min.; *The Story of Jazz.* 90 min.; *Yugoslavia: The Death of a Nation.* 165 min.

CREDITS

Color Plates

A1 © 1994 Jean Clottes/AP/Wide World Photos **A2** Metropolitan Museum of Art, Rogers Fund, 1930 **A3** © R. Sheridan/The Ancient Art & Architecture Collection **A4** Scala/Art Resource, NY **A5** Eric Lessing/Art Resource, NY **A6** The Fitzwilliam Museum, University of Cambridge, Cambridge, England **A7** Giraudon/Art Resource, NY **B1** Scala/Art Resource, NY **B2** Scala/Art Resource, NY **B3** Vatican Museums Photos, Vatican City, Rome **B4** Detroit Institute of the Arts **B5** Alte Pinakothek, Munich/Joachim Lavel Krotothek **B6** Bridgeman/Art Resource, NY **B7** Eric Lessing/Art Resource, NY **C1** Eric Lessing/Art Resource, NY **C2** Bridgeman/Art Resource, NY **C3** National Gallery, London **C4** National Gallery, London **C5** Giraudon/Art Resource, NY **C6** © Board of Trustees, National Gallery of Art, Washington, D.C. **C7** Vincent van Gogh Museum **C8** Jackson Pollock, *Number 1, 1950 (Lavender Mist)*. Ailsa Mellon Bruce Fund, © 2000 Board of Trustees, National Gallery of Art, Washington, D.C. 1950, oil, enamel, and aluminum on canvas. 2.210 × 2.997 (87″ × 118″); framed: 2.235 × 3.023 × .038 (88″ × 119″ × 1 1/2″)

Photos

15 Kestner Museum, Hanover, Germany **26** Oriental Institute, University of Chicago **28** Hirmer Fotoarchiv, Munich, Germany **35** © The Ancient Art & Architecture Collection **38** © SuperStock **39** Trans World Airlines **42** King Mycerinus and a Queen, Egypt, Giza, Mycerinus Valley Temple, Old Kingdom, Dynasty IV, 2599–2571 B.C.E., Greywacke with faint remains of paint; H: 54 11/16″ × W: 22 3/8″ × D: 21 5/16″ (139 × 57 × 54 cm). Harvard University—Museum of Fine Arts Expedition, 11.1738. Courtesy Museum of Fine Arts, Boston. Reproduced with permission. Copyright © 2000 Museum of Fine Arts, Boston. All rights reserved **48** Reproduced by the courtesy of the Trustees of the British Museum **49** Reproduced by the courtesy of the Trustees of the British Museum **54** British Information Service **57** © Oscar Savio, Rome, Italy **64** © Alison Franz **75** Foto Marburg/Art Resource, NY **90** © Frederick Ayer III/Photo Researchers **93** Alinari/Art Resource **94 (top)** © George Holton/Photo Researchers **94** Marburg/Art Resource **96** Reproduced by the courtesy of the Trustees of the British Museum **97** Alinari/Art Resource, NY **98 (left)** Alinari/Art Resource, NY **98 (right)** © Réunion des Musées Nationaux, Paris **99** Alinari/Art Resource, NY **123** Reproduced by the courtesy of the Trustees of the British Museum **141** French Government Tourist **143** Alinari/Art Resource, NY **144** National Gallery of Art, Washington, D.C., Samuel H. Kress Collection **145** Hirmer Fotoarchiv, Munich, Germany **147** Courtesy of the Prints Division, Astor Lenox and Tilden Foundation, New York Public Library **148** © Leonard von Matt/Rapho-Photo Researchers **149** Alinari/Art Resource **153** © The Ancient Art & Architecture Collection **178** Scala/Art Resource, NY **197** The Italian State Tourist Office **200** © A. F. Kersting **213** Bibliothèque Nationale of France **217** © H. Armstrong Roberts **229** Kaufman-Fabray Photo, Chicago **233** Dr. Harold Busch **237** Erich Lessing/Art Resource, NY **241** Universitetets Oldsaksaming, Frederiksssqt. 1,0164, Oslo, Norway **259** Plan of a manor from *An Introduction to English Industrial History* by Henry Allsopp, G. Bell & Sons, Ltd. **267** Archives Photographiques, Paris, © SPADEM, Paris **275** Bibliothèque Nationale de France **287** Marburg/Art Resource, NY **288** Marburg/Art Resource, NY **289** Marburg/Art Resource, NY **291** Clarence Ward **292** © R. Lamb/H. Armstrong Roberts **293** Aerofilms, Ltd., London, England **294** Giraudon/Art Resource, NY **295** Clarence Ward **306** Henry E. Huntington Library and Art Gallery **306** Courtesy of the Trustees of the National Gallery, London **323** Bibliothèque Nationale of France **332** Reproduced by the courtesy of the Trustees of the British Library **336** The Granger Collection, New York **340** The Granger Collection, New York **384** Alinari/Art Resource, NY **385** George Holton/Photo Researchers **386 (left)** Alinari/Art Resource, NY **386 (right)** Alinari/Art Resource, NY **387** Alinari/Art Resource, NY **388 (top)** Courtesy of the Trustees of the National Gallery, London **388 (bottom)** Courtesy of the Trustees of the National Gallery, London

INDEX

A page number in *italics* indicates an *illustration*. No separate number is given for related text on the same page.

Years shown in parentheses ( ) following the name of a *ruler* are the years of reign. For other individuals, years shown are for *birth* and *death*.

Index entries marked by an asterisk (*) are *important historical terms*. The meaning of each term is explained on the pages of text shown for that entry.

Byzantine Empire, 50, 107, 128, 156;
architecture and art, 216–218; and the
Crusades, 309, 310, 312–313; as custodian
of classical culture, 216; decline and fall,
312–313, 325; and the Franks, 238–239;
Greek Church and, 214, 220; and the
Arabs, 222, 224; and the Slavs, 218–220,
312, 327, 458–459; and western Europe,
215–216, 220, 308–309. *See also* Orthodox
(Greek or Eastern) Christianity
Byzantium. *See* Constantinople

Cabot, John (1450–1498), 361
Caesar, Julius (100–44 B.C.), 50, 121–122, 123,
127, 135
Calder, Alexander (1898–1976), *748*
Caliph (Muslim) and caliphate, 222, 226, 309
Calvin, John (1509–1564), 177, 182, 418–424,
435, 583
Cambodia (Kampuchea), 677, 734
Cambyses (Persia, 528–521 B.C.), 50
Camelot, (Lerner and Loewe), 754
Camp David, 672
Canada, 507, 689, 694
Candide (Voltaire), 483
Cannon. *See* Firearms
Canon of Avicenna, 227
Canterbury Tales, The (Chaucer), 306–307
Capet, Hugh (France, 987–996), 244, 252
*Capitalism: early modern, 369, 419, 434;
Hellenistic, 106; medieval, 321, 329–335;
modern, 552, 554–565, 569–572,
602–603, 626, 630, 637, 638, 642–645,
667. *See also* Bourgeois; Capitalist class
Capitalist class: early modern, *335,* 343, 349;
medieval, 329–335; modern, 552, 554,
560–561, 571–572, 626, 634, 642, 667;
Roman, 118. *See also* Bourgeois
Capuchin order, 431
Caracalla (emperor, 211–217), 132
Carcassonne, walled city, 266, *267*
Cardinals, College of, 280, 408, 729, 730
Caribbean, 364, 367
Carnot, Sadi (1837–1894), 574
Carolingian dynasty, 230–233, 239–240, 244
Carolingian empire, 233–242
Carolingian renaissance, 236–238
Carrack (late medieval ship), *336–337*
Carter, Jimmy (b. 1924), 663, 672, 676, 680, 681
Carthage, 117–118. *See also* Phoenicians
Cassatt, Mary (1845–1926), 589
Castiglione, Baldassare (1478–1529), 377
Castlereagh, Lord (1769–1822), 522
Castro, Fidel (b. 1926), 676–677

Catch 22 (Heller), 741
Cathedral schools, 296
Catherine II, the Great (Russia, 1762–1796),
459–460, 480, 625
Catherine of Aragon (1485–1536), 425–426
Catholicism. *See* Christianity
Catullus (84–54 B.C.), 134
Cellini, Benvenuto (1500–1571), 400
Celts, 57, 121, 130, 210
Central Intelligence Agency (CIA), 676, 679
Central Powers. *See* Triple Alliance
Central Treaty Organization (CENTO), 661
Cervantes, Miguel de (1547–1616), 401
Ceylon. *See* Sri Lanka
Cézanne, Paul (1839–1906), 589–590, 745,
Color Plate C6
Chaldeans, 44, 52, 166
Chamorro, Violeta (b. 1939), 699
Chanson de Roland (Song of Roland), 86, 236,
251, 304
Charismatics, 695
Charlemagne (Franks, 768–814), 230,
233–239, 240, 242, 283, 304
Charles I (England, 1625–1649), 499–500
Charles II (England, 1660–1685), 501
Charles I (Spain, 1516–1556), 233. *See also*
Charles V (emperor)
Charles V (emperor, 1519–1556), 353, 415,
417, 426
Charles II (West Franks, 840–877), 239
Charles VII (France, 1422–1461), 333,
347–349
Charles X (France, 1824–1830). *See* Artois,
Count of
Charles the Bold (Burgundy, 1467–1477), 349
Charles Martel (689–741), 222, 230–231
Charters (medieval), 256, 267–268, 298
Chaucer, Geoffrey (1340–1400), 306–307, 373
Chechnya, 708
Chernobyl, Ukraine, 698
Chiang Kai-shek (1886–1975), 662
Children's Crusade (1212), 312. *See also*
Crusades
Chile, 678–679
China, 17, 128, 158, 206, 227, 335, 337, 354,
355, 360, 362, 366, 459, 653–654,
662–663, 664, 667
Chirac, Jacques (b. 1932), 694
Chopin, Frederic (1810–1849), 538
Chrétien de Troyes (12th cent.), 305
Christ Blessing (Lectionary), *275*
Christian Era: defined, 7 (n. 2)
Christianity: adoption by Roman Empire,
155–156, 189; architecture and art, *143,*